Base Ball on the Western Reserve

Base Ball on the Western Reserve

The Early Game in Cleveland and Northeast Ohio, Year by Year and Town by Town, 1865–1900

James M. Egan, Jr.

McFarland & Company, Inc., Publishers
Jefferson, North Carolina, and London

LIBRARY OF CONGRESS CATALOGUING-IN-PUBLICATION DATA

Egan, James M., 1953–
Base ball on the Western Reserve : the early game in
Cleveland and northeast Ohio, year by year and town
by town, 1865–1900 / James M. Egan, Jr..
p.   cm.
Includes bibliographical references and index.

ISBN 978-0-7864-3067-3
softcover : 50# alkaline paper ∞

1. Baseball — Ohio — Western Reserve — History —19th century.
2. Baseball — Ohio — Cleveland — History —19th century.
I. Title. II. Title: Baseball on the Western Reserve.
GV863.O32W474   2008   796.35709771'3 — dc22   2007052127

British Library cataloguing data are available

©2008 James M. Egan, Jr. All rights reserved

*No part of this book may be reproduced or transmitted in any form
or by any means, electronic or mechanical, including photocopying
or recording, or by any information storage and retrieval system,
without permission in writing from the publisher.*

On the cover: The Forest City Baseball Club, 1869 (Photography
Collection, Miriam and Ira D. Wallach Division of Art, New York
Public Library; Astor, Lenox and Tilden Foundations)

Manufactured in the United States of America

*McFarland & Company, Inc., Publishers
Box 611, Jefferson, North Carolina 28640
www.mcfarlandpub.com*

Table of Contents

Preface *1*
Introduction *3*

PART I. THE EARLY YEARS, 1865–1877
    1865 *5*
    1866 *7*
    1867 *9*
    1868 *23*
    1869 *32*
    1870 *43*
    1871 *55*
    1872 *66*
    1873–1877 *72*

PART II. THE MIDDLE YEARS, 1878–1889
    1878 *77*
    1879 *85*
    1880 *96*
    1881 *105*
    1882 *113*
    1883 *122*
    1884 *131*
    1885 & 1886 *140*
    1887 *144*
    1888 *155*
    1889 *169*

PART III. THE CLOSING YEARS, 1890–1900
    1890 *181*
    1891 *193*

1892	*204*
1893	*215*
1894	*221*
1895	*230*
1896	*242*
1897	*259*
1898	*270*
1899	*278*
1900	*281*
Afterword	*291*
Chapter Notes	*293*
Bibliography	*299*
Sources by Chapter	*301*
Index	305

Preface

This book is about nineteenth-century baseball in Greater Cleveland (northeast Ohio) following the Civil War. The first of its three main sections documents the rise of the organized game on the Western Reserve, covering its spread from town to town, and the advent of professional play; the second section focuses on baseball in Cleveland, then undergoing a dramatic increase in population, and follows the six-year run of the National League Blue Stockings, 1879–1892, as well as selected events from the larger Reserve-area cities such as Akron, Canton, and Youngstown; the final section looks at regional amateur and minor league play, though the emphasis is squarely on the major league Cleveland Spiders. With a few exceptions, chapters cover one season each and together span the years 1865–1900.

Because the book covers a great deal of ground, both historically and geographically, the main text forgoes conventional narrative in favor of an episodic arrangement. Each chapter consists of free-standing, chronologically arranged write-ups about local baseball-related events. As most of these write-ups are only loosely related to any that immediately precede or follow, the result is a book that is more nearly a chronicle of events than a narrative history.

The first section, covering the years 1865 to 1877, proved the most difficult to research, requiring visits to 14 cities and nine counties outside of Cleveland and countless hours spent poring over small-town newspapers. Coverage in these newspapers, which were often weeklies, was spotty at best, and sometimes there might be no more than a line or a paragraph to be found in a month of issues. For the years after baseball had become better established, both as sport and as business, the challenge involved choosing from among the many stories and news items that appeared in first the sports columns and then, eventually, the sports pages of the daily newspapers.

Almost all of the information in this book comes from primary resources, which are listed in a bibliography following the main text.

Introduction

> If Edith wishes to see "a great strike" and "lots of fun," let her walk down Water Street some pleasant afternoon towards "set of sun" and see the "Bachelors" make the ball fly.[1]
> — *Cleveland Herald*, 1841

Baseball has been a part of life in Ohio for a century and a half. This book is the story of the game in Greater Cleveland and on the Western Reserve (northeast Ohio) from the end of the Civil War to the end of the nineteenth century.

In 1810 the population of Cleveland was all of 300; by 1840, aided by the opening of the Ohio & Erie Canal in 1832, the population had reached 6,071. By the close of the century Clevelanders numbered an amazing 381,768.

The historical origins of baseball are obscure; throwing, hitting and catching a ball were already old skills in the early nineteenth century. One-eyed-cat, barn ball, goal, wicket, base, and town ball were all names given to a game of "ball." The modern game of baseball traces its organized roots to 1845, when Alexander Cartwright drafted a list of rules for his New York City "Knickerbockers" baseball club. By the 1850's the records of the proceedings of Cleveland City Council show that ball games, at least those being played on Public Square, had already become enough of a nuisance to warrant regulation by law.

By 1857 the New York game of baseball had become so popular along the Eastern seaboard that an organization was formed in an attempt to regulate the clubs and their players. This first sanctioning body was called the National Association of Base Ball Players (NABBP).

For most of this period, the game was in theory a game for amateurs; however, the NABBP's work to keep money out of the game met with limited success. A lot of money was floating around the game under a number of guises: travel expenses, hotel bills, meal money, a little pocket money, uniform upkeep, etc. The better players were also getting cash under the table, and gamblers of all stripes were wagering openly at the ball grounds and in local "poole" halls.[2] Within a few years of the Western Reserve's entry into the ranks of amateur baseball, these questions of money would be confronting teams in that area too.

Part I. The Early Years, 1865–1877

1865

Organized Baseball

Soldiers during the Civil War played the popular New York brand of baseball. Following the end of the war, their return home launched a wave of baseball mania that in the second half of the 1860's swept the nation. In Cleveland that wave arrived in September of 1865, when the Forest City Base Ball Club organized for "match play." The wave, however, first swept through a college town west of Cleveland.

Oberlin, Ohio: April 3, 1865

On Monday evening, the "old six pounder" cannon boomed and boomed against a bonfire lit sky—the "jubilee" went on all night till dawn.[1]

The celebrants had gathered on the Tappan Square following a series of dispatches from the telegraph office. General Robert E. Lee, head of Confederate forces, had capitulated at Appomattox, putting an end to America's bloodiest conflict—the Civil War.

A few days later, three young men, in gray uniforms of the Confederacy, jumped from an inbound train at the Oberlin train depot and quickly headed out of town. The local paper speculated that "they might be local county men looking for work in the country side."[2]

Mr. Daniel Russell of Henrietta, Lorain County, was walking around downtown Oberlin that April when—without warning—a bat loosed from the direction of Tappan Square hit him between the eyes. The college boys were practicing baseball on the commons at the time. Mr. Russell recovered, but "his nasal bone was broken."[3]

The Oberlin College team, formed this April, took the name "Penfields." A former team member recalled in his memoirs that Professor Penfield of the school inspired the choice of name.

Cleveland, Ohio: September 19, 1865

The Forest City Cricket Club, inactive since the start of the war, played a "match game" against Meadville, Pennsylvania, on the Kinsman Grounds. Cleveland won, but in the October return match at Meadville they lost.

Some of the cricket team began playing intramural games of a second sport—baseball. Utilizing the rules of the NABBP, they felt after several weeks of practice ready to challenge the only other "organized club," the Penfields of Oberlin. The ritual match game challenge was issued and Oberlin accepted. Each team used its "first nine," or the best club members by position.

Warned the *Lorain County News*: "Look Out Clevelanders."[4]

Kinsman Grounds

The Kinsman Grounds were on the northeast corner of Case Avenue (E. 40th St.) and Kinsman Street (Woodland Avenue). Nearby, within sight of the grounds, were the Jewish Orphan Asylum, the Water Cure (health retreat), and the Female Seminary (a well-to-do girls' boarding school). The ball players were quite aware of the girls' school, and its view of their ball field. These were the only buildings of note on what, at the time, was the outskirts of urban sprawl.

The field itself was nicely manicured but had no other improvements. The State Fair had been held there in the past, and a Civil War camp once existed near by. The first match game of baseball in Ohio was held there at 4 P.M. on October 20, 1865.

The Oberlin Penfields arrived on the morning train and found their own way out to the ball field. The choice of ups—a coin toss—went to the Forest City. They chose to take the field. A large crowd, numbering several hundred, braved the cold, "[a] keen west wind chilly and cutting."[5] The sky was clear and the sun an autumn bright.

During the game, on an infield pop fly, the Cleveland catcher A. R. "Pikey" Smith lost the ball in the sun, causing him to run head first into another player. When the melee was untangled, Pikey's smile was minus two teeth.

This was not the only mishap in this hard fought game. Right from the start injury was part of the game. Cleveland's left fielder had to leave the game when he damaged his arm on a throw in. The Penfields did not go unscathed either. Mr. Ryder, while in the field, managed to stop a batted ball the hard way—with his face.

Gathering darkness, and the close of the seventh inning, brought the contest to an end by mutual agreement. In this era of barehanded fielding, the final tally was Oberlin 67 and Cleveland 28.

In the spirit of good sportsmanship, and embracing tradition, the two teams and friends adjourned to Garrets Hall downtown, where the Clevelanders treated the winners to a sumptuous dinner. A good time was had by all.

1866

Cleveland

Baseball fever raged throughout the nation in 1866 with organized teams popping up in the smallest of hamlets. Cleveland by year's end could boast of eleven new clubs. They were High School (nicknamed "Occidental"), Eagle, Young America, Alert, Peconic, Star, Mohawk, University, Eureka, Defiance, and Union Railway. The last-named team was composed of the employees of the Union Railroad Terminal, newly opened on the Cleveland lakefront this year.

In the late 1860's, the Union Railway (though not an official company team), along with the Forest City, brought national attention to Cleveland baseball.

The Forest City and the high school team played an early spring game on the Kinsman Grounds. The high school boys had an outstanding pitcher, L. C. Hanna, who later played for the senior Forest City. (His brother, Marcus Hanna, was destined to be a powerful industrialist and Republican Party boss—the man who would put William McKinley in the White House).

The Forest City ball team still shared its grounds with the Forest City cricket team. In early June the latter hosted the Windsor, Canada, cricket team.

In the middle of June, the Forest City Base Ball Club made their first road trip. They went to Hudson, Ohio, to play the "Reserve" team of Western Reserve College. Cleveland won the game 40–26. Along with their compatriots, they enjoyed the traditional post-game banquet, served by the ladies of Hudson.

Mansfield

In Mansfield, Ohio, the Exercise Base Ball Club and the Mansfield Base Ball Club were formed. The following year, the Mansfield Base Ball Club became the Independents of Mansfield, and, with the importation of John Clapp, Mansfield became in the closing years of the decade a nationally ranked team.

Reserve College at Hudson, Ohio, in 1866. Note the college nine at play on the campus green (Historical Society of Hudson, Ohio).

Ashtabula and Painesville

East of Cleveland, Ashtabula had a team in the field. They hosted the Painesville "Athletics" in early September, winning in front of a large crowd of ladies and gentlemen. They then took Painesville out to dinner at the Fisk House.

The *Painesville Telegraph* reported that on the Grand River Grounds, in mid–October, the High School Club won a close game against the "second-nine" of the Athletics, 42–36.

The *Telegraph*, in the last days of October, told of a game played at Painesville by the "Contest" (a team with but eight players in the field) against the "Remnant." The "Contest" won 40–33.

The Silver Ball and Rosewood Bat

The baseball event of the year took place at the Kinsman Grounds on the Fourth of July. Cleveland businessmen, having caught the baseball fever, and following a practice of their East Coast counterparts, initiated a trophy prize game. Open to all the teams of the Western Reserve, a challenge match (required at least once every thirty days) would determine the holder of the valuable silver ball and rosewood bat.

John Sargent, the popular local merchant, secured the silver ball and silver-in-laid rosewood bat from famous Tiffany's of New York. The $120 cost for the prize bat and ball was about a year's pay for a good working-class job.

The Forest City club was the original prize custodian. In order to win the prize permanently, a team must remain undefeated for a year's worth of challenges. Having accomplished that, their names would then be engraved on the bat's silver shield, and it and the silver ball would become permanent items in the winning team's trophy case.

The first challenge was scheduled for the Fourth of July at the Kinsman Street Grounds. The

Forest City club was now a much more practiced group of players. But were they ready for their old nemesis the Penfields of Oberlin? In both towns, the papers predicted a much closer contest this time.

Parade, Balloon, and Ball Game

Cleveland newspapers listed a number of events planned for Wednesday the Fourth of July:
- The brightly uniformed Fenian Cadets will march in downtown.
- The steam fire department will route their parade through downtown and the near west side.
- An always-popular balloon ascension, wind willing, will be held.
- The long awaited baseball match for the trophy prize will be at the Kinsman Grounds.

A match game on a holiday, the press ballyhooing the expensive baseball prize, and baseball fever in general would bring out an unprecedented crowd from all walks of city life. Reports put the number in the thousands, and at the Oberlin depot over one hundred supporters, in company with the Penfields, boarded the morning train and went to Cleveland.

Loud cheers greeted the players as they took the field. Attired in uniforms of black pants, black belts, black caps and contrasting white shirts, the Penfields faced the Cleveland Forest City, who wore blue pants, white belts, white shirts, and white caps.

A tent, the only structure on the grounds, had been set up for the comfort of the scorers. Everyone else stood.

It was a slugfest, and the hometown boys did most of the slugging. Inning after inning they rolled up the score. The eighth inning, with approaching darkness and Oberlin hopelessly behind, would be the last. Revenge took the form of an unexpected pasting of the visitors, 48–14. Cleveland's hitting was of the efficient base hit variety, only McEwen and Hurlbut of the home team having hit home runs. In the spirit of good sportsmanship, Captain Smith led the Forest City in "three ringing cheers" for the Penfields.[1]

The Oberlin players responded in kind, but due to an early train they were unable to join in the traditional post-game repast.

Earlier in the day the high school boys played a game with the second-nine of the Penfields at the Kinsman Grounds. Oberlin won the match 16–9.

On August 25, the Penfields returned to the Kinsman Grounds to give the Forest City men their last serious challenge to their right to hold the prize trophy in 1866. Once again, the Oberlin entourage came in on the early train. This time, to make sure the train schedule didn't cost the visitors a meal, the Forest City gave the Penfields a pre-game banquet at the Kennard House.

There was a large crowd on hand as Oberlin sent Fisher, their second-string pitcher, to the box—their regular man having taken ill. Cleveland countered by sending their man Stockley in to pitch. The visitors kept the game close through four innings. At that time, Cleveland had 16 runs and Oberlin 11. Thereafter, Cleveland put the game out of reach.

The scoring:

Inning	1 2 3	4 5 6	7 8 9	Final
Forest City	3 2 8	3 6 0	7 5 2	36
Penfield	5 0 4	2 0 1	0 6 0	18

Winner: Stockley. Loser: Fisher. Home run: "Pikey" Smith. Time of game: Three hours and twenty minutes. Umpire: R. K. Paige, Athletic Club—Painesville.

Notes • Despite their loss, the Oberlin team was reported to have left on the evening train in high spirits. • According to the *Cleveland Leader*, the bat and ball were exhibited for a few days in the window of Sargent's, a store just west of Public Square in the Marble Block, on Superior Street.[2]

1867

Diamonds in the Cornfields

Throughout the Western Reserve ball clubs were sprouting in many a farm town. Travelers in wagons and trains would often see a familiar sight in the countryside: a ball diamond, cut out of a cornfield at the edge of town. And often the local "nines" were to be seen hard at practice, or playing a match game against some other town's team.

THE MAHONING VALLEY

In 1803 the first blast furnace in Ohio was built on the outskirts of Youngstown. The limestone deposits, and the famous Briar-Hill block coal found in the area, were instrumental in the rapid development of Youngstown as a major American center of iron production prior to the Civil War. Appropriately, the first organized team of ball players in town chose the name "Ironsides." Youngstown also fielded two lesser nines—the "Rough and Ready" and the "Youngstown Stars."

In nearby Warren, the "Mahoning" team formed; along with the Youngstown team they were considered one of the region's "crack" teams—the best of 1867. Four more teams called the Mahoning valley home: Girard had its "Social," Lowellville its "Active," and, surprisingly, tiny Poland fielded two teams—the "Resolutes" and the "Stars."

Competition being somewhat thin, local teams challenged clubs from across the nearby Pennsylvania state line. Sharon was a frequent Ironsides foe, Edinborough and New Castle also sent teams into the valley this year.

In the spirit of good sportsmanship, the ball clubs from the Youngstown area continued the Eastern tradition of providing and sharing a post-game meal. In Youngstown, the baseball grub was often served at Mr. J. P. Martin's—the preferred dining room of the Ironsides. In that hotbed of baseball activity, Poland, Ohio, teams supped on the food dished out at the Sparrow House. Teams venturing across the Pennsylvania line to play the "Peerless" of Sharon could look forward to a nice plate put out by the Iron City House.

The newspapers of Youngstown were the *Courier* and the *Register*—both weeklies. From mid-April till September, they carried the scores of 9 games, and occasionally a few more details of the match games that drew large crowds.

PORTAGE COUNTY

The *County Democrat*, the newspaper covering the news of Portage County, gave a surprising number of column inches to the game of baseball in 1867.

The city of Ravenna occupied center stage in the sport of baseball in Portage County this year. Its team, the "Stars," was formed on July 10, 1867. They played their home games at the Ravenna Driving Park (racetrack). Players named Webber, Campbell, M. Phillips, Vance, Alcorn, G. Phillips, Coolman, Witter, Swain, Wadsworth, Oakley, Ranney, Gardiner, Mason, Cotter, King, Butler, Harris, Collins, Ney, Musson, and Leffingwell played in match games for the Stars of 1867.

The Ravenna Stars, in their first three match games, scheduled games with superior competition from across county lines. The Stars, a team of but two weeks' standing, played their first game against a year-old club from Summit County, the Hudson "Enterprise."

On Monday, June 24, at 1 P.M., umpire A. J. Mack of the Western Reserve Club of Hudson called for start of game.

For three hours the Enterprise drubbed the novice Stars, and at close of play the visitors had 82 runs and the hometown boys but 26.

Comments on the Game: • "The Ravenna boys played a straight, square game..."[1] • "There was quite a large attendance of spectators at the Driving Park, who enjoyed the sport with a keen relish."[2] • "...the two clubs partook of an elegant supper at the Gillette House, thus concluding the exercise of the occasion in the happiest manner."[3]

The Stars' second match game at home was scheduled against a crack team, the Warren "Mahoning." However, members of each club's second string, or "second-nine," would play this game. The *County Democrat* printed the bad news July 31. The Mahoning second-nine had demolished the Stars' second-nine 91–28. The high point of that day for the Stars was another trip to the Gillette House for the good-sportsmanship dinner.

The Ravenna Stars went to Hudson on Saturday, August 10, for the return game with the Hudson Enterprise. They were outscored almost two to one, losing 91–54. The winners banged out five home runs during the four-hour fifteen-minute game. Professor Barrows of the Hudson Reserve Club gave good service as umpire, and once again the high point for the Stars was dinner — this time at the Mansion House.

The ladies of Ravenna, proud of their Stars team even in defeat — or perhaps trying to help them find some teams they could beat — offered a prize for Portage County teams only. The prize was a silver ball and silver bat of undisclosed value. It was to be held by their local team until some other team could win it from them. The prize was to rotate, its final disposition to be determined.

A mini-baseball tournament for the trophy's first challenge was held at the Fair Grounds on Wednesday, September 18. Due to a shortage of organized teams in the county, only two teams registered to take on the Stars— the "Island" of Kent, and the "Ledge" of Nelson. The last two named were to play first. The winner would then try to take the prize from Ravenna in game two— if they could.

Game one started at 9:00 A.M. The Island won the coin toss and chose the field. It didn't take long to realize Kent had the superior team. When the runs stopped, the Kent Island had 63 and the Nelson Ledge 22.

The trophy game started at 2:20 P.M., the Stars going to the field. Experience earned in the severe beatings they took from out-of-county teams paid off. Ravenna sank the Island with 79 runs; Kent had 33. Ravenna took their prize home to admire some more, and Kent went home to practice some more.

The Island put their practice to the test when on Monday, October 14, they were in Ravenna to play a second match for the trophy.

The game started at 2:30 P.M. at the Driving Park and was played into darkness.

The score seesawed back and forth early on, but by the middle of the seventh Ravenna had amassed 53 while Kent had managed but 31. With little light left, it was agreed the bottom of the seventh would be the last.

By the time two men had been retired it was quite dark, and Kent was still 13 runs behind. Rather than risk injury, they called it a day.

The unofficial score was 53–40. However, following match game rules, the score reverted to the last full inning of play. The official score of six innings was Ravenna Stars 42, Kent Island 31.

The last attempt to move the prize out of Ravenna came in late October, from an unheralded team: the Streetsboro "Buckeye." The visitors rolled into the Ravenna Driving Park on a very cold October 23. In front of a very thin crowd, game start was called at ten after one. The game was close for four innings, then the visitors started to pull away. The thin crowd became thinner each inning, until in the ninth it was all but invisible. The Buckeye surprised the Stars with excellent batting and frequent base stealing — the keys to their success. Score: Streetsboro 63, Ravenna 38.

The clubs took dinner at the Gillette House. Following supper, the Streetsboro boys promised to take good care of the bat and ball until the next match game — next year. They then loaded up their trophy and headed home.

A few days later, the weekly paper, in its account of the game, roasted the Ravenna Stars. Every aspect of their game came under fire. It was even implied that, by letting the prize provided by the local ladies get away, they had insulted womanhood itself. It would be a long winter for Ravenna's fallen Stars.

A final game of baseball involving junior nines was played October 26 at Kent. The juniors were boys ages thirteen to sixteen who were understudies of the Ravenna Stars and Kent Island. The Kent youngsters went by the name "Active." The Ravenna lads called themselves the "Star Club Juniors." The Ravenna boys bludgeoned the Kent juniors 118–19.

Chardon

The center of government in Geauga County today and in 1867 was Chardon. It was also the local epicenter of the baseball epidemic of 1867.

Chardon fielded three clubs of ball players that summer. The best by far was the "Lightfoot." A second club was called the "Independents," and all that is known of the third team is that it was organized in mid-August.

The Chardon Lightfoot team was born on Saturday, July 20, 1867; that day it elected nine officers. From July 31 through September 7, the team played 6 match games.

The Chardon Lightfoot players whose names appeared in box scores were Adams, Alle, G. Bestor, H. Bestor, Bickle, Bruce, Canfield, Canfield (once two Canfields appeared in the same game—no first initial), Clapp, Clark, Eggleston, Ellicke, Folder, Metcalfe, Munsell, Squire, H. Randall and W. Randall.

Game one: Chardon crossed over the county line to play its first game at Rock Creek in Ashtabula County on July 31, a Wednesday. They were not ready, losing 84–35. Mr. Kellogg of the Jefferson B.B.C. called the game in three hours and twenty-one minutes.

Game two: Saturday, August 2, was the home opener for Chardon. The experienced Willoughby "Sorter" team from Lake County was the opponent. Chardon did better than expected, but the Willoughby team still prevailed 39–26. The *Geauga Democrat*: "It will be seen that our boys played well, and were not badly beaten—but 'Sorter.'"[4] Converse Cowles umpired the game of three hours and twenty-one minutes.

Game three: The "Eureka" club of Hamden rolled into Chardon, and when they rolled out, the Lightfoot had their first victory. The margin of victory was 21 runs and the score 56–35. Mr. J. Radcliffe of the Painesville Athletic B.B.C. came down to perform the umpiring duties. Time of game: three hours twenty minutes.

Game four: A five-inning game at Willoughby saw the Lightfoot come home with their second victory, having defeated the Willoughby Sorter 18–12. G. B. Hudson was the arbiter. The shortened game took an hour and forty-five minutes to complete.

Game five: The Chardon boys went over to Hambden Center to play the return match with the Hambden Eureka. They won a quickly played game 20–16. Umpire: E. Patchin. Time: one hour and forty-five minutes.

Game six: The season finale was in Chardon on September 7. A large crowd was on hand to see if the hometown favorites could make it four wins in a row. The Willoughby Club was in town to see that they didn't.

This game was anything but fast. Inning after inning the score piled up. By the middle of the eighth the team from Willoughby had 52 runs and a 15-run lead. The Lightfoot, with the encouragement of the partisan crowd, refused to crawl into the hole that had been dug for them. They responded in the bottom of the eighth with 13—their largest inning output of the day. The score now stood at 52–50.

In the top of the ninth Willoughby added 2 runs. Trailing by but 4 runs, the hometown crowd was in high spirits when their boys came to bat in the bottom of the ninth. Their spirits soared even higher when Chardon quickly plated run number 51. But before any more runs came in, three men were made outs, and the Chardon Lightfoots' season was over. Score: Willoughby 54, Chardon 51. A very tired Roll St. John of the Rock Creek B.B.C. umpired the game that lasted five hours.

The last game of the year reported was the beating the "Independent" club of Chardon received at the hands of the visiting "Yankee" club of Willoughby, losing 70–33.

The Chardon paper also mentioned the names of a few other town teams playing ball in the general area: Hartsgrove (Ashtabula County); Chester (Geauga County); and the "Pioneer Club" at Waite Hill in Kirtland (Lake County).

Akron

The Akron newspaper record for 1867 is incomplete. From records of surrounding towns we learn that Akron had a very strong club. They were referred to as the Akron City Club. At home in July, Akron beat Mansfield 46–30.

Mansfield: "Our correspondent speaks very highly of the way in which the Mansfield people were treated by the Akronites, which we are pleased to put on record."[5]

The record of the game also included the Akron lineup: Babcock, rf; Hudson, 1b; Smith, 3b; F. Hanford, ss; Fred Hanford, 2b; Hanssom, cf; Perkins, lf; Angel, c.; and Rawson, p.

Akron played the Forest City at Cleveland on August 15; a good-sized crowd of Akronites rode the train into Cleveland with the ball players. A delegation of Cleveland players met them at the depot, and escorted their Akron guests to the Kinsman Grounds for the 3 o'clock game. Akron took the field in handsome uniforms of white shirts and caps, red belts, and red pantaloons with white cords—"a la militaire."[6] The Forest City opened up the game with 5 runs in the first. At the end of the fifth inning they led 34–16. Akron never could catch up the rest of the way. The final score was Cleveland 52, Akron 33. The teams then dined at the Kennard House. In the evening a special train took the visitors home.

The audience numbered over two thousand for a game which was not for the trophy. Akron used the same lineup as in Mansfield, excepting Buchtel, who played left field. Pitcher Rawson of Akron had the only home run. The *Herald* on Akron: "They are a very fine looking club, active and vigorous, and with experience will become a hard club to encounter at base ball."[7]

A second Akron team of lesser quality, nicknamed the "Excelsiors," played a game in August against a team from Middleburg, losing by a score of 89–38.

Canton

"Stark" was the name of the first ball club to organize in Canton, at least in terms of what they understood "organize" to mean. Following their first game with an outside club, the *Canton Repository* observed that the game "was purely a social one played for the mutual improvement of the clubs and should not be regarded as, in any sense, a 'challenge' game."[8] The Canton paper also suggested the Canton players pay "most careful attention to the rules of the game, as under the new regulations of this year many of the old customs in Base Ball have changed."[9]

The "social game" took place in nearby Massilon, Ohio, versus the but-days-old "Sippo" team.

Batting orders and positions

STARK	SIPPO
Pierong, ss	Dobson, lf
Piero, cf	Sharpnack, .p
Kuhn, c	Humberger, c
Essig, 3b	Brown, 1b
Miller, 2b	Heckman, rf
Alexander, lf	Rider, 3b
Harter, 1b	Breks, cf
Williams, rf	McClymonds, 2b
Underhill, p	Melain, ss

C. A. Kelly of the Sippo started the game as umpire; he was relieved by G. S. Lester of the Stark for the last few innings.

A rain-threatening sky delayed the start of game until rather late in the afternoon; then the clouds blew away, the sun came out, and there was almost no wind. A fair-sized crowd had waited out the weather. The game itself was less than stellar, fielding blunders being a regular feature of the contest. It was not so much lack of practice on the part of the players as it was the embarrassing condition of the field — "very rough and uneven."[10] The spectators enjoyed the convivial nature of the day and weren't to concerned about the level of play. Those in the crowd who liked scoring, especially in double digits, were the most pleased. Due to coming evening, the game was called after five innings, by which time Canton had a commanding lead. The only home run was hit by Canton shortstop Pierong. The solitary round-tripper was even more amazing when one reflects on the score: Canton 72 and Massilon 25.

A Big-time Social Game

Everyone was surprised when it was announced that Canton baseball would present a very special event for the Fourth of July. The nationally known and highly experienced Allegheny Base Ball Club, based near Pittsburgh, would play a friendly exhibition game against the hometown team.

The *Canton Repository*:

We find so complete a report in the Pittsburg Leader that we append it in lieu of remarks of our own.

On the afternoon of the 3rd inst., the Allegheny club made a pleasure excursion to Canton, Ohio to play the Stark club of that place a match game of ball. They started from Allegheny depot at half-past three o'clock P.M., and arrived at Alliance about seven, where a committee from the Stark club, who accompanied them to Canton and escorted them to the St. Cloud Hotel, met them. Arrived at the hotel, supper was ordered for our hungry travelers, and comfortable quarters engaged for the night. At noon on the 4th a heavy shower of rain came on, and it was feared the match could not be played. The rain however, lasted but a short time, and the sun coming out gloriously, in a couple of hours the ground was in excellent condition for the game. At about 2 o'clock the teams repaired to the Commons, and at 3 p. m. play was called. A large and brilliant assemblage had gathered on the field to witness the contest, including quite a number of the fair sex, and although they were by no means wanting in local pride, yet they were decidedly impartial in their criticism on the game. The weather continued favorable up to the seventh inning for the Stark. The Allegheny had finished their seventh, and the others had just commenced theirs when a heavy shower of rain came on, dampened the ardor of the contestants, and effectually stopped the play. The game, therefore, rested on the sixth inning....

[Totals: Allegheny 45 Canton 13]

At 8 o'clock in the evening a grand supper was given in the hall of the G.A.R. [Grand Army of the Republic] at which about sixty were present. Here also the young ladies were out in full force, and by their pleasant smiles and kind attentions spread happiness and pleasure broadcast. Taking into consideration the exercise of the afternoon, it is hardly necessary to state that ample justice was done to the repast. After supper the table was cleared away, the musicians came, and the dance commenced, which was kept up till the "wee sma'" hours, when after exchanging goodbyes and mutual well-wishes, the happy party separated.

Too much praise cannot be given the young ladies and gentlemen of Canton for the untiring energy and kindhearted hospitality they displayed on this occasion. The manner in which the Allegheny B.B.C. were treated during their sojourn to Canton, and the many kindnesses that were heaped upon them, gave ample evidence that the heart of the Canton people is in the right place. Nothing was left undone that could be done to add to their comfort and enjoyment. It seemed as if the ladies and gentlemen had entered into a kind of joint partnership with determination to make their visitors enjoy themselves and feel that they were among friends. How well they succeeded we will attempt to state. All their wants and wishes were anticipated by their host and their every pleasure was the order of the day. We feel assured that the Allegheny club entertains the warmest feeling of gratitude for their Canton friends and feeling themselves so greatly in debt for the entertainment that they enjoyed, they only hope for a speedy opportunity to reciprocate the kindness and at least for their honors sake to make a partial payment.[11]

* * *

Medina County

From the pages of the *Medina Gazette* we learn of the outbreak of baseball fever in and around Medina County. Using our imaginations, let us read a letter that a couple of young travelers might have sent home.

Base Ball in a Farm Town

Medina Village, October 1867: Driving our wagon toward Medina we noticed a ball club hard at work in a field just south of town. Coming into town we stopped at the local general store, tied up our rig, and entered the emporium of one A. I. Root. We immediately noticed a sign behind the men sitting at the pickle barrel, it said: "We have base balls of every description direct from New York City—fifteen cents each, one hundred twenty five dollars takes all."[12] A casual comment to the clerk about the ball game at the edge of town woke up a couple of the old timers at the pickle barrel and they started bending our ear about the team we saw in action. They told us the team was formed officially on Monday, July 22, at the courthouse in town, C. G. Codding being voted in as president at that time—practice starting Wednesday of that very same week. They said: "To this very day they still ain't got no nickname—just Medina Base Ball Club." They recalled some of the players on the club: "There be Alden, Floyd, Fenn, Larson, Frazier, Hard, Reese, Ainsworth, Sexton and Hobart. S. B. Woodward's a member too but not on the first nine. He lots of times umps the games 'cause he knows the rules pretty good. It was on his land that you saw the boys playin.'" Taking turns the men recited the details of games past. We learned that the first game was against the "Star" team from Seville. It was a road game for Medina. The game was on a Tuesday, August 27, at 2 o'clock P.M. The game was characterized as a "social game" rather than a match game. The usual match game conventions, however, were followed. Medina's 17 runs in the first and 30 in the sixth kept Seville from entertaining any hopes of victory. The final was Medina 95, Seville 44. The Star team gave their visitors three cheers and then escorted them down the road to the American House where they shared a congenial meal. Tuesday, the 27th of September, a crowd of a thousand Medina people came out to see the much-talked-about game of baseball with the team from Wooster, Ohio—the "Hope." E. B. Rawson of the Akron Club was on hand to umpire this highly publicized game. Wooster's team should have been called the "hopeless." Medina ran up a scoring tally of 138 runs to Wooster's 41. There was no mention of a friendly dinner following this game. The Seville club came to Medina for a return game at the end of August. One of the locals showed us a newspaper account of the game, here's an exact quote we wrote down: "Notwithstanding the wind blew a strong gale from the north west, both clubs played finely, and about three hundred spectators witnessed the athletic and nimble performance of both clubs."[13] Medina outscored the visitors three to one and at the close of game had a 93–32 advantage. Time of game: three hours and fifteen minutes. Mr. S. B. Woodward of Medina club performed the umpiring duties. Both teams once again adjourned to feast at the American House. The Seville club, following dinner, and we again quote from the local paper, "gave the Medina Club an approving meritorious toast, with three hearty cheers."[14]

The sales clerk was adding up a few items for us, including a couple of base balls, while the hangers-out gave us a final word on baseball in Medina. "There's plans for the fat boys in town to start a team. You have to be at least a hundred and eighty pounds to get in. They sure enough can use the exercise if it don't kill 'em." They then told of some other teams and plans in the county: "There's a team in York," said one. "The town of Wayne has a club too," recalled another. And a third said, "I heard tell of a rumor that at the fair grounds over in Seville two $50 prizes would be put up if a tournament of county ball clubs could be got together." We then said our good-bys and thanked them for the conversation. One fellow then asked us, "Where's ya bound." "Mansfield," we told him. "That's a way in a wagon," says he. "We ain't in no hurry, besides we got a letter to write," says we.

Your Correspondents,
Zeke and Eb

Mansfield

In the first week of May 1867 the Exercise B.B.C. and the Mansfield B.B.C. (both formed in 1866) combined to form the new "Mansfield Club." Hedges Grove on East Market Street had a large empty lot next to it. The ball team moved its playing field to that space, abandoning their field near the old depot. The better location, with a superior diamond, would host a number of first class match games in 1867. Serious combat, to test the mettle of the reconstituted "Mansfields," was planned against the "Washington Club," the pride and joy of Ashland, Ohio. The Mansfield boys arrived in Ashland on Friday, May 24. A large crowd was on hand when J. C. Stubbs of Raleigh, North Carolina, the umpire, called for the start of play. For three hours Mansfield rolled up the score. A final outburst of 14 runs in the ninth gave them an even 100. Ashland managed but 30.

The list of batting orders and runs scored per player, as it appeared in the Mansfield paper:

MANSFIELD CLUB	Runs	WASHINGTON CLUB	Runs
G.W. Blymer, rf	11	S. B. Jacobs, 2b	4
G. Thomas, ss	11	Pancoast, 3b	3
R. H. Rowland, p.	13	L. S. Saner, p.	4
L. A. Strong, c.	12	John Landis, cf	3
J. Bell, 3b	12	C. E. McCluskey, lf	3
J. Hade, lf	12	J. McClusky, ss	2
Geo. Snyder, 2b	10	A. F. Ford, 1b	4
J. Cobean, 1b	7	H. A. Saner, rf	5
W. Dougherty, cf	12	E. Skeets, c.	2
Total:	100	Total:	30

"The Mansfield Club will have 'foemen worthy of their steel.'"[15] That's the description given to the "Lenape" club from Delaware, Ohio. They were coming to Mansfield in the second week of June. A crowd estimated at "not less than two thousand"[16] showed up at the East Market Street ball field. All the people were surprised at the result, including the Mansfield ball players: they easily beat the Delaware team 70–28. There was now some giddy talk of Mansfield being able to beat any team in Ohio for a state championship. Galion, Ohio, was the site on Saturday, June 29, of Mansfield's next game in its drive for state recognition. The game started a little late, at three o'clock, in front of a large audience. A much smaller audience saw the finish. The seventh inning was the final due to darkness. The reason it was dark was because Mansfield was so busy crossing the plate they had used up all the daylight. Score: Mansfield 106, "Resolute" of Galion 39.

Akron was scheduled to be Mansfield's next victim at the end of July. The game was in Akron. Akron, however, proved to be no pushover. Somewhere along the line those Akron boys had learned to play ball too: Akron 46, Mansfield 31.

Schism: A split between the first nine of the Mansfield club and the balance of the club membership ended in late August, when the first nine withdrew and formed a new team called the "Independent." Dr. J. N. Mowry was elected president and George H. Bowman vice-president. The team quickly became known around Ohio as the "Independents of Mansfield." Starting in 1868, they would head down the road to professionalism and national recognition.

Norwalk

The Firelands region is formed by Erie, Ottawa, and Huron counties. The city of Norwalk is in the heart of Huron County. Originally, the state of Connecticut held land rights to the area, and had granted property parcels to its citizens who lived in towns burned by the British in the American Revolution, thus the Firelands name. Platt Benedict and Elisha Whittlesey led the settlers from Norwalk, Connecticut, who founded Norwalk, Ohio. With an eye toward history, the group that gathered in the offices of T. H. Kellogg to start a ball team decided the club would be called the "Firelands." The team elected officers, and agreed to play by the rules now governing baseball as a national amateur sport. These rules, from the National Association of Base Ball Players, were printed in the town paper, The *Norwalk Reflector*. One rule — number eleven — specifically defined a professional player, simply: one who played for money. It went on to state that members were not allowed to use professionals, and that umpires must not allow them in games. If an umpire could not enforce the rule he must quit the game in question, and the results of such a game would not count as an officially sanctioned match game. Non-members of the Association were encouraged to follow the spirit of all the rules and the ideal behind them. The Firelands had some rules of their own. Each member of the club was required to show up for practice, and to pony up a dollar to cover membership, equipment, and other cost. Formed at the beginning of August, the Firelands challenged a neighboring town to a "home and home match" (best two out of three) in the second week of August. The match would start on the road against the Fremont club known as the "Croghan." Practice now took on an air of serious urgency.

There were in Norwalk, that summer, others in need of practice of various types. The young son of Mr. C. V. Fay needed practice in the art of dodging wagons. The youngster, age seven, was playing baseball near the Presbyterian Church — in the street. A vehicle coming down Main Street hit him square on. He was badly shaken up but fortunately not seriously hurt.

The "Terribles" and the "Horribles" were "muffin nines," and their need for practice was acute. They were the respected retailers of Norwalk. The former were from the south side and the latter from the north side of Main Street. They played at the Fair Grounds. Home runs were so numerous no one bothered to count them, or if they did, they soon quit. The same went for errors. It was enough work keeping track of the "Terribles'" 78 runs and the "Horribles'" 59. The large crowd laughed from start to finish. When the tired teams called an end to the show after but six innings no one complained. After all, it had taken them four hours to get that far.

NORWALK AT FREMONT

Ready or not, on August 9 the Firelands were in Fremont. They were not ready. The Croghan pitcher, Mr. Downs, had a pitch "very swift and peculiar."[17] The pitch, perhaps an early curve ball, gave Norwalk difficulty all day. *Norwalk Reflector*: "...and as a chronicler of passing events, it becomes our duty to record, at least, the result; otherwise we might be induced to drop the matter in disgust."[18] Whatever the Fremont pitcher was pitching, it was better than whatever Mr. Perkins of Norwalk was throwing. The final score was Fremont 74 and Norwalk 27.

MONROEVILLE AT NORWALK

Norwalk Reflector: "This being the first amusement of this kind ever offered our citizens, a large crowd was on the grounds to witness the sport."[19] August 19 was a Monday, and at 2:25 P.M. the visiting Monroeville "No Names," having won the coin toss, chose to take the field. The day started with a bright sky and a hot temperature. By game time clouds had rolled in and left it overcast for the rest of the day, making the fielders happy about not having to fight the sun on fly balls. There were one thousand spectators, "a majority of the number being composed of the fair sex,"[20] who were glad to leave their sunbrellas folded. Captain Keenan, the Norwalk catcher, stepped into the batter's box, in the pitcher's box, Brown, the Monroeville pitcher, gave the umpire a nod and the game began. Kennan stroked a beautiful single into right field for the Firelands— the first match game hit in the city of Norwalk. The game was close for three innings. In the fourth the hometown team put up 27 runs. The game was never in question after that. The Norwalk pitcher, Read, was the hitting star of the day—he hit five home runs. His teammates chipped in with nine more. The "No Names" had no home runs, and with their pitcher Brown giving up 89 runs, they had no win.

Score: Norwalk 89, Monroeville 50. Umpire: John G. Hamilton, Penfield Club.

FIRELANDS		MONROEVILLE	
Players	*Runs*	*Players*	*Runs*
Kennan, c	12	Lewis, c	6
Read, p	12	Gann, 2d. b	5
Penfield, 2b	9	Cooner, lf	7
Wickham, rf	8	Brown, p	3
Randolph, ss	11	Carabin, rf	6
Culp, lf	8	Stenz, ss	7
Hoyt, 1b	7	Houston, 3d. b	4

FIRELANDS		MONROEVILLE	
Players	Runs	Players	Runs
Perkins, cf	11	Bennett, 1st. b	6
Parker, 3d. b	11	Prentiss, cf	6
Total	89	Total	50

Inning	1	2	3	4	5	6	7	8	9	Final
Firelands	3	6	11	27	1	6	5	15	15	89
Monroeville	10	5	11	11	0	7	0	4	2	50

CLYDE AT NORWALK

Saturday, August 24, the "McPherson" ball club of Clyde, Ohio, came to Norwalk to play the "Firelands." The hometown favorites handily won the tilt with 71 runs to the visitors' 40.

Batting orders

FIRELANDS	McPHERSONS
Kennan, c.	Blanchard, c.
Reed, p.	Odell, p.
Penfield, cf	Eaton, ss
Wickham, rf	Manger, 1b
Case, 2b	Stark, 2b
Culp, lf	Harkness, 3b
Hoyt, 1b	Hatfield, lf
Perkins, ss	Parker, cf
Parker, 3b	Welker, rf

Inning	1	2	3	4	5	6	7	8	9	Final
Firelands	9	8	4	17	8	0	10	10	5	71
McPhersons	5	9	3	3	1	4	6	3	6	40

FREMONT AT NORWALK

With two solid wins, was the Firelands club now ready for the return match with the Croghans?

September 3, 1867: It was a high-scoring affair and a close game till the finish. The Firelands knocked out eight home runs to the Croghans' three. After eight innings the Firelands clung to a one-run lead, 74–73. They then pushed 10 across the plate in the top of the ninth to take an 11-run lead. Fighting back in their last at-bat, the Croghans added 5 to their 73 — then the fight went out of them and it was all over.

Final: Norwalk 84, Fremont 78. Umpire: W. H. Cutter of the Occidental Club of Cleveland. Time of game: Four hours and five minutes.

The teams then retired to the local edition of the American House for an enjoyable dinner. The esteemed Mr. Rainey, manager of the American, was their host. Fremont departed for home on the 10:45 P.M. train.

The "Arctics" was a second Norwalk team, formed in the closing days of August. The nickname, a popular one around the country this year, was attributed to Secretary of State William Seward's purchase of the territory of Alaska (dubbed by the popular press as "Seward's Folly"). It was also a humorous response to "Firelands." Two victories of the Arctics were recorded. They beat the Monroeville "No Names" 73–43 and a team from nearby Peru 57–15.

In late October, the Norwalk ball clubs merged to form a new team called the "Maple City" — the nickname for the city of Norwalk itself.

The area in and around Norwalk had a higher concentration of ball clubs than did other sections of northern Ohio in 1867. There were "Bay City," of Sandusky; "Eureka," of Fremont; "Union," of Shelby; "Nameless," of Plymouth; "Stars," of New London; a team in Brighton, and all those mentioned earlier.

TOLEDO AT NORWALK

Toledo had a team of two years' standing called the "Quicksteps." They had gained a measure of notoriety by knocking off the nationally recognized Detroit Club of Detroit, Michigan. The Quicksteps came to town to play the Firelands on Friday, September 14, 1867. The game started under a deep-gray overcast sky. The Quicksteps, as expected, dominated. In the fifth inning it started to rain. When the rain came down even harder in the sixth, it was decided, with the Toledo team well in command of the contest, to call it a day.

Score: Toledo Quicksteps 44, Norwalk Firelands 15. Mr. Knapp, of the Alert Ball Club of Rochester, New York, filled the job of umpire.

Norwalk would host a baseball tournament in late autumn — more about that later.

Cleveland

Employers and their employees in Cleveland and its suburbs fell victims to the baseball fever and formed teams this year. The Lakeshore and the C & P railroads had teams. The *Leader* and *Herald* newspapers had teams. So did the shoe manufacturers: O'Hare, Petty & Bruce, along with Griffith Bros. & Kennard, played for an in-house bat-and-ball prize.

Institutions also succumbed to the epidemic. In the suburb of Newberg workers at the mental hospital had their "Asylum" team, and the tax collectors of the Internal Revenue (with headquarters in the Customs House) had their "Infernals" team.

The Forest City Base Ball Club in April elected James Clark president and William Hudson vice-president for 1867. The Railway Club conducted a little business of their own. They joined the National Association of Base Ball Players, thereby further enhancing their image as a first-rate club.

Game Day

Friday, May 30, 1867, was the first exciting baseball match of the year. The Forest City and the Railway contested for the prize bat and ball.

The club members prepared the grounds for the late afternoon start. Using stakes and wire, they formed a circle around the playing area to hold back the crowd (a standard procedure). Benches were set out for the club's special guests — the ladies. It was impossible by 2 o'clock to find any kind of seat on the Kinsman line. The horse-drawn busses were full — their platforms packed, even the roofs heavy with humanity. Hundreds more were seen walking toward the ballpark. The more prosperous sporting bloods and their guests arrived in carriages and buggies of all description; they parked around the circle and watched the game in comfort.

At the park, friends of the Forest City gathered on the right side of the field, and those of the Railway on the left. As for the youngsters, they were "in tree tops, on fences and other eligible positions."[21]

The *Herald* counted a crowd of about three thousand. The *Plain Dealer* said four thousand.

FOREST CITY	RAILWAY UNION
Clark, c.	Doubleday, c.
Gorham, rf	Scotten, p.
McEwen, 2b	Spade, ss
Stockley,	Hardenberg, 1b
Scates, cf	Hattersley, 2b
Hurlbut, ss	Davis, 3b
Hamms, lf	Rouse, lf
Smith, A. J., 3b	Baker, cf
Vilas, 1b	Melton, rf

John Van Valsor, of the powerful Niagara Club of Buffalo, was umpire. Police and "specials" (security guards) worked the game. When they had "set back"[22] the crowd the contest began.

Deafening cheers, clapping hands, thrown hats, and women waving handkerchiefs followed each success of a favored club.

The Railway men, accustomed to physical labor, were muscular in build. Throughout the game they powered long fly balls to the deepest part of the outfield. The Forest City men, sons of the gentry, had a more wiry appearance. Their fielding, place hitting, and base stealing showed they had mastered the "science to the game."[23]

The Forest City took an early lead and kept it. The Railway patronage took heart in the seventh, when their team scored a bundle of runs, but in the end they couldn't catch up.

Final: Forest City 51, Railway 26.

The two clubs celebrated their sporting comradeship by dining together at the Kennard House.

Inning	1	2	3	4	5	6	7	8	9	Final
Railway Union	1	2	4	1	8	0	7	3	0	26
Forest City	11	7	2	1	6	9	12	3	6	57

Notes: • Forest City—Captain A. R. "Pikey" Smith was unavailable for the game. • Once again, as was common in the first few years of match game play, the accounts dwelt more on the social setting surrounding the event than on the game itself.

The College Boys Come to Town

It was a very hot Friday in Cleveland on June 29, 1867. The Reserve team of Hudson, Ohio, composed of the college men of that place, had just finished two weeks of duties leading up to commencement ceremonies. They had had little time for ball practice, but they were in good spirits as they arrived in Cleveland to challenge for the trophy bat and ball. The Forest City, if victorious, would (according to the somewhat puzzling rules) retire the trophy.

At twenty-three after three the circle was formed and the bases laid out. The Forest City, the coin toss winners, chose the field. The crowd, estimated at three thousand, let out a resounding cheer as the teams took their positions.

The Cleveland Forest City would now try to win a second victory over the Hudson visitors. Cleveland took the lead from the start and kept it until the final inning. Then Hudson managed to forge ahead, taking a 3-run lead.

Cleveland came to bat in the bottom of the ninth determined to win their prize. One run crossed the plate, then another. One more would tie it, but before that third run could be earned, the third out was made. The Forest City had lost their first-prize game, and had also lost a chance to retire the trophy.

Score: Reserve of Hudson 37, Cleveland Forest City 36.

The Forest City challenged the Reserves to a rematch on the spot, and it was accepted.

The teams retired to the Kennard House for dinner. Following that meal, the winners marched out the door with the trophy and headed home to Hudson. Earlier in the day the Occidentals (close associates of the Forest City Club), using their "second-nine," defeated the "second-nine" of the Hudson team 67–55 at the Kinsman Grounds.

Nines: Black and White

The land area near the Forest City grounds, between Kinsman and Scoville streets, provided space for many of the local teams to practice. One Saturday in late September, a *Plain Dealer* reporter counted twenty-two different teams working out there. He noted that "Two of the clubs were composed of Negroes."[24]

The first Cleveland Negro baseball teams were named "Twilight"[25] and "Manhood."[26] The new Cleveland Caucasian teams for 1867 were "Amateur," "Athletic," "Benicia," "Comet," "Contest," "Cuyahoga," "Dramatic," "Mechanics," "Mystic," "Shakespeare," and "Zouave."

The "Iron" and "Ironside" were playing southeast of Cleveland in Newberg. The original East

Cleveland had its "Clumsy" club. Collamer to the northeast called its team the "Academy," and present-day Bedford fielded the "Mayflowers" and the "Ivanhoes."

Too Small a Revenge

The local press was not very amused by the return match between the Forest City and the Reserves, held at the Kinsman site. Cleveland did not bludgeon the Reserves for the humiliating loss they suffered in late June. As a result, the papers were very sparing in their July 27, 1867, accounts of the game. There was an estimated crowd of five thousand watching as Cleveland barely recovered its prize, hanging on to win by a mere two runs, 40–38.

The papers, however, did go out of their way to highlight one incident of the game. One reporter said that Captain Smith of the Forest City had been injured recovering a ball that had gone under a horse. Another added that the horse had kicked him, and a third stated that the kick was in the arm, but that the captain was expected to recover.

August

The mid–August Forest City home game against Akron (chronicled in the section on Akron) was the warm-up game for the August 23, 1867, trophy challenge from the Railway Union. Concerning the prize bat and ball, the *Herald* wrote: "[the Railways have] an itching, or more properly a 'hankering' after them."[27] Five thousand friends of the two teams were at the game, many of them of the "fairer sex."

The *Herald's* man thought it would be rather witty to tell the public of overheard female comments on the game: "Such expressions as: 'why don't you catch it you silly thing!' 'Why, what a spooney to risk so much!' 'Run, run, you great dunce!' 'You dear fellow, that was fine!' 'Don't miss it you scamp!' ... and a thousand others...."[28]

The Railways played well for the first half hour, then the scoring all went the Forest City's way. The Forest City's play in the fourth inning was singled out for base stealing, a talent they were becoming noted for.

The Railways in the last inning made a gallant run at the Forest City. The game had to be delayed a number of times until the cheering died down. The Railways plated 12 runs in this comeback, but their total of 40 fell short of the Forest City's 48.

Cleveland Herald: "[the game] on the whole presented an animated and lively scene."[29]

A September to Remember

The Forest City booked some outstanding clubs for the month of September. The "crack" team from Buffalo, New York — the "Niagaras"— was booked for the fifth of September. The Toledo club, the "Quicksteps," was due September 12, and Detroit would play a rubber match in Cleveland the eighteenth. Detroit had come to town last fall and won 36–18; in Detroit, on the Fourth of July, Cleveland had won 30–22.

Niagaras

September started poorly for the home team. The *Cleveland Herald*: "B.B. Items— The Forest City Club was defeated by the Niagara club, yesterday, by a score of 66–11."[30]

Quicksteps

Things improved the following week. "A beautiful day and a field in fine condition...drew to the Kinsman street grounds yesterday afternoon one of the best crowds of the season." The game started at 2:45. The fielding by both teams was excellent. In what was a relatively low scoring game Cleveland won 32–22, with the players "remembering throughout the contest that a ball-player could likewise be a gentleman."[31] As was customary, the contestants dined together at the Kennard House after the game.

DETROITS

In the Detroits game, Cleveland played well in the field, keeping the score close until the eighth when Detroit made ten. Captain "Pikey," Hurlbut, and Scates homered — the latter having hit 2. Detroit hit 7 home runs and won the game.

Umpire: D. M. Ferry, Detroit Club. Time of game: 2h. 45m.

Junior Trophy

September 5, 1867: "The prize bat and ball for the Western Reserve Junior Clubs, presented to the Occidental by citizens of Cleveland, and which they are to hold for one year before becoming permanent owners, has arrived from New York. The ball is made of silver and the bat is silver mounted rosewood."[32] The prize cost $75.

The "Penfields" of Oberlin came to town on September 26, 1867, to play the Forest City, but not for the trophy.

Oberlin had now been declared a junior organization. This fact pleased the senior Forest City, but vexed their understudies, the Occidental, who would eventually have to defend their "junior" prize against a very good Oberlin club.

A large crowd had assembled on the Kinsman Grounds, and at a quarter to four the Oberlin versus Cleveland game began. The visitors took to the bat first. For four and a half innings fielding dominated, with the Forest City up by only a run, 8–7. The Forest City, however, then started to pull away, starting with 5 in the fifth.

A most unusual home run occurred in the sixth. McEwen, as he was heading for the plate, ran into second baseman Churchill of Oberlin, "their heads coming together like those of belligerent rams.... McEwen fell stunned, and for a moment insensible, when captain Smith, with an eye to the score, seized him by the foot and deposited the brogan on the iron plate."[33]

The Forest City continued to score, and at the close of the eighth, both teams agreed to call the match over, Cleveland winning by a final score of 36–13.

Cleveland Herald: "Scates of the Forest City was in his element and made some most magnificent fly catches over in his corner, in the left field.... But he had a dangerous rival in the person of a colored man, named Younger, who played left field for the Penfield nine, and played it well; creditable to any club."[34]

Younger was the first black man, known by name, to play baseball on the Western Reserve and in Cleveland. (More about the illustrious life of Mr. Simpson Younger on and off the field appears in chapters to come).

Time of game: 2 hrs. Umpire: Mr. Riley, Railway Club.

The Great Baseball Tournament at Norwalk

The people of Norwalk were much taken by the baseball fever. Several leading citizens decided that what was needed to close out the year of 1867 was a baseball tournament. They formed the Western Reserve Base Ball Association. It was a stock company and it raised $775 for "premiums" (cash prizes).[35]

It was hoped the substantial offer of money would draw teams of national, state, and regional reputation. The prizes would be awarded by category in a playoff format.

First prize — Open to the world, $300.00; Second prize — Open to the world, $200.00; Third prize — Confined to Ohio, $100.00; Fourth prize — Congressional district (9th), $75.00; Fifth prize — Huron County, $50.00; Sixth prize — Best thrower of a base ball, $25.00; Seventh prize — Best runner of bases, $25.00

The late October tournament was scheduled for Tuesday the twenty-first through Friday the twenty-forth. The games would be held at the Norwalk Fair Grounds.

Teams took trains to Norwalk from Cleveland, Toledo, and other places. One of the other places was Mansfield. The decision of the "Independents" to compete in the tournament was last-minute: Thursday evening at 8 P.M., accompanied by a number of citizens, the Mansfield players went to nearby Monroeville to jump a Norwalk-bound freight, not scheduled for passengers.

The train slowed enough for all to board except "our friend 'Cal' the scorer of the Independents, who was not nimble enough, but joined us next morning."[36]

Hotels in Norwalk were filled. Wandering the streets at a late hour, the Mansfield team and friends were on their own. Luckily, most of the boys were given a place to sleep by the obliging landlady over at the Farmer's Exchange.

At the Norwalk Fair Grounds, "Two games can be played at the same time without at all interfering with each other, while a thousand can be seated while watching the progress of the game."[37] The local teams played for the smaller prizes on Tuesday and Wednesday. The big boys went after the big money on Thursday and Friday.

The New London "Star" surprised the average baseball expert by making it into the final rounds, but the big-boy Cleveland Railways quickly disposed of the upstart locals by a 20-run margin (no score given). The Railways then met the "Union" of Toledo and lost 38–24.

Friday was the final round for the $300 first prize. Mansfield versus Forest City was the elimination game for the right to play the Toledo team for the big money. Laboring under the disadvantages of not having his regular catcher, and of injuries to three of the starting nine, Mansfield pitcher Rowland pitched a very fine game but was not supported in the field. In the end the Forest City won 32–16.

In the afternoon the Forest City and Union of Toledo played the final game: "The playing of both clubs was magnificent, and well worth going a long way to see."[38] The Forest City lost 39–27.

The Union of Toledo came in for some criticism for having combined, just before the tournament, the best players of the "Quicksteps" and of the "Union," and then playing under the name of "Union of Toledo." The Norwalk-based "Association" let the Toledo merger stand (after all, their Norwalk ball club had done the same thing somewhat earlier). The two Cleveland teams, that had not combined, complained the loudest.

The base-running and ball-throwing contests were held off until Saturday, in hopes of recovering some of the expected box office losses by scheduling an additional day of tournament.

William Hollinger of the Mansfield Club, using a lighter-than-usual baseball and throwing into the wind, won the throwing contest and the $25. His toss was 285 feet and 9 inches. Trembly of Toledo took the running prize of $25 by rounding the bases in fifteen and a quarter seconds.

The Cleveland teams didn't stick around for Saturday. Their train arrived at the Cleveland Union Station at 9:45 Friday evening. Cleveland baseball enthusiasts had had very high hopes for the Cleveland teams at the tournament. Their disappointment was summed up by the *Leader*'s sportswriter: "We pause for a few moments to permit our lachrymal organs to distill a few silent tears, and then rush on the pencil."[39]

WINNERS AND LOSERS
COUNTY PRIZE—$50.

Nameless, of Plymouth; Alert, of Bellevue; Star, of New London; Maple City, of Norwalk.... Taken by the Star.

DISTRICT PRIZE—$75.

Croghan, of Fremont; Star, of New London; Resolute, of Galion; Maple City, of Norwalk.... Taken by the Resolute.

STATE PRIZE—$100.

Union, of Toledo; Maple City, of Norwalk; Railway Union, of Cleveland.... Taken by the Union, of Toledo.

CITIZENS PURSE — $200.
Railway Union, of Cleveland; Star, of New London.... Taken by the Railway Union.
FIRST PRIZE — $300.
Union, of Toledo; Forest City, of Cleveland; Independent, of Mansfield.... Taken by the Union.[40]

The tournament was well managed, with all of the games played and prize money awarded. It was not a financial success, however. The very cold weather and the non-attendance of a number of first-class clubs, notably the "Niagaras" of Buffalo and the "Excelsiors" of Rochester, were blamed for the light crowds.

The tournament in Norwalk was preceded by a local mini-tournament in Medina, and another one downstate in Cincinnati. The popular idea was imported from back East.

Prize money would be a first step in the inevitable evolution of baseball into a professional game. Those who lamented the gradual loss of traditions surrounding the amateur "gentlemen's" game of baseball would soon have to find what measure of contentment they could in watching another less popular but unchanging sport: cricket.

1868

Case Commons

Leonard Case Jr. is the Case in today's Case Western Reserve University. He was also the Case in yesteryear's Case Commons — a large area of green land that he owned and allowed the public to use as a park. His father, Leonard Case, Sr., is credited with giving Cleveland the nickname Forest City.

The Forest City Base Ball Club and the Union Railway Base Ball Club, operating officially as the Cleveland Base Ball Association, built an enclosed ballpark on a parcel of land within the Case Commons. The newspapers usually referred to the park as the Association Grounds.

Plans for 1868 included a series of showcase games. The two Association teams would play the best baseball teams in America. Cleveland was a city on the move up, and Cleveland baseball, with a little help from its friends, hoped to join that upward movement and be in the inner circle of the country's elite teams — soon.

The Association and the press worked together to convince the public that the rather costly 50-cent admission charge to these special games was not too high. They argued that the expense already incurred erecting the facility, the ongoing cost of maintenance, and the money needed to cover the "incidental" cost of the famous visiting teams, made the close-to-break-even charge a reasonable one. They felt certain that if the public would support their efforts this year, admission prices could be rolled back in the not-to-distant future.

They had done their civic duty. Would the citizens of Cleveland now do theirs?

THE ASSOCIATION GROUNDS

The ballpark bordered Scoville Street (Community College Avenue) to the south, and was surrounded by a tall board fence interrupted only by two large entry gates. Running about a hundred or so feet beyond the northern wall was Garden Street (Central Avenue). To the west was Putnam Street (E. 38th) and near the east fence ran Case Avenue (E. 40th).

A portion of Osborne Street (E. 39th) actually ran through the grounds. This north-south route was closed off and would be the source of controversy later on.

The Association let construction contracts for a covered stand with a seating capacity for several hundred. It went up in the northwest corner of the grounds behind home plate, where it helped protect the batters' as well as the patrons' eyes from the glare of the evening sun.

The nearby players' clubhouse had two masts on its roof, from which the colors of the two association teams were flown. A tall "elegant" flagpole went up in the southwestern corner of the grounds.[1] On important game days the banners of the competing teams were raised — visitor's flag flying high on top with the home team's floating just below. The ballpark went up quickly; started in early spring; it was ready for games by the beginning of May.

Cleveland clubs played some games at the new ballpark prior to the special 50-cent games that were to start in June. Some were free and some cost a quarter. A free game between the Willoughby Sorter and the Forest City, and a "junior championship" game between the Peconics and the Occidental, drew some interest in late May.[2]

On June 3, the Railways went to Hudson and defeated their traditional rival the Reserves 44–9. The next day they were scheduled to open their new ballpark.

The Forest City vs. The Union Railway

A large crowd took in the sights of the new ballpark. The beautiful banners flying over the clubhouse gave color to an otherwise gray overcast sky. The Forest City flag was a white field trimmed in blue with an English-style F. C. on it. The Railway flag, also on a white ground, was trimmed in red with the design of a locomotive in the center.

The assembled throng cheered as the players left the clubhouse and entered the field of play. The Forest City wore white short-collared shirts, long dark pants with the cuffs rolled up, white hats, white belts, and spiked brogan shoes. The only description of the Railway outfit was that "The Railway uniform is simply checked caps and pantaloons."[3]

The Forest City won the coin toss and chose to take the field. The game started at 3:15, with the "bat and ball" trophy at stake. The Railways took the lead with 5 runs in the first and never relinquished it. The seventh inning was the last inning played due to threatening weather.

Inning	1	2	3	4	5	6	7	Final
Railway Union	5	2	3	5	1	0	5	21
Forest City	0	4	0	2	1	7	0	14

The Railways now held the prize bat and ball for the first time.

The Brooklyn Atlantics vs. The Union Railway

Wednesday, June 17, 1868, brought Game I of the showcase series. Transportation to the big game was available on the street railway lines of the East Cleveland and Kinsman companies (these streetcars were pulled by horses over railway tracks set in the street). Horse-drawn wheeled omnibuses called "specials" were also run game day.[4] They left from the Weddell House hotel downtown and went direct to the park. Fare was a quarter.

The Association charge of 50 cents was lowered to a quarter for ladies. They made up a sizable portion of a crowd estimated to be three thousand. A second crowd of mostly youngsters was in the trees overlooking the western fence — they were a capacity crowd. The free branches also offered shade, while most of the paying customers inside had to stand and endure the unbearably hot weather.

From a distance the arriving customers could see the colors of the two teams flying from the tall flagpole. Drawing closer to the mast, they could make out a crouching tiger on a field of blue — the striking symbol of the Atlantics— and below this the flag of the Railway.

Shortly after 2 o'clock, several players of the two "nines" took the field, "practicing with a ball, throwing to each other to get their 'hands in.'"[5]

The Atlantics won the coin toss and took the field attired in "white woolen caps and shirts, trimmed with blue; blue flannel pantaloons, and leather brogans, with several long spikes in the soles."[6] Pitcher Zettlein often played the field on days when the competition was judged to be less than "crack." This day, Atlantics player Mr. Pratt got the call to face the Railways' pitcher Mr. Riley.

Harvey Brown of the Forest City, acting as umpire, called start of game at 2:30, and Cleveland baseball enthusiasts settled in to enjoy the talented play of the former "Champion of America."

The *Cleveland Plain Dealer*: "The play of the Atlantics is marked with remarkable coolness and precision, and great skill in every point of the game; each is strong and well proved and the whole work together with the exactness of a machine."[7]

Some of the well-known parts of that machine included twenty-three-year-old Brooklyn-born pitcher George "The Charmer" Zettlein (playing in right field this day); Joe "Old Reliable" Start, at first base; and at third, the outstanding infielder Bob "Death to Flying Things" Ferguson.

The Atlantic Base Ball club of Brooklyn was two years removed from its most recent championship, but their game against Cleveland's Union Railway Base Ball Club in July of 1868 drew a sizable crowd.

Inning after inning the Atlantics circled the bases. Despite the sweltering heat, most of the crowd stayed for the full nine innings. When the last hit had been made and the last run scored, the Atlantics had outscored the Railways by nearly a four-to-one margin. The final: Atlantics 47, Railways 12.

Score

ATLANTICS		RAILWAY UNION	
Players	Runs	Players	Runs
Smith	6	Melton	2
Start	5	Doubleday	3
Chapman	7	Riley	1
Crane	6	Hardenberg	2
Mills	6	Bradbier	2
Ferguson	6	Bouse	2
Pratt	4	Davis	0
Zettlein	5	Frame	0
McDonald	2	Crumbie	0
Total	**47**	**Total**	**12**

Time of game: two hours and forty-five minutes.

Notes: • "The side show consisted of a young man with a very uninviting 'mug' upon his shoulders, selling pictures of the Atlantics for $3."[1] • After the game the Atlantics caught the boat for the next day's game in Detroit.

Teams and Tidbits

Company men: The organization of company teams, a trickle in 1867, was now a flood. The professions, the trades, and the merchant houses fielded ball clubs. Everywhere, there were teams of doctors playing teams of lawyers, teams of plumbers playing teams of streetcar conductors, shoe store clerks playing cigar store clerks, and hardware companies putting uniforms on their men and playing baseball against other men from other hardware companies.

Road game: The Cleveland printers went to play baseball against their brothers—the printers of Detroit.

Word game: The *Cleveland Plain Dealer* and *Cleveland Herald* writers promoted their impending clash with a prose fit for a royal coronation. The *Plain Dealer's* "Ironclads" beat the "Red Hots" of the *Herald*, 29–18. Had the winners had their way, the account of the glorious day would have been front-page news.

"Muffin" games were popular this year. Several games featured local celebrities, with the gate money going to some favored charity.

Throughout the region the names of small towns and their teams made print for the first time. Ads in Cleveland and Oberlin newspapers trumpeted this or that retailer's superior supply of baseball equipment. Sporting news items now told of one promising young player's addition to, or another popular older player's retirement from, this team or that team. Teams were referred to as "junior" or "senior" organizations based on age, with the exact criterion being less than clear.

The "Independents" of Mansfield, led by John Clapp ("imported" from across state lines) were lining up "match game" dates with the best competition they could find. There was little doubt as to Mansfield's being a "senior team"—one looking for national recognition.

Mansfield won several games against top competition, including defeating Akron 39–16 and the Cleveland Railways 27–13.

Mansfield, however, was embarrassed in early August in a 40–19 drubbing by their strongest opponent—the Cleveland Forest City. In a return match, in late August, they came close to upsetting the Forest City, losing by only 4 runs, 26–22.

Nicknames, such as the "Farmer," the "Banker," "Japanese Tommy" (he wasn't), "The Man From Morgan County" and others, helped personalize the players and, with the aid of the press, develop a loyal following. A typical Mansfield Independents lineup:

>"Banker" Rowland, p
>John Clapp, c
>"Farmer" Hade, 1b
>Burns, 2b
>Jimmy Cobean, ss
>"Japanese Tommy" Deitz, of
>Clugston, of
>"The Man from Morgan County" Strong, of
>Webber, of
>Hunt, of

The Philadelphia Athletics vs. The Cleveland Forest City

Wednesday, June 24, 1868 — Game II of the showcase series: "The weather was pleasant, but cloudy enough to cool the atmosphere."[9] The game started late, due to the absence of one of the Forest City men. The Athletics took the fifteen-minute delay to demonstrate their throwing, hitting, and batting skill. The Athletics were also known for superior base-stealing skill, and for not chatting too much on the field. Their uniforms too were noteworthy: "Their dress is peculiarly characteristic of the Quaker City [Philadelphia], being a grey shirt and pants, decidedly the most neat and least ostentatious uniform ever worn in this city."[10] The uniform also had a large letter A on the front.

Six Athletic players—Ned Cuthbert, lf; John Radcliff, c; "Cherokee" Fisher, 3b; "Count" Sensenderfer, cf; Dick McBride, p; and Al Reach, rf—would go on to careers in the major league when it started in a few years. Al Reach would also go on to a career as a sporting-goods magnate; the line of sporting goods today called Reach bears his name. Mr. Reach, however, missed this game due to an injury.

Having won the toss, the Athletics went into the field at 3:15 to start the game. In the pitching box was hard throwing Dick McBride. Many believed he was the best pitcher in America, as well as the fastest. His catcher could offer testimony as to his speed. In the first inning McBride nailed his battery mate with a fast one on the knee: "He remained upon the ground trembling for a minute or two, as though he would faint."[11] He recovered, but in the second inning switched positions with the left fielder Cuthbert.

The Forest City man chosen as the pitcher and sacrificial lamb was Charles Brown. The Athletics answered the Forest City's 2 runs in the first with 10 in their half of the inning.

And so it went — with every Forest City score the Athletics responded in their turn, putting up double digits in five of the frames. "It was evident, from the beginning, that the Athletics were playing to make all they could, and in this respect they pleased the spectators to a greater degree than did the Atlantics—a club that played to win, but not to win all that could possibly be made."[12] And win they did, the score 85 for Philadelphia and but 11 for Cleveland.

Despite all the run-scoring, only one home run was hit. Tom Berry of Philadelphia hit a 3-run homer in the seventh. The men in the audience gave him a nice round of applause, and the ladies waved their handkerchiefs.

Oberlin Resolutes

The Oberlin "Resolutes" were considered by baseball insiders as the best of the junior organizations. The team was formed from the best players on last year's "Penfields" and "Business" clubs. There was another Oberlin ball club this year called the "Fairchilds," but they were no match for the new "Resolutes."

Simpson Charles Younger of the former "Penfields" was now a member of the "Resolutes," and the only black man on the only integrated ball club on the Western Reserve.

Simpson came to Oberlin in 1854 at age four, along with his sister Katherine and mother Elizabeth, after being freed from slavery in Missouri by the children's father, white slave owner Charles H. L. Younger. Simpson was educated in the Oberlin schools, and at age thirteen, after several attempts to join the army, was made a member of the United States Colored Troops in January of 1864. He was one of the youngest soldiers to tote a gun and see action in the Civil War. He wrote a number of poems in later life about his beliefs and experiences concerning the war.

The Resolutes came to Cleveland on July 21, 1868, to play the Occidentals for the junior trophy. Simpson Younger pitched and they won the game. The Oberlin-based *Lorain County News*: "Bat and ball are ours, Score 43 to 13. 'Hip!' The exultant monosyllable is pardonable. Well done, Resolutes."[13]

Throughout the summer the Resolutes won all the trophy games. Their only problem seemed to be which store window in Oberlin — the one of Goodrich Co. or the one of Fitch & Fairchild — would display the bat and ball from week to week.

Some Resolutes wins along the victory trail: The Occidentals, visiting Oberlin, were defeated on the Tappan Square. The local city of Brighton was beaten. The strong Charter Oaks of Cleveland lost 58–12. And in a game played at Sandusky, the Maple City of Norwalk was defeated 31–24. An extract from a poem written by a player from the champion Resolutes team of 1868, "How the Resolutes Won the Junior Championship":

> Have you heard of the educational Hub
> And its old time, invincible, Resolute Club?
> Of Anson Burwell and Stevens and Good,
> Of Younger and Austin Burwell and Todd,
> Of Reed and Grannis and L. B. Platt,
> And the things they did with the Ball and Bat —
> How they set the Western Reserve ablaze
> In the redden, golden, Oberlin days?
> To the college faculty, then, athletics

> Was a mild form of sin like the use of cosmetics.
> They smiled, we must own, at the Club's renown
> But the smile was O'ercaste with the shade of a frown.
> Compare with your elegant campus, please
> The old little ball ground bordered by trees.
> The infield that kept us all 'in the air,'
> The backstop that we wished was there.
> The plank walk in right that was all too real
> When we hurled it backward with nimble heel,
> The gravel path through the left field laid,
> The young tree in center that gave a good shade,
> And tenderly looking down on all
> The vagabond form of old Tappan Hall,
> Which led the batsmen to boast in vain
> 'By thunder I'll knock out a window pane.
> No mask and no gloves, and no trainer ar' teacher,
> The sod for a grandstand, the walk for a bleacher,
> Cheered on by the students who came out to view,
> And the eyes of the sweet girls, tender and true...."[14]

The silver ball is lost, but the rosewood bat of the junior champions, with the players' names engraved on the silver shield, still survives in the archives of Oberlin College.

The "Champions of America"

The Union of Morrisania vs. the Forest City of Cleveland: "The third of a series of games between the principal clubs of the United States and the leading clubs of Cleveland...."[15]

Friday, July 31, 1868 was a great day for a ball game. The weather was cool with some cloud cover. This was not only a ball game but also a social event. The crowd was large with many ladies and a number of prominent citizens attending — many never having been seen at a ball game before.

The Union was from the town of Morrisania, known today as the Borough of the Bronx of New York City, and was the NABBP's current champion from 1867.

The Union was great at throwing, catching, and stealing bases. The outstanding left-handed pitcher Charles "The Old Woman in the Red Cap" Pabor, future Hall of Fame shortstop George Wright, and that defensive gem, catcher Dave Birdsall, led them.

Remarkably, after four innings had been played, Cleveland led by a run, 6–5. In the fifth the Union plated 8 and they continued to pull away after that.

The Union defense blanked Cleveland in six of the innings including the last three.

Score of the game — Union 25, Forest City 7. Time of game: two hours and thirty-five minutes. Umpire: Mr. Hardenberg of the Railway Union Club.

UNION	Runs	FOREST CITY	Runs
Goldie, 1b	3	J. White, ss	0
Austin, cf	4	Clark, 1b	1
Martin, 2b	2	H. Brown, 3b	1
Pabor, p	2	Hanna, 2b	2
Wright, ss	4	Kirkwood, rf	0
Birdsall, c	1	Smith, c	1
Shelly, 3b	3	Sheffield, c	0
Smith, lf	4	Branch, lf	1
Reynolds, rf	2	C. Brown, p	1
Total	25	Total	7

The Union was so pleased with the turnout in Cleveland, that they agreed to stay and play a game the next day against the Railway Union.

The National Game
The Champion Club vs. Railway Club
Score 43 to 8 — B. B. Notes.

The *Cleveland Herald*: "The Union Club was hardly in as good a condition for playing as upon the previous day, when it defeated the Forest City by a score of 25 to 7. The catcher, particularly, was in bad condition and changed places with the short stop before the close of the game.... Stealing bases is one of the favorite sources of amusement with the champions. They risked much in doing so frequently making the result very exciting.... They had two men put out in succession at the commencement of the fifth inning on fly catches, and joined with the spectators in applause for the brilliant play of the Railway Club. Goldie of the Union Club, made the only home run on the day.... The game was umpired with very good judgment. The day was not very warm, and the attendance was quite large."[16]

Score

UNION	Runs	RAILWAY UNION	Runs
Goldie, 1b	5	Melton, rf	1
Austin, cf	5	Scates, 3b	2
Martin, 2b	4	Riley, p.	1
Pabor, p	3	Crumbie, 2b	0
Wright, ss	6	Bouse, lf	1
Bidsall, c	4	Phelan, ss	1
Shelly, 3b	7	Hardenberg, 1b	0
Smith, lf	6	Hattersly, cf	1
Reynolds, rf	3	White, c	1
Total runs	**43**	**Total runs**	**8**

Inning	1	2	3	4	5	6	7	8	9	Final
Union	5	12	4	3	3	8	2	4	2	43*
Railway Union	0	0	1	2	1	2	1	0	1	8

*The runs for the Union in the box score add up to 43, but in the by-inning graph they add up to 44, though the 43 total was printed in the original paper.

The Western Reserve

To the east, there was no shortage of ball clubs in Ashtabula and Lake counties this season. Painesville had the "Rough and Ready" club; they played a game against the "Eureka" club of Hambden. "Grand River" played in Austinburg; "Tuscan," in Mechanicsville; "Dexter," in North Madison; "Muscle," in New Lyme; and "Athletics" in Hartsgrove. The Geneva "Times" and Geneva "Spencer" each played the "Union" of Ashtabula at the Fairgrounds in Jefferson for a $60 prize put up by the Agricultural Society. Ashtabula took the money with its win over the "Spencer" 51–12.

To the west: Sandusky had a pretty good club called the "Bay City" they also had a not so good club called "Germania." When "Germania" played "Bay City" they were destroyed 117–16. Following this game, the *Sandusky Register* ran a poem about the trials and tribulations that are sometimes connected with

BASE BALL

The noonday sun was pouring down
Upon a meadow sere and brown,
Where stood a youth with bat on high,
Loud to his comrades rang the cry,
        "Base ball!"

He hopes to win himself a name,
By playing soon "a great match game:"
For him 'twill be the greatest fun

To hear the words "Bay Citys won."
        "Base ball!"

His brow was bumped, his eye was black,
His coat was torn from off his back;
But still, like battered bugle rung,
The accents of that swollen tongue,
        "Base ball!"

Around the field he saw the light
Of friendly faces beaming bright,
Just by his head a ball has flown,
And from his lips escapes a groan,
    "Base ball!"

"Now stop the game," the old man said,
"The 'second base' has smashed his head;
The 'pitcher,' too, has sprained his wrist,
The 'umpire's' brains are in a mist,"
    "Base ball!"

"Oh, drop that bat!" the maiden said,
"And make a long 'home run' instead;
A "hot ball" hit him in the eye,
But still he answered with a sigh,
    "Base ball!"

"Beware! you'll soon be out on foul!"
This was the fielder's awful howl;
But still re-echoed in his ear,
In that deep voice, so thick and queer,
    "Base ball!"

"Used up," he sinks upon the ground,
While pitying comrades gathered round,
And in the awful throes of death,
He murmured with his latest breath,
    "Base ball!"

There on the cold earth, spent and gray,
To perfect jelly smashed, he lay,
While o'er the summer fields afar
Was heard the victor's loud huzza,
    "Base ball!"[17]

Big Game Number Four

THE EXCELSIORS OF CHICAGO VS. THE FOREST CITY OF CLEVELAND

The last of the 50-cent games featuring the leading teams of America was to be with the New York "Mutuals." The "Mutes" canceled, but the Association was able to present a pretty good team as a late replacement — the "Excelsiors" of Chicago.

It was cold on September 20, 1868, but the Forest City's bats were even colder. The crowd size was not published, but those who were there became cynical after Chicago had scored 11 unanswered runs in the first two frames. When the Excelsiors had blanked the home team for the first three innings, the crowd started cheering for the Excelsiors to keep up the "goose eggs." In this wish they were not disappointed; Cleveland was shut out in six of the innings.

Score

EXCELSIORS	Runs	FOREST CITY	Runs
Foley, 3b	3	White, c	1
W. Stearns, ss	2	Herse, lf	0
Simmons, 2b	4	Sheffield, c	0
Lex, p	2	Brown, 3b	0
Tracey, lf	3	Johnson, 2b	1
G. Stearns, 1b	1	Smith, ss	1
Lennon, c	1	Hanna, 1b	1
Goodrich, rf	1	Burt, cf	1
Oberlander, cf	2	Taylor, rf	0
Total	19	Total	5

Inning	1	2	3	4	5	6	7	8	9	Final
Excelsiors	4	7	0	2	5	0	0	0	1	19
Forest City	0	0	0	1	0	0	0	2	2	5

The series of games against some of the nation's best teams demonstrated that in order to compete at that level, players must play full time, and in order to play full time they needed to be paid.

In 1868, the National Association of Base Ball Players (NABBP), in effect, recognized the existence of the professional by not banning its members from "match play" for having played on teams that had their paid "ringers"—a practice that had been going on in the East for quite some time anyway.

Cleveland would add professionals, officially, in 1869, but a team in Ohio had gotten a big start in that direction the year before. Cleveland played that team twice in 1868; they were called the Cincinnati "Red Stockings." Six of the nine players who would become famous throughout the nation the following year were in place for the Cincinnati season of 1868.

Two with Cincinnati

CLEVELAND AT CINCINNATI

On Tuesday, August 13, 1868, Cleveland played the "Buckeyes" of Cincinnati — a team of locals considered the town's second best. The Forest City was defeated 18–8. The next day Cleveland had to play Cincinnati's best team — the "Red Stockings."

They lost again.

Inning	1	2	3	4	5	6	7	8	9	Final
Cincinnati	3	5	6	4	3	7	10	2	4	44
Cleveland	4	4	0	0	2	4	2	0	6	22

CINCINNATI AT CLEVELAND

A large audience was in attendance on October 12, 1868; Cleveland won the toss and put Branch in the pitcher's box.

Branch gave up 15 runs in the first inning — "The Red Stockings struck a streak of luck and just knocked the ball all over the field where no one was playing."[18]

The visitors' "streak of luck" kept Mr. Branch from a second inning of work. Riley and White finished the pitching chores. White — perhaps throwing curves (?) — was the more effective of the two because "They couldn't knock them crooked balls [White's] all to pieces no how."[19]

If Cincinnati had played as hard as they could have after the second inning, the game would not have been such a competitive one for seven innings.

Due to the early darkness of October the game was called after eight innings.

Score: Cincinnati 33 Cleveland 14. Time: 2:45. Umpire: Mr. F. J. Phelps of the Detroit Club — Detroit, Michigan. Scorers: Bascom and Rawson.

Inning	1	2	3	4	5	6	7	8	9	Final
Cincinnati	15	6	0	4	3	0	3	0	2	33
Cleveland	1	0	2	2	2	6	1	0	0	14

In addition to the Cincinnati games, Cleveland also played a number of regional games against good "nines" from Detroit, Mansfield, Xenia, and Pittsburgh. The game against the last-named team was particularly gratifying. The Forest City, in front of a home crowd, hit three home runs, beating the Pittsburgh "Mutuals" 39–18.

Columbus Convention

The National Association of Base Ball Players set up state chapters in 1868. To join the NABBP a team had to first join its state chapter. Nine dollars covered a team's entrance fee and dues for the first year of membership. In Ohio teams made application to Recording Secretary Frank Harvey, P. O. Box 711, Cincinnati, Ohio.

On Wednesday, September 30, 1868, the Ohio Association of Base Ball Players held its first convention at Columbus, Ohio. Teams that attended the annual meeting with at least one representative were entitled to two votes.

State conventions made it more convenient for teams to meet than did national conventions. Such meetings were needed; the large explosion of new teams, and questions of professional and amateur status, as well as the regulation and future direction of their sport, demanded more input from the participants.

The "Fats" and "Leans"

A "Muffin Game"—1868

They boarded three omnibuses, of the open-air kind, in front of Dave Price's downtown establishment. They were all local celebrities to one degree or another. Their mission was to have a baseball game for charity.

A muffin game of baseball was meant to be humorous, the players possessing no particular skill for the sport. With the addition of a substantial amount of beer, this muffin game promised to have less skill than most.

Each wagon flew a large flag promoting the game. The first wagon was loaded with Papworth's Band, the musical entertainment for the day. The second wagon carried the "fats," averaging two hundred pounds per man. They wore chipped hats circled with a red ribbon, on which was printed "Heavy Bobs." The third wagon had the "lean" team—they averaged one hundred forty pounds each. They wore the same style chipped hats, but their ribbon was blue and said "Light Bobs."

At 10 A.M., with the three flags flapping in the breeze, the horses pulling the omnibus wagons heard the crack of the whips, and the procession started. To best promote the game the parade was routed through all the principal streets of the downtown, and then out to the Association Grounds. Along the way, stops were made at the newspaper offices, the large hotels, and a restaurant.

Keg party: At the ballpark a barrel of beer was waiting by each of the bases.

Originally they were to be put on top of sawhorses by the bags, but the crowd stole the wood horses for seats.

The Heavy Bobs batted first. Upon arriving at a base or advancing to the next one, a player was allowed to have a drink of beer. In the first inning the "fats" drank a lot more beer than did the "leans."

Notes: • "At the end of each inning both teams adjourned for beer." • "As the game progressed and the frequent libations began to work...supremely ridiculous...stumble and rollover in the dust ... the spectators in a roar of laughter continually." • "Every few minutes appeals were made to the umpire, until he became so annoyed he refused to act."[20]

Winners all: Somewhere around the fifth inning the game came to an end, each team claiming victory. But by that time, no two players could give the same score, much less have a clue as to what the true score might possibly be.

On the way home, some one in the Lights' bus put up a broom to indicate that they had "swept," i.e., won the game.

The Heavys, upon seeing this, put up two brooms on their wagon. The band now joined in the fun, showing six brooms. And rightly so—after all, they were the only ones doing any real playing that day. "The company drove to Dave Price's and separated, each side jubilant over its victory."[21]

1869

The Fence Must Go!

Osborne Street was originally fenced off in 1868 where it passed through the Association Grounds. The action started an ongoing heated debate between residents near the ballpark and the Cleveland Base Ball Association.

Cleveland City Council and Cleveland Board of City Improvements, for reasons of their own, also wanted the obstruction gone. The baseball people claimed they were given permission by

Leonard Case to enclose a portion of his property for a ball field. Residents and their allies said "you just don't close off a street because some powerful individual says you can."

The matter remained in the hands of the city attorney for a year. In May of 1869, City Attorney T. J. Carran decided: "Mr. Leonard Case, being the owner of the property, has given the Base Ball Association permission to occupy it. The property has never been appropriated for a street. Until such a step has been taken, Mr. Case and the association are sole owners and occupants."[1]

The Occidental Base Ball Club was a junior organization that in practice served as a developmental squad for the senior Forest City. They, as well as the Forest City, used and maintained the "old" Kinsman Grounds as their official club field; the Forest City, however, played their important games at the enclosed Association Grounds.

The Forest City Base Ball Club had clubrooms in the Lyman Building. They met there in April, at which time a new constitution was adopted, copies of it being put up at the headquarters and at the ballpark. The club also decided to provide copies for all the membership: "The recording secretary was instructed to cause 300 copies to be printed."[2]

An interesting policy was enacted for the three hundred members (a sort of season ticket):"A certificate of club membership will entitle the holder and ladies to admission in all cases, in carriages and on foot."[3] All others were to pay the posted rates. It was also noted that horses and vehicles, this year, were to be parked outside of the grounds by Case St. (E. 40th).

The waters of the pro game were tested this year. The Forest City Club, however, only went in waist-deep, paying for four "new" men brought in from the outside; a fifth was added later. The rest of the "nine" was drawn from the best of the club's amateurs—the "old" men. Getting paychecks were new men: Arthur Allison, John Ward, John Riley, and Al Pratt. James White, who had been "unofficially" paid in 1868, quit the team after the season. He returned in early August as the fifth "officially" paid player.

The Forest City played amateur teams, including the "Sorters" of Willoughby and the American Club, to prepare for their first big game in June.

* * *

The *Cleveland Herald*: • "The famous Red Stockings, of Cincinnati, will be here in a few days, and the boys will make every exertion to 'warm' them."[4] • "policemen will be in attendance to preserve order."[5]

Cleveland Leader: • "the nine of the Cincinnati Club is, to-day perhaps the most perfectly disciplined organization of its kind ever seen in this country."[6] • "the contest today between the two leading clubs of Ohio will be an event of no secondary interest."[7] • "Tickets of admission are for sale at Rawson's book store and at the entrance gates of the grounds."[8] • "Visitors will take the Kinsman street or Garden street cars both of which run near the grounds."[9]

Cleveland Plain Dealer: • "it is quite probable that the Cincinnati Club may bring the championship west of the Allegheny Mountains [for the first time]."[10]

The Red Stockings

All of the players had extensive baseball credentials as well as some interesting other skills: marble cutter, jeweler, bookkeeper, hat-fancier, engraver; two of the men were in the insurance business. Only one player was from Cincinnati, the rest were from the New York City and Philadelphia areas.

Cincinnati, after beating Mansfield 48–14, took the train to Cleveland, arriving on the morning of June 3, 1869.

The Weddell House at Superior and Bank N. W. (W. 6th), upon its opening in 1845, was called the most magnificent hotel west of the Alleghenies. A delegation of Clevelanders met the Red Stockings at the depot, and escorted them to the Weddell House, where they were entertained and treated like visiting royalty.

The Red Stockings were transported to the grounds in time for the three o'clock start. The weather was beautiful and the several thousand people there, including many of the city's elite, were ready for a ball game.

Cleveland wore their uniforms from 1868; their fancy new ones had not yet arrived. The Red Stockings wore an all-white uniform, with a stylized letter C on the front, and red stockings showing below their knickerbocker pants. Cleveland's new uniform would be identical to Cincinnati's, with the exception of blue stockings, an English-type letter F over C, and a star on top of the white hat.

Al Pratt took to the pitcher's box for Cleveland, George Wright stepped into the batter's box for Cincinnati, and with the umpire's signal the game began.

Al pitched well for six innings, spreading out 15 runs. However, Asa Brainard, in the pitcher's box for Cincinnati, pitched exceptional ball. Cleveland was shut out in four of the first six frames, scoring but single runs in the third and fourth.

Pratt weakened in the seventh, allowing 7. In the bottom of the seventh Cleveland thrilled the assembly as it mounted a two-out rally.

A "splendid stroke" was made by Arthur Burt[11]: he ended up on third, sending two runners across the plate. Burt soon scored and the man behind him, Eb Smith, soon followed. With "Pikey" Smith and John Ward having reached base, the number-three batter, Arthur Allison, now came to the plate:

"Allison went to the bat, sanded his hands, blew his nose, took an extra reet of three inches in his left shirt sleeve, and gave other indications that he 'meant business.'"[12]

The Cincinnati man behind the plate was amused by Arthur Allison's antics; after all, he was his brother Doug Allison.

Arthur waited on Asa for the right pitch, and when he got it, he put the ball in play. But alas, he was "slaughtered" at first base by the fielding of the "remorseless Gould."[13]

With 2 in the eighth and 1 in the ninth the Red Stockings finished their scoring having amassed 25. Cleveland went down meekly, being "whitewashed" in their last two chances. They had managed but 6 runs for the day's work.

Score

FOREST CITY	Runs	RED STOCKINGS	Runs
"Pikey" Smith, 3b	0	George Wright, ss	5
John Ward, c	0	Charles Gould, 1b	1
Arthur Allison, 1b	0	Fred Waterman, 3b	3
Johnson, 2b	0	Douglass Allison, c	3
Branch, lf	1	Harry Wright, cf	3
Al Pratt, p	1	Andrew Leonard, lf	2
John Riley, rf	1	Asa Brainard, p	4
Arthur Burt, cf	2	Charles Sweasy, 2b	1
Eb Smith, ss	1	Cal McVey, rf	3
Total	**6**	**Total**	**25**

Inning	1	2	3	4	5	6	7	8	9	Final
Forest City	0	0	1	1	0	0	4	0	0	6
Red Stockings	2	2	3	2	2	4	7	2	1	25

MANSFIELD INDEPENDENTS VERSUS CLEVELAND FOREST CITY

An "immense audience" was at the Association Grounds on Tuesday, June 29, 1869, at 3 o'clock.[14] Wearing their new uniforms, the Forest City went to the "ash" and the game began.

Any illusions the Mansfield men had about doing better against Cleveland than they had against Cincinnati were quickly snuffed out. Cleveland opened the game with an 8-run inning.

Mansfield to the bat: "In the first inning they went out 1, 2, 3, order, not able to do anything with those dreadful balls that Pratt sent in red hot."[15]

The visitors were able to do very little against Pratt this day, scoring 4 in the second and 3 in the fifth. They put up "goose eggs" in the other seven innings. Cleveland pitcher Al Pratt hit the only home run.

The 1869 Cincinnati Red Stockings. Clockwise from the top right are Asa Brainard, Charlie Sweasy, Andy Leonard, Charlie Gould, Harry Wright, Doug Allison, George Wright, Cal McVey and Fred Waterman (Library of Congress).

Cleveland scored in every inning but one, ending up with 44 — or was it 45? The box score said 44, but the numbers listed added up to 45. The thing of importance is they won, and won by a lot.

Inning	1	2	3	4	5	6	7	8	9	Final
Forest City	8	7	4	0	3	3	9	4	6	44? or 45?
Independent	0	4	0	0	3	0	0	0	0	7

The *Herald* complimented two players for their fielding:

Burns of Mansfield: "He would throw a ball from the centrefield to the home base as straight as an arrow."[16]

Allison of Cleveland: "at first base was 'sure as taxes.'"[17]

FOREST CITY	Runs	INDEPENDENT	Runs
A. R. Smith, 3b	8	Hade, p	0
Riley, rf.	5	Smith, c	0
Ward, c	4	Deitz, 3b	1
Sheffield, lf	5	Manchester, ss	0
Allison, 1b	2	Strong, rf	2
Hanna, 2b	4	Clapp, 1b	2
Pratt, p	4	Clugston, lf	0
Burt, cf	6	Littler, 2b	1
E. Smith, ss	7	Burns, cf	1
Total	44 or 45	Total	7

Umpire: Mr. E. C. Voltz, of "Ours" Club of Philadelphia. Time of game: three hours and fifteen minutes.

"BLUESTOCKINGS"

On July 1, 1869, the sporting scribes at the *Herald* nicknamed the Forest City Club the "Bluestockings." The similarity, by design or accident, of the Forest City's new uniform (excepting the color blue) to that of the "famous Red Stockings" made the choice of the name "Bluestockings" a natural one.

Formally the Forest City would be called Blue Stockings (Bluestockings), less formally Blues, and more casually Blue Legs (bluelegs). The name Blue Stockings and its variants, whether in quotation marks, as one word or two words, or in capital or small letters, would be used almost exclusively by Cleveland's professional teams until the arrival of the Spiders in 1889.

The Blue Stockings' first game, on July 1, 1869, was at home against their old rival the Western "Reserve" College team of Hudson.

Inning	1	2	3	4	5	6	7	8	9	Final
Forest City	7	8	8	11	1	6	10	21	3	75
Reserve Club	2	0	0	1	3	6	4	0	1	17

The Fourth of July on the Fifth

Cleveland baseball celebrated Independence Day—with its Blue Stockings in Detroit for a game—on the fifth.

Cleveland's Association Grounds celebrated the holiday by hosting the Scottish games (an early version of a track and field event)—on the fifth.

The Fourth of July fell on a Sunday in 1869. The politicians, with the coaxing of most of the ministry, scheduled Monday, the fifth of July, for the official observance in Cleveland. The same scenario occurred in Detroit. In both cities the German communities, however, insisted on celebrating Independence Day on Sunday the fourth. And they did, their activities being patriotic in practice, but "decorously conducted" with the Sabbath always in mind.[18]

The Forest City Club took the steamer *R. N. Rice* out of Cleveland, and under the capable hands of Captain McKay was dropped off in Detroit on Sunday. They looked around for a reception committee. Finding none, they waited for a time, then made their way into town and made their own arrangements at that "model hotel the Russell."[19] They discovered that chief hotel clerk L. A. McCreary was a former Clevelander. He helped entertain the team and in general made them feel comfortable while in Detroit. Another Cleveland expatriate, A. M. Vanduzer, played the role of tour guide during the team's stay.

On Sunday the boys attended the German celebration.

CLEVELAND VERSUS DETROIT

The *Cleveland Herald* sent their man up to Detroit to cover the game. An unprecedented inning-by-inning account of the game was published, with every run and every out explained in detail. One detail was left out of the box score, however: the field position of the players. In the written account of the game the name of the Detroit pitcher was also missing. A sample of the recapitulation:

"First innings.

"The toss of the nickel sent the Forest City to the willow, and Smith A. R., commenced the business by sending a safe one to left field and went to first, stole second and third and came in on Riley's hit to left field. Ward sent a reaper to left field sending Riley to second; then stole a base. Sheffield hit hard going to second and sending Riley and Ward home. Allison got to first Sheff coming home. Hanna hit lightly to second and died at first. Pratt fouled out. Burt sent a creeper to first but did not follow it. Allison left on third. Four runs.

"Brown (the pocket Hercules) sent a grounder to Eb Smith but found it at first when he got there. C. Ward sent a daisy to centre went to first, stole along to third, and came home on a passed ball. Collins fouled out, and Hall rolled one down to Allison. One run."[20]

When all the innings had been closed, Cleveland had 25 runs and Detroit but 10. "The Detroit boys accepted the situation and received their defeat with three hearty cheers for the 'Blue Legs.'"[21] Al Pratt was the winning pitcher.

Score

FOREST CITY	Runs	DETROIT	Runs
A. R. Smith	5	Brown	1
Riley	3	C. Ward	2
Ward	3	Collins	2
Sheffield	3	Hall	1
Allison	0	Bowler	0
Hanna	3	Mahon	1
Pratt	3	Shearon	1
Burt	3	M. Ward	0
E. Smith	2	Sprague	2
Totals	25	Totals	10

Inning	1	2	3	4	5	6	7	8	9	Final
Forest City	4	1	2	1	4	4	3	2	4	25
Detroit	1	2	2	1	0	1	1	0	2	10

Umpire: F. D. Standish, of the "Alerts Club," Detroit. Scorers: Forest City, D. M. Graham; Detroit, James Vernon. Time of game: 3 hours and 20 minutes.

Another Clevelander, the noted actor and opera house operator John Ellser, took the Forest City men to the Opera House in Detroit after the game. Mr. Ellser himself had just finished an engagement there.

Following a custom of the day, an admirer of the ball club showed up at the boat with "an enormous bouquet just about the size of a bushel basket."[22] "Pony" Gardner, representing the club, gave a speech of thanks to Mr. W. H. Sullivan for the thoughtful gift. With everyone waving, the boat headed home.

Base Ball
Olympics of Washington vs. The Forest City
The Tourist Laid Out — Score 28 to 20.[23]

Cleveland won this game against the nationally recognized baseball powerhouse on Thursday, July 8, 1869. A large crowd, including many ladies, witnessed the upset victory. The game, however, was not without its controversies. The Olympics were down 10–3 after the third, when they demanded that Edward Voltz, the umpire, be removed because of partiality to the home team. The umpire in question had arbitrated many games in Cleveland, his integrity never before questioned. Mr. Clugston, of the Mansfield club, happened to be on hand; he agreed to umpire, and the game went on.

Cleveland, incensed because the visitors had "went back" on the umpire, exploded for 13 runs in the top of the fourth inning, and that would prove to be enough to win.[24]

Inning	1	2	3	4	5	6	7	8	9	Final
Forest City	2	4	4	13	2	0	2	0	1	28
Olympics	1	2	0	0	3	1	6	7	0	20

SCORE

FOREST CITY	Runs	OLYMPICS	Runs
A. R. Smith, 3b	3	Force, ss	3
Riley, rf	5	Reach, ss	2
Ward, c	3	Malone, c	2
Sheffield, lf	4	Young, rf	1
Allison, 1b	3	Billings, 3b	3
Hanna, 2b	2	Emmett, 1b	1
Pratt, p	4	Woods, cf	4
Burt, cf	2	Robinson, lf	3
Eb Smith, ss	2	Leech, p	1
Total	28	Total	20

"Match Game of Base Ball between the Olympics and Forest City to— day."[25] Because a second game against the Olympics on July 9 was a last minute scheduling, this ad was taken out in the *Cleveland Herald*— perhaps the first paid ad for a professional baseball game in Cleveland.

Hanna, Sheffield, Ward, and A. R. Smith, citing business engagements, begged out of the second game. The *Plain Dealer* felt that the truth was that they were still angry about the umpiring incident from the day before, and they would not play "with a club that could so offend the dignity of the game."[26]

If that was indeed the case, then in the name of dignity, the short-handed home team was heavily defeated 44–19. (The box score of the game was omitted in the Cleveland papers.)

Inning	1	2	3	4	5	6	7	8	9	Final
Forest City	0	5	2	0	5	2	1	3	1	19
Olympics	5	5	4	4	11	3	6	2	4	44

Diamond Dust

The ball diamonds of amateur ball had a number of new entries in the field this year. Among teams representing their towns for the first time were the "Royaltons" of Royalton Twp.; the "Rough and Readys" of Olmsted; and the "Dexters" of Columbia.

The name "South Side" was replacing the name University Heights in the newspapers this year (today this area of Cleveland is best known as Tremont).

The South Side of 1869 had the best new amateur team in town; they were named the "Red Jackets." They had a snazzy uniform: red cap and shirt, blue and white belt, white woolen pants, and red stockings worn with white shoes. In their first game, the Red Jackets trounced a team named the "Orientals." The score was 81–10.

Then there were the legal eagles: "...the Court House Base Ball Club, an organization that flashed like a blazing meteor into the base ballic sky, dazzling the amateur world with its brightness and then came as suddenly down, like a sky rocket into a goose-pond."[27]

When the Court House gang in its first game, a muffin game, beat a team of players attached to Cleveland City Hall (score 60–10), their egos, and to a degree their sense of humor, got the best of them. They picked officers and otherwise started organizing. They adopted a motto paraphrasing a biblical quotation: "Let every man blow his own bugle, for whosoever bloweth not his own bugle his bugle shall be not blown, but whosoever bloweth his own bugle his bugle shall be blown with a muchness!"[28]

They then started boasting that they could beat any team in town. They beat none. After their first few "organized" games, the Court House bugle was blown no more.

In the southeast part of Cleveland, a picnic was held at Forest Hills Park on August 2. The black community sponsored it in remembrance of West Indies Emancipation: "On Monday morning a colored base ball club marched up from the depot, in full uniform, with all the implements of warfare. They probably came to play with the colored club of this city."[29]

Who were they? They were the "Orientals" of Akron, and they were heading for the picnic to play a ballgame with the Cleveland "Excelsiors." They performed double duty this day: as ball players they played ball, and as musicians they played music.

In August, near the Association Grounds, "two colored clubs"—the "Oriental" club of Akron and the "Bannaker" club of Cleveland—played a baseball game.[30] The Akron club was victorious by a score of 58–53. On August 23, 1869, the Excelsiors of Cleveland went to Akron to play the Orientals. "Both clubs are composed of colored young men of the respective cities, and have reached a considerable proficiency in the game of base ball."[31] Cleveland won the match 58–16.

Cleveland versus Syracuse

Cleveland went on a road trip at the end of July. It was described as its western tour. The tour, however, started somewhat to the east.

The state champions of New York were the "Central Cities" of Syracuse. One of their men was native to nearby Canton, New York; in 1868 his address had been Cleveland, Ohio. He was James "Deacon" White. Fortunately, Jim did not play this July 31 game. The Blue Stockings had their hands full as it was, finally winning 29–23.

A few days later, Jim showed up wearing a Blue Stockings uniform; he was now the fifth man on the payroll.

River Run

The Forest City Club took several trains to Cincinnati, arriving at the Queen City, on the banks of the Ohio River, on Wednesday, August 4, to play the rematch against the Cincinnati Red Stockings. They discovered that, because of a scheduling snafu, the Central Cities were playing the Red Stockings that day. Their game was rescheduled for Saturday.

They spent the day taking in the sights of the city. In the evening they went down to the docks, where they boarded the paddle wheeler *Fleetwood*, a steamboat of the Accommodation Line Co., for a tour of the Ohio River.

For 125 miles, Captain Charles M. Holloway guided the boat up the river. The hills above the Ohio side were largely devoted to raising peaches, apples, and grapes. The Kentucky side had its vineyards and cultivated fields—but mostly there was a "stunted growth of bushes and the occasional straggling town."[32]

The boat stopped wherever a signal fire indicated freight was wanted, or had been brought to the river's edge ready for loading.

At each stop — from twilight and on through the night — the well-muscled crews of ebony-skinned Negroes ran down planks dropped from the boat onto the mud banks. The passengers watched, amused, as the laborers wrestled loads of barreled or boxed produce on and off the boat till dawn.

On one occasion, several of the black men doing the backbreaking, grueling work took a tumble off the work plank, and fell into the thick, dark river mud. At this, some low humor was heard from those standing and watching from above at the railing.

Kentucky — "the dark and bloody ground." The watchers and the workmen were also being watched. All along the way, on rises above the river, on the river's southern side — the Kentucky side — were log houses. When the *Fleetwood* was close enough to this side the passengers could make out more details: squalid cabins (tin roofed) with ramshackle porches, and the locals smoking away on corncob pipes, watching, and some waving.

Thursday morning the steamer pulled into the dockage at Portsmouth, Ohio. The "Riversides" ball club, of that place, met them and escorted them to the Taylor House. The weather was cloudy and threatening, but a large crowd, including many ladies, came to the game.

The home team won the toss of the nickel and took the field at 2:45. The result was predictable, and not unexpected by the crowd. The Forest City scored 48 and the Riversides only 12. The Riversides would have done even worse had not Riley been allowed to pitch the seventh. His wildness allowed 6 runs, and also allowed six balls to get past catcher Jim White.

Inning	1	2	3	4	5	6	7	8	9	Final
Forest City	4	0	9	15	4	0	10	4	2	48
Riversides	3	0	0	0	1	0	6	0	2	12

Home runs: Forest City — Hanna 1, Sheffield 2.

Commendations: "Of the Riversides, the play of Lewis, catcher; Bratt, shortstop; and Davis, left field, was very fine."[33]

Cleveland at Cincinnati

The Cleveland club was headquartered at the beautiful Gibson House. From there they headed out to the Union Grounds where a large crowd of one thousand was already on hand to see the game. When the visitors entered the field the crowd also got to see the new uniforms of the newly named "Blue Stockings."

Pratt, who was feeling "unwell," started the game for the Forest City.[34]

Cincinnati quickly showed just how ill Pratt was in the bottom of the first. They whacked him around for 9 runs. Al recovered somewhat in the next four innings, allowing only 9 more runs.

Cleveland was "whitewashed" in the first inning, but got back into the game with 6 runs in the second and 8 in the third. Cleveland was very much alive after their sixth inning, trailing the "Porkopolitans" by a solitary run, 18–17.[35] However, when Cincinnati batted in the sixth they faced Riley not Pratt. Pratt was now too sick to go on. Quickly following the exit of the starting pitcher also went any chance — short of a not-to-minor miracle — of Cleveland's rallying. "Like 'giants refreshed with new wine,' one [Cincinnati player] after another ... grasped the bat, and sent the ball spinning in every direction...."[36] The Red Stockings added 19 more to their run column.

Final: Red Stockings 43, Blue Stockings 27.

Inning	1	2	3	4	5	6	7	8	9	Final
Red Stockings	9	4	0	3	2	19	3	2	1	43
Forest City	0	6	8	0	0	3	5	1	4	27

Cleveland had a game lined up for Saturday with the less-prestigious Cincinnati "Buckeyes." Cleveland handled them pretty well, winning 53–31. The trio of Burt, Sheffield, and White stood out on the day with three home runs. Darkness ended the game after eight innings.

Inning	1	2	3	4	5	6	7	8	Final
Forest City	6	0	11	5	3	9	11	13	58
Buckeyes	3	4	3	4	9	0	5	3	31

The game with the Buckeyes was, for a time, of secondary interest to "the players and everybody else," the primary interest being focused on an unfolding astronomical phenomenon:

The eclipse performed splendidly for three quarters of an hour, a little more than three fourths of the sun's disc being obscured. The stars shone out, the swallows flew about in a perfect flutter of bewilderment, and one could well say [quoting *Macbeth*],

> By the clock 'tis day,
> And yet dark night strangles the traveling lamp.
> Is it night's predominance, or the day's shame,
> That darkness does the face of earth entomb,
> When living light should kiss it?"[37]
> — The *Cleveland Herald*

The Herald's man had obviously lost interest in the ballgame—more so than most.

Champion Cheaters

"The Game Between the Eckford, Champion Club of the United States, and the Forest City"[38] brought three thousand to the Association Grounds on August 12, 1869. It was the largest crowd of the year. As reigning champs, the New York City—based Eckfords were absolutely certain of victory. Their big-headedness was to cause them some embarrassment at the end of the game.

The Eckford ego seemed justified when they batted first and tallied 15 runs off of Pratt.

Cleveland had its problems with "Martin's 'slow pitching' of which so much has been said. He delivers the ball with a kind of 'jerk,' at moderate speed, but with a peculiar twist that makes him the terror of batters."[39]

The Eckfords had 29 runs after their fifth inning and the Forest City had 15. In the fifth, Cleveland saw right-hander Martin—who seemed to have the game well in hand—pulled, and left-handed Pinkham put in. The real reason for the Eckfords' "change" pitcher came to light in the eighth: "Some of their financial managers had staked loose scrip on a score of two to one," i.e., gambling on the game.[40] Pinkham was an insurance policy for the bettors, and the Eckford players were in on the betting. The lefty Pinkham did his job, allowing but 2 runs in three innings.

At the close of the seventh the score was 37–17. This was a not-to-safe three-run cushion, in the 2-to-1 betting. The Eckfords decided to try to play it safe by taking advantage of a technicality in the rules: When a game is called because it is too dark to continue, and an inning has not been completed, the score reverts to the last inning of complete play.

A now-twilight sky, and the start of the eighth inning, seemed to have inexplicably coincided with the Eckfords' developing a severe case of "dropsy," and arm problems. Everything hit their way was dropped and then thrown wildly. Cleveland scored 10 runs, but the umpire, despite the darkness, would not call the game; he knew what was up, and wasn't game for the angling. The Eckfords suddenly rediscovered their lost skills, and the Forest City was soon retired. Now it was truly dark, and try as they could, the New York men just couldn't see the ball very well; they somehow managed 4 runs—but they needed 13 more. Though they won the game, they had clevered themselves right into losing the betting.

There were no wet Cleveland eyes in the stands, but there were some smiles—some wider than others—and some wallets now fatter than they use to be.

Score: Eckfords 41, Blue Stockings 27.

Score

FOREST CITY	Runs	ECKFORD	Runs
White, c	4	Allison, 1b	3
A. R. Smith, 3b	3	Patterson, cf	5
Ward, 2b	0	Martin, p	5
Allison, A., 1b	3	Nelson, 3b	4
Pratt, P	3	Hodes, ss	6
Burt, cf	2	Jewett, c	5
Riley, rf	3	Tracey, lf	6
Sheffield, lf	5	Woods, 2b	5
E. Smith, ss	4	Pinkham, rf	2
Totals	27	Totals	41

Inning	1	2	3	4	5	6	7	8	Final
Forest City	1	2	5	7	1	1	0	10	27
Eckford	15	1	10	0	3	7	1	4	41

The Troy "Haymakers" of New York State came to town for a game on Monday, August 23, 1869. From the Weddell House they came to the grounds in a large wagon. As they entered the gate they regaled the crowd with their favorite song — the "song of the haymakers."[41] When they climbed down from their vehicle, the spectators saw that, with the exception of the monogrammed H on the breast of their uniform, their outfit was identical to that of the Forest City.

It was a close contest, but the "bluestockings" with the H beat the "bluestockings" with the F C. Score: 34–31.

Inning	1	2	3	4	5	6	7	8	9	Final
Forest City	2	9	5	3	10	2	0	0	0	31
Haymakers	6	6	5	0	1	1	6	7	2	34

The Resolutes of Oberlin were invited to come to Cleveland to play the Forest City on October 9, 1869. Following a gorgeous week of weather, a storm front followed the visitors into town. The overcast weather shrunk the crowd and shortened the game.

Oberlin won the coin toss, and took the field "in the reddest pants ever seen in Cleveland since the old Railway club changed its uniforms."[42]

Al Pratt pitched for Cleveland, Simpson Younger for the Resolutes. Al Pratt, the professional, limited Oberlin to but 2 runs. Simpson Younger gave up 17 runs, but he spread them out well. The *Leader* was a bit condescending when it said: "The Resolutes play admirably so far as they have had experience, but before such pitching as Pratt's they are yet but children."[43]

The *Herald* writer perhaps thought he was being liberal with his comments on the "colored" Oberlin pitcher, but today his words seem quite patronizing: "The popular traditions in regard to Oberlin are sustained, the pitcher of the Resolutes being one of those whose forefathers and foremothers came from 'Afric's sunny fountains'.... He fought 'nobly' however, his play being inferior to none in the nine."[44]

The Old and the New

Symbolic of change was a ball game played October 6, 1869; it paid homage to the passing day of the "gentleman player," and acknowledged the arrival of the "professional player." Led by "Pikey" Smith, one of the original Forest City men of 1865, the old guard played the new guard. The new guard was the regular lineup, which included the five professionals. The weather was nice and the audience sizable. "For an inning or two the old boys made things 'hot' for the champions, but they finally struck their gait, and thence the game was just like the handle to a jug — all one side."[45]

Score: The "New" 43, the "Old" 12.

Inning	1	2	3	4	5	6	7	8	9	Final
The Old	2	3	0	1	1	0	3	1	1	12
The New	1	1	13	4	1	10	4	2	7	43

Score

THE OLD	Runs	THE NEW	Runs
Smith A. R., c	2	WHITE, c	7
Hurlbut, ss	0	WARD, 2b	6
Gorham, rf	2	PRATT, p	5
Brown, 2b	2	ALLISON, 1b	7
McEwen, lf	2	Burt, cf	5
Stockley, p	1	Melton, lf	3
Clark, 1b	0	RILEY, rf	3
Hanna, 3b	1	E. Smith, ss	4
Truesdale, cf	2	Sheffield, 3b	3
Total	12	Total	43

The professional players' names are capitalized.

Next year the Forest City Club would field an all-professional "nine," and the amateur and the professional game from that point on would never mix again.

1870

Professionals All

The Forest City Base Ball Club came up with the cash needed to pay a professional team. They got it from the businessmen; many were club members already and others were friends and baseball lovers from the ranks of commerce and industry at large. The six paid men of 1869 were back, and some new blood was added. The Alert team of Rochester lost two players to Cleveland — John Kimball and Ezra Sutton (Sutton being destined for greatness).

Cleveland thought they had a deal with a Mr. Pennington of Long Island, New York, and with Elmer White of Canton, NY. The deals, however, fell through at the last moment. In their stead George Heuble, a former member of the great Philadelphia Athletic Club, and James Carleton, an excellent amateur from Chicago, were signed. The spring roster now had ten professionals plus Harvey Brown, one of last year's amateurs, who agreed to be available on an as-needed basis— monetary considerations not being mentioned. Elmer White, Chick Fulmer, and a player named Parker played some games for the Forest City later in the season.

The money raised by "subscription" was $3000, and most of it went for payroll. Some friends of baseball in Cleveland, acting in the role of a booster club, helped raise funds for items not in the budget. Baseball equipment was such an item. A benefit fund-raiser was planned, to be held at the popular Central Rink downtown. It was "an ice skate with competition."[1] Donations were collected and prizes given out to the best skaters in a variety of categories, and it was a success.

Warmed by this outpouring of generosity on their behalf, the players decided to do something for Cleveland in return. They decided to help the ball-playing youth of the city. Specifically, they adopted promising young players as understudies. They instructed them one-on-one, as a group, and by training in practice games. A small fee was sometimes charged for these games, with the money going to help the young team. To make the practice games more fair and interesting, the adults often used the juniors' pitcher, and the youngsters usually had Al Pratt working for them.

The big boys didn't relish facing their own man, fastballer Pratt, and the young men didn't fancy hitting against their teammate, thirteen-year-old pitching phenom Johnny Bohn. One writer who saw Johnny said he pitched at a level "that would do credit to a first-class adult player."[2]

The Forest City and their young players hosted a youth appreciation day this year, inviting all the young players of the city to attend for free. Hundreds did. The high point of the day was a game between the pros and their young trainees—the "Eastern Rocks"—the best darned amateur team in town! And their undefeated match game record at the end of the year proved it.

The Eastern Rocks were victorious over all comers:

From Cleveland:	April 16	Amateurs
From Cleveland:	May 25	Niagaras
From Chagrin Falls:	June 4	Quicksteps
From Cleveland:	June 11	Amateurs
From Glenville:*	June 25	Independents
From Cleveland:	June 29	Niagaras
From Cleveland:	July 8	Excelsiors
From Painesville:	July 27	Bed Ticks
From Cleveland:	July 30	Carpet Baggers
From Oberlin:	August 3	Resolutes
From Cleveland:	August 18	Grove Citys
From Cleveland:	August 24	Grove Citys
From Cleveland:	August 29	Athletics
From Cleveland:	October 1	Eries

RECORD: 14 WINS, 0 LOSSES. **

*The 1870 city of Glenville is the Glenville neighborhood of Cleveland today.

**The record of the scores of a number of these games is damaged. The legible record shows that the Eastern Rocks outscored most opponents by a nearly 3–1 margin.

The Resolutes of Oberlin came to town on May 10, 1870. It took two hours and ten minutes for the Cleveland professionals to whip the "juniors" of the college city 31–14. The game worked out some of the Forest City's kinks in their muscles, and they were now ready to go to Cincinnati for what was advertised as "The First Grand Game of the Season."[3] It wasn't the first ball game there but it served as the season opener.

The Blue Stockings vs. The Red Stockings

The crowds approaching the Union Grounds were somewhat smallish, due to an overcast sky and a rather high-priced ticket of 50 cents. The beautiful grandstand—"The Grand Duchess"—however, had a full crowd of ladies and their escorts.

A brisk shower, just before the game, soaked the field pretty well and that helped keep the scoring down. The sun came out and the lively crowd of 2,000 saw a well-played game.

Cleveland won the coin toss and chose the field. Al Pratt, pitching for Cleveland, and Asa Brainard, for Cincinnati, were magnificent. After five innings the two pitchers had kept the scoring down to an amazing Cincinnati 3, Cleveland 2.

Cleveland was very much in the game, but could the Blue Stockings break the Red Stockings' winning streak from having played all of 1869 undefeated?

Al Pratt had a reputation of being a six-inning wonder (a man whose arm would tire after six innings), a charge he claimed was not true.

This day his pitching came undone—in the sixth.

Defensive stalwart Jim White could not handle Pratt's sudden wildness and 9 runs scored. Pratt managed to shut out the Red Stockings for the last three innings, but the damage was done. After the fifth, Asa Brainard allowed no more scoring.

The final was 12–2. Jim White and Al Pratt scored the only Cleveland runs.

Inning	1	2	3	4	5	6	7	8	9	Final
Red Stockings	1	0	1	0	1	9	0	0	0	12
Forest City	0	0	0	1	1	0	0	0	0	2

Note: • Cleveland was commended by the Cincinnati papers for its excellent fielding, having shut the Cincinnati team out in five innings—an unheard-of feat against the great juggernaut.

Thursday, May 12, 1870:
    I congratulate you upon the magnificent game played by your club to-day. Hundreds of our citizens want your boys to stay and play.... Arrange it by all means and telegraph immediately.
                                                         J. P. Joyce[4]
                                   [Secretary of the Cincinnati Base Ball Club]

    The good gate on Thursday, and an outlook for better weather the next day, convinced the two ball clubs to play an unscheduled second game. Despite the high 50 cents charge, and the rush to advertise the contest, the crowd was double that of Thursday — upward of four thousand.

    It was a great game for four innings, the Red Stockings up by a solitary run, 4–3. Pratt weakened after that, and change pitcher Jim White, brought in for the eighth and ninth inning, was fast but without command. His wild pitches and walks, as well as the passed balls of third baseman Ezra Sutton (now catching) helped put the game out of reach for Cleveland.

    Score: Red Stockings 24, Blue Stockings 10.

    Note: • "[Eb] Smith [of Cleveland] at right field, played brilliantly yesterday, making the finest one hand catch ever seen on these grounds in the third inning."[5]

In Cleveland

    An amateur group of youngsters, on the west side of the city, had convinced themselves they were a pretty good bunch of ball players, and were doing a lot of bragging about it—claiming they could beat anybody. "Anybody" heard about it, and that anybody was named the Forest City Blue Stockings. The amateurs named themselves after that famous team from Brooklyn, New York—the Atlantics.

    The Cleveland "Atlantics" played the Forest City Blue Stockings May 17, 1870. The Forest City batted first and scored 52. The Atlantics in their turn scored 0. In the second inning the professionals showed mercy, scoring only 16. The Atlantics then scored a run—and celebrated. The Forest City now continued to administer their object lesson, scoring a total of 64 more. The youngsters were made to chase the ball all over the field for five innings, at which time the adults called an end to the "game."

    Final: adults 132, braggarts 1. Lesson learned!

Inning	1	2	3	4	5	Final
Forest City	52	16	53	1	10	132
Atlantics	0	1	0	0	0	1

The Red Stockings Are Coming!

    The Cincinnati Red Stockings Club was scheduled to come to Cleveland for the return match on May 31, 1870, the first game of note on the Cleveland grounds this year.

    In the week prior to the arrival of Cincinnati, Cleveland, hoped to get in some practice games—possibly with the "crack" team from Oil City, Pennsylvania.

"Knights of the Crimson Hose"[6]

    The incredible success of the Cincinnati Red Stockings unleashed a national wave of "stocking fever": "The penchant for naming ball clubs Red, White, Blue, Pink, Yellow, and Black Stockings ... Clean Stockings or Dirty Stockings ... is becoming epidemic."[7]—*Buffalo Express.*

    The Cleveland Forest City "Blue Stockings" had contracted the stocking malady in 1869. A prominent team in Illinois, the Rockford Forest City, joined the footwear frenzy by adding the nickname "Green Stockings." This other Forest City club would play a role in Cleveland's baseball fortunes next year.

    Van Wert, Ohio: Word spread faster than a fast telegrapher could telegraph: "the famous Red

Stocking club" will be passing through town on their train.[8] Hundreds of the locals rushed to the train station in hope of catching a glimpse of the famous ball players. With a whistle and a puff of smoke the train came into view. It slowed but slightly as it approached the platform, and then all too quickly passed on by. So where were the friendly faces of all the smiling, waving, ball players? The people looked at each other with puzzled expressions.

Someone pointed, then another, soon everyone was looking toward the platform of the last passing car. A man was standing there with a great big wide grin on his face; from his hand dangled a small pair of red stockings that he was slowly waving back and forth. It took a moment to sink in — the famous red stockings!

Cincinnati left home at seven o'clock Monday morning. Their train rolled into Cleveland lake front station early that evening. At the depot, they were immediately taken into hand by a delegation of Clevelanders, who escorted them to the water's edge, not too far from the depot, for a sunset cruise on the sailing yacht *Phantom*, built by wealthy Cleveland young men the previous fall.

During the boat ride, the visitors noticed a plume of smoke floating over the city and stretching into the far distance.

"What is it?" they asked. The Clevelanders replied, "We call it 'the Cleveland comet'" (pollution spewing from an already emerging industrial giant).[9]

The Red Stockings were fed: cheese, bread and lemonade. Spirits were offered, "but these were disdained."[10] Cigars, however, were acceptable and were quickly passed around and a nice post-meal smoke had by all. The breeze, which had been light, quit, and a tug had to be signaled to haul the boat to harbor.

The two-hour sea voyage concluded with a pretty sunset. The Cincinnati team spent the night at the prestigious Weddell House — Cleveland's best.

They came by the thousands: the young, the old, and many ladies too. They came from the small towns, and the countryside. By train they arrived out of the southeast, on the Mahoning and Pittsburgh roads. Along the lake they rode the Lakeshore line. And up from the southwest, they took the Cincinnati way. They rode the regular streetcars and extra streetcars. They drove their carriages and they walked. And when they all got to the grounds, there were four thousand of them.

It was the largest throng ever assembled to see a ball game in Cleveland.

The *Cleveland Herald*: "At a quarter past two the conquering Red Legs, wearing the crimson hose that were typical of a hundred victories, marched into the grounds with Captain Harry Wright at their head, and were greeted with loud and long continued applause from the assemblage. Harry acknowledged the compliment by a graceful wave of his 'castor.'"[11]

Tuesday, May 31, 1870: The teams took their warm-ups, and just before the start of play, they were photographed together on the field. Policemen patrolled the ropes holding the standing crowds back in the outfield, and many ladies in the grandstand, brightly dressed, gave the place a nice color.

At 3 o'clock, Umpire W. R. Ellis signaled the start of game — Cleveland at the bat. James "Deacon" White stepped into the batter's box, and Asa Brainard took his place in the pitching box. Mr. White quickly singled one into center, took second on an error, and unhappily was left stranded on third — his teammates going out in one, two, three order. The visitors failed to tally in their turn. Cleveland failed to score in the second but Cincinnati got 5.

In the third Cleveland fought back. George Heuble had a scratch single, and Eb Smith brought him in with a "tremendous hit to right field," good for a triple.[12] James White then hit a triple of his own over the center fielder, bringing in Smith. And John Ward hit a grounder into left, plating White. Three runs. The Cincinnati team then showed their winning mettle, putting up 8 runs in the bottom of the inning.

Cleveland scoring highlights: In the fifth inning, Kimball took first on an error and stole second; Smith drove him in with a single to center. Smith moved to second on a fly out, and scored on a pitch that eluded the catcher. Two runs.

James L. "Deacon" White, shown here as a member of the Detroit Wolverines. White was a great fielding, hard-hitting catcher and Cleveland's first star (1868–1872). White went on to a stellar career in the National League for fifteen seasons.

Eighth inning: Harry Wright relieved Brainard. White and Ward beat out slow rollers to third. "Pratt hit feebly," getting first on a fielder's choice at third.[13] Sutton earned first to make the "bases all full."[14] Ward and Pratt came in when Carleton put one between the legs of the game's best infielder, shortstop George Wright. Sutton scored on miscues. Three runs.

The exciting ninth inning: Brainard came back in to pitch, and center fielder Doug Allison, the regular catcher—nursing a mangled hand—came in from center to catch for the first time. Arthur Allison, the brother of the Cincinnati catcher, led off for Cleveland. Arthur doubled to left field, Kimball took first on the pitcher's error, and Allison came home on a Heuble single to right. Smith then singled to center, and "White essayed Leonard to muff."[15] Bases full. Ward then singled in Heuble and Smith, White came in on a passed ball, and Ward came in on a Pratt fly to center. Cleveland had scored 5 runs, but there were now two outs. Sutton next came to bat, and continued the fun by stroking a single to right, but he got greedy and tried for second—and the umpire called him out on the game's only controversial play.

As the rules required, the Red Stockings now had to finish their half of the ninth despite the fact that they had in effect already won the game.

They rang up 7 runs to make the official score Cincinnati Red Stockings 27, Cleveland Forest City Blue Stockings 13.

Inning	1 2 3	4 5 6	7 8 9	Final
Forest City	0 0 3	0 2 0	0 3 5	13
Cincinnati	0 5 8	1 4 0	2 0 7	27

CINCINNATI	Runs	FOREST CITY	Runs
G. Wright, ss	3	White, c	2
Gould, 1b	0	Ward, ss	2
Waterman, 3b	3	Pratt, p	1
Allison, rf	3	Sutton, 3b	1
H. Wright, cf	5	Carleton, 1b	0
Leonard, lf	5	Allison, cf	1
Brainard, p	3	Kimball, 2b	1
Sweasy, 2b	2	Heubel, lf	2
McVey, c	3	Smith, rf	3
Totals	27	Totals	13

Time: Two hours and fifteen minutes. Umpire: W. R. Ellis of the Athletic Club, Philadelphia.

Notes: • The *Herald* newspaper gave a pair of spiked brogans to the player who had earned the most bases. Forest City's Eb Smith, with five total bases, claimed the shoes. • The Red Stockings left town on the 10:40 P.M. train for a game in Rochester the next day. • On June 14, 1870, the Red Stockings played the Brooklyn Atlantics at the Capitoline Grounds (Brooklyn). There were 20,000 spectators on hand. The game could have ended in a 5–5 tie after nine innings, but Harry Wright insisted on playing it out. In eleven innings, Cincinnati's winning streak of 84 games came to an end—Atlantics 8 and Red Stockings 7.

Cleveland Blue Stockings vs. Chicago White Stockings

Cleveland arrived in Chicago on Thursday afternoon, June 2, 1870, for a game with the professional Chicago White Stockings, to be played Friday. That evening they attended McVicker's Theatre by invitation. The next morning they ate early and went sightseeing. A number of Clevelanders, having come in by train, also showed up that morning, and they had plenty of money in their pockets to wager on the game.

The game was on the ball field at the Dexter Trotting Park. The steam cars, or a drive up beautiful Wabash Avenue, were the recommended routes to the game. Dr. John Draper, of Cincinnati, was suggested as a neutral umpire, but Chicago said no. Captain Eb Smith agreed to let

S. D. Phelps of Chicago umpire. The close game played out fair for seven innings, despite what appeared to be the general incompetence of the umpire.

Cleveland led 9–8 when Chicago came to bat in the bottom of the eighth.

The umpiring at this point became so bad that Clevelanders were convinced that something sinister was at work. Chicago, with the help of Phelps, was able to ring up 7 runs, and as it turned out that was enough to decide the game.

Inning	1 2 3	4 5 6	7 8 9	Final
Forest City	0 1 0	2 0 3	3 0 0	9
Chicago	3 1 0	0 0 0	4 7 0	15

The *Cleveland Plain Dealer*: "It will take but very few victories like this to wipe the Chicago Club out of existence, as the job was so evidently 'put up' that nobody on the grounds who knew anything of the game, could fail to see it."[16]

The *Chicago Journal*: "The agony of Cleveland over the defeat of its pet club is at once pitiable and ludicrous. The newspapers are blind with fury, and strike out in very impotence. Their columns are filled with distorted and lying reports of the game between the Chicago club and the Cleveland pet lambs. Cleveland lost its money and its temper at the same time, and that embryo city can ill afford to lose either."[17]

The *Cleveland Plain Dealer:* "The Chicago club is a 'mushroom nine.'"[18]

The *Chicago Journal*: "So long as Cleveland was ahead the greenbacks were ready, and so until the seventh inning it was cat and mouse. In the eighth and ninth the mouse got hurt, and its friends who lost their money and their temper have been squealing ever since."[19]

The *Cleveland Plain Dealer*: "We perhaps may be allowed to suggest to that umpire to steer clear of Cleveland, and advise the White Stockings to play 'square' if they ever come here, for if they ever try to play any fraud in this city the whole nine and their satellites will be thrown out of the grounds bodily."[20]

It would soon be seen if the White Stockings heeded this advice — Chicago was scheduled to come to Cleveland on June 20.

Score

FOREST CITY	Runs	CHICAGO	Runs
White, c	1	King, c	3
Ward, ss	1	Hodes, ss	2
Pratt, p	0	Flynn, lf	3
Sutton, 3b	0	Cuthbert, cf	2
Carleton, 1b	0	McAtee, 1b	1
Allison, cf	2	Treacy, 2b	0
Kimball, 2b	0	Meyerle, p	0
Heuble, lf	3	Craver, rf	3
Smith, rf	2	Pinkham, 3b	1
Total	**9**	**Total**	**15**

JUNE NEWS

June 11: John Ward will miss a few games this year due to business.

June 13: The Rockford, Illinois, Forest City Green Stockings ball club arrive at the Euclid Avenue and Wilson St. (E. 55th) train station and are taken directly by carriages to the ball park for a game with the Blue Stockings.

June 14: Cleveland beats Rockford 21–12 in game one. June 15: Rockford beats Cleveland 24–18 in game two.

June 17: Captain Eb Smith hands in his resignation, fueling suspicions he was in on the Chicago "fix"— Carleton elected captain in his place.

June 20: Cleveland goes to Oberlin and defeats the Resolutes 54–24.

The White Stockings vs. The Blue Stockings

Several thousand people came to the Association Grounds under a gray-clouded sky on June 21, 1870, a Monday. They wanted to see the Blue Stockings seriously muddy up those cheating White Stockings from that big-shot-nothing Chicago town!

Cleveland, however, wasn't in good shape to do any serious getting even. Jim White's hands were so banged up he had to wear gloves with sponges in them (an undermining of the barehanded style of play that was regular and expected). Sutton was playing with a migraine, and Harvey Brown—replacing Eb Smith, who had quit the team—was kept from playing. Brown had not played in a match game for sixty days, a technical violation of the rules that Chicago—being bad guys—demanded be enforced. Parker took his place in right field, but "did not distinguish himself."[21] Chicago wasn't in the best of shape either, several of its men nursing this or that ailment. They made a fair number of errors, but Cleveland's fielding was worse. And when the sick Sutton went behind the plate to relieve White, who could not continue, his play was the worst of all, accounting for many of Chicago's 24 runs. The Forest City, even with the generous "muffing" of the visitors, managed to score only 8 runs.

The game was characterized by disgust on the part of the crowd—not by the revenge they had hoped would be taken wholesale upon the Chicagos. No one complained when the game was called after the fifth inning when the rain came.

Score

FOREST CITY	Runs	CHICAGO	Runs
White, c, 3b	2	King, c	4
Ward, ss	0	Hodes, ss	3
Pratt, p	0	Wood, 2b	2
Sutton, 3b, c	0	Cuthbert, cf	4
Carleton, 1b	0	McAtee, 1b	2
Allison, cf	0	Flynn, lf	2
Kimball, 2b	3	Meyerle, p	0
Heubel, lf	2	Craver, rf	3
Parker, rf	1	Pinkham, 3b	4
Total	8	Total	24

Inning	1	2	3	4	5	Final
Forest City	1	4	2	0	1	8
Chicago	4	2	6	6	6	24

The New York Mutuals vs. The Cleveland Forest City

July 2, 1870

There was a good crowd on hand at the Association Grounds to watch Cleveland play the famous Mutual team from New York City.

The visitors took the field first. The crowd took in the details of the well-known uniform of the "Mutes"—the stylized letter M on the breast of their shirts, and the high green stockings below the knickerbocker pants. Cleveland's Jim White came to bat, and the umpire called for the start of game.

Rynie Wolters, the visiting pitcher, quickly disposed of the home team without a run. Al Pratt, pitching for Cleveland, soon returned the favor in the bottom of the inning, giving the New Yorkers a "goose egg" of their own. Cleveland was shut out in the second, but New York in their half managed a run.

Cleveland surprised the Mutuals with a 4-run third. New York got serious and came back with 3 in their turn. The game now settled into a pitching duel and fielding contest.

Sutton, Kimball, and White scored a run in the fifth, seventh, and eighth, respectively, for the home team. Dave Eggler made a run for the visitors in the eighth. The surprisingly low score now stood at Cleveland 7 and New York 5.

Cleveland was not expected to win this game, and the crowd prayed for some insurance runs in the top of the ninth. Those prayers were not answered. To the bat, in the bottom of the ninth, came the determined Mutuals. The crowd held its breath. Right fielder McMahon stepped into the batter's box and "after considerable cautious skirmishing succeeded at striking out."[22] Loud applause. Captain Charlie Mills now brought his "ash" to the plate. He knocked a high fly into center; Allison got under it and there were two outs. More applause.

The pitcher Wolters was next, and maybe last. He took a couple of called strikes; then he knocked one high into the air over the center field:

> As the ball rose high in the air and turned earthward the vast crowd rose to their feet in the intensity of the excitement. Allison was again the cynosure of all eyes and everyone held their breath as he gathered under it. As it yielded gracefully to its inevitable fate the crowd went wild with joy. They sprang over the ropes, old men and young, flung their hats into the air, and shouted till compelled to desist from sheer exhaustion. No such scene was ever before witnessed on those grounds.
> As the victors came in from the field they received compliments, cheers and hand shakings by the hundred.[23]

The Cleveland Forest Blue City Stockings had just won a game — its first over one of the nation's best ball clubs.

Note: • In honor of the win the *Herald* printed a new-style box score with a key describing much added detail:

Key: Batting — O., outs; R., runs; 1B., first base on hits; TB., total bases on hits; E., bases on errors; L., left on bases; S., struck out. Fielding — F., flys caught; B., put out on bases; LD., foul bound catches; T., total outs secured; A., assisted to put out; E., errors on muffs, wild throws, etc.[24]

FOREST CITY: CLEVELAND PLAYERS

	Batting Score							Fielding Score					
	O	R	1B	TB	B	L	S	F	B	LD	T	A	E
White, c	3	2	1	3	1	-	-	2	1	2	6	1	3
Ward, ss	3	1	1	1	1	1	-	-	1	-	-	3	-
Pratt, p	3	1	1	1	-	1	-	1	1	-	1	2	-
Sutton, 3b	1	2	1	1	2	1	-	-	1	-	-	4	2
Carleton, 1b	3	0	1	1	1	-	1	-	1	-	10	-	1
Allison, cf	4	0	-	-	-	-	2	4	1	-	4	-	-
Kimball, 2b	3	1	-	-	-	1	1	3	2	-	4	2	1
Heubel, lf	3	0	1	1	-	1	-	1	-	-	1	-	-
Fulmer, rf	4	0	-	-	-	-	1	1	-	-	1	-	-
Total	27	7	6	8	5	5	5	12	8	2	27	12	7

MUTUALS: NEW YORK PLAYERS

	Batting Score							Fielding Score					
	O	R	1B	TB	B	L	S	F	B	LD	T	A	E
Hatfield, ss	4	0	1	1	-	-	-	1	4	-	1	1	1
Eggler, cf	2	2	2	2	-	-	-	2	2	-	2	2	1
Patterson, lf	2	1	1	1	1	1	-	2	2	-	2	2	-
Nelson, 3b	2	1	2	2	1	1	-	2	1	-	3	2	1
E. Mills, 1b	4	0	1	1	1	1	-	1	1	-	8	1	-
McMahon, rf	3	1	1	1	1	1	1	-	1	-	-	-	-
C. Mills, c	4	0	-	-	-	1	-	8	-	1	9	8	-
Wolters, p	3	0	1	1	-	1	-	-	-	-	-	-	1
Swandell, 2b	3	0	-	-	-	-	-	2	1	-	2	2	2
Total	27	5	9	9	4	6	1	18	12	1	27	18	6

Inning	1 2 3	4 5 6	7 8 9	Final
Forest City	0 0 4	0 1 0	1 1 0	7
Mutuals	0 1 3	0 0 0	1 0 0	5

A Poem to Celebrate Victory

THE GAME VERSIFIED

From the Empire City,
The Mutuals with pity,
To Cleveland, on Erie, have wended their way,
Determined to *beat* us,
But never to cheat us,
For ne'er has their fair fame been slandered
     at play.*

'Tis an afternoon charming,
And the players are arming
For the contest approaching so deadly and near;
While the grounds are fast filling,
And the weather seems willing
That the day should be fresh for our victory
     dear.

Now the nickel is tossed,
And our boys have lost,
So the green-legged heroes are called to the
     field-
Sending White to the bat,
And then Ward and then Pratt,
Who, with Sutton and Carleton, the inning
     doth yield.

Now the greens are awake,
And the lads of the lake
Take a "whitewash," but give them the same
     in return;
And the cheers fast are flying,

When the Mutuals in trying,
Stow away one sweet tally that McMahon did
     earn.

How the balls fast do fly
From the bat to the sky!
And the score, it is even as the third inning
     ends;
But the fifth leaves us leading
By the tally, that's needing
To place us ahead of our famed Eastern friends.

Now the ninth is at hand,
And the brave Mutual band,
Has "Chicagoed" our boys, leading seven to
     five;
So with two they will tie,
But that centre field fly
Must leave them a "goose egg," how hard
     they may strive.

Now the cheers loud are ringing,
While brave Allison's flinging
That ball that has beaten them high in the
     air;
And the hands round are shaken,
For the flies that were taken,
And for Scotten, who umpired "all on the
     square."   B. B.[25]

The reference to cheating and slandering has to do with an 1865 game in which an investigation found three Mutual players had conspired to throw a game against the Brooklyn Eckfords.

July doings

• A crowd of 1,500 celebrates the Fourth of July at the Association Grounds, as Cleveland knocks off the Rochester, New York, "Flower City" 28–13.

• Elmer White — said in some histories to be James "Deacon" White's cousin (they were both from Canton, New York), is now hired as change catcher/right fielder. He had declined the job at the start of the year.

• Fremont, Ohio, holds a baseball tournament. First prize is $50; second prize $30; and third prize a bat and ball. The "junior" Grove Cities of Cleveland take first prize.

• Chick Fulmer is the second new Forest City to sign a contract in July.

• Novel team names: The "Shoo Fly" play in Geauga County; the "Carpet Bag" is a Cleveland-picked nine; Wapokeneta has its "Bloody Lions" and Painesville its "Bed Ticks."

The Great Eastern Tour of August

Cleveland started the tour in Buffalo, but before they played, they visited the souvenir shops near Niagara Falls, and then had a team photo snapped with the falls in the background. (Several other teams' photos with Niagara Falls in the background survive — the Cleveland photo, however, is lost.)

New York City: The team was wearing their uniforms— very fancy uniforms when compared to the usual such items— and they were walking to the ballpark with President Evans, who was also decked out in a nice set of clothes. A passer-by approached Evans and wanted to know if he was the English lord whose yacht was docked in the harbor, and if these men were his crew. President Evans and the Cleveland players all had a good laugh.

THE ROAD RECORD OF THE FOREST CITY

Niagaras of Buffalo	5	Forest City	26
Flower City of Rochester	2	Forest City	29
Haymakers of Troy, NY	19	Forest City	11
Atlantics of Brooklyn	15	Forest City	9
Mutuals, NYC	10	Forest City	9
Eckfords of Williamsburg*	0	Forest City	13
Unions of Tremont**	15	Forest City	19
Stars of Brooklyn,	7	Forest City	9
Athletics, Philadelphia	19	Forest City	11
Mutuals, N.Y.C.	16	Forest City	15
Pastimes of Baltimore	18	Forest City	22
Olympics of Washington, D.C.	17	Forest City	18
Nationals of Washington, D.C.	12	Forest City	67
Alleghenys of Pittsburgh	5	Forest City	16
Alleghenys of Pittsburgh	3	Forest City	26

Totals: Forest City 10 wins and 5 losses.

*Williamsburg is a section of the borough of Brooklyn, New York.
** Most likely a part of New York City.

The success of the 1870 tour cemented the issue. Cleveland would have a professional team in 1871.

In late September, management held a meeting at the Weddell House to raise funds for the next season. In a departure from the so-called subscription system, shares of stock were offered. At $50 a share, $10,000 was raised.

It was decided to legally incorporate the club. Incorporators were chosen, and on October 16th a certificate of incorporation was filed with the Secretary of State's office.

THE ROAD WEST

• The Forest City stopped in Kalamazoo, Michigan, on Sept. 16. They stayed long enough to whip the ball club there 47–5.

• Two days later, the Blue Stockings played the White Stockings in Chicago. This time 4,000 watched a game played "on the square."

• In one of the finest games of the year, the visiting Clevelands beat the home team Chicagos 9–7. Good feelings between the two rivals were restored. But next year Chicago would be up to its old tricks again.

Cleveland at Cincinnati

OCTOBER 6

"A fair crowd of 2,500 watched from the 'Grand Duchess.'" [26] The partisan red colors worn by many in the grandstand contrasted nicely with the gray sky. The temperature was quite chilly; Al Pratt, however, was red hot, giving the Red Stockings but 3 runs through six frames. The bats of Cleveland also had some fire in them this cold day, knocking out 15 runs in the first six innings.

Al Pratt's reputation as a six-inning wonder once again began surfacing in the seventh. It also didn't help that he was working with a substitute catcher, Jim White's hands having become so sore by the end of the sixth that he had to be moved to another position.

Cincinnati had rallied by the start of the ninth, netting 10 runs to tie the game at 15. Cleveland failed to score in their turn. But in their turn, Cincinnati quickly scored a run to win. The inning, as the rules required, was played out, and the Red Stockings added 2 more runs of no consequence.

The official score of the incredible comeback was Cincinnati 18, Forest City 15.

Note: • Asa Brainard started for Cincinnati and was relieved in the later innings by Harry Wright. • "The game was umpired in an admirable, intelligent and impartial manner by Dr. John Draper, of the Cincinnati Club."[27] • The contest ended as darkness gathered at precisely 5:30.

Cincinnati at Cleveland

The *Cleveland Plain Dealer*:

Base Ball

The last base ball game of the season, as far as the Red Stockings and Forest Citys are concerned, was played on the Association grounds Saturday afternoon. The sky was clear, but the weather was so chilly that both players and spectators were uncomfortable. So, taking it all in all, the game was a very unsatisfactory one. Neither nine played well, very many errors being made in the field. Pratt, becoming tired, pitched very wildly in the last three innings and this, together with muffs and bad throwing, allowed the Reds to add so many tallies to their score.[28]

Score

FOREST CITY	Outs	Runs	RED STOCKINGS	Outs	Runs
J. White, c	2	3	Geo. Wright, ss	1	6
Heuble, lf	3	2	Gould, 1b	3	3
Parker, rf	4	2	Waterman, 3b	1	5
Sutton, 3b	4	1	Dean, rf	3	3
Ward, ss	3	1	H. Wright, cf	4	2
Kimball, 2b	3	1	Leonard, lf	5	1
Allison, cf	2	2	Brainard, p	4	1
Carleton, 1b	4	1	Sweasy, 2b	3	3
Pratt, p	2	3	McVey, c	3	3
Total	27	16	Total	27	27

Time of game: two hours and forty-five minutes.

Inning	1	2	3	4	5	6	7	8	9	Final
Forest City	2	2	0	5	0	5	1	0	1	16
Red Stockings	4	1	0	5	0	0	7	4	6	27

Umpire: Mr. Ellis, of the Athletic Club of Philadelphia.

The win in Cleveland was the 67th win of the season for the Red Stockings. In two years, the club had compiled an astounding record of 124 wins, 6 losses, and a tie. The convoluted rules governing the so-called national championship, however, gave the title to the far inferior New York Mutuals. But no one cared. In the hearts of America, the Cincinnati Red Stockings were the greatest team ever—the true champions.

As it turned out, the most successful team of all time had played its last game—at least as the Cincinnati Red Stockings—on that cold November day in Cleveland.

In late November, the Cincinnati Base Ball Club decided not to field a paid team in 1871. Harry Wright then took most of the team back with him to his home town of Boston, where they would have a future as the Boston Red Stockings.[29]

The Forest City Blue Stockings' future would be in Cleveland.

1871

The First "Show"

Traveling from as far away as Illinois, they came to New York City to gather at Collier's pub on St. Patrick's Day, 1871. Representing nine different ball clubs, they formed the National Association of Professional Base Ball Players. Henry Chadwick, famous sportswriter, historian, and statistician was there, thus giving the proceedings a look of official approval.

That day, the Cleveland Forest City Base Ball Club joined the National Association — baseball's first major league.

Joining Cleveland were the Boston Red Stockings, Chicago White Stockings, Fort Wayne Kekiongas, New York Mutuals, Philadelphia Athletics, Rockford Forest City, Troy Haymakers, and Washington Olympics.

All Aboard for Fort Wayne!

The Cleveland ball players got on board the T. W. & W. at 3 P.M. With a toot on the whistle, the release of a cloud of steam, and a slow turning of wheels, the train pulled out of the station. Traveling through a damp overcast night, the Forest City men arrived at Fort Wayne in the early morning hour of 1 A.M., and took refuge in the downtown Aveline House. All day the weather continued to look like rain, and when the team headed out to the grounds for the 3 o'clock game the sky was still a dark gray.

The Hamilton Field ballpark was built for the 1870 season, on land that had served as a Civil War camp; it was called the Rockhill Addition, and was near to the St. Mary's River.

Fort Wayne City Council, in June, granted the ball club's petition to fence off portions of unpaved Walnut, Fair, and Center streets where they crossed the ball field.

In honor of the beautiful grandstand at the Union Grounds in Cincinnati, known as the "Grand Duchess," Fort Wayne built their own "Grand Duchess" a lesser version of the original, but a pretty and solid structure none the less.[1] The players' clubhouse served as the foundation on which the grandstand seats and the roof were added. An open stand went up on either side of the grandstand. The field was completely fenced in, and in one corner of the park the official team pennant flew from an impressive 125-foot-tall pole. And for the first game with Cleveland, "Two beautiful new flags have been made to mark the foul lines, They were shown in Moderwell & Fowler's shop windows last evening."[2]

In a game a few weeks before the arrival of the Cleveland team, a spectator surnamed Barr, watching from his rig, decided it would be fun to drive his four-horse team all over the diamond, delaying the game. To prevent this, a "long railing"[3] crossing the outfield was put up to keep the vehicle trade in their rigs, and in their place: off the field of play. It would also help control any standing-room crowd. The threat of rain, however, eliminated any concern about standing-room problems at the Cleveland game.

The famous ball players of the Boston Red Stockings and Washington Olympics were meant to play in the new league's showcase inaugural. Rain ended that idea. Thus the Cleveland Forest City versus the Fort Wayne Kekiongas became, by default, the first major league game. The historical significance of this was lost on the players, as well as the patrons. They may not have even realized it was a *first*. The media after the game also failed to make note of it.

The crowd was only 200, a sprinkling of what had been anticipated had the weather looked more favorable. The game, however, was quite memorable, and the local and national sporting pages made much of it.

The Forest City Blue Stockings left their hotel and headed for Hamilton Field, hoping — against the dreary looking sky — that a game could be played. From quite a distance they spied the banner of the Fort Wayne Kekiongas, flying high and flapping hard atop its gigantic flagpole.

Nearer to the park, they could see the pennant in detail: on a field of red bunting was printed "Kekionga" in white letters, and along the outer edge of the banner was a border of blue trim.

The Cleveland team then entered the enclosure, and the Kekiongas, wearing their white uniforms with red stockings, escorted the Forest City, wearing their white uniforms with blue stockings, to the clubhouse.

Everything about the game promised to be a very red, white, and blue affair.

After warm-up practice, the teams assembled in front of the grandstand, and the coin was tossed. Fort Wayne won and chose to take the field.

The players (in opening-day batting order):

FORT WAYNE KEKIONGAS*

	Place of Birth	Date	Year	Age
Frank Williams, 3b	—	—	—	—
Robert T. Mathews, rhp	Baltimore, Md.	Nov. 7	1851	19
James H. Foran, 1b	New York	—	1848	22
Wallace Goldsmith, ss	Baltimore, Md.	—	1849	21
William F. Lennon, c	Brooklyn, N.Y.	—	1848	22
Thomas John Carey, 2b**	Brooklyn, N.Y.	—	1849	21
Edward John Mincher, lf	Baltimore, Md.	—	—	—
Joseph McDermont, cf	—	—	—	—
William Kelley, rf	New York, N.Y.	—	—	—
T. J. Donelly (sub.) (did not play)	—	—	—	—

*Kekionga is an old Indian name for Fort Wayne.
**Carey would play shortstop for Cleveland in 1879.

CLEVELAND FOREST CITY BLUE STOCKINGS

	Place of Birth	Date	Year	Age
James Laurie White, c	Canton, N.Y.	Dec. 7	1847	23
Eugene Kimball, 2b	Rochester, N.Y.	Aug. 31	1850	20
Charles Henry Pabor, lf	Brooklyn, N.Y.	Sept. 24	1846	24
Arthur Algernon Allison, cf	Phila., Pa.	Jan. 29	1849	22
Elmer White, rf	Canton, N.Y.	Dec. 7	1850	20
Al Pratt, rhp	Pittsburgh, Pa.	Nov. 19	1847	23
Ezra Ballou Sutton, 3b	Seneca Falls, N.Y.	Sept. 17	1850	20
James Carleton, 1b	New York	—	1849	21
John E. Bass, ss	Baltimore, Md.	—	1850	20
Caleb Clark Johnson (sub.) (did not play)	Fulton, Ill.	May 23	1844	26

The First Major League Game

Umpire John L. Boake, of Cincinnati, handed the baseball to catcher Bill Lennon, who tossed it to Bobby Mathews in the pitcher's box—45 feet away from the home plate. James "Deacon" White stepped into the left side of the batter's box, and prepared to receive one of right-handed Mathews' famous fast underhand deliveries. After a few quick "shoots" to the plate, White spotted one to his liking—he rifled it into right. By the time Bill Kelley had fielded it in, the "Deacon" was standing on second base; he had just made the major league's first hit—a double. White was then doubled up on a pop out to second and Pabor ended the inning with a foul out to the catcher.

Nothing further happened until the bottom of the second. Lennon led off with a double to left field. Carey hit a hard one toward center. Arthur Allison in center tumbled, fell hard, but hung on, as he made the catch of the game—a spectacular one-handed, far-reaching grab of Carey's slicing liner. Mincher flied out to Kimball at second. With two outs, McDermont came to bat. He hit a single, and from second, Lennon galloped home with the first run for Fort Wayne, and the first run in major league history.

The average ball game of that era, because of barehanded play, was a rather high-scoring, double-digit affair, but this game defied that norm.

When Fort Wayne came to bat in the bottom of the fifth the score was still 1–0 — an unheard-of feat. Kelley, with one out, hit a single. Williams now batted, and he watched as White let two pitches get by him to put the runner Kelley on third. Williams did his job, he put the ball in play, and his sacrifice plated Kelley with the game's second run.

Great pitching and great fielding kept both teams from scoring in the sixth, seventh, and eighth. The score was still an unbelievable 2–0 when Cleveland came to bat in the ninth.

Jim White, the man who had doubled to start the game, led off. He stroked a pitch for a hit that McDermont chased after. Goldsmith, the shortstop, quickly ran into the outfield for a relay from McDermont. White, picking up steam, rounded first and headed for second. Goldsmith got the ball, fired it to Carey covering second. He snagged it and tagged out White. One down. Kimball meekly fouled out to the catcher Lennon. Two outs. Pabor, the last chance, was next. He put a fly up to the center fielder McDermont who got under it, caught it, and dropped it. With Pabor on first Allison now came to the bat. Could he bring glory to Cleveland, in this, the first major league game of what is now one hundred and thirty plus years of major league games?

He struck out!

This ended what was believed by many to have been the lowest-scoring professional game on record. As the rules required, Fort Wayne had to bat in the meaningless bottom of the ninth. They went through the motions, going out in one, two, three order.

Final: Fort Wayne 2, Cleveland 0.

Ft. Wayne Gazette:

SCORE BY INNINGS

Inning	1 2 3	4 5 6	7 8 9	Final
Cleveland	0 0 0	0 0 0	0 0 0	0
Fort Wayne	0 1 0	0 1 0	0 0 0	2

Umpire: Mr. J. L. Boake, of the Live Oaks, of Cincinnati. Scorers: B. Johnson for Cleveland and Wright Rockhill for Fort Wayne. Passed balls: White 2, Lennon 1. Time of game: Two Hours.

The following inning-by-inning account of the game is from the *Fort Wayne Gazette:*

First Inning—Cleveland. J. White lead off by going to 2nd on a fine hit. Carey made a double play, catching a fly from Kimball and putting J. White out at 2nd. Lennon took a foul from Pabor. No runs.

Fort Wayne. J. White took a foul fly from Williams and a foul from Mathews. Foran hit to 1st; Goldsmith foul fly to J. White, leaving Foran on 1st. No runs.

Second Inning—Cleveland. Allison after three got to 1st; E. White struck out; Allison to 2nd, Foran and Carey failing to run him out between bases; Pratt foul fly to Foran; Sutton out on a fine fly catch by Mincher; Allison left on 2nd. No runs.

Fort Wayne. Lennon going to bat, made 2nd, by a fine hit to left field; Carey struck a fly to Allison, who took it finely with one hand, reaching far for it, and falling down; Mincher struck a fly to

Al Pratt, the flame-throwing Cleveland pitcher (1869–1872), was in the pitching box for the first National Association game, as he and Cleveland lost, 2–0, at Ft. Wayne on May 4, 1871.

Kimball; McDermont hit to 1st, sending Lennon home; Kelley foul fly to J. White. McDermont left on 1st. One run.

Third Inning — Cleveland. Carlton going to the bat strikes out; Bass struck a high fly to Mincher; J. White gave a foul fly to Lennon. No runs.

Fort Wayne. Williams foul bound, and Mathews foul tip to J. White, both fine catches; Foran out on a foul fly to E. White. No runs.

Fourth Inning — Cleveland. Kimball and Pabor out on fine flies to Williams; Allison out on a fine foul fly catch by Lennon. No runs.

Fort Wayne. Goldsmith to 1st on called balls; Lennon out on a foul tip finely taken by J. White; Carey to 1st, forcing Goldsmith out at 2nd; Carey to 2nd on passed ball; Mincher fly to Pratt; Carey left on 2nd. No runs.

Fifth inning — Cleveland. E. White struck out; Pratt to 1st on called balls; Sutton hits to 1st, sending Pratt to 3d; Sutton out at 1st, after a foul; Mincher caught finely a high fly from Carlton; Pratt left on 3d. No runs.

Fort Wayne — McDermont out on 1st by Kimball and Carlton; Kelley hits to 1st and reaches 2nd; he goes to 3d on passed ball; Williams out at 1st, sending Kelley home; Mathews out on foul bound to J. White. One run.

Sixth Inning — Cleveland. Mincher put Bass out by a beautiful foul catch; Goldsmith muffed a fly from J. White, who went to 1st; Kimball out on fly to Foran; J. White to 2nd on passed ball; Pabor a fly to Mathews; J. White left on 2nd. No runs.

Fort Wayne. Foran a fly to Kimball; Goldsmith a foul tip splendidly taken by J. White; Lennon a fly to Bass. No runs.

Seventh Inning — Cleveland. Allison to 1st by poor play of Goldsmith; E. White struck out; Allison out running to 2nd; Pratt fly to Carey. No runs.

Fort Wayne. Carey out at 1st by Pratt to Carlton; Mincher out at 1st, by Sutton to Carlton, McDermont out at 1st. No runs.

Eighth Inning — Cleveland. Sutton out on foul fly well caught by Lennon; Carlton out at 1st by Williams to Foran; Bass struck a fly which was finely taken by Goldsmith. No runs.

Fort Wayne. Kelley fly to Allison; Williams fly finely taken by Kimball; Mathews out at 1st. No runs.

Ninth Inning — Cleveland. J. White out at 2nd by a fine strike to centre field, fielded in by McDermont to Goldsmith and he to Carey; Kimball foul fly to Lennon; Pabor to 1st on a fly muffed by McDermont; Allison struck out leaving Pabor on 1st. No runs.

Fort Wayne. Foran and Goldsmith out at 1st by Pratt to Carlton; Lennon out at 1st by Bass to Carlton. No runs.[4]

Note:

This is undoubtedly the best game on record. We know of nothing like it that has ever happened before. Just think of it, only two runs made in nine full innings![5]

—*Fort Wayne Gazette*

The First Dose for 1871— A Whole Nest of Goose Eggs
0 0 0 0 0 0 0 0 0 [6]

—*Cleveland Leader*

... the darkly glorious game of Thursday.[7]

—*Cleveland Leader*

Al Pratt's counterpart was the great curveballer Bobby Mathews, who shut out the Forest Citys on five hits.

The Cincinnati Commercial speaks of the game at Ft. Wayne, between the Forest Citys and Kekiongas as 'the greatest game on record.' Its correspondent speaks in the very highest terms of the play of both clubs.[8]

—*Cleveland Herald*

A Rainbow for all the Baseball Tomorrows

Within ten minutes after the game was finished, the good news had gone through the city like wild fire and everyone was congratulating his neighbor. Then down came the rain. The sun came out of the clouds, and a magnificent double rainbow appeared, in two perfect arches, promising a bright and victorious future for both of the contestants on this hard fought field.[9]

—*Fort Wayne Gazette*

Downtown the crowd gathered at the National City Bank Building. They watched as the score came in over the telegraph, live and direct from the ballpark, and was posted inning by inning on the bulletin board. It was game two of the championship season, and Cleveland was playing in Illinois against the Rockford Forest City Green Stockings. At the ballpark, the cold weather kept the crowd at around a thousand.

Rockford had some good ball players. Among them was Adrian "Cap" Anson, a product of Marshalltown, Iowa. He would become a member of the National Baseball Hall of Fame, and be the first major leaguer to reach a career three thousand hits (1897). Fastballer William "Cherokee" Fisher was the Rockford pitcher, and Al Pratt the pitcher for the Clevelanders.

Cleveland, from the very start, hammered Fisher's swift pitches on a regular basis. In the first inning Kimball, Allison, Pratt, Elmer White, Sutton, and Carleton crossed the plate.

The Blue Stockings never looked back: "The score of the final inning finally came, and with the cheering total of 12 to 4 in mind, the happy gathering went home to tea."[10] Cleveland had just won its first major league game!

Chicago was the next stop before heading home. Here Cleveland, though they played a good game, came up on the short end of the score. The bad feelings between the two clubs from the year before were put aside after this fair and well-played game. Ezra Sutton distinguished himself, his team, and the city of Cleveland, by hitting the major league's first and second home runs.

Score: White Stockings 14, Blue Stockings 12.

The Forest City Base Ball Grounds

Lovers of the national pastime were invited to come out in the first days of April, and have a look at their new ballpark. Many did.

Riding the East Cleveland streetcar line out Garden Avenue (Central Ave.), the curious soon arrived at Wilson St. (E. 55th). Looking across the street from Cleveland into the original city of East Cleveland, they saw, on the southeast corner of the intersection, the wooden skeleton of the new grandstand, and noted that it was almost all the way up.

Leaving the cars they crossed the street, where they were escorted into the facility through a gate-tunnel cut through the grandstand itself and began their tour.

They noticed that the diamond had been marked out, and all of the playing field, as well as the sidelines, had been made flat with heavy horse-drawn rollers. To the left and to the right of the grandstand, the view showed the auxiliary stands going up.

The public was told that the grandstand of course will be roofed, and that the side stands are to be "open" ones (not roofed), and that altogether they will seat 750 people. It was pointed out that a tall wooden fence, covering five hundred square feet, would surround the grounds. Their guide said that gates to serve pedestrians, yet wide enough to allow the carriage trade in to watch the games from their rigs, will be put into the north and west walls of the outfield fence. And finally, that near the park's north gate, the players' clubhouse will be built.

The visitors were invited to come back for the beginning of the baseball season in May by which time, it was believed, there would be nice green grass to go along with a hopefully very nice spring day.

Opening day details:

The new rules of 1871 allowed the visitors to name five potential umpires in advance of the game.

Cleveland telegraphed the recommended choice of Mr. Willard, a Chicagoan they knew and felt would be competent and impartial. Chicago, however, brought Mr. Haynie to town instead. He was an unknown entity in Cleveland, but was an office holder in the National Association — its secretary. And since the "straight" game in Chicago the week before had seemed to erase any enmity left over from the controversial contest of 1870, Cleveland — with an eye to the large crowd in the stands, and telling themselves that Mr. Haynie was after all a league official — readily agreed to the replacement. Had they been aware of Mr. Haynie's alleged unethical maneuverings at league headquarters, they might have anticipated that a "fix" was indeed a possibility.

Cleveland's First Major League Home Game

The Chicago White Stockings versus the Cleveland Forest City Blue Stockings: The weather was perfect and the audience large. The Chicago White Stockings arrived in the morning, and later made it out to the grounds for the three o'clock game start.

The visitors took warm-up practice first. The crowd watched, and commented on the stylish uniforms of the Chicago club. The "western" men wore blue caps with a white star on top. Their blue-trimmed white flannel shirts were inscribed with a blue C on the breast. A blue-and-white belt held up their knickerbockers of bright blue lined with white cord. The famed white stockings themselves were made of pure British thread, and worn with spiked shoes of white goatskin — very nice.

The crowd came to its feet and applauded when the Cleveland team came out for their warm-up time. The Forest City Blue Stockings were wearing their usual outfit of white hat, white shirt, white pants above blue stockings, and, on the shirt front, the fancy English F-over-C monogram.

The pitchers: George "The Charmer" Zettlein of Chicago and Albert "Uncle Al" Pratt of Cleveland. Mr. Haynie refereed the coin toss that sent Chicago to the bat.

First inning:

"Bub" McAtee, the first baseman of Chicago, stepped to the plate and the umpire signaled for the action to start. Jim White fired the ball to his pitcher, Al Pratt, and Al went into his windup. McAtee ignored a few offerings before he laced one, a hard liner, for a clean triple. An out later, Charlie Hodes brought him home with a ground out to third for the first run of the game and the first run at the new grounds. One run.

Cleveland came to bat for the first time. Jim White, Gene Kimball, and Charlie Pabor all hit rollers to the pitcher, and were out at first. No runs.

This listing from the W. S. Robison Co. City Directory shows the Forest City Base Ball Grounds (National Association 1871–1872) to be just outside of Cleveland, in old East Cleveland, a city that Cleveland annexed in 1873.

The only record of the Forest City Grounds exact location

Second inning:

Elmer White made a great catch in right on a Joe Simmons long fly, and Ed Duffy got an infield scratch past second base. Ed Pinkham came to bat, and chose this moment to do something that he would do but once all year—he hit a home run. It went deep into right field and all the way to the fence. He crossed the plate to a gracious round of applause. No more damage. Two runs.

Art Allison led off with a single, stole second, and moved to third on a fielding miscue. Ezra Sutton hit a grounder that was dropped, allowing Allison to score Cleveland's first run. The next three men were retired. One run.

Third inning:

Mart King led off the inning by hitting "a splendid home run."[11] His effort was also applauded. Charlie Hodes flied out to second. Jimmy Wood knocked a long hit to the outfield, but in trying to be a hero, he was tagged out at the plate by Jim White on the relay from second. Joe Simmons, next, tried the hero game too. He hit a deep one to center, but Art Allison tracked it down and fired a beauty to the plate, and Simmons, on a close play, was out at the "winning post."[12] One run.

Chicago, known for hitting but not for fielding, showed why. After a number of errors in the bottom of the third, Cleveland scored 4 and went up by a run. During the inning, Al Pratt hit a triple, but was left stranded on third. Four runs.

Fourth inning:

Tom Foley, the first man up, walked but was forced at second. The umpire now discovered that Pratt couldn't throw a strike. The Chicago players walked and continued to walk until 2 runs had come in—this put them up by 1. McAtee and King, however, couldn't wait for the umpire's help. Pratt's pitches were looking very juicy now—too good for any patience. A foul tip to White, and a fly to second, and the visitors headed for the field. Two runs.

James White came to bat to lead off, and soon put a charge into a George "The Charmer" Zettlein pitch—all the way to the wall in center. With the assembled throng yelling and shouting and clapping as much as they could, "[Jim] came home bound on a gallop"[13]—plating the first major league home run for Cleveland, at Cleveland—tying the game at 6. The ecstatic cheering was as loud as it was long. Then, with 2 outs, Pabor and Kimball earned singles, but Allison failed, flying out to the shortstop. One run.

Fifth inning:

Both teams were denied any runs by excellent fielding. No runs.

Sixth inning:

Duffy started the frame by flying out to short stop Bass. Pinkham and Zettlein walked—and then the trouble began. McAtee hit the ball to Sutton at third and he forced out the runner there. His relay caught McAtee wandering too far off first for the third out—or so it appeared to almost everyone.

To the Chicago rescue came Umpire Haynie: he called McAtee safe at first. The floodgates then opened, and with two outs, the White Stockings, with a little help from their friend, continued to score: "At this [juncture] the spectators, a very unusual thing for Cleveland, exhibited their intense disgust vociferously. Shouting or hissing at an umpire is to be deprecated at all times, but the crowd seemed quite unable to refrain when they saw that the Forest Cities, with their usual meekness, would submit to such gross injustice without a murmur."[14]

Five runs.

Cleveland quietly went out. No runs.

Seventh inning:

The reporter covering the game didn't bother to explain how Chicago scored their runs in the seventh. Three runs.

Cleveland was shut out. No runs.

Eighth inning:

Chicago added the last of its 18 runs. Four runs.

Cleveland was losing 18–6 but continued to play. They somehow managed 4 runs to keep it alive, but "a flagrant error of judgment put Pabor out at third."[15] This ended the inning. Four runs. However, "This last decision was the straw that broke the camel's back and the officers of the Forest City club coincided with Captain Pabor in surrendering the game as it stood."[16]

Umpire James Haynie then called the game a forfeit, and by the rules it was declared a 9–0 win for Chicago. (The official score of a forfeited major league game remains 9–0 to the present day.) The Chicago players expressed regret at the cause of all the trouble. Cleveland said nothing as it handed the game ball — a trophy for the winners — over to Captain Wood of the White Stockings.

According to one history of the proceedings, the crowd then swarmed onto the field and had their say.

Notes: • Al Pratt, and his relief pitcher Charlie Pabor, were said to have been very accurate with their pitches to the plate this day. The umpire, however, called nine walks on them. • The game was protested to the league office, but no more was heard of it.

The score by innings (unofficial runs):

Inning	1	2	3	4	5	6	7	8	Final
Chicago	1	2	1	2	0	5	3	4	18
Cleveland	0	1	4	1	0	0	0	4	10

Cleveland had an exciting game at home with Rockford at the end of May. They were up by a run after eight, 10–9. Rockford sent their pitcher Cherokee Fisher up to start the ninth. He did it once all year, and he did it now: he hit a home run. It tied the game.

Cleveland ninth:

Kimball smote viciously to Ham [the shortstop], but he let the ball go between his feet and Kimball made first, stealing second a few moments later. Pratt made first by Anson's wild throw, Kimball to third. On Sutton's beauty Kimball came sailing in, making the winning run amidst loud and prolonged applause.

Score: Rockford 10, Cleveland 11[17]

— *Cleveland Herald*

The Successful Eastern Tour

June and July:

		Forest City	Opponents
Oswego, NY	W	40	8
*Haymakers of Troy, NY	W	20	11
Lowell, MA	W	23	17
*Red Stockings of Boston, MA	W	8	7
Eckfords of Brooklyn, NY	W	7	1
*Mutuals of New York City, NY	L	6	10
Stars of Brooklyn, NY	W	6	0
Resolutes of Elizabeth, NJ	W	24	3
Experts of Philadelphia, PA	W	10	9
Nationals of Washington, D.C.	W	12	2
*Olympics of Washington, D.C.	L	3	16
Pastimes of Baltimore, MD	W	22	9
*Athletics of Philadelphia, PA	L	9	22
Eckfords of Brooklyn, NY	L	3	4
*Mutuals of New York City, NY	W	6	5

* A member of the National Association and an official major league contest. All the other games were with either independent professional or strong amateur teams. The American public, at this time, judged their teams' worth by overall game performance, not just by their major league game record.

JUNE

Cleveland played an amateur Boston team, the Lowells, before they played the Boston Red Stockings. Hardly anyone showed up to buy a ticket; they were all at the free International Order of Odd Fellows parade.

Therefore, Cleveland was quite happy when a crowd of six thousand showed up, with their money, for the follow-up game with the Red Stockings (half of the Boston players were from Harry Wright's Cincinnati team of the year before).

They were also quite pleased with the game results. In a major upset Cleveland won the game 8–7.

JULY 4

The Forest City Juniors (a.k.a. the Eastern Rocks) played the Resolutes of Oberlin in front of a large holiday audience at the Forest City Grounds, and won 38–25. The senior Forest City, however, was in the home of the Liberty Bell, Philadelphia. And the people there were in the spirit for a baseball game — all eight thousand of them.

Philadelphia was led by third baseman Levi Meyerle, second baseman Al Reach, and pitcher Dick McBride. Levi Meyerle was to be the league's batting champion of 1871 (.492); he was also the major league's first player of Jewish ancestry. Al Reach was born in London, England, and would be the founder of a sporting goods empire (the Reach brand name of today comes from his company). Dick McBride would lead the league in wins (20) in 1871 and lead the Athletics to the pennant.

The best team in the country showed the Forest City men why they were the best, by clobbering Cleveland 22–9.

The last game of the tour was against the New York Mutuals.

The game was exciting and well played until "A drizzling rain commenced to fall in the eighth inning and it was difficult to hold the ball."[18]

Cleveland was on top 4–3 when they led off the ninth — in the wet. They scored two insurance runs. Now the "Mutes" came fighting back. They had scored 2 runs by the time two were out. They were now trailing 6–5 and the bases were loaded. Dick Pearce walked slowly to the plate, as the Mutuals' friends shouted for "Dickey to knock the cover off."[19] Dickey didn't knock the ball, he nipped it instead — right into the waiting hands of catcher Jim White. Game over.

Inning	1	2	3	4	5	6	7	8	9	Final
Forest City	0	0	0	1	1	1	1	0	2	6
Mutuals	0	1	0	0	0	0	2	0	2	5

The *Cleveland Herald:* "The boys have acquitted themselves splendidly, far exceeding the expectations of their friends, and we hope they will receive a cordial welcome on their return."[20]

August: The Road West

Cleveland was to begin its road trip in Fort Wayne — that was, if the team could get to Fort Wayne. Team president Peter Rose and Captain Kimball got off the train to telegraph for overnight berths on the change train. They missed the train. Unfortunately, they had the team's tickets in their pockets. However, the railroads accepted their telegraph messages as vouchers, and the team was allowed to ride on through.

At the Fort Wayne game, Cleveland got their ticket punched by the Kekiongas, losing 15–3.

Cleveland went to Chicago to play the White Stockings. But first they played a neutral site game there against Rockford, and another against the amateur Aetnas of Chicago. The Rockford team traveled seventy miles hoping for a nice payday. What they got was a win, but the payday was average — only 1,500 showed up for the game. Score: Rockford 11, Cleveland 5.

Cleveland was now ready for a tune-up game with the Aetnas. They almost lost, but squeaked by 16–15.

Chicago had chosen Eb Smith of Cleveland as an acceptable umpire. Cleveland brought Frank Peake of Pittsburgh instead, claiming Smith was unavailable due to pressing business. Captain Wood of the White Stockings, after being assured by Al Pratt, who was from Pittsburgh, that Peake was well respected there, accepted the substitution on one condition: if Peake was found wanting in the skill department, a man of their choosing would be allowed. Cleveland agreed.

Chicago, August 10, 1871—The Chicago game, Cleveland style: "The game was witnessed by three or four thousand people. Play commenced at 3:30. Kimball's ill luck stuck to him and he lost the toss."[21]

There was a large crowd of rowdies at the game, and they booed everything Cleveland did, and cheered anything Chicago did. They went out of their way to harass the umpire, trying to keep him rattled.

Cleveland scored 5 runs to start the scoring in the second. Chicago had lived up to its reputation for less-than-stellar fielding—4 of the runs were unearned. The earned run was a Jim White home run.

Concerning the Cleveland-sponsored umpire: "When, after a little, Mr. Frank Peake had plainly shown that he knew rather less of base ball than he did of Sanskrit, Captain Wood applied to Mr. Kimball to redeem his promise, and put in another man."[22] Kimball said he had changed his mind on that score, and President Peter Rose, when asked to intervene, said "Peake stays."

Chicago now realized that they had been outmaneuvered by the rubes from Cleveland. They had two options: walk off the field and let Peake forfeit the game to Cleveland (and protest it to a "do nothing" league office), or play it out and hope for the best. They chose the latter.

Peake really didn't know much about the rules of the game; the crowd and sometimes both teams were upset by his calls. However, he knew his job, and his ignorance fell intentionally (and sometimes unintentionally) most often in favor of Cleveland.

The high point of Mr. Peake's career may have come in the fifth inning, when his sponsor, Al Pratt, went about the business of stealing second and was plainly tagged out by Jimmy Wood.

The umpire said safe, and Al, encouraged by this, immediately took off for third. He had to run way out of the base line to avoid Wood, who still had the ball. Wood stood there waiting for the umpire to call the runner out for leaving the base line: "Pratt's friend said 'No' and the consequence of this and eleven other like decisions was the defeat of the Chicago's."[23] Cleveland won the game 12–10.

The *Cleveland Herald* man on the scene had no problem containing his glee over the game. Quoted from a "Special Dispatch to the Herald"[24]:

Of the umpire: "Considered mathematically, it may be said of Mr. Peake [of Pittsburgh]: scored four runs for Cleveland, assisted six times, and put out four of the opposing side. He made no base hits."[25]

Of the crowd: "The average Chicago base ball crowd affords strong evidence in favor of Darwin's theory of the descent of man, with the alteration that he came from an animal having much longer ears and much less sense than the monkey tribe."[26]

In a few weeks all these shenanigans would be forgotten in the face of tragedy and a call to help.

Selected Games by Opponent and Standings

PHILADELPHIA ATHLETICS won the pennant at 22 and 7.
July: Forest City L-9 at Philadelphia W-22
(Crowd—eight thousand)
July: Philadelphia W-18 Forest City L-10
(At neutral site—Cincinnati)
July: Philadelphia Athletics W-13 at Forest City L-8
(Crowd—two thousand)
July: Forest City L-8 at Philadelphia W-11

CHICAGO WHITE STOCKINGS finished second at 20 and 9.
May: Forest City L-12 at Chicago W-14
(Ezra Sutton of F.C.s hit the major league's first and second home runs.)
May: Chicago W-9* at Forest City L-0*
(*The controversial game was forfeited in the eighth; Cleveland was losing at the time 18–10. James "Deacon" White hit the first home run at the home grounds to right field in the fourth inning.)
Aug: Forest City W-12 at Chicago L-10
(Crowd — estimated at three to four thousand)

BOSTON RED STOCKINGS finished third at 22 and 10.
June: Forest City W-8 at Boston L-7
(Crowd — six thousand)
July: Boston W-12 at Forest City L-8
Sept.: Forest City L-10 at Boston W-31
(Crowd — eight hundred)
Sept.: Boston W-10 at Forest City L-7
Oct: Boston W-24 at Forest City L-5

WASHINGTON OLYMPICS finished fourth at 16 and 15.
May: Washington W-13 at Forest City L-9
June: Forest City L-3 at Washington W-16
Oct.: Washington L-3 at Forest City W-22

TROY HAYMAKERS finished fifth at 15 and 15.
June: Forest City W-20 at Troy L-11

NEW YORK MUTUALS finished sixth at 17 and 18
June: Forest City L-6 at New York W-10
July: Forest City W-6 at New York L-5
(Crowd — two thousand)
Aug: New York L-5 at Forest City W-10
Sept.: Forest City L-8 at New York W-11
Sept.: Forest City W-7 at New York L-5

FORT WAYNE KEKIONGAS finished eighth at 7 and 21
May: Forest City L-0 at Fort Wayne W-2
(The first major league game)
May: Fort Wayne W-16 at Forest City L-7
Aug.: Forest City L-3 at Fort Wayne W-15

ROCKFORD FOREST CITYS finished ninth and last at 6 and 21.
May: Forest City W-12 at Rockford L-4
(Cleveland's first major-league win; crowd — one thousand; weather very cold)
May: Rockford L-10 at Forest City W-11
Aug.: Rockford W-11 Forest City L-5
(At neutral site — Chicago; crowd — fifteen hundred)

Catastrophe in Chicago

Chicago, October 8, 1871— It started on DeKoven Street in a barn. A cow lived there — Mrs. O'Leary's cow, and legend says the cow kicked over a lantern and started the "Great Chicago Fire." There had been a drought in Chicago and the fire spread quickly. Property damage in 1871 dollars was estimated at an incredible $187 million. The known loss of life was set at two hundred and fifty.

But the true human tragedy was that one hundred thousand Chicagoans were retreating from their burning homes and struggling through the blocked and crowded arteries, hoping to get far enough ahead of the advancing flames so they could lie down in the streets and get some sleep.

The people of the city of Cleveland were among the first in the nation to respond. Extracts from the *Cleveland Herald*:

The job:

"... cooked victuals, clothing and other necessities will be received at the [train] depot ... collecting wagons will go around and get what is most needed."[27]

The response:

"Bread, crackers, cheese, cooked meats, blankets, bedding and other articles in the present emergency were brought out in liberal quantities and piled into the boxes ... others were taking their contributions directly to the depot."[28]

"[With] ... many of the poor actually giving their last loaf and dividing their scanty blankets ... those who gave did so without desire of notoriety."[29]

"Up to Tuesday night nine full car loads [boxcars] of supplies had been sent from Cleveland."[30]

"The surrounding townships have begun to send in ... the workmen in the rolling mills gave their pay for yesterday amounting to three thousand dollars."[31]

Many of the Cleveland notables went with the first relief train to Chicago to see to the distribution of supplies, and to see first hand the damages, and figure out what was the best action to take next.

Eighteen seventy-one, a year with a May sky showing a double rainbow of hope and good will following the first major league ball game. Eighteen seventy-one, a year that saw an October sky over Chicago burning bright red, fueled by countless homes and buildings, including the Chicago baseball park itself.

Eighteen seventy-one was quite a year!

1872

The Second Time Around

The National Association dropped three teams for 1872 and added four. Chicago was gone because of the Great Fire. Fort Wayne and Rockford left because of travel cost and poor attendance. Added were the "Lord" Baltimores, Brooklyn "Atlantics," Brooklyn "Eckfords" Middletown (CT) "Mansfields." (The Mansfields were named after General Joseph Mansfield, who died at Antietam in the Civil War. He was from the Middletown, Connecticut, area.) Cleveland now remained as the only team from the Midwest. Cleveland, however, with a bankroll of $15,000, had no problems to limit them from putting a top nine on the field.

The seven directors elected for 1872 were: Peter Rose, N. B. Prentice, N. B. Sherwin, J. N. Frazee, Marcus Alonzo Hanna, Charles Bulkley, and Clay H. Doolittle. They represented wealth, industry, national politics, and, most of all, their class. The men who had played baseball in its amateur gentlemen's days, now ran it in its business days—hiring the lower classes to play it.

James F. Evans was a vice-president on the board of the National Association and a Clevelander. His one-year term was about to end at the league's annual meeting. Mr. Evans arranged for that meeting to be held in Cleveland, on March 5, 1872, at the Kennard House. The president of the Association, Mr. James N. Kerns of Philadelphia, was unable to attend, so Mr. Evans served in his place.

Evans sponsored H. Clay Doolittle of the Forest Citys as a candidate for league vice-president. He was elected.

Evans was also able to get the league to adopt a code of player conduct. This was in essence the same set of so-called model rules of behavior that the Forest City team played under in 1871. The league's players, as had been the case for the Forest City men earlier, had no say in the matter.

Scott Hastings traded in his green stockings for blue ones. He was still a Forest City, but no longer an old Rockford Forest City Green Stocking, but a newly signed Cleveland Forest City Blue Stocking. He split catching duties with Jim White.

Charles Sweasy had been one of the famous Cincinnati Red Stockings. In 1871 he played with the Washington Olympics, who wore blue stockings. Cleveland gave him some fresh blue socks, and he signed up for 1872.

Cleveland had a new-look infield this year. They added Joe Simmons, a former White Stocking, to play first; Charley Sweasy was sent to second, and Jim "Long Jim" Holdsworth was put at short. And baseball's first player of Dutch birth, Rynie Wolters, came on board as an extra pitcher and outfielder.

The officials of the Forest City Base Ball Club hired J. H. Murch, and gave him the title of Superintendent of the Forest City Base Ball Grounds. Mr. Murch owned a restaurant downtown on Bank Street (W. 6th). This experience would help him in his job of running a concession at the grounds. He was also responsible for groundskeeping among his other chores.

The improvements by Mr. Murch were largely aimed at increasing the female patronage. The list below is extracted from the *Cleveland Herald*'s reporting of April 20, 1872:

1. Free ice water will be in the grandstand at all times.
2. An usher will see the ladies comfortably seated.
3. Lemonade, creams, candies and fruits—in their season—will be available in the grandstand.
4. No intoxicating liquors will be sold on the grounds. [Beer, however, was made available in the outfield clubhouse.]
5. Elegant refreshment rooms [restrooms] for the ladies have been fixed up.
6. Police protection inside and out of the park has been increased.

Mr. Murch, on the last Sunday of April, decided to take a ride and, while at it, pass by the ballpark. As he neared the grounds, he noticed a big plume of smoke rising from near the south fence. He hurried his team and found quite a fire under way as he arrived. Also under way were two youngsters, running from the fire as fast as they could run.

He put out the fire and became a hero in the papers for having saved the fence, and possibly the ballpark itself. Murch promised, "A good watch will be kept hereafter around the grounds and buildings."[1]

Perhaps a bit heady with notoriety, J. H. Murch took it upon his own authority to announce to the *Herald*: "The headquarters of the Association for the receiving of news of the games of the tour will be at J. H. Murch & Co., Bank street, where a bulletin board, with innings as they are played, will be for inspection."[2] President Peter Rose took exception to this promotion of Mr. Murch's personal place of business as an Association headquarters. No more claims of being any kind of headquarters of the Forest City Club were heard from Mr. Murch after that.

The First Eastern Tour of 1872

The season started on May 14 in Washington, D.C., and moved up the East Coast until winding up in New York on May 25. The schedule had 10 games, 9 of which were for the pennant. Game one was an exhibition game with the independent professional Washington Nationals club. It was not an auspicious start for the baseball season. Cleveland lost 13–10. The official opener for the pennant, however, had a much happier ending. Cleveland won in convincing fashion over the Washington Olympics 16–2.

The next game was in Baltimore. The Lord Baltimores had stocked their National Association entry with a number of men from the three abandoned Midwest franchises: Bill Craver,

Cherokee Fisher, Lip Pike, Tom Carey, and — most important of all — home-town hero and fastball phenomenon Bobby Mathews.

The Lord — or, rather, the owner — of the Baltimore team had a thing for the color yellow — a very bright, gaudy yellow. He made it the color of the players' uniforms. The men hated it. The national press loved it (in a derisive sense), calling the Lord Baltimores at various times the "sunflowers," the "mustard legs," and the "canaries" (perhaps the first of the Baltimore "birds" — Orioles coming at a later date).

The "mustard legs" were better than the "blue legs" this day. Score: Baltimore 21, Cleveland 12.

A lot of money was bet on ball games in Cleveland. Many friends of the Forest City, not excluding newspapermen, enjoyed betting in "poole halls." By using live telegraph reports from a ball game, they could bet on the score by inning.

Many a bettor was not too happy when, during the May road trip, the Philadelphia Athletics beat Cleveland heavily 31–7. The next day, the Forest City bounced back with a win in New York over the Atlantics 16–7. The next four games were losses: Mutuals 15, Cleveland 6; Mansfields 10, Cleveland 5; Troy 10, Cleveland 2; Eckfords 12, Cleveland 4. The game in Boston was rained out. The road trip of 2 wins and 6 losses was seen as a total failure.

The sportswriters now began to crucify the team in print:

How Shall We Receive Them?

A triumphal arch will be constructed over the canal where it joins the Cuyahoga, and through this the survivors will march following the canal bed (which will contain only mud and dead cats) to the dog pound, where they will receive an address from the policeman on duty there, and then will be conducted in carriages through the back alleys to the jail, where they can receive that rest and quiet they need.

There are a thousand occupations for such young men as compose the Forest City ball club.... Let them become bartenders, and catch tumblers on the fly or flies on the tumblers as they see fit.... Men who can handle a club are wanted to fill the ranks of the Colorado potato bug killers, there is glory for the boys anywhere outside of the ball field, will they reach for it?"[3]

In Memoriam

The Nine of Nines is about to return to its native heath, "picked" as thoroughly and completely as any Thanksgiving turkey.

Upon their arrival at the depot the remains of the 'F. C. B. B. C.' will be tenderly gathered up and deposited in the 'Black Maria,' which the Workhouse authorities have generously offered for the occasion, to obviate the expense of a hearse. The funeral procession will then form in the following order.

"Black Maria," surmounted by a rooster
with his head wrung off.
"Eastern Rocks," or Forest City Juniors,
with bats reversed, pall bearers.
Papworth's Band, playing the "Rogue's
March."
Brigade of market women, with baskets of
goose eggs.
Whitewashers of Cleveland in a body, with
pails and brushes, singing "John
Brown's Body."
Sprinkling carts, in operation, typifying the
blessed rain that saved a defeat in
Boston.
Gray's Band, playing the tune on which the
aged cow shuffled off this mortal coil.
President and other officers of the F. C. B. B. C.
upon cots in ambulances.
Members of the Club, arrayed in sackcloth
and ashes.

> Victims of misplaced confidence, who stacked
> and lost their money, with crape on
> their hats and arms, singing,
> "Let me hit him for
> his mother."
> Miscellaneous assortment of mourners, wiping their eyes with
> red bandannas.
> Small but wicked boys, singing. "That's the
> way the money goes— Pop goes
> the weasel."

The procession will move by a circuitous route, through the suburbs of the city, to the base ball grounds, on Wilson avenue. The remains will be decently interred in one corner of the field. A tombstone will be erected over their last resting place bearing the inscription:

> Here lie
> The earthly remains of the
> FOREST CITY PICKED NINE
> They have reached the
> HOME BASE.[4]

With all the vilifying in print going on, management decided that, rather than open in Cleveland with Baltimore as scheduled, a few neutral-site games at Chicago might be a good idea. Chicago, recovering from the Great Fire, would not field a major league team of its own until 1874. Dexter Park, a racetrack north of the fire zone, was the site of the games in Chicago.

After the Forest City lost both games to Baltimore at the Chicago venue — 5–2 and 13–3 — the two clubs headed for Cleveland and an uncertain welcome at the opener.

Home Opener

> "BASEBALL! Grand Championship Game!
> First of the Season
> BALTIMORES VS. FOREST CITY
> Saturday, June 1st, 1872. game called at 3 P.M."[5]

FOREST CITY	*BALTIMORE*
Scott Hastings, rf	John Radcliff, ss
Ezra Sutton, 3b	Bill Craver, c
Joe Simmons, 1b	Dick Higham, rf
James "Deacon" White, c	Tom York, lf
Al "Uncle Al" Pratt, p	Bill "Cherokee" Fisher, 3b
Jim "Long Jim" Holdsworth, ss	Lipman "Lip" Pike, 2b
Charley Sweasy, 2b	Tom Carey, 1b
Art Allison, cf	George Hall, cf
Charley Pabor, lf ("The Old Woman in The Red Cap")	Bobby Mathews, p

Baltimore went to the bat first. Two fly-ball outs, a single, and another fly out, and they went to the field.

Twelve hundred cheered as the Blue Stockings came to bat for the first time. Scott Hastings led off and earned first. Next up was Sutton. His grounder forced Hastings at second, but Sutton, in running to his base, ran into the first baseman — who was standing in the way. In the collision, "Both men were considerably bruised and the game was stopped for awhile."[6] Sutton returned to his base, but played the rest of the game with an injured throwing arm that affected his play. Simmons flied out to short, and Sutton made the last out trying to steal second.

Neither team scored in the second or third. Baltimore made the first run of the contest in the fourth, when Craver was able to score on a Sutton error. Cleveland responded with 3 runs in their turn. With some timely hitting, and the help of an error, Hastings, Sutton and Simmons reached home. Three runs.

No runs in the fifth. In the sixth, the Baltimores, with runs from Higham and Pike, tied the score at three. Cleveland in their half of the sixth went out in order.

In the seventh, champion umpire-baiter Bill Craver — unusually restrained to this point of the game — now entertained the crowd with some "chin music" (arguing chin-to-chin with the umpire).[7] Then he was called out on a foul bound to the catcher. He claimed the ball had hit one of the bats laid out behind the home plate, and the current rules said he was therefore not out. The umpire thought about it for a while, and told him to go back to bat. He then fouled the next pitch into Jim White's hands. The next two men went out easily.

In the bottom of the seventh Simmons got on base for Cleveland, and Jim White knocked him in for the go ahead run. One run.

Neither team scored in the eighth. The ninth began with Cleveland up 4–3. Hall led off by flying out to Sweasy at second. Mathews got on base because of a Holdsworth error, and when Allison dropped Radcliff's "sky raker" to center, Mathews came home with the tying run.[8] Cleveland then went down easily with two fly balls and a grounder to the pitcher. Score: 4–4.

The Baltimore manager proposed to call the game a draw, but Cleveland said — let the game go on! Baltimore tenth: York hit a long fly that Hastings in right field hung on to, "Cherokee" Fisher struck out, and "Lip" Pike grounded out short-to-first to end Baltimore's chances.

Cleveland tenth: "White took first on called balls (intense excitement); Pratt earned first; Holdsworth flew [sic] out to Fisher; Sweasy first on an error by Radcliff and White home; (great cheering)."[9]

Cleveland finished out the inning as the rules required. They added scores by Pratt and Sweasy to make the official score a 7–4 Cleveland victory. "There the joy began. Everyone stood up and yelled. Many shook hands and said they had told some one so. 'How was that for pitchin' and ketchin'?' was a popular conundrum among a certain class. Many went over to the clubhouse for lemonade; others, alas! for beer. The Baltimores climbed into their chariots and left the field, and the most fortunate victory ever won by the Forest Citys was secure."[10]

June

There were only 3 championship games played in Cleveland in June. Cleveland won the opener against Baltimore, and on June 17, made it 2 in a row by beating the New York Mutuals 11–4. The finale would be with the pennant-holding Philadelphia Athletics on Saturday, June 22.

The huge crowd — it would be the largest of the year — hoped their Blue Stockings might upset the champions, or at least make a good game of it.

Cleveland batted first, but on four hits, they scored only one run. The fielding on both sides was very sharp, but Philadelphia kept pecking away, and at the end of the fifth had a 7–1 lead. Cleveland, for the next three innings, played superb defense, not allowing the visitors a single score. Cleveland in that time managed to add 2.

"The ninth opened with a very unpromising score of seven to three," but the Forest City would not say die.[11] They scored a run, and then another. "The excitement became intense, every hit being greeted with tremendous cheers."[12] They scored a third run, Pabor scored the fourth and tying run of the inning, and Pratt crossed the plate with the go-ahead run. Cleveland had scored 5 runs in the miracle ninth to go up by an 8–7 score. Now, they only needed to shut down Philadelphia one more time for a glorious win.

Cuthbert led off, and with great patience earned a walk. Then McBride hit a little pop up to Sweasy, that under the rules he could have dropped accidentally on purpose in order to make a double play. He chose to play it safe and catch it for one out. Then Meyerle hit an easy fly ball to Pabor in the outfield, "which he would surely have taken but for the fact that the sun shone squarely in his eyes and he could not see the ball."[13]

Cuthbert came all the way around to score and tie the game, and Meyerle ended up at third.

There was one out, when something that had not happened for the entire game happened: Jim White, Cleveland's great back-stop, let a pitch get by him, and the passed ball allowed Meyerle to come home and win the game. The next two men went out to end the already lost game.

Clevelanders were not bitter about the game, they took it as a sign that the Forest City might yet live up to expectations.

Cleveland, on a high note now, prepared for its second East Coast trip. A good showing would be critical to show the home backers their worth if they hoped to draw good crowds when they came back home in August.

The Road Record II

Lost: Cleveland Forest City	0	Boston Red Stockings	17
Lost: Cleveland Forest City	8	Boston Red Stockings	9
Lost: Cleveland Forest City	1	New York Mutuals	20
Lost: Cleveland Forest City	3	Brooklyn Atlantics	10
Won: Cleveland Forest City	24	Brooklyn Eckfords	5
Lost: Cleveland Forest City	3	Brooklyn Atlantics	13
Lost: Cleveland Forest City	5	Lord Baltimores	7
One win.		**Six losses.**	

The road trip was a total disaster. After getting blown out of the first game 17–0, Cleveland lost the next one — a real heart-breaker — by a single run to Boston in the ninth. And Cleveland lost it, in the same fashion they had lost the Philadelphia game in Cleveland, by giving up 2 runs in the bottom of the ninth. The Boston game could be pointed to later as the day the real funeral march for Cleveland baseball began.

Al Pratt had lost most of his effectiveness, and Rynie Wolters, his substitute, was pitching longer and longer, but still the team lost. In the middle of the trip, when Wolters' old team the New York Mutuals whipped Cleveland 20–1, Wolters took the occasion to go AWOL. He was suspended. Charley Pabor, the third-string pitcher, tried to right the sinking ship — but he couldn't.

Low morale and injury — some self-inflicted with alcohol — were destroying discipline and unity. The team even took the field in two games with but eight men.

Their one victory was against the Eckfords, a team destined to finish in the cellar of the standings.

August Funeral

The players returned home to find that management, with the encouragement of the stockholders, had canceled their contracts. The players, however, voted to continue as a co-op venture, paying themselves solely from the gate receipts. This had been done in a few other places, unsuccessfully, but had provided a few more paydays. Cleveland went to Oil City, Pennsylvania, for two games against their "Senecas." Cleveland won 28–9 and 21-3. The games made a little profit. A third game with the Senecas was rained out in the third inning. The new Blue Stockings then announced that two championship games would be played with the Boston Red Stockings at the Forest City Grounds in mid–August. The Red Stockings came to town on Saturday, August 17. Mr. Ellis of Philadelphia was the umpire, and in 2 hours and 10 minutes Cleveland had lost another game.

Score: Boston 18, Cleveland 7.

Inning	1	2	3	4	5	6	7	8	9	Final
Forest City	2	0	0	0	0	3	1	0	1	7
Bostons	5	1	1	2	3	0	0	6	0	18

A small crowd of only three hundred showed up for the second game with Boston on Monday. Cleveland won the toss and sent Boston to the bat. Boston went out. Cleveland in their turn made 2 runs. At the close of the seventh the game was very close, Cleveland trailing by but two, 5–3. In the eighth Boston finally broke through, figuring out Wolters' pitching and ringing up 7 runs. Cleveland was shut out in the eighth and Boston in the top of the ninth also failed to score. Now all that was needed was for Cleveland to go out quickly, so the smattering of people left at the park could go home. However: "The Forest City surprised everybody, including themselves and the Red Stockings ... by making four runs."[14] But now there were two outs, as Cleveland's last hope, Joe Simmons, came to the plate.

The *Cleveland Leader*'s man on the scene wrote: "Simmons went out on a fly; the audience went out on that fly, and we fear base ball, in Cleveland, and the Forest City base ball club, all went out on that fly."[15]

The Farewell Innings

Inning	1 2 3	4 5 6	7 8 9	Final
Boston	0 0 1	2 2 0	0 7 0	12
Forest City	2 0 1	0 0 0	0 0 4	7

The sports headline of the *Cleveland Leader* said it all: "Funeral of the National Game in Cleveland — The Muffers Disband To-day."[16]

It was Cleveland's last game as members of the National Association — baseball's first major league — and it was Cleveland's last professional ball game for quite some time.

There is some confusion as to what the official versus actual won-loss records for teams were at this time, due (among other decisions) to the league's decision not to count disbanded teams' games in the pennant race. And there was less than total reporting in the papers of decisions on what games were later ruled exhibition rather than championship, or on what the final decisions on some games that were protested were.

One contemporary official baseball encyclopedia shows Cleveland wining 6 and losing 15, while another gives the record as 6 wins and 16 losses.

1873–1877

Having given up its franchise in the National Association in the late summer of 1872, Cleveland now entered a dormant period in baseball activity that coincided with the national economic downturn called the Panic of '73. The National Association itself lasted as a major league only from 1871 through 1875.

1873

As with the country's economy, the baseball recovery also came slowly. So complete was the demise of baseball in the Cleveland area in general that only a handful of games were reported.

A group of ball players from the Cleveland Western Union Telegraph had to go all the way to Toledo to find a ball game with their brother operators there. The Toledo "Duplex" defeated the Cleveland "Dashes" 17–14 on June 7. Both clubs' names were telegraph-related. "Duplex" referred to a technical innovation by which messages could be sent over a single telegraph wire in two directions at the same time. "In the evening an elegant banquet [sic] was given by the Toledo operators in honor of the occasion, which is described as an exceedingly pleasant affair."[1]

Cleveland ball players put together a "picked nine" to go to Lake County to find some ball games. One player failed to make the trip, but the "picked nine," of eight players managed to beat

In 1920, the *Cleveland Sunday News-Leader* commemorated the 50th anniversary of major league baseball in Cleveland with two front-page articles and this large illustration, in which a mustachioed Forest City ballplayer stands between a Cleveland Indian and Father Time (Courtesy John Thorn).

the full teams of Willoughby and Painesville. Cleveland was victorious over the former 17–11 and the latter 27–20.

A ball game between the Robison and Sanford companies was scheduled in early June, and a game was to be played in August, on what was left of the Forest City Grounds (the salvage crews having done their work/damage), between the Forest City Juniors and the Western Rocks of Elyria. No scores from these scheduled games were printed.

1874

Some company games were played this year in June. The St. Clair machine shop claimed victory over the Malleable Iron Works 35–25. A letter sent to the *Herald*, supposedly from the "Malleable" players, claimed they had actually won the game. The truth remains unknown.

Employees of two businesses, located in today's downtown Warehouse District, had a ball game at the old Forest City Grounds. Kennard & McKinney of Bank Street (W. 6th) won over Adams & Ford of Water Street (W. 9th) 42–32.

The Cleveland, Columbus, and Cincinnati (C.C.C.) railway workers had a Sunday ball game in the Flats. No score given.

The Olympics: "A challenge has been published by the Olympic Base Ball club (colored) requesting any other city nine to play them a game of base ball."[2]

Monday, August 24, at 2:30 P.M., on a vacant section of the Case Commons between Garden Street and Scoville Avenue, was the time and place the Olympics played a game against a picked nine composed of players from the old Eastern Rocks (the understudy team of the former Forest City Blue Stockings).

This was the only game this year that received any detailed coverage. The two following articles giving an account of the above game were suspiciously similar (the *Leader* on occasion would accuse the *Herald* of stealing its sports articles).

The *Cleveland Leader*: "The game of base ball between the Olympics and a picked nine was won, yesterday, by the latter by a score of 41–22. Some very good playing was done by both sides, but the Olympics were outplayed from the start, the score being 18–2 by the second innings. Among the pale faces the batting of Castor and Bohen was up to the mark, and in the field, Bohen in the position of pitcher, played the game in his old fine style. Not knowing the names of the Olympics, and their scorecard being 'non est comatibus,' it is impossible to particularize with reference to their playing. Their uniforms are neat, and their behavior is that of gentlemen. Being the only organized nine in the city, it is thought they are deserving of this little recognition."[3]

The *Cleveland Herald*: "The game of base ball, Monday, between the Olympics (shades) and a picked nine of pale faces, was won by the latter by a score of 41 to 22. Some very good playing was done by both sides, but the shades were out-played from the start, the score being 18 to 2 at the end of the second inning. Among the pale faces the batting of Castor and Bohen was up to the mark, and in the field Bohen played his position as pitcher to perfection. Not knowing the names of the shades, and scorecards not being at hand, I cannot particularize with reference to their playing. Their uniform is neat, and their behavior that of gentlemen. Being the only organized nine in the city, I think they are deserving of this recognition."[4]

With baseball looking like a truly dead sport in Cleveland, a new sport was played in a game at the Northern Ohio Fair Grounds in September. A large crowd watched the Victoria Lacrosse club of London, Ontario, play a club of Tuscarora Indians. (The Tuscarora Indian tribe originated in South Carolina, but in the early seventeen hundreds joined Iroquois Confederation and settled in the area of New York and Ontario, Canada.) "The principal object of the Victoria club coming here seems to have been to create an interest in the game, with a view to the formation of a Lacrosse club in Cleveland and prospective vibrations back and forth between this city and London for the purpose of play."5

Their hopes proved futile; lacrosse has never caught on in Cleveland.

1875

This may have been the darkest of the dark years in Cleveland baseball, the score of but one game having been found. On June 8, 1875, East Cleveland (which had become part of Cleveland a few years earlier) scored a victory over the East High School team 24–20. The game was played on the grounds at E. Madison (E. 79th) and Cedar.

The organized game of baseball in and around Cleveland was almost gone, but pickup games on the Case Commons showed there was at least still the ghost of a ball-playing spirit alive — somewhere.

1876

America celebrated its centennial this year, and in baseball the National League replaced the National Association as the only major league.

Cleveland was slower than the nation in general in showing a revival in the popularity of baseball. Some good signs: The Slow and Easy team played a game on Case Commons in May against a "picked nine." Everyone was pleasantly surprised when a crowd of several hundred came to watch.

Inning	1 2 3	4 5 6	7 8 9	Final
Picked Nine	1 0 4	2 0 2	0 0 0	9
Slow and Easy	0 0 0	0 1 1	7 3 6	18

Former Forest City star Austin "Pikey" Smith, and other interested parties, formed a group to bring big-time baseball back to Cleveland — unfortunately their plans fell through.

At the end of May, a game between the varsity teams of the Brooks School and the High School resulted in victory for the latter, 18–14.

Western Reserve, led by Clarence Emir Allen, was the terror of the college circuit this season. Allen would become a professor of the classics at Western Reserve College. In 1876 he was a pitcher for that school's ball club. It was the year he developed a curve ball. For those playing intercollegiate games against Reserve, it was something they had never seen before, and also something they could not hit. It was said the school never lost a game until he graduated. Opponents of the Reserves included Buchtel, Kenyon, Hiram, Mt. Union, Oberlin, and Wooster colleges.

Because of ill health, Clarence Allen moved to Utah, where he managed mining operations, and served terms in the Utah legislature and United States Congress. He was the father of Florence Allen, the first woman elected to the Ohio Supreme Court, and the first woman appointed to the United States Circuit Court of Appeals.

After May, no record of any local games appeared until August.

August 22: The Brown Stockings of Cleveland went to Youngstown and beat the Mahonings 18–3.

August 24: After their victory in Youngstown, the Brown Stockings ran into the Slow and Easy team on the Case Commons in Cleveland, and were beaten by a 10–6 score.

1877

The variety of groups playing baseball this year was a hopeful sign that the dark ages of Cleveland baseball might indeed be coming to an end. At the Western Reserve College, in May, the ball team had notched wins against Akron, Newberg, and Gambier. The *Leader*, May 29: "A game of base ball was played yesterday [on Case Commons] between, the Picked Nine and the Olympics (colored) and won by the latter in a score of 15 to 14."[6]

Two pharmaceutical concerns played a ball game on the Case Commons on May 30th. The "Bad Medicine," of Strong Cobb & Co. won over the "Pills" of Benton, Myers and Canfield, 43–26. A. J. Etlein of the first club was awarded a prize ball for his performance.

Neighbors on Main Street, and others, complained about young boys playing baseball in the afternoons. The *Cleveland Leader* thought these was nothing wrong with this, but they did ask that the beat policeman in the vicinity of Superior Street and Payne Avenue look into the charges of "outrageous language being used by the young ball players on that corner.[7] And on the west side of town a group of youngsters was chased by the police for illegally playing ball on Sunday — they managed to elude capture.

The dark years of Cleveland baseball were indeed coming to an end.

Part II. The Middle Years: 1878–1889

1878

Hollinger

William Hollinger: Who was he? Was he the same William Hollinger who once played ball for Mansfield? Perhaps. Was he a man from high society? No. But he was a friend and neighbor of Doc Prentice, a man who did walk in elite company. Hollinger knew baseball, and when he convinced those with money and connections that he knew baseball, Cleveland had a man and a manager who would bring the professional game back home, leaving the dark years of amateurish ball behind.

Hollinger's men:

Emil M. Gross: very tall at 6'2"; an excellent catcher.
Harry Salisbury: medium height, a very muscular 200 pounds; a hard-throwing pitcher.
Charley Eden: a strong-armed outfielder who occasionally pitched.
"Bones" Ely: a promising young outfielder.
Bill Phillips: a second baseman with a long Cleveland career ahead; first Cleveland pro born in Canada.
"Pigtail Billy" Riley: a center fielder who filled in at shortstop.
Tom McGinley: hired as a shortstop, he proved too slow and so was made a fill-in outfielder.
Art Allison: the old Forest City star was a walk-on who landed himself a roster spot.
Charley Morton: a third baseman by trade, he also filled in at short. A native of North Kingsville in Ashtabula County, he would become a major league manager.
Andy Cummings, *Jack Glasscock*, *Henry Luff*, *George Strief*, and *Mike Burke* would also join the team over the course of the year.

Art Allison and Charley Eden had been there, and—with the exception of Tim McGinley and Andy Cummings—all these men would someday be there. "There" was the major league—a testimony to just how good a judge, recruiter, and developer of talent William Hollinger was.

A Place to Play

A parcel of land large enough to house a ballpark was getting scarce in Cleveland. Most of the parcels large enough had been given over to some niche or another in the once again expanding economy of Cleveland.

A field was found. It was shaped like a rectangle, with trees in the northeast corner. The short ends of the rectangle ran north to south between Sibley Street (Carnegie) and Cedar Avenue. The long ends ran west to east and were not too distant from both Kennard Street (E. 46th) and Wilson Street (E. 55th).

The layout of the field was an odd one, because of a house and trees which the property owner would not cut down.

The fence was up by May 3, and the grandstand work was rushed to completion for the May 7 game with Erie. The grandstand started near the northwest corner (the corner itself had the house on it) and ran flush against the fence following Kennard Street (E. 46th). Next to it, heading south, flat against the same wall, was an open stand.

The diamond's layout was such that the batter's position was dangerously close to the grandstand, where a batted foul or high pitch could wreak havoc on the customers. It was a long way down the right field line into the corner of the rectangle, and the short left field line disappeared into the small grove of trees.

Preparations were going along just fine for the first game. The boys were out practicing in their new uniforms—bought from the Albert Spalding Company: "They look as slick as a new dollar."[1] The telegraph wire to the ballpark was completed to the office downtown, and details on getting to the game on public transit, as well as seat pricing, were announced. Also a change of game time: "In order to accommodate a large class who desire to see the full game and can not get away from business much before 4 o'clock the time of commencement has been fixed at that hour."[2]

This was a tactful way of saying that, for the first time, the admission quarter of the factory worker was now as welcome as that of the office clerk.

Some limited parking was available at the park's carriage enclosure. It was suggested that an excellent alternative route to the ballpark was the Garden Way or Prospect Way streetcars—both lines coming within five minutes' walking distance. And a reminder: "The blue flags on the Prospect street cars always indicate a game."[3]

One and a Half Openers

A "large throng" came out on May 7, despite the threatening weather, to watch Cleveland play its first match game against the independent professional "Eries" of Erie, Pennsylvania.[4]

They saw four and a half innings of baseball before the rain ended it. The rules required the Eries to bat in the bottom of the fifth, despite the fact they were ahead 2–1. The rain would not allow this, so the game was called null.

Cleveland opened the road season on May 8, shutting out the Eries 8–0.

The honor of playing in the first official opening game at home now fell to the amateur ball club of Geneva, Ohio.

May 10, 1878

Geneva Blue Stockings versus Forest City Blue Stockings

Batting orders

GENEVAS	FOREST CITY
Wagner, 3b	Gross, c
Green, 1b	Eden, rf
Bohn, ss	Ely, lf
Johnson, 2b	Phillips, 1b
Mullane, p	Riley, cf
Strick, c	McGinley, ss
Stewart, lf	Allison, 2b
Dorman, cf	Salisbury, p
Camp, rf	Morton, 3b

The crowd, larger than the weather would have predicted, braved a continuous cold wind and occasional rain sprinkles throughout the two-hour game.

At 4 o'clock sharp, Wagner led off the game against Salisbury, who had cut off his long curls in the name of professionalism and luck. Wagner got a hit anyway, but the visitors failed to score. Cleveland got 2 in the first, 2 in the second, and 2 in the fifth. Geneva put up goose eggs through the first six.

The sixth inning excitement: "Eden sent a beauty away down to the fence in the rear of the right fielder, and made a clean home run amidst the greatest applause from the spectators."[5]

Cleveland's Charley Eden now owned the first home run at the new ball grounds. Cleveland plated 4 runs in the inning.

Eden left the outfield and came in as the change pitcher for Cleveland, and Bohn became the change pitcher for Geneva. Geneva failed to score in the seventh, and in the bottom of the frame the Forest City added a run. Geneva broke up the shutout with a run in the eighth. In the ninth Cleveland scored runs 12 and 13. Geneva in the ninth closed out the game with a consolation run.

Final: Cleveland 13, Geneva 2.

Inning	1 2 3	4 5 6	7 8 9	Final
Genevas	0 0 0	0 0 0	0 1 1	2
Forest Citys	2 2 0	0 2 4	1 0 2	13

Umpire: Charles Morgan, formerly of the Yale College Club.

Game note: • "Strick, the Geneva catcher, wears a face protector in the shape of a wire muzzle. Gross tried it on, during a part of the game, just for fun."[6] (A catcher's mask was something new in this part of the baseball world.)

Some games:

Date	Place			Results	
May 7+	Cleveland			The opener versus Erie (PA) was rained out after four and a half innings—Erie was up 2–1.	
May 8+	Erie	Forest City	8	Eries (PA)	0
May 10*	Cleveland	Forest City	13	Genevas (OH)	2
May 16+	Cleveland	Forest City	3	Eries (PA)	7
May 23*	Geneva	Forest City	26	Genevas (OH)	6
May 24*	Cleveland	Forest City	16	Atlantics	2
June 25+	Cleveland	Forest City	21	Independents (OH)	3
July 4*	London, Canada	Forest City	9	Atlantics	4
July 23*	London, Canada	Forest City	3	Atlantics	5
Aug. 27*	Indi'apolis	Forest City	5	Capital Citys (IN)	0
Aug. 28*	Indi'apolis	Forest City	5	Capital Citys (IN)	3

Won — 8 Lost — 2

+ Versus independent professional club
* Versus amateur ball club

The Atlantics were from London, Ontario, Canada. The Independents were deaf and dumb players from the state institution in Columbus, Ohio.

Bumps and Bruises

The Forest City Club had serious concerns about the safety of spectators—especially the ladies and the youngsters—in the grandstand, where the danger of foul tips and overly high pitches was high. In a workout session open to the public in early May, a schoolboy was hit in the side of the head by a foul ball—he came around after being out for a few minutes.

Something had to be done! A rather novel solution was found. A foul-ball screen was put up in front of the grandstand—perhaps the first such screen at a professional park.

But on May 15, any kind of screen would have been useless to the folks over in the open stands. The game was against Erie, and at one of the high points in the game, the loud crack of timber was heard — everybody in the place turned toward the open stands as they went down under the weight of several hundred paying customers.

As the last of the crowd crawled from the debris — with no more than bumps and bruises — concern quickly turned to a hearty laughter, with even the victims joining in, pleased to have escaped in one piece.

The game continued, Erie rallied to forge ahead in the late innings, and Cleveland felt the sting of its first loss on the year, 7–3.

Reconstruction of the fallen stands included a brilliant construction idea (originally ignored) — enough poles to support the weight.

There was a two-story house on the corner of Kennard and Cedar. Its roof gave a good view for watching a ball game for free. During an early May game a boy named Pettee, sitting on the edge of the roof, was overcome by a fit: "He had just time to gasp to a friend, 'Good bye, Charlie, I've got to go,' when he fell to the ground a distance of some thirty feet. The limp condition of his body undoubtedly saved him from severe injury, as he is reported not badly hurt."[7]

Roofs can be unsafe places, but flat ground can be a dangerous place too, as Oliver Koppler found out. Youngsters were often allowed to play ball on the field after a Forest City game. During just such a game in May, involving high schoolers, Mr. Koppler was hit so hard by a line drive that it knocked him down. He was so badly hurt that he had to be carried home to his mother. He recovered.

It was around this time also, after all these exciting episodes, that Doc N. B. Prentice generously volunteered his services as team physician — and presumably as an emergency doctor for anyone else in or near the ballpark.

There were some changes that helped Cleveland before it played its first game of the year with a National League team. Three or four of the trees in the left field corner were cut down. However, the worst offender of all, a giant elm, was not.

In mid–May Cleveland added Andy Cummings to the payroll. He was called one of the country's premier shortstops. Cleveland was taking a chance on the Cincinnati native; his drinking problem was the reason he had remained unsigned for the year.

The Alleghenys franchise from Pittsburgh had folded its tent, and Jack Glasscock, a superb third baseman, and Henry Luff, a pitcher, left there to become Blue Stockings. With the demise of the Alleghenys, Cleveland was invited to fill their vacated spot in the International League; however, they would play as a non-pennant-competing member, at least this year.

High Point

The Game that was "The Game"!
batting orders —

| *Chicago* | *Cleveland Forest City* |
White Stockings	Blue Stockings
Bill Harbidge, c	Emil Gross, c
Joe "Old Reliable" Start, 1b	Charley Eden, rf
Cap "Pop" Anson, lf	Bill Phillips, 1b
Bob "Death to Flying Things" Ferguson, ss	Bill "Pigtail Billy" Riley, lf
Bill McClellan, 2b	Jack "Pebbly Jack" Glasscock, 3b
John Cassidy, rf	Andy Cummings, ss
Terry Larkin, p	George Strief, 2b
Frank Hankinson, 3b	Charley Morton, cf
Jack Remsen, cf	Harry Salisbury, p

June 11, 1878

Cleveland went to bat first and went down in order. Chicago "came here confident of a 'walk away' and when they went to bat in the first inning nearly every man picked out his bat and sat down to wait his turn."[8] Only Anson got on base; Salisbury was a better pitcher than they had thought. That thought would last all day.

Cummings got the only Cleveland hit in the second and was left stranded. The Chicago second inning was the weird one of the game. The first man was out, on a dropped "strike 'em out, throw 'em out" pitch. Cassidy, next, "scratched" a base on a Glasscock miscue at third; he stole second and on the wild throw from catcher Gross ended up at third. Cassidy, on a grounder to Strief at second, broke for home; he eluded the catcher's tag, but he ran at least four feet out of the base line to do it.

H. J. Delhman was the umpire; he had lost his job as a player when Erie had gone out of business a few weeks earlier, and was now trying his hand at umpiring. The crowd was shocked when he said Cassidy was safe.

Some people thought the umpire was getting even with Cleveland, because there was a rumor that Cleveland had wanted him as a player but had changed its mind. The *Cleveland Leader* said they didn't think that was the case. They felt it was just that Delhman was a better ball player than umpire — though he wasn't all that good a ball player either. The run stood.

Neither team scored in the third or fourth. Larkin, after blanking Cleveland through four, gave up his first run in the fifth: "In the fifth inning Morton made a good base hit and was helped along by Salisbury's hit and Remsen's error, which brought Morton home."[9] Chicago failed to score in its turn.

Cleveland: "In the sixth inning Phillips made a capital two base hit and Riley followed with another, which earned a run for Phillips and made the score two to one."[10]

With great defense behind him, Salisbury did not allow a single run after the incident in the second inning. With the final out, Cleveland became the first International League team this year to beat a major league team. Score: 2–1.

Charley Morton was singled out for his superior play in center: "It seemed as if the crowd [by far the largest of the year] would never tire of applauding him."[11]

Cleveland Plain Dealer: "We are compelled to omit very much which we should be pleased, if space would permit, to give in regard to the fine points of play by both sides, as it was a remarkable game. Manager Hollinger is loaded down with congratulations and accomplishments for having secured so good a nine."[12] After this great game, Hollinger's load of congratulations was never so heavy, and his nine never again so good. It was the high point of 1878 in Cleveland baseball, Forest City Blue Stocking — style.

The year's exhibition record through August 23 versus the teams of the International League and National League — baseball's best two professional circuits:

DATE	WHERE	CLEVELAND		OPPONENT	
May 30*	Pittsburgh	Forest Citys	1	Alleghenys	7
May 31*	Pittsburgh	Forest Citys	0	Alleghenys	1
June 1*	Pittsburgh	Forest Citys	4	Alleghenys	3
June 3*	Cleveland	Forest Citys	4	Alleghenys	0
June 4*	Cleveland	Forest Citys	7	Alleghenys	15
June 7*	Cleveland	Forest Citys	1	Tecumsehs	5
June 10+	Cleveland	Forest Citys	2	Milwaukees	4
June 11+	Cleveland	Forest Citys	2	Chicagos	1
June 13*	Cleveland	Forest Citys	3	Rochesters	1
June 15*	Cleveland	Forest Citys	2	Rochesters	13
June 18*	Cleveland	Forest Citys	1	Rochesters	3
June 21+	Cleveland	Forest Citys	1	Bostons	2
June 22+	Cleveland	Forest Citys	0	Cincinnatis	4
July 6*	Cleveland	Forest Citys	8	Tecumsehs	0

DATE	WHERE	CLEVELAND		OPPONENT	
July 11*	Cleveland	Forest Citys	7	Hornells	21
July 14*	Cleveland	Forest Citys	8	Stars	6
July 16*	Cleveland	Forest Citys	2	Stars	8
July 17*	Cleveland	Forest Citys	4	Stars	11
July 19+	Cleveland	Forest Citys	3	Milwaukees	9
July 20+	Cleveland	Forest Citys	3	Milwaukees	8
July 23*	London	Forest Citys	2	Tecumsehs	5
July 27*	Buffalo	Forest Citys	0	Buffalos	3
July 29*	Buffalo	Forest Citys	2	Buffalos	3
July 30*	Cleveland	Forest Citys	4	Buffalos	2
July 31*	Cleveland	Forest Citys	9	Buffalos	0
Aug. 1+	Cleveland	Forest Citys	2	Indianapolis	4
Aug. 2+	Cleveland	Forest Citys	9	Indianapolis	6
Aug. 5*	Cleveland	Forest Citys	8	Springfields	0
Aug. 6*	Cleveland	Forest Citys	1	Springfields	4
Aug. 9+	Cleveland	Forest Citys	8	Cincinnatis	3
Aug. 20+	Cleveland	Forest Citys	4	Chicagos	4
Aug. 21*	Cleveland	Forest Citys	11	Tecumsehs	8
Aug. 22*	Cleveland	Forest Citys	4	Tecumsehs	12
Aug. 23*	Cleveland	Forest Citys	9	Uticas	3

Record: May–August 23, 1878. Games: 35. Wins: 13. Losses: 21. Ties: 1.
Versus National League: Wins: 5. Losses: 8. Ties: 1.
Versus International League: Wins: 8. Losses: 13.
Key — Forest Citys' opponent: + National League team; * International League team.
Source: The *Cleveland Leader*.

Notes: • The Alleghenys are from the city of Allegheny that was located across the river north of downtown Pittsburgh (now a neighborhood of Pittsburgh). • The Tecumsehs are from London, Ontario, Canada. • The Hornells are from Hornellsville, New York. • The Stars are from Syracuse, New York (International League pennant winners of 1878).

Let Me Entertain You

Billy's game: When you are a celebrity you get free things. Sometimes they come from other celebrities. Entertainer Billy Emerson was at the June 13 game when Cleveland beat Rochester 3–1. He was so pleased by the sport that he insisted both teams be his guests that evening, and come watch him perform *his* game at the Euclid Avenue Opera House.

AMUSEMENTS
MAKE NO MISTAKE
Euclid Ave. Opera House.
One Night, Thursday, June 13.
The Elite Attraction
EMERSON'S MINSTRELS
and the only original
BIG 4 BIG
BILLY DAN JOHNNY MAST
SMITH WALDRON MORTON MARTIN
The Opera Quintet
Sig. Fred Chas. Jos. Chas.

> Abecco, Waiz, Heywood, Garland, Moore
> 21 STAR ARTIST 21
> Direct from Broadway, New York, led by the
> inimitable and envied
> BILLY EMERSON
> Monarch of Minstrelry.[13]

Another freebie: The manager of the *Pearl* and *Alaska* steamboat line wasn't the monarch of anything, but he was the boss, and he loved baseball. The Blue Stockings were his guests for a Lake Erie excursion to the Black River (Elyria, OH) on the steamer *Alaska*.

The gracious ways of yesteryear:

> At the opening of the game yesterday a little boy climbed into the grand stand and handed over to Manager Hollinger a large basket filled with some of the most delicious fruit that ever grew. Further than saying it was given to him by a young lady, who would not tell her name, the little fellow could give no information. Accompanying the gift was a card, upon which was penned, by a female hand, the words "To our Forest City nine, with compliments. Care of Captain Strief."
> *To the editor of* the *Leader*:
> In behalf of the Forest City Base Ball Club I, as captain, take pleasure in returning sincere thanks to the donor of the beautiful basket of fruit at the grounds this afternoon. By our conduct on and off the field we hope to merit the same. Most respectfully, George Strief, Capt. F.C.B.B. Club.[14]

The Drunken Buggy

Ball players often stayed in groups at some boarding house near the ballpark during the season, unless they were married, in which case they would usually lease an apartment. Only three of the Forest City players had wives.

Bachelor Charley Eden rented a buggy from Castor's stable one early September evening, and went to his boarding house. He waved at fellow player Emil Gross and two of Emil's pals, whom he spotted walking toward the house as he went in for the dinner hour.

When Charley came out to take his evening ride, the buggy was gone. The easy-going Charley figured the three men probably just took his ride down to the corner on some errand or another. After about half an hour it dawned on him that they weren't coming back — he had been the victim of a mean trick! Eden later remarked: "Along about 8 o'clock they drove by the house and shouted tauntingly to me, but they did not stop. They acted as if they had been drinking a great deal."[15]

The revelers picked up a fourth rider and somewhere, probably a tavern, they loaded up with a fifth — Andy Cummings.

Down Garden Street at full gallop sailed the happy crew, until they came to the Perry Street crossing, where they crashed into a wagon. All five men were thrown from the buggy. "The rig was badly wrecked, but none of the men were hurt much."[16] A policeman showed up about then, and had to "hook on" to Andy Cummings for disorderly conduct.[17]

Eden decided that Emil Gross and Tom Johnson, two of the original culprits, would have to pay for the damage to the buggy, and to make sure they did, he went down to the Central Police Station and swore out a warrant.

The driver, Fenney, a fireman from Number 9's house, and the man who actually wrecked the buggy, was mysteriously left out of any legal proceedings.

Andy Cummings was fined two dollars in police court for disorderly conduct.

Manager Hollinger, hearing of the affair, immediately expelled Cummings from the team. And maybe the worst fate of all for Andy Cummings was that he now had the job of explaining it all to his wife. For Cummings, the loss of his job seemed to undermine any chance to truly develop his great talent. Andy Cummings — perhaps the player with the most potential of any of the Forest City Blue Stockings — never played one day in the major leagues.

City Lots

The ranks of amateur ball around Cleveland were quite full in 1878, an indication that the popularity of the game had rebounded after five years of hibernation. One summer afternoon, an observer at the Case Commons counted twelve games in progress at the same time. At other times, even the old Forest City cricket team was out playing on the Commons.

Companies were again fielding employee ball teams. Hower and Higbee, the department store, had a team. George Worthington, the hardware concern, had a team. The Standard Oil Co. played in the flats near Broadway — pitting the office and the works employees against each other. And the Rolling Mills and the Rhodes Co. played each other and other industrial teams.

The Cleveland firemen, in order to raise funds for survivor benefits, posted bright advertising all over town announcing a game with the firemen from Buffalo, New York.

In the suburbs, the "Zephyrs" played in Berea, and a team from Newberg called the "Crickets" held an amateurs' prize — a new trophy bat.

And outside of the county, the "Etnas" of Warren played the "White Stockings" of Garrettsville.

Some of the better Cleveland sandlot teams were named Slow & Easys, Brown Stockings, Niagaras, Favorites, Atlantics, and White Caps. In addition to Case Commons and Forest City Grounds, games were being played at Case (E. 40th) and St. Clair, at Stones Flats, and, for the first time, at today's Woodland Hills Park.

The Big Blue Stockings versus the Little Red Stockings:

In the manner of the old "Eastern Rocks," the Blue Stockings had an understudy "nine" named the "Red Stockings."

Will Bohn, the Red Stockings' pitcher, amazed the good-sized crowd by shutting out the Blue Stockings for the first three innings. Harry Salisbury, pitching for the Forest City, was surprised when the youngsters erupted with 4 runs in the third. The embarrassed pitcher then shut them out for the rest of the game. The Blue Stockings, down by four, began to take charge in the fourth, scoring runs in every inning after that.

Final: adults 14, youngsters 4. Date: July 18, 1878.

Inning	1	2	3	4	5	6	7	8	9	Final
Red Stockings	0	0	4	0	0	0	0	0	0	4
Forest City	0	0	0	1	3	2	3	2	3	14

Additional scores of some National League and International League games after Aug. 23:

DATE	WHERE	CLEVELAND		OPPONENT	
Aug. 24*	Cleveland	Forest City	5	Uticas	6
Aug. 26+	Cleveland	Forest City	9	Indianapolis	4
Sept. 16+	Cleveland	Forest City	0	Providence	5
Sept. 17+	Cleveland	Forest City	2	Providence	7
Sept. 19+	Cleveland	Forest City	2	Bostons	3
Sept. 20+	Cincinnati	Forest City	6	Cincinnatis	15
Sept. 23*	Cleveland	Forest City	2	Stars	10
Oct. 3+	Cleveland	Forest City	2	Cincinnatis	10

Wins—1 Losses—7
Versus National League: Won—1 Lost—5.
Versus International League: Won—0 Lost—2.
Key: + = National League team. * = International League team.

Note: • Cleveland's professional team of 1878 was credited with having played 111 or 112 games, according to a short history of the team in a 1908 newspaper.

In a meeting held at the office of C. H. Bulkley, it was decided that the Forest City Base Ball Association for 1879 would be based on the stockholder model, rather than the 1878 subscription plan. The new original fifteen stockholders represented wealth and leadership in Cleveland.

William Hollinger was also admitted as a stockholder and was hired for the next year as manager, and given authority to contract players. Elected to the executive committee were Mr. C. Wesley, Mr. Charles A. Brayton, and Mr. A. B. Hough.

Intriguing Ending

The weather was terrible for the second-to-last game of the year against Cincinnati on Oct. 4. The small crowd, however, gave the Cincinnati catcher a nice welcome. He was James "Deacon" White—the popular old Forest City player. His brother, Will White, was with him—he was the Cincinnati pitcher.

Cincinnati beat Cleveland handily 10–2. This first game in the series of two was the only one played. There were two reasons why the game the next day—a Saturday—could not have been played. At 2 o'clock game time, the cold and wet weather would have prevented a game. But that didn't matter, because Cincinnati didn't wait around for the umpire's decision—they were already on the train heading out of town and home.

James F. Evans was an official of the old National Association and a friend of sporting goods manufacturer Albert G. Spalding, who was a major figure in the only major league—the National League. Mr. Evans owned Evans, Van Epps & Co., the well-established Cleveland stationery-goods company. The Evans store now also carried a complete line of Spalding uniforms and baseball equipment.

William Hollinger was out of town signing ball players for the Forest Citys' planned up-coming year in the International League. James F. Evans took advantage of his absence to gain control of the team; he then orchestrated a successful bid for a National League franchise in Cleveland for 1879.

In mid–October, the ball club, with James F. Evans as its newly elected president, notified Hollinger that his services were no longer required as manager, and that he was to turn over his player contracts to the club. Hollinger fired back that said contracts were actually with him, and not with the directors or their president, and that he, with "his" players, might very well be looking for another city to play ball in for the upcoming year.

Evans then went about the business of getting all the signed players to sign a second contract with him. All did. Mr. Evans was able to prevail because the players wanted to play in Cleveland, where they were sure of a stable market and a financially secure ownership.

William Hollinger then surfaced in Detroit as the man behind a new, strong, independent Detroit Base Ball Club. Hollinger would be a prominent figure in Detroit baseball for many years to come.

Evans would be remembered as the man who put Cleveland baseball in the National League for the first time.

And, of course, Mr. Evans would have been sure to remind you not to forget that next year you could get your tickets for any National League game at Evans, Van Epps & Co.—located at 200 Superior Street.

1879

Back in the Big "League"

Cleveland was back in big league baseball after being gone for six years—back in the "League." The National League, the only major league, was called the League, and Cleveland's new team in it was the Blue Stockings.

In 1876 the Declaration of Independence was one hundred years old. That centennial year, owners of the National Association teams in Boston and Chicago launched a rebellion of their own — they left. As they were the Association's strongest members, their absence killed off an already shaky league.

The two rebels hooked up with new franchises in Cincinnati, Hartford, Louisville, New York, Philadelphia, and St. Louis, and so the National League was born.

Morgan Bulkely served as president for the first year. William A. Hulbert followed him, and served from 1877 until his sudden death in 1882. Hulbert was an owner of the Chicago White Stockings, and the acknowledged political architect behind the start of the National League.

There were thirteen changes in League membership under Hulbert. These changes were needed to create a successful league of financially stable franchises, accountable to a centralized authority (major shortcomings of the old National Association).

Cleveland and Buffalo came on board in 1879 as replacements for the weak markets in Indianapolis and Milwaukee. When linked with Chicago and Cincinnati, they were referred to as the "western" (circuit). Syracuse and Troy were expansion teams this year; when associated with Boston and Providence they were known as the "eastern" (circuit).

Changing Places

The new ballpark of 1878 had served its purpose, but membership in the prestigious "League" called for a complete remodeling of the now obsolete structure. The ballparks in National League cities were often called League Park, to indicate their major league status. These parks also had local names. The Cleveland League Park was best known to Clevelanders as the Kennard Street Ball Park, so named because the entrance to the grandstand was there.

Leasing a lot that fronted on Kennard Street enlarged the grounds. It would be used to park the carriage trade. The ball diamond, moved to the southwest corner of the field, now faced the northeast.

An anchored grandstand went up directly behind home plate. It contained 450 numbered seats separated by iron bars. For extra comfort, one grandstand concession rented seat cushions for a nickel. In the back of the grandstand a stairway gave easy access to the horse pen and vehicle lot.

Along the first base line and the third base line ran covered stands, each separated from the grandstand by a walkway. Each stand had room for a thousand people.

The fences of 1878 were removed and the wood recycled into the new fences. Part of the left field fence was shortened to avoid a house on the corner of Sibley (Carnegie) and Kennard (E. 46th) streets. Balls hit over this short fence were ruled ground-rule doubles.

Several trees in the new outfield were cut down. One very large tree in center field, however, was not — the owner of the land felt the cost of its removal too high. To the dismay of the ballplayers, the tree stayed for the whole season.

J. Ford Evans, as president of the Cleveland Base Ball Association, had a job that was similar to such a position in our day: he had an assistant, named Mr. Wesley, and Evans had to answer to a board of directors.

The position of manager, however, was closer to what the responsibilities of front office personnel would be in our time. The manager would contract players, hand out pay checks, and enforce discipline. He was also responsible for booking exhibition games, and taking care of all travel arrangements. Joe Mack — a theatrical agent — who knew nothing of baseball matters — was chosen manager. The job of running an actual ball game was given to a captain — a player named by President Evans.

President Evans accepted bids for the rights to establish a restaurant at the ball grounds under the grandstand. All interested parties had until Tuesday, April 29, at 6 P.M. to apply. There was, however, one rather large catch — no whiskey or alcohol of any kind could be sold.

Mike Carrol was hired to be groundskeeper. His crew had the infield sodded and the entire field rolled and leveled by mid–April. The job of watering, and again rolling the area outside the

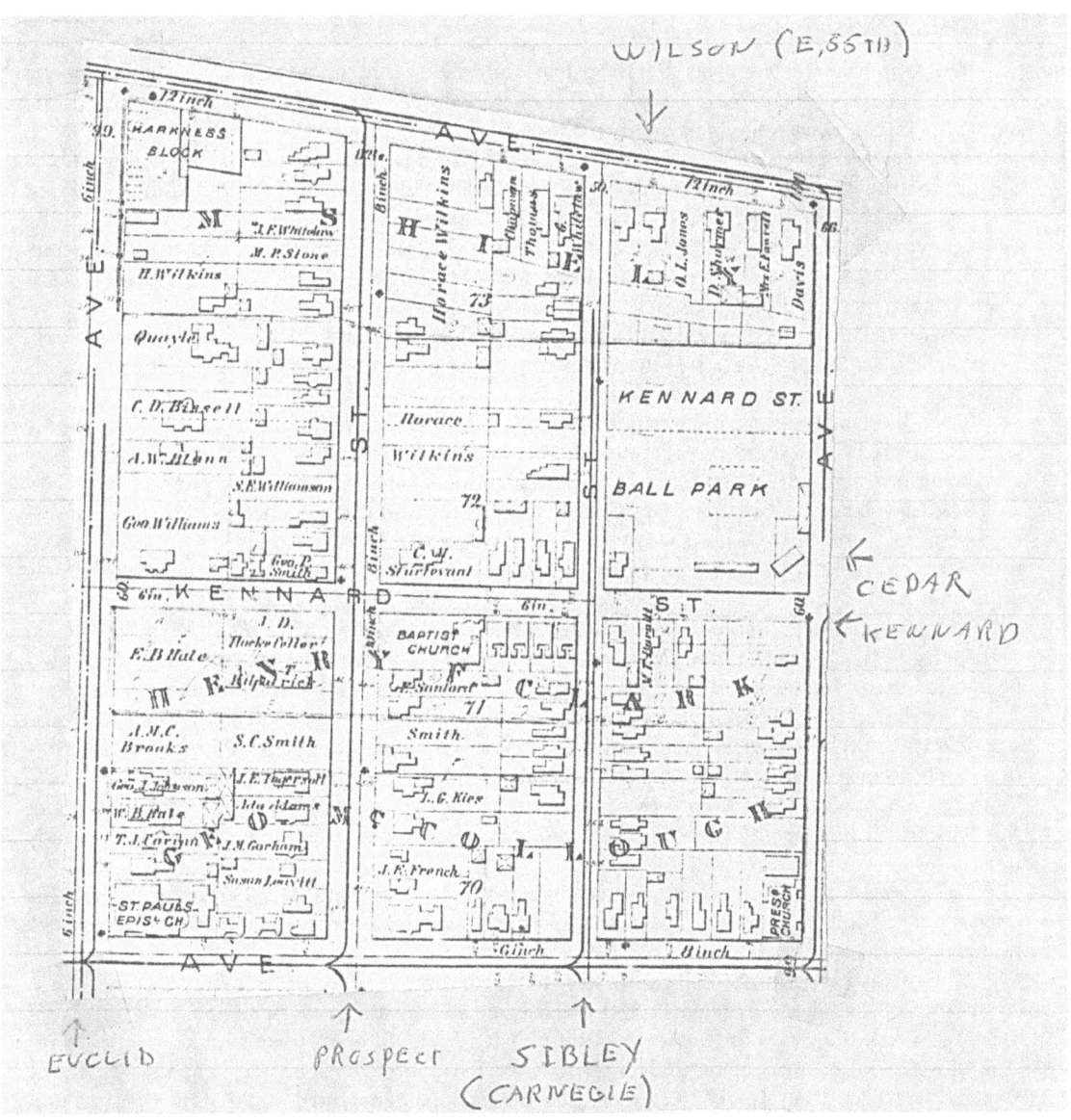

The Kennard St. Ball Park, shown on this Platt map, was home to the National League Cleveland Blue Stockings from 1879 to 1884. A short walk from the park was the home of the famous millionaire John D. Rockefeller. The location of the Rockefeller residence is shown at the intersection of Euclid and Kennard.

infield, commenced on April 23rd. The final touch was "the sprinkling of the field with three or four barrels of grass seed."[1]

Work on the grandstand continued right up to the start of opening day. In 1878 there had been a number of serious injuries in the grandstand as a result of foul balls. A new innovation put an end to that: a foul-ball screen. In 1879 the idea was revisited: "a wire screen [perhaps a major league first] extending the entire length of the stand, and from the floor to the roof, has been erected to protect spectators from the foul balls."[2]

A final item installed in the grandstand, as required by National League rules, was a turnstile.

Training Sessions

The captain of the team was shortstop Tom Carey. He came to town April 2 — the first player to arrive. The rest of the men soon reported for duty, and were issued practice uniforms; they were navy blue in color, set off by a pair of brown stockings.

Practice was immediately started on the Case Commons. This was one of the playing sites of the old Forest City team. Large crowds of the curious and the enthusiastic attended the workouts. Practice moved to Kennard, and the first exhibition game was held there April 26, between the new League team and the best of Cleveland's amateurs — a "picked nine." To make the game interesting, the amateurs were allowed to use Cleveland ace Jim McCormick, while the professionals used "change pitcher" Bobby Mitchell.

Season ticket holders for official games were allowed to attend this unofficial game for free. Everyone else had to pay a quarter and pass through that new thing — the turnstile. The press estimated the crowd to be around five hundred.

The Clevelanders played like major leaguers. Their scoring highlight, a George Strief home run, was greeted with a loud roar of approval. The "picked nine" received polite applause when they scored; unfortunately for them, that was not often enough. Final: Cleveland 7, "picked nine" 2.

The Cleveland baseball club still followed some of the tradition attached to the word "club" — they had a players' clubhouse. It was set up in rooms behind Swartzenberg's cigar store, which was located in the lobby of the Forest City House on Public Square (the Renaissance Hotel is now on the site).

Mr. Swartzenberg, a great lover of the game, set up a chalkboard in his store. With the aid of the telegraph, Cleveland's road games could be followed live inning by inning. The scores would be marked up or "bulletinized" at the close of each inning. The public was welcome to watch.

The front office issued a number of decisions in the closing days of April. It was decided season tickets would be $15 for men and $10 for women — the ladies to be given preference for seats in the grandstand. Season tickets were to go on sale at nine in the morning of opening day at Evans, Van Epps & Co. (President J. Ford Evans' company). A final move: "Those attending the games this season will be presented with a score card [and] fan combined. It will prove to be a handy item."[3]

Ball games were to start at three-forty-five. The East Cleveland streetcar company, starting opening day, would run baseball specials from downtown every three minutes from three o'clock to three-twenty.

Out-of-towners going to ball games were happy to discover that the train depot, at the southeast corner of Euclid and Wilson (E. 55th), was but a short walk from the ballpark.

On May 1, the Grays of Providence, Rhode Island, would be in town to take on the Cleveland Blue Stockings in the inaugural. A few days earlier another providence came into the life of Captain Tom Carey. On April 28th, a message from back East informed him that his wife had presented him with a handsome new son — born at Providence, Rhode Island.

Game One: The Providence Series

PROVIDENCE GRAYS	CLEVELAND BLUE STOCKINGS
James "Orator Jim" O'Rourke*, rf	Charlie Eden, rf
Joe "Old Reliable" Start, 1b	Bill Phillips, 1b
Paul Hines, cf	Jack "Pebbly Jack" Glasscock, 3b
Lew "Blower" Brown, c	"Doc" Kennedy, c
Mike McGeary, 2b	Tom Carey, ss
George Wright*, ss	Fred Warner, cf
John Montgomery Ward*, p	George Strief, 2b
Tom York, lf	Billy "Pigtail Billy" Riley, lf
Bill Hague, 3b	Jim McCormick, p

* (Hall of Fame)

It was chilly on May 1, 1879, but that didn't matter to fifteen hundred Blue Stockings loyalists.

At three-fifty P.M., Umpire E. G. Fountain signaled the start of the game. The heavy-hitting "Grays" sent Jim O'Rourke to the bat. Jim wasted no time in hitting a Jim McCormick offering over the short left field fence — a ground-rule double. He then sat down on second and waited for the boys stationed outside the fence to field the ball in. O'Rourke scored the first run when Joe Start singled. On the throw home, Start took second, and then came home on a sacrifice fly by catcher Lew Brown.

Future Hall of Fame member Jim O'Rourke had the first hit and first run scored at the new major league park, and Providence had a 2–0 lead as Cleveland came to bat for the first time.

Eden struck out, Phillips grounded out to short, but then Jack Glasscock became the first Blue Stocking to reach base, when Hague, the third baseman, threw high to first for an error. Kennedy, however, ended the inning with a fly out to center. In the second, Fred Warner got Cleveland's first hit, a single, but he was left stranded.

Providence put on a hit parade in the third — scoring 5 times. Cleveland then scored its first runs. McCormick led off with a double to right, moved to third on a wild pitch, and came home on a hit by Eden. Eden and Glasscock also scored during the inning.

"Pigtail Billy" Riley, in the fourth, scored Cleveland's fourth run. It was the last of the day for Cleveland. Providence, however, continued to show off its power hitting till the end. Providence had twenty-six hits and Cleveland nine. It took two hours and twenty minutes to play.

Game final: Providence 15, Cleveland 4.

Cleveland may still have been wearing that "practice" uniform, issued in April, of blue shirt and flannel pantaloons over brown stockings. A few days later the *Cleveland Leader* announced that: "The uniforms are to be 'shot' and new ones ordered."[4]

Friday drew a small crowd of 557 to the second game of the series with Providence. John Montgomery Ward (Hall of Fame) pitched for the visitors, and Jim McCormick once again handled the sphere for the home team. Those there saw a great game.

Providence scored in the first, and then the game remained scoreless until Cleveland scored 2 in the seventh to retake the lead. The visitors then responded with 3 of their own in the eighth. Cleveland came back with 2 more in the bottom of the eighth to tie the game.

Word had spread throughout the neighborhood about the close game; when the ninth inning started there were more people in trees and on shed tops watching the game for free than were in the stands.

Providence dampened the spirits of the spectators, in and out of the park, when they pushed across 2 runs to start the ninth. Cleveland, however, was up to the job, and amidst the wildest of cheering, managed 2 runs to send the game into overtime.

The tenth was a whitewash for both teams.

Many present, in the park and elsewhere, felt that the umpire blew the call, and that James O'Rourke should have been out on an inning-ending double play. He ended up scoring, and when Cleveland failed to tally in its turn — that was the ball game.

Score: Providence 7, Cleveland 6.

Jim McCormick took the loss, and John Montgomery Ward notched the victory. The eleven-inning game took two hours and thirty minutes to play.

Friday's exciting extra-inning game helped double the crowd count for the Saturday finale to around a thousand or so. The weather was much warmer than for the first two games, and the fielders were pleased not to have to fight the sun, the sky staying overcast throughout.

Jim McCormick vs. John Montgomery Ward was the pitching match up once again. Cleveland won the coin toss and chose the field.

The first inning was uneventful. Providence: second inning, no scoring. Cleveland in the second did some damage after the first two men went out. Riley beat out a grounder and went to third on a bad throw to first. A single off the bat of McCormick brought him in. Eden hit a single, Phillips hit the ball into right field to score McCormick, and right on the heels of the

Cleveland pitcher, burning up the base-paths, was Charley Eden. The element of surprise was Eden's—and he was safe at the plate. Three runs in.

Third inning: no runs.

Fourth inning: no runs.

Fifth inning: no runs.

Sixth inning: still no runs for either club.

Seventh inning, and yet no runs for the Providence base ball "pounders." Cleveland finally earned another run in the seventh, when Glasscock drove in Phillips who had singled earlier.

Phillips was proving to be the hero of the day. In the fifth inning, catcher Kennedy, playing close to the batter, took a wicked foul tip off his finger: "Time was called ... the bruised hand was washed and done up in a rag."[5] Kennedy was then sent to first to replace Phillips, who was now behind the plate. Phillips played like he was born to catch, not giving Providence any chance to score on his account.

Eighth inning: no runs.

Cleveland ninth: no runs.

Providence ninth: two outs, and into the batter's box stepped the Grays' last hope, the great shortstop George Wright (once a member of the legendary Cincinnati Red Stockings).

George the great "failed to make a base, and a scene not to be described on paper followed. Suffice it to say that the air rang with the cheers and noise for fully five minutes, and as the crowd slowly filed out, congratulations were in order on every hand."[6]

Cleveland had won its first game as National Leaguers, shutting out the powerful team from Providence 4–0.

Time of game: two hours.

THE GIANTS* FELLED

0 0 0 0 0 0 0 0 0

Nine Goose Eggs for the Providence Pounders.[7]

—*Cleveland Leader.*

Cleveland played most of the month of May at home, closing out with Troy, New York.

Cleveland management said the new uniforms it had promised would be available for Cleveland's approaching month-long road trip. At least the ball players would look good—in front of strangers. Friends of the club, however, were given a little surprise—a sneak preview of the new uniforms.

The *Plain Dealer*: "On Saturday [the last home game of the month] the Cleveland team will appear in the new uniform—white cap, shirt and breeches, blue jacket, belts and stockings."[8]

The boys did—and they looked good—but they still lost 7–2.

Amateurs of 1879

The Cleveland Base Ball Amateur Association met in April at the Weddell House. Mr. N. S. Cobleigh, as secretary, presided over the get-together. His first item of business was to resign. Mr. Frank Wright was then elected in his place.

Some revisions for the organization's constitution and a schedule for the year were discussed. A number of inactive teams were dropped from the rolls, while a list of ten clubs was finalized to compete for the championship of 1879. The teams were Forest City, Southern Rocks, White Caps, West Side Reds, Alerts, Grove Boys, Press Nine, Crickets, XYZs and Stars.

ODDITIES & CURIOSITIES

- The Malleables of the iron works played the prisoners of the "Work House Nine."
- The "Fifth Ward Snakes" played the "Hungry Men from Glenville."

---

* The word GIANTS here is descriptive and not a nickname.

- The "Nine Snides" played the "Snide Nine."
- The "Forest City Troop" played the "Gatling Gun Nine."
- The "Independents"—a team of deaf-mutes from the state institution in Columbus—barnstormed around the Western Reserve. They played the amateur Forest City at the Kennard Grounds, and were recorded playing ball in Seville to the west, and Garrettsville to the east.

Kennard Street Ball Park: In the grandstand, Mayor Herrick, a Republican, hosted a delegation of visiting Detroit city officials. On the field, Cleveland City Council divided into "nines" by party. The players wore white caps with a red or blue star on top—red for Republican, blue for Democrat. The crowd itself was composed largely of company-sponsored ticket holders and city workers. The ball game was a benefit for the Children's Aid Society.

The game started a little after three, with W. H. Voltz umpiring. In the fifth inning, a tired Councilman Leonard tried to get the umpire to call the game. His colleagues voted him down.

The *Cleveland Leader* noted that Councilman Lamprecht needed more than rest after the game: "with a few more falls like the ones he took in the game there might be a vacancy in the Eighteenth ward."[9]

In the stands, the Detroit officials enjoyed the game thoroughly, and there was even some talk of sending a "nine" from the council up there, to play our council down here.

The Republicans were the better ball players, winning the game 40–24. Republican Dave Morison called the win a sure sign of Democratic defeat in the fall.

Time: three hours and thirty-three minutes.

After subtracting $24.55 for expenses, representatives of Cleveland City Council handed President T. P. Handy of the Children's Aid Society $155.95.

Expansion "Blues"

The Cleveland Blue Stockings experienced the same struggles as most new teams. The team managed but 1 win per 3 games, staying near the bottom of the standings all year. The public expected this, identifying more with personal favorites then with actual games won. But the season itself was not without its interesting moments.

Boston, June 10, 1879:

"The Bostons won an easy victory over the Clevelands today.... Kennedy was again disabled, his finger injured at Syracuse being again broken by a foul ball."[10] Cleveland, however, had an exciting moment in the game: "The Clevelands made a triple play in the second inning, Warner, Glasscock, Phillips and Kennedy doing the work, putting out Burdock, Bond and Snyder."[11]

The final score was 11–1.

Cleveland protested 2 losses this year. A 1–0 loss against Boston was blamed on runner Sadie Houck's running into Tom Carey, who was trying to catch a fly ball at the time.

An 8–7 game loss was blamed on Jack Farrell of the Syracuse team, who deliberately knocked a thrown ball out of Glasscock's hand when he might otherwise have been out.

These incidents were violations of the rules—supposedly. At League headquarters the written protests were received, filed, and forgotten.

In a home game against Syracuse, the visitors were up after five by a score of 5–3. In the sixth the umpire examined the ball and decided it was too worn. He called to the manager to bring him a new ball. Manager Mack didn't have a new ball, or any ball—he had forgotten to get one.

While the manager stalled, a youngster sitting high up in the stands took it upon himself to solve the problem. Quickly he ran down the steps, across the field, and out the gate toward his home, which was nearby. And just as quickly he ran back—a baseball clutched in his hand. Allowed back into the park, he brought his ball onto the playing field and handed it to the manager.

Playing to the crowd, the kid shouted gleefully: "I just made a home run for Mack."[12] The crowd took it as a pretty good pun and the game went on.

The new ball was a fair one: each team squeezed 3 runs out of it. Unfortunately for Cleveland, the visitors had gotten 2 more runs than Cleveland had out of the original ball.

Score: Syracuse 8, Cleveland 6.

In the game where "Doc" Kennedy originally broke his finger, first baseman Phillips was forced to work behind the plate. He got banged up so badly that, after several innings of gutsy play, he was sent into Eden's spot in right field — unlucky Charlie Eden then closed out the game as the second emergency catcher.

Something had to be done. Cleveland scouting found a catcher playing in the New England League on the Clinton, Massachusetts, team, and made a deal to bring him to Cleveland.

Cleveland folks thought that management had lost their minds when they first saw Barney Gilligan — a one-hundred-thirty pound, five-foot six-and-a-half inch catcher.

How could this lightweight possibly catch the hard-throwing Jim McCormick?

Within a few days the *Cleveland Leader* said of Barney: "He hops from side to side to meet McCormick's twisters, snaps them like the grip of fate, throws to second base with wonderful quickness and precision and picks up foul bounds away off in the crowd and along the fence where no other catcher would think of looking for them. 'Gillie' is a brave boy."[13]

Cleveland had a new catcher and an instant hero.

A Different Kind of Game

The Rev. S. L. Blake of the Woodland Avenue Presbyterian Church delivered a sermon at the YMCA's tenth lecture series. His topic was "All work and no play makes Jack a dull boy."[14] He praised the game of baseball, reminiscing about playing the game in his youth. He of course had to warn the audience about a sinful aspect of the game: "The chief abuse is pool selling [i.e., betting, apparently legal, conducted in taverns around town], which is no more a necessary incident of the game than an Atlantic voyage, which are largely occupied by a certain class with the making of pools."[15]

The "certain class" referred to was the Irish. When the minister was talking about not letting Jack become a dull boy, he left out that other class of person — Jill. The clerical-collar crowd was quite opposed to girls' playing baseball.

In Utica, New York, two touring teams of female ball players played a game of baseball, for pay. On August 13, the *Cleveland Herald* said of these girls: "The Amazonian teams are to afflict Buffalo with a game."[16]

If the ministers and their supporters had been paying attention to geography, they might have realized that a dose of "Amazonian affliction" might well be heading in their direction.

Girls got game: They attempted to book a game at the Kennard Grounds but were denied permission. They were successful, however, in securing grounds on the east bank of the Rocky River by Detroit Avenue.

On Friday, August 15, the Red Stockings of New York and the Blue Stockings of Philadelphia took the field in front of a thousand people. Greater Cleveland was about to see its first game featuring "female base ballists."

George Stephens was a young man who had agreed to umpire the game. It was said he seemed rather embarrassed at times, but in spite of that he still called a fair game. The Blues went to bat first, scoring a run; the Reds responded with 4 in their turn. The Reds scored 24 more and the Blues scored 15 more. The game was called after only five innings because it was raining.

Final: Reds 28, Blues 16.

The *Cleveland Herald's* man on the scene wrote: "One very remarkable thing was the presence of so many gray-haired and middle-aged men in the crowd."[17] It is hard to see why this surprised him, when earlier in his report he called the game little more than a variety show, the kind that would attract someone to a can-can dance.

He also wrote: "One other feature that raised a ripple of excitement was when the gentle

Georgia Bell spread her wings and started for first base, running over the damsel who stood guard there, and tumbling head over heels into the field."[18]

The game was, in fact, little more than a comedy, with not too much attention paid to the rules. However, it was a groundbreaking event for more serious girls' teams at the close of the century.

RED STOCKINGS	BLUE STOCKINGS
Laura Gray, c.	____ Clifford, c.
Retta Howard, 1b	Georgia Lostabum, 1b
Tillie Sheldon, p.	Josie Howard, 2b
Mirnie Stacy, 3b	Lizzie Brooks, p.
Georgia Bell, 2b	Josie Arnold, 3b
Kate Moore, rf	Maud Pierce, lf
May Addison, lf	Nellie Harding, rf
Jennie Taylor, cf	Hattie Howard, cf

* The girls' teams played without shortstops.

The *Cleveland Leader* gave a fair account of the game, but editorial policy compelled this rider at the end of the story: "Cleveland has no room for such games. They are not what might be called indecent, but are sadly out of taste. Hereafter the Reds and Blues are requested to go West via Columbus."[19]

More Sandlots

Local ball player Will Bohn landed himself a job as a professional minor league ball player. He was signed by Davenport, Iowa, of the Northwestern Association. Bobby Watson, another Cleveland sandlotter, having recovered from an injury, was catching for the Yale University team.

East of Cleveland, the city of Geneva boasted of a local star named John Lee Richmond. He was playing baseball at another Ivy League school — Brown University in Providence, Rhode Island.

Geneva, Ohio, had a team of white players, and a team of colored players, this year. They played each other.

Cleveland had a very good new team of white players, named the "Red Stockings," and a very good new team of colored players, without a name but referred to as the "new colored nine."[20] They played each other. In a publicized game on the Case Commons, at the end of August, the "new colored nine" upset the Red Stockings by a score of 24–17.

Ruffen, Dewey, Mack, Warden, Gilbert, Oswalt, Kurtz, Hartman, and Brassell were the Red Stockings. Milligan, Smith, J. Morris, Wilson, Henderson, Doctor, Brown, W. Morris, and Alexander were the "new colored nine." (These players would in the future be on teams that not only had names but were as good as the best "crack" white teams.)

The White Caps not only had a name, they had two names. The topnotch sandlot club decided they liked the theatrical production *H. M. S. Pinafore* (on tour in America this year) so much that they changed their name to Pinafores. They then complained loudly to the papers when another team purloined the White Caps name. This in their mind, if not the papers, was a shameless attempt to ride the coat tails of their famous retired name.

This year two new baseball names appeared in the suburbs — Parma "Reds" and Berea "Stars."

Whitewashing "White Stockings"

Cleveland had a lucky charm — an old broom kept in the bat bag. So as not to use up its luck, it was brought out sparingly. It came out on Friday, August 15. The White Stockings were in town.

Cleveland won the coin toss and chose the field. Chicago batted and went down. Cleveland now came up. Carey singled, went to third on a passed ball, and scored on another. No runs went up on the scoreboard for the next four and a half innings. In the sixth Cleveland got its second run, when Gilligan singled and Glasscock ran home from second. For Chicago, goose eggs continued to go up on the scoreboard until there were nine of them, and no more innings.

There is a baseball term for a shutout dating from the 1870's and still used today. That word is "Chicago."

Big Jim McCormick "Chicagoed" Chicago.
Final: Cleveland 2, Chicago 0.
Cleveland made no errors.
McCormick allowed the visitors but four hits.
Time of game: two hours.
Umpire: Albert G. Pratt (the old Forest City pitcher).
From the inspired pen at the *Cleveland Herald*:

For some time past we have been reading and hearing talk of a town somewhere in the West on the shore of Lake Michigan. They say that more people live there, and that they can buy more wheat, do more business, jump higher, dive deeper and come out dryer than any set of white men on this mundane sphere, and the people who live out there say they have more water, broader prairies and better land than can be found anywhere.... They concluded that this year they would put the base ball business in their pockets just to show the people of America that there was nothing which they could not excel in.... They thought they'd have an easy thing ... with the tail end of the League, so they came to Cleveland ... you should have seen the Cleveland boys play in nine innings without an error. Those great Chicagoans, so called, the big silk-stockinged Suckers from Illinois, the fellows who were said to have the championship banner within their grasp to a dead certainty, coming here to take a dose of the worst kind of whitewash from the club that had been struggling all the season at the tail end of the League. You ought to have seen how they struggled and kicked as the bitter dose was being administered, and the wry faces they made would have put into shadow the puckering countenances of a seven-year-old child under his first dose of 'ile and turpentine.' [21]

Jim McCormick led all of baseball with 45 wins in 1880, establishing a record for Cleveland pitchers. He was a Cleveland Blue Stocking (N.L.) from 1879 until late 1884, when he deserted the team to join the upstart Union Association.

Booze Ball

The Cleveland team had a record of 9 and 22 by the first week of July. Their record two months later on September 1 was 21 and 41.

Cleveland management was embarrassed by charges, in late July, that some team members were not doing their best to win because they were nursing too many hangovers.

The *Cleveland Leader* was unusually bold when it blamed a specific July loss on players' being under the influence of "calamity water." When Bill Phillips flipped over a buggy during this anti-drinking crusade, the paper implied that strong beverage was at play. The notorious incident of the year before, involving Cleveland ball players crashing their wagon and going to jail to sober up, made the Phillips incident all the more plausible. Mr. Phillips, however, was not disciplined by the ball club or held by the authorities. The over-all issue faded away.

In September, the club officials had a meeting at the Weddell. They had decided earlier to continue the team for next year, and to go about the business of beefing up the offense.

Blondie Purcell, a ball player with great potential, was available. His signing for 1880 was announced at the meeting. Cincinnati, however, had a prior claim to his services, a position the League upheld. A year later, Cincinnati was happy that Cleveland still wanted him. If Mr. Purcell's drinking habits had been as famous as they would become in the future, he would not have played even 20 games for Cleveland in 1881. He played for twelve seasons and for almost as many different teams.

Cleveland was in Syracuse when the team posed for a photograph in the studios of P. S. Ryder. A copy of this photo appeared in a Cleveland newspaper in the early part of the twentieth century. It is the only likeness of the National League Blue Stockings to have survived their stay in Cleveland.

What did not survive the season of 1879 was the franchise in Syracuse. The National League frowned on drinking at its ballparks, but Syracuse, complained one Cleveland writer, not only had a bar, but had it in plain sight where everyone in the stands could watch drinks being tossed down during a game. In the second week of September, Cleveland was at Syracuse for a game. The crowd was sparse, and Cleveland's cut of the gate was a very thin $4.30. Syracuse managed to win the game 6–5. It was their last win and final game as a major league town. After the game the franchise folded.

Syracuse had a record of 22 and 48 when they quit, and a .314 winning percentage. They finished one place above the cellar, in seventh, 30 games behind first-place Providence.

"Red legs," "blue legs," and the battle of Ohio

Cincinnati came to town on August 28. *Cleveland Leader*: "It was the dirtiest, noisiest game played in Cleveland this year."[22]

Will "Whoop-La" White was the "red-legs'" pitcher, and former Cleveland Forest City star James "Deacon" White was his battery mate and older brother. They were the only two Cincinnati players not making loud abusive noises, due to their religious views. Cleveland's "blue-legs" sent Jim McCormick to the pitcher's box, and the wiry Barney Gilligan was his catcher.

Twelve hundred people attended the game, and their mood "swayed between excitement, enthusiasm and disgust."[23]

Cleveland scored the first run in the bottom of the second. Cincinnati came back with 2 in the top of the third. Cleveland again took the lead with 3 in the fourth. The visitors gained a 1-run advantage in the sixth, scoring 3 to go up 5–4.

Cincinnati was really getting into its noisy game at this point. Whenever Cleveland batted a ball into the air, "eight captains yelled the name of the player who was to catch it."[24] A little later, the crowd was subjected to a red-legs yeller of somewhat more indecorous comments: "Gerhardt talked back insultingly in the last inning, and the indulgence cost the frisky young man $30."[25]

It looked like a Cincinnati day when but one out was needed to end the contest. Captain Tom Carey was now Cleveland's last hope. The captain clubbed a clutch two-bagger into the outfield that sent pitcher McCormick trotting home from third with the run that sent the game into extra innings.

After ten and a half innings the game remained tied; "in the eleventh the 'blue-legs' went to bat with blood in their eyes and a determination to end the agony."[26] George Strief led off, but popped out to Hotaling in center. Cleveland pitcher McCormick then launched the ball high into the infield air; Barnes, the shortstop, got under it, but he let it slip through his fingers. Lead-off batter Phillips now singled McCormick into scoring position. Up to the plate with a confident swagger walked Charlie Eden. He took his place in the batter's box and waited patiently for a pretty pitch. Finally, "Whoop-La" gave him one, and Charlie turned it into a single—big Jim McCormick came around, stomped his foot on the plate, and the game was won—but not over. The reason, once again, was that under the bizarre rule of the day, the game could not officially end until there were three outs. The practice had but statistical value and lasted only a few more years. Warner and Glasscock quickly made the last two outs.

Final: Cleveland 7, Cincinnati 6.
Will White allowed sixteen hits, struck out three.
McCormick scattered seven hits, striking out five.
Umpire: Albert G. Pratt.
Time: four hours and forty-three minutes.

Late Dates

Joe Mack left the team in mid–September. He went to his home in Columbiana County, Ohio, to rest up for business he had in Chicago.

September 30 was a Tuesday, and Cleveland beat Cincinnati at League Park 9–6. The highlight of the game was a home run. Barney Gilligan, the sentimental favorite of the home crowd, hit it. It was the last game of the regular season, but the newspapers made little of it.

Club president Evans, at season end, wasted no time in getting two Albany ball players under Cleveland contract for 1880 — left fielder Ned Hanlon (Hall of Fame) and second baseman Fred "Sure Shot" Dunlap. The latter would become an all-time Cleveland great.

The Cleveland team, rather than going home, now opened a mini post-season of exhibition games. They played the amateur "Forest City" at League Park. They then went to Akron, and the papers of October 7 and 8 reported Blue Stocking wins over the Akron team of 9–2 and 12–5.

The last game was October 13, and in a shortened six-inning game, Cleveland beat Western Reserve College 15–2.

Lovers of the national pastime who couldn't get enough baseball now had to be content to follow the post-season games of pennant-winning Providence. There was no "World Series" in 1879, but the famous Joe Haverly booking agency, out of Chicago, arranged a tour for the "Grays." They played the best teams the sunny state of California could throw at them.

The Blue Stockings for their part now disbanded, and did the best they could to stay warm until spring.

STANDINGS OF 1879

	W	L	PCT.	GB
PROVIDENCE	59	25	.702	—
BOSTON	54	30	.643	5
BUFFALO	46	32	.590	10
CHICAGO	46	33	.582	10.5
CINCINNATI	43	37	.538	14
CLEVELAND	27	55	.329	31
SYRACUSE	22	48	.314	30
TROY	19	56	.253	35.5

1880

Rumsey's Gym

The worst of winter was over in early March of 1880. At the ballpark workmen were removing the retaining walls from the ice skating rink and preparing the field. In a few short weeks the ball team would be starting its spring practice.

Some of the players had wintered in Cleveland, and others had arrived early to get a head start on getting in shape. Thoughts of using space under the grandstand as a workout facility, however, were nixed when the concessionaire objected. A happy solution was found right downtown.

The players were told to report to Room No. 15 of Waring Block Building on March 15 to start getting in shape. They would be under the instruction of Professor Rumsey, the self-proclaimed "king of exercise."

Rumsey was known by his illustrated ads of a boxer working out in a gym (the professor's head was superimposed on the boxer's body). The boxer was striking Rumsey's invention — his patented air punching bag.

The regimen for the players at the downtown gymnasium included the throwing of Indian clubs, use of the rowing machine, sparring to improve "the pins" (the players' footwork), and, of course, use of the patented air punching bag.

On the second day at the gym, three club officials stopped by — Charley Sheffield, Lem Rawson, and the old Forest City star, L. C. Hanna. They met newcomers Ned Hanlon and Fred Dunlap.

The new men said they were quartered at the Johnson House, and so far had found Cleveland to their liking. The officials were impressed by the two and were certain they would do well.

A local reporter seconded the opinion: "The players are fine looking, healthy gentlemen and exceedingly intelligent in conversation. They are complete strangers to Cleveland but they should have no trouble making friends here."[1]

Ned Hanlon played only one season in Cleveland — his rookie year. His playing career lasted for thirteen years, but he was a highly respected manager for nineteen years— seven as skipper for the great Baltimore teams of the 1890's. He was also a major activist in the labor movement for ball players' rights. The Hall's special committee on old timers put him into baseball's Hall of Fame in recent years.

Fred "Sure Shot" Dunlap played four of his twelve seasons with Cleveland; he would be one of the great Cleveland stars of the nineteenth century. In 1880 he led the League with 27 doubles. He was a member of the St. Louis Maroons, a team in the one-year major league — the Union Association of 1884. Fred Dunlap batted .412 that year, which was the highest average ever recorded in the major leagues up to that date, and which would be the sixth-highest single-season batting mark of the nineteenth century.

Baseball business announcements

• A season ticket is $15 and for the first time its use is transferable to a friend or business associate for any game. The pass is also good for all other non–League games. April 20th is the last day to purchase your season tickets.

• A new twenty-game package, good for choice of any twenty games, has grandstand privileges if desired.

• Ticket outlets include Evans & Van Epps, Short & Foreman, Swartzenberg's Cigar Emporium, and Bruce's Drug Store (on Prospect Avenue).

• Patterson and Brunell have published a pamphlet complete with a schedule of Blue Stocking games and other items.

Funny business

In the spring, a certain captain of police made an appearance at the ballpark and announced, "here after a $3 license fee will be required for each game."[2]

President Evans was not long in hearing about the pronouncement, and neither was the press. The *Plain Dealer's* nose for news detected a stale fish smell coming from City Hall. The paper observed that the mayor apparently equated baseball games with "circuses and fat women shows. Wonder if he will require a candidate to have a music permit when he is serenaded."[3]

Evans went into City Hall, said hello to no one, and made a straight line to the office of licenses. The bureaucrat in charge was soon engaged in intense study, to determine just what kind of a license was called for. Finally, after some time and consultation, it was decided that a combination skating rink/bathing house permit came closest to the definition of the "required" ballpark license.

A $50 fee was assessed and paid on the spot. With his license in hand, President Evans went public. He stated that a provision under the law governing licenses such as he had been issued entitled him to free police protection at taxpayers' expense.

Considering that he had been hiring four to six "moonlighting" policemen, at the cost of $1.50 per game per cop, Evans' rough math calculated a savings of about $300 a year!

No more was heard from City Hall.

The public was invited to see a "picked nine" practice game on April 21. A dime was charged. Upon arriving, some in the audience were quick to point out a major improvement: that giant tree—an outfield obstruction for two years—was gone. Many ladies came to the game, most choosing to watch from their vehicles inside the now sturdier carriage enclosure.

The "picked nine" featured the talented brothers Will and Charley Bohn. Will turned professional ball player before the year was out, and his brother Charley would be the first Cleveland sandlotter to wear a major league uniform.

Cleveland wore last year's worn-out uniforms to practice in. The new uniforms from Spalding were due in from Chicago in a few days. Cleveland gave their old uniforms a good workout, scoring in every inning. Score: Cleveland 21, "picked nine" 9.

Inning	1	2	3	4	5	6	7	8	9	Final
Cleveland	4	2	6	3	4	1	0	1	*	21
Picked Nine	0	0	0	0	2	2	0	2	3	9

First Games

The Washington Nationals were not members of the National League, but they were one of the nation's most prominent professional teams, being famous even before the advent of major league play. Their game with Cleveland was considered a season opener.

The threatening weather of Friday, April 30, put a damper on the crowd, but 750 hardy souls still showed up, hoping for a game. The game went for five drizzly innings, and then a serious cloudburst ended it. Cleveland was up 1–0 when the game was called. The highlight of the game was when new player Fred Dunlap knocked the ball out of the park over the short left field fence. However, it only counted as a long ground-rule double.

GAME ONE OFFICIALLY

The championship season for the pennant opened on Saturday, May 1. Al Pratt, the beloved former Forest City pitcher, was now working as an umpire. As a player he was well respected; as the umpire for the day, he was not. Cleveland lost to Buffalo 7–4, and many thought Mr. Pratt was partly to blame.

The *Plain Dealer* put the fault elsewhere: "Buffalo beat Cleveland on Saturday. After the game our people were industriously inquiring the reason. In our opinion the defeat may be explained this way, McCormick did not pitch with his usual effectiveness and some bad errors, particularly in throwing, were made in the field. The Buffalos played an admirable game."[4]

BUFFALO	AT BAT	RUNS	BASE HITS	ERRORS
Bill Crowley, cf*	5	0	1	0
Jack Rowe, c	5	1	3	0
"Hardy" ("Old True Blue") Richardson, 3b	4	2	2	0
Oscar Walker, 1b	5	1	3	0
Joe "Ubbo Ubbo" Hornung, lf	5	1	2	0
Davy Force, ss	4	1	0	0
Sam Crane, 2b	4	1	0	1
"Dude" Thomas Jefferson Esterbrook, rf*	4	0	1	0
Bill "Gunner" McGunnigle, p*	4	0	1	0
Total	40	7	13	1

* These Buffalo players would eventually spend time in a Cleveland uniform.

CLEVELAND	AT BAT	RUNS	BASE HITS	ERRORS
Fred "Sure Shot" Dunlap, 2b	5	1	1	1
"Orator" George Shaffer, rf	5	0	1	0
Pete "Monkey" Hotaling, cf	5	0	1	1
"Doc" Michael Kennedy, c	4	0	1	2
"Ned" Edward Hanlon, lf	3	2	1	1
Bill Phillips, 1b	4	0	2	0

CLEVELAND	AT BAT	RUNS	BASE HITS	ERRORS
Frank Hankinson, 3b	4	0	1	0
Jack "Pebbly Jack" John Wesley Glasscock, ss	4	1	1	1
Jim McCormick, p	4	0	2	1
Total	38	4	11	7

Cleveland: three-base hits (Hankinson) 1, bases on balls (Hanlon) 1, left on base 8, McCormick struck out 5.

Buffalo: two-base hits (Rowe, Richardson) 2, three-base hits (Walker) 1, bases on balls (Richardson, Force) 2, left on base 7. McGunnigle struck out 0 and walked 1.

Time of game: Two hours.

Umpire: Al G. Pratt, of Pittsburgh. [This is an early instance in the nineteenth century of the letter "h" being used in the spelling of Pittsburgh.]

Pending amateur games

- The White Sewing Machine Company versus the Malleables of the iron works plant.
- The Cleveland Fire Department to play the Detroit Fire Department.
- The High School versus the Brooks Academy.
- Cleveland Young Rattlers to face Young Idlers.
- The Richmond Twp. Settlement team to play Collamer Reds (Collinwood area).
- The Berea Anchors versus the Seville Anchor (at Berea Fairgrounds).
- The Rockwells versus the Red Hearts of Painesville.

Two stories

Al Hall

Al Hall played 67 games in 1879 for the Troy franchise in the League. Now a Blue Stocking, he was out to prove his worth. In practice he played with all his heart, even knocking a fingernail off somehow. He made spectacular over-the-shoulder catches running at breakneck speed; he was desperate to win a starting outfielder's job. Management was impressed, and gave it to him.

Cleveland was playing in Cincinnati and Al was in left field — it was his third game. Pete Hotaling, the captain, was playing center. The Cincinnati batter stroked a screamer toward left center. Both men converged on the ball, with Hotaling yelling Hall off the ball all the way. Hall heard nothing; everybody else heard the thud of colliding bodies. For a minute the two men lay on the ground tangled in a motionless heap. Hotaling recovered his wits first; he took one look at Al, and like a crazy man, came running in, wildly waving his hands high, shouting over and over for a doctor.

When help arrived in the outfield, they saw the ugly and frightening sight of a bone sticking out of Al's leg between his ankle and knee. His leg was very obviously and very badly broken.

Al was removed from the field by ambulance, and shortly sent back to the Johnson House in Cleveland to recover for a few days. Then it was arranged to send him home to Oil City, Pennsylvania. Al knew that his season was likely over; the doctors thought that his career was likely over. They said that if the healing went well, perhaps by fall Al would be able to walk again — after a fashion.

President Evans, the next day, was at a champagne breakfast with Cincinnati big shots. During the course of dining, he casually mentioned that the players of Cincinnati and Cleveland had expressed a desire to stage a benefit game for the wounded Al Hall following the current series of scheduled games, and that he had decided to grant such permission.

The game raised $400 for Al Hall. Sadly, after 3 games with Cleveland, Hall's big league career was indeed over. Later, for a time, he tried his hand at managing minor professional teams around Western Pennsylvania.

By 1885, five years after a broken leg had ended his baseball career, Al Hall was in Warren, Pennsylvania — a resident of the sanitarium there. And that February, on the tenth of the month, he died. Was it a broken heart, caused by his early forced retirement from the ball diamond he loved so well? Some thought so.

Lee Richmond's Perfect Game

John Lee Richmond was born in Sheffield Twp., in Ashtabula County, on May 5, 1857. At a young age the family took up residence in the city of Geneva.

John was a lefthander and he took to baseball pitching as if born to it. As a young teenager, he would often be a guest pitcher for some of Cleveland's best sandlot teams. Mr. Richmond was a bright lad, and when he reached the proper age, he was accepted for enrollment at Oberlin College, where of course he pitched for the college "nine."

John Richmond loved baseball, but he wanted to serve the community in the best possible way his intelligence would allow: he wanted to be a doctor. He made application to Brown University in Providence, Rhode Island. He was accepted and enrolled in pre-medical courses. Brown had a baseball team, and with the arrival of John Lee Richmond they soon had a great pitcher — one that would lead them to a championship.

There was no rule against it, so in order to make some money for school, Richmond pitched professionally during the summer recess. He got a summer job pitching for the 1879 edition of the pro team out of Worcester, Mass. He made quite an impression in an exhibition game against the National League's Chicago team: he pitched a no-hitter. The Worcester crowd was absolutely delighted.

That same summer, in what was the accepted practice of renting a pitcher for a day, the National League Boston team hired John Richmond to pitch one of their games. In this solitary appearance the record shows that John won the game, giving up but 2 runs in nine innings while striking out eleven.

In 1880 Worcester replaced Syracuse, New York, in the National League. They wasted no time in signing Richmond to a contract for the summer. Worcester, however, wanted Richmond right away; they didn't want to wait till June. The officials at Brown University were persuaded to make special arrangements, and John Richmond was able to leave school in May.

John pitched in 74 of Worcester's 83 games and posted a 32 and 32 record, leading the first-year Worcester National League team to an impressive fourth-place finish. Far more impressive was his performance in the June series against a visiting Cleveland.

Cleveland versus John Lee Richmond

June 11, 1880 — "Lee" Richmond showed why many considered his left-handed "drop curve" the best in the country. Cleveland scratched out but four hits off the clever lefty as they were whitewashed 5–0.

Saturday, June 12, 1880 — date future generations of serious baseball fans would memorize. Jim McCormick pitched for Cleveland and was opposed by John Lee Richmond. Both men were pitching masterpieces — not a run had scored up until the fifth. The critical inning: "Irwin led off with a hit and was advanced to second on Bennett being given his base on balls; Whitney then hit to McCormick, who threw to Dunlap for a double play, but the latter muffed the ball and then in attempting to cut Irwin off at the plate threw high over Kennedy's head."[5]

One run scored for Worcester, and that would prove to be enough. McCormick gave up no earned runs, struck out seven, and allowed but three hits. Richmond struck out five and walked none. The most important statistic: Cleveland sent twenty-seven men to the plate, and none of them saw first base. "Worcester, Mass., June 12 — The game between the Clevelands and the Worcester today was the most wonderful game on record. The two nines might have played indefinitely had not Dunlap's double error presented the Worcester with the winning run.... Rain stopped the play eight minutes in the eighth inning. The attendance was good."[6]

Incredible! Twenty-three-year-old John Lee Richmond had just pitched the major league's first perfect game.

Score: Worcester 1, Cleveland 0.

Time: One hour and twenty-seven minutes.

Umpire: G. H. Bradley.

As a reward Richmond was given the next day off. He could have used two. His next outing was described as the worst performance of his professional career. Cleveland lit him up for twenty-four hits in a 7–1 victory. But no one would remember June 14, 1880.

Some years after his perfect game, a story was told that was said to have originated out of Providence: John Lee Richmond was fresh from having completed his exams at Brown University when an urgent telegram arrived. The dispatch ordered him to rush to Worcester to pitch that very afternoon. He hurried to the train station where a special train was standing by—just for him. All trains along the route, so the story goes, had been sidetracked to clear the way. The express roared off toward Worcester at full steam, making it in record time. John, who had dressed on the train, was rushed onto the field and into the pitcher's box just as the umpire called for start of game—the perfect game.

John Lee Richmond was born and spent most of his life in the Cleveland area. As the hard-throwing, crafty left-handed pitcher on the Worcester, Massachusetts, team of 1880, he pitched the National League's first perfect game, winning 1–0. His unlucky opponents were the visiting Cleveland team.

It's a great story; the only problem with it was that the newspapers at the time forgot to tell it.

What did happen shortly after the historic pitching performance was that Harvard University sent word that John Lee Richmond had been accepted to attend medical school there. He could now complete his dream of becoming a doctor.

Except for that one glorious day in June, the pitching career of John Lee Richmond was rather mediocre. In six years he pitched in 191 games and had a record of 75–100.

John Lee Richmond's true contribution to the world was in the classroom. Forsaking his medical degree, he became a teacher. He taught in Geneva, Ohio, becoming a principal at one point. The majority of his teaching days, however, were in the city of Toledo. He worked in the high schools there for many years. In his final years as an educator he was a faculty member at Toledo University, where he was a mathematics instructor.

"Lee" Richmond took an active interest in the affairs of baseball after he left the game, and all through his retirement years. In 1929, John Lee Richmond suffered a heart attack, and on September 30, just a few weeks before the start of the Great Depression, he passed away. The "perfect pitcher" and beloved schoolteacher was 72.

Akron Adventures

Gid Gardner, in his one year as an extra pitcher for the Blue Stockings, posted a record of 1 and 8. In five years he pitched but 15 games, winning 2 and losing 12.

An episode in Akron may help explain why he achieved so little with his talent. The twenty-one-year-old Gardner was called on in July to pitch an exhibition game against the professional Akrons. To the shock of everyone, perhaps including himself, Gardner pitched a 14–0 shutout.

The team returned to their quarters at the Empire Hotel. Gardner stepped into the hotel tavern with a few teammates for a victory drink or two. He soon lost track of his rounds, and his buddies lost track of him. After a time, they were called to come pick him up off the floor — it wasn't the bar room floor he was laid out on, it was the lobby floor. Gardner had gotten there by falling through the skylight in the ceiling. He was more stunned than hurt. The real pain would come when his manager found out.

A Chicago tumbler

Chicago had clinched the pennant in September, and, with a day off in the series at Cleveland, decided to go down to Akron to show the people there what the "right stuff" looked like. The large crowd thoroughly enjoyed what they saw, and that was their Akron team victorious in an exciting 4–3 game.

The Good, the Bad, and the Law

THE GOOD

The Cleveland White Sewing Machine Company team was judged one of the best in town. They learned what the Chicago White Stockings learned — that Akron had a very good ball club. A quarter was charged for admission to the game, and a nice crowd came out to League Park in late September to watch Akron rip the "Whites" 21–2.

THE BAD

Unlike Akron, Cleveland had a group of ball clubs that were terrible, but they always had a helluva good time anyway. They were the muffin nines from "The Big Bonanza Beerguzzling Association."[7]

THE LAW

When Chicago ball player Joe Quest came to Cleveland with his team, he discovered that the wheels of justice had gotten there ahead of him. Leaving his room at the Weddell, he went into the lobby, where the rest of the team was getting their paychecks from the club's manager, but there was no envelope for Joe. His check had been garnished in full by court order. The manager had just been telegraphed of the fact, and was instructed not to distribute the Quest check.

Quest owed an Indiana man $80, and the man had gotten an order of attachment from the Superior Court of Warren County, Indiana. The entire award including damages and so forth was $220. This was more than Joe's check.

Depressed, Joe returned to his room, where a Cleveland policeman was standing by overseeing the hotel workers who were hurriedly removing the last of Mr. Quest's personal property.

By sending a telegraph to police headquarters, the Indiana court had legally directed the Cleveland police to implement its wishes, which included confiscation of property to meet debt obligations.

No Fireworks on a Sunday

Holiday ball:

CLEVELAND	TROY, NY
Fred "Sure Shot" Dunlap, 2b	Ed Cogswell, 1b
George "Orator" Shaffer, rf	Pete Gillespie, lf
Pete Hotaling, cf	Bob "Death to Flying Things" Ferguson, 2b

CLEVELAND
Ned Hanlon, lf
Bill Phillips, 1b
Frank Hankinson, 3b
Jim McCormick, p
"Pebbly Jack" Glasscock, ss
Barney Gilligan, c

TROY, NY
John Cassidy, rf
Roger Connor, 3b
Ed Caskin, ss
Louis "Buttercup" Dickerson, cf
Mickey "Smiling Mickey" Welch, p
Bill Holbert, c

The Fourth of July fell on a Sunday in 1880, so the popular Independence Day ballgame was played on Monday the fifth. It looked like rain, and Jim McCormick pitched like it was a certainty. Troy went to bat, and after four straight doubles and some lousy fielding, Troy had the lead 3–0. In their turn, Dunlap started the Cleveland offense by leading off with a walk, went to second on a grounder, and then came around to score on a Hotaling single.

McCormick got his rain; in the second inning play was halted for ten minutes before Troy could bat. McCormick appeared to be a new man after the rain, quickly retiring Troy.

In the second, Hankinson doubled and moved to third on a rare balk call. McCormick came up and singled him in. Cleveland added the tying run in the fifth.

The game would last for fourteen innings. From the second through the thirteenth inning McCormick was a master. He allowed no runs, and his game totals would show nine strikeouts and an amazing fifteen assists on outs. After the fifth, Mickey Welch of the Troys would keep Cleveland off the board for eight innings.

Troy now moved ahead 4–3 by scoring a run in the top of the fourteenth. Dunlap led off the bottom of the frame. He hit a single, and with the help of some bad fielding ended up on second. Shaffer hit a grounder to shortstop Caskin, who let the ball play him, and Dunlap grabbed third. Shaffer next stole second, but did not draw a throw from the catcher. Hotaling then performed what today we would call a suicide bunt, and Dunlap was in with the tying run. Shaffer was on third and Hotaling on first, when Hotaling tried a little trick—trying to get caught in a rundown between first and second to allow Shaffer to score—but it didn't work. He was out and Shaffer kept the base at third.

In the words of one who was there:

Hanlon went to bat. Three balls passed, to which he paid no attention. The fourth he arrested in its flight and handsomely turned its course backward, and landing it in the left field where nobody was, Shaffer ambling home at his ease and making the winning run and under the new League rules that ended the game. A wild shout went up from the vast crowd and presently the cushions, peddled about the stands for five cents each game, began to fly thick and fast through the air. For ten minutes the scene was ludicrous in the extreme. The first to throw a cushion was doubtless someone who let it go in the frenzy of joy. The cue was quickly taken by others and soon hundreds of cushions were sailing through the air and presently people began to pelt each other with them. Some of the Troy players joined in the sport and for a few minutes the great crowd reveled in one of the most comical sprees ever seen. People forgot all about their suppers and the game and stopped to see and heartily laugh at the fun. Take the game all through, it was one of the most entertaining, most satisfactory ever played in this city.[8]

Inning	1	2	3	4	5	6	7	8	9	10	11	12	13	14	Final
Troy	3	0	0	0	0	0	0	0	0	0	0	0	0	1	4
Cleveland	1	1	0	0	1	0	0	0	0	0	0	0	0	2	5

Time of game: three hours and twenty minutes. Umpire: G. H. Bradley.

Notes: • Troy third baseman Roger Connor was the nineteenth century's greatest home run hitter (138). He is in the Hall of Fame. • Troy's Mickey Welch was the sixth or seventh pitcher with the most wins in the nineteenth century. The Baseball Encyclopedia (New York: MacMillan, 1974) says sixth—311 wins. Total Baseball (Warner: New York, 1991) says seventh—307 wins. He is in the Hall of Fame.

Ripped Off

In mid–July Worcester was in Cleveland to play a game. The visiting team was entitled to 15 cents of every ticket sold, and by League rules the cut was to be turned over to the visitors at the start of play.

Worcester took the field, and after Cleveland batted it started to rain a bit. Everyone figured there would be a short delay. Worcester, however, had their money and refused to play any more. Cleveland took the field, but the umpire refused to call a forfeit — he called it a "no game." Cleveland would appeal that decision to the League officials.

The entire executive committee of Cleveland's management allowed their names to be attached to a shameless, lengthy document telling why there could be no refund. Some of the richest men in town, in essence, cried poverty as far as the baseball customer was concerned. They cited losses to the shareholders from the year before; they went on to make it sound like the baseball business was a charity — that they kindly agreed to operate — and that asking for a refund was a violation of the patrons' civic duty to support a baseball team.

The public didn't buy it; but the owners had the only major league game in town, and fortunately for the owners the team was doing pretty well, so attendance didn't noticeably slide.

The only Hall of Famer to have played for the Cleveland Blues is Ned Hanlon, who spent only the 1880 season with the team and made it to Cooperstown on the strength of his managerial record (Library of Congress)

In the second week of August, Worcester was back in town. Walking out again would probably not be a good idea — the stunt pulled in July was still too fresh in the public's mind. The visitors played the entire game this time. No runs scored until Worcester got 2 in the fifth. Cleveland came to bat in the bottom of the ninth losing 2–0. They scored a run, and then they tied it. And then the payback was completed — another run scored, and it was officially over (no need to complete unnecessary outs any more).

And then "a cushion spasm seized the crowd."⁹

A Critical Series

The baseball public was in a good mood as the second-place Providence team prepared to come to Cleveland in the third week of August. Cleveland was in third place.

Game one was the best; it took thirteen innings but Providence prevailed 4–3.

Game two: Providence 5 Cleveland 0.

Game three: Providence 6 Cleveland 0.

Cleveland had hoped to change places in the standings — and they did. After two shutouts and three straight losses they were now in fourth place. After the Providence series Clevelanders lost interest in their team.

There was a doubleheader with Cincinnati at the beginning of September. A sparse crowd showed for the morning game, and a small crowd of four or five hundred for the afternoon. It took Cincinnati 2 hours and 15 minutes to whip Cleveland 5–4. Cleveland shut out Cincinnati in the later contest 6–0, doing it in quick time: 1 hour and 35 minutes.

September 22 was the last home game of the regular season. Cleveland beat Buffalo 8–1. They were in third place and would finish there — not bad for a second-year franchise. In an effort to show some good will to their followers, management had Cleveland and Buffalo play an extra exhibition game at a discounted price. Cleveland won 10–1.

The season ended up on the road September 30, when last-place Cincinnati shut out Cleveland 2–0.

Inning	1	2	3	4	5	6	7	8	9	Final
Cincinnati	0	0	1	0	0	0	1	0	0	2
Cleveland	0	0	0	0	0	0	0	0	0	0

1880 Final Standing:

	W.	L.	PCT.	G.B.
CLEVELAND	47	37	.560	20

The official season ended September 30, but the Cleveland front office decided to take the team to New York and play some exhibition games for as long as they could make some money at the box office. Their opponent was the New York Mets, a team that wanted to join the League. The games therefore served as a sort of barometer for market potential. The Cleveland papers said they considered the season over, and so didn't bother reporting on the New York games.

They did mention, however, that the Cleveland team officials had decided the subscription plan would finance the 1881 ball club.

During the off season, the League officials came up with an idea that did not go over well with the players. Each team would have a right to reserve five players for its roster (an early form of the reserve clause). This was one way of saving the bosses from themselves, because they were all busy cutting sneaky deals to get the better players away from the competition.

With issues of their own, the disgruntled bosses of the Cincinnati team, which would not return to the League next year, attended a meeting in New York to consider forming another major league. The building discontent would lead to difficulties for the arrogant League owners, but they would be given a year of grace before the "chickens came home to roost."

1881

Personnel and Policy

St. Malachi's Hall had some visitors every morning in March. They were John Clapp, Edward Sylvester "The Only" Nolan, William Aloysius "Blondie" Purcell, and Jim McCormick. They used the facilities at the hall to practice their baseball regimens, and in the afternoon they took a ten-mile walk. The first three were new to Cleveland, and new to the Blue Stockings, but they had McCormick, the star of the team, to show them around town. The rest of the ball club was getting in shape at rooms set up for them at the Kennard Grounds.

The church hall gang was staying at the Weddell Hotel, and right around the corner, on Frankfurt Street, was Mat Wolford's tavern, and fairly close over on Prospect was Danny Catoir's bar, the Arch.

Both places had a connection with the telegraph company to receive live reports of baseball games by inning, a very helpful thing, since both businesses operated sports betting "pooles." In the case of baseball, bets were often based on per-inning results. Ball players were often to be found in such places in their leisure time.

Baseball business: The League notified Cleveland that lineups for the day must be posted by nine o'clock so that scorecard printers could be assured their list of batters was accurate. In the same note, teams were told that no policeman out of uniform was ever to be allowed into a game without being charged.

The league also notified its members that they were not to arrange any games of any nature with the "National" team of Washington, because they had not lived up to their obligation as a member of the League's "alliance" to provide Cleveland with players.

Cleveland developed a relationship with the company team of the White Sewing Machine Company as a possible source for players. Many of its supposedly "amateur" players had professional experience. White Sewing Machine would eventually become the White Motors Company and compete for national baseball championships.

The Blue Stockings played most of their training games that spring with the Whites—about a dozen.

Twelve thousand posters, featuring a ball player in the act of pitching, arrived at the ballpark. They would be posted all over town to advertise upcoming ball games.

The East Cleveland Street Railroad made a 60-cent package available for sale on its cars; it was good for admission to the ball game and a round-trip ride.

THE IRREGULARS

McGeary and Purcell, who were both in the opening day lineup, didn't last long. Mike McGeary, who started the season as captain and third baseman, stayed 11 games and resigned. "Blondie" Purcell, the center fielder, lasted 20 games (he had a history of drinking problems). Bill Taylor, Pop Smith, John Doscher, Phil Powers, and Rudy Kemmler were the occasional substitutes, playing from 1–24 games each.

Jack Glasscock was a fixture at shortstop throughout the six-year history of the Blues. An above-average batsman, Glasscock was also an outstanding defender (Library of Congress).

THE REGULARS

George Washington "Grin" Bradley, 3b:
Born July 13, 1852; games this year—60 (48 at 3b); 5th major league season—1st year in Cleveland; pitched the first no-hitter in major league history (Washington, D.C., defeating Hartford, CT, 2–0 in 1876).

John Edgar Clapp, c:
Born July 17, 1851; games this year 68 (48 at c); 5th major league season—1st in Cleveland. *Frederick C. "Sure Shot" Dunlap, 2b:* Born May 21, 1859; games this year 80 (79 at 2b); 2nd major league season—2nd in Cleveland; best average on team, .325—5th best in League.

John Wesley "Pebbly Jack" Glasscock, ss:
Born July 22, 1859; games this year 85* (79 at ss); 3rd—major league season—3rd in Cleveland.

James McCormick, p:
Born 1856; games this year 70 (59 at p); 4th major league season—3rd in Cleveland.

Michael Moynahan, lf:
Born 1860; games this year 33 (32 of); 2nd major league season—1st in Cleveland.

William B. Phillips, 1b:
Born 1857, St. John, New Brunswick, Canada; games this year 85* (85 1b); 3rd major league season—3rd in Cleveland.

John J. Remsen, cf:
Born 1851; games this year 48 (48 of); 5th major league season — 1st in Cleveland.

George "Orator" Shaffer, rf:
Born 1852; games this year 85* (85 of); 5th major league season — 2nd in Cleveland.
* Some records credit Cleveland with 84 official games in 1881.

The Chicago Games

The League season started for Cleveland with a late April trip to Chicago. Games between Chicago and Cleveland involving controversy had become somewhat of a tradition.

Cleveland led 5–4, in what to that point had been an entertaining game, when Chicago came to bat in the top of the ninth inning. There were soon two outs and but one man on base; the odds favored the Blue Stockings. "King" Kelly, always a tough out, got a base, and Dalrymple tried to turn it into a scoring play; the ball beat him to the plate but he evaded the tag by running out of the base line (an out under the rules). Umpire Herman Doscher, however, had a wider concept of what a base line looked like than Cleveland had ever seen before, and called Dalrymple safe.[1] Captain McGeary was furious and protested the game on the spot. But the game was now tied. Cap Anson then knocked in Kelly with the go-ahead run, and then the White Stockings added 3 more, all with two outs.

In the bottom of the ninth the disheartened Cleveland club went out meekly to end the game. Score: Chicago 8, Cleveland 5.

Chicago would visit Cleveland to "break open" the season there, in about a week.

THE HOME OPENER WITH CHICAGO

J. F. Evans was a happy man on May 6. He had made the ball club $500 before the regular season had even started; that was their cut of the skating rink operation he ran at the ballpark over the winter. The practice games had gone well and the players were physically fit. The ballpark, with the help of a good grounds crew, and a little rain the day before, was also in excellent shape.

And when the boss checked, there were early lines outside the park at the box office, waiting to buy an opening day ticket — including a fair number of the ladies. All that was needed to complete his day was a victory over Chicago to even the score for the opening day calamity there.

Chicago arrived at 2:30. At 3:00 Cleveland came onto the field sporting their new uniforms: white caps, blue neckties, white shirts with a letter inscribed on the front, blue belts, white pants, and, of course, blue stockings.

They were greeted with unusually long applause: "At 3:30 o'clock his royal nobs, Herr Herman Doesher, who had been chosen to officiate as umpire, stepped out into the ring, the band struck up 'All on account of Eliza,' and the show began."[2]

Neither team scored in the first.

Shaffer led off the top of the second for Cleveland and, "with music in the air," promptly rapped a double into right center. Glasscock, next, singled him home with the game's first run. Phillips then hit a double into center to put Cleveland up 2–0.

McCormick kept Chicago off the board for the first six innings, while Cleveland failed to score in the third, fourth, fifth, and sixth innings.

The seventh inning:

The *Cleveland Leader*:

SEVENTH ACT
The circus during this act was where the crowd got their money's worth — Shaffer led off with a daisy two bagger into left; Glasscock reached first....[3]

The *Cleveland Herald*:

Phillips stepped up and a buzz went through the crowd. Once before he had not been found wanting and this time he again proved equal to the occasion, sending the ball out to right field, Shaffer scoring and Glasscock going to third. McCormick next stepped out. His hit went directly towards second but Quest failed in his attempt to cut off Glasscock at the home plate, though no error was made, fleet running once more coming into play. With Phillips on second and McCormick on first Moynahan was retired on strikes, making the first hand out, McGeary popped up a fly towards second which Quest purposely muffed, expecting to double up a couple of base runners. A treacherous bound, however, spoiled his little plan, leaving the bases full. At this juncture the interest ran high, and a hush fell upon the crowd as Clapp appeared at the plate. The first ball was a good one and he landed onto it with all his might. It flew a way out between center and right and every man scored, Clapp taking second. The cheers that followed this magnificent drive were long and lusty and everyone now regarded the game as won, a point about which many had felt considerable anxiety until now. Dunlap then hit to left field, advancing Clapp to third. Purcell's grounder to short stop spoiled the chances for any more runs, Burns, Quest, and Anson accomplishing a clever double play, retiring the side with Clapp on third."[4]

In the bottom of the seventh frame Chicago tallied twice. Kelly singled, stole second, moved up on a ground out, and came in on a passed ball. Burns then hit a solo home run. The last two innings were scoreless.

Final score: Cleveland 7, Chicago 2.

The *Cleveland Leader*: "At no game was the excitement so intense as on yesterday. The fielding was so pretty, and the batting so heavy, at intervals, that it set the crowd wild with delight. Both teams placed their strongest men in the field, and the fight from the outset was full of interesting points."[5]

Inning	1	2	3	4	5	6	7	8	9	Final
Cleveland	0	2	0	0	0	0	5	0	0	7
Chicago	0	0	0	0	0	0	2	0	0	2

Time of game: 1 hour and 50 minutes. Attendance: 1,500.

CLEVELAND

	At Bats	Runs
John Clapp, c	5	0
Fred "Sure Shot" Dunlap, 2b	4	0
William "Blondie" Purcell, cf	4	0
George "Orator" Shaffer, rf	4	2
Jack "Pebbly Jack" Glasscock, ss	4	2
Bill Phillips, 1b	4	1
Jim McCormick, p	4	1
Mike Moynahan, lf	4	0
Mike McGeary, 3b	4	1
Total Runs — 7		

CHICAGO

	At Bat	Runs	Avg.*
Abner Dalrymple, lf	4	0	.326
George Gore, cf	4	0	.298
Mike "King" Kelly, rf*	4	1	.323
Cap "Pop" Anson, 1b*	3	0	.399
Ned Williamson, 3b	4	0	.268
Tom Burns, ss	3	1	.278
Fred Goldsmith, p	3	0	.241
Frank "Silver" Flint, c	3	0	.310
Joe Quest, 2b	3	0	.246
Total Runs — 2			

The Chicago players' averages for the year validated why the White Stockings were considered the team to beat at season start — Kelly and Anson are both in the Hall of Fame.

Oberlin and Akron

Oberlin: The place that originated organized baseball in Ohio in 1865 continued its tradition of outstanding teams and liberal politics.

This year intercollegiate baseball would come into its own at Oberlin. Oberlin College had scheduled games with the college teams of Hillsdale, Ann Arbor, Kenyon, Delaware, Wooster, Hudson, Marietta, and Yale (when that famous team came west).

The team was open to all. Weldy Walker made the club as a catcher—his brother was former Oberlin player Moses Fleetwood Walker. This was in keeping with the continuing tradition of allowing blacks and other disenfranchised groups to participate in all aspects of college life at Oberlin College.

Akron baseball: Akron took its highly respected ball club on the road. They went to Louisville and St. Louis—two cities that secretly had big baseball plans for the not-too-distant future.

The Louisville "Eclipse" team drew a large crowd on St. John's Day, June 21, to see "The best game played here this season, and the Akrons have the honor of being the first team to waltz the Eclipse this year."[6] Akron surprised Louisville, winning 9–1. The next day Louisville salvaged some pride, winning 11–6. In August, Akron went to Louisville again, and once more surprised the Eclipse, winning a close game 6–4.

Later that summer, Akron was in St. Louis for games on Sunday and Monday. St. Louis that Sunday produced the largest baseball crowd seen there in years. Many of the 7,000 had to be restrained behind ropes in the outfield.

It was a hard-fought game: "Several men on both sides were hurt Piercy getting a black eye from the ball and Jones, the Akrons pitcher, spraining his arm. 'If this keeps up,' said a boy in the crowd, 'the Akrons will all be dead men before they leave St. Louis.'"[7]

A couple of fielding gems were quite memorable: "Maskrey from the visitors played a splendid game at left, going clear into the crowd twice and taking the ball on the run."

When it was over St. Louis was on top 18–14.

Inning	1	2	3	4	5	6	7	8	9	Final
St. Louis	0	3	3	8	2	1	0	1	*	18
Akrons	3	1	0	2	0	0	6	2	0	14

On Monday, Akron bounced back with a 10–5 win.

Got to go show Akron! Chicago in 1880 had clinched the pennant, and then went down to Akron to play an exhibition game—they lost. During their series in Cleveland, League members Buffalo and Detroit, recalling the large attendance for the Chicago game, decided to show the "crack" Akrons how to respect major league teams. On August 12, a Friday, Buffalo beat Akron 17–4. The following Monday, August 15, new League member Detroit also beat them, 4–0.

Buffalo liked the Akron outfielder Ed Swartwood, and later borrowed him for one of their regular season games. Over the following eight years, Swartwood played 724 major league games for five different clubs.

The Independence Day game

PROVIDENCE GRAYS AT CLEVELAND BLUE STOCKINGS

The coverage of the Fourth of July game was somewhat squeezed this year, due to a larger than ordinary amount of national news: "The day was hot and sultry, and fans and coatless men were numerous. The grand stand and part of the right side stand were crowded with ladies. The side stands and the field were also filled, making it very uncomfortable for the fielders."[8]

The start of the game was held up a bit to accommodate the late rush from a crowd of five thousand. Jim McCormick pitched for Cleveland. Kennedy, the regular catcher, was injured and did not play; John Clapp substituted as catcher, and despite his own bad hands caught well. Hoss Radbourn pitched for Providence; his catcher was the former Cleveland player from 1878, Emil Gross.

Comments on the game: • "The work of McCormick was brilliant, and to him is partially the victory due for his excellent delivery. The fielding of Moynahan, Remsen and Shaffer was unusually fine." • "Radbourn was hit freely, but most of the runs were gained through the wretched fielding of the visitors." • "The umpire was strict with both sides, especially in calling strikes, but he was as hard on one side as the other."[9]

Inning	1	2	3	4	5	6	7	8	9	Final
Cleveland	0	2	0	2	0	3	1	1	0	9
Providence	0	0	0	2	0	0	1	0	0	3

Cleveland	Runs	Hits	Providence	Runs	Hits
Dunlap, 2b	1	1	Hines, cf	0	1
McCormick, p	0	0	Start, 1b	1	2
Bradley, 3b	0	1	Farrell, 2b	1	1
Shaffer, rf	0	1	York, lf	1	1
Moynahan, lf	1	1	Ward, rf	0	2
Phillips, 1b	3	2	McClellan, ss	0	0
Clapp, c	2	2	Gross, c	0	0
Glasscock, ss	1	2	Radbourn, p	0	0
Remsen, cf	1	2	Denny, 3b	0	0
Totals	9	12*	Totals	3	7

Providence errors: Fumbled grounder—Denny. Passed grounder—Denny, Start, York. Muffed thrown ball—McClellan. Passed balls—Gross, 4. Time of game: one hour and fifty minutes. Umpire: Bradley.

* The *Herald* gave Cleveland 12 hits, the *Leader* 13, and the *Plain Dealer* 11.

Dealing with Detroit

Detroit was in Cleveland July 19, and so was a goodly portion of Detroit's "sporting" types—the grandstand being filled with Detroiters.

The *Cleveland Plain Dealer*: "Jubilant at the success of the Detroit nine Saturday [in Detroit] and encouraged by the winnings of the Detroit bettors then, they are said to have come to Cleveland with an abundance of shekels, which they freely wagered."[10]

The visiting crowd was very noisy for an inning and a half, at which time Cleveland scored 5 runs. The grandstand became "solemnly quiet and orderly after that."[11] The Blue Stockings won the game and many a Clevelander won some money.

Score: Cleveland 5, Detroit 2.

A discounted ticket to see the ball game in Detroit was offered by one Cleveland steamship line; for $3 a round trip and berth could be had on either the *City of Detroit* or the *Northwest*.

Cleveland was in Detroit August 3, and so were a substantial number of the Cleveland "sporting" types.

The *Cleveland Leader*: "Two or three hundred Detroiters came here on the first visit of the Detroit Club, took seats together in the grand stand and stamped and howled like mad at every successful play of the Detroits and every error of the Clevelands. About as many Clevelanders have now gone up to Detroit to return the compliment—and with interest, for the party took along about a hundred fish horns, which they will carry concealed about their persons until the first time the Clevelands make a hit: then the people of the City of the Straits will think that Mother Shipton's alleged prophecy has come true and that Gabriel has begun his overture."[12]

The *Detroit Post & Tribune* reported the arrival of the Cleveland crowd Wednesday morning:

> That Cleveland club, supported by the lungs and badges of three hundred representative citizens, fell upon this peaceful city yesterday morning with the venomous determination of vengeful warriors glistening in their eyes and diffusing itself in their aggressive manners. The quiet people of Detroit

viewed them with awe and hastened to Recreation Park in the afternoon to see how much more warlike and awe inspiring they would be with their paint and feathers on.... The phenomenon became complicated and the spectators disgruntled but through it all and above it all the penetrating voice of the instructive Clevelander could be heard from the grand stand. The Cleveland voice is something of a phenomenon itself. He speaks a various language and there was really more excitement and amusement to be found in listening to its varied accents then in the ups and downs of the menagerie exhibiting on the diamond."[13]

Cleveland lost this error-filled game 13–11. Cleveland lost the second game on Friday, but won the finale on Saturday 10–3.

Detroit's ball players:

Name and Position	Total Years–M.L.	Avg.–1881	Age
George A. "Dandy" Wood, lf	2nd of 13	.297	22
Lon (Alonzo) P. Knight, rf	3rd of 7	.271	28
Ned (Edward) Hugh Hanlon, cf (He was with Cleveland the year before.)	2nd of 13	.279	23
Martin J. Powell, 1b	1st of 5	.338	25
Charley Wesley Bennett, c*	3rd of 15	.301	26
Stephen Arnold Douglas "Sadie" Houk, ss	3rd of 8	.279	24
John Joseph "Move Up Joe" Gerhardt, 3b	5th of 12	.242	26
Art Wilson Whitney, 3b	2nd of 11	.182	23
George H. Derby, pitcher	1st of 3	–	–

Won — 29 Lost — 26

* (His career ended when he lost his legs jumping a train; the Detroit ballpark was named after him for a time.)

The *Cleveland Plain Dealer*:

The Detroit *Free Press* perpetrates this:

> McCormick's crown it came to town,
>   With a big broom stuck upon it;
> But Bennet's bat soon knocked it flat
>   And Derby sat upon it.
>
> Hanlon doodle doodle do;
>   Houck a doodle dandy;
> The Detroit nine they play so fine,
>   Oh, they're the boys so handy.

(Handy twice out of three times.)[14]

Of Race, Racing, and "A $2-a-Week Brain"

RACE

Moses Fleetwood Walker, the black ball player from Oberlin College, was added to the roster of the White Sewing Machine Company team in August.

The Louisville Eclipse invited the White Sewing Machine Company to play them in Louisville in August. They were not aware the team had a Negro catcher. Walker, on arriving at the park, was told he could not play, and so he agreed to take a seat in the stands. When the Cleveland first baseman replacing him proved to be no catcher, the people in the stands started yelling for Walker's return.

Walker came out and made some practice throws to the bases, to the amusement of the crowd. One Louisville player, however, was not amused, and said he would not play with the Negro he found objectionable. After some more discussion, it was decided Mr. Walker would watch from the stands again. This wasn't good enough for Charles Fuller, the aggrieved player. He rushed up to Walker, "and endeavored to eject him summarily from the park. Some gentleman standing near interfered and prevented this, so he took a seat among the crowd, and watched the game throughout."[15]

The *Louisville Commercial* wrote of the incident: "Louisville is the first city whose base ball club has refused to allow him to play [it was also the first Southern city Walker had tried to play in]. He is well educated, and probably more intelligent than sixteen out of eighteen of the players. His parents are highly respectable [this may have been true within his parents' limited circle] and wealthy citizens of Cleveland [they were not rich and the family was from Mt. Pleasant, Ohio]. All the League clubs have played against him [not true]. It is hoped he will be allowed to play in today's game [he wasn't]."[16]

Lost in the story of prejudice were any details of the game, other than that the team from Cleveland lost.

Racing

The Northern Ohio Fair Association had its eleventh annual show at the racetrack in Glenville from September fifth through the ninth. The racetrack was located near St. Clair Avenue and M.L.K. Boulevard (formerly Liberty Blvd.).

> Trotting, Running, and Pacing Daily!
> Four-in-Hand Roman Chariot Races!
> Four-in-Hand Trotting Race!
> The Amateur Bicycle Club Race!
> Indian Chase For a Bride!
> SPECIAL ATTRACTIONS DAILY.
> The Famous CHICAGO BASE BALL CLUB, Champions of the United States vs. the
> Cleveland Base Ball Club, will play a match game of Ball for a
> purse of $300.00 TUESDAY AFTERNOON.[17]

"Grin" Bradley won the exhibition game for Cleveland and Fred Goldsmith took the loss for Chicago.

Score: 9–0.

Ball game write-up in those days bore little resemblance to today's. A *Plain Dealer* sports writer calls for the reporting of the facts—simply the facts:

> The slangy gush which disfigures so many base ball departments in the newspapers is a positive drawback to the popularity of the game. It is not demanded by any class of people we know of or by any agency of the sport. It is simply the effervescence of a $2-a-week brain in a struggle with a much higher priced subject. One day, when a player has made a run by the aid of called balls and wild pitches and has caught an easy fly, he is depicted in the report as Battering ram Bob, the highknockerknock of Knocktown, a 22-carat angel in disguise, with gold dust from the pavements of the New Jerusalem still sticking to his shoes. The next day, after a fierce line ball has broken two of his fingers, knocked four teeth down his throat and rolled spitefully away into field, he is held up to public scorn as Butterfinger Bill, the double-back action muffer from Muffdom, a bald-headed, squint-eyed hypotenuse of a reverberating sulfur fed ichthyosaurus. The reporter who would write up the performance of a policeman at a street fight or a fireman at a fire in the same style would be placed in a guardian's care; and yet ball players are only another class of hired athletes and are entitled to be treated in the same business like way.[18]

From August on, Cleveland gradually slid into the lower regions of the standings—the spirit had gone out of the team. The newspapers thought this was because too much spirit was going into the team, in the form of alcohol, and that those in charge were to blame for their inability to enforce discipline. A housecleaning of personnel was called for in the off-season.

* * *

An ongoing national story, with a Cleveland connection, came to an end shortly before the close of the baseball season.

On the second day of July, in the morning, a man from Ohio had been shot in the back. The tragic ordeal of this man, born and raised near Cleveland, was watched by a shocked and saddened nation. Late in the evening of September 19, he died after weeks of "suffering the greatest agony but bearing it with a magnificent fortitude that won the admiration and sympathy of the civilized world."[19]

The life of James Abram Garfield, twentieth president of the United States, had been taken by an assassin's bullet. He was 49. President Garfield had been at the Baltimore and Potomac train station in Washington, D.C., preparing to go to Williams College in Massachusetts for a commencement address, when Charles Jules Guiteau, a disappointed office-seeker, shot him.

Cleveland played its last home game a few days later, losing to Boston 10–3.

Standings 1881

	Won	Lost
Chicago	56	28
Providence	47	37
Buffalo	45	38
Detroit	41	43
Troy	39	45
Boston	38	45
CLEVELAND	36	48
Worcester	32	50

1882

A New League and Some Crazy Clothes

The National League lost its monopoly on major league baseball this year. It would now have to fight to retain the services of its better players. The Louisville and St. Louis clubs that played the Akrons last year were now in the new league. They were joined by Baltimore, Cincinnati, Philadelphia and Pittsburgh.

The American Association was the new league, and, unlike the old League, you could buy a beer at the games and see a game on Sunday—the working class loved it!

The new league also halved the National League's admission price by charging a quarter.

Many of the new owners were saloon operators who had gone on to make beer manufacturing their primary business. The newspapers, with the encouragement of the new league's detractors, popularized a nickname for the American Association. They called it "The Beer and Whiskey League."[1]

For the National League, current problems and new ones just over the horizon were made worse in April, when president William A. Hulbert, the man who had started the National League, died suddenly.

The Cleveland Base Ball Association met in March and a new regime was elected to power. Mr. Charles H. Bulkley (of the locally powerful Bulkley family) was chosen president. Customs collector George W. Howe was made the new vice-president; Howe would be a popular figure in Cleveland baseball circles for the rest of the century.

Charles T. Wesley, B. F. Wade, A. B. Hough, and Charles A. Brayton were also elected as directors.

New players:

"Fatty" ("Alderman") Charles F. Briody, c (53 games; age 23; average .258; 2nd League year)

"Dude" Thomas Jefferson Esterbrook, lf (45 games; age 22; average .246; 2nd League year)

John ("Father") Francis Kelly, c (30 games; age 22; average .135; rookie)
Mike Muldoon, 3b (84 games; age __; average .246; rookie)
John H. Richmond, cf (41 games; age__; average .171; 4th League year)
David E. Rowe, of (24 games; age 26; average .258; 2nd League year)
John C. Tilley, of 15 games; age 25; average .089; rookie)
Julius Willard, of (9 games; age __; average .139; rookie)
William ("Gunner") Henry McGunnigle, of (1 game; age 27; average .200; 3rd year)
John Dwyer, of (1 game; age __; avg. .000; only major league game)

Those returning from 1881 were *Phillips, Dunlap, Glasscock, Shaffer, McCormick, Bradley, Doscher and Kennedy.*

The directors hired Herm Doscher as a player-manager.

Chilly weather greeted the first exhibition game in early April, but the baseball faithful, a couple of hundred of them, showed up anyway — the game between the Blue Stockings and the White Sewing Machine Company promised to be an interesting one.

The National League had adopted a new uniform policy for 1882. The idea was taken from the sport of cricket. Teams throughout the League would now wear nine different uniforms — one for each position.

Cleveland wore the new clothing for the first time in this "Whites" game: "The men appeared to be embarrassed by their masquerade style of dress and when they came on the field in bright colors and stripes they were greeted with prolonged laughter and shouts, especially from the small boys."[2]

Here's the rundown on the sartorial display:
Catcher: Scarlet cap and shirt.
Pitcher: Blue cap and shirt.
First Base: Scarlet and white striped cap and shirt.
Second Base: Orange cap and black shirt.
Third Base: Gray cap and white shirt.
Short Stop: Maroon cap and shirt.
Left Fielder: White cap and shirt.
Center Fielder: Red cap and black shirt.
Right Fielder: Gray cap and shirt.
Substitutes: Green cap and brown shirt.

Cleveland didn't hit the ball as well as expected but they still won the game 8–2. The *Plain Dealer* reminded its readers that the "Whites" pitcher Arundel and his catcher Ardner were the best amateur battery in town, and that cold weather wasn't that conducive to hitting in any case.

The Colorful Opener

Cleveland versus Detroit: Color and more color hit the eyes and blurred the minds of the 1,500 people on hand for the first game. Cleveland practiced and Detroit practiced, but they both wore the same uniforms — nine different uniforms — the *same* nine different uniforms. Which team was which? The announcer would have to help with that one.

The weather had been nice all morning, but right before game time it clouded up and started to rain. The ground wasn't too wet when the rain, after a short shower, stopped for good. Umpire Higham looked over the grounds and nodded to proceed. Detroit won the coin toss and sent Cleveland to the bat.

First inning: Dunlap led off the game by flying out to left. Kennedy then coaxed a walk. Phillips dropped a hit into short center, and Kennedy thought about going to third but changed his mind. Heading back to second, he tripped over the base and was tagged out. Richmond ended the first with a foul tip to the catcher.

Detroit started their batting game off with Wood hitting a double to left center. Hanlon grounded out, pitcher to first. Powell then struck out. Two down. Knight was next, and he knocked in Wood with a single to center and moved to second on the throw home. Bennett walked, and when he was heading for a steal of second, Kennedy's bad throw allowed Knight to come home. Farrell then singled, plating Bennett with the third and last run of the inning.

Second inning: Cleveland got a break when Hanlon dropped a Muldoon fly to center. The Cleveland runner then stole second, and pitcher McCormick helped himself with a single to left that scored Muldoon. Shaffer struck out. Glasscock, with a full count "staring him in the face, banged the leather over the left field fence, scoring a home run and sending McCormick in ahead of him. This was greeted with tremendous applause, and with the score a tie the spirits of the crowd went up to a normal degree once more."[3]

Third and fourth innings: Goose eggs.

Fifth inning: No runs for Cleveland. Detroit's Powell singled with two outs; he then tested Kennedy's arm with a dash to second, and was rewarded with another wild throw from the Cleveland catcher. Bennett then singled Powell in to give the visitors a one-run lead.

Sixth inning: No runs.

Seventh inning: Glasscock and Dunlap were on base when Dunlap started taunting the pitcher with huge leads. Derby overthrew first base, and Glasscock scored, with Dunlap also going from first to home. Dunlap, however, cost Cleveland the lead: in his hurry to home, he never touched third, and the umpire called him out. Score again tied at 4 each.

Eighth inning: Blanks. Kennedy's problems on the day continued when he sprained an ankle running into second and had to be replaced at catcher by Kelly. Ninth inning: Cleveland disappointed the crowd by going out in order on three easy grounders.

Now, if Detroit would only cooperate, the game could be decided in extra innings. Derby and Wood cooperated, making two easy outs. Hanlon, however, showed some patience and earned a walk off McCormick, who wasn't throwing anything too close to the plate. Hanlon then started jumping around at first, and McCormick figured he could pick him off and end the inning. What he did was what he didn't want to do. He put Hanlon on third with a wild throw past Phillips at first.

Powell was the batter, and he got a little wood on a McCormick pitch, and the dinky blooper, dropped in for a hit; a moment later Hanlon put his foot on the plate — and it was Detroit's game.

Score: Detroit 5, Cleveland 4.

Joe H. Mack, the Blue Stockings' manager back in 1879, was in town managing what he was trained to manage—a troupe of stage performers. The evening of the opening game, at the invitation of Mr. Mack, the team attended a performance at the Euclid Opera House:

> J. H. Haverly's Consolidated
> MASTODON MINSTRELS
> The largest, the strongest, and absolutely the
> greatest and very best the world has ever seen.
> Every Act, every scene, every song, every Sketch,
> every joke positively and truly new and original.
> The greatest achievement of the century. Earth
> has never seen its like. The only company in the world
> that can change its program nightly for a week.
> THREE NIGHTS ONLY[4]

The *Plain Dealer's* amusement critic was taken by the quality of the singing; as for the rest of the show, he called it your average claptrap of the kind an unsophisticated public in general demanded.

A Ticket to Kennard

Baseball-sparked bickering between Cleveland newspapers flared up regularly. The *Plain Dealer* came right out and accused the *Herald* of not even trying to cover its theft of *Plain Dealer* sports columns. Later, the *Leader* was heard to complain about not getting enough free passes for the Fourth of July game. The *Plain Dealer* argued that the *Leader* was already getting four admissions per game, and that alone added up to 168 passes in a season. And for the holiday game the ball club had even given them four extra ones, but they were not happy with that and wanted ten more. The *Plain Dealer* called it "greedy."

Extra attractions at the ball yard: The Kennard Grounds was the scene of a number of non–League ball games this year, as well as some other events.

The Scottish gymnastics games were held Decoration Day, and the Cleveland Forest City Cricket Club played a match against the Maumees of Toledo, defeating them by a score of 138–78.

The best two amateur teams in town, the White Sewing Machine Co. and the Red Stockings, played a game at Kennard in June — the former winning 7–4.

Detroiters seemed to like Cleveland; two teams composed of their citizens came and played at Kennard. The Detroit Light Guard challenged the Cleveland Grays (reserve military units) and Cleveland won the battle 4–3. Detroit jewelers and Cleveland jewelers fielded company "picked nines"— Detroit's diamond men won 27–8.

The Democratic members of Cleveland City Council got in shape for their big upcoming July 18 benefit game with their Republican colleagues at the Kennard Grounds by playing a "picked nine" at Case Commons. They won.

C. H. Bulkley, president of the Cleveland Blue Stockings and a major figure in Republican Party politics, donated the use of the Kennard Grounds for the City Council's ball game for charity. There was to be no "free list" for this game — even the players were to pay an admission. The council, however, would have a free ride from Public Square to the game: a special streetcar would be waiting for them. The service was donated by the East Cleveland Street Railway Company.

The Republicans had 18 runs and the Democrats 16 when the latter came to bat in the bottom of the eighth. The tying runs had reached base when down came a hard shower and ended the sport.

Black ball

The Southern Stars were the outstanding "colored" team in Cleveland, but they had problems trying to find quality teams willing to play them. One exception was the ball club of Kent, Ohio. The game was played in Kent on September 13. The *Herald* gave a brief report of the game.

"The Southern Stars of Cleveland is composed as follows: Smith, p; Stanley, c; Doctor, 1b; Wilson, 2b; Oswalt, 3b; Williams, ss; Husten, rf; Jones, cf; Milligan, lf."[5]

Inning	1	2	3	4	5	6	7	8	9	Final
Kent	3	0	1	1	3	4	1	1	3	17
Southern Stars	3	0	3	1	0	2	1	0	0	10

Buoyed by Briody

The Cleveland ball club started the month of May with a 1 and 7 record. Catching problems threatened to keep things bleak. When the regular catcher, Kelly, was not available to catch in a mid–May game, first baseman Bill Phillips was forced behind the plate.

Phillips managed to lose a fingernail playing the unfamiliar position. Doc Kennedy was telegraphed for as an emergency measure, but before he could arrive John Dwyer got his chance. In his only major league appearance, he became a Blue Stockings catcher for six innings. He had no hits.

Doc Kennedy came to town and caught one game for Cleveland, but the catcher who came to the rescue and saved the day was "Fatty" Charles ("Alderman") Briody. "Fatty" had played one major league game for Troy in 1880, and the 23-year-old youngster would prove to be the right medicine for a team with injuries to key players and an anemic record. Briody had an Irish brogue, temperament, and sense of humor, and with his skillful catching he became an immediate favorite with the Blue Stockings' faithful.

Right before the big Fourth of July doubleheader, the team, with Briody under contract, had turned themselves around and won 17 games. They were in a three-way tie for fifth but were only half a dozen games from the top.

Two for "The Fourth"

The Providence Grays versus the Cleveland Blue Stockings: The outlook for the 1882 Independence Day doubleheader was gloomy in the morning; it was a rather brisk day by July standards and it was raining. Game one was scheduled for an eleven o'clock start. At nine the rain stopped and the sky started to clear. The grounds crew threw a number of bushels of sawdust on the worst of the wet spots, and soon the field was reasonably ready for play.

The veteran "Grin" George Bradley was given the starting assignment. In nine days he would turn 30. The Providence pitcher was future Hall of Famer John Montgomery Ward. He was 23 years old. Cleveland won the coin toss and the thousand people on hand cheered as they took the field.

Batting orders

Providence	*Cleveland*
Paul A. Hines, cf	Fred ("Sure Shot") Dunlap, 2b
George Wright, ss	Jack ("Pebbly Jack") Glasscock, ss
John A. ("Moose") Farrell, 2b	Bill Phillips, 1b
Joe ("Old Reliable") Start, 1b	"Orator" George Shaffer, rf
John Montgomery Ward, p	"Dude" Thomas J. Esterbrook, lf
Tom J. York, lf	Mike Muldoon, 3b
"Old Hoss" Charles Radbourn, rf	John H. Richmond, cf
Jerry Denny, 3b	"Grin" George W. Bradley, p
"Sandy" Vincent P. Nava, c	"Kick" John ("Father") Kelly, p

THE EARLY EVENT

Excellent fielding by both teams, along with a lot of weak hitting, kept the score a whitewash for three innings. Providence drew first blood in the fourth. Start singled and York dropped a beauty down the left field line for a double and a run batted home.

The fifth was uneventful. No runs.

The next inning was something else: "The sixth was a disastrous one for the local club. Muldoon started a regular muffing match by fumbling Wright's grounder and throwing wild to Phillips. Then Farrell hit for two bases, Wright going to third. At this point Start sent up a high fly to Esterbrook which he muffed, letting Wright in. Ward followed this with a hot one past Muldoon, both Farrell and Start coming home. York's hit to Muldoon forced Ward out at second, but another wild throw by the solid but terribly rattled Muldoon gave Radbourne a life and advanced York to third, from where he scored on Glasscock's pass of Denny's grounder."[6] Four runs.

Cleveland drew a blank in their half of the sixth but in the seventh they broke up the shutout.

"Dude" Esterbrook got a gift base when his easy grounder was botched by second baseman Farrell. Richmond sacrificed the runner to second. Muldoon made up for some of his bad play in the field by lacing the ball down the left field line for a double that plated the "Dude." One run.

It was the last run either team would score.

Final: Grays 5, Blue Stockings 1.

Time of game: One hour thirty minutes.

Umpire: Dickey Pearce.

THE AFTERNOON AFFAIR

The morning crowd filed out at 12:30, and the separate admission crowd for the afternoon 3 o'clock game started to trickle in. The day now held no threat of unpleasant weather and a flood of humanity descended on the ballpark.

It was the largest crowd ever to attend a Cleveland ball game. It was so big the start of game was pushed back to 4 o'clock. The stands had capacity crowds: "Even the roofs of the stands were black with spectators."[7] The grandstand itself was packed with fashionably dressed ladies, and the carriage enclosure was filled with every class of vehicle. Inside the park, all along the fences, stood the overflow crowd.

Estimates from the three dailies put the total numbers between 4,500 and 5,000.

Batting orders

Providence	*Cleveland*
Hines, cf	Dunlap, 2b
Wright, ss	Glasscock, ss
Farrell, 2b	Phillips, 1b
Start, 1b	Shaffer, rf
Ward, rf	Esterbrook, lf
York, lf	Muldoon, 3b
Radbourn, p	Richmond, cf
Denny, 3b	McCormick, p
Gilligan, c	Briody, c

Barney Gilligan, former Cleveland catcher, was behind the dish for Providence; his first at-bat received polite applause. "At 4 o'clock the penny was hoisted into the air by Wright, who lost the toss and was sent to the bat."[8]

Hines quieted the crowd by leading off with an opening double, but his teammates left him stranded. Then nothing of note happened until the Cleveland third, when the first runs were made.

The home third started with "McCormick getting first on a line hit over second. A wild pitch advanced him to third and Briody took the place he had just vacated on called balls. Dunlap's single helped send McCormick home, and Glasscock's timely drive did the same for Briody. Phillips followed it up with another, and Dunlap scored."[9] Three runs.

Nothing happened in the scoring column for the fourth, fifth, and sixth innings. In the seventh, McCormick beat out a single on a weak grounder to second base. Dunlap came up next, swung, and nicked a pitch that died in front of the plate. He quickly took off for first; by the time catcher Gilligan got a throw off, Dunlap was arriving at first base, where he became entangled with "Old Reliable" Joe Start. The ball got loose. Start looked everywhere for it but he couldn't find it — and it was only ten feet away. Farrell, the second baseman, finally recovered the ball, but it was too late — McCormick, running at full speed, was already crossing the plate. The laughing crowd loved it. One run.

Eighth inning: No runs scored.

Ninth inning: The last chance for Providence. Farrell got a single; the next man up — Start — singled, and then a wild pitch allowed Farrell to score, and McCormick was denied his shutout. The crowd felt a twinge or two of nerves at this point, but the damage was over, and soon Cleveland had a split on the day:

"Following the close of the game the spectators shouted until they were hoarse, cushions were thrown into the air, and the scene was one of wild excitement."[10]

Score: Cleveland 4, Providence 1.
Time of game: One hour and forty minutes.
Umpire: Dickey Pearce.

The "Dude's" Swelled Head

Dude Esterbrook was known for being a bit of a peculiar character and very much stuck on himself. One day, a short time after the Fourth of July, Esterbrook carelessly left his jacket lying around where his teammates could go through its pockets. They were rewarded with a letter, addressed to a friend, concerning the second game on the Fourth of July. It was a total fantasy.

The Blue Stockings all read it, and were thoroughly entertained before placing the purloined correspondence back in Esterbrook's jacket pocket.

Several years later, in 1889, Curry Foley, a writer for the national magazine the *Sporting Times*, let the whole country in on the "Dude's" letter:

> The recent marriage of Tommy Esterbrook to an estimable Brooklyn lady reminds me of a little story about the dude when he played in the Cleveland club in 1882....
>
> Here is the part of the letter that tickled the Cleveland players.
>
> "Three men were on the bases, two hands were out and Estie at the bat. 'One strike!' cried the umpire. Then there was silence. 'Two strikes!' shouted the umpire. 'Why don't he hit at it?' shouted some nervous Clevelander. Ah! little they knew that Tommy was cool as an iceberg. But, as I have said before, they were excited—I mean the spectators. But was that a good reason for me to get excited? The spectators now held their breath, some of them, no doubt thinking I would fall victim to the pitcher's many curves. Here comes a good ball: Estie sees it and lets go, and away she flies over the left fielder's head. Three runs were scored and Estie safe on third. Talk about excitement! Men went wild; they cheered until they were hoarse; the ladies rose en masse and waved their handkerchiefs and the echo from 6,000 throats could be heard a mile away. Only for Estie it would have been all day for Cleveland."[11]

Estie hit his triple in the morning game in front of the smaller crowd of a thousand. He was left stranded. He did score Cleveland's only run in that 5–1 loss, when he reached base on an error and was knocked in by a double.

Dude Esterbrook was a member of the Cleveland Blues for only one season, but teammates would remember him years after — for his imagination if not his play (Library of Congress).

Contrary to his claim, he was not involved in the run production of the second game at all.

The Rules and Rowe

The ever-evolving rules involved with conducting a baseball game in the nineteenth century were drawn up in committees, but they needed to be tested on the field of play to determine their actual value for improving the game.

The number of balls and strikes allowed to a batter—something one might think of as an easy rule to establish—actually changed for a number of years. From 1876 to 1887, a player needed from five to nine balls for a walk. The number generally moved in the direction of fewer balls, until in 1889 the number was permanently affixed at four. The number of strikes needed to retire a batter was three, though there was for a while, under special-game circumstances, a required fourth strike. The process of fine-tuning the rules has never stopped, but by the 1890's most of the rules we take for granted today had been field tested over time and proven to be the best for their intended purpose, and would remain solidly in place.

Today, if the fans saw certain things go on in a baseball game, many would say, "that can't be — the rules don't allow it!" But at one time the rules did allow it. Here are two examples from Cleveland games in 1882.

Jim McCormick threw a brilliant one-hitter against Buffalo in June — an event as rare in the nineteenth century as it is today. With some clever help, his one-hitter also remained a shutout.

In the second inning Orator Shaffer, the right fielder and current team captain, took advantage of the rules, "and by means of keen tactics made a double play which ended the inning."[12] Hardy Richardson of Buffalo had made it to third without the benefit of a hit. There was one out, when Davy Force lifted a high fly to right field; as soon as Hardy saw it settle into Shaffer's hands he tagged up and headed for home. In his mad dash for home, he didn't see Shaffer immediately throw the ball back up into the air before catching it again. This meant the runner had left base before the out on Force was legally made. Shaffer then casually threw the ball to his catcher, Kelly, who walked over to a baffled — and soon to be stunned — Richardson and tagged him out.

Another game with a peculiar twist saw Cleveland playing Troy in the early days of June. Fortunately Cleveland had a 7–0 lead in the eighth inning, when Troy, with some help from an unexpected quarter, was able to break up the whitewash and get two runs.

Two men were on base when an overthrown ball bounded away and went under the seats. The fielder quickly headed for the spot where he saw the ball disappear. But before he could reach for it, a small dog that had been hiding under the stands grabbed the live ball and ran off — allowing the men to score.

Despite the canine caper Cleveland won 7–2.

A change of clothes: "The Clevelands have thrown away their circus uniforms."[13] About a week after the Fourth of July, the Cleveland team received a shipment of new uniforms to replace the controversial "clothes of many colors." They hoped the change would do them good.

All the League teams soon had new uniforms. An edict by League headquarters required the new uniform of each team to be completely of one color — a color the teams would choose. The Cleveland Blue Stockings chose blue.

Cleveland had a change of center fielders shortly after they had a change of uniforms. John H. Richmond had to go on the "hospital list," after having badly injured his leg in a game where he collided with Detroit's catcher Bennett.

He was released from the team a week later because, it was said, the injury was "worse than at first thought."[14] The real reason for his release may very well have been his .171 batting average. The strong-armed Dave Rowe now became the regular center fielder. A strong arm in and of itself does not mean a man has the right stuff to be a pitcher. Cleveland would discover that, in the case of center fielder Dave Rowe, this was all too true.

Cleveland's two regular pitchers needed some rest, and it was announced that Dave Rowe would pitch a game at Chicago.

The *Cleveland Plain Dealer*: "Rowe ... has been held in reserve by the management for a long time for a surprise when the proper time should come. It came yesterday. He was a surprise."[15]

The *Cleveland Leader*: "the poorest batters [hit] him with ease. The Chicagos literally knocked the cover off two balls, so savagely did they hit."[16]

The *Cleveland Herald*: "Today's game between Cleveland and Chicago was a circus indeed for Chicago, Rowe, the Cleveland pitcher, being hit for a total of fifty bases. No such batting was ever seen since the League was established."[17]

Rowe allowed 29 hits. There were sixteen singles, nine doubles, one triple and three home runs. Rowe walked seven, struck out none, and had two wild pitches. His team helped out by making nine errors.

Final score: Chicago 35 runs, Cleveland 4 runs.

The *Cleveland Plain Dealer*: "The Chicago game yesterday is best described by Dundreary — 'a wiot, a wumpus and a wowe.'"[18]

The performance of Dave Rowe on July 24, 1882, is today still pointed to as the worst-pitched game in major league history.

The *Cleveland Herald*: "Fifteen hundred people saw the picnic Chicago had with Cleveland. Following is the score."[19]

Chicago	At Bats	Runs	Hits	Cleveland	At Bats	Runs	Hits
Darymple, lf	8	4	4	Dunlap, 2b	5	1	1
Gore, cf	6	5	4	Glasscock, ss	4	0	1
Kelley, ss & c	8	4	4	Phillips, 1b	4	0	0
Anson, 1b	6	5	1	Shaffer, rf	3	0	0
Williamson, 3b	6	5	4	Esterbrook, lf	4	0	0
Burns, 2b	6	5	4	Muldoon, 3b	4	1	0
Corcoran, p	6	1	0	Willigrod, cf	4	0	1
Flint, c & rf	7	3	4	Rowe, p	2	1	1
Nicol, rf & ss	6	3	4	Briody, c	4	1	1
Totals	59	35	29	Totals	34	4	5

Inning	1	2	3	4	5	6	7	8	9	Final
Chicago	5	0	4	9	2	4	1	7	3	35
Cleveland	0	3	0	0	0	0	0	0	1	4

Umpire: Dickey Pearce. Time: 2 hours and 40 minutes.

The *Cleveland Plain Dealer*, London, Canada, July 27, 1882:

Having tried Rowe as a pitcher in a game with Chicago the Clevelands plunged into the wilds of Canada to try him on a strictly amateur team outside the boundaries of the United States and beyond the jurisdiction of the League.

The amateur Tecumsehs of London succeeded in making more base hits off his pitching than the Cleveland professionals made off the pitching of the Canuck amateur and we presume the association will consent to allow Rowe to retire on his laurels.[20]

They did.

Summer Slide

Cleveland had a grueling six-week road trip from mid-July through the last days of August. During the last week of the trip, with the pennant out of sight, they decided they would like the antics and ego of "Dude" Esterbrook to be out of sight as well. Esterbrook was given his walking papers.

Cleveland's fight to retain respectability in the standings had been helped a good deal by one team — Worcester. That Massachusetts team was nice enough to lose 11 straight games to Cleveland before September.

Worcester was on the Western Reserve at the start of September. They had arranged an exhibition game with the city team in Wakeman, Ohio. Wakeman gave the big leaguers a good fight. Against Frank Mountain, the Worcester change pitcher, Wakeman came up with 11 runs. They lost, however, as was expected: the final was 19–11.

One Cleveland paper criticized Worcester for not doing better against a "country" club.

Worcester responded to that jibe the next day, ending its losing streak against Cleveland, with a 10–3 victory in front of a small crowd of 700.

The small crowds in September did not represent the usual geniality of a Cleveland gathering. The Cleveland crowd blamed the umpire when Cleveland lost a close 4–3 game against Providence a few days after the loss to Worcester. So incensed were they with the work of Mr. Sullivan, he had to hide in the Providence bus to get away from the park in one piece.

September weather did not smile on the plans of the men organizing a baseball tournament for the week of September 19. The *Herald* carried the story of the upcoming baseball tournament to be held at Bucyrus, Ohio. Prizes were to be $100, $50, and $40.

The weather front that moved into the Bucyrus area the week of the tournament had stalled. The likelihood of heavy rain, at any time, limited the field of a planned twelve-team tournament to one of only four clubs. The games were all played on Tuesday, and the promoters, even in the face of certain financial losses, awarded all the prize money.

Columbus won the $100, Galion the $50, and Ada College took the $40 premium.

When a crowd of 1,200 showed up on September 9, it was a happy moment in the affairs of September baseball in Cleveland. The crowd included three hundred children who were given a special rate of 10 cents. Cleveland managed to lose yet another game, to Providence 5–0.

The last game of the season was played on the last day of September. It was the third game of the series here against Detroit. The grounds were very slippery from an earlier rain, and the wet ball made for many errors and a sloppy and generally boring game. The game dragged on. In the top of the seventh Detroit scored 2 runs to tie the game at 7 each. Cleveland failed to score in their turn, and asked the umpire to call the game a draw because it was dark. The umpire didn't think it dark enough and ordered the eighth to start. Cleveland then used an old stall tactic; they suddenly couldn't field any ball put in play. Detroit soon ran up 6 runs before they were retired. It was definitely too dark to finish the eighth, and the score, according to the rules, reverted to the last complete inning played.

The 7–7 tied game was the second tie of the year for Cleveland.

The last game of the season that had a winner and loser was the one from the day before. That was the best game Cleveland played in September — the Blue Stockings winning 9–0.

Inning	1	2	3	4	5	6	7	8	9	Final
Detroit	0	0	0	0	0	0	0	0	0	0
Cleveland	0	1	2	1	0	0	0	5	*	9

Winning pitcher: Jim McCormick. Losing pitcher: George "Stump" Weidman.

Cleveland finished the season with a record of 42 wins and 40 losses in 84 games played. That put them in fifth out of eight, and 12 games behind pennant-winning Chicago (55–29).

Cincinnati (55–25) won the pennant in the new American Association.

1883

The "Gilt-Edged" Boys

The most exciting and successful season in Cleveland organized baseball history since its inception in 1865 was about to unfold.

In the American era which Mark Twain called the "Gilded Age," Cleveland sportswriters gave the Blue Stockings of 1883 the honorific "the gilt-edged."

New Ball Players	1883 Games	Age	M. L. Season
Pete ("Monkey") Hotaling, cf	100	26	5th*
Tom York, lf	100	35	13th
Jake ("Bloody Jake") Evans, rf	90	—	5th
"Doc" Albert Bushong, c	63	27	5th
"One Arm" Hugh Daily, p	45	26	2nd
Will Sawyer, p	17	19	rookie
Bill Crowley, of	11	26	5th

Cecil Broughton — 4 games; Charles Cady — 3 games; Lem Hunter — 1 game.

The returning men: Bill Phillips, Fred Dunlap, Jack Glasscock, Mike Muldoon, Jim McCormick, Fatty Briody, and George Bradley. Pete Hotaling had played the season of 1880 for Cleveland.

Spring Notes
• Behind the walls of the Kennard ballpark, nearby neighbors and passers-by heard hammering against wood, as groundskeeper Tom Lawrence and crew busied themselves knocking together "framed hangers" (billboards).
• Management announced that a season ticket would be priced at $18, and that children would be charged but a dime at a special entrance behind the grandstand.
• S. P. Nevins became the official peddler of scorecards at the ballpark: "They will be very neat with a colored lithograph base ball design on the back, a different design for each day."[1]
• On game days, after 2 o'clock, the flagpole on top of the dome of the Weddell Hotel will fly a white flag with a red ball. Remember: after 2 P.M. flag up — game; flag down — no game.
• W. H. Voltz, a sportswriter in Cleveland, went to Toledo to publish the *National Pastime* — a baseball magazine.
• Director George Howe was promoted to vice-president of the Blue Stockings.
• The John McCullough acting company was at the Cleveland Opera House in March. Frank Lane, a player with the troupe, would take his leave to make wardrobe changes in a different kind of dressing room: the League had hired him as an umpire.
• John Clapp, ex-Cleveland catcher, was a partner in a New York City business venture: "The Club"— a sports bar.
• New Cleveland manager Frank Bancroft had barely started his job when, at the end of March, he was called home to Massachusetts — his wife had died.

The Season Opens

MAY 1, 1883

Buffalo at Cleveland

Batting orders

Clevelands	*Buffalos*
Dunlap, 2b	O'Rourke, lf
Hotaling, cf	Shaffer, rf
Muldoon, 3b	Kennedy, cf
York, lf	Brouthers, 1b
Glasscock, ss	Richardson, 2b
Phillips, 1b	Rowe, c
Evans, rf	White, 3b
McCormick, p	Force, ss
Bushong, c	Derby, p

Two thousand people came out and shivered throughout the game under a bright sun that put out no heat.

First inning: O'Rourke led off the game for Buffalo by hitting an easy one to McCormick, who tossed him out at first. The next two men to bat were former Cleveland players, George Shaffer and Doc Kennedy. Each man as he came to the plate was greeted with cheers and presented with a beautiful basket of flowers. Shaffer walked and Kennedy struck out. Brouthers, with a wicked shot at short, ended the inning when Glasscock threw him out. Dunlap led off for Cleveland and was walked, as was the number-two hitter Hotaling. Muldoon's ground out advanced the runners. York fouled out to Brouthers at first, and Glasscock's grounder to the shortstop closed out the first.

Second inning: Buffalo failed to score. Cleveland first baseman Phillips rubbed his good luck charm and led off with a double. Evans, up next, struck out. Tally time: "McCormick stepped in and hit for a base, and galloped down to second while Force was doing an Indian corn dance with his hit, and Phillips scored the first run."[2]

Third inning: No Buffalo runs. Cleveland scored two runs this inning, but the writer for the *Plain Dealer* forgot to explain how.

Fourth inning: Both teams put up zeroes.

Fifth inning: Nothing for Buffalo. Glasscock rapped a single into left. Phillips reached first and McCormick "hammered a buttercup thumper" into right field, where Shaffer juggled it, and compounded his mistake by throwing the ball past the hands of Brouthers at first.[3] In the confusion Glasscock and Phillips quietly slipped across the plate. Bushong made the second out by fouling to the catcher. Dunlap hit a dandy baser to center. McCormick next came home on a passed ball, and Dunlap followed him in when Hotaling hit one into left field. Fielding blunders allowed Hotaling to get to third, but he went out in an attempt to steal home. Four runs.

Sixth inning: No runs.

Seventh inning: O'Rourke singled, Kennedy singled, and Brouthers doubled — and with a lot of bad defense in between, they had two runs. Cleveland didn't score.

Eighth inning: No runs.

Ninth inning: Buffalo, as they had done in the previous at bat, went down in one, two, three order — and that ended the game.

Victory in the opener went to Cleveland by a 7–4 score.

Inning	1 2 3	4 5 6	7 8 9	Final
Clevelands	0 1 2	0 4 0	0 0 0	7
Buffalos	0 0 2	0 0 0	2 0 0	4

Time of game: 2 hours 20 minutes. Umpire: W. E. Furlong. Earned runs: Cleveland 3, Buffalo 0.

Mascottes: A Collection of Lucky Charms

Bill Phillips was said to be bringing his lucky pet alligator to town. However, by the time he actually arrived in Cleveland, the pet alligator story had become a short story. Phillips showed up with an "ornate" alligator tooth. He had acquired the tooth while wintering down South, where he had been fortunate enough to find a Negro — practiced in the arts of the arcane — to put a "voodoo" curse on it for good luck.

Manager Bancroft, on the way to the ball grounds, spotted a horseshoe in the street — an extra fortunate find. He grabbed it quick; a horseshoe found in the street has more luck in it than one found elsewhere (as everyone knows).

To increase the power of the "mascotte," Bancroft had the horseshoe galvanized — then he nailed it above the clubhouse door.

One dark stormy night ...

Tom York arose from his slumbers, bothered ... the boys all wanted a mascotte, and he was worried about it. Not being the seventh son of the seventh son, he knew not how to go about it to procure one, so he arose and went out in the elements to meditate. The wild winds were a pleasing accompaniment to the hurricane raging in his own bosom. He wandered along the lake shore, and the swashing of the heavy sea on the beach was melody in his ears, while the dark clouds and rumbling thunder gave life to the thoughts that flashed through his brain that some supernal occurrence might put him in possession of the coveted mascot ... but ere long he found himself in a thick wood, near a little hut that for years had been looked upon as haunted by unquiet spirits. [With] ...unearthly yells and a rattling of chains; the door of the hut flew open, and a bright flash of lightning revealed, crouching at his feet, a white and yellow bull pup, while following close on a clap of thunder came an awful voice saying 'Take your mascot young man.' Tom seized the pup in his arms and speeded down the shore for home as though he had made a three-base hit....[4]

(A little later)

"He called the pup Champion, and the pup looked up in his face with a merry eye and smiled."[5]

"During the Philadelphia games last week Champion was there and the gilt-edged won every day."[6]

Characters and "Blackberriwyne Row"

Cleveland had its share of players and patrons who were quite the characters both on and off the field.

A grin and a dhundeen: • "'Grin' Bradley's smile gets away from him and it disappears behind his ears."[7] • "Give Jake Evans plenty of pie, a comfortable siesta and his favorite dhundeen [cigar] and he'll play right second to none."[8]

A barker, a barber—a Briody: • "Briody makes one of the dandy ticket takers. When he gets his derby over his right eye and reaches for a ticket every time the turnstile creaks he looks every inch a fit partner for Forepaugh [the circus owner]. He ought to hallo at the gillies, though, to 'pur—chase your tickets before entering the door.'"[9] • "Briody wandered into Charley Notry's barber shop in Ontario Street yesterday just as Ed Dooley, the lion trainer, sat down in a chair for his daily shave. 'Ah, ha, watch how nice I can shave him,' said Briody, as he snatched up a razor, seized Ed firmly by his pretty nose, and made a swipe with the shining steel down one side of the cheek that brought out the day's growth of beard by the roots. The yell Ed gave would have made one of his lions blush, and Briody threw up his hands."[10]

A whipping boy: • Sometimes ball players considered dwarves to be good luck charms. There was a small man, of indeterminate age, who frequently rode out to the ballpark in a little cart pulled by a dog. Once in the park and seated, he always began a continuous cracking with a small whip, never ceasing his noise throughout the game. • His routine was really getting on the nerves of some of the players, and the superstitious among them began branding the fellow a "jonah" (a bad luck charm)—one to be banned. Management, however, paid no attention to all the "jonah" talk, and the team continued to win despite the distraction.

THE BOYS OF "BLACK-BERRI-WINE-ROW"

They were at every Blue Stockings game; they sat up in the right field stands, and from there they loudly critiqued every aspect of the game being played below, while all along sipping their beverage of choice—blackberry wine.

This collection of devoted "croakers" (fans)—composed of local celebrities and their followers—was the first (though unofficial) booster club for Cleveland baseball.

With the help of the *Cleveland Leader*, and through a number of spelling changes, they became "blackberriwyne row."[11] They were led by a very large man, Al Johnson, who along with his brother Tom Johnson (a future mayor of Cleveland) owned the Brooklyn Street Railway streetcar line.

Al's lieutenants in "blackberriwyne row" were Charles Le Marche—proprietor of the Weddell House Hotel; George Wilson—a cigar manufacturer located a stone's throw away from the Weddell, on Water Street; and Mat Wolford—tavern owner, and noted, or notorious, seller of sporting "pooles" (in essence gambling). His place was on Frankfurt Street, also near the Weddell.

The antics of the wine-tasting gang were part of the fun throughout this exciting season of 1883.

The Owl Club and Baseball

Located near Public Square, the rooms of the Owl Club were the social center of the sports-minded black population of Cleveland; among the regular clientele were most of the best black ball players in town. Drinks, billiards, and the regular items found in any men's club were available. The Owl even boasted of a "tonsorial department" (barber shop).

Mr. Bridgewater, an out-of-town visitor at the Owl Club, played a match game of billiards there. He was also the business manager of the barnstorming St. Louis Black Stockings—the country's best team of black ball players.

Bridgewater offered a challenge to the Owl Club to put together the best group of Cleveland "colored" players they could muster, and, at a time and place of their choosing, his team would beat them.

An emergency meeting was called. Special invitations were extended to William W. Wilson, Edward Wilson, James Morris, Charles Stanley, and Edward W. Doctor (all superb ball players) to attend a meeting at the Phoenix club to work out details for the up-coming match game with the St. Louis Black Stockings.

Rather than just get together a "picked nine," the team organized itself and elected officers. George Meyers was chosen president, William Sabb the secretary, and William Wilson became both treasurer and manager.

The game was to be played May 9 at the Kennard Grounds. The National League Cleveland Blue Stockings (white) were invited to watch the "new Cleveland Blue Stockings" (colored) defend the honor of Cleveland baseball against the visitors from St. Louis.

George Strief played amateur baseball in Cleveland, and in 1879 was on the Cleveland League team. In 1883 he was with the American Association team in St. Louis. He was familiar with the St. Louis Black Stockings team, and just happened to be at the ballpark for the "colored" match game.

The *Cleveland Plain Dealer*: "Briody and Glasscock were both wanted by the colored clubs to umpire yesterday. They did not want any of it."[12]

George Strief (in a likely pre-arrangement) allowed himself to be talked into umpiring the game.

The *Gazette* (the local black weekly), the *Herald*, and the *Plain Dealer* gave sparse accounts of the game other than the score. The *Leader*, however, devoted an unprecedented half column to the contest between the black athletes.

The Cleveland Blue Stockings
Versus
The St. Louis Black Stockings

"About 400 people witnessed the game at League park [Kennard Grounds], mostly comprised of the colored population."[13] Most of the white minority in the stands came from the Cleveland League team. The *Leader* noted that "There were many handsome black eyes watching the home team from the grandstand."[14] The reporter felt that all the attention from the ladies was one reason the Blue Stockings were trying too hard to make an impression at the beginning of the game.

The Blue Stockings' shortstop, Wilson, led off with a smash to his counterpart, who couldn't handle it, and he was safe at first. Stanley then tried to be a hero by knocking a ball — with home run distance — high into the air, but the high hit started to curve foul, and the fleet-footed Black Stocking in left was able to catch up with it for the first out. Back-to-back errors allowed Doctor and Smith to get bases, with Wilson scoring the game's first run: "Milligan came up, looked at the ladies' stand and smiled a smile...." But then "He fanned the air with his timber three times in the most desperate manner and took his seat on the player's bench."[15] Trip smiled at Milligan as he headed for the batter's box, but he wasn't smiling when he left the batter's box. He too had struck out.

St. Louis took advantage of the nervous fielding of Cleveland in their first turn at bat: "Black Stockings jumped in and walked on the canvass bags until they had scored four runs, all of them coming in on errors."[16]

The rest of the innings were not recapped individually.

Score: St. Louis 11, Cleveland 5.

The *Cleveland Plain Dealer*: "The Blue Stockings only scored in four innings while the Blacks chalked up runs in every inning with the exception of two. The game could have been much worse, but it was not. In fact it was better than looked for, some really good plays being made by both sides."[17]

The *Plain Dealer* closed its coverage by saying the two teams deserved a larger attendance.

Inning	1	2	3	4	5	6	7	8	9	Final
Blues	1	0	1	0	0	0	1	0	2	5
Blacks	4	1	0	0	1	3	1	1	*	11

Blue Stockings	Runs	Hits	Black Stockings	Runs	Hits
William W. Wilson, ss	2	1	Gordon, rf	3	1
Charles Stanley, c	0	0	Canter, ss	2	0
Harold C. Smith, p	0	1	Rodgers, 1b	1	1
Edward W. Doctor, 1b	0	1	Davis, p	2	1
W. Milligan, lf	0	0	Sutton, cf	1	1
Tripp, 2b	2	3	Hannis, c	2	2
William Sabb, rf & 2b	1	0	Art "Ike" Carter, 2b	0	0
Edward Wilson, 2b & rf	0	1	Obouvon, 3b	0	2
Sam Smith, cf	0	0	Bracy, lf	0	0
Totals	5	7	Totals	11	8

Time of game: one hour and thirty minutes. Umpire: George Strief.

OTHER BLUE STOCKINGS

In May, the Toledo Blue Stockings of the Northwest League played an exhibition game at the Kennard Grounds with the Cleveland National League Blue Stockings.

One of the Toledo players, their catcher, stood out more than the others. He was the black man who had once played for Oberlin College, and later, in 1881, for the Cleveland White Sewing Machine Company: Moses Fleetwood Walker.

The crowd treated him politely. As for the game itself, Cleveland won 4–1.

Material Men

The Excelsior Clothing store put up four prize medals for the Blue Stockings to compete for. The *Cleveland Leader*: "They are beauties, and make no mistake, rich, and neat, composed of solid gold, with three bars on gros grained silk and round pendant, the size of a silver half-dollar, attached."[18]

Each pendant had a unique design of a ball player in action, representing best batting, best fielding, best base running, and most sacrifice hits. Made by Brunner Bros. of Cleveland, the prizes would be awarded at season end.

The Cleveland police stationed at the park decided they would like some material stuff too: more money. The *Plain Dealer* couldn't believe they had the nerve to ask for $1.25 for only two hours' work at the ball grounds—that was more than the vast majority of workers made in a full twelve-hour day.

One writer at the *Leader*, feeling under-appreciated for his value to the business of baseball, and perhaps with an eye to the superior seating accommodations baseball management provided for themselves, penned: "The Cleveland Club has just received from Constantinople an elegant Turkish carpet woven in one piece, to fit the reporters stand at the ball park. The easy chairs for the scribes will be elegantly upholstered with fine Russian leather. Beautiful ottomans, profusely embroidered with silk have been ordered, one for each chair ... and the desk will be a long plank of richly finished ebony furnished with a profusion of finely pointed pencils ... champagne and imported cigars will also be prodigally strewn around—in your mind."[19]

The Blue Stockings' Record

Cleveland's fortunes followed the weather in 1883. As the weather warmed up so did the Blue Stockings. At the beginning of June they were in seventh. In July, for the first time in their history, they were not only fighting for first place but had actually been there for a few days.

With change pitchers "One Arm" Daily and Will Sawyer giving ace Jim McCormick more days off than he had ever had before, the team continued its winning ways. At home and on the road, the Cleveland club consistently whipped the League's best teams.

A tendency to let down somewhat against the circuit's tail-enders, and management's heavy booking of exhibition games, were negatives; the newspapers expressed some concern.

There was also concern about player drinking, but since the team was doing so well the criticism in that area was limited. However, the drinking of two players, to the detriment of their play in the field, earned this comment: "We do not wish to get personal but the initials of the players are Muldoon and Hotaling."[20]

A few games of rather flat fielding and lackluster batting, in the heat of mid-July, inspired this submission to the *Cleveland Leader*:

> It is terribly sad,
> And makes me feel very bad,
> To see any one out in a toot;
> But the gilt-edged they say
> Were led slightly astray,
> By the juice of the forbidden fruit.
> (To be sung in mournful monotone with
> ice water accompaniments.)[21]

Amateurs around Town

Downtown: Employees of both the Grand Arcade (still standing) and National Bank played ball at the League Park.

East: "The 'Academy' Base Ball Club of Collamer [today part of the Collinwood neighborhood in Cleveland] have organized for the season.... They would like to hear from all clubs whose players are under seventeen years of age. Address, F. B. McCrosky, Collamer, O."[22]

West:

To the editor of the Leader:

The citizens of Rockport [Lakewood and Rocky River area], particularly those in the vicinity of [the] Rocky River, were annoyed last Sabbath by a base ball game at the park.... There is no reason why the residents of Rockport should allow a parcel of roughs from Cleveland or elsewhere come into their midst, make the air hideous with their curses and foul language, and their pleasure drives dangerous, because of the reckless driving of drunkards and disreputable characters, and they do not mean to quietly submit while their rights to a quiet Sabbath are being trampled, and there is law to protect those rights.

A RESIDENT[23]

The Solid-Gold August of "The Gilt-Edged"

After returning home in mid-July, Cleveland stayed in or near first place, and their public was starting to believe the unbelievable. The crowds at Kennard, from the first day of August till the end of the home stand on August 23, all had one thing in common — pennant fever.

A golden opportunity: The popularity of the Blue Stockings was a financial bonanza for one lucky property owner, "a man who owns a little frame house that stands bang against the center field fence...."[24] Now, instead of the regular fifty cents, the thrifty minded baseball watcher could see a game from a private roof top seat for a dime.

The directors of the Cleveland team ordered a heightened fence to block the view. The owner of the renegade seating responded to this by ordering a heightening of his own. The bleachers were raised up on scaffolding — and the dime racket was back in business.

While the directors contemplated their next move, an incident played into their hands. On August 13, during an exciting moment in an otherwise rather tedious game, the occupants of the discounted seating discovered that not only were the seats cheap but that the scaffolding supporting those seats was even cheaper.

The crowd in the park heard the crack as the first of the shoddy scaffolding failed. Heads turned toward the scary scene as the restraining rail gave way. The crowd held its breath as three spectators were thrown out, and down some thirty feet onto the field of play. Those watching winced as wooden debris now began to rain down on top of the unlucky trio.

Two victims disentangled themselves quickly, got up, and ran away, "but John Slager, of No. 68 Croton street, was so stunned that he lay unconscious for several minutes."[25] The Hogan & Harris ambulance was called by phone, the crew arrived shortly, crossed the field, gathered up the victim, and took him downtown to their Bank Street facilities. Examination showed no broken bones and Mr. Slager was sent home. What was broken was the seating scheme.

The *Cleveland Leader*: "Officers of the law should see to it that the man who rents this roof is restrained from allowing people to risk their lives there again."[26] With the *Leader* and the team owners crying for action, the police put the roof top business out of business.

Blackberriwyne row celebrated at the last home game of the year as "The necks were knocked off of several bottles of wine and many bumpers were swallowed to the success of the Gilt-edged on their trip West and East."[27]

Though the team lost the last home game to Chicago, they remained in first place with a record of 47 and 26. With several more weeks of games yet to be played, Cleveland now had the tough job of trying to win a pennant on the road.

The Golden Arm of "One Arm"

"One Arm" Hugh Ignatius Daily stepped into the pitcher's box at Philadelphia on September 13. Philadelphia sent Manning up to start the game. He grounded to Glasscock, who threw him out. Harbidge hit the ball in front of Hotaling, who scooped it up, and from center field threw him out at first. Gross ended the first with the second ground out to Glasscock. Philadelphia failed to score in the second and third. They threatened in the fourth when Manning and Harbidge walked, but Daily worked out of that jam. Cleveland did not score for six innings, but in the seventh they scored an unearned run. York made a hit and stole second base, Crowley hit the ball to left, and when Purcell let the ball go between his legs, York was able to score. Cleveland went out in the eighth and ninth. Daily had pitched well all day, and had kept Philadelphia off the bases in the first, second, third, fifth, sixth, seventh, and eighth. In the ninth, Daily won the game, by once again, retiring Philadelphia in order.

Score: Cleveland 1, Philadelphia 0.

Cleveland had one unearned run on six hits.

Philadelphia had two walks, no runs and no hits.

Many in the crowd at Philadelphia didn't realize what had just happened. Then it sank in — no hits! As in, no-hit game! "One Arm" Daily had just pitched Cleveland's first no-hitter (it was the eighth such game in League history).

The *Cleveland Leader:*

Base Ball
NOT A HIT[28]

The *Cleveland Herald:*

THE 'PHILLIES' FAIL
TO MAKE A SINGLE HIT OFF DAILY[29]

PHILADELPHIA	Runs	Hits	CLEVELAND	Runs	Hits
Manning, rf	0	0	Dunlap, 2b	0	1
Harbidge, cf	0	0	Hotaling, cf	0	0
Gross, c	0	0	Glasscock, ss	0	0
McClellan, ss	0	0	York, lf	1	1
Purcell, lf	0	0	Phillips, 1b	0	1

PHILADELPHIA	Runs	Hits	CLEVELAND	Runs	Hits
Farrar, 1b	0	0	Crowley, rf	0	1
Coleman, p	0	0	Muldoon, 3b	0	1
Ferguson, 2b	0	0	Bushong, c	0	0
Warner, 3b	0	0	Daily, p	0	1
Totals	**0**	**0**	**Totals**	**1**	**6**

Inning	1	2	3	4	5	6	7	8	9	Final
Philadelphia	0	0	0	0	0	0	0	0	0	0
Cleveland	0	0	0	0	0	0	1	0	*	1

As things would turn out, the Daily no-hitter would be the most memorable feature of the year of the "gilt-edged" boys.

The long road trip to close out a long season that was too full of exhibition games finally caught up with the Blue Stockings' pitching. By the end of the road trip that closed out the season, the Cleveland club was in fourth place. However, they still set a club-high mark of 13 games over .500, which put them 7.5 games out of first place with a .567 winning percentage. Jim McCormick made 43 appearances and had a record of 28 and 12. His winning percentage of .700 led the League. Hugh Daily pitched 45 games and had a record of 23 and 19 with a .548 winning percentage. Will Sawyer pitched in 17 games; he won 4 and lost 10 for a .286 winning percentage.

National League Standings of 1883

	W	L	PCT	GB
Boston	63	35	.643	—
Chicago	59	39	.602	4
Providence	58	40	.592	5
CLEVELAND	55	42	.567	7.5
Buffalo	52	45	.536	10.5
New York	46	50	.479	16
Detroit	40	58	.408	23
Philadelphia	17	81	.173	46

Gold Digging

Contrary to usual practice, "One Arm" Daily was not paid in August while recovering for a short time from a shoulder injury. The directors had arbitrarily decided he was not hurt, but was being sulky, and so they gave him no money for games missed.

The large number of exhibition games the Cleveland players were required to play in, without a voice in the matter, and the lack of redress in any matters similar to the Daily incident, spurred talk of some kind of union. Such talk was taking place on other teams as well.

The post-season exhibition schedule took Cleveland to St. Louis to play the American Association franchise there. Cleveland lost the game 4–2. Had management realized that more than a game might be at stake in St. Louis, they would never have taken the team there. The National League players didn't get a union, but another opportunity came their way—and it came out of St. Louis.

Henry Lucas was a wealthy man in the streetcar business. He wanted to be in the baseball business too, but the two major leagues kept him out. Lucas, not deterred, then went about the business of starting the third major league. He ignored any agreements and understandings the two leagues had with each other concerning territory and personnel. He hijacked players with big chunks of cash and set up teams in the other leagues' markets. Lucas was from St. Louis and he was there when Cleveland came to town in late October.

The Cleveland directors looked forward to a great season in 1884. What they didn't know was that their star hitter, Fred Dunlap, would be in the Union League of 1884, and that he would be wearing a new uniform with the words St. Louis written on it.

While in St. Louis, Dunlap had secretly met Lucas—and, for more money, he had agreed to desert his Cleveland bosses. The first shot of the baseball war of 1884 had been fired, and the first team to be hit was Cleveland.

1884

The Baseball War of '84

The entrance of the Union Association into the major league baseball business created the largest number of big-league franchises to play in any single season in baseball history.

In 1883, sixteen franchises represented fourteen cities. Thirty-three franchises, located in twenty-four cities, started the season of 1884. Seven cities had two teams, Philadelphia had three, four cities made their only major league appearance, and four teams played from eight to twenty-five games before going out of business. One Union Association franchise became the first of only three teams to play in two different cities in the same year: Chicago moved to Pittsburgh in mid-season.

During the baseball war many players, including quite a few stars in the National League and American Association, totally ignored their signed contracts. With the agents of Henry Lucas waving a lot of up-front money around, and promising the best long-term deals, players quickly "jumped" to the Union Association.

The situation for many players was better than having a labor union. However, the situation—like any war—had its inevitable fallout. The business of baseball suffered, the patrons saw a diminished product, and starting the next year all the players would pay a high price for this one year of excess.

The major leagues and their cities in 1884

NATIONAL LEAGUE	AMERICAN ASSOCIATON	UNION ASSOCIATION
Boston	Baltimore	Altoona, PA*
Buffalo	Brooklyn	Baltimore
Chicago	Cincinnati	Boston
CLEVELAND	Columbus	Chicago/Pittsburgh #
Detroit	Indianapolis	Cincinnati
New York	Louisville	Kansas City
Philadelphia	New York	Milwaukee
Providence	Philadelphia	Philadelphia
	Pittsburgh	St. Louis
	St. Louis	St. Paul, MN*
	Richmond, VA*	Washington
	Toledo	Wilmington, DE*
	Washington	

*That city's only major league season.
The Chicago franchise moved to Pittsburgh in mid-season.

The "Colts"

The National League, in order to deal with the on-going raids on its players by the Union Association, set up a system of "reserve" teams in the spring of 1884.

The teams stocked promising minor leaguers and sandlotters as emergency replacements for position players who might desert to the Union Association. Each League team had its own "reserve" team that would play its home games in the big league park. The Cleveland papers nicknamed the Cleveland Reserves "colts."

Politically, the Cleveland papers leaned in the direction of local baseball ownership, and tried their best to promote "colts" baseball as a worthy adjunct to major league baseball.

The Cincinnati Union team wanted him, but Charley Hackett signed on with Cleveland to manage the Blue Stockings of 1884. The new manager took his troops to the roller rink downtown and held his spring training workouts there.

Because of budgetary restraints caused by the need to conserve funds for the baseball war, a very limited schedule of road practice games was played. The parent team, and its "colt" team, played a fair number of exhibition games with their ally in the baseball war, the American Association.

The Blue Stockings would spend most of May on the road before finally coming home. It was hoped that during their absence from the Kennard Grounds the public would go see the new "colt" team.

The Blue Stockings headed east in the second week of April. They played the American Association teams: Pittsburgh Alleghenies, New York Metropolitans, and the new franchise in Richmond, Virginia — winning at the last place 6–3. They also played a game at Trenton, New Jersey, winning 15–4. And in a final warm-up prior to the road opener at Providence, they beat the famous Yale College team at New Haven, Connecticut, by a score of 13–9.

THE COLTS

Joe Ardner	Arundel, p
Curry	Darragh, p
Lyman D. Drake	Hoyle
Morrison	Mulholland
O'Rourke	Parker
Shippy	H. Smith
Sommer	

The "colts" also went on the road in the second week of April, starting in the damp weather of Ohio, and heading into the worse weather of Michigan. They lost at Dayton (Ohio League), and were shut out at Columbus (AA) as well as at Toledo (AA). Finally, with a little help, they won a game at Muskegon, Michigan (Northwest League).

Cleveland was winning the Muskegon game 2–0 when, in the home fifth, Muskegon took exception to a ruling by the umpire, and in a temperamental fit stormed off the field. Cleveland was awarded the game; the "colts" then headed home with most of the team nursing colds.

At Providence, the Cleveland Blue Stockings won the first championship game of the year by defeating the Grays 2–1. They followed up this opening victory with six straight losses.

The "colts'" road record did little to stimulate advance ticket sales either. On April 28, at the Kennard Grounds, they lost to Grand Rapids, Michigan (Northwest League) 17–2.

Mr. Voltz, the former Cleveland sportswriter turned baseball manager, wanted the Cleveland Reserve team to be based in Akron, where he believed it would be more financially successful if he were in charge. His idea was turned down — so he organized his own Akron team.

The Cleveland management, however, soon realized that their "colts," as presently constituted, would be lucky even to draw flies. They announced a plan to combine the best of the Akron players and the best of the "colts" in order to form a new team, to be based in Akron and managed by Mr. Voltz (though some home games would be played in May at the Kennard Grounds). The team would function as a Cleveland "reserve," and honor the schedule of home and away games against the American Association clubs and the League's "reserve" squads.

Manager Voltz played out the "Akrons" home games, and on May 21, embarked on a very ambitious road trip planned to last through mid–June.

In late April, about the time it was decided to merge the Cleveland "colts" and Akron teams, the best player for Akron was expelled for intoxication. Billy Bohn, the great sandlot pitcher from Cleveland, was the player fired.

A few days after Bohn was gone, Manager Laney of the Springfield, Ohio team came to town looking for Bohn, but found he had left. A newspaper story had broken just before his arrival that stated that Mr. Laney's brother Ben had been Bohn's drinking companion, and was using Springfield money to help get Billy Bohn fired so he could be lured to Springfield.

Manager Laney claimed he sent train fare to his brother for Bohn, in order to secure the pitcher's services, because he thought he was free of Akron obligations.

Mr. Laney's story rang hollow when the *Herald* reported that, having missed Bohn, Manager Laney then went behind Manager Voltz's back trying to seduce some other Akron players—but at this he was unsuccessful.

Home at Last

Chicago versus Cleveland

May 21, 1884: Pitching for the visiting Chicago White Stockings: Larry Corcoran, born Aug. 10, 1859, now in the fifth season of an eight year career (177 wins and 89 losses lifetime).

Pitching for the hometown Cleveland Blue Stockings: Jim McCormick, born 1856, Glasgow, Scotland, now in the seventh season of a ten-year career (263 wins and 214 loses lifetime).

The White Stockings wore their usual white uniforms, but also wore what were called "particolored" hats. The Blue Stockings' uniform was the familiar white and blue of past seasons.

By game time the crowd was 1,500—with an additional 300 having wandered in by the close of the second inning. Cleveland lost the coin toss and Chicago chose to send them to the bat first.

Batting orders

Chicago	Cleveland
Abner Dalrymple, lf	Pete ("Monkey") Hotaling, cf
George Gore, cf	Jack ("Pebbly Jack") Glasscock, ss
"King" Mike Kelly, c	William ("Gentle William") Murphy, lf
"Cap" Adrian Anson, 1b	Bill Phillips, 1b
Billy Sunday, cf	Mike Muldoon, 3b
Ned Williamson, 3b	Jake ("Bloody Jake") Evans, rf
Fred ("Dandelion") Pfeffer, 2b	Jim McCormick, p
Walt Kenzie, ss	"Fatty" Charles ("Alderman") Briody, c
Larry Corcoran, p	Joe ("Old Hoss") Ardner, 2b

Inning one: Hotaling led off and hit a nasty bounder over the head of Corcoran for a single. His teammates, however, left him stranded. No runs. Kelly earned the only Chicago base in the first, by a hit to short right, but was out in a run-down when McCormick picked him off first. No runs.

Inning two: Phillips grounded out hard to Anson. Muldoon coaxed a walk, shortstop Kenzie let Evans' "red-hot" grounder get through, Muldoon advanced to third on a McCormick fly out to Billy Sunday in right field, and a half-passed ball by catcher Kelly allowed Evans to gain second. With two outs, and the weak-hitting Briody due up, Cleveland decided to try trickery. By taking an outrageous lead at second, it was hoped Kelly would try a throw down there to get Evans, while Muldoon broke for the plate and Evans scampered for third. Kelly was game and took to the bait, throwing the ball as hard as he could, but it sailed into center, giving Cleveland 2 runs. Briody walked but Ardner forced him out. Two runs. Chicago failed to score.

Third inning: Cleveland was blanked. Chicago's man Pfeffer gained first, when Ardner fumbled his grounder at second. Kenzie lifted a high lazy fly to left center, but Murphy, with an aching leg, couldn't catch up with it and took it on the bounce; he then made matters worse with a wild throw to third, giving the runners second and third. Pfeffer had a good lead at third, and when Corcoran hit a rocket-shot at the pitcher, he broke for home; McCormick somehow snagged it on a bounce and threw out Pfeffer at the plate, Kenzie taking third. Dalrymple delivered a single to right, plating Kenzie. Gore then hit into an inning-ending Ardner-to-Phillips double play. Chicago: one run.

Score after three innings: Cleveland 2 and Chicago 1.

Fourth inning: Goose eggs for both sides.

Inning five: Nothing for Cleveland. Chicago led off the fifth with Ned Williamson taking his base on balls. Pfeffer hit a single to right, and on the throw in Williamson smartly grabbed third. Pfeffer then stole second, and there were runners in scoring position with no one out. McCormick now worked his best magic of the day. He struck out Kenzie, and then McCormick's counterpart stepped in — both pitchers knew that the game might very well be on the line right now. McCormick, after an intense battle, prevailed, striking Corcoran out. Dalrymple then cooperated by ending the inning with a fly to Glasscock at short. No runs.

Sixth inning: No runs.

Inning seven: Evans' red-hot single went for naught when a double play erased him and ended the inning. No action of note by Chicago.

Eighth inning: Cleveland went out easily. After Corcoran led off with an easy fly out to McCormick, Chicago threatened. Back-to-back singles by Dalrymple and Gore brought "King" Kelly to bat—the man who would be the League's batting champion (.354). Kelly didn't do what he wanted, but got credit for a sacrifice roller to the pitcher that moved up both runners. Now "Cap" Anson, the clean-up batter, came to the batter's box—he would be fourth in League hitting this year (.335). McCormick, however, was equal to the task, inducing Anson to ground one to Ardner, who threw the ball to Phillips to end the frame. No scoring; Cleveland was still clinging to a 2–1 lead going into the last inning.

Ninth inning: Cleveland went down quickly. Chicago, however, refused to surrender. The last chance for Chicago started nicely for Cleveland, with Billy Sunday flying out to center fielder Hotaling. Ned Williamson spoiled the fun by hitting safely to center for a single. Pfeffer made an out, and an easy grounder off the bat of Kenzie to Phillips at first looked like a game-ender. Phillips, however, juggled the ball, and then compounded his mistake by shoveling the ball to McCormick, instead of running to the bag himself. Kenzie was safe and the game continued. Corcoran now had a second chance to aid his own cause. He hit it high to center. Hotaling got under it—and the ball dropped right into his waiting hands.

The win to Cleveland! The crowd responded in a wild spasm of cheering and nervous relief.

Inning	1 2 3	4 5 6	7 8 9	Final
Cleveland	0 2 0	0 0 0	0 0 0	2
Chicago	0 0 1	0 0 0	0 0 0	1

Note: • Chicago center fielder Billy Sunday became a famous evangelist after his baseball career. He was on a par with Billy Graham of our own time in terms of recognition. There is a line in the Frank Sinatra song "Chicago, my kind of town" that calls Chicago "the town that Billy Sunday couldn't shut down" (referring to Sunday's attempts to rid the city of alcohol and other sins)."

Voltz of the "Colts"

William ("Billy") Voltz was a former Cleveland sportswriter. Before managing the Akrons, he was in Toledo, where he published a sporting magazine and managed the Toledo ball club. Chris Von der Ahe was a German immigrant, beer brewer, owner of the St. Louis Brown Stockings of the American Association — and the most eccentric and colorful character who ever was boss of a baseball club.

BILLY VOLTZ'S LUCK

"It's hard to die young, isn't it!" said Billy Voltz, of the defunct Akrons, last evening, as he entered the HERALD office, at the same time shaking Hamilton dust from his boots. "You see we left Akron on the 21st of May, full of life — but little money. We arrived in Chicago at 4:40 p. m. the next day, and beat the home nine by a score of 5 to 4. The three games at Chicago netted us $113. We left Chicago for Rock Island on the 26th, where we played the 27th and 28th. There we received $150. We next struck St. Louis, and oh, Lord! I trust the next time I strike that town it won't be with a base ball nine. We played two games on Decoration Day, and I received $8.60 for my share. It cost me $12 to get to the grounds and back. Saturday afternoon I telegraphed home for money, but they failed to recognize my voice and I was compelled to call good and kind Chris Von der Ahe, who loaned me $100, with nothing but my face for security. We played in Evansville [Indiana] next day and I received $109 for my share. I was waiting at the bank's door next morning and when it opened I bought a draft for $100, which I sent Von der Ahe. I had $9 left, and a cloudy sky. It did not rain and the show went on. At Vincennes [Indiana] we got enough to carry us to Louisville, where we got $15 for our share. I stayed up until 2 o'clock in the morning waiting for more money from Cleveland, but it came not. I met a friend and borrowed enough to get us to Cincinnati. At that place we got $9.45. This was the unkindest cut of all. All my hopes vanished. Cincinnati, the great and only ball town in the West, gave me $9.45 and a dreary road ahead. We left Hamilton [Cincinnati suburb] last Saturday, where we played a sixteen inning game. Fifteen dollars was what I got, and was sure of 2,000 people next day—Sunday. I retired early that night after I saw all the players in bed, and dreamt of bags of gold and grand stands black with people, brass bands at the depot in Akron, etc., but imagine my disappointment when I woke and peeped out the window and saw it was raining. It rained hard all day, and those two thousand were compelled to go to Sunday-school and spend their quarters, while a poor little base ball club from Akron was suffering at the hotel. I sent to Akron for money that day, and they replied they had none, and my heart in my mouth, I told the landlord, and he, good soul that he is, told me not to worry but do the best I could, and I did. I disbanded the club and here I am, anxious for other pastures green."[1]

Winning ways continued to elude the Blue Stockings. On May 25, their record was reported at 5 wins and 13 losses; on June 8, it stood at 9 and 22. It was hoped the addition of some new men would help turn that around.

A French Dentist and Some New Blood

Fatty Briody was Cleveland's only legitimate catcher in the months of April and May. The excellent defensive catcher Doc Bushong (1883 Blue Stockings), at the wish of his family in Bordeaux, France, had given up the diamond to pursue his trained profession of dentist.

Vice-president Howe announced he had asked Bushong to reconsider his choice and come back to Cleveland. On April 3, Bushong cabled that as soon as he could tie up personal affairs in France he would set sail for Cleveland. This was considered quite a coup, because rumor had it that the St. Louis Union club was hotly pursuing Bushong too. Doc's affairs took longer than expected to iron out (on his arrival in America he quietly slipped off to Providence and got married). His name started appearing in the Cleveland box scores at the start of June.

Also arriving in June, as an extra outfielder, was Mike Moynahan, another former Blue Stocking (1881). As soon as he arrived he had to fill in for Jake Evans. On a throw in from right field Evans' arm had popped completely out of its socket. The bizarre accident left his arm in a fragile condition that would plague him for the rest of the year.

Joe Ardner, a Cleveland native, was taken off the "colts'" roster early on to play second. By June, his .174 batting average was found wanting and another second baseman was secured.

The Altoona, PA, franchise of the Union Association lasted 25 games before folding. Their rookie second baseman, George "Germany" Smith, hit .315 in those 25 games. He was signed as the new regular second baseman for Cleveland

From the June record of 9 and 22, Cleveland by the Fourth of July had improved to a record of 20 and 27—a mark of 11 wins against 5 defeats during that span.

A YOUNGSTOWN INTERLUDE

Cleveland opted out of a game in Akron on July 3, against Youngstown. Manager Brownlee of the Youngstowns was reported angry enough to threaten a lawsuit. Cleveland then agreed to play a game in Youngstown a week later, and the lawsuit story was called just so much newspaper nonsense.

Cleveland won the game 11–5. James McAleer, a man with a very bright future in Cleveland, played for Youngstown — his home town.

A week after the game with Cleveland, it was announced that a Youngstown local streetcar company had signed a deal to service the new Youngstown ball grounds on West Federal Street. It was hoped material assistance from the transit company would stabilize the Youngstown minor league franchise and help in the sale of stock.

Holiday Ball

Things seemed to be heading in the right direction, as the sixth-place Blue Stockings prepared to host the second-place Grays of Providence for two games on Independence Day:

4TH JULY,
BASE BALL
CLEVELAND VS. PROVIDENCE
Two games 10:30 a. m., 3:00 p. m.
GRAND DISPLAY of FIREWORKS
In the evening.
MESSNER'S BAND will be in attendance
Admission, Base Ball 50 cents: Fireworks 25
cents: Reserved Seats 15 cents, can be obtained
at Van Epps & Co's store.[2]

* * *

The early morning game on the Fourth of July was rained out. The sun, however, by coming out in full force shortly thereafter, made the soaked field presentable, and the now gorgeous day promised a good holiday crowd for the later game. It wasn't a good crowd — it was a stupendous crowd!

The *Cleveland Herald* wrote: "The largest crowd that ever assembled at a ball game in this city crowded the stands and their roofs and all the fields long before game was called. Nearly 7,000 people paid for admission and their presence rendered necessary an agreement that any hit among them should be good for but two bases."[3]

Batting orders

Providence Grays	*Cleveland Blue Stockings*
Paul Hines, cf	Bill Phillips, 1b
Jack ("Moose") Farrell, 2b	Pete ("Monkey") Hotaling, cf
Joe ("Old Reliable") Start, 1b	"Germany" George Smith, 2b
"Old Hoss" Charles Radbourn, p*	Jake ("Bloody Jake") Evans, rf
Arthur Irwin, ss	Jim McCormick, p
Jerry Denny, 3b	Jack ("Pebbly Jack") Glasscock, ss
"Cliff" Carroll, lf	Willie ("Gentle Willie") Murphy, lf
"Barney" Gilligan, c	Mike Muldoon, 3b
Paul Radford, lf	"Fatty" Charles ("Alderman") Briody, c

* "Old Hoss" Charles Radbourn is in the Hall of Fame.

The *Cleveland Herald*:

Cleveland, Ohio July 5 ... Providence opened at the bat, and Farrell got around the bases in the first inning on his single to left, a passed ball, Start's put-out and Radbourn's hit to center. In the fourth the visitors earned two runs. Radbourn opened with a hit but Irwin forced him out by his grounder to Smith. Then Denny hit to the center field fence for three bases, sending Irwin home, and Gilligan's second double made Denny a run getter....

Fourth inning: Cleveland got one tally in this inning. Smith started in with a single to left and got second on Gilligan's high throw to catch him stealing. Jake Evans' hit to left sent Smith to third and

McCormick's grounder to Radbourn gave Jake second. Smith rushed for the plate, while Murphy was at bat, and when Gilligan had thrown down to catch Evans off. There was a mix-up. Gilligan dropped the ball and Smith was safe. Evans got to third but no further.

In the fifth Providence got another tally. Mac gave Paul Hines his base-on balls and a big lead off to steal second, which Paul accepted. He went to third on Farrell's put out and Start's single to right sent him home.

Not until the eighth did the local men add to their score. Phillips got around in that inning on his single to center, Evans' double into the crowd at left field, and a passed ball. After that they could do nothing and the game resulted in a reversal of the score Wednesday....[4]

PROVIDENCE 4, CLEVELAND 2

Inning	1	2	3	4	5	6	7	8	9	Final
Providence	1	0	0	2	1	0	0	0	0	4
Cleveland	0	0	0	1	0	0	0	1	0	2

"Gentle" Willie

William N. Murphy: "Murphy again batted as if he didn't care a cuss whether the game was won or lost."[5]

Cleveland, O., July 18, 1884:

For the past month he has been guilty of drunkenness and insubordination. He has refused to appear for practice several times, and besides quarreling with the other players and abusing Manager Hackett in return for advice, has been drunk on the streets and generally acted in a ruffian manner. Last Sunday night he put in his plea for release.

While under the influence of liquor he went into Duncan C. Ross' saloon on Ontario street and there met Mervin Thompson and O. E. Pooler. The trio began arguing and Murphy lost his temper. He told Thompson that he was no good and that anybody could lick him, etc. Thompson laughed at him and got a blow in the chest in return. The big pugilist was about to hit Murphy, when Pooler took a hand. Telling Thompson not to fight with a bad hand, the big wrestler sailed into the ballplayer, hit him twice in the face falling him and then giving him another blow while down. Murphy left vowing vengeance and threatening to return with a pistol and shoot.

Murphy was released on Monday last and yesterday went to Pittsburg to join the Washington Americans with whom he will play when the ten days interval between engagements, provided by the rules, have expired. The young man had a narrow escape from the black list.[6]

Murphy lasted five games with Washington and one game with the Boston Unions — his big-league career was then over after but 48 games. It is not known what ever became of "Gentle Willie" Murphy — no obituary notice of his death has been found.

Health and safety matters of ball players made for some concerns, interesting notions, and clever inventions this year. Several local ball players were unavailable as possible replacements due to illness.

Concerns

- Amos Cross came home from Pittsburgh in April with a case of typhoid fever.
- Then, in early June, Cleveland pitcher Will Sawyer was placed under a doctor's care in Grand Rapids, before being sent home to finish his recovery from an undisclosed ailment.
- And, in July, Ed Seward was in a Minneapolis hospital — the second player to contract the typhoid fever.

Interesting notions

- For a sore arm or strained arm — try a crude-oil rub.
- For sore limbs — a rub of sweet oil, liquid ammonia, and rye whiskey will do the trick.
- Thirsty? Try a lemon or an oatmeal-water drink — separately or together.

Clever inventions

- A new version of a catcher's mask appeared this year. It was spring-loaded, allowing the face wires to open so the catcher could scratch his face, sip fluid, or see with less obstruction.
- Ball players James O'Rourke and James "Deacon" White were collaborators in testing an air-filled chest protector.

A few of the Blue Stockings came up with some clever equipment too

- Briody in June was sporting a chest protector of his own; he called it his "liver pad" and his personal mascotte.
- Jake Evans was wearing some sort of a fitted rubber cap on his arm to keep it from popping out of its socket. It must have been effective because he played a full season.

The Traitorous-Trio

Cleveland lost five games in a row from July 21–26 and hearsay around town had it that the team was about to fold. Adding water to the rumor mill were stories reputed to be from the ball players themselves. McCormick, it was said, felt that despite good pitching on his part, he had lost games because of a lack of support from his teammates, and wanted to be released because his heart was no longer in the Cleveland game. Another report was that Glasscock was also disappointed by the team's overall level of play and that he too wanted out.

Vice-president Howe was confident and assured the public that everything would work out fine with the players. He also spoke hopefully of new grounds—for next year.

The *Herald*, commenting on the poor attendance: "Cleveland is a good base ball city if good play is done by the team, but the success of 1883 cultivated a high taste from which it is hard to step down."[7]

Secret agent man: Cleveland was in Buffalo and so was Frank B. Wright. Mr. Wright was secretary and special agent for the Cincinnati Unions. He was a former sports editor at the *Cincinnati Enquirer* and the *Buffalo Express*. His experience in Buffalo allowed him to expertly entertain his main target, Jim McCormick, in whose company he was often seen while the Cleveland team was there.

There was an above-board effort by Mr. Wright, while in Buffalo, to purchase the three Cleveland players he wanted. Management, however, said no, because they felt it was probable the players would not desert their legal obligations under contract, and anyway they weren't in the business of selling players.

Wright then hung to the Cleveland team until it reached Chicago, where "President Thorner took Wright's place in McCormick's affections."[8] McCormick, Glasscock, and Briody were offered $1,000 cash each, plus a deal to pay them close to their regular full-season salaries for playing the last two months of the Cincinnati Union schedule. They secretly sold out—and "jumped."

The hijacking completed, "The precious trio played their last game with Cleveland yesterday [August 8] and left it last night in company with President Thorner of the Cincinnati Unions, for Cincinnati."[9] "The only excuse the traitors offered for their action is that they wanted the money offered. It is the excuse of the pick-pocket."[10]

There had been talk of selling the right-of-release from the contracted McCormick and Glasscock to either another League team or an Association team. But the Union Association, at war with both leagues, had sent in its agents and carried off "the precious trio" of Jim McCormick, Jack Glasscock, and "Fatty" Briody.

The angry Cleveland sportswriters demanded ownership fight it out in the courts till the bitter end. The Cleveland owners said they planned to use the services of baseball activist and attorney John M. White, in suing Cincinnati to get back the players who left—legal fees to be raised by subscription.

The sportswriters then commenced a campaign of bad-mouthing the three deserters:

- Of McCormick for the team of 1883: "...the failure of his arm cost it the championship.... [But] He was paid every dollar of his salary."[11]
- On Glasscock: "... [he] had been petted by the public, and with reason, for his equal as a general player is scarce. But this year his fielding has been off and his batting poor. His heart was undoubtedly not in the work."[12]
- "Glasscock has been 'lushing' this season on the cheap plan — when others would pay for his intoxicants."[13]
- About Briody: "Briody was picked up in 1882 by the club, and a very seedy pick-up he was. He was umpiring games and regarded as a played-out catcher. He would play for anything...."[14]
- And one writer was bitter enough to inform the public that "Chris Wagner [is] the owner of the saloon on Wilson avenue, where the traitorous trio used to fill their skins with beer and get in prime condition to lose a game the next day...."[15]

Repent, the End Is Near

Cleveland now scrambled to find players to fill three immediate holes in the roster, as well as protect themselves against future desertions and injuries.

George Pinckney was found playing for Peoria, and agreed that, should the Peoria team disband, he would play for Cleveland.

Terms of employment were telegraphed to Pinckney and he wired back acceptance. He was unaware that "This under the national agreement, answers the same purpose as a written contract."[16]

Peoria collapsed and George Pinckney went to Chicago to meet manager Hackett. Henderson, manager of the Baltimore Unions, was staked out at the train depot; he buttonholed Pinckney and hurried him off to Baltimore under contract.

A short time later the Baltimore Unions visited the Boston Unions for a series of games; by coincidence the Cleveland League team was also in town, playing games with the Boston League team.

Cleveland representatives got hold of Pinckney (who had not yet played in a Baltimore game), and explained that he could be blacklisted by the League and Association for breaking their rules on contract acceptance, in spite of Pinckney's ignorance of those rules.

When Cleveland left Boston they took their new infielder, George Pinckney, back with them. He would play in 36 Cleveland games.

Baltimore was not happy, and a few days later the Union Association floated a story about possible entry into the Cleveland market in 1885 with quarter tickets—half the League price.

Ernie Burch, an outfielder, also came to Cleveland via the disbanded Peoria ball club route. He took Moffett's place in the outfield for 32 games, freeing up the latter man to be the new change pitcher and allowing the old change pitcher, John Harkins, to take Jim McCormick's place. These were the only two replacements of note after the "trio" left. Half a dozen or so other less-notables played in a few games.

On October 8, at the Kennard Grounds, 400 spectators got to watch the Blue Stockings help the Providence Grays clinch the pennant by losing 9–7. On October 12, the Clevelanders who showed up saw Providence whip Cleveland 8–1 in the last game of the season.

What those on hand didn't know was that they were watching the Cleveland Blue Stockings' last major league game, and that they were also at the last major league game to be played at the National League's Cleveland Kennard Grounds. Cleveland finished their sixth and final year in seventh place with 35 wins and 77 losses—a record that left them 49 games out of first place.

Aftermath of the war: The Cleveland Blue Stockings went out of business after the war of 1884—the only National League franchise to fold. The American Association went out of business in five cities, including Columbus and Toledo. The Cincinnati Unions also went when the entire Union Association closed up shop. Thus Ohio, in one year, lost four major league teams!

Henry Lucas, the Union Association's money-man and general, who caused the baseball war to be fought, was allowed to buy the rights for the Cleveland franchise slot in the National League for $2,500, and in 1885 he used it to field the St. Louis Maroons.

Brooklyn of the American Association got the rights to most of the Blue Stockings' men, and in 1885 they put Bill Phillips, "Germany" Smith, Pete Hotaling, John Harkins and George Pinckney on their roster.

At East Madison (E. 79th) and Cedar a new ballpark for local ball clubs had gone up in April. It would become the home of the best sandlot baseball in Cleveland. The Kennard Grounds, after a short interlude in 1885, was abandoned and left to decay. Cleveland would not see another major league franchise call the city home until 1887. An era had ended!

1885 & 1886

1885

The year saw the birth of the Western League, a minor circuit. It went through a number of deaths and rebirths until finally evolving into a major league in 1901. We know it as the American League.

After 1884 the Cleveland Blue Stockings were no more, and in 1885 the new Western League's Cleveland "Cardinals" arrived. Brothers Al and Tom Johnson (streetcar magnates) owned the team. Tom Lawrence, groundskeeper from the Kennard Grounds, was hired as manager.

Cleveland went into league with Toledo, Milwaukee, Indianapolis, Kansas City and Omaha, NB (Keokuk, IA, was a late addition). A quick sweep of games through the South served as spring training: Nashville, Memphis, Birmingham, Atlanta, Macon, Chattanooga, and Louisville were the cities visited.

The original roster players were J. A. Sommers, "Doc" Bill Kennedy, Will A. Reid, Joe V. Battin, Ed Hogan, John E. Carroll, Harry W. Wheeler, Mike R. Mansell, Moses Fleetwood Walker (the famous "colored" player), Walter S. Walker and pitchers Ren Deagle and "Chuck" Lauer. Pitcher Sweeney, as well as some fill-in players, were added during the season.

Walter Walker was a mysterious character of whom little is known. If he was in reality Moses Fleetwood Walker's brother Weldy Wilberforce Walker, the reason for changing his name to Walter, and the Cleveland papers' not revealing his race (black), is not known. The Negro Leagues Book: S.A.B.R. 1994, list Weldy Wilberforce Walker as a member of the 1885 Cleveland Western League team (original Cleveland sources do not).

Brooklyn Park

The Johnson brothers decided that their team would draw best on weekdays and Saturdays at the old Kennard Grounds. However, they felt confident that a new park on the west side, dedicated to Sunday games (the city law against them being considered unconstitutional by the brothers), could equal the money made the rest of the week. To do this, they constructed "Brooklyn Park," half a block south of Clark Avenue and west of Rhodes Avenue (Fulton Rd.), on the land called the "Selden farm" in the Cleveland area then usually called Brooklyn. (Several parts of Cleveland's west side had the word Brooklyn as part of their name at one time or another: Brooklyn Village, Brooklyn Township, and South Brooklyn.)

Johnson streetcars supplied transportation direct to Brooklyn Park. A route deviation and an auxiliary track brought cars within a hundred feet of the gate, allowing them to be conveniently lined up for the trip home.

For an investment of $3000, it was envisioned that Cleveland would have a new ballpark seating 5,000 and the improved grounds to go with it. Several weeks before the grand opening, a sizable force of men went to work on the park. They enclosed the site with a ten-foot board fence, and finished open-side stands of plank seating for four thousand. The thousand-seat, two-story, covered grandstand, however, was not ready for the April Sunday opener against Toledo.

No intoxicating drinks of any kind — not even soda pop that looked the color of beer — was to be sold at the park. Large signs were posted throughout the park asking the public to be on its best Sunday behavior. A large force of "special police" was hired to ensure that the instructions on the signs were followed.

The first Sunday game at Brooklyn Park: Toledo versus Cleveland. The side stands were filled. A standing row three deep circled the field, and the crowd of 3,500 was graced by the presence of many of the ladies.

The Toledo team wore gray and blue outfits, and the Cleveland club sported dark gray uniforms detailed in tasteful cardinal. (In mid–May they gray uniforms were replaced with white ones, also trimmed in cardinal.)

Cleveland lost the coin toss and was sent to the bat. The game was called at 3:30 P.M. sharp, and Harry Wheeler stepped in against the Toledo hurler Bill Stemmyer — a former sandlot star from Cleveland.

The *Cleveland Plain Dealer*—

Cleveland —first inning:
Wheeler was called out on strikes, but Hogan got first on balls, promptly stole second, went to third on a wild pitch and by good footing scored on a passed ball.

In their first essay the visitors got a run, Rainey going to first and second on balls, stealing third and scoring on a wild pitch.

In their third inning Cleveland got two runs on Hogan's beautiful drive to right center for three bases, Carroll's single which went to Rainey far too hot to be handled, and some of the most daring, speedy and well judged base running that has ever been seen on a local ball field, the exhibition making both men prime favorites at once.

In the fourth inning Captain Battin got a run on his base on balls and Lauer's drive to the left field fence for three bases— a clean, pretty hit.

In the fifth Hogan rallied for the home team on his red hot snick over third, some more pretty base running, a passed ball, and Faatz' muff at first of Stemmyer's assist on Mike Mansell's grounder.

In the fourth inning Toledo looked dangerous. Some uneven pitching and singles by Stemmyer and Cook twice filled the bases. McDonald, who reached first on balls, scored. But Hogan by two pretty pickups and throws to Walker cut off both Stemmyer and Buckenberger at the plate, each play being heartily applauded.

The Clevelands earned two runs in the fifth by a fine streak of batting, Reid's double to right, Battin's baser to left and a "corker" for two bases to the same field by Harry Wheeler doing the work.

In the seventh Toledo got three runs. Faatz got to first on balls and Stemmyer by being solidly hit by a pitched ball. McDonald sent Faatz home by a single to left and Cook's red hot line fly to the same field caught Mansell with the sun in his eyes and got away, yielding the batsman two bases and sending Stemmyer and McDonald over the plate. Then the Toledos stopped, and as Lauer began to get control of the ball they scored no more. Neither did the Clevelands until the ninth, when as a parting shot, they made four tallies, and earned three of them. Mike Mansell opened the work. He got to first on balls and second on "Doc" Kennedy's sacrifice hit to Stemmyer. Then Walker and Reid contributed singles and Battin and Lauer doubles to the collection, which, with a timely sacrifice by Wheeler, sent Mansell, Walker, Reid and Battin home.[1]

Final: Cleveland 11, Toledo 5.

The *Plain Dealer*'s view of the game: "The star plays of the day were a pretty one-handed stop and quick throw to first by Captain Battin, and a 'lily' in the way of a double play by Mansell, who in the first inning caught a fly from Stemmyer's bat in deep left and threw home to Walker, retiring Wright as he tried to score. Walker's catching was better than good. Mr. Brennan's umpiring was very fair and certainly impartial, but he should study the rules of the Western League. They provide that seven and not six balls shall send a batsman to his base."[2]

Inning	1	2	3	4	5	6	7	8	9	Final
Cleveland	1	0	2	1	1	2	0	0	4	11
Toledo	1	0	0	1	0	0	3	0	0	5

Time of game: 2 hours 15 minutes. Umpire: Mr. John Brennan.

CLEVELAND	Runs	TOLEDO	Runs
Wheeler, cf	0	Rainey, 2b	1
Hogan, ss	3	Wright, rf	0
Carroll, rf	1	Morrison, cf	0
Mansell, lf	1	Faatz, 1b	1
Kennedy, 1b	0	Stemmyer, p	1
M. F. Walker, c	1	McDonald, ss	2
Reid, 2b	2	Cook, c	0
Battin, 3b	3	Buckenberger, 2b	0
Lauer, p	0	McArthur, lf	0
Total	**11**	**Total**	**5**

Manager Tom Lawrence was not, as had been expected, arrested for playing Sunday baseball. Patrolman Lennahan, on Monday morning, swore out a warrant for the arrest of Moses Fleetwood Walker on the charge of Sunday ball playing. Whether this was scripted, a matter of political pressure, or just plain prejudice cannot be said. However, the first test of the constitutionality of the law against Sabbath baseball would now fall to the Clevelands' "colored" catcher.

That Monday, Cleveland won the ball game at Toledo 11–9. Walker was with the team but did not play; after the game he headed for Cleveland.

At 4 o'clock Tuesday afternoon, in the company of Al Johnson and attorney Jay L. Athey (who was also a Cleveland councilman), Walker turned himself in at the central police station. Walker was released on $100 bail, Henry Beckman acting as surety for the money. Walker then rejoined his team on their western road trip.

A few days later, legal counsel for the defendant argued the case in the court-room of Judge Hutchins, who delayed his decision. At the time of the proceedings, the defendant — Moses Fleetwood Walker — was playing ball in Omaha, Nebraska.

The team was out of town, so on Sunday, May 3, Brooklyn Park featured an exhibition game between the local Forest City and the team from Youngstown. The Forest City would feature a guest pitcher, the newly signed Sweeney of the Cleveland Cardinals.

While announcement of the judge's decision was being awaited in the press, a second Sunday incident took place. Leading up to the Sunday game, Cleveland played an exhibition game Friday with Brooklyn of the American Association; half of the visitor's lineup were old Cleveland Blue Stockings. The crowd warmly welcomed them.

Saturday: "In the eighth Deagle sent the pigskin over left field fence for two bases."[3] Despite being shortchanged by the ground rules at Kennard, Cleveland pitcher Deagle soon scored run number nine. Cleveland won over Omaha 19–3, and the team now left its east side park for a Sunday game on the west side.

Sunday May 17: "The Clevelands fairly 'murdered' the Omaha team in yesterday afternoon's game."[4] The three thousand people there enjoyed themselves thoroughly, as Cleveland was victorious by a 10–1 score — but the excitement wasn't over yet.

Enter Sergeant Johnson, leading a squad of police. The Cleveland battery of Sweeney and Sommers was arrested, and while the cops were at it, they grabbed up third baseman Jimmy Say of Omaha. The trio was taken to the Main Street station and they posted bail. On Monday, Say and Sweeney appeared in court and their cases were disposed of.

Attorneys Athey and Kline then used the Sommers case on Wednesday as the one with which to test the Sunday anti-ball law. When Judge Hutchins didn't buy the argument in their demurrer — that there was insufficient information in the warrant to constitute an offense — they asked for a jury trial, and a date was set.

Captain Joe Battin, on May 20, became the new Cardinal manager. Tom Lawrence had quit to look after his other baseball business, but any keen observer knew he was more like the rat that jumps from the sinking ship. Despite the recent Sunday crowd of three thousand, the team was taking a financial bath — its future quite uncertain.

The Weddell House tried to help the team by flying a big white flag with a red ball on it on game days. The company policy of charging extra for carriage parking and for admitting ladies to the grandstand (holidays excepted) was dropped.

A particular pet peeve of the team involved Cleveland native Bill Stemmyer, a pitcher with Toledo. Stemmyer liked to cheat a little by erasing the front line of the pitcher's box. Marble slabs in front of the pitcher's box were installed at both ballparks just before the Toledo series came to town.

It would be interesting indeed to see "Stemmys'" reaction to the reconstituted box, and quite entertaining should his spikes ever hit flat stone.

Decoration Day put the Cardinals on the road, but for the Kennard Grounds a holiday extravaganza was announced:

THE GREATEST SHOW ON EARTH!
Pain's Wondrous Fireworks
MARVELOUS AND UNPARALLELED
RESULTS ACHIEVED
At Kennard St. Base Ball Park,
Decoration Night
The Monitor and Merrimac Fight
18 Set Pieces and 1,000 Rockets
A Display Costing $2,000,
AND
Grand Concert by the Gray's Band.
Fireworks at 8 O'clock.
ADMISSION 50 CENTS[5]

A second spectacular non-baseball event was planned for Brooklyn Park the second week of June. The ad hit the papers June 5.

Buffalo Bill!
"He is king of them all,"—General E. A. Carr.
Brooklyn Park, Cleveland,
Three days commencing Monday, June 8, two
performances daily. Gate open at 12, noon and 6 p.
m. Performances at 2:30 and 8 P.M., rain or shine,
BUFFALO BILL'S WILD WEST!
Reconstructed, enlarged, and improved.
Admission 50 cents. Children 25 cents.
Street cars to the grounds every 3 minutes from all
parts of the city. Grand street parade 10 A.M. Monday.[6]

* * *

Joe Sommers was found guilty, by a jury of his peers, of playing baseball on a Sunday — and any thoughts of an appeal were dropped because of emerging events.

Two days before the Wild West Show came to town, Cleveland beat Kansas City 4–3. It was to be the last hurrah. After the game the team announced it was folding its tent. Even the arrival of Buffalo Bill couldn't save the Cardinals now.

Professional ball was gone from Cleveland, but local baseball games and special events were staged throughout the summer at Brooklyn Park.

A semi-pro/semi-amateur game between the Forest City and West End Grays was held on June 28, a Sunday. On September 11, another Sunday game was played, featuring world boxing champion John L. Sullivan (the last of the bare-knuckle fighters) as a guest pitcher in a semi-pro game.

Buffalo Bill showed up again at the end of the summer for another series of shows. Part of the show included the Sioux Indian chief of "Little Big Horn" fame, Sitting Bull.

1886

The sandlot game was the only game in town this year. In April, the Cleveland police were given instructions that no ball games of any kind would be played on Sunday: "In the suburbs the ball tossers can play as they like, but within the city limits they will be liable to 'five dollars or five days.'"[7]

The limited number of games and teams showed a definite drop in the popularity of baseball this year.

The Unions were the only "colored" team mentioned as existing in 1885. Well-known black baseball activist Will Wilson, of that same Union team, was trying to put together a "colored" team for 1886 to play exhibition games with the new national circuit, the Southern League of Colored Baseballists, and other Ohio teams of color. Results of his efforts are not known.

The handful of teams around town were Crescents, Sanfords, Adelbert College, Brooks School, Malleables, Graphics, Shamrocks, and Lakesides. The last two named teams played in a game on September 5 at Brooklyn Park. It was a benefit game for the mother of Bill Smith, a Cleveland sandlotter who had recently died at Toronto. To raise more money the game was held on a Sunday. Due to the charitable intent behind the game the police decided to look the other way.

Free admission for ladies attracted a large contingent of them to a Thursday, September 16, game at Brooklyn Park between the Malleables and Graphics.

Gathering storm clouds, however, threatened the game. When the rain came the crowd sought shelter in the grandstand. The weather brought high gusting winds — and all of a sudden the roof was ripped off! Everyone got good and wet and the game was called.

Damage to the grandstand and park from the storm was never repaired. In a few years, the Selden farm succumbed to the pressures of progress. New housing and new streets completely covered the land, and soon no sign whatsoever remained of the proud and pretty ball field once known as Brooklyn Park.

1887

A New Park for a New Team

The Cleveland Base Ball Park went up in 1887. It was the home of the new Cleveland team in the American Association — the other major league. It was located at the dead ends of Douglas (E. 36th) St. and Perkins Avenue. The land was in the heart of the Weddell estate — the same family that built the Weddell House Hotel.

President Frank De Haas Robison and Treasurer George W. Howe, along with businessman Davis Hawley and *Plain Dealer* sportswriter Frank E. Brunell, were the principal partners. They secured the franchise (winning out over bids from Kansas City and Detroit), arranged a lease on the land, signed the players, operated the facility, and promoted the games. They had an operating stock of $20,000.

A local architect, the "bright young," Edward P. Ruprecht of the Euclid block, designed the buildings and the noted contractor Foote & Co. did the landscaping.[1]

The park had three types of connected stands: grandstand, pavilion, and open (bleacher). Grandstand seats started eight feet above the ground and numbered a thousand. These seats cost fifty cents. Ladies escorted by paying gentlemen were admitted to these stands free. A special upper section was set aside for ladies only. The grandstand had a foul-ball screen stretched across its higher half where the ladies sat. Also, in the center of the grandstand was reserved a section of private boxes. They were arranged in two rows of ten running from top to bottom. Each box held six and cost $100 per year. The roof of the grandstand was a four-sided peaked affair, with a flagpole on top; its trussed construction eliminated obscuring poles and pillars. To enter, patrons went up the stairs in back of the grandstand to a platform, and then went down the aisles to their seats.

Five doors were built into the front of the grandstand. Viewed facing the grandstand, the end doors were for the dressing rooms (far left visitors, far right home team). The three in the center led to private ground-level field boxes. The left-center door led to the scorers' box. The right center door admitted the VIP "kranks" into the "kicking pen" (a box to keep the rabid rooters isolated from normal people). And the middle door was for President Robison.

Also under the grandstand were the club offices and rooms for the press (with individual desks and personal door keys for the writers) and, lastly, the most popular room — the public bar room.

Frank De Haas Robison, a director and later a powerful owner and authoritative president, was connected with Cleveland baseball from 1887 to 1899. One of his horse-drawn streetcar lines and a subsequent cable car route took the fans out to two different big league parks.

The grandstand itself angled across the northwest corner of the property. The intersection of E. 36th Street and Perkins Avenue crisscross the grounds of the original park.

Running south from the grandstand, following the first base line, was the pavilion. Its short-backed bench seating started three feet above the playing surface. For forty cents each, two thousand people could sit here under the pillar-supported flat roof. Gates at the back of the stands could "be thrown open at games end."[2]

The plank-style open stands ("bleachers") were along the third base line. At a quarter a head, there was room for fifteen hundred.

There was "Renegade seating," too: a large toboggan slide, on private land outside the park, gave about 200 spectators a free view for the first few games, but it was a short-lived deal.

Two rows of twelve-foot picket fence enclosed the park behind the stands. Space between these fences was fifty feet wide — more than enough for pedestrian and carriage traffic.

The fence surrounding the park was clipped on its corners, giving the field an uneven octagon form. The *Plain Dealer*: "Inside its fences it is 475 feet broad by 680 feet long. From the home plate to the left field fence — the only point a ball is likely to go over — is 390 feet, and to the right field fence about 590 feet."[3]

Advertising on the inside of the fence had a space available of about 1,200 feet. Harry Doyle, a Cincinnati native and nephew of Manager Jimmy Williams, was in charge of selling the fence space. He was also responsible for scorecard sales.

The diamond was a "skinned" one, i.e., all dirt, with the infield behind it sodded for fifty feet before meeting the grass-seeded outfield. Footing on the base paths, and in the pitcher's and catcher's box, was a combination of sand and cinders. Individual tarpaulins covered these areas when not in use.

Heavy horse-drawn rollers repeatedly rolled the entire field. These leveling devices were on loan from the Cleveland Driving Park race track.

The outfield had horse and carriage space for three hundred. Rigs, with advance sale tickets in hand, could enter the park through a more convenient gate, a large one cut in the outfield fence. This route was a direct connection from Euclid Avenue, via the new alley built between the Sterling and Williamson estates.

On and around the original park now stand several light-industrial warehouses and factory buildings, including a soft-drink distributor and an air-conditioning company, as well as a number of small and new-tech companies in the old Gould plant.

Politics

With a ballpark in place, management now moved to ensure the financial success of the team. The American Association, with a blue-collar customer base, owed much of its success to its willingness to play on Sundays and make spirits available at its games. The more conservative, middle-class-oriented National League did not favor these practices. Cleveland had its grandstand bar licensed and operating by the time the season was under way.

With the goal of Sunday games in mind, management tapped one of its political connections. Cleveland Councilman Daly introduced Ordinance No. 269 to amend section 600 of the law enacted in 1882. That was the law that prohibited baseball within city limits on a Sunday. Some city officials thought the amendment's language conflicted with the state law against Sunday sport — in which case the state law would prevail. The legislation was pigeon holed, but the issue itself did not go away.

Items

• Frank Brunell was elected the team's scorer; his writing background made him a good choice.

• A. F. Drake & Company, a Cleveland concern, provided uniforms: "The Cleveland club will have two uniforms this season. One will be of white and the other of blue-grey, both with dark blue stockings and dark blue belts and blue hats with white bands."[4]

• The Cleveland sports pages in 1887 continued a love affair with the color blue that had started in 1869; they called the team the "Blues," or more informally "blue legs" or "navy blues."

Spring Training on the Cheap

To get in shape, players exercised the best they could at home; those who came to town early were trained in gyms.

One Cleveland player, John "Cub" Stricker, didn't work out at home or in Cleveland. He joined some other ball players and went to train in Cuba.

"Cub" Stricker was at a loss in Cuba: he knew no Spanish until one day he went to a bullfight. Then, every time he went out to eat, he would call out to the waitress in the only Spanish he knew: "Bring in another bull."[5] And onto his plate would flop another steak.

"Athletic park," "bicycle park," and "driving park" were interchangeable names to describe a number of locations around Cleveland that featured sports. One such location was at the northeastern corner of the intersection of Cedar Avenue and East Madison (E. 79th St.). Officially it was named the Cleveland Driving Park.

In April, the Cleveland Driving Park became a temporary practice site. The Cleveland Base Ball Park's new drainage system, under a heavy rain, had failed miserably, leaving the whole field one big sloppy mess.

The "Shams" faced the "Blues" at the Cleveland Driving Park. The Shamrocks, one of the best amateur teams, played on the west side at the old-river-bed grounds near Whiskey Island.

Having crossed the Cuyahoga River, the Shamrocks put any thought of turning back out of their heads. At the Driving Park, the Cleveland professionals showed the "Shams," and the crowd of two hundred, why they were paid professionals. From the *Plain Dealer*: "A description of the game would be useless and tiresome."⁶ Final: Blues 28, Shamrocks 1.

The paper, however, did say that the west-siders, in their new brown-and-white uniforms, looked quite fashionable in defeat. Having beaten perhaps the best team on the west side, the Blues now had an exhibition with the team many thought was the best on the east side — the Malleables. The Malleables did do somewhat better than the west siders: they lost 33–6.

The first exhibition game promoted at the new park was against the International League team from Toronto, Canada. The Northerners looked good in their pretty "Canadian blue and gray uniforms"—but not pretty enough to win.⁷ They lost the game 20–3.

It was hoped that some of the typically inclement April weather in Cleveland could be avoided by heading a bit further south for practice.

Ohio League, 1887

The Ohio league was a minor league that met in Mansfield, Ohio, in April to announce its starting circuit of Akron, Columbus, Mansfield, Steubenville, and Zanesville, and out-of-state teams in Wheeling, West Virginia, and Kalamazoo, Michigan.

Cleveland, in April, played Ohio League teams a number of times. The first game they played opened Mansfield's brand new ballpark, and featured Mansfield's just-signed rookie, Ed Delahanty—the sandlot hero of Cleveland. The Blues, however, showed no sentimental feelings on this special day, knocking off Mansfield 20–0.

Heading south, Cleveland showed up in Zanesville for a game. This Ohio League team had an unusual star in the person of one Richard Johnson. Zanesville fought a hopeless cause against Cleveland, but in the closing moments of the ninth inning, Mr. Johnson gave the "kranks" a last hurrah—a home run. What was unusual about Mr. Johnson was that he was the star on a team that was otherwise all white—he was a black man. The Blues won 16–7 as twelve hundred watched.

HOT-STOVE LEAGUE STORIES

The Cleveland papers, in order to keep whetted the public's spring fever for matters baseball, reprinted short stories of a lightly amusing nature from around the country. Here are two:

The first (reprinted by the *Plain Dealer* from the *Cincinnati Enquirer*) involves the great ball player, Pete "The Gladiator" Browning, a native son of, and player for, Louisville of the American Association. Pete was illiterate, not all that uncommon at the time, and rather naive to anything outside the world of baseball. He also drank.

"Pete Browning of the Louisvilles will be surprised when he sees what young men compose the Cleveland club. Pete it will be remembered recently saw a picture marked 'Cleveland and his cabinet' [a reference to Grover Cleveland, then president of the United States]. Turning to his side partner Reddy Mack, Pete remarked, 'Ain't them Clevelands got an old lot of ball players, though?' 'Ain't dey!' said Reddy. 'Say Pete, we kin knock dem old duffers out, can't we?'"⁸

The other, from the *Pittsburgh Courier*, described a ballgame in progress while nearby a circus was leaving town: "At Bridgeport [Connecticut] on Saturday, in the sixth inning Jones of Bridgeport batted the ball over Portlands' left fielder. It was a three-bagger. One of Barnums' elephants engaged in pushing one of the circus cars out of the enclosure saw the man fall and left the car. The ball bounded near the animal and he seized it in his trunk, waved it over his head and then hurled it across the field towards the first base. The ball passed over the first basemans head and Jones made a home run."⁹

The Cleveland Base Ball Park Opens

Five thousand nicely bound game schedules, starting opening day, were passed out to the ladies upon entering the grandstand. Management hoped the ladies would lineup dates in advance, resulting in an increase in attendance.

Club official Davis Hawley came up with an idea of his own to help the box-office count. As owner of the Hawley House downtown, he ordered that, for home games, a large banner be stretched across the face of the hotel. It read: "Ball Game Today."

To liven up the opening series, the players with the best overall single day in batting, fielding, and base running were each to be given an award. In order: A diamond on a gold-and-platinum scarf pin, a pair of solid-gold sleeve buttons, and a diamond stud (to be worn with evening clothes). The items came from Mr. August S. Ilg of the Crittenden Jewelry Co.

Wednesday, May 4, 1887: At two o'clock, the White Sewing Machine Co. Band struck up the music; the gates were opened and the crowd filed in. The crowd continued to swell until it reached five thousand. All the stands filled (the grandstand itself being half taken up by the ladies), while hundreds more stood behind barrier rope strung along the left field line.

A caravan of carriages entered the ballpark at 3 o'clock. It was the Cincinnatis, and they received a warm round of applause from the Clevelanders. The visiting players were dressed "in pinkish grey flannel with scarlet belts, caps and stockings."[10] They took field practice first.

From the front of the grandstand, at three fifteen, the Cleveland players ran out of their dressing room and into the thunderous roar of the crowd. Then the Cleveland "Blues" began their warm ups. They were outfitted in uniforms of "white flannel with rich navy blue belts and stockings and made a fine appearance."[11]

CLEVELAND
Opening Day Lineup
Team High Stats* and Personal

Pete "Monkey" Hotaling, cf	13 triples—.299 avg.—rookie—bats left born: Mohawk, New York
Ed McKean, ss	13 triples—60 walks—rookie—born: Grafton, Ohio
Charlie Sweeney, 1b	only 36 games—born: San Francisco
Fred Mann, lf	went to Phily (AA) after 64 games bats left—born: Sutton, Vermont
Myron Allen, rf	4 homers—born: Kingston, New York
Ed Herr, 3b	only eleven games—rookie—born: St. Louis
John "Cub" Stricker, 2b	86 stolen bases—team captain—born: Philadelphia
Charlie Reipschlager, c	played in 63 games—born: New York City
Mike Morrison, p	led league with 205 walks—second in league with 4.49 strikeouts per nine innings—record in 40 games 12 and 25 born: Erie, Pennsylvania.

* Offensive stats are based on one hundred-plus games.

CINCINNATI
Opening Day Lineup

Hugh Nicol, rf	John "Pop" Corkhill, cf
"Bid" McFee, 2b	Warren "Hick" Carpenter, 3b
Frank Fennelly, ss	Clarence "Kid" Baldwin, c
Charley Jones, lf	Tony "Count" Mullane, p
"Long John" Reilly, 1b	

CINCINNATI AT CLEVELAND

The rules of 1887 allowed the home team to choose ups—Cleveland chose to bat first. Tony "Count" Mullane walked out to the pitcher's box, and waited for Umpire E. E. Cuthbert to put in an appearance. He arrived at 3:25 P.M. At 3:30 P.M. the game bell rang, and Pete Hotaling stepped into the batter's box.

"Hotaling and McKean went out on easy chances...."[12] Charlie Sweeney then became the first man to reach base at the new park when he worked the "Count" for a walk. He was caught stealing to end the inning.

Cincinnati's Nicol struck out. McPhee earned a walk, moved up on a wild pitch and stole third. McPhee scored when Charley Jones got the game's first hit and run batted in with a line single to center.

Fred Mann opened the second with the Clevelands' first hit at the new park — a single to left. Mann managed to get as far as third by stealing, but Cleveland did not score. Cincinnati failed to score in their turn.

Cleveland pitcher Morrison began the third with a grounder to first baseman Fennelly, who muffed it for an error. However, with only one out, Morrison died at third. The visitors were blanked in the bottom of the third.

The fourth was Cleveland's inning. Cleveland sent seven men to the plate. Mann led off with a single. Allen walked and moved up on a passed ball. Herr slapped a hard one to second and McPhee made a nice stop, threw home, and just did get Fred Mann as he slid into the plate. Allen moved to third on the play. Herr on first via the fielder's choice then stole second. Now captain Stricker stepped into the batter's box. He waited, waited some more, he swung and the ball flew into center for a hit — Allen and Herr scurried home. Cleveland had grabbed the lead 2–1. The crowd loved it!

The captain wasn't finished yet: he stole second and moved to third on a ground out. With two outs, pitcher Morrison helped his cause by walking, then he attempted to steal second. Catcher "Kid" Baldwin was so determined to gun down the gutsy pitcher that he threw the ball all the way to the center fielder on the fly. "Cub" walked home with the third run and Morrison took third. The fun ended with "Peter J. Hotaling 'fanning' as they say in the south."[13] Cleveland 3, Cincinnati 1. Cincinnati in their half of the fourth went down in order.

The fifth inning and top of the sixth were uneventful. It all started out well enough in the bottom of the sixth, with Fennelly striking out. Jones, however, hit a first-pitch single, and then Morrison hit Reilly with a pitch — an "erratic curve."[14] Corkhill hit to right, and when Allen fumbled it for an error, Jones scored. Cleveland now tried to play clever ball. When Corkhill broke from first to steal second, Stricker took the throw, but decided he might catch Reilly breaking from third for home, and so he quickly threw to his catcher Charlie Reipschlager. Whether the man on third was breaking or not did not matter, because the throw by "Cub" was so wild the run scored easily. Corkhill was on third when Herr booted an easy grounder off the bat of "Hick" Carpenter to give Cincinnati their third unearned run — and Cleveland their third error of the inning. Cincinnati 4, Cleveland 3.

The pitcher hit Hotaling to lead off the seventh. The next two men were easy fly outs. Hotaling moved to second on a Mann single and then stole third. Allen, however, left him stranded by striking out to end the threat.

Cincinnati quickly scored a tally in the seventh: "Bid" McPhee coaxed a walk, and Jones tripled him in Cincinnati 5, Cleveland 3.

"Cub" Stricker singled to start the Cleveland offense in the eighth. This was followed by a Charlie Reipschlager single that turned into a run-down between first and second. While Charlie played pickle, "Cub" hot-footed it all the way home to pull the Blues within a run: Cincinnati 5, Cleveland 4.

Then came the ugly eighth: "the total team fell to pieces in the face of a little hitting and a good deal of pretty and daring base running by the visitors."[15] Corkhill hit an innocent-looking grounder to McKean at short, he botched it, and it was off to the races for the red-legs. Corkhill broke for and stole second when Reipschlager's throw went wild, "Hick" Carpenter's "daisy to left" brought him in, and "Kid" Baldwin's "cracking double" into right center plated "Hick."[16] The "Kid" helped Cleveland when he tried to steal third when the strikeout on Mullane was dropped — Reipschlager nailed him, Mullane getting first. McKean botched another grounder, giving Nicol his base, and Reipschlager followed with a bad throw trying to catch Mullane stealing third. Fennelly then singled him in. Errors by Reipschlager and Herr allowed Nicol and Fennelly to score. Cincinnati 10, Cleveland 4.

In the ninth a few heads were turned when Hotaling patiently earned a walk off Mullane — perhaps the "Count" was tiring. Ed McKean put an exclamation point on that thought, by getting the home team's first extra-base hit — a deep one into right center. Hotaling came in and McKean strolled into third. The exodus from the stands slowed, and when McKean scored on a wild pitch it slowed some more. Mullane, however, now showed his mettle — and put an end to it.

Final: Cincinnati 10, Cleveland 6.
Mullane struck out ten and walked eight.
Morrison struck out nine and walked four.
Time of game: two hours and twelve minutes.

* * *

Group tickets

The Travelers Protective Association made a bulk purchase of tickets for an "outing" at the end of May. The front office encouraged such group events. When the Association showed up for their ball game, they marched into the grounds and up to their grandstand seats, led all the way by the Knights of Pythias Band.

One group of "kranks" (the term "fan" was still a few years away) showed up for their ball game but found they had been led astray. They were victims of a practical joke. Someone had put up the banner in front of the Hawley House indicating ball game today. There was no ball game that day. Upon investigation, it was learned that the Louisville team, in Cleveland for an early summer series, had arrived a day early and had checked into the Hawley House. The villain was not hard to find — an intoxicated, and not infrequently so, Thomas Ramsey, the Louisville pitcher, was the prankster. Ramsey's nickname was "Toad."

Two Games and Fireworks

To maximize profits on Independence Day, separate admissions to the games were charged. The Park Theatre was the Blues' regular ticket outlet, but to accommodate the holiday crowds, "Mr. Newton will sell all kinds of tickets at the west entrance of the Excelsior Clothing store on Superior Street Monday morning — from 7 A.M. to 9 A.M."[17]

THE BROOKLYN TROLLEY DODGERS	THE CLEVELAND BLUES
George Pinckney	"Cub" Stricker
Bill McClellan	Ed McKean
Jim McTammany	Pete Hotaling
Ed Swartwood	Charlie Sweeney
Bill Phillips	Myron Allen
"Germany" Smith	James Toy
Ernie Burch	Phil Reccius
"Adonis" Terry	"Pop" Snyder
Ed Greer	Mike Morrison

Pinckney, Phillips, and Smith were former Cleveland players on the 1884 National League franchise that was, some felt, unfairly driven out of business.

Early game

The day was very hot and the ground very parched: "Clouds of dust at times hid the drama from view."[18] The pitchers were "Adonis" Terry for Brooklyn and Mike Morrison for Cleveland. Four thousand watched.

Cleveland scored first in the first with 2. Stricker led off with a hit, McKean walked, and a bad throw on a grounder plated both.

The Cleveland fifth looked like a replay of the first. This time, though, Stricker walked, McKean got the hit, and pitcher Terry committed the 2-run error with a wild pitch.

The visitors made 5 tallies in the middle innings. Cleveland responded in the seventh with 2. Morrison made first on a dropped fly, Hotaling was hit by a pitch, and Charlie Sweeney doubled them both in. Cleveland was now up 6–5.

Jim Toy singled in the eighth, and catcher Bill Greer was kind enough to give up three passed balls to allow Toy in with an insurance run.

Brooklyn, in the ninth, started trouble when Bill McClellan earned his fourth walk of the day, Jim McTammany tripled him home, and a sacrifice fly tied the game at 7. The game went into extra innings.

The two teams—between bouts of inhaling dirt—battled for twelve innings. With the players hungry, and in need of rest for game two, the 7–7 deadlock was postponed. It had taken three hours and fifteen minutes to play. It would be played out from the twelfth inning before the following day's game. Both pitchers finished all twelve innings, as did Umpire McQuaid—who, unlike the starters, still had another game to work.

Late game

Cleveland went to the bat first, and quickly roughed up John "Pa" Harkins, the Brooklyn starter. Stricker doubled, moved up on a McKean out, and scored on a Hotaling single. Sweeney, on via an error, was followed by an Allen hit, and a Reccius double. When the smoke cleared, or rather the dust, Cleveland had 4 runs. Brooklyn got 1 run back in the third off of Cleveland pitcher Hugh "One Arm" Daily.

Cleveland erased that in the fifth with the hitting highlight of the day, a Hotaling triple. He scored on a sacrifice fly moments later. Two more in the seventh and 1 in the ninth gave Cleveland 3 more and a total of 8.

Brooklyn with a run in the eighth ended their scoring for the day. Cleveland had in effect won the game in the first inning.

The parched crowd cheered as best they could.

Score: Cleveland 8, Brooklyn 2.

Time: 2 hrs.

Umpire: John McQuaid.

Attendance: 6,000.

Because of bad weather, the game against Brooklyn ended in a tie. Cleveland played 133 games (two were ties) of the 135-game schedule for 1887. No record of the Fourth of July tie game's having been played at a later date has been found.

Other Games

The home of the Blues was also the site of many amateur activities—not all of which involved baseball. In the outfield, areas were marked off for lawn tennis and cricket. And one ball game between the great Malleables and Graphics featured an extra attraction: "After the game Professor Hayden will go into the clouds in his balloon 'The Graphic.'"[19]

Located on the city's southeast side, the Beyerle Amusement Park offered boating, bowling, dancing, vaudeville shows, and, on Sunday, the best amateur baseball in town—including one contest featuring a rather interesting "amateur."

Cleveland sandlot star Bill Stemmyer reached a goal he had dreamed of since childhood, when the Boston Red Stockings of the National League added him to the pitching roster. Two years later the Boston press reported that their Red Stockings' pitcher Bill was using his right hand for more than pitching. He was pushing a pen around as an aspiring author. His writing project even had a title—*Adventures in Baxter Street*.[20] What the book was about, or if it ever saw print, is not known.

Bill, on one of his visits home to Cleveland, took part in a little charade. The Cleveland Police Department had a ball game with their brother officers from Detroit. The Cleveland police sent their "officer for a day" Bill Stemmyer to the mound. They would have succeeded at the scheme if not for the detective eye of one of the Detroit cops. In 1887 Cleveland policemen wore long-sleeve uniforms—even in warm weather. Bill's arms were sporting a very nice tan. When pressed on the matter, the Cleveland men in blue came clean—and the ringer took a seat.

Phineas T. Barnum and his freak sideshows were quite popular at this time. Ball players with disabilities appealed to this macabre interest in the unusual and unfortunate and were used as drawing cards.

The sporting crowd read:

- Sandusky signs mute catcher Ryn to a pro contract.
- Mansfield releases their one-arm pitcher England.
- Cleveland kranks are buoyed by news that Hugh "One Arm" Daily is now a Blue.

Pitcher England was gone from Mansfield, but pitcher Charley Bohn was there, and on August 21 every Mansfield krank was glad he was. The game was against Canton and Bohn pitched a beauty. He struck out nine batters, and though the other eighteen batters didn't strike out neither did they reach base. The well-known sandlot star from Cleveland had pitched a four-to-nothing perfect game!

On the city's east side, one nationality was showing its pride in being part of the American culture. Called "Germania," the new ball club was looking for games with any team willing to be beaten.

On the city's west side, the brothers Al and Tom Johnson were still supporting amateur baseball and running their streetcars to the games. Tom was a great lover of theater and loved to perform on stage himself. One of the games played this year featured his friends the Park Theatre troop. They played the Little Tycoons and won.

The nineteenth century was a time of great scientific advancement. Social progress however was much slower. Ball players were generally products of the white lower classes, and were often illiterate and superstitious. One belief, concerning race, was that young "colored" boys were good luck charms; therefore, they were often used as mascots on white teams.

With this mind-set in place, the Cleveland Blues (no one was on record as having objected) obtained the services of one such "lucky" black youth: He was "a fat colored boy who acted as mascot for the Torontos' of 1886 and the Syracuse Stars when they won the New York League pennant in 1885...[he] will be maintained as long as the team wins."[21]

The youngster was eventually replaced in a move that did not conform to the usual practice. The young son of owner Davis Hawley was made the new mascot. It is not known if Hawley Jr. was a fat white boy, but pictures of him as an adult banker show him as rather portly.

A story, based supposedly on the scientific method rather than on superstition, was drawn from the thoughts of Doc Bushong, a dentist and former Cleveland catcher: "Doc Bushong advises all ball players to wear a mustache, that is if they can. He says 'I'm positive that the shaving of the upper lip is a big drawback to a man's sight. I have watched the thing closely and I'm sure that I'm right. Take my case for instance. When I shave my upper lip it always makes my eyes discharge more or less water, and a man can't see in such a condition. The day I had my finger broken in Louisville by a pitched ball I had no mustache. It had been taken off the day before, and I truly believe this alone was the cause of the accident.'"[22]

OF LEGS, ARMS, AND EYES

Legs: Harry Doyle believed that "this alone will bring the team luck." The *this* was "a very dirty very ugly and very bow legged bull pup"— the mutt cost an astronomical two dollars.[23]

Arms: "One Arm" Daily wore a leather stub on his left arm to protect what was actually more a missing hand than arm. Daily used a short bat, because he used only his right hand for batting, and as a result his pitching hand was frequently hit. To counter this, George Howe cleverly fashioned a wire-screen hand protector; it fit well, and more importantly it worked.

The screen, however, couldn't prevent Hugh Daily from sidelining himself on a regular basis. He was as good at drinking with his right hand as he was at throwing with it.

Eyes: John "Scrappy" Carroll caught the attention of the kranks at the ballpark one sunny afternoon. The Cleveland outfielder was wearing something no one had recalled ever seeing before. He wore "a pair of colored spectacles and thinks of adopting them for good. Not a bad idea."[24]

Never on a Sunday

Cleveland management, due to legal problems, personal preferences, and strong opposition by church groups, was hesitant to introduce the American Association policy of baseball on the Sabbath. The squeeze at the box office, and the lure of large Sunday gates, had, by August, overcome any reluctance to attempt Sunday ball. The problem of management was now how best to get away with doing it.

Church groups were actively looking for ways to prevent the planned Sunday games. However, City Council, for its part, had lately passed some modifying legal language regarding Sunday entertainments.

Thinking legal loophole, or possible test case, team officials decided to stage a Sunday game at the Cleveland Driving Park. This was at the middle eastern edge of town, an area humorously referred to as "suburbia."

August 21 was a Sunday, and on that day Cleveland's first major league Sunday game was played at Cedar and East Madison (E. 79th) "before 2,500 people and in a drizzling rain."[25]

THE NEW YORK METS Versus THE CLEVELAND BLUES

METS	BLUES
Eddie Hogan, ss	Cub Stricker, 2b
Al Mays, lf	Ed McKean, ss
Charley Jones, cf	Pete Hotaling, cf
Frank Hankinson, 3b	Myron Allen, lf
James "Chief" Roseman, 1b	John "Scrappy" Carroll, rf
Jim Donahue, c	Charles "Pop" Snyder, 1b
George "Stump" Weidman, rf	Charlie Reipschlager, c
"Move Up Joe" Gerhardt, 2b	Jimmy Say, 3b
Ed Cushman, p	Hugh "One Arm" Daily, p

New York's man Hogan started the game with a walk. Following a wild pitch and a single by Mays, the Mets took a 1-run lead. Cleveland did not score in their turn.

The second inning was a disaster for Cleveland. Costly errors by Snyder and McKean were central to the visitors' 5-run outburst.

Both teams went without a run in the third, fourth and fifth. Cleveland finally scored in the sixth. Stricker was hit by a pitch, then the hero from Grafton, Ed McKean, hit a ball over the carriages parked on the racetrack. He made it to third and Stricker scored. McKean then came in on a Hotaling out.

"Pop" Snyder started the seventh with a single to right. Reipschlager, a slow runner, made second when he put the game's second ball over the carriages, driving in Snyder. Jimmy Say capped off the scoring by singling in Reipschlager.

Cleveland had kept the Mets scoreless for the last five innings, and with 4 runs was creeping up on the Mets, who had 6.

Weidman of the visitors led off the eighth with a double, and in an example of classic clutch ball, the next two men sacrificed him in for an insurance run.

The Cleveland eighth: Pete "Monkey" Hotaling led off with a grounder to Gerhardt, whose wild throw to first was an error. A wild pitch put him on second. "Scrappy" Carroll hit a light single to center, and Hotaling, unwisely, headed home and was out at the plate by yards. Carroll, on the play at home, advanced to second and then easily stole third. Snyder singled him in for Cleveland's fifth run. New York went down in the ninth, and Cleveland followed their example — and that was the game.

Score: New York Mets 7, Cleveland Blues 5.

Umpire: Al Bauer.

Inning	1	2	3	4	5	6	7	8	9	Final
New York	1	5	0	0	0	0	0	1	0	7
Cleveland	0	0	0	0	0	2	2	1	0	5

The *Plain Dealer*: "The crowd was a very respectable one and there was no unnecessary noise during the game...in the later part of the game...excitement ran high" (but not too loud).[26]

All this would seem to be fortunate from the standpoint of showing that Sunday baseball was not a raucous desecration of the Lord's Day.

However, J. C. Bachelor, a coal merchant and resident on nearby Bolton Avenue, was not impressed by the "respectable crowd" and lodged a complaint.

Lieutenant Thompson was on hand and, following orders, arrested Cub Stricker right after the last out was made, and charged him with Sunday ball playing. The case was to be tried in police court, with the Honorable John C. Hutchins acting for the defense. The ball club took care of Mr. Stricker (he missed no ball games as a result of his arrest). The press thereafter ignored the whole affair. It all had the feel of a lot of backroom maneuvering.

No more Sunday games were attempted this year. Next year would be a different story.

The Season Winds Down

Teams in their first year, or with a roster full of rookies, were often nicknamed "babes" or "babies," "infants," "colts," etc., by sportswriters. The puzzling statement "The babies have both a toy and a cub"[27] makes sense when one knows that James Toy and "Cub" Stricker are Blues players. The Cleveland "baby-infant" ball club was playing with much bigger boys. The team floundered around the basement in the standings for most of the year, eventually securing the cellar.

Most teams fielded a roster of no more than a dozen men during a season. The Blues, however, issued uniforms to twenty-six different players in 1887.

The Cleveland team had two future stars on their roster. Ed McKean in his first few seasons was noted for his hot-headed temper, and was often on the *outs* with umpires and just about everyone else. Ed settled down, and in a stellar career with Cleveland for twelve campaigns became one of the city's great stars of the nineteenth century. Many students of nineteenth-century baseball feel the great-hitting and -fielding shortstop Ed McKean has been overlooked by the Hall of Fame.

Charles "Chief" Zimmer was acquired from Rochester late in the season. He was not of Indian ancestry but rather German. The "Chief" would play ball for thirteen years in Cleveland and would be a solid .269 career hitter. His defensive skills as a catcher were often said to be second to none. He would become Cy Young's personal catcher.

The Blues played the Brown Stockings of St. Louis on October 9, a Sunday. They lost the game 6–2. It was their 92nd loss against but 39 wins. It was also the last game of the official season. Cleveland finished in last place, 54 games behind their host, pennant-winning St. Louis. The Blues stuck around the "Mound City" to watch the start of the "World Series." St. Louis eventually lost this early post-season series against the National League's Detroit "Wolverines."

Unfortunately for Cleveland, the end of the season was not the end of their year. Management had arranged a schedule of exhibition games (the local sports-writing fraternity was not impressed). In Indianapolis they split two, losing 12–0 and bouncing back with a 9–5 win.

They now had to play a contrived state championship series with Cincinnati. Three thousand showed for game one in the Queen City. Cleveland was shut out 8–0. They then lost the best-of-three series by losing game two 13–8. An unnecessary third game drew but four hundred (no score was given).

On October 19, the Cleveland "very blue" team was busy getting beaten in Pittsburgh 9–6. Cleveland came home and, in their final ball game here, beat Pittsburgh 11–8. Then once again back to Pittsburgh, where the "Smoky City" boys this time won 11–8.

Finally, the Pittsburgh rooters had enough baseball. A dwarfish crowd of one hundred watched their home team whip Cleveland 16–7. The Cleveland cut of the gate was only $3.75. There was now no more bleeding enough bucks out of the exhibition racket to go on, so management sent the men home — before it snowed.

1888

Year Two of the "Blues"

MARCH HAPPENINGS

Howard White joined the Blues' board of Frank Robison, George Howe, and Davis Hawley.

Tom Lawrence, the former groundskeeper at the Kennard Grounds and manager of the 1885 Cardinal team, was hired as superintendent of grounds for the Cleveland Base Ball Park Association Park).

Returning Cleveland manager Jimmy Williams was put in charge of the Association's transportation committee at the annual meeting of the American Association.

Harry Doyle was once again the club's media agent. Harry's job included distributing "1,500 handsome lithograph bills of the home games."[1] The large schedules contained the home games within a frame of advertisements, and were placed at all news depots and hotels within 50 miles.

The pavilion seats for the year cost $28, and for the grandstand $35. Season and individual tickets for all the games could be purchased at Secretary George Howe's office, in Room 5 in the Lehman Block; Hexter's news depot, at 303 Superior Street (near the post office); and Drake's, at 186 Superior Street.

At the end of March, Jimmy Williams took most of the ball club to his home town of Columbus, Ohio, to start training.

Cleveland outfielder Ed Hogan and catcher Charles "Pop" Snyder were already in training. They were members of a co-op team that played the Chicago White Stockings at the latter's training site in Hot Springs, Arkansas.

THE PLAYERS

A collage of pen and ink drawings, based on photographs of the Cleveland Blues ball players, appeared in one of the dailies this spring. It showed 16 of the 23 men who would play for the team this year. With the exception of pitcher "Darby" O'Brien, it included all the season regulars.

The original big group photo was on display in the window of Webb C. Hall's store. For a $2 copy, one was instructed to see Harry Doyle over at the Hawley House Hotel.

Most games played by position, and other statistics, 1888 —

	Games*	Age†	M.L. Year	At Cleve.
Pitcher: "Jersey" Edward Bakely	(p-61)	24	3rd	1st
Pitcher: "Darby" John O'Brien	(p-30)	21	1st	1st
Catcher: "Chief" Charles Zimmer	(c-59)	27	4th	2nd
Catcher: "Pop" Charles Snyder	(c-59)	33	12th	2nd
First Base: Jay Faatz	(1b-120)	27	2nd	1st
Second Base: "Cub" John Stricker	(2b-122)	28	6th	2nd
Short Stop: Ed McKean	(ss-78)	23	2nd	2nd
Third Base: Gus Alberts	(3b-49)(ss-53)	26	2nd	1st
Third Base: John McGlone	(3b-48)	?	2nd	1st
Outfield: Pete ("Monkey") Hotaling	(of-98)	31	9th	5th
Outfield: Bob Gilks	(of-87)	20	2nd	2nd
Outfield: Ed Hogan	(of-78	?	4th	1st
Outfield: Mike Goodfellow	(of-62)	21	2nd	1st
Others:				
Deacon McGuire	26 games, 17 at catcher	24	5th‡	1st
Bill McClellan	22 games, 15 in outfield	32	8th	1st
Bill Crowell	18 games at pitcher	22	2nd	2nd
Dick Van Zunt	10 games at third	?	1st	1st**
George Proesser	7 games at pitcher	23	1st	1st**
Ed Keas	6 games at pitcher	25	1st	1st**
Mike Morrison	4 games at pitcher	19	2nd	2nd
Hart Oberlander	2 pitcher; 1 first base	23	1st	1st**
Ed Knouff	2 games at pitcher	20	4th	1st
Bill Stemmyer	2 games at pitcher	24	4th	1st

* Games by position (most players also filled in a few games at other positions).
† Age — Before May 1, 1888.
‡ Deacon McGuire would play in 26 seasons.
** Only major league games.

Cleveland played a series of spring practice games with Wheeling, West Virginia.

Wheeling, Saturday, April 14: "The weather was cold and raw, but 1,000 people bravely faced it and remained till the close of game."[2] Maybe the reason they stayed was that, right from the first pitch, Cleveland was making it hot for everyone — especially Umpire Sheppard.

Led by field captain Jay Faatz, Cleveland kept up a game-long chorus of insults and bush-league antics. "There were quite a number of ladies present and they were highly incensed at the ungentlemanly conduct of the visitors."[3]

Following the game Jay Faatz was arrested and charged with disorderly conduct. Cleveland won the game 5–4, but Captain Faatz had to leave a deposit of $15 at the central police station in order to leave town that night. Faatz was fined the maximum in police court — $20 and $5.10 court cost. If he wished to play ball — or even be — in Wheeling again, he would have to pay the balance of $10.10 or risk arrest.

Inning	1	2	3	4	5	6	7	8	9	Final
Cleveland	1	2	0	0	0	0	2	0	*	5
Wheeling	0	0	0	3	0	0	0	0	1	4

Notes: • The Cleveland sandlot star Ed Delahanty played second base for Wheeling; he had a double and scored a run. • A few days before this game the *Plain Dealer* reported: "Frequenters of the base ball matches here ... will remember the bright, fair-haired little fellow who often used to play in the promenade, of the grandstand, and will as sincerely sympathize with Mr. and Mrs. Faatz in their terrible bereavement...."[4] Mrs. Faatz became so ill at the loss of her child that it was seen as the reason for the divorce of the Faatz couple some months later.

Homecoming

April 16 was a cold Cleveland Monday, but over 600 people showed up to check out the new "Blues" and comment on changes to the field of play, as well as take in a practice game between Cleveland and a picked nine.

Groundwork: The diamond was reoriented toward the south to avoid the late afternoon sun on the left side of the field (the cause of numerous errors and some collisions the year before).

The infield, once again a "skin" one (all dirt), was smooth and level. New sod had been put down behind the bases, "running back thirty feet of the line from third to second, and then crossing diagonally from second to right field, eighty feet back of first base."[5] It remained only for a few "sun baths" to make the rest of the grass-sown field a beauty.

The Blues played a practice game with a picked nine composed of four roster players and five local ball players. The "team-for-a-day" dubbed themselves the "Gymnasium."

With George Bell umpiring, the very chilly game started at 3:40 P.M.

The Blues batted first and scored early and often. No complaints were heard, from either the players or the crowd, when it was decided in the seventh inning to call the game with Cleveland ahead 15–5.

Mike Morrison and Bobby Gilks pitched for the winners, and Bill Stemmyer and "Jersey" Bakely for the losers.

Inning	1	2	3	4	5	6	7	Final
"Blues"	3	0	3	0	4	2	3	15
"Gymnasium"	1	0	0	1	3	0	0	5

Cleveland started the season on the road by losing 7 straight games. Included was the bad beating they took at Philadelphia on April 23, where Blues pitcher Bill Stemmyer (the Cleveland sandlot star) pitched the entire 27–7 loss. Cleveland was scheduled to open at home against Philadelphia on May 2. On May 1 they had a 2-and-9 record.

Before the home opener, Cleveland opened a new ballpark at the Presque Island, near Toledo, on Sunday May 1. There was a shortage of boats to transport the crowd, but 2,000 people saw Cleveland beat Toledo 4–2.

The Home Opener

The Philadelphia Athletics
Vs.
The Cleveland Blues

Cleveland, O., Wednesday, May 2, 1888: The Philadelphia team took the field. They wore a uniform of dark-blue pants, white jersey with the word ATHLETIC across the breast in light-blue letters, light-blue stockings, a white cap trimmed in blue on the top, a white belt, and a dark-blue jacket.

The Cleveland players were dressed in pants of dark-blue flannel, a shirt and cap of that same color, stockings of a darker blue than the rest, and worked on the breast of the shirt was an "Old English" letter C in black. Drake & Co., a local merchant, made the Cleveland opening-day uniforms.

Both teams wore black crepe in memory of Charles Ferguson, the 25-year-old Philadelphia League pitcher ('84 –'87), who had died April 29.

Cleveland, because of their road trip, was a bit late in getting into town, and this caused a slight delay in the start of game. At 3:40, in front of an audience of 1,000, Umpire Gaffney started the game with Cleveland at the bat.

Ed Hogan faced Philadelphia rookie pitcher Bob Gamble. It was the 20-year-old Gamble's first major league appearance, and it would prove to be his only one.

First inning: Hogan was walked and then McKean walked; second baseman Bierbauer let a Hotaling grounder slip through his fingers, allowing Hogan to reach home. McGlone flied out. Alberts drove one to right center, it got past Tom Poorman, and McKean and Hotaling crossed the plate. Number-eight batter Zimmer closed the inning with a fly out to third. Three runs.

Second inning: Hogan was hit by a pitch and stole second with a "pretty diving slide."[6] On a wild pitch he took third and kept going — with another diving slide, onto the plate, he was safe. One run.

Fifth inning: McKean led off with a single to center but was out trying to make it a double. Hotaling singled and stole second. McGlone was thrown out by shortstop Gleason. Alberts popped up the ball to outfielder Welch, who dropped it. A double by Stricker to left, followed by a double to center by Faatz, scored Hotaling, Alberts, and Stricker. Three runs.

Eighth inning: Philadelphia broke up the shutout, when Sullivan hit a triple to the left field fence and Bierbauer singled him in. One run.

Ninth inning: McKean and Hotaling singled. McGlone's fly to the outfield was caught. Gus Alberts, who was having a good game, tripled over the head of outfielder Poorman to drive in his third and fourth run for the day. Alberts scored on a sacrifice fly by Stricker. Three runs.

Philadelphia was retired without any damage in their last turn — and the people were very happy.

Score: Blues 10, Athletics 1

Inning	1	2	3	4	5	6	7	8	9	Final
Philadelphia	0	0	0	0	0	0	0	1	0	1
Cleveland	3	1	0	0	3	0	0	0	3	10

The clothier Drake also provided a second uniform and a variation to go with the outfit worn at the opener. The second uniform was one of white pants and shirt (with the "Old English" C in blue), and blue stockings and blue caps. And in June, "While the Clevelands are away on their long trip, blue and white barred caps [vertical stripes] and white stockings will be built to fit the blue uniforms."[7] (A shirt of vertical one-inch-wide blue and white stripes was also added later).

As the season progressed the uniforms took a beating, and one writer complained that the players were wearing a variety of shirts in the same game — undermining the very idea of a uniform.

Manager John Ellser of the Park Theatre invited both ball clubs to be his guests in the evening after the opening ball game. The entertainment was a performance of *Article 47*, starring Lilian Lewis as Cora.

The *Plain Dealer* review: "'Article 47'" was the play produced at the Park theatre last evening, with Miss Lillian Lewis as the wicked, heartless and vengeful Cora. Miss Lewis' conception of the part is somewhat at variance with that of the average Cora, and the text is changed by George Duhamel inflicting the wound upon Cora's throat instead of her face. This rather robs some of the most telling lines of their significance, for Cora's despair, madness and consequent action is principally caused by the horrible wound on her face, which mars her beauty. Miss Lewis' Cora is able to conceal her wound with a perfectly natural looking lace collar, which would not attract attention, while the motive of the dramatist in compelling Cora to cover her face and disfiguring her beauty is really the motive of the play. Miss Lewis' Cora is on a par artistically with her Mercy Merrick and Lena Despard. She was at her best in the third act, where she faints at the top of a flight of steps and rolls down to the floor after the fashion of Pauline L'Allemand, Margaret Mather and Grace Hawthorne. Miss Lewis' best piece of acting of the week was in the third and fourth acts, where she depicted step by step the gradual approach of madness."[8]

May notes: • A bulletin board, put up behind third base, would post the scores of all Association and League games as results came in. • A new inner fence was put up along the right field line, to be used as a controlled viewing area for the carriage trade. • At the end of the month:

"Some thieves broke into association park on Monday night and stole ten balls, several white uniforms and several pair of shoes, Crowell is shoeless."[9]

"Stem's" Story

Bill Stemmyer was born in Cleveland on May 6, 1864. He spent three years pitching for the Boston League team, winning 22 games in 1886. His first game as a Cleveland pitcher was that disastrous 28–7 loss in Philadelphia. Before that road trip was over, Manager Williams told Stemmyer to go home.

As soon as the rest of the team arrived home, Stemmyer found the team's ace pitcher, "Jersey" Bakely, and talked him into accompanying him on a little business trip to the west side.

A saloonkeeper had borrowed $100 from "Stem," and he went to the tavern to collect his money. The story told is one of Bakely and Stemmyer shaking dice at the bar, and some customer interfering with their fun by repeatedly insulting Stemmyer until he lost his temper. Whatever the truth might have been, Stemmyer was fined $25, and required to pay another $75 for the insulter's doctor bill to repair a leg broken in two places. So much for "Stem's" $100. Bakely went on to get very drunk, and in the game with St. Louis the next day gave up 18 runs on 26 hits.

Stemmyer was suspended without pay until late June. On July 13, it was reported that "Stemmyers's hand, hurt on a man's hard head, is not as strong as it once was and he has eschewed pitching and doesn't think he will play in fast company this summer."[10]

Stemmyer did some pitching for the sandlot team the Shamrocks that summer. Later in the summer, a local amusement park promoted Stemmyer as a guest pitcher for the west side Athletics team. The crowd was disappointed when he failed to show up.

After having pitched and lost but two games for Cleveland, Bill Stemmyer's major league career was over.

Two from Cleveland

Frank Knauss was a promising pitcher from Cleveland and was recommended to the Wheeling team by their catcher, Cleveland sandlot star Ed Delahanty. The two men, who lived near each other in the downtown St. Clair neighborhood, enjoyed playing professional ball together for Wheeling until May 17, when they were separated after a game at Toledo.

Delahanty was the toast of the "Nail City" (Wheeling), where it was said "[he] has as much pie as he can eat."[11] With a batting average of .450 he became the "apple of the eye" of Al Reach, the Philadelphia League team owner, who was in Toledo on May 17. At the end of the day, Delahanty was a new major leaguer on his way to Chicago, to play a game as a member of the Philadelphia Phillies team. The Reach purchase of the Delahanty contract from Wheeling would turn out to be one of the best baseball decisions any buyer of ball players ever made.

The revolving door

At the end of May, Cleveland was in sixth place. A few days later the *Plain Dealer* counseled: "If a good pitcher can be found it will pay the local club to buy him, even though the price be high. With reliable pitchers the Cleveland team will make an important showing in the association race."[12]

An attempt to sign pitcher Ed Beatin of Allentown, Pa., failed when Detroit (NL) refused to give up rights on him.

Following the death of a sister in Cleveland, Billy Bohn, the Cleveland native, was given his release from Charleston, South Carolina. He failed to show up for a tryout with Cleveland, so was not signed. He joined Sandusky for a short time, but was released — an ongoing drinking problem blamed.

On June 18, Cleveland paid Lima of the Tri-State League $3,000 for the services of a pitcher with 17 wins in 19 tries, and an earned run average under 1.00. His name was John F. O'Brien.

Outfielder William D. O'Brien played for Brooklyn (AA). His nickname was "Darby." Within a few weeks of his joining Cleveland, the *Plain Dealer* had turned John F. O'Brien into the American Association's second "Darby" O'Brien.

Cleveland tried to help its pitching situation further by releasing and adding more pitchers. They got rid of Bill Crowell (18 games, 5–13) on July 18. Ed Knauff was obtained from St. Louis (AA) on July 21— Knauff's Cleveland record would be 0–1 in 2 games. On June 22 it was learned that Bill Stemmyer had been released. Ed Keas came to Cleveland from the Dubuque, Iowa, team August 16 — Keas' final Cleveland record was 3–3 in 6 games.

However, "Jersey" Bakely (61 games) and "Darby" O'Brien (31 games) were the mainstays of the staff, appearing in 91 of the 132 official games played. Ten others helped with the pitching chores on the year.

The Newsboys' Championship

"The object for which the newsboys' league was organized is to raise a fund to improve the newsboys' homes in the different cities."[13] These homes served as a half-way home/orphanage for many of the paperboys, who needed such help in supporting themselves. The players themselves were not required to be newsboys, and were generally drawn from the ranks of the best amateur youths in each town.

The *Plain Dealer* sponsored the Cleveland team, and did much to promote their charity game at the Cleveland Base Ball Park. Other cities sponsoring teams in the newsboys' league were Rochester, Syracuse and Albany in New York State, as well as Boston, Massachusetts, and Detroit, Michigan — the reigning champion and the visiting club for the fund-raiser in Cleveland June 18.

The sponsors and the boys in each city took the championship game quite seriously. The sponsors had their newspaper's and city's pride to consider, and the boys had bragging rights for motivation. The boys' team that became national champion also became custodian of the beautiful N. S. Wood cup, and would remain in charge of it until defeated.

Professional ball players in the individual cities were training many of the young teams. Jay Faatz put the Cleveland team under his personal tutelage. Someone even suggested that extra training — at night under electric lights—would improve the boys' chances.

In Cleveland, the *Plain Dealer* team was given two extra incentives: They would be given a percentage of the gate receipts, and would compete for "the Holden pennant, a handsome banner of red silk and bullion trimmed, offered by President L. E. Holden of the PLAIN DEALER company."[14]

Brainard's Band started playing in front of the *Plain Dealer* office at one in the afternoon, with the newsboys gradually gathering behind and in front of the musicians, until their numbers reached five hundred. The band then moved out over the parade route, with the boys falling in behind; next came the large bus carrying the two teams, followed by a number of hired hacks conveying officials.

The procession proceeded "along Water and Superior streets and on the square and Euclid avenue crowds of people watched the boys as they yelled along and enjoyed themselves hugely."[15] The parade arrived at the ballpark at 2:20 P.M.

The players took the field and practiced hard. The Detroit uniform was light gray with green trimmings, and under their light-gray shirts they wore white ones. The Cleveland outfit was gray with wine-colored hats, belts, and stockings. Cleveland, however, exchanged their gray shirts for comfortable white ones just before the start of play.

Wakefield, the Detroit manager, protested that some of the *Plain Dealer* boys were over age — Robert P. Bell, O'Brien and E. C. Murphy sat down. When Tom Delahanty, Stanford, and Gaffney were offered in their place, the visiting manager agreed to play the game.

The crowd of 1,500 started clapping as Umpire Joe Carr received Wakefield's lineup card. Carr glanced at it quickly, checked his watch, and shortly thereafter called for start of game at 3:30 P.M. exactly.

Batting orders

Detroit Journal	*Plain Dealer*
J. Cohen, 1b	Tom Delahanty, 3b
McDonald, p & ss	John McMahon, ss
Kellogg, cf	William Bell, 2b
Dinsmore, 3b	J. Kiernan, 1b
Darsey, rf	Ed Cuddy, c
J. Gallagher, ss & p	E. Horan, cf
Sheehan, 2b	Stanford, rf
B. Cohen, lf	Gaffney, lf
Downer, c	M. Gallagher, p

First inning: Delahanty led off with a single to left, McMahon beat out a hot one to J. Gallagher at short, who helped with a bad throw to first. Billy Bell smacked a triple to left for two runs and scored on a wild pitch. Cleveland: Three runs.

Third inning: Delahanty, leading off, singled; McMahon walked, and Bell got a base when McDonald messed up a pop fly. With the sacks filled, Kiernan's out brought in Delahanty, then Cuddy singled to plate McMahon, and when he went for a steal of second, the bad throw of catcher Downer let Bell score the final run of the inning. Cleveland: Three runs

Fourth inning: Gaffney walked, stole second, moved to third on Downer's bad throw, and came home on a Delahanty single. Cleveland: One run.

Errors by Delahanty, Gaffney, and Cuddy allowed Kellogg, Darsey, and Sheehan to score — the last two named also having had singles. Detroit: Three runs.

Fifth inning: Cuddy was safe on a grounder to short that was muffed at first. Horan singled him over, Cuddy then stole third and came around to score on a hit by Stanford into short left field. Cleveland: One run.

Sixth inning: Kellogg made first when McMahon threw his grounder wild. Delahanty botched a Sheehan ground ball, Darsey singled to right; another wild throw by McMahon, and a wild pitch by Gallagher, sent Kellogg and Sheehan in. Detroit: Two runs. M. gallagher and McMahon scored for Cleveland, two runs.

Seventh inning: A throwing error by McMahon, and two more by Delahanty on grounders, plated Kellogg. Detroit: One run.

Eighth inning: Catcher Cuddy dropped a third strike, giving Sheehan a base. A passed ball, and a scratch hit to left by Downer, brought Sheehan around. Detroit: One run. Ninth inning: No scoring.

Final score: Cleveland 11, Detroit 7.

Inning	1 2 3	4 5 6	7 8 9	Final
Plain Dealers	3 0 3	1 1 2	0 1 0	11
Evening Journals	0 0 0	3 0 2	1 1 0	7

Time of game: two hours. Umpire: Joseph Carr of the Shamrocks.

The Fourth of July

Two games at Kansas City. If you made the mistake of sneaking into the Kansas City "Cowboys" ballpark by climbing over the ten-foot fence, you would find yourself at the bottom of a forty-foot pit — fifty if you counted the height of the fence.

Center field had a pile of rocks along its length — forty feet high — to hold up that part of the hole. The right side was made of the rock that had been blasted back to widen the park.

Behind the grandstand was a pond, held back by a clay bank, that diverted water to keep the grounds from turning into a swimming pool. When the weather was warm, the heat made the park one very hot hole to be in — and the grounds themselves were very rough too.

Cleveland lost the morning game 8–5. They lost the afternoon game 14–10. At the end of the day, Cleveland had a record of 19 wins and 37 losses — which had them in sixth place, two spots above the cellar.

Amos and Jimmy

Amos Cross, a catcher by trade, was the third Cleveland resident sandlotter to enter the big leagues (Louisville, AA, '85–'87). Charlie Bohn, p (Louisville, AA, '82) was the first Clevelander in the major leagues, Sim "Derby" Bullas, c (Toledo, AA, '84) was the second.

Amos Cross was also the first, and oldest, of Cleveland's first group of brothers to play in the major leagues. He was also the first major leaguer born in Czechoslovakia; his brothers were born in Cleveland. Brother Lave Cross played in the major leagues for 21 seasons (1887–1907); brother Frank Cross played for Cleveland (AL, 1901); and Joe Cross, another brother, never played in the major leagues but was a local star.

It was reported that Amos had sustained an injury while working out in a gymnasium early in 1887, and that his lungs were affected. This was believed to have been the cause of consumption (tuberculosis) setting in.

Amos was sent home to his family home on Clark Avenue to recover. On July 16, brother Lave, who had replaced Amos as the Louisville catcher, was summoned home — his brother was near death. Amos Cross died that same day. He was 25 years old.

"Cleveland, July 18. Amos Cross, the old catcher of the Louisville club is dead.... He was especially noted for his throwing to second, sending the ball down like a rifle shot, and few runners were able to steal the base on him.... Manager Davidson, of the Louisville Club, at once telegraphed Director Hawley, of the Cleveland Club, to have an elegant design of flowers made with the description — 'From the Louisville Team.'"[16]

Jimmy Williams, the 41-year-old Cleveland manager, resigned in mid–July; a number of things forced his hand.

Personal family matters: The manager's wife was in ill health, and a few days earlier, his father, Dr. James Williams, age 66, had passed away at home in Mechanicsville, Ohio.

On the field: The "Blues" under Williams had an abysmal record of 19 and 41.

Williams retained a 20 percent interest in the Cleveland franchise, and was expected to get the job of secretary in the Association's office in Columbus. Instead, in August, the Columbus office of the Ohio Centennial Commission hired him.

At the July 17 game Jimmy Williams officially handed over the reins of the team to 31-year-old Tom Loftus, who had been with the Dubuque, Iowa, team.

Williams, popular with his players, was in the estimation of many of the baseball pundits too easy-going. Loftus was expected to wield a tougher whip, and indeed Loftus' winning percentage, for the balance of the season, would end up 100 points higher than that of the man he replaced.

Playing Fields

Brookside

The Albions ball club was one of the best teams around. This year, and for quite a few more, they made the area of today's zoo, in the Brookside Park valley, their playing site. In 1888 they played on a parcel of land called the Foster's grounds.

Newberg

The sports-minded people of the city of Newberg, in June, organized "The Newberg Athletic Company."[17] A charter with the state allowed them to form a stock company. Shares numbering 2,500 were offered at $1 each; within days 1,300 had been grabbed up.

Shortly thereafter, a site was secured a half-mile from Broadway at the west end of Howard Street, and ten acres were leased for ten years at a very modest price. Plans called for grounds surrounded by a ten-foot-high "tight-board" fence.[18] The multi-use facility was to have a grandstand, racetrack, and baseball and cricket grounds. The in-house ball team was to be composed of the best players who lived in Newberg. A big hoopla was planned to open the grounds on the Fourth of July.

Beyerle Park

Baseball, presented throughout the week at the Beyerle Amusement Park, was a recent addition to the park's many activities. It featured the best sandlot teams around, and on Sunday the City League played their games there. Somehow this Cleveland-located business was able to skirt the city law against Sunday ball playing. This situation would have some interesting consequences later in the summer.

Black ball

The Z team, managed by Charles Black, was the best "colored" team in town; they challenged any nine in the city to a ball game. They could be contacted through their business manager — Charles Black, Public Square. A team named Zulu appeared in print, once, before the Z team did. The name Zulu may have been, for political reasons, changed to Z by the papers. The Zulu warriors of Africa, at this time, were quite controversial from a white point of view.

The Walker brothers were the only black men to play in major league baseball in the nineteenth century. They played in 1884 for the Toledo Blue Stockings of the American Association. They also played for Cleveland-area companies and minor-league teams. Moses Fleetwood Walker, now of the Syracuse Stars, was said to have taken exception to a remark from a spectator at a game in Toronto, and as a result was taken into custody by two policemen. He reportedly was about to pull a gun at the time of the incident. He had to post bail at the police station. Weldy Walker, a recent manager of the independent Pittsburgh Keystones, was released from his job after accusations of fixing a game at Butler, PA; he shortly thereafter returned to his family's home in Steubenville, Ohio.

Heat Stroke and Yellow Fever

Cleveland started August in sixth place with a 29 and 48 record, but Tom Loftus had his team playing close to .500 ball since taking over as manager. What he didn't need now was to lose his number two pitcher, "Darby" O'Brien.

It was a very hot day in Cincinnati on Friday, August 3, 1888. O'Brien pitched the whole pot-boiler of a game, but afterwards he was seized with cramps and was taken to the team's residence at the Grand Hotel. He had no appetite for supper and retired to his room.

Zimmer, the catcher, checked up on him an hour later, and found him lying on the bed, unconscious and breathing heavily. Dr. Minor was rushed to the hotel, and before long he requested that a priest be summoned. It took an hour, but the doctor brought a very weak O'Brien around. O'Brien was lucky. He had survived a very bad case of heat stroke. He would pitch again after some days' rest — but he had scared everyone.

Less fortunate than O'Brien were the victims of the yellow fever outbreak in Jacksonville, Florida. A benefit ball game was organized to help. It would be played at the Cleveland Base Ball Park in late September. The game, planned for a Sunday (for a larger gate) would allow Mr. Frank Robison to make a political statement concerning Sunday ball, as well as perform a charitable act. He also allowed the event organizers free use of the grounds.

Despite resident opposition, the benefit game between the Hudsons and Shamrocks went on, the latter winning 3–0.

The *Plain Dealer*, on September 29, received a letter from Mayor C. B. Smith of Jacksonville, acknowledging the receipt of $130 and thanking the teams and individuals involved for their help. The newspapermen, from their game later, also sent money to Florida.

The Newspaper Funnies

Proceedings of the Board of
Councilmen
OFFICIAL
Petitions.
Sept. 17, 1888. To the Honorable Board of Councilmen:
GENTLEMEN: your presence at the base ball contest between the daily and weekly newspaper men at association park on Tuesday afternoon, Sept. 18, is earnestly requested.

The grand stand will be open to you and a coterie of slaves will attend to your every requirement.

> Elmer E. Bates
> Sam T. Hughes
> Charles P. Salen
> Committee[19]

In the manner of a "muffin" game, the newspapermen put on an annual comical championship game.

"There was a funny scene in the first inning. Bates pitched a ball that hit the backstop. It was called a ball whereupon the entire nine rushed in from the field, protesting the decision, which Umpire Athey promptly reversed and then, seizing a huge musket, drove the fielders back to their positions."[20]

The weeklies won the game and the championship banner.

"After the game Dr. Arthur Ware amused the audience with a number of remarkably clever card tricks without the assistance of apparatus."[21]

Inning	1	2	3	4	5	6	7	Final
Weeklies	4	3	2	1	5	7	6	28
Dailies	2	1	1	0	1	5	3	13

WEEKLIES	DAILIES
Tello, 2b	Bell, c
Ganz, c	Foster, 2b
Dewald, c	Hughes, ss
Ewell, 3b	Wright, 3b
Hall, lf	Goggin, 2b
Salen, 1b	McCoy, lf
Rob'n, cf	Williams, 1b
O'Neil, rf	Wald'ke, cf
Buffett, ss	Mul'y, p & rf
Byrne, p	Bates, p & rf
Rose, p	

Cleveland weekly newspapers: *World, Universe, Grip, Graphic, Town Topics, Sun & Voice,* and *Cuyahogan.*

Cleveland daily newspapers: *Herald, Leader, Plain Dealer,* and *Press.*

Sunday Ball at Geauga Lake

Cleveland, finally, got around to following the policy of the American Association by playing games on Sunday.

Mr. Kent, owner of the Geauga Lake picnic grounds resort (the same place as today's well-known amusement park), had been staging amateur Sunday games, and he proposed to build a new ball grounds where the Cleveland Blues could play Sunday games. Cleveland eventually agreed, and the first Sunday game was scheduled against Baltimore on July 22.

Plans called for a 550-foot-square fenced ballpark, with a "skin" (dirt) diamond, and bleacher stands for 6,000. However, only 2,000 seats were up by game day, but another 1,500 were promised for the following week's game.

For those coming from Cleveland, the New York, Pennsylvania, and Ohio Rail Road (N.Y., P. & O., nicknamed Nypano) offered a 75-cent round trip train ticket and admission to the ball game. The Nypano depot, on Water Street, sold the special yellow tickets. The company advertised trains for the 22 mile ride to the 3:00 P.M. game leaving at 9:30 A.M., 10:45 A.M., 12:15 P.M., and 1:15 P.M.

The 1:15 P.M. train was late in being hooked up and those people arrived at the start of the third inning. The crowd of 3,500 included 400 ladies. The trains brought 2,500.

BALTIMORE	CLEVELAND
"Oyster" Burns, lf	"Cub" Stricker, 2b
"Blondie" Purcell, rf	Ed McKean, ss
Mike Griffin, cf	Jay Faatz, 1b
Jack ("Moose") Farrell, 2b	Pete ("Monkey") Hotaling, cf
Chris Fulmer, c	Bob Gilks, lf
Tommy Tucker, 1b	Mike Goodfellow, rf
Bill Greenwood, ss	John McGlone, 3b
Bill Shindle, 3b	"Pop" Snyder, c
"Phenomenal" Smith, p	"Jersey" Bakely, p

Cleveland led off. Stricker grounded out pitcher to first, McKean grounded out second to first, and Faatz flied out to Purcell in right. Baltimore started the scoring in the bottom of the inning. Burns went out short to first, Purcell then hit a single past McKean, Bakely walked Griffin, Farrell beat out a hit to second that scored Purcell and put Griffin at third — from where he scored on a passed ball. Two runs.

Cleveland got rolling in the third. McGlone popped out to first. "Phenomenal" Smith now hit a streak of wildness— in succession, he loaded the bases by hitting Snyder and walking Bakely and Stricker. A McKean grounder past third brought in Snyder and Bakely. A Faatz single past second brought in Stricker and McKean; Faatz then stole second and also third, but a fly out to second base, and another to left field, left him stranded. Four runs.

Cleveland earned a tally in the sixth, when Hotaling hit a double, stole third, and — not waiting for any help — stole home. One run.

The sixth and final Cleveland run, an unearned run, came in the eighth. Greenwood, at short, juggled a Faatz grounder, then made his problems worse with a wild throw to first, allowing Faatz to get to third, from where he scored on a Hotaling ground out to first. One run.

Baltimore led off the ninth with a Purcell single, but he was out trying to make second. Griffin beat out a single he hit at the second baseman. But then: "Farrell struck out and Snyder caught Griffin napping at first, ending the game 6–2 in favor of the home nine."[22]

Inning	1 2 3	4 5 6	7 8 9	Final
Cleveland	0 4* 0*	0 0 1	0 1 0	6
Baltimore	2 0 0	0 0 0	0 0 0	2

* The only written recapitulation of Cleveland's 4-run inning states that those runs scored in the third. The box score in that paper and another show those runs scoring in the second inning.

Notes: • The trains were advertised to leave right after the game, but they waited an hour. The company promised better service in the future. • The next day, Monday, the Nypano railroad company held a company picnic at Geauga Lake. Over six thousand attended.

The opposition to the Sunday games was strongest in the nearby towns. The *Chagrin Falls Exponent* reported on some of the pro and con sentiments over the Sunday games:

• An injunction to stop the games is being talked.[23]

• There is considerable kicking over these Sunday games, it being held by many that there are enough days in the week for base ball besides Sunday.

- The advocates of Sunday ball claim that it brings thousands out of the city where they can spend a day in pure air and away from saloons and other low influences.

The *Exponent* had announced earlier that the Kent House at the Geauga Park had voluntarily stopped serving alcohol (local religious forces, promoting prohibition and opposing Sunday ball, hailed the move).

Though claiming to be neutral concerning Sunday ball, the *Exponent* promoted a Saturday, July 28th, game in Chagrin Falls—the day before the second Sunday American Association game at Geauga Lake—as an alternative. The sandlot game between a Cleveland team from Kinsman Street and the Chagrin Falls "Invincibles" would cost only a dime and be played at the Washington Park grounds managed by the home club.

THE ST. LOUIS BROWNS VERSUS THE CLEVELAND BLUES

Geauga Lake, Ohio, July 29—

The second Sunday game of 1888 was over in the first two innings. The poor fielding and throwing of the Blues gave the Browns four unearned runs of the five scored in the first. St. Louis added two more in the second. "Darby" O'Brien allowed no more runs the rest of the way, but it was too late. "Silver" King kept Cleveland off the board till the last innings, when Cleveland managed 2 runs, but the umpire was blamed for killing a rally in the ninth, by cheating Cleveland out of 1 run and at least one hit. Final: St. Louis Browns 7, Cleveland Blues 2.

The crowd was estimated at 3,500 including 400 ladies.

Notes: • The *Cleveland Leader*: "No one doubts [umpire] Ferguson's honesty.... It's eyesight that we complain about."[24] • Umpire Ferguson: "One day they will give you a ride in a chariot, and the next day they will drive the chariot over you."[25]

After a few weeks' absence a third Sunday game was played at Geauga Lake. It would be the last.

A few days earlier, on Thursday, a seven-inning exhibition game composed of sandlotters and some Blues backup players was played against the St. Louis Browns. Because of the Knights of Labor picnic the exhibition game had a good gate. Score: Cleveland 7, St. Louis 6.

Another Sunday-alternative sandlot game was played in Chagrin Falls between the strong Cleveland "Browns" and Chagrin Falls "Invincibles."

SUNDAY: GEAUGA LAKE, OHIO, AUGUST 26, 1888

St. Louis Browns versus Cleveland Blues:

Cleveland, in the second, got a hit from Bobby Gilks, who stole second, moved up on an Alberts out, and was singled home by Zimmer. With two outs, Cleveland had the bases full, and "Cub" Stricker came to the plate. He hit a fly ball—but it was caught. One run. The scoring started in the fourth for St. Louis, when "Jersey" Bakely walked Arlie ("The Freshest Man on Earth") Latham and "Yank" Robinson. Both men then scored on "Tip" O'Neill's triple. Two runs. In the seventh, Charles ("The Old Roman") Comiskey tripled, followed by scratch singles from Harry Lyons and Jack ("Honest Jack") Boyle to load the bases. Then a passed ball, by new catcher "Chief" Zimmer, allowed Comiskey and Lyons in. Two runs. St. Louis, in the eighth, earned their last run on singles by O'Neill and Comiskey, and a sacrifice fly by McCarthy. One run. Cleveland, in the ninth, scored a run when Hotaling and Gilks singled, and Lyons and Latham made errors, allowing Hotaling to come in—but that was the end of the scoring. One run.

Ball game: St. Louis 5–2.

Inning	1	2	3	4	5	6	7	8	9	Final
Cleveland	0	1	0	0	0	0	0	0	1	2
St. Louis	0	0	0	2	0	0	2	1	0	5

The Cleveland directors were not pleased with the crowd of only 1,000 at the third Geauga Sunday game. They were seriously thinking of taking up the proposition by the owner of the

Beyerle Park Amusement Company to move the games there — starting Sunday next, against the Louisville "Colonels." Since the park was in Cleveland, and the City League had been playing Sunday games there since April, and the public was being charged to attend, it was felt that the law could not stand in the way of the Blues' making it their Sunday site too.

Beyerle Park

An 1886 ad:

G. WM. BEYERLE
owner and proprietor of
BEYERLE'S PARK,
    office —
    13 PUBLIC SQUARE, ROOM 3.
    telephone 1839.

For the information of Families, Social Parties, Societies, Sunday Schools and Churches that it is no longer necessary to travel fifty or one hundred miles to reach a suitable and beautiful place for a Picnic or Excursion. I have built this park as such a place. It is situated only three miles south of the public square, near Independence and Petrie Streets, and contains over thirty acres, consisting of beautiful woods, adorned by walks, promenades and buildings, pavilion and tower; of valleys beautified by an artificial lake, which has an area of over seven acres; of hills, which are connected by bridges crossing the lake, one of the bridges being 300 feet in length and 60 feet above the surface of the lake. There will be twelve new boats on the lake, kept ready for the pleasure seeking public. The pavilion is a very large building and will accommodate 5,000 people, it is carefully built, with a first class floor for dancing and skating. The tower will rise fifty feet above the highest spot in the grounds, wherefrom the public can get a beautiful view of Lake Erie, and the romantic surroundings.

The Connotton Valley Depot, at Independence Street is seven minutes walk distant. On short notice, conveyances will be furnished from any point direct to the park, at reasonable prices. The Park adequately supplies a long needed want of our citizens, and I intend, year by year, to add to its beauties, curiosities and attractions.

Any inquires will receive prompt attention by writing, telephoning or calling at the above address.[26]

LOUISVILLE VERSUS CLEVELAND

The ball grounds were located north of the artificial lake in the middle of the park. The fenced-in grounds were small and the seating was very limited. Most of the crowd of three thousand stood around the area of play, unrestrained by ropes or police.

There were no official ground rules for the game. When McKean hit an easy fly into the crowd in right, he rounded the bases. Louisville protested the unfairness of it, so it was agreed he would return to second base so that the game might continue.

Pitcher Bakely hit the ball over the short right field fence, where it landed in the lake near the steam yacht, but this time the round-tripper was allowed to stand. It was Bakely's only home run for the year. "Hub" Collins hit the only home run for the "Colonels" — a two-run blast in the eighth over the left field fence.

Cleveland native Lave Cross was the visitors' shortstop. When he slid into first base, in the fifth, he cut his knee and lodged a pebble in the wound — he left the game and was expected to miss some playing time.

Final: Cleveland 11 Louisville 4.

Inning	1 2 3	4 5 6	7 8 9	Final
Cleveland	1 0 1	0 4 0	4 0 1	11
Louisville	0 1 0	0 0 1	0 2 0	4

Winner: "Jersey" Bakely —11 hits; 6 strikeouts; 3 walks. Loser: "Toad" Ramsey — 23 hits; 8 strikeouts; 3 walks. Time: 2:23. Substitute Umpire: William T. Crowell, former Cleveland Blues pitcher. (The Association's regular umpire, Bob Ferguson, was a no-show.)

There was a second Sunday game played at Beyerle Park the next week against the Kansas City "Cowboys." There was, however, a problem:

> Tom Loftus tried hard to have the game counted as a championship contest, but the Kansas City management evidently anticipating the defeat that they suffered refused to play anything but an exhibition game, so the Cleveland victory does not count in their Association record.[27]
>
> Secretary Clough refused to play a championship game. Permission to do so had not come from President Wikoff and without it Cleveland could not insist. So an exhibition game was played.[28]

Inning	1 2 3	4 5 6	7 8 9	Final
Cleveland	3 0 0	0 0 0	1 3 0	7
Kansas City	2 1 0	0 0 2	0 0 0	5

A crowd of 2,000 saw Cleveland win an exhibition game instead of a real one, as had been advertised. The Cleveland game with Louisville was to be the only major league game ever played at Beyerle Park.

Lave Is Lost

The Cross family was quite upset when word reached their home at No. 668 Clark Avenue in October that Lave Cross was missing—especially after the death of son and brother Amos that past July.

During a reporter's interview, a sister said he had recently sent some quail home, and that they were tending the birds till his return. When questioned further about a girl in Louisville named Emma Hyberger, the sister said that, at 22, Lave was too young to marry, and that she had heard that "he had given her up."[29]

Lave in love: The family got a message from Ed Seward, a Clevelander playing for the Philadelphia AA team. Lave was in Philadelphia, and while there had eloped with the now former Miss Hyberger. In 1889, Lave Cross would play for Philadelphia's Association team.

The Cleveland Blues closed out their final season in Cleveland with a number of East Coast games, including a few on Sundays:

Sunday, October 7, Ridgewood Park (in New Jersey): Brooklyn 8, Cleveland 4—crowd 7,000.

Sunday, October 15, Glouchester, New Jersey: Philadelphia 7, Cleveland 3 (a six-inning game).

The playing season was reaching an obvious end when only 84 people showed up to watch Cleveland lose at Baltimore 7–4.

1888 American Association Standings

	W	L	GB
STL	92	43	—
BKN	88	52	6.5
PHI	81	52	10
CIN	80	54	11.5
BAL	57	80	36
CLE	**50**	**82**	**40.5**
LOU	48	87	44
KC	43	89	47.5

1889

Hot Springs, Arkansas

A distant bugle sounds—then again, closer. Down the tracks, at the edge of town, rolls a big double-pump handcar. A man up front waves a large American flag, while another in back lets out another bugle blast. Between them sits a group of uniformed men. They roll into town. Someone yells out: "Look! It's the Cleveland baseball club." And it was! On through town and back they ride, and all along the way, they wave, smile, and call out to the people—"Hey! Come watch us play ball today."

Switching sides

In 1886 Detroit spent a lot of money to land the contracts of Jack Rowe, "Deacon" White, and "Big Dan" Brouthers a future Hall-of-Famer. Added to their man "Big Sam" Thompson, Detroit had what was called baseball's "big four." The team finished second, but in 1887 the four led Detroit to its first pennant. The following year, the same high-priced team finished fifth. After that season, Detroit went out of the baseball business.

Cleveland won the right to replace Detroit in the National League—a circuit many considered more prestigious than the American Association—while Columbus took Cleveland's place in the American Association.

Cleveland did not sign any of the "big four," but they did pay for the rights to eight Detroit players. Four of the eight would make the team.

In March, it was hard to find people connected with Cleveland baseball anywhere near Cleveland. Director George Howe was in Europe with NL President Albert Spalding's showcase tour of American ball players. And Frank Robison, team president, was busy in Washington, D.C., at the winter meetings of the National League.

While attending a party in Washington, at the Welkers, Mr. Robison and the other baseball magnates met a Mr. Halford, the private secretary of a government official. Later that evening Mr. Halford escorted them all over to his boss's house—the White House, where they met and shook hands with President Benjamin Harrison.

On March 11, the Cleveland team, under the leadership of returning manager Tom Loftus, arrived by train in St. Louis, where they spent the night at the Lindell House. The travelers switched rail lines in the morning, and within a day the men rode into Hot Springs, where they settled in at their home base—the Plateau Hotel. Workouts started almost immediately.

Training tales

Jim Buckley was a pitcher of average talent, but an above-average ego when it came to the ladies. He went to camp with the Cleveland team, but during the trip, his trunk full of lady-killer clothes was "[lost] out in the wilds between Malvern Junction and El Paso,"[1] joked the *Plain Dealer*. For two weeks he wore what outfits he could put together. Jim was described as looking like a poor white dressed in clothes that looked part Ohio ball player, part Cleveland dandy, and part Arkansas farmer. His sullen mood improved when his luggage arrived—but his pitching didn't.

Welch was a young Cleveland sandlotter whom the team took along so he could study how to be a ball player. Welch showed that he was not one to be easily rattled. At the Plateau, during dinner, Darby O'Brien passed Welch a bottle of vinegar, and said: "Have some maple syrup."[2] Welch then smothered his full plate of pancakes with the vinegar, and ate every one of them as if absolutely nothing was wrong! The veterans were impressed.

The seating at the first spring training game at Hot Springs cost 25 cents to stand, 50 cents to sit on a wooden plank, and a whole dollar for a comfortable chair in the grandstand. The 800 people present all enjoyed the game.

Inning	1 2 3	4 5 6	7 8 9	Final
Cleveland	1 0 0	2 2 1	3 0 *	9
"Picked Nine"	0 0 2	0 0 2	0 0 2	6

Jayhawkers and "Globetrotters"

Following a few weeks of a tough and thorough exercise schedule, and some practice games, the team left Hot Springs at the start of April. A series of exhibition games were played as the team slowly worked its way back north to Cleveland. During a Missouri stop-over, a bush-league team embarrassed Cleveland. The loss inspired a St. Louis writer to pen this little gem:

The *Cleveland Leader*:

> The Cleveland 'Hand Me Downs' went to St. Joe after the series with Kansas City, and St. Joe gave them a grand razzle-dazzle, defeating them by a score of 3–1. This Cleveland team is none other than the one, which in the minds of the Cleveland writers, is going to win the League pennant, and smash Chicago, Boston, and New York into smithereens. Any man who is so short sighted as to place Cleveland well up in the League race should wear telescopes on his eyes for a century or two. The remains of the representative ball players of the Lake Erie grease spot will be here in a few days to meet the Browns on the field of honor. Before they arrive here they will meet the St. Joe team, and the boys of the latter organization have promised to send the Cleveland jayhawkers down to St. Louis in nice coffins and a refrigerating car. The Cleveland club has a special refrigerating car of their own in which they travel the entire season in order to keep fresh. The Cleveland club is very strong; so strong in fact that the health authorities will have them quarantined and disinfected before allowing them to enter the town. ['Extracts from the Printing of the Precocious and Vulgar Infant who wastes Good Lead Pencils on a Kindling Wood Sheet Known as the *St. Louis Sayings*.']"[3]

Cleveland may have gotten back to Ohio a bit too soon. On April 15, in front of 500 shivering Mansfield faithful, they won 11–1. A few days later, they played in front of a crowd of 800 at Canton's Pastime Park, defeating Canton in a close game 4–3.

Clevelanders were given a quick glance at their new National League team when the Milwaukee team of the Western Association dropped into Cleveland for a game April 18. The 1,000 people who went through the gates saw the hometown club win 3–1.

"The Globetrotters"

Al Spalding's tour of Europe with American ball players ended. An exhibition tour of American cities to welcome the conquering heroes home was arranged. It would go from New York to Chicago. On April 17, it came to Cleveland. The "Globetrotters" or the "Tourists" were newspaper names used to refer to the Spalding baseball show. The teams were the regular Chicago White Stockings, and an all-star selection called All America. Six of the players would become members of baseball's Hall of Fame. Advance tickets to see this early form of an all-star game went on sale at Van Epps the week before game day. After playing in Pittsburgh the day before, the team reached Cleveland in the forenoon of Wednesday April 17. Local baseball men took them to the well-known Weddell House for refreshing. A few hours later, the players paraded the principal streets with a band. At three o'clock they entered the ballpark to the cheers of the huge crowd of 4,000 (only Boston had turned out more).

Batting orders

CHICAGO	ALL AMERICA
Jimmy Ryan, ss	Ned Hanlon, cf*
Marty Sullivan, lf	John Montgomery Ward, ss*
Hugh Duffy, rf*	Tom Brown, cf
"Cap"("Pop") Adrian Anson, c*	Fred Carroll, 1b
Fred ("Dandelion") Pfeffer, 2b	George ("Dandy") Wood, 3b
"Oyster" Thomas Burns, 3b	Jim Fogarty, lf
Fred Tenney, 1b	Jimmy Manning, 2b
Tom Daly, cf	Billy ("The Little Globetrotter") Earle, c
"Lady" Charles Baldwin, p	"Cannonball" Edward Crane, p

* Member of the Baseball Hall of Fame.

Chicago batted first but failed to score. Hanlon then led off for All America with a slow grounder that the pitcher couldn't handle. Ward sent Hanlon to third but was out trying to stretch a single into a double. "Lady" Baldwin next let loose with a wild pitch and a run scored. Brown followed with a walk, stole second, and scored on a single to center by Carroll to give All America a 2-run lead.

Pfeffer walked, advanced on a wild pitch, and came home on two sacrifice outs to give Chicago its first tally in the second. All America went scoreless in the bottom of the frame.

In the top of the third inning, Chicago was kept off the boards, but All America, in its turn, put up its third run when Brown thrilled the crowd with a long home run to center.

Both teams drew blanks in the fourth.

"Cannonball" Crane had allowed but 1 run on three hits through four innings, "but in the fifth he got a dose of the rattles, gave the Chicagos four bases on balls and almost as many hits and chances to win the game — advantages taken and held to the end of the game."[4] The Chicago advantages taken in the fifth added up to 6 runs.

All America added a final run in the eighth when Jimmy Wood knocked a triple to center field, and scored on an out by Manning.

It wasn't the greatest game ever seen in Cleveland; both teams were obviously fatigued from their long trip. Chicago with some good base running, and All America with some displays of hitting prowess, kept the game from being too tiring. The true attraction of the day was the pageantry surrounding the event, and the presence of so many great players.

Inning	1	2	3	4	5	6	7	8	9	Final
Chicago	0	1	0	0	6	0	0	0	0	7
All America	2	0	1	0	0	0	0	1	0	4

The Sandlot Game

The H. R. Jacobs theatre put together a ball club, and it was announced that "The uniform selected is a white shirt with the initials H. R. J. across the breast in white, white pants and blue stockings and a blue and white cap. This being the favorite club its members will tour through the eastern circuit in Mr. Jacobs' private car. Prior to June 24, they will practice and play on Beyerle's park."[5]

The best teams in town were, on the west side, Shamrocks and Albions, and on the east side, Forest City, Woodlands and Z Club (the premier club of black players).

The Z Club received as much newspaper coverage as the best of the white teams. This was the first year that any black team was given the publicity it deserved.

The Shamrocks had put more of its members into the ranks of professional baseball than any other club in town. With $100 from a benefit, they fixed up their field at the old-river-bed grounds (near Whiskey Island). This is why they declined to join the City League organized to play at Beyerle Park.

The Albions played at the Foster grounds, one of the ball fields found in the Brookside valley. Encouraged by their level of play, they formed a stock company at the end of the season. They also put up a baseball facility, with a grandstand and other improvements, near the end of the Brooklyn streetcar line (the ballpark was in the current parking lot of the Rain Forest building at the zoo). Due to a number of Albion players' having German surnames, one newspaper suggested they should be called "Limbergers" not Albions.

Best of the west
Rosters

Shamrocks	*Albions*
Landy, lf	H. Kaufman, ss
J. Gilman, ss	H. Schlee, p
Carr, cf	W. Smith, 2b & p
Moran, 1b	Koll,
Murphy, 1b	C. Siegerist, c

Shamrocks	Albions
Brooksmith, p	L. Voeike, 1b
Bell, 3b	O. Hummel, 3b
Rogers, 2b	J. J. Butcher, cf
Ryan, c	Spurney, 3b
Martin, rf	Treat, lf
Huntington, 1b	Frey, cf
	Tom E. Mouks—secretary
	Geiger Mouks—manager

The Forest City played many games at Beyerle Park as members of the City League. The gate split at the amusement park was 70 percent for Mr. Beyerle and associates, and 30 percent for the ball clubs. In September, the east side Forest City finished out their year by securing the west side Brighton grounds, at Brookside valley, as their home field for the balance of the season. The Woodlands was the new name of the St. Edwards team. The *Plain Dealer* declared them amateur champions when they defeated the Forest City 5–4, in a Sunday game in early September, at the rubber works grounds.

Forest City	Woodlands
Fringer, 2b	Burke, c
Hofer, 3b	Snider, 1b
Berchtold, ss	Weber, lf
Brower, 1b	Male, ss
A. Miller, lf	Whitney, 3b
Riley, c	Oergel, 2b
Hardwick	Mahon, cf
Allen, cf	Seiple, rf
G. Miller, p	Roach, p
Davis, cf	Nevil, rf
O'Donnel, 1b	Bullas, c
Hughes, p	

In March, it was announced that the colored Z Club had reorganized for the year. The officials were Charles Black, manager and treasurer, and William Gordon and Frank Doctor, who took turns as secretary.

An account of one Z game this year: "The Woodlands defeated the great colored team from the Z Club yesterday afternoon on the Rubber's grounds by a score of 22–12. The game was a very amusing and at times very exciting one. The funny coaching of the Z Club brought peals of laughter from the crowd that numbered nearly two thousand people. Both sides did some hard hitting and it was impossible for the fielders to get any balls in the field, owing to the people."[6]

The Z Club played to some huge crowds, against the best white clubs in town, and on the best fields—but on any given day they could be found anywhere on any available sandlot in the city. On September 15 they were booked at Beyerle Park for the park's usual Sunday ball game. Another attraction billed that day was:

Steve Brodie
The Champion Jumper and Swimmer of the World
Fresh from the Terrific Plunge Over Niagara Falls[7]

Fresh from Geneva, in town to challenge the Z Club, was the Geneva Grays—the other great colored ball team of northeast Ohio.

Batting orders

Geneva Grays	Z Club
Grant Perkins, c	W. Nelson, c
John Hamilton, p	Jas. Jackson, p
R. Miller, 1b	F. Johnson, 1b
O. C. Cameron, 2b	C. Griffin, 2b
R. Holland, 3b	J. Lindsay, 3b

Geneva Grays	*Z Club*
S. Mitchell, ss	W. Wilson, ss
J. Gordon, lf	John Jackson, lf
C. Cameron, cf	W. Stanard, cf
J. Johnson, rf	R. Gross, rf
C. Adams, sub.	O. Hall, sub.

The Grays weren't so great this day; the Z Club, in front of a large crowd, batted them all over the lot, winning by a score of 20–5. The work of the Jackson brothers and Johnson the first baseman were noted as fine features of the winner's game.

A novelty game: There were no ads run for the game, but the *Plain Dealer* noted that Beyerle Park had a group of Chicago ball players scheduled to play the local Forest City team on Sunday, August 11. The novelty was that the visiting team was an all-girls' team (the first such girls team to play in Cleveland in a decade). The twist this time around was that these girls played against men rather than each other. These games were carnival acts—and, as planned, the ladies miraculously won, beating the men 32–16.

The Season Begins

They paraded in carriages through the streets of Indianapolis led by a fine band. Then the entourage of ball players, press, and baseball officials arrived at Athletic Park. It had rained in the late morning, but by noon the sun was out, and by game time a crowd of 4,000 was on hand. The band played while the teams practiced, and at 4 o'clock Umpire G. W. Barnum signaled Indianapolis to the bat, and the game started. "Jersey" Bakely pitched for Cleveland, and "Pretzels" Getzein for Indianapolis. The early rain left high winds behind, and Cleveland had more difficulty with wind-blown balls than did the Hoosiers. A little luck got Cleveland on the board for the first time in the sixth. Following a McAleer hit, McKean lined the ball over first. It landed a few inches foul, but the umpire called it fair; McAleer scored, and a moment later McKean scored on a Faatz single. Cleveland scored a final run in the bottom of the ninth when Faatz came home on a sacrifice fly. Five errors gave the Hoosiers 4 unearned runs to go with their 6 earned ones. Indianapolis won the game 10–3. The quick game took one hour and thirty minutes. The *Plain Dealer's* analysis of the game: "the Cleveland team was outplayed at every point and the local club won the game with ease. Bakely was batted hard and often and his support was very indifferent."[8]

Inning	1	2	3	4	5	6	7	8	9	Final
Indianapolis	0	1	1	2	2	0	3	0	1	10
Cleveland	0	0	0	0	0	2	0	0	1	3

The Cleveland uniforms for 1889 consisted of black belts, stockings, caps, and cardigan jackets set off by gray flannel pants with black side stripes. Drake, the Cleveland sporting goods retailer, made the uniforms.

The outfits had been expressed to Hot Springs in time for the first game there. Each player was issued two identical uniforms to be worn for road and home games. The all-one-style uniform assured a professional look; in the past players had often mixed and matched uniforms as they saw fit. The players, however, soon called the gray-and-black uniform bad luck—a "jonah"— and blamed the new clothes for light hitting and some injuries in April.

The directors of the team decided they didn't like the Drake uniforms either, and decided to order new ones from the prestigious Philadelphia firm of Reach & Co. The two new uniforms, made of jersey cloth, were navy-blue pants and shirt, and black pants and shirt. Both were trimmed with black stockings, a white belt, and a cap of black and white vertical stripes. The shirts had white trim around the cuffs and white collars, were laced at the top (rather than buttoned), and across the shirtfront—in white raised letters—was the name CLEVELANDS. An optional jacket of black, with thin white stripes, was also issued.

The outfits arrived in time for the home opener. Cleveland won a pair and lost a pair in the Indianapolis series, followed by two wins and two losses at Pittsburgh. Cleveland now brought its 4 and 5 record home to open the season against Chicago on Friday May 3.

Clevelands of 1889

"Jersey" (Edward Enoch) Bakely, p
Ed (Ebenezer Ambrose) Beatin, p*
Jay Faatz, 1b
Bob (Robert James) Gilks, utl
"Hen" (Henry John) Gruber, p*
Jimmy (James Robert) McAleer, cf
Ed (Edward John) McKean, ss
"Darby" (John F.) O'Brien, p

Paul (Paul Revere) Radford, rf
"Pop" (Charles N.) Snyder, c
Charlie (Charles Wellington) Sprague, p
"Cub" (John A.) Stricker, 2b
"Sy" (Edward Elmer) Sutcliffe, c
"Patsy" (Oliver Wendell) Tebeau, 3b
Larry (Lawrence Grant) Twitchell, lf
"Chief" (Charles Louis) Zimmer, c

* Players acquired from the former Detroit franchise.

CLEVELAND VERSUS CHICAGO

Cold! Cold! Cold! The players, the band, and the crowd all shivered and froze all the way through the whole show.

The band led the parade, and the players rode close behind in carriages. The route crisscrossed Cleveland and ended up at the ballpark. The band entertained from the grandstand, while the players took practice and tried to warm up. The audience, a bone-chilled 4,000, loudly voiced their anger because the game started late.

At 4 o'clock, "Cub" Stricker stepped up to the plate, and the umpire signaled the Chicago pitcher, "Wild Bill" Hutchison, to start the game.

The first three innings were goose eggs. The first runs came in the Chicago fourth. Anson batted with one out and hit a vicious liner to center, good for a triple. The infield moved up, but Pfeffer fooled them when he "dumped" the ball into right, scoring his man. Pfeffer helped the Cleveland cause by getting caught stealing second. Farrell hit a long one that bounced off the left field fence and put him on third. Burns' grounder eluded both Bakely and McKean, and the visitors got another run. Cleveland was shut out in the fifth and sixth. For the White Stockings, "The fifth yielded Chicago nothing but in the sixth, after Anson and Pfeffer had been retired on a pretty and rather lucky double play, that unpleasant person from Marlboro, Mass.— Charles Farrell — drove the ball out to the fence at left center and scored before it could be handled by Snyder."[9]

Striker went out to start the eighth. McAleer coaxed a walk but was forced out by McKean. Twitchell kept faith and moved the runner to second with a hit to center. The crowd then thrilled at the loud crack off the bat of Jay Faatz. The liner screamed into left, but bad luck sent it right into the hands of Van Haltren, who hung on to it. In their turn, Chicago hit three singles to earn their fourth and final run. Radford, up first in the ninth, gained a base when second baseman Pfeffer juggled his grounder. Radford then committed a sin of his own, by getting nailed trying to steal second with his team down by 4 runs. Tebeau then flied out and Snyder struck out. Score: Chicago 4, Cleveland 0.

CHICAGO:	AT BAT	RUNS	HITS	ERRORS
Ryan, cf	2	0	1	0
Van Haltren, lf	4	0	2	0
*Duffy, ss	4	0	0	0
*Anson, 1b	3	2	2	0
Pfeffer, 2b	4	0	1	1
Farrell, c	4	2	3	1
Burns, 3b	4	0	2	1
Tener, rf	4	0	1	0
Hutchison, p	3	0	0	1
Totals	**32**	**4**	**12**	**4**

CLEVELAND	AT BAT	RUNS	HITS	ERRORS
Stricker, 2b	4	0	1	0
McAleer, cf	3	0	0	0
McKean, ss	4	0	1	0
Twitchell, lf	3	0	1	1
Faatz, 1b	4	0	0	0
Radford, rf	4	0	0	0
Tebeau, 3b	4	0	1	0
Snyder, c	4	0	2	0
Bakely, p	3	0	0	0
Totals	32*	0	6	1

Hutchison walked 2 and struck out 4, Bakely walked 3 and struck out 5, Farrell hit a home run for Chicago. Time of game: 1:45. Umpire: G. W. Barnum.

* Hall of Fame
** The Cleveland hit column adds up to 33, but the totals show 32.

Call 'em "Spiders"

> The 'Spiders.'
> Cleveland, O., May 18.—Editor *Sporting Life* -
> The Cleveland Spiders—so called on account of their peculiar appearance in their suits of black and blue—are in the East fighting their way along as well as a team ever fought....
> Beat the Spiders if you can.[10]

Frank Brunell, a club official, a *Plain Dealer* writer, and the Cleveland correspondent to the national magazine *Sporting Life*, was the first to call the team "Spiders" in print. Coincidentally, at this time, newspapers across the country were headlining the American tour of the world lightweight boxing champion, Ike Weir, the "Belfast Spider."

The *Plain Dealer* started using the name Spiders on May 12. The other papers called the team the Clevelands or the "babies" or the "infants" (these last two being generic terms used to identify a new franchise or club of young players).

As the weather warmed up so did the "Spiders." Cleveland closed out the month of May in Washington, D.C., on Decoration Day.

Cleveland scored two runs in the first inning. It was all "Hen" Gruber needed to win his first game of the year, and put Cleveland four games over .500, at 17 and 13, and in fourth place.

Score: Spiders 2, Senators 1.

June Is Red-Hot

Cleveland got even hotter in June. The "infant' was growing a lot faster than the experts thought possible.

The defending champion New York Giants came to Cleveland in late June for a four-game series. On Saturday the Cleveland battery of O'Brien and Zimmer faced the battery of Welch and Ewing—two future Hall of Fame members. Cleveland took the lead in the first with three runs, courtesy of three consecutive walks, a single, and a bad throw from catcher "Buck" Ewing.

Ewing in the third inning made up for his error in a big way. A fielder's choice and two walks loaded the bases: "At such a stage "Buck" caught one of O'Brien's fast balls on his bat and drove it high over the left field fence."[11]

It was a grand slam. The crowd was stunned into silence until they realized this was the longest ball ever hit at the park. As Ewing rounded third the crowd rose to its feet and gave him a hearty round of applause. The *Plain Dealer* noted: "The present plate is 410 feet from the fence and the ball went over it at the chewing gum sign and six feet above its top."[12]

Cleveland fought on, and scored its seventh and eighth runs in the seventh and won the game 8–6. The 4,000 in the stands rejoiced as the red-hot Spiders' record went to 30 and 18, a mark that put them in second place.

Beaneaters on the Fourth

Cleveland was still in second place with a 36 and 20 record when the League's leader, the Boston Beaneaters, arrived in town for a four-game series, starting with a Fourth of July doubleheader. The Beaneaters threw two future Hall of Fame pitchers at the Spiders— John Clarkson and Hoss Radbourn. Cleveland countered with Ed Beatin and Darby O'Brien.

GAME ONE

Bright and cool weather accompanied the holiday crowd as they clicked through the turnstile:

There were 9,500 people at the league park to see the Clevelands and Bostons fight for their places in the league race. Cleveland was beaten and never cut a figure in the game. It was all centered around Clarkson, who held the Clevelands in the hollow of that very skillful and high priced right hand of his. At no time was he in any danger of runs and the four hits made off his delivery were scattered through four innings. When he was hit with men on bases the ball went at a fielder or into the air. He had the luck of the game with him, too, the errors of Nash being made when they cost nothing. For Cleveland Beatin was in the box. For four innings nothing like a hit was made off him.

In the fifth the Stars got one scratch but after that Beatin was unsteady and four bases on balls, badly distributed, five hits and some sloppy fielding sent in six runs. Beatin got fair support. Stricker was not at his best. The slippery infield cost two hits, McKean getting the ball and slipping with one. Only one Spider got as far as third. That was Sutcliffe in the eighth. But he was left.

Boston began scoring in the sixth, when Clarkson's ugly bounder, well taken by McKean, didn't give an out, because Mac slipped down. Brown's sacrifice sent Clarkson to second, a wild pitch advanced him to third, and Johnsion's [sic] sacrifice let him in. Kelly followed with a hit, making the run earned.

In the seventh Beatin fell apart and three bases on balls and two hits gave Boston three runs. Brouthers led off with a hit to short left and bases on balls to Richardson and Nash filled the unfilled corners. Quinn's grounder to McKean caused Brouthers to be put out at the plate. The bases were still full and Beatin gave Bennett four bad balls and forced Richardson. Clarkson's fly was taken by Stricker. It now looked all right, for Tom Brown hadn't hit the ball safely. But this time he scratched it into the crowd at right for two bases and Nash and Quinn scored. That was all in this inning.

In the eighth the Stars got two more runs on bad fielding. Tebeau threw Kelly's grounder into the crowd and gave the runner second. Beatin hit Brouthers with the ball and Richardson sent a two-baser into right, on which Kelly scored. Nash flew out to Tebeau and the throw of Quinn's grounder to McKean killed Brouther's at the plate. Quinn stole second, Bennett got a base on balls and when Stricker was off second and missed taking McKean's throw on Clarkson's grounder, which would have forced Bennett, Richardson scored. Then the trouble stopped. The score follows:[13]

BOSTON	AT BAT	RUNS	BASE HITS	ERRORS
Brown, rf	5	0	1	0
Johnston, cf	4	0	0	0
Kelly, rf	3	1	1	0
Brouthers, 1b	3	0	1	0
Richardson, 2b	3	2	1	0
Nash, 3b	2	1	1	3
Quinn, ss	4	1	1	0
Bennett, c	2	0	0	0
Clarkson, p	4	1	1	0
Totals	30	6	7	3
CLEVELAND	AT BAT	RUNS	BASE HITS	ERRORS
Stricker, 2b	4	0	1	2
McAleer, cf	4	0	1	0
McKean, ss	4	0	2	0
Twitchell, lf	4	0	0	0
Faatz, 1b	3	0	0	0
Radford, rf	3	0	0	0
Tebeau, 3b	3	0	0	1
Sutcliffe, c	3	0	0	1
Beatin, p	2	0	0	0
Totals	30	0	4	4

The *Plain Dealer*'s observations on game one:

Clarkson on the third base line, to Nash, in the seventh: "Now, Billy, make him put them over." Mike Kelly at first base: "Never yer mind, Billy! Do wot yer like. Boston! Beans! Culchah!"

Mike Kelly is no longer a symmetrical beauty. He resembles a bumboat woman in his style and demeanor, is unpleasant in his methods, and indicates in a blue gray way that all other denizens of the earth are small creatures compared to Mickey Kelly....

General Dixwell, famous for his enthusiasm and love of anything baseball and Bostonese, was on the stand and made the crowd mad by his continual Hi! Hi! Hi! Hi! when anything good for Boston turned up. The general cannot help it, and does not want to if he could. Other cranks are small and insignificant beside Dixwell, who pays for his weakness and ought to enjoy it.[14]

Game two:

There were 10,200 paying people within the fences, when Umpire Curry called "play" for the afternoon game ... 8,000 were strangers and 1,000 well dressed ladies. They were in all stands and [it] was worth a trip to the park to see the crowd and worth ten trips to see the game. It was a model only marred by a spasm of wildness by veteran Radbourn in the sixth inning. There was hard, clean batting, pretty fielding and prettier base running in abundance and Cleveland got the best of it. The Spiders outbatted the Stars and that was all there was to the game. The bat swung hard and fast all through it. To beat the Bostons was glory enough, but to beat them at their own specialty—batting—was ecstasy indeed. The crowd recognized this and cheered the batting wildly. The grand stand responded with Hi! Hi! Hi! when the bloody fifth was in progress, and General Dixwell was crushed. He started to Hi! Hi! in the third, but the fifth settled him, and he was heard no more.

Radbourn and Ganzel were the Boston battery. Rad couldn't fool anyone with his ins and outs, though he occasionally showed his old time superfine curves. Ganzel caught him admirably, and his field support was perfect. The runs Cleveland didn't earn he gave himself.

For Cleveland O'Brien and Zimmer did the battery work. Darby wasn't at his best, and was hit pretty hard, but he pitched easily during the last half of the game. His field support was stiff, and Boston had to earn four of its seven runs.

The Spiders began to make runs in the second, when two earned runs came in, the result of singles by Faatz and Tebeau and Zimmer's double—a mighty fly almost to the fence at left center.

In the fourth Cleveland got two more earned runs, Tebeau and Zimmer scoring them on their own singles and two more by O'Brien and Stricker.

When the fifth opened the score was 4 to 4, but Cleveland won the game right there and got six runs off Radbourn before the side was retired. McKean hit the ball to left for two bases as a starter. Twitchell's bounder earned him first, the ball glancing off of Radbourn's left hand so no one could field it to first before the runner. McKean went to third. Faatz got a base on balls and the infield corners were full. Radford's base on balls forced McKean in and left the bases full. Tebeau flew out to Nash. Zimmer waited for his base on balls and got it, forcing Twitchell in. Still the bases were full. O'Brien flew out to right, and Faatz beat Kelly's throw home. Zimmer stole second. Stricker's single to left sent in Radford and Zimmer. "Cub" took second on Brown's throw in and scored on McAleer's hit to left. McKean got another hit, but Twitchell's fly to center retired the side and left McAleer and McKean on the bases.

Another and the last run came to Cleveland in the seventh on Zimmer's base on balls, O'Brien's sacrifice and Stricker's single. Then the side was retired on a peculiar double play, Stricker and McAleer being killed off at the plate.

Cleveland had ten runs after the fifth inning and O'Brien took it easy. Boston got its first runs in the third. Three, two earned, came in a bunch and all centered on Brown's base on balls. With one out, Brown was sent to first. He stole second and ran on to third on Zimmer's high throw down. Then Johnston got a scratch hit and Brown scored. Johnston stole second and scored on Kelly's hit to left. Kelly ran to second on the throw in and scored on Richardson's double into the crowd at right.

In the fourth Ganzel earned a run and tied the score. He got first by fast running on a bunt, went to second on Radbourn's out at first and scored on Brown's double into the crowd at right.

Hopelessly in the rear Boston got a run in the seventh. Twitchell dropped Johnston's fly and gave the runner two bases and Kelly's double to right finished the run. But the great Mike was joshed off second while McKean had the ball and a quick throw to Stricker caught him off. The fall of Mickey the mighty was hugely enjoyed.

In the ninth the Bostons earned two more runs on Johnston's single to left, a wild pitch, Kelly's chop hit to right, some loose throwing in returning it, Brouther's red hot one through Faatz, the ball caroming off his legs like a glancing shot, and Richardson's sacrifice. The score follows:[15]

CLEVELAND	AT BATS	RUNS	HITS	ERRORS
Stricker, 2b	6	1	3	0
McAleer, cf	5	0	2	0
McKean, ss	3	1	2	0
Twitchell, lf	5	1	1	1
Faatz, 1b	4	2	1	0
Radford, rf	4	1	0	0
Tebeau, 3b	5	2	2	0
Zimmer, c	3	3	2	1
O'Brien, p	5	0	1	0
Totals	40	11	14	2
BOSTON	AT BATS	RUNS	HITS	ERRORS
Brown, lf	4	1	1	0
Johnston, cf	5	3	3	0
Kelly, rf	4	2	3	0
Brouthers, 1b	5	0	1	0
Richardson, 2b	3	0	2	0
Nash, 3b	5	0	0	0
Quinn, ss	4	0	1	0
Ganzel, c	4	1	1	0
Radbourn, p	4	0	0	0
Totals	38	7	12	0

Time: 1:52. Umpire: Wesley Curry.

FURTHER PLAIN DEALER COMMENTS

Notes: • Kelly dallied with the crowd by pretending to muff flies he had caught. Before the series is over he'll drop one or two. He is not a superfine field anyway. • In the second inning Zimmer got a basket of flowers and responded with a two-base hit which sent in two runs. Stricker got a silver trophy, but could only send a grounder to Brouthers. But he got even later and drove in four runs. • Jay players get caught off a base once in a while. But stars do not. Kelly was caught off very nicely in the seventh, through not knowing where the ball was. McKean had it after Kell had made his two-base hit and when he walked off second an easy throw to Stricker caught the mighty one off so far that there wasn't even a wrangling chance. He went to the bench with the whistled music of Rogue's March in his Sixth Avenue ears.[16]

The East Coast and a Cool-Down

Cleveland won the next two games 2–0 and 9–6 to win 3 of 4 of the series with the league leader. They were now 18 games over .500 with a record of 39 and 21. Cleveland and Boston now headed east to open the next series of games against each other in Boston.

Cleveland lost the first 2 Boston games, but took the third, before continuing on their tough East Coast trip. The team finished with a 3 and 7 road record against Boston, New York, Philadelphia, and Washington. From a high point of 18 games over .500, the Spiders by month's end had cooled down somewhat, to 8 games above .500 at 43 and 35.

The team played break-even ball for most of August, but after they went to a 48 and 49 mark, in the last week of August, they never again rose above the respectable .500 mark. As September weather cooled so did the Spiders.

Saturday, October 5, was the last day of the season. New York had a chance to clinch the pennant, if Boston, playing over in Pittsburgh, would lose, and the Giants, playing here, should win. Tim Keefe of the Giants was helped with some great fielding in a very tight game that went right with Jim

Keefe pitching the Giants to win 5–3. The Giants hung on to win 5–3. The telegraph soon signaled: Pittsburgh 6, Boston 1; Jim Galvin winning pitcher. (Galvin and Keefe are in the Hall of Fame.)

The Giants had won the National League pennant. They went downtown to the Holenden Hotel and had their first victory party. Cleveland ended up in sixth place — but it had been the most exciting season in Cleveland baseball since 1883.

The future looked sunny for the Spiders, but behind the scenes storm clouds were gathering that threatened the game itself with a heavy rain.

National League 1889

	W	L	Pct.
New York	83	43	.659
Boston	83	45	.648
Chicago	67	65	.508
Philadelphia	63	64	.496
Pittsburg	61	71	.462
CLEVELAND	61	72	.459
Indianapolis	59	75	.440
Washington	41	83	.331

Post-Season Exhibitions

The Youngstown baseball association built a new ballpark for its fall-season Ohio League team; among the improvements were a twelve-foot fence and a grandstand for 700.

In his 12 years with Cleveland, Ed McKean enjoyed several strong seasons at the bat. In half of those seasons McKean would finish in the top 10 in total bases.

In October, the association hoped to raise some operating funds by staging an exhibition game between Cleveland and Pittsburgh of the National League.

Jimmy McAleer, a Youngstown native and former sandlot star, was in town recovering from a game injury — a torn ligament above the ankle. His friends wanted him in the game, so they drafted him to umpire, and he agreed. Despite the cold weather, the game drew 1,000 to the new West Side Park. In the seventh inning, another former Youngstown player, Ed McKean, drove in 2 runs with a triple to put Cleveland up 4–3; it would be the final score of the game.

The players wanted to go home but they were under contract till the end of October. In the middle of October, the team now started its ill-conceived Ohio series. Columbus and Cincinnati of the American Association would be the opponents.

It cost 500 shivering Clevelanders 50 cents to see Cleveland beat Columbus 5–3.

A "cold proof" Cleveland crowd of 400 endured seven innings before darkness ended the second Columbus game — the visitors winning it 9–6.[17] During the game, one warm drunk in the bleachers got sent home for "over insulting" the umpire.[18]

Jimmy McAleer was well enough to play in the game here against Cincinnati; he caught six flies in the 4–0 Cleveland win. The venue for the second game with Cincinnati moved a bit south, to Akron. Score: Cincinnati 8, Cleveland 5.

The games now moved to Columbus: Cleveland

won the next game with Cincinnati 4–1. Columbus then played Cincinnati, winning in front of 1,500 people, 5–2. Columbus made it 2 in a row at home, by beating Cleveland 6–2.

On to Cincinnati: Two hundred paying customers watched Cincinnati beat Cleveland 7–2. The next day, a band and marchers with placards made the rounds of the Cincinnati streets to promote the ball game. The game, although played on wet grounds, was a good one. Cincinnati won the contest 3–1. What wasn't so good was that, despite the advertising parade, only 50 people bought tickets. The baseball owners now mercifully ended the Ohio series and sent the men home.

A Major Change in the Wind

Fed up with years of abuse by baseball ownership, players, in order to better their lot, had formed a mutual beneficial society called the Brotherhood of Professional Base Ball Players.

The organization, in but a few short years, had secretly become the cornerstone of a protective labor movement. However, after the season of 1889, rather than go on strike in the manner of a union, the players quit the National League in large numbers, and to a lesser extent they also left the American Association.

Under the auspices of the Brotherhood of Professional Base Ball Players, they formed the Players National League — a new major league, with new owners, new ballparks, and progressive labor contracts. The new league, based on an employee-ownership model, was launched over the winter months.

Al Johnson, the Cleveland streetcar magnate, became the leader of the new money men backing the Players League. On October 21, it was revealed that land east of Wilson Street (E. 55th) at the end of Diamond Park Street (on the bluff to the north overlooking the RTA rapid tracks) had been leased from Dr. Barr and Michael Woolrich by Al Johnson and associates, for the purpose of building a first-class ballpark.

On November 21, 1889, the Cleveland Players League club incorporated at Columbus, Ohio.

Part III. The Closing Years: 1890–1900

1890

The Brotherhood War

In 1884 baseball owners waged war against each other. In 1890 the players waged war against the owners.

Through the agency of the Brotherhood, new owners had been brought on board, and they built competing ballparks in every National League city except Cincinnati. To complete an eight-team league, a team was placed in Buffalo. The Players League of the Brotherhood of 1890 was now in business as a rival to the National League.

Albert Spalding, founder of the Spalding sporting-goods empire, led the war for the National League. Albert Johnson, a national streetcar magnate, with headquarters in Cleveland, was the general for the Players League (Al's bachelor apartment at Superior and Bond (E. 6th) was called the birthplace of the Players League).

The Cleveland National League team lost all of its stars except two—Ed McKean and "Chief" Zimmer. Zimmer, having agreed to play for the Brotherhood, recanted, and went back to the Cleveland League club. The Brotherhood felt they had a legal case against Zimmer and promised to go after his financial assets to set an example.

Starting in January, President Robison and his new manager, Gus Smeltz, began signing ballplayers, especially pitchers, from all over the place, to find replacements for the club's depleted roster. Their hopes were that a few might make the cut. Pitchers John W. Wadsworth (Cleveland); Ezra Lincoln (Rockland, IL); Will Garfield (Pittsburgh, NL-1889) and Charlie Parsons (New York, AA-1887) were early signings. Smeltz, who recruited Parsons, said, "Parsons has better command of the ball than any other left hander in the country."[1]

Parsons, who had been out of baseball for a while due to illness, finished his major league career in 1890 as a Cleveland Spider—going 0 and 1 in two appearances with an earned run average of 6.00 for 9 innings work.

Over in the Brotherhood camp, the plan was to land the contracts of some of the game's greatest stars. To this end, Al Johnson had the help of his cousin J. J. Coleman,

J. A. Fawcett, and Doc Beeman (founder of the Beeman Gum Co.).

Coleman made the first big media splash when, in the last week of January, he penned Pete "the Gladiator" Browning" to a Brotherhood contract. Browning, a native of Louisville, had played for no other major league team but Louisville. He hit between .313 and .402 in seven of eight seasons there—leading the American Association twice in hitting. His ninth season, however, would be played in Cleveland.

Browning ended an interview with the *Plain Dealer* by saying:

> Well, goodby. You want to keep an eye on the Cleveland outfield. I guess I'll play left field and McAleer will play center. Why, we will have an outfield that you can't beat. Goodby! Keep yer eye on old Pete!...
>
> The old "Gladiator" tendered his big brawny right to the newspaper man, and as he shook a hearty farewell there was no quiver in his muscles of steel. [There was always concern about the "Gladiator's" health due to his fight with alcoholism.] His eyes were clear as crystal, his complexion white with no tinge of the red and his stout frame erect as ever it was in the proud days of yore when the

M'ALEER. DELEHANTY. BROWNING. LARKIN. HEMING. TWITCHELL. SUTCLIFFE. GRUBER.
O'BRIEN. BAKELY. TEBEAU. STRICKER. BRENNAN.
THE TEAM OF THE CLEVELAND PLAYERS' LEAGUE BASE BALL CLUB.

The Brotherhood benefit association of the players formed the Players' League of 1890 as a rival to the two major leagues. Though they signed most of the game's star players, the league folded after one season. This drawing of the league's Cleveland entrant appeared in *Sporting Life*.

men yelled themselves hoarse when he sent the sphere whistling over the green turf for a clean home run hit, and the ladies cried with pride when the champion crossed the plate and won the game with his prowess.[2]

President Robison solidified the left field position with the re-signing of Cincinnati native Bobby Gilks. Though not a hitter for average, Gilks could get on base. As the regular lead-off man for the Spiders in 1890, he would lead the league in at-bats and steal 38 bases. He even chipped in with four pitching starts, going 2 and 2.

Gilks was interviewed in Cincinnati shortly after signing with Cleveland for his fourth campaign:

> Bob Gilks, the great all around player of the Cleveland team, paid a visit to the Enquirer office yesterday. Gilks was in excellent humor. He had just received notification that he was entitled to $150 that he knew nothing about. Bob led the league players last season in fielding and won a prize offered by a New York chewing gum firm. He had never heard of such an offer, and it was not until yesterday, when he received a letter asking where the check should be sent, that he knew that he had won the money. "That $150 comes at a good time," said Bob. "I can use it very nicely just now. I won't have to break in on my little roll that I had put away for a rainy day."
>
> "Where have you been keeping yourself?"
>
> "Hunting of course. I like to flush a covey of birds as well as any man in Cincinnati. I have put in nearly two months quail hunting in Indiana, Ohio and Kentucky. I bought one of the best dogs in the country and he has paid his way already. Birds are very plentiful this fall and it was a poor day in season when I did not get twenty or thirty quail."[3]

Spring Training

The National League team left for Hot Springs on March 11. The Panhandle train out of Cleveland, running late, left the players stranded in Cincinnati for a time awaiting a later connection to St. Louis, and the final transfer into Hot Springs.

On arriving in Hot Springs the entourage set up house keeping at:

THE HOTEL EASTMAN
Hot Springs, Ark.

The largest and finest hotel in America will open for the season of 1890 January 15, under the management of O. G. Barron of White Mountain hotels. This house has 482 large, well lighted and ventilated guest rooms, elegantly furnished, heated with steam, lighted with 1,500 incandescent and 50 arc electric lights, palatial parlors for ladies and gentlemen, cuisine of the very best; the finest bath house in the world, supplied with water from the Hot Springs connected with the hotel. Buy tickets by St. Louis. Iron Mountain & Southern railroad.[4]

* * *

The first game was March 13 against the professional team from Denver. On St. Patrick's Day, the Cleveland squad split into an "all Irish" and an "all American" team for an intramural practice game.

On March 12, the Brotherhood club left Cleveland with eight of its roster players. The balance of the team was to join up at various convenient points throughout the South. Rather than have a base city for spring training games in 1890, the Cleveland and Chicago Brotherhood teams planned to play games against each other in a number of Southern cities. It was hoped this scheme would prove financially advantageous.

The schedule, printed in early March in the *Plain Dealer*, called for games in New Orleans, April 16; Mobile, April 18, 19; New Orleans, April 20, 21; Houston, April 22, 23; and then appearances at Austin, Waco, Fort Worth, Dallas, Texarkana, Pine Bluff, Hot Springs, Little Rock, and St. Louis.

Philadelphia's League team had its spring training in Charleston, South Carolina. On March 21, Cleveland native Ed Delahanty, with a $1000 advance on a $3500 contract from Al Johnson, jumped the Philadelphia ship, and became a member of the Cleveland Brotherhood team. Despite the best efforts of Philadelphia management to make him stick, he left town on the 4 o'clock train to join Cleveland.

With the signing of Pete Browning and Ed Delahanty (the greatest ball player ever to come off a Cleveland sandlot), the Cleveland Players League now had two major box office attractions.

Will Johnson, a brother of Al Johnson, ran a streetcar company in St. Louis. If St. Louis could demonstrate, in a series of spring exhibition games, that they could turn out a crowd, there were plans to place Will Johnson in charge of a St. Louis franchise to replace Buffalo. The spring training schedule was arranged so that on Saturday, April 5, Cleveland and Chicago would be in St. Louis for an exhibition of the first Players League game in that city.

The teams arrived at the Union Depot via the Cairo short line, their train having braved an early spring snowstorm that was still raging outside. A tallyho met the players and escorted them from the depot to their lodgings at the Lindell Hotel. The parade was led by the Emerald cadet drum and fife corps; following them were the Walsh Zouaves under the command of Captain Heyman, as well as the Olympic and other local ball clubs. Four white

Remembered today nearly as much for the mysterious circumstances surrounding his death as for his excellent play, Ed Delahanty starred in the National League for parts of 16 seasons. His first full session came in 1890, as a member of the Cleveland Brotherhood.

horses, with Will Johnson handling the driving ribbons, pulled the carriages carrying the players. Accompanying the visitors were several of the more popular St. Louis (A.A.) ball players from the 1889 roster.

The corridors of the Lindell were crowded with well-wishers, and while it snowed outside, the happy party continued on inside. Some games were lost to the weather, but those that were played drew large crowds. The game on Saturday drew 5,000 — and the game on Sunday had a flash-crowd of 15,000. Unfortunately, the turnstiles weren't fast enough to handle such a Sunday mob, and a good number of the people rushed the gates and got in free. Sunday's score: Chicago 7, Cleveland 5.

Diamond Dust Around the Reserve

Representatives of the Tri-state League met March 25, 1890, in Akron. W. H. McDermith (Columbus)— president, secretary, and treasurer of the league — gaveled the meeting to order at 10 A.M. precisely. Seated around the table in the parlors of the Hotel Buchtel were Nate Fiel (manager), of Wheeling, West Virginia; J. P. Neil and Frank W. Torreyson, of McKeesport, Pennsylvania; C. H. Vogele (president) and J. H. Burns, of Mansfield; Harry C. Fisher (manager), of Springfield; T. D. Donovan (manager), of Dayton; M. J. Gilbo, L. C. Miles, C. M. Hundley, and A. E. Miller, of Akron; and Walter Marvin, of Canton.

After a heated debate, the meeting settled on a $700 a month salary cap for players. Next, representatives of the Spalding and Reach sporting goods companies showed their samples, and were allowed to enter bids to provide the league with uniforms and equipment. At about this point in the day's work, an interesting requirement was enacted, stating: "umpires shall appear on the field in a neat uniform."[5]

At 1 o'clock the group adjourned for lunch.

The afternoon discussion was taken up with the schedule, with officials taking turns arguing for and against certain dates assigned to their respective team. However, after but a few modifications, the overall list of league games was approved.

During the meeting it was learned that Akron planned to build a new elegant grandstand — 100 feet long and 10 feet high. It was hoped it would be ready for the opening game with Springfield on April 30 —"Labor Day."

The Tri-state League champion of 1889 was Canton. On May 5, 1890, their pennant arrived. The large bunting banner was 15 x 30 feet. It was white, with the edge trimmed in deep red, and in large black letters said "CHAMPIONS OF 1889."[6] It was scheduled to fly over the ballpark on May 15.

At the start of April, the first amateur game of note took place — St. Ignatius College hosted St. Patrick. The game was played on the college grounds, and the batteries were, for St. Ignatius, Lavelle and Shea, and for St. Patrick, McNerney and Dempsey. The college boys won 26–10.

There were a number of amateur leagues in action this year. The East End League was for players ages 13–18. Its teams were the Athletics, Prospects, Sunsets, Unions, Young Americas, and Young Clevelands. The Northern Ohio Athletic Association was for colleges. The membership included Adelbert, Case, Hiram, Oberlin, and Mt. Union.

The Brotherhood amateur league and Hellers league acted as developmental organizations for the Players League and the National League respectively.

The City league, once again based at Beyerle Park, initially accepted application for membership from the Forest Citys, Troys, Woodlands, Rocks, Mets, and Kinsmans. The Z club, composed of black players, was told that their application for membership would be honored should a vacancy occur in the six-team league.

Cleveland businesses promoted and outfitted their fair share of company ball teams for 1890. Standard Oil, Warner & Swasey, Goldsmith, Joseph, Feiss & Co. (clothier), Cleveland Twist Drill, Kennard House and Weddell House (hotels), as well as Society for Savings and National City Bank all fielded strong teams. On a bit of an odd note, at the start of the amateur season, President S. E. Seymour of the Cleveland Burial Case Company asked for teams to please come forward and challenge his lively nine.

Brotherhood Park

Since January, the public had been reading reports about the doings near Wilson (E. 55th) and Diamond Court, in the city's 25th Ward. The site was the home of the new Brotherhood Park.

Crews were already out in January leveling the grounds in preparation for construction. At month's end, an additional parcel of property was leased, making possible an add-on of 130 feet to the left field and room for a carriage field of 70 feet.

By mid–April, the papers reported that the heavy timbers for the three stands were all in position, and that iron rods and pine scantling were being used to frame out the construction. It was estimated that between 75 and 100 carpenters were hard at work on the project.

The grandstand was shaped in a semicircle and was taller than the pavilion on either side. The grandstand's 2,500 seats were of an Al Johnson design and built in Chicago. They were cushioned and wider than your standard "folding opera chairs."[7]

A short access space separated the grandstand from its flanking stands, where the strongly pitched roofs were intended to make high infield flies easier to see. These side stands employed wooden-backed benches and could accommodate 2,500 people each. All of the seating in all three sections was angled more sharply than at other parks, again with the aim of improving the view.

Al Johnson was inspired by an idea after visiting some ballparks back East. When he came home, he ordered contractor Slattmeyer to put private boxes all along the top of the grandstand. Each of the twenty-one luxury boxes contained several of Al's special chairs.

As the leader of the money men trying to improve the players' lot, Al Johnson set a wonderful example by providing facilities to serve the men at his ballpark that were unheard of in the past and that were truly fit for kings.

Under the grandstand, the players' clubhouse was outfitted with Brussels carpet, plate glass mirrors, and individual wardrobe areas and lockers. The bathroom had a big marble plunge pool, hot and cold showers, and a number of individual tubs. A side room was outfitted with "two or three gymnastic appliances."[8] There were also a number of rooms under the grandstand available for lease by private groups.

Getting ready

The Spiders finished out their spring training on April 17, in Quincy, Illinois, by beating the Quincy team 15–10. They were in Cleveland the next day for an exhibition game against Youngstown. The price for the Youngstown game was 25 cents, and on a very cold day, a surprise crowd of 1,500 came out to watch Cleveland win 12–3.

Plans for the opener included giving out pocket schedules and allowing the ladies in for free. Ticket agencies this year were A. F. Drake, Bennett & Fish, England on Euclid, Goff and Kirby, Hexters, Larwood & Day, and Meyer & Glein.

The construction of Mr. Robison's new cable car line, on Superior and Payne, made it necessary to reroute the horse-line a bit, but by running a spur track down an alley off of Payne, the public could be taken all the way directly to the park.

The players and a brass band made a little parade around town before arriving back at the ball yard for the 4 o'clock game.

Opener: Chicago at Cleveland

The 1890 season began ceremoniously on April 26:

> The band-wagon and the players' carriages arrived at the grounds at about half past 3, and the men formed in two columns. Then they marched up to the plate, where Anson took off his cap and made a polite bow to the cheering people.[9]

The pitching match-up for the day was "Wild Bill" Hutchison for the Chicagos and Ed Beatin for the Clevelands.

There was an audience of 1,800 shivering souls gathered in the stands, and "It was exactly 4 o'clock when umpire Jack McQuaid walked up to the home plate at the National League park and called: 'Play ball.'"[10]

Ed McKean, wearing a white flannel uniform trimmed with black hat, belt, and stockings, came to bat to start off the game. He received a nice round of applause and said thank you with a nice single into right—followed by a swipe of second. After Smalley flied out to right, Dailey hit a single into right that scored McKean and put Cleveland on the board first.

Chicago warmed up by scoring 4 in the lower half of inning one. In the third, both teams scored again: a pair for Cleveland, one for Chicago. Chicago got a run in the fourth to take a 6–3 advantage. Cleveland turned up the heat by plating 3 in the fifth to tie the game up at 6 apiece.

Cleveland forged ahead in the ninth. McKean led off with a single, but was forced at second on Smalley's short hit to right. Smalley advanced to third on passed balls. Dailey walked, and when Zimmer's grounder to first was dropped, Smalley scored. Hutchison then loaded the bases with a walk to Davis. All three runners eventually scored to give Cleveland a 4-run ninth. Three flies made easy-pie of Chicago in the ninth. Final: Cleveland 10 and Chicago 6.

Cleveland	*Runs*	*Chicago*	*Runs*
Ed McKean, ss	2	Jimmy Cooney, ss	0
Will Smalley, 3b	2	Cliff Carroll, lf	1
Vince Daily, rf	2	Walt Wilmot, cf	1
Chief Zimmer, c	1	Adrian "Pop" Anson, 1b	2
George Davis, cf	2	Jim Andrews, rf	0
"Peek-A-Boo" Veach, 1b	1	Tom Burns, 3b	0
Joe Ardner, 2b	0	Howard Earl, 2b	1
Joe Sommers, lf	0	"Wild Bill" Huchison, p	0
Ed Beatin, p	0	Malachi Kittredge, c	1
Totals	**10**	**Totals**	**6**

The *Plain Dealer* poked fun at the mood of Manager "Pop" Anson following the loss to Cleveland: "At the end of the game it wasn't necessary for him to swing his arms about. He was warm enough without doing so. The fact of the matter is that the old man, after the ninth inning, in which his crowd of coming pennant winners fell down and allowed a crowd of unknown players who make no pretensions to being pennant winners take a game from under their very noses was decidedly hot. He was so hot that the cool air from off of lake Erie had no effect on him, and riding down town after the game he threw off his sweater and even then he was in an uncomfortable state of warmth."[11]

At the end of April, the Cleveland Nationals had a record of 3 and 4 and were in sixth place. The Cleveland Brotherhood opened on the road, and came home to start the season with a 2 and 5 record that had them in seventh place.

Opening Day II

May 1, 1890: There were a number of ways for the crowd to get to the Brotherhood opener. The west side Brooklyn streetcar line, owned by Al Johnson and his brother, had negotiated route privileges for their electric cars to go directly to the park from the square, a distance of five miles. The Scoville electric streetcar also had a direct route from the square. Al Johnson augmented his streetcars with covered wagon-specials, picking up people on Case (E. 40th) and on Wilson (E. 55th) streets. And the Beefsteak Club had organized a tally-ho to the grounds.

Al Johnson ran the following ad in the papers to promote the opener at the new ballpark: "Endorsed By the American People, The Greatest Base Ball Talent in the World. The Men of Honor and Skill. The Finest Ball Grounds on Earth! Lightning Express Trains to the Grounds Without a Stop! Running Time From the Square to the Grounds Sixteen Minutes. Two Great Umpires; Therefore, No Disputes. Base Ball on a Higher Plane. A Larger Collection of 'Stars' than Ever Known. 'We are the People.' All the Great Favorites. Brotherhood Park Cleveland vs. Chicago. Game 4 o'clock. April 30, May 1 and 2."[12]

As the crowds neared the park, they noticed one enterprising individual was ready for the opener; he had a big banner — in "startling English" — stretched all the way across the front of his tavern, declaring his business "Brotherhood Headquarters."[13]

At the park, a private alley near Diamond Park Street to the north had been leased, and a spur track constructed in order to drop riders off not three hundred feet from one of the gates. The alley's late-night movement of streetcars led to a lawsuit being filed by Wilamina Kehres, a nearby property owner, but the cars continued to roll.

A house and a lot on Diamond Street were leased, and a gravel path was put down to give pedestrians easier access from the north side. The south side of the park was flanked by the tracks of the New York, Chicago & St. Louis Railroad Company, better known as the Nickel Plate. One newspaper wag suggested that the young boys station themselves by these tracks in order to retrieve balls hit over the short right-field fence — and thus earn a "pass to de bleacher."[14]

The west side of the park was a few hundred feet behind the car barns of a rival streetcar magnate on Wilson Street (E. 55th). There was a little room here for some horse-hitching posts to be installed. The Nickel Plate depot, to the southwest, was but a few hundred feet from the field — convenient for out-of-town visitors. To the east, behind the outfield fence and an orchard, was Kinsman Street. Entrances on every side of the three stands — a total of twelve — helped expedite the large inaugural crowd.

Chicago at Cleveland

According to the *Cleveland Leader*: "There were 3,490 people, turnstile arithmetic, at the Brotherhood grounds."[15] According to the *Plain Dealer*: "By actual turnstile count there were 4,157 people on the three big stands of the new park."[16]

The public, once in the park, took in a number of details. A house, not two hundred feet from the home plate, came within a few feet of the left field foul line (many a foul ball was certain to end up in this neighbor's yard). The catcher's position was ninety feet in front of the grandstand, making passed balls a serious problem. There was foliage planted in front of the grandstand, and to either side, behind the catcher's box, there were brightly colored plants in the shape of stars (symbolizing the Players' League as one consisting of "all-stars"). The field was completely sodded with the exception of a strip along the back fence near the scoreboard, where somebody "who doesn't fear the hereafter" had helped himself to about three hundred yards of Mr. Johnson's green.[17]

The stands themselves were not yet painted, but in a few weeks: "When the Players' league club returns from the east June 5 and the local park is again thrown open to the public it will hardly be recognized. The new stands will all be painted a pretty shade of olive, with bright red trimmings. The interior woodwork will be pink and the decorations will be carried still further by hanging baskets of flowers in the grandstand."[18]

It was a beautiful day for baseball, and high above the grandstand three flags flew from the tall towers: "Old Glory" in the center, flanked by the burgees of the two contending clubs. Chicago's flag was black with a border of white stars, and CHICAGO in white. Cleveland's flag was bright blue with white braid, with CLEVELAND in white.

Majordomo Thomas Mears struck up the band, and: "It was just about 3:30 p. m. when the big gates leading to the old orchard in left field opened and a brass band followed by half a dozen carriages, in which the players were seated, entered. There was a preliminary cheer as the procession drove across the field and halted. The players alighted and in company front on the left and right of the band the two clubs, as perfectly well timed military companies, marched toward the stand. Meanwhile there was a deafening amount of cheering and hand clapping, mingled with the shrill whistling of the small boy. The players doffed their hats and then scattered for their benches."[19]

There were a number of ladies throughout the grandstand, many wearing colorful Easter bonnets, as well as a contingent of well-known society ladies and their escorts up on the roof in the private boxes. Also, most of the administrative staff of City Hall had seats in the grandstand.

Frank Brunell, editor of the official *Players' League Guide*, and George Mears, the Cleveland writer working for the *Sporting News* of St. Louis, as well as the rest of the local press corps, had a nice view of the game from the new press box in the lower grandstand, directly behind the catcher's position.

Following warm-up practice and some music from the band, Al Johnson rang the big gong to announce the game was about to begin. Dressed in blue, the double umpiring crew of Knight and Jones now took their places (they would alternate by inning behind the plate and in the near outfield).

Dressed in a bright-white new uniform, George Stricker came to the plate amidst a loud round of applause to lead off the game for Cleveland. The umpire gave the signal, and Frank Dwyer, of the new Chicago Brotherhood "Pirates," went into his windup. Stricker smashed one at third, Latham made a nice stop and threw him out. Delahanty's grounder on the rough ground fooled Pfeffer, and he was aboard. Pete Browning was next — but first "'Pietro Gladiatorio' was presented with quite a gorgeous basket of hothouse flowers when he came to bat and acknowledged it with a bow that would have made a French dancing master green with envy."[20] He forced Delahanty out at second. Lon Knight stopped Larry Twitchell on his way to the plate; the umpire pulled something out of his pocket and handed it to Larry — a gold case, and inside it a handsome watch. A smiling Twitchell singled to left but was out trying to stretch it into a double. Hen Gruber, pitching for Cleveland, retired Chicago in the first inning.

Chicago put the game's first run up on the board in the bottom of the second. Comiskey started with a fly out to Browning in left. Pfeffer singled into right, Farrell walked, and Boyle's hit scored Pfeffer.

Cleveland first scored in the third. Gruber dropped a double near the foul line in right, and when the ball off the bat of Delahanty was misplayed by Bastian at short, Gruber came home. In the Chicago third, Latham walked and was moved over on a sacrifice by Duffy. He made it around to third, and on O'Neil's hit to Tebeau at third, Latham headed home and beat Tebeau's throw to the plate with a nice hook slide.

Cleveland, with two out in the fourth, got a single past the pitcher from McAleer. Gruber hit his second short hit into right, and while Duffy fumbled around with the ball in the outfield, McAleer ran all the way home. Chicago led off in the fourth with a single from Farrell, but Doyle forced him at second. Gruber uncorked a couple of wild pitches, and Doyle was standing at third. Bastian, however, didn't let him stand long; he drove him in with a hit into right.

In this early action photo, Bid Ed Delahanty swings at a pitch. The ball can be seen at right, coming in at shoulder level (Courtesy John Thorn).

Singles in the fifth, by Stricker, Delahanty, and Twitchell, gave Cleveland a run. Tebeau then drove in Delahanty with a second run, and a third run was added when Larkin's sacrifice brought in Twitchell from third base.

No runs in the sixth. Inning seven: "In the seventh by a combination of old gold errors Cleveland permitted Chicago two runs."[21] A wild throw from Delahanty gave Dwyer a base, Latham singled, Tebeau fumbled a weird-hopping grounder from Duffy, giving him a base, and Dwyer went out at the plate on an O'Neil hit to the outfield. Delahanty's error on Comiskey scored Latham, and Duffy made the final run of the inning to tie the game at five apiece.

The eighth was scoreless. The ninth: Stricker led off the tied game for Cleveland by flying out to Latham at third. Delahanty's hit into deep right screamed of extra bases, but "Del" fell down rounding first, and had to stay at first. Browning hit a single into left, and Delahanty legged it over to third without falling. Twitchell lifted a high fly to right, and Delahanty tagged up and scored the go-ahead run. In the bottom of the ninth, "The Chicagos went easy and the game was over."[22] Score: Cleveland 6, Chicago 5.

Inning	1	2	3	4	5	6	7	8	9	Final
Cleveland	0	0	1	1	3	0	0	0	1	6
Chicago	0	1	1	1	0	0	2	0	0	5

Cleveland	Runs	*Chicago*	Runs
George Stricker, 2b	1	Arlie Latham, 3b	2
Ed Delahanty, ss	2	Hugh Duffy, cf	1
Pete Browning, lf	0	Tip O'Neil, lf	0
Larry Twitchell, rf	1	Charley Comiskey, 1b	0
Patsy Tebeau, 3b	0	Fred Pfeffer, 2b	1
Henry Larkin, 1b	0	Duke Farrell, rf	0
Jimmy McAleer, cf	1	Jack Boyle, c	1
Hen Gruber, p	1	Charlie Bastian, ss	0
Jim Brennan, c	0	Frank Dwyer, p	0
Totals	6	**Totals**	5

The end of May saw an amateur doubleheader take place at League Park. A balloon ascension was the pre-game entertainment. The first game featured the college teams of Adelbert and Case. The many lady supporters of the collegiate clubs wore ribbons and clothing in the school colors—yellow for Adelbert and orange for Case. Yellow won. The Standards and Forest City played the nightcap.

Both Cleveland teams had mediocre records at the end of May, and nothing earth-shattering happened at either ballpark—that is, until June 5.

Frightening Lightning

It was a Thursday, and the third game of a series with Buffalo at the Cleveland Brotherhood Park; Alex "Colonel" Ferson was pitching for the "Bisons," and Willie "Kid" McGill for Cleveland.

Neither pitcher was having a good day; at the start of the third Cleveland led 6–4:

The game continued merrily enough for Cleveland, despite the fact that from the beginning of the game an ugly looking mass of clouds had been gathering over the field.... Charley Snyder had been given his base on balls in Cleveland's half of the third inning when without a warning drop, sheets of water began pouring down. The players hurriedly gathered up their property and broke for the cover furnished by the grand stand.

It rained steadily for five minutes and more and then the lightning, which had been flashing constantly, approached dangerously near. Bolt after bolt descended and to the seven or eight hundred spectators who had paid to see a ball game it looked as if the dangerous electricity would surely strike the building.... Finally there was a crash and roar as if a cannon had been fired into the stand. At the same instant a trail of blinding fire flashed down a pillar, which supports the stand, and splinters and shingles flew in all directions. In a minute there was a scene of confusion. When the building was struck nearly everybody in the stand received a shock more or less severe, and one or two gentlemen toppled over as if shot. Several ladies fainted and it was an exciting moment.

Another flash and a big apple tree over in left field tipped over, cut in two by the lightning as clean as a whistle...."[23]

The rain stopped after a little while and Al Johnson wanted to proceed with the game. Umpire Robert Ferguson would have no part of it. He walked out onto the field, and, in a loud voice, announced to the crowd that the game was over. It then started to rain heavier than before.

The *Cleveland Press* of Friday claimed, concerning the lightning: "So swift was its flight homeward that it collided with the flag staff on the roof and broke it off."[24] From Friday's *Cleveland Leader*: "'Did you get a rain check or a lightning check?' said one facetious young man as he walked out of the Brotherhood Park yesterday."[25] A few days later, when announcing that a free ladies' day was scheduled at the Brotherhood Grounds, the *Leader* mentioned that "The grounds are gay as ever, and seven new lightning rods are warranted to draw the attention of the lightning from any dangerous clouds that may loom up in the future."[26]

A short time after the lightning storm, the *Plain Dealer* gave the Brotherhood team a nickname — they called them the "Electrics." The name, however, didn't catch on and was dropped from print, perhaps because a pretty good amateur team around town had, of late, been calling themselves the Electrics too.

Five for the Fourth

Both clubs had been suffering from anemic attendance overall through June, thus making the upcoming Fourth of July doubleheaders, to be staged in Cleveland, critical for the war chest of both teams in order to continue waging the baseball war of 1890.

The National League doubleheader was scheduled for a 10 A.M. and a 4 P.M. start. The Players' League advertising called for games at 10 A.M. and 3:30 P.M.

Early morning rain, from 9 until 10 o'clock, changed all the times around some. Tom Lawrence had his bucket, sponge, and sawdust crew out at League Park, and the first game there started at 10:45 A.M., against the New York Giants, in front of a very disappointing crowd of only 1,200.

The first game against the Philadelphia Brotherhood men also started late at 10:30, the rain-shrunk crowd number was 1,600.

The scores:
Brotherhood morning game: Cleveland 8, Philadelphia 7.
Winner: Darby O'Brien.
Loser: Charlie Buffinton.

Inning	1	2	3	4	5	6	7	8	9	Final
Cleveland	4	0	2	1	1	0	0	0	0	8
Philadelphia	1	1	3	0	1	0	0	0	1	7

League morning game: Cleveland 11, New York 7.

Inning	1	2	3	4	5	6	7	8	9	Final
Cleveland	2	7	0	0	1	0	0	1	0	11
New York	0	2	1	1	1	0	1	0	1	7

The afternoon games were a pleasant surprise for both franchises. With the inclement weather gone for good and the sun shining, large crowds came out for the afternoon games. The League put 3,000 in the seats, but the game of choice was the one at the Brotherhood Grounds. Their largest crowd of the year put in a show — over 5,000.

The scores: • Brotherhood afternoon game: Philadelphia 15, Cleveland 6. • On the day, Delahanty accounted for nine errors. • Winner: Ben Sanders. • Loser: Jersey Bakely. • Umpires: Knight and Jones. • Time: 1:57.

Inning	1	2	3	4	5	6	7	8	9	Final
Philadelphia	0	0	0	2	0	6	2	5	*	15
Cleveland	0	0	2	0	0	0	0	1	3	6

League afternoon game: New York 3, Cleveland 2.

Inning	1	2	3	4	5	6	7	8	9	Final
Cleveland	2	0	0	0	0	0	0	0	0	2
New York	1	0	0	0	0	0	0	1	1	3

The holiday was full of advertising in one form or another. Frank Brunell, the Players' League's publicist, used the day to announce the launching of his new magazine, *The American Sportsman*. It would emphasize horse racing but would also do some stories on baseball and other sports. The paper cost a nickel, and if need be you could get in touch with Mr. Brunell in Room 3 of the Blackstone Building.

Beyerle Park had a little public relations stunt of its own for the Fourth: a baseball game featuring the "Champion Young Ladies' base ball club No.1."[27] The game was against the men of the Forest City team, and was played out before an audience of 3,500. The captain of the team was May Howard; the rest of her nine were Nellie Williams, Lulu Grant, Edith Mayres, Maggie Marshall, Bertha White, Annie Grant, Alice Morrow, and Rose Mitchell. The pitcher, Nellie Williams, had the distinction of being the first female base ballist to have her likeness appear in a Cleveland paper. She is shown in a pose ready to deliver a pitch to the plate. The girls wore vertically striped hats, blouses, and skirts (below the knee), and full-length leggings.

A few quotes from the *Plain Dealer's* man at the game:

- "Where are your girls from?" was asked Manager Franklin.
"Oh," he said, "some of them are from Cincinnati. Many of them were picked up nearer Cleveland than Cincinnati."
- The game was interrupted [meaning the police shut it down] and had to be brought to a close at the end of the seventh inning....
- What the score was it was almost impossible to find out, there being no official scorer there, but it was understood the girls were not defeated.[28]

The Spiders, in mid–July, changed managers— Smeltz was out, and Bob Leadley of the defunct Detroit franchise was in.

The Brotherhood announced, at the end of July, that they would have a one-price doubleheader, and that an upcoming series of three games would be free to the ladies (in the first week of July, the League team had started admitting all ladies free for the rest of the year).

An August Find

There was a pitcher whose work down in Canton had come to the attention of the decision makers over at the Cleveland League offices. This particular pitcher was reputed to be wearing out several catchers per game. It was even speculated that one of his catchers, named York, who had been fined for drinking, might have been doing so out of pain and fear for his life — so fast was the fastball of this unknown pitching prodigy. In addition to speed, the pitch repertoire of this hot prospect included — in the terminology of the day — a good rise, outdrop, and inshoot.

President Robison and his advisers contacted the Canton baseball club, and for a consideration (reputed to be $300) their star pitcher became a Cleveland Spider.

He was given his first Cleveland trial in the first game of the August 7 doubleheader against Chicago. He was a big farm boy, and his hurriedly thrown together uniform made him look all the more a hayseed. Some of the young boys in the stands took to teasing him, calling him "Jed Prouty" and "Josh Whitcomb"—country bumpkin characters in two popular plays of the time about rural life.

The Chicago batters were totally baffled, not getting a run through the first five innings. The new pitcher weakened a trifle in the sixth, and Chicago put up a solitary run. It was to be their only run, as they went down to defeat 8–1: "The ex-farmer boy had become the idol of the hearts of Cleveland's base ball cranks."[29]

It was a masterful three-hitter the rookie pitcher threw that day. It was win number 1, there would be 510 more. Welcome to Cleveland, Mr. Cy Young!

Inning	1	2	3	4	5	6	7	8	9	Final
Cleveland	3	0	0	0	0	2	2	1	0	8
Chicago	0	0	0	0	0	1	0	0	0	1

"Wild Bill" Hutchison was Young's opponent. McDermott was the umpire. Chicago won the second game 7–1.

In a Brotherhood game in mid–August against Buffalo, Cleveland won 12–8: Delahanty, McAleer, Sutcliffe, and Faatz all hit home runs—not one of them was a cheap shot. Maybe the heavy hitters had *borrowed* one of Ed McKean's barrels of miracle mineral water, brought over to the League clubhouse from his home town of Grafton, Ohio.

September Luck

Wonder-water wasn't working for either team on September 1, when Cleveland accomplished an ignominious feat that they will never again be able to duplicate. They lost 4 ball games in a single day!

The Cleveland League team lost to the New York Giants 4–0 and 5–1. The Cleveland Brotherhood team lost to the Boston Reds 11–7 and 11–2. Cleveland's two teams were both in seventh place at the beginning of September.

It wasn't known what it would take to improve the luck, or the place of either team in the standings—perhaps a proper talisman could be found for the job. At the National League park, a big pile of horseshoes in the outfield wasn't doing its job in the luck department—a few Spiders had even tripped over the stack during play. And the lucky horseshoe some young ladies had hung up in the grandstand wasn't so lucky either, so they cut it down—and it fell into the passageway behind the grandstand and almost brained a spectator.

The goat-and-terrier mascot team at the League Park was doing more eating than luck-making, and the two mascots (former streetcar mules of the Johnson brothers) over in the outfield at the Players' League were doing a better job of being retired than producing wins. Despite serious efforts by all the experts in such matters, no new winning mascot was forthcoming in either baseball camp.

Frank Robison, not waiting for the right lucky charm to come along, was quietly working on a change of venue and mode of transportation that would hopefully bring fortune his way next year. The four-year lease on the present League facility was up after the year, so Robison, in order to protect his baseball interest, had signed a long term lease for the use of the amateur grounds at the northeast corner of Lexington and Dunham (E. 66th) streets. He also arranged that his currently being built Payne cable car line would have a licensed extension to the doors of his new ballpark on Lexington, as well as a further right-of-way out to the edge of University Circle.

The War and the Season Ends

The baseball war was winding down, because President Al Spalding of the National League had bluffed the Brotherhood's magnates into believing that he had the far greater resources to continue the battle. The Brotherhood players were suspicious, but they could do nothing to stop their money-men from cutting individual private deals behind the scenes with the National League powers.

Al Johnson talked a brave fight, while at the same time arranging a cash purchase of the League franchise in Cincinnati for $38,000. He claimed it

Cy Young started his famous career in Cleveland in August of 1890 and remained a Spider through 1898. He pitched in Cleveland post-season championship series in 1892, 1895 and 1896.

would be a good market for the Brotherhood to be in next year, but it really gave him leverage for being a franchise owner in the National League, or being bought out by the League's owners for a tidy little profit.

The season ended in Cleveland for both teams on Saturday, October 4, 1890. Both of Philadelphia's teams were in town for the finales. The National League "Phillies" had a shot at second place if they could defeat the Spiders in a doubleheader. They lost both games.

The first score was 5–1 and the second 7–3. The second contest was called after the seventh due to darkness. Cy Young pitched both ends of the twin-bill victories.

The Brotherhood "Quakers" from the City of Brotherly Love trounced Cleveland 16–4. Hen Gruber took the loss, giving up 14 hits in the final game at the Brotherhood Grounds.

"Good by, old season of 1890; may we never see such another."[30]

—*Cleveland Plain Dealer.*

The National League would be back in Cleveland in 1891. The Brotherhood of Professional Base Ball Players would not. The Cleveland Base Ball Park (1887–1890) and the Cleveland Brotherhood Park (1890) had just seen their last major league games.

Frank Robison was committed to his new ball grounds and was not interested in moving into the Brotherhood location. All of the Brotherhood parks, with the exception of Cleveland and Buffalo (which did not have a major league team), eventually became home to an American Association or National League franchise in their city.

The two Cleveland ballparks hosted a few additional games before the year ended. On October 11, the Brotherhood Park hosted Cleveland's first soccer game. The Cleveland Wanderers beat the Bay Citys (probably Sandusky) 5–4. The Albions and Standards also played a ball game at the Brotherhood Park at the end of October.

In November, a football game was played at League Park. The Cleveland football team, wearing olive green, defeated the Crescent football team 10–0. It was a benefit game for Lakeside Hospital.

Al Johnson took his team down to Cincinnati for three exhibition games only a few days after the regular season ended. Cincinnati won game one 11–6; Cleveland won game two 8–2; and game three went to Cincinnati 14–1.

It was rumored that a load of Al Johnson's famous folding opera chairs from the Cleveland Brotherhood Park—as well as some other pieces of the park—had followed him down to Cincinnati. Frank Robison was seen nosing around the Brotherhood grounds in late October, trying to get some good deals on some of the fixtures that were being sold off. He was also helping the Cleveland Athletic Club (of which he was an official) search for a suitable site for their new athletic field. It was to feature baseball, bicycle racing, and track and field.

The Players' League hung on for a while, in name only, following the last games. The smarter players knew they had lost, and that their lot in the future was going to be the lesser for it. It would take more than three-quarters of a century for major league ball players to get a labor organization that meant anything—up until that day, the owners called all the important shots.

1891

Cable Cars

Cleveland was to have its second new ballpark in just two years because Frank Robison could not get a lease extension on the land of the Cleveland Base Ball Park.

A few years earlier Robison had decided to replace his horse-drawn streetcars. To his chagrin he had dismissed electric streetcar technology as a distant dream. In its place he had gotten himself locked into contracts for the construction of a San Francisco–style system of cable car lines.

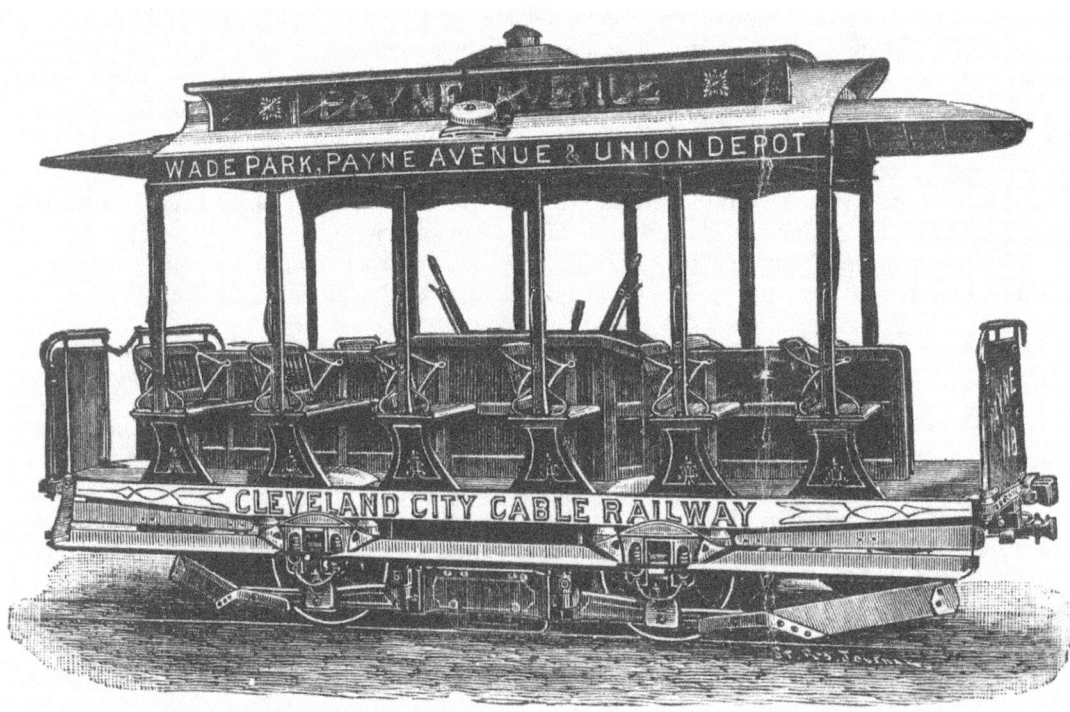

An illustration of the cable car that from 1891 to 1899 went to League Park.

Due to recent advances in electric motor technology the cable car system was obsolete before it was even built. If Robison wished to have his baseball patrons ride his cable cars, he had to have a park somewhere along his franchised right of way. This ruled out taking over the Brotherhood Park.

The Payne Avenue cable car line was designed to terminate on the edge of the University Circle area near today's Martin Luther King Blvd. The route of the Payne cable car going east was: from the Union Terminal on the lakefront, south on Water St. (W. 9th), east on Superior to the intersection of Payne, out Payne to its dead end at Wilson (E. 55th), south on Wilson, east via Lexington, south on E. Madison (E. 79th), and finally east on Hough to its ending at Cable Park — a picnic area with an outdoor amphitheater (current site of the Rockefeller Park lagoon).

Cable cars were mechanical in nature. A device called a grip accessed a continuously moving cable set in a pipe below the center of the tracks. The grip was in the center of the car and was basically a long flat piece of metal that extended through the bottom of the vehicle and into the openings of the split center rail and cable tube below. At its tip it opened like a pair of hands that were closed by the operator in order to "grip" the moving cable.

As the cable was gripped, passengers would be pressed hard against the back of their seats by a sharp forward lurch, as the car immediately matched speed with the moving cable. The Payne cable moved at twelve miles an hour over its route, with the exception of a short span from Public Square to the Union Depot, where the speed was six miles an hour (this was made possible by reduction gears in a vault under Public Square). Releasing the grip and applying the manual brake could stop cable cars.

The complete system of the Superior cable and Payne cable lines consisted of four cables each operating as a separate independent loop. Collectively the cables stretched for 20 miles under the street. The powerhouse was on the northeast corner of Superior and Kirtland (E. 49th) where the back annex of the original structure still stands. The Cleveland architectural company of Cudell & Richardson designed the beautiful buildings.

Two William Wright–model oil-burning steam boilers, built by Babcock and Wilcox, generated 1,600 horsepower for the cable. The flywheels of the operation were twenty-four feet in diameter and weighed in the tens of tons. The six drums holding the cables were twelve, fourteen and sixteen feet in diameter and were grouped in equal pairs.

At the height of the baseball war of 1890, Robison had secured a ten-year lease for the land on the northeast corner of Lexington and Dunham (E. 66th). This is where the Cleveland Base Ball Grounds was to be built. The Payne cable cars could then drop off passengers near the entrance. In February the baseball company was issued a building permit. Work on the site began at once.

The Cleveland Base Ball Grounds (League Park)

Walter Rice, the former city engineer, and an architect designed the stands, and Tom Lawrence, the veteran groundskeeper, was put to work supervising the building and landscaping of the new park.

The grandstand had a single deck; it was a semi-circle with unobtrusive iron pillars supporting the roof. It was 90 feet long, 40 feet deep, and averaged 18 feet in height. On the front right corner of the roof were six private balcony boxes with seating for 20 each. The boxes sold out for the year before opening day. On the left front roof corner was a smaller box that was pressed into service in mid-season as the reporters' stand. The club directors reserved a section of seating in the center of the grandstand to serve as their own private box. The front of the stands was broken at field level for gate openings between the grandstand and the pavilion on the left and the open-air bleacher on the right. This was to expedite the crowds from and into the promenade under the grandstand.

This drawing from the *Plain Dealer* shows League Park as a mostly wooden structure. The park was rebuilt for the 1910 season, the wooden grandstand giving way to a two-deck concrete and steel structure.

The structures were ready for the painters' final touch by the end of March.

The base paths had a foundation of gravel and were topped with a covering of hard clay. The pedestrian walkways in front of the stands and the warning track along the outfield fence were of gravel. Most of the lumber for the twelve-foot-high fences, and all of the three thousand yards of sod used to cover the field and diamond, were hauled over from the old park.

Due to budgetary restraints an abbreviated spring training took place this year. Cleveland hooked up with the team from Pittsburgh, and under the care of George Howe went to Jacksonville, Florida, to work out and plan some exhibition games. They arrived at the end of March. Press coverage of spring training was sparse, but in one of the games at Jacksonville, in front of a crowd of 500, Cleveland was credited with a win. The teams headed north after April 13 and were reported as having played in Macon, Georgia, and Atlanta, Georgia. Cleveland won over Pittsburgh at the latter place on Saturday, April 8. Cleveland's catcher Charley "Chief" Zimmer hit a home run in the 6–5 victory.

Cleveland opened on the road with series at Boston and Pittsburgh:

> The opening day at length is come,
> The gladdest of the year;
> Of muffing flies and dodging fouls
> And swatting of the sphere.
> Grouped in the shadows of the stands
> The cranks, with faces red,
> Send execrations swirling down
> Upon the umpire's head.
> The preacher and the laymen swear.
> Likewise the restless Jay.
> And Davy Jones has much to do
> Upon the opening day.[1]
>
> —*Cleveland Press*

Getting Ready

The Spiders came home for the May 1 home opener with a record of 8 and 6. The Cleveland players got to the ballpark early in order to change into their uniforms for an early afternoon appointment. They checked out their new clubhouse under the pavilion and found it to be well lit and ventilated. They found the showers to be good and hot and the lockers to be nice big ones, and hung up inside each of these lockers was a fitted and freshly pressed new white uniform, with "Cleveland" printed across the front in black letters, awaiting its owner.

To advertise the opening of the season and the new ballpark, a cable car train, done up in American flags and patriotic colors, was stationed by the Lexington Avenue exit of the pavilion. At one o'clock, the sixteen-piece brass band on board began to play, and the Payne cable train started on its way east.

On its return trip west, it stopped at the ballpark and loaded up with ball players and headed downtown. At the Hollenden Hotel, Cincinnati Manager Tom Loftus and his players in their fresh blue uniforms climbed on board and joined the happy parade. They rode to the end of the line by the Union Depot and then back to the ballpark. Through the lively music, and with the flags whipping in the breeze, they shouted and waved at everyone they saw.

The papers suggested that those attending the opener take the cable or the rerouted Wade Park electric, because the new ballpark had only a pavilion parking lot and that had but twenty spaces.

The public, after purchasing their pasteboard tickets, passed through the two turnstiles into the corridor in the back of the grandstand. A wooden walkway led to the bleachers on the left and to the pavilion on the right. A revolving door of the metal-bar type at the entrance to each side stand prevented sneaking back into the grandstand after the ushers went off ticket duty. The combined bench seating of the two stands was three thousand. Two broad stairways, one on the right and another on the left, underneath the rows of the grandstand, led up to 1,800 cushioned chairs. With the exception of a small section in the far right of the grandstand, no smoking was allowed.

The man stationed at the outfield gate took one more look at the bright scene in front of him. The grass was a vibrant green and all over the outfield it held swarms of bright yellow dandelions in full bloom. Sunlight glistened off the fresh paint, red and white for the stands and blue-gray for the fences. And high above the grandstand, on top of the balcony boxes, red, white and blue bunting was strung between the four flagpoles, from each which floated "Old Glory."

The man now gazed at his watch and it was exactly 2:45 P.M. He threw open the gate:

Then up spake the band in an
OUTBURST OF JOVIAL HARMONY,
and with the Cincinnati club on the right and the Cleveland club on the left, marched as gaily as Paddy Rooney on the 17th of March down through the center of the field to the front of the stands, where everybody bowed, the crowd not being outdone in courtesy by the players, and the craft was launched.[2]

The band went into the grandstand and for the next hour performed a delightful program of music for the people.

The game was scheduled for a 3:45 P.M. start, but early on, every train of streetcars was bringing its full load of humanity.

The two ticket offices quickly proved inadequate. At two thirty the line was ten feet long, by two forty-five it had reached 40 feet, and at three it went all the way from the ticket windows at Beecher and Dunham to Lexington Avenue, a distance of over 400 feet. With an estimated thousand people still outside in line, it was decided to delay the start of game until four o'clock.

At 4 P.M. the umpire called for a short delay while the man in center field with the big camera took a picture of the crowd. He then called another delay and summoned local lad Frank Knauss, now a Spider, to come forward and be honored with a bouquet of flowers from his admirers. Frank flushed red, as the drummer in the band beat his drum half to death in tribute.

By this time the audience had grown so large that two of every three people were standing in the field. The crowd in front of the pavilion was ten feet thick. From there it extended outward near to the foul line, and out to and all along the outfield fence. Another large bunch was in front of the bleachers just past third base.

It was a good thing the crowd proved to be a good-natured one, because the shorthanded force of policemen could never have handled all the people now gathered on the grass and in the stands — an audience numbering nine thousand.

Former Cleveland manager Tom Loftus decided to put James Whitney Duryea in the pitcher's box for Cincinnati. Second-year Cleveland manager Bob Leadley picked Denton True Young as his hurler for this special day. Both pitchers had interesting nicknames — "Jesse" (Cyclone Jim) Duryea and "Cy" (Cyclone) Young.

CINCINNATI AT CLEVELAND
Batting orders

Cleveland	Cincinnati
McAleer, James, lf	McPhee, "Bid," 2b
McKean, Ed, ss	Latham, Arlie, 3b
Davis, George, cf	Marr, "Lefty," rf
Childs, Clarence, 2b	Holiday, "Bug," lf
Johnson, Ralph, rf	Reilly, "Long John," 1b
Alvord, Billy, 3b	Slattery, Mike, cf
Virtue, Jake, 1b	Smith, "Germany," ss
Zimmer, "Chief," c	Keenan, Jim, c
Young, "Cy," p	Duryea, "Jesse," p

The umpire sounded the game gong, and "Bid" McPhee, the Cincinnati second baseman, took his place at the plate:

At eight minutes past 4 o'clock yesterday afternoon Denton Young, ex-rail splitter, put a double reef in his trousers, wet a brand new Spalding base ball with his fingers, smiled grimly and then propelled his arm through space, releasing the ball as he did it. It sailed gently, toward a rubber plate firmly fastened in the ground some feet in front of him and passed directly over the center of the plate.[3]

Umpire Phil Powers gently murmured "one strike." The baseball season of 1891 was open in Cleveland and the heart of the lover of the game was glad.[4]

McPhee went down on two more strikes. Latham fouled out to Virtue at first. Marr walked and "Bug" Holiday's fly to Davis closed out the first for the visitors.

Jimmy McAleer doubled to left but got greedy and was out trying for three. McKean then grounded out to McPhee at second. The umpire then called another delay of game; another bouquet of flowers had made its appearance—this one with George Davis' name on it. Davis made his thanks, went to bat and paid for his flowers with a little patience and a walk. Childs whacked a double, scoring Davis, and moved up to third on a bad throw. Ralph Johnson then popped a little cheap hit over second that plated Childs. Johnson went for a steal, but Alvord meekly rolled the ball out to McPhee at second to close the inning. Two runs.

The Cleveland Spider, left, shakes hands with a representative of the pork packing, beer brewing City of Cincinnati, at Cleveland's new League Park on Opening Day May 1, 1891. The cartoon ran in the *Cleveland Press.*

There was no scoring in the second, third, and top of the fourth. Johnson got the action going in the fourth by getting hit by a wicked curve from Duryea. While Johnson recovered from being stunned, Childs was allowed to go in for him as a courtesy runner. Alvord singled, and the crowd looked up just in time to see a speedy Childs sliding into third. With a sacrifice hit off the bat of Virtue, the courtesy runner had circled the bases. One run. Johnson went back to his position in right field in the fifth inning.

Pitcher Young got aboard via a Reilly error at first base, Jimmy McAleer followed with a single, and the pride of Grafton, Ohio, Ed McKean, loaded them up with a single into right field. Davis hit one right to Reilly at first, who misplayed it but recovered to salvage a force out of Young at the plate. Childs singled. Clever base running by the Spiders now led to poor choices by the visitors concerning which base to throw to in order to catch which Cleveland runner. In the orchestrated confusion three Spiders came home. Three runs.

In the sixth Cleveland padded the lead by two, with a Virtue triple, a Zimmer double and a Young single. Two runs. In the seventh, the score boy chalking up the runs on the big scoreboard to the right of the pavilion added his seventh consecutive zero for Cincinnati.

The boys in blue came up in the top of the eighth, determined not to get totally skunked in the run department. Keenan got them going with a lead-off double. The replacement pitcher Rhines, up next, hit a fly above second base, but Childs dropped it. "Bid" McPhee stepped in and was nice enough to strike out. Arlie Latham, called "The Freshest Man on Earth" due to all his crazy antics on the field, came up next. With two strikes on him, Arlie looked like he might play the role of a nice guy and strike out too. Young put his fastest fast ball right over the center of the plate, and Latham put it right over the left field fence for a three-run homer. Marr flied out, Holiday singled, and Reilly closed out the inning by going out to Childs. Three runs.

In the lower half of the eighth, Cleveland, with an 8–3 lead, was taking no chances of Cincinnati's coming back and spoiling the opener at their new ballpark. They went to work with a Virtue triple, followed by a Rhines wild pitch that allowed Virtue to walk home. A rattled Rhines then gave back-to-back walks to Zimmer and Young. McAleer moved the runners over with a sacrifice. McKean's hit brought in Zimmer. Davis lifted a fly to Marr in right but he dropped it, and Young crossed the plate. McKean got nailed trying to pilfer third, and Davis moved up to second on the out. Childs was given first on balls, and the weak-hitting Johnson came up. Johnson got his second anemic hit over the infielder's head on the day. On the safe hit, Davis ran in with the final run. Four runs.

Cincinnati failed in the ninth and that was the ball game. Cleveland 12 and Cincinnati 3.

Inning	1	2	3	4	5	6	7	8	9	Final
Cincinnati	0	0	0	0	0	0	0	3	0	3
Cleveland	2	0	0	1	3	2	0	4	*	12

Notes: • "Three wild geese sailed over the ground in the fifth. 'That means three runs,' shouted a crank and just three runs were made."[5] • A young boy up in a balcony box was dressed in an exact duplicate of the Spider uniform: "He was the mascot for the day."[6] • "McAleer wore dark glasses but Holiday didn't. Zimmer got a 'sun' two-bagger because Old Sol was stronger than the Bug's eyes."[7] • Latham and Virtue, by having the longest hits on the day for their respective team, each won a box of cigars from Walter Smith, the news dealer on Superior Street. • Mr. White, one of the club directors, was out in the street with the police working diligently on getting the crowd inside. • "'What a funny little fat man,' said a young lady as Childs walked to the plate for the first time. Then, as the chubby second baseman hit the ball for two bases, she said: 'He's a perfect angel, anyhow,' and the people around her smiled audibly."[8]

Amateur Ball

Some of the more interesting names for teams this year included Wideawakes, Growlers, Balance of Power, Bryan's Bill Posters, Young Green Flags, Puzzlers, Fakirs, and Favorites.

A call went out for the best colored players to come to a meeting at the home of William Wilson at No. 442 Sterling Avenue (E. 30th) to form this year's version of the Zs. Invited to attend: Jackson, Griffin, Wilson, Mitchell, Johnson, Dennis, Lindsay, Dean, Consens, R. Johnson, Williams and interested others.

In May a "shop baseball league" was being formed[9]; early members were W. S. Tyler, American Wire Works, Brush, and Cleveland Twist Drill companies.

Out on the west side, between Dover Station and West Dover, an excursion train of the Nickel Plate road carrying six hundred passengers jumped the tracks. Six of the passenger coaches were heavily damaged. People were evacuated to area hospitals but no fatalities were discovered until the repair train lifted one of the coaches. Zachariah Rogers was found under a car, dead from massive head injuries: "Evidently he had either jumped hoping to save himself or had been thrown from the car's platform, and in either case been crushed beneath the falling coach."[10]

The Shamrock ball club called a meeting to attend to details for the funeral of Zachariah Rogers, their second baseman. Rogers, who was in his late twenties, was single and worked at the Cleveland Burial Case Co.

Life After the Brotherhood

J. J. Coleman was a signing agent and George Sliney the treasurer of the defunct Brotherhood league. The two Cleveland men found new jobs in 1891. Coleman became the manager of the ball team that his cousin, Al Johnson, strongly supported. Under his leadership the Albions won the city championship. George Sliney was now an entrepreneur at his new cigar emporium on Superior Street.

Al Johnson, following the demise of the Brotherhood, was stuck with a ballpark where, by the terms of surrender with the National League, he was not allowed to stage baseball games. Al thought the ruling didn't include amateur teams (which were often really semi-pro). The League said no regular-season sandlot games are to be played, period; however, they would allow an exception in the case of strictly amateur exhibition games.

At Brotherhood Park most of the articles of value, such as interior room furnishings, and exterior items in the rooftop boxes and grandstand — including Johnson's special design chairs — had been auctioned off or removed. The park, however, was in general still a viable facility for the holding of public events in 1891:

Lacrosse.
THE CLEVELAND CLUB IS BOOMING
The Cleveland Lacrosse club has secured Brotherhood park for practice and games, and the members feel very elated over this fact. The club has now thirty members and in playing strength is very strong...[11]

"A SHAM SHAM BATTLE"
"A fireworks display and sham battle was advertised for Brotherhood park last night and several thousand people assembled to witness the sight."[12]

This was supposed to be a Fourth of July extravaganza. However, the fireworks, which were "good but not elaborate," were sent up before half the people arrived.[13]

The main event, however, was the real dud. The Fifth Infantry sent Companies A and F under command of Capt. Zimmerman to fight it out with Company B led by Captain Whitney. The problem was that the light provided by the fires at either end of the field was insufficient. When combined with ground fireworks of different colors, the dim light had a weird look to it, "the appearance of the soldiers was more ethereal than material. They looked like spooks."[14]

Half the time, the location of the soldiers was revealed only by the firing of their guns. The battle was haphazard because the captains' orders could not be heard over the fireworks. Half the crowd left before the show was over; the other half stayed and cracked jokes about the farce on the field.

Get the Leadley Out

The record in May and June of the Spiders under manager Bob Leadley was mediocre. By mid–June the writers were running a not-too-subtle campaign for his ouster. They had Pat Tebeau in mind as a replacement. As last year's captain of the Brotherhood team, and as one of the ringleaders of the roughhouse antics of the 1889 Spiders, they felt Tebeau had the intellect and fire-in-the-belly attitude to make a go of the 1891 Spiders.

A number of stories favorable to Tebeau started showing up in mid–June. In one story his fast thinking was credited with saving a man from drowning. The man had gotten drunk in the bar at the Kennard House — the players' hotel — and Pat had pulled him out of the lobby fountain just in time.

The reprinting of this poem after some humiliating losses in New York City didn't help Leadley's cause:

> The Spiders came smiling out of the West,
> Out of the West where the sun goes down—
> There were Davis, McKean and all the rest
> O; the sluggers bold from Cleveland town:
> But the goose did sit and the goose did lay
> And her eggs all went in the good old way
> And the Cleveland boys are mourning.[15]

HOLIDAY TWIN BILL

Philadelphia was the attraction for the Independence Day doubleheader. Seven thousand showed up for the early game. Cleveland batted first, and had the game well in hand when, in the top of the ninth, they scored four runs to take a commanding 14–4 lead. Cleveland's starter Lee Viau then had a total cave-in and had to be relieved by outfielder George Davis, who barely held on to save the game. The visitors' ten-run outburst fell just short of tying. Final: Cleveland 15, Philadelphia 14. Lee Viau won and Duke Esper lost.

THE SECOND GAME

The late game drew 10,000, but second-year pitcher Frank Knauss was no match for the Philadelphia hitters, and veteran Kid Gleason was more than a match for the Cleveland batsmen. Final: Philadelphia 9, Cleveland 1.

Tebeau had been on the hospital list for ten weeks but had returned in time to play in both games for the Fourth of July. A week after the sloppy play in the holiday doubleheader, R. H. Leadley was out as manager and Oliver Wendell "Patsy" Tebeau was in.

August "Fighters"

By August first, Cleveland's new player-manager had taken the team from sixth place up into fourth place with an over-all record of 42 and 42. But most of the games were in front of friendly crowds; August would be a month of road games.

By mid–August the Spiders' record was 44 and 50. At this low point, Tebeau led the team to a moral victory at Boston in its first extra-inning affair of the year. With two out in the twelfth he drove in Childs to secure a 6–5 win.

In the meantime the papers had been pushing a pet name for Pat's boys. They called them "the fighters." The *Chicago Tribune* said of the Cleveland team, after almost a month on the road: "The latter are known as 'the fighters' along the circuit, and at Cincinnati and other places they are so full of ginger that they waste it in chasing opposing players around with bats and doing other kittenish tricks. But when they find the hustling Colts in front of them they are as meek and humble as a band of Trappist monks."[16]

When the Spider "fighters" came home at the end of August there were some changes on the team and at the park. Ralph Johnson had been released and replaced by somebody named Jesse

Burkett. They found their field in a hard and scorched condition, due to the severe drought conditions in August; the thousands of barrels of water thrown on the field had done no good.

One player noticed that on top of the grandstand there was now a wire screen (this to cut down on the loss from foul balls). And in the grandstand, trying to cut down on some of his losses, was Al Johnson. Johnson and his new bride were at all the games now. Johnson, getting back in the good graces of President Robison, had even donated the Brotherhood uniforms to amateur ball. They ended up on the backs of the Stars, a team that just happened to have grounds at the end of Mr. Robison's Superior cable line.

Finally, the last holdouts in the press corps had left their dangerous seats in the first row of the grandstand and joined the rest of the boys up on the roof.

Keen on McKean

A *Sporting Life* correspondent out of Cleveland took exception to the flowery prose of a colleague at a rival publication, and wondered what made him qualified, over himself, to sit in the press box at the ballpark. He quoted an example of what he meant:

> McKean walked to the front like a major in the face of a fierce charge from the cavalry, and saved the game when the bell was tolling in the distance. It was not a game of any particularly gorgeous plays, but it was one that had great slabs of excitement plastered to nearly every inning. Errors counted faster than milestones from the window of a fast mail train, and the few bases on balls that were given were as conspicuous before the fray was over as a diamond ring on the lily white hand of a sweet little maid who will persist in feeling for the dimples in her dainty cheeks with delicately manicured fingers.[17]

Cleveland's keystone combination of shortstop Ed McKean and second baseman Cupid Childs were not with out their off-the-field ambitions—these being of an artistic nature. Childs, whose personal attire ran in the direction of loud and garish, was spotted in the audience of some theatrical production on an almost nightly basis. He had ambitions of being an actor, possibly, in a minstrel show. McKean fancied himself as the player-poet of baseball. A small extract from his "epic" baseball poem appeared in the column of a writer friend at the *Sporting Life*:

> The Season's Over; or, 'The Short Stop's Reverie'
>   The sun shone bright in the ball field,
>   And all nature seemed so gay,
>   When a batter, who a bat could wield,
>   Stepped forth like a baleful bay;
>   And smashed the ball with power immense,
>   And it came down fast and sweet;
>   Some thought 'twas going through the fence,
>   But I got there with both feet.
>   That night when we went to our suppers
>   My steak and tea were cold,
>   The girl turned on her uppers
>   And said I was bad and bold,
>   It was her fellow who made the smash,
>   And she wasn't going to see
>   Warm tea, and bread and steak and hash
>   Fed to a brute like me.[18]

September Spoilers

On September 16, Chicago was in first place at 76 and 46, and close behind them was Boston, their record 70 and 50. Cleveland was out of the pennant race and in sixth place with a record of 55 and 69, but could possibly play a role as spoiler with a series against Chicago coming up at the end of the month.

On the 17th Cleveland was in Brooklyn, where a win could move them into fifth place ahead of Pittsburgh:

> Brooklyn, Sept. 17.—[Special]—Just as the mantle of night was about to spread its folds over the green field of Eastern park, just as the last train of returning race-going 'suckers' was passing the grounds; just as the night force of policemen went on their beat, Tom Daly caused wrinkles of joy to enlighten the countenances of George W. Howe and Davis Hawley this evening. They sat in the grand stand and through the gathering dusk they could be seen nervously twirling their mustaches. It was the last half of the ninth inning. The Brooklyns had scored five runs, so had the Clevelands. Three blue robed westerners ornamented the bases and one was out. The ladies, and there were many of them present, for it was ladies' day, earnestly hoped that dear Mr. Inks would strike Burkett out. But Burk did not see it in that light. He missed two good balls, 'tis true, but he lit on the third one all right. Tom Daly was playing first base owing to an injury to Foutz's finger. The ball came at him with a hop. But Tom mistook a lump of darkness for the ball and the latter bounded off his shin. Shearon ran in from third, thumped to home plate with his big right foot and the game was over.[19]

Cleveland 6, Brooklyn 5. Cleveland moved into fifth with the win.

The Spiders' last hurrah came at the end of September when they helped knock the White Stockings out of the pennant race. *Chicago Tribune*—Monday, Sept. 28: "Verily are we undone. A fresh scalp which rested snugly on our baseball pates this morning dangles at the Cleveland belt tonight. The dreaded Spiders, who up to the present time had won two out of seventeen games played with the Colts, have snatched the third contest and at this time, too. The Colts can afford to despise no club now."[20]

Boston won the pennant with a record of 87 and 51. Chicago was three and a half behind them at 82 and 53. Cleveland finished behind New York and Philadelphia with a 65 and 74 record that left them twenty-two and a half games out of the top spot.

The Cleveland Athletic Club

Frank Robison, always interested in the affairs of amateur baseball and amateur athletics in general, was an official and a driving force behind the establishment of the new Cleveland Athletic Club. The C.A.C. would join several other cities as part of the American Athletic Union (A.A.U.).

The baseball component of the club—the "CACs"—was mostly the roster of the renamed Standards club (the team sponsored by Standard Oil). The CACs had been playing the best teams around town all year, many of the games being played at the YMCA grounds at East Madison (E. 79th) and Cedar. But on October 14 there would be a grand opening of their new athletic grounds on Payne Avenue and Alabama Street (E. 28th).

The athletic park's clay track faced north and south, with two straight stretches of a hundred yards and two banked curves of 120 yards. In the center of the oval, the ball diamond and football field as well as a jumping path were marked out. Tennis courts were also planned. There was bleacher seating for 600, and as soon as funds would allow a grandstand was to go up next to the bleachers.

An American flag and blue pennant flying over the main gate welcomed the thousand "fans" to the first field day and opening of the Cleveland Athletic Club's new park. Streamers of navy blue and white, the club colors, were floating in the breeze from many of the bicycles parked in one corner of the park.

There had been a cold drizzle earlier in the day but the sun was out when things got started at about 3 o'clock. The first event and only bicycle race was "a one mile novice for safety wheels."[21] This was followed by ten different foot races consisting of several dashes, relays, and a mile run. There was also a high-jump contest, and "The Cleveland lady cyclists were there with their wheels, and after the races were over the ladies tried the track themselves and found it to be a good one."[22]

The new athletic park, however, wasn't the only place where serious exercise was taking place in October. At the end of the month, Woods Gym on Sheriff Street was full of exercising ball players who were wintering in Cleveland. They were seen dumb-bell lifting, doing chin-ups on the horizontal bar, pounding on the heavy bag with their fists, and getting out the kinks in the muscles with Turkish bath massages.

There was also word that, in order to stay in shape during the off season, several players, including the "poet" McKean, had joined local amateur football teams. It was all a good sign for Cleveland baseball. Just wait, *next year* will be the year!

1892

Split Season

The National League became a monopoly in 1892 when the American Association, severely wounded in the baseball war of 1890, gave up the ghost. The League absorbed Louisville, Washington, St. Louis, and Baltimore of the Association, and made arrangements for Boston, Philadelphia, Columbus, and Milwaukee to shut down permanently.

The new twelve-team league was a bit unwieldy. To maintain interest in the pennant race a format of a split season, with a spring and a fall pennant winner, was introduced. There was also the possibility, if it looked profitable to the owners, of a post–season championship series between the pennant winners.

The public did not know until the end of the season, but Frank DeHaas Robison and his brother M. Stanley Robison had become absolute owners of the Spiders. During the off-season they bought all the shares of stock held by George W. Howe, Davis Hawley, Charles J. Sheffield, Howard White, and Charles A. Brayton—the principal partners. Howe and Hawley, the most active directors in the day-to-day activities of the business, agreed to continue in their traditional roles for the remainder of the year.

The main pitching staff for 1892 was Cy Young, rookie George Cuppy, George Davies of the failed Chicago Milwaukee (A.A.) team, and John Clarkson, the veteran pitcher of nine campaigns, who came over in mid–season from Boston. With the addition of Jack "Peach Pie" O'Connor in the outfield—a man who could also catch—Cleveland looked to have improved its chances over last year.

Hot Springs

The Cleveland team had a nice send-off party with friends and admirers before leaving on the Sunday, March 13, train bound for Hot Springs. Hot Springs turned out to be colder than Cleveland and under ten inches of snow. Training was temporarily moved indoors.

Cy Young sent a description of part of the training at Hot Springs home in a letter:

On our arrival at the springs...we did not find the weather quite as pleasant as we had expected. Coming here we were followed by a snowstorm...and the rest of the way there was a heavy sleet—something unusual in this part of the country. Previous to this they have had fine weather all spring. The weather being unfit for out–door practice, we were ordered to take a bath, it being provided by our management. The bathhouse is about two blocks from our hotel.

This is the way you take a bath. First you hire an attendant for whose services you will pay $1.25 a week. After nine to 12 minutes in the regular bathroom you are rubbed perfectly dry. Next you are put in the sweat room where the temperature is kept at from 115 degrees to 125 degrees. You stay there 20 minutes, and from there you are again taken to the rubbing room where you are rubbed and given a shower bath. The next place is the cooling room where you are thoroughly cooled, and your bath is completed. As this is my first day here, will not attempt to write anymore this time for fear of waste basket consequences. If this is appreciated by friends at home you may hear from me again.

Cy Young.[1]

Chicago and Cleveland trained together this year; a pennant to take home and display as the champions of spring training was at stake.

It took a few days to get the snow off the field, but in the first game on March 21 Cy Young prevailed over "Wild Bill" Hutchison, 18–15. At one point, in the rather short stay at the Hot Springs, the Spiders won three in a row over Chicago but then lost the next two. However, they managed to win the spring pennant.

During a break from training some of the players recollected stories of former Cleveland Blues and Spiders pitcher Darby O'Brien. On March 11, in his home town of West Troy, New York, his life had been cut short by pneumonia. He was 24.

At the end of the month there was another funeral, as the nation mourned the passing of the great American poet Walt Whitman.

Opening Festivities

Having opened the season on the road, Cleveland left St. Louis with a record of 1 and 2. The boys arrived home Wednesday, April 20. The next day Cleveland met up with Cincinnati at the Hollenden Hotel and, at 2 p.m., got on board with the brass band for a musical cable car parade to promote the opener.

The cable train was decked out in its traditional red, white and blue, but this year, flying from the roof of the lead car, was the championship pennant won at Hot Springs. A shorter than usual route went down Superior Street then up Water Street (W. 9th) and back.

The game, if the threatening gray sky permitted, was scheduled for a 3:45 p.m. start. In preparation for the Thursday opener the grandstand chairs had a new coat of varnish, and to the left of the old bleachers, a new set of bleachers had been put up. They had room for a thousand, cost only a quarter, but required entry through a special turnstile on Beecher Street. The turnstiles in the regular fifty-cent stands, as by league agreement, owed a quarter per click to the visiting team.

CINCINNATI AT CLEVELAND

Cleveland	*Cincinnati*
Childs, 2b	McPhee, 2b
Burkett, lf	Latham, 3b
O'Connor, rf	Halligan, rf
McKean, ss	Holiday, cf
Tebeau, 3b	O'Neil, lf
McAleer, cf	Comiskey, 1b
Virtue, 1b	Smith, ss
Zimmer, c	Murphy, c
Young, p	Chamberlain, p

Cincinnati, in road gray uniforms and red socks, took the field. Cleveland, in last year's uniform of home white, took their places on the bench. And the sun — which had been hiding all day — now took its proper place in the sky.

Five thousand hometown partisans yelled their approval as "Kid" Childs headed for the plate. Umpire Lynch checked his watch, looked to the pitcher, nodded at the batter, and called "Play ball." The "Kid" then continued the festivities by coaxing a walk from "Icebox" Chamberlain. Jesse Burkett sacrificed him over to second, and "Peach Pie" O'Connor sent Childs over the plate with a drive into left. McKean came up next and the umpire called a halt to the proceedings to present Mr. McKean with a gift from friends. It was a little box that contained a diamond-studded watch charm. McKean, usually unnerved by such things, smiled and hit a single into center field. Tebeau made an out, and McAleer ripped a double past O'Neil in left field, allowing O'Connor and McKean to score without breaking a sweat. Virtue smacked the ball over Holiday's head in center, and McAleer jogged home at a comfortable pace. Zimmer put the boys back on defense by fouling out. Four runs.

Cincinnati started their batting game with "Bid" McPhee going out short to first. Latham got lucky when he popped a dying quail into center that McAleer, despite a wonderful run and dive, let slip through his fingers for a double. Halligan, with a rap to right, singled in Latham — but then, taking a snooze at first base, got himself picked off before Holiday singled to left. And at second base, Childs got a little third-out fly ball off the bat of "Tip" O'Neil. One run.

Second inning a goose egg apiece. The third inning started with an O'Connor double into left and a McKean single into right. O'Connor, a fast runner, only made third on the play, but soon dashed home on Tebeau's single into left. McKean, having advanced to third during the scoring play, came in when McAleer put the ball into play on the right side, going out McPhee to Comiskey. Two runs.

The chalk boy marked up five more round numbers on the scoreboard, until the Cleveland sixth. Zimmer banged a curve into left. Pitcher Chamberlain struck out pitcher Young. Childs doubled into deep left, plating Zimmer. Another swat into left, this one by Burkett, brought Childs around to score. The popularity of left field as a place to deposit hits continued, when O'Connor put his double out there to drive in Burkett. McKean made the mistake of hitting the ball to right field, and right at Halligan for an out. O'Connor stole third and Tebeau walked. A delayed double-steal was next in the Spiders' strategy. Tebeau broke for second and on the throw O'Connor headed for home, but on the relay he was caught in a run down. Tebeau advanced to third and Chamberlain, finally realizing what was going on, ran to cover the plate, but dropped the throw from Latham and O'Connor was safe. McAleer's triple scored Tebeau. Virtue walked and the Cleveland boys tried the double-steal stunt again, only this time McAleer, according to Umpire Lynch, was out at home on a close play. Five runs. There was no more scoring after this.

Final score: Cleveland 11, Cincinnati 1.

Inning	1	2	3	4	5	6	7	8	9	Final
Cleveland	4	0	2	0	0	5	0	0	0	11
Cincinnati	1	0	0	0	0	0	0	0	0	1

To celebrate victory, "the band struck up that stirring air 'Ta-ra-ra Boom-de-ay,' after the Clevelands had knocked Comiskey's discouraged players down and metaphorically then tramped all over their bruised and bleeding forms."[2]

> We are a merry little crew,
> Each of us made a hit or two,
> We also made Comiskey blue,
> Just what we started out to do.
> It could not have been otherwise,
> Because we've found our batting eyes;
> They thought we were just their size,
> And so we gave them a surprise.
> Ta-ra-ra Boom-de-ay![3]
>
> — *Cleveland Press*

Robison Doings

Frank DeHaas Robison had his fingers in a number of baseball pies this year. He owned a minor league team in Ft. Wayne, Indiana, that just happened to have its grounds by a streetcar route he also owned.

His friend the architect John Richardson, who had designed his cable car powerhouse, landed the job of designing the C.A.C. gymnasium on lower Euclid Avenue. The 800-seat grandstand, put up this year at the club's Payne Avenue grounds, was also from a plan drawn up by Richardson.

Another friend of Robison's, and an activist in C.A.C. affairs, John F. Kilfoyl, went to New York to represent the club at a meeting to consider replacing the A.A.U. with another sanctioning sports body, perhaps to be called the "American league." This was mostly a political move to get a stronger voice in the East Coast–dominated A.A.U.

Robison allowed the use of League Park for a ball game between his Superior Street and Payne Avenue cable car employees in June. During the game an interlude was called so that a little bit of Keystone Kops–style fun could be played out. One of the companies' spotters was spotted on the grounds and all the players chased him around the field two or three times until catching him.[4] He was then hastily loaded into a fake ambulance and sent home. The game itself went to the Superior Street team 30–13, with Supt. F. C. Wheal acting the role of umpire.

The May record of the Cleveland team was rather mediocre. On June 7, with a record of 20 wins and 21 losses, the *Cleveland Press* sports headlines started calling the Spiders the "Alleged Clevelands."[5] This seemed to spark the team into some better play. By June 20 their record had improved to 30 and 24 with wins in seven of their last eight games.

At the end of the month they had a tiring 16-inning game in St. Louis that ended in a 3–3 tie due to darkness. Soon, however, they would start a home stand that included the weak Washington Senators club, due in for the Fourth of July separate-entry doubleheader.

The Fourth Times Two

Morning Game
Washington at Cleveland
Phil Knell, lhp versus George Cuppy, rhp

The weather was moderately warm and a total of 11,000 people put in an appearance at the two games.

The first run of the day came in the bottom of the second, when Washington catcher Jocko Milligan got a good swing on a Cuppy pitch: "The ball struck the slats on top of the left field fence and went through, much to the disgust of Burkett who had jumped a rope, turned a couple of somersaults and run fifty yards in order to make a phenomenal catch."[6] One run.

Cleveland got on the board in the third. Childs, on first via an error, stole second; Burkett struck out and Davis hit a double into left field to score Childs. Davis moved to third on a McKean out at first and on a passed ball he came home. Two runs.

In the Senators' third, pitcher Knell, batting eighth, singled, Robinson sacrificed him to second, Radford walked and Dowd knocked in Knell with a hit. One run.

The Cleveland fourth got going with a Cuppy hit, a walk to Childs and a Burkett double that brought in Cuppy. Davis plated Childs from third with a single, and on the same play Burkett got nailed at the plate. Two runs.

Cleveland added a run in the sixth with a Cuppy double, a sacrifice by Childs, and a Davis single that sent Cuppy over the plate. One run.

Phil Knell's pitching problems started in the eighth: "He didn't seem to know if he was afloat or on horseback. A film came over his eyes, and he couldn't see the plate, while the nerves and muscles in his business arm flapped around like unscrewed fiddle strings."[7]

Knell's flapping arm started to flap with back-to-back-to-back walks to Zimmer, Cuppy and Childs. Burkett helped out Knell by going out on strikes, but Davis, up next, knocked in two men with a double. Two runs.

In the top of the ninth, with two men down, McAleer got a base on balls. Singles by Zimmer and Cuppy sent McAleer in with a run, and when Duffee fumbled the pickup on the Cuppy single, Zimmer grabbed third and scored on a wild pitch. Two runs.

Washington, who had not scored since the third frame, continued its streak of scoreless innings by going out easily in the ninth to give the early game to Cleveland.

Final: Cleveland 9, Washington 2.
Crowd: 4,800.
Umpire: Tim Hurst.

Inning	1	2	3	4	5	6	7	8	9	Final
Cleveland	0	0	2	2	0	1	0	2	2	9
Washington	0	1	1	0	0	0	0	0	0	2

Washington	Runs	Hits	Cleveland	Runs	Hits
Radford, rf	0	0	Childs, 2b	2	0
Dowd, 2b	0	1	Burkett, lf	0	1
Hoy, cf	0	1	Davis, rf	1	4
Larkin, 1b	0	0	McKean, ss	0	1
Milligan, c	1	3	Tebeau, 3b	0	1
Duffee, lf	0	1	Virtue, 1b	0	1
Richardson, ss	0	1	McAleer, cf	1	3
Knell, p	1	1	Zimmer, c	2	1
Robinson, 3b	0	0	Cuppy, p	3	3
Totals	2	8	Totals	9	15

AFTERNOON GAME
Washington at Cleveland
Frank Killen, lhp versus George Rettger, rhp

Childs led off the game with a single but was caught stealing second, and Burkett flied out to Larkin at first. Davis came up, got a single, stole second, and when catcher McGuire, in his hurry to get him, threw the ball all the way into center field, Davis made it all the way home. One run.

Rettger began the game with walks to Radford and Dowd. Hoy sacrificed the runners into scoring position. Larkin hit a slow roller to McKean, but his throw to nip Radford at the plate was late. Larkin broke for second, stopped, and when the ball was thrown to Virtue at first, Dowd made a mad dash for home; in his haste Virtue threw the ball over catcher O'Connor's head to give the Senators another run. McGuire then doubled in Larkin. Three runs.

The next scoring action took place in the Washington third. Larkin hit a single and scored following errors by McKean and Virtue. One run.

Cleveland got back in the game in the sixth. Burkett opened the inning with a hit to center, Davis dropped a single into right, and then both men moved up a base on a wild throw from McGuire. Burkett ran home when McKean got a hit, and Tebeau's sacrifice fly sent Davis over the dish. Two runs.

The run by Davis would turn out to be the last of the day, as six more zeroes went up on the scoreboard to make it Washington's game.

Washington 4, Cleveland 3.

Inning	1	2	3	4	5	6	7	8	9	Final
Cleveland	1	0	0	0	0	2	0	0	0	3
Washington	3	0	1	0	0	0	0	0	*	4

Crowd: 6,100. Umpire: Tim Hurst.

Cleveland	Runs	Hits	Washington	Runs	Hits
Childs, 2b	0	2	Radford, rf	1	1
Burkett, lf	1	1	Dowd, 2b	1	0
Davis, rf	2	3	Hoy, cf	0	0
McKean, ss	0	1	Larkin, 1b	2	1
Tebeau, 3b	0	1	McGuire, c	0	2
Vibtue, 1b	0	1	Duffee, lf	0	2
McAleer, cf	0	0	Richardson, ss	0	1
O'Connor, c	0	0	Killen, p	0	0
Rettger, p	0	0	Robinson, 3b	0	0
Totals	3	9	Totals	4	7

Baltimore came into town after the Washington games and lost 11–5. The *Press* wrote that their play was poor because, while in Pittsburgh over the holiday, "Monongahela river water and unripe bug juice consumed by some of them had a bad effect."[8]

Another visiting team suffered a bad defeat in Cleveland, this one not attributable to alcohol:

Sandlot Baseball

The *Cleveland Gazette*, August 3, 1892: "The game of base ball Sunday afternoon at Forest City Park between the Old Leaguers (white), of this city, and the Keystones (Afro-American), of Pittsburg, was a farce."[9]

The Old Leaguers cheated legally by using a guest pitcher. In this instance, that was George Rettger, until recently a backup for the Spiders. He pitched a four-hitter in the 18-to-nothing shutout. Jim Lindsey, of the victimized visitors, received an honorable mention for his superior play in center field. Lindsey was originally from Cleveland. Two thousand spectators witnessed the spectacle.

The *Cleveland Press* newspaper boys' championship baseball game was held July 16 at League Park. On Saturday, at 9 a.m., the players (13 to 16 years old) climbed aboard a cable car train on Water Street. With a brass band playing and the flags and bunting waving in the breeze, they set off for the ten o'clock game at League Park.

The teams wore the uniforms they had won as the champions of their respective sides of town: "The East-siders were dressed in light gray suits, with blue stockings and belts, while the boys from across the river wore dark gray, with maroon trimmings."[10]

Second baseman Cuoid Childs helped the 1892 Spiders to the post-season series, leading the league in on-base percentage and runs, finishing second in walks, and third in runs created.

The pavilion was reserved for young friends of the players, but anyone who wanted to go could get a free ticket at any press agency. Twenty-five hundred people went to the game. In a corner of the grandstand the band of "southern colored boys"[11] provided music throughout.

The East-siders wasted no time in showing why they were the favorites. Seven runs in the first and seven more in the game, and they were the champions. Final: 14–5.

There were two home runs in the game. In the seventh the East-side catcher Auger hit one, and "In the eighth inning, Tommy Leach, captain of the East side, demonstrated that he is a coming base ball player by knocking out a home run."[12]

Tommy Leach was 14 years old when he pitched this game. In 1898 he would go on to fame as a National Leaguer, first as a third baseman and later in the outfield. His career lasted eighteen years.

Some strong semi-pro clubs with regional reputations this year included the Duebers of Canton, the Russells of Massillon and the city team from Alliance. The Old Leaguers were the strongest team out of Cleveland, and the Sunday house team at Forest City Park. Their roster was replete with the names of the best old professionals and perennial sandlotters. The Alliance team, however, defeated them six times over the course of the season.

The Cleveland Athletic Club played around twenty home games this year. The Boston Athletic Association (B.A.A), the Michigan Athletic Association (M.A.A.) and the Detroit Athletic Club (D.A.C.), under former Cleveland N.L. manager Bob Leadley, were regular opponents.

The Cleveland Athletic Club had their big field day in August and their bicycle members threw a "lantern parade."[13] The wheelmen decorated the spokes of their bikes and wore costumes: some dressed as peacocks, horses, and Japanese acrobats, while others rigged up their rides as boats, windmills, and other clever things.

End of the First Half

On July 7 the *Press* reported: "John Clarkson 'the erstwhile' king of pitchers has been signed by Cleveland."[14] Also in that day's *Press*: "The lemon squeezer has been operated by Cleveland and the players salaries reduced owing to the indebtedness of the club."[15]

Having no real power, the players had no say over such a decision, and not wishing to antagonize Mr. Robison, they all signed the new reduced-salary contracts immediately. Robison at this time also cut the purse strings of his money-strapped Ft. Wayne ball club. The players planned to try to survive as a team on the shaky co-op plan.

The third week of July brought an end to the first half of the split season. The first-half pennant winner, with a 52 and 22 record, was the Boston Red Stockings. Cleveland would have to do better than their first-half fifth-place finish of 40 and 33 if they wanted a shot at the second-half pennant.

The Second Half

Cleveland played very well the remainder of July, and on August 2 the *Press* hailed the news:

The 1892 Cleveland Spiders at League Park.

> Ring out, ring out, wild bells ring out,
> The joyful news proclaim;
> We're in first place because we beat
> 'Der Browns' in Monday's game.
> Go toot the fog-horn, fire the guns,
> And drive your cares away;
> Forget all save the fact that we
> Are in first place today.[16]

Cleveland continued to do well in August, drawing holiday size crowds to a number of games. A particularly satisfying and well-attended home series in mid–August saw the Spiders take two of three from the first-half winner Boston.

Cleveland had two games to play in Philadelphia on Labor Day. George Cuppy won the first game 7–3 and Cy Young won the second game 6–0. Back home "In a number of resorts [bars] three cheers were given the boys."[17]

Cleveland continued to do well in September, including winning eight out of nine at the end of the month, including the last three wins in a row at Cincinnati. On October first they were in first place.

Cleveland was in Pittsburgh on October 11, and Boston was at Brooklyn for two. In the eighth inning of the Cleveland game the score was tied one to one. Childs and Davis got walks, and then Pat Tebeau stepped in against Adonis Terry, and hit a 3-run homer to put Cleveland up by 3. However, in the bottom of the ninth Pittsburgh rallied for 3 and the game was tied. Umpire Gaffney felt that was enough game for the day and called the contest a tie.

Boston won their first game 4–3, but in the second game, with darkness approaching and Brooklyn up 9–2 after five innings, Umpire Emslie called the game officially over. The Boston loss made Cleveland the mathematical winner of the second- half championship:

> Hurrah for the pennant winners!
> Hurrah for Captain Tebeau!
> Hurrah for the plucky base ball management.[18]

A nine-game World's Championship series was agreed to. The first three games would be in Cleveland, the next three in Boston, and if needed three more would be held at a neutral site in New York City.

Cleveland played its last regular game in Louisville and won 11–2.

The Championship Record for the Fall Pennant

	Won	Lost	Percentage
CLEVELAND	53	23	.697
Boston	50	26	.658
Brooklyn	44	33	.571
Pittsburgh	43	34	.558
Philadelphia	41	36	.532
New York	40	37	.519
Chicago	39	37	.513
Cincinnati	38	38	.500
Louisville	33	42	.440
Baltimore	26	46	.361
St. Louis	25	52	.373
Washington	23	52	.307

"World's Championship"—Game One

"World's Championship Games,
CLEVELAND VS. BOSTON"[19]

Six thousand people came out to League Park to watch Cleveland play its first "world series game." The day was bright and warm as Cy Young (W.36 — L.11) and Jack Stivetts (W.35 — L.16), prepared to face off against one another at 3 p.m. sharp.

Childs started the game with a walk, but was erased when Burkett hit into a double play. Davis then went out on a fly to left. Despite two hits Boston failed to score in their first try: "The contest was, above all and everything, a pitchers' battle. The stout, well-seasoned bats that had helped both Cleveland and Boston onto many a victory were powerless when opposed to the ball scurrying through space with the swiftness of a meteor, or writhing and twisting like a mammoth snake as its curves carried it one way or another."[20]

No runs had scored in the entire game through eight, and then it got exciting in the Cleveland ninth. Childs flied out to Lowe in left; Burkett's bunt for a hit hugged the third base chalk line and finally hit the bag for a single. Davis' hard smash at Tucker, the Boston first baseman, handcuffed him and Davis beat it out for a hit. On a three-and-two count McKean scorched a ball that unfortunately went right into the hands of shortstop Long, and enabled him to toss to Quinn at second and force Davis. However, Quinn felt that Davis had interfered with his chance at a double play, and "While he was arguing Burkett was edging off third, and suddenly made a dash for the plate. Quinn recovered his wits just in time, and threw the ball to Kelly. A foot farther and Burkett would have won the game for Cleveland."[21]

The scoreless game would go twelve innings, at which time, it was declared a nothing-to-nothing tie.

Game: #1

Inning	1	2	3	4	5	6	7	8	9	Final
Cleveland	0	0	0	0	0	0	0	0	0	0
Boston	0	0	0	0	0	0	0	0	0	0

Time: three hours. Umpires: Emslie and Snyder. Cy Young gave up four hits and no walks; Jack Stivetts allowed five hits and four walks.

Game Two

John Clarkson (W.25 — L.16), the man who pitched for Boston in the first half of the season, took on the pitching chores for the Spiders in game two. His opponent was Harry Staley (W.22 — L.10). Boston started the game at the bat and got a run in the first inning. Both teams put up a run in the third, but Cleveland's chances were hurt in the third inning because the bum leg of George Davis would not allow him to continue. Tebeau took his place. Cleveland tied the game at 2 with a run in the fourth. Boston again regained the lead with a tally in the fifth. The sixth and seventh were scoreless. With another solo run in the eighth Boston was on top 4–2. With two outs in the bottom of the ninth Cleveland staged a rally. O'Connor put a single into center, "Then Zimmer nearly drove a board out of the left field fence. The hit was a three bagger and O'Connor was across the plate in an instant."[22] With 7,000 fans cheering like 20,000, Clarkson came to bat with a chance to save his own game. He didn't keep the people waiting. He hit the first pitch on the nose, right into— and then out of — pitcher Staley's hands. The ball bounded away, and, as fate would have it, went right into the sure hands of shortstop Long, who threw to first in time to get Clarkson and end the game.

Game: #2

Inning	1	2	3	4	5	6	7	8	9	Final
Cleveland	0	0	1	1	0	0	0	0	1	3
Boston	1	0	1	0	1	0	0	1	0	4

Time: 1:35. Umpires: Gaffney (balls and strikes) and McQuaid (field decisions). John Clarkson gave up 10 hits, struck out six, and walked one. Harry Staley allowed 11 hits, had no strikeouts, and walked one.

Game Three

This game would be another nail biter. Cy Young and Jack Stivetts, the pitchers in the first game, were again matched up for game three. Cleveland began the action with 2 runs in the first. Boston in the lower half of the inning got one back. In the second inning Boston knotted the score at 2 each. The next four innings were scoreless. The seventh saw Boston score one to earn a 1-run edge. The eighth was blanks for both sides. Cleveland's last chance again played out like the day before. They had two outs, a man on third, and the pitcher due up. This time manager Tebeau decided to have George Davis come off the bench and bat in Cy Young's place:

> The sound of the ball as it met the bat was not heard in the noise that the breaking of that bat made. Of course the breaking of the bat killed the force of the ball. Even as it was, it was hard hit and Tucker had to squeeze the ball hard to hold it. But hold it he did, and again Cleveland was beaten by the narrowest possible margin, one single run.[23]

Game: #3

Inning	1	2	3	4	5	6	7	8	9	Final
Cleveland	2	0	0	0	0	0	0	0	0	2
Boston	1	1	0	0	0	0	1	0	*	3

Time: 1:30. Umpires: Snyder and Emslie. Cy Young gave up 9 hits, struck out none, and walked none. Jack Stivetts gave up 7 hits, struck out 6, and walked one.

Game Four

The Boston-bound train carrying the Spiders was about to pull out of the station when manager Tebeau received a last minute delivery. It was a pair of lucky jack-rabbit ears, come up from Bellevue, Ohio.

The Columbus Day parade disrupted streetcar service and the wind brought a chill, but still 6,000 made it out to the Boston ballpark. Cleveland's George Cuppy (W.28 — L.13) and Boston's Kid Nichols (W.35 — L.16) were the men called on to take their turns in the pitcher's box in game four of the World's Championship.

Cleveland batted first, and put up the first of four zeroes on the scoreboard before Boston broke through in the third with 2 runs. There were two outs when McCarthy walked to give Hugh Duffy his chance with the ash, and wouldn't you know it, bang! Over the short right field fence went a Cuppy pitch for a home run. Cleveland missed a chance for a run in the top of the inning. Tebeau and Cuppy had been called out on strikes, but Childs kept hope alive with a drive deep into the outfield that ended with him standing on third. He was still standing there when Burkett fouled out to Tucker at first.

Both teams put up zeroes in the fourth and fifth frames. In the Boston sixth two more runs went into Boston's scoring column to put them up 4–0. Nothing happened in the seventh or eighth.

The Cleveland bats shook off some of the day's cold as the ninth inning started. Childs hit safely, Burkett hit safely, but then Virtue went and forced out Burkett. McKean and McAleer were next in the batting order. But there would be no Irish uprising today because Stivetts threw strikes and those strikes were not hit. Score:

Boston 4, Cleveland 0.

Game: #4

Inning	1	2	3	4	5	6	7	8	9	Final
Boston	0	0	2	0	0	2	0	0	*	4
Cleveland	0	0	0	0	0	0	0	0	0	0

Time—1:40. Umpires—Gaffney (behind the plate) and McQuaid (in the field). George Cuppy: 6 hits, struck out 1, and walked 4. Kid Nichols: 7 hits, struck out 6, and walked 1.

Game Five

"Tonight with solemn and mournful ceremony the rabbit's ears were burned and the ashes scattered to the four winds of heaven.... Now the Cleveland players swear they can't lose."[24]

With the bad bunny ears having been disposed of the night before, Cleveland now put its chances in the hands, and the right arm, of John Clarkson. The hopes of Boston were pinned on the strength to be found in the right arm of Jack Stivetts.

Cleveland batted first but failed to score, as did Boston in its turn. In the Cleveland second inning Zimmer doubled to right and Tebeau got aboard on an error by Long. Clarkson went to the plate, and, remembering that short right field fence that Boston's Duffy hit one over the day before, put one of Jack Stivetts' pitches over it for a home run of his own. Cleveland didn't stop with 3 runs. Childs singled, and Long booted another grounder to give Burkett a base, Virtue earned a walk, and with the bases juiced McKean's single to right brought in 2. The last run scored when the catcher Ganzel tried to get McKean stealing, and Virtue took off from third on the throw and made it home. Six runs.

With Cleveland now up by six, the burning of those hoodoo rabbit ears the night before was starting to look like a pretty good bet.

No runs crossed the plate in the third. The unlucky fourth had the help of two errors, along with two hits and two sacrifices, to enable three Boston men to cross the plate. Three runs.

In the Cleveland fifth McKean singled, he moved to second on a sacrifice, and Zimmer delivered him home with a nice single through the infield past second. One run.

Boston now started to get some run momentum going with 2 runs in the fifth, 4 runs in the sixth, and 3 runs in the seventh (including a lead-off homer by Tucker). They took a break from run scoring in the eighth. Cleveland answered with no runs in the sixth, no runs in the seventh nor eighth, and none in the ninth.

Final score: Boston 12, Cleveland 7.

Game: #5

Inning	1	2	3	4	5	6	7	8	9	Final
Boston	0	0	0	3	2	4	3	0	*	12
Cleveland	0	6	0	0	1	0	0	0	0	7

Time: 1:50. Umpires: Snyder and Emslie. Home runs: Clarkson and Tucker. Triples: Stivetts and Childs. John Clarkson: 4 hits, struck out 3, and walked 4. Jack Stivetts: 9 hits, struck out 3, and walked 2.

Game Six

"Monday Cleveland will make its last stand."[25]

Pitchers: Boston — Kid Nichols; Cleveland — Cy Young. No runs in the first two innings. Then: "Cleveland was the first to score. In the third inning Young hit to right field and, on two strikes and three balls on Childs, started for second base. Then Childs hit safely to right field and McCarthy let the ball get away from him, Young scoring and Childs taking third. The fat boy scored on Burkett's hit to right. Jesse stole second, took third on Bennett's low throw and scored when McKean hit to center after Virtue had struck out."[26]

Three runs for Cleveland. Boston responded to the Cleveland runs in their half of the inning, as Nichols, with one man out, got on with a single and moved to third on two wild pitches. Long flied out but McCarthy was walked. McCarthy got caught off base, but Virtue, not realizing there were two outs, threw to third to get the lead runner and the bad throw scored Nichols. McCarthy then came in on a Duffy double. Two runs.

In the Boston fourth, Tucker, with one man down, hit for a base. Quinn fouled out, but singles by Bennett and Nichols brought in Tucker and then Bennett. Two runs.

Single runs went up for Boston in the fifth, sixth, seventh, and eighth. The run in the sixth was a shot off the bat of Bennett that went way high and way long over the right field fence. Cleveland from the fourth through the ninth put up the proverbial goose eggs on the scoreboard and lost the game and the World's Championship: "Young alone is responsible for the defeat. He had no speed at all and when the Boston players began to hit him, they kept it up until the end of the game."[27]

Game: #6

Inning	1	2	3	4	5	6	7	8	9	Final
Boston	0	0	2	2	1	1	1	1	*	8
Cleveland	0	0	3	0	0	0	0	0	0	3

Time: 1:55. Umpires: McQuaid and Gaffney. Home run: Bennett. Triple: Quinn. Stolen bases: Cleveland 1, Boston 7. First base on errors: Boston 3, Cleveland 3. Cy Young gave up 11 hits, struck out 3, hit 3 and walked none. Kid Nichols allowed 10 hits, struck out 8, hit 2 and walked none.

It would take 56 years and a Cleveland team in another league to get even with the descendants of this Boston franchise: In 1948 the Cleveland American League club beat the Boston National League team 4 games to 2 in a best-of-seven series.

1893

Money Woes

The Panic of 1893 was a nationwide economic recession. In addition, tight money and financial fall-out left over from the baseball war of 1890 forced the ball club to operate on a budget that had taken some heavy hits. George Davis, a promising twenty-two-year-old infielder/outfielder, was traded for an aging thirty-three-year-old Buck Ewing, a former catcher. Observers were convinced that President Robison had received a nice chunk of unreported cash in the deal.

Spring training was a short tour of the South from late March through mid–April, with games planned against Atlanta, Macon, Charleston, Savannah, and Chattanooga. After the spell in Dixie, the team was to come home to Ohio for more practice games at Findlay and Lima, but rain canceled that idea. Finally, on April 24, a game for the contrived Championship of Ohio was played at Columbus against Cincinnati. Cleveland won 7–4. "Peach Pie" O'Connor, who had played for Columbus at one time, delighted the audience with a home run; Buck Ewing also hit a home run for the good guys, and Arlie Latham hit one for the bad guys.

The road opener was scheduled for April 27 in Pittsburgh. For three dollars, those in Cleveland wishing to attend the game could take a train ride with the team — round trip to Pittsburgh. Seventy-five people went.

On April 25, another train, this one out of Philadelphia, came to Cleveland, and the public was invited to come downtown to the lakefront tracks and see what was mounted on a flatcar bound for the World's Fair in Chicago. With a contingent of armed soldiers standing on guard, Clevelanders were given an opportunity to view America's Liberty Bell.

This year, the pitching distance was lengthened to 61 feet 6 inches, and the pitcher's box was eliminated. In its place was installed a 12-inch-long and 4-inch-wide pitching slab made of rubber.

At Exposition Park, across the river from downtown Pittsburgh, right-handed Cy Young toed the "rubber" for Cleveland and lefty Frank Killen for Pittsburgh. Cleveland won the game 7–2, and some Clevelanders returned home with heavier wallets than they had left with: "Pittsburg is quite a town for sports, and some who think speculation is a part of base ball hadn't money enough left after the game to pay the toll over the bridge to Pittsburg."[1]

Inning	1	2	3	4	5	6	7	8	9	Final
Pittsburg	2	0	0	0	0	0	0	0	0	2
Cleveland	4	0	1	1	1	0	0	0	0	7

Home run: Childs (fourth inning). Attendance: 4,000. Time: 1:50. Umpire: Lyn.

Breaking Open the Home Season

"COLD AS BLUE BLAZES: ...the air was laden with pneumonia and the crowd with furs and winter flannels."[2] There was the usual cable car parade, complete with flags and bunting and music. Five thousand hardy lovers of the national pastime braved the cold, and came out to watch Cleveland take on "Uncle" Adrian Anson and his Chicago Colts.

President Robison was host to a number of guests and family members invited to share his private box. Among those enjoying the game with him: his wife, daughter Marie, Mr. Monahan, of the *Fort Wayne Journal*, and Senator Bell, of the Indiana Legislature.

Enjoying the game, as he worked, was the famous scorecard salesman Harry Stevens, who had landed the contract for his firm to print and sell scorecards, as well as run the soft-cushion concession at League Park: "Everyone who attended the game and got one of Harry Stevens' score cards could not help remarking that it was the neatest and most convenient score sheet they had ever seen. The cover of the card, lithographed in several colors has in the center the photo of a ball player. Thursday, Tebeau's picture adorned the card. A different picture will be published each day. Harry disposed of nearly 2,500 cards and his methods of selling them and 'jollying' up the crowd at the same time, while new to this city, are clever and pleasing."[3]

Cy Young, and the one-time Cleveland Brotherhood man Willie "Kid" McGill, were the pitchers for opening day.

Hitting orders

CLEVELAND	CHICAGO
"Fatty" Childs, 2b	Jimmy Ryan, cf
Jesse Burkett, lf	Bill ("Bad Bill") Dahlen, ss
Ed McKean, ss	Sam Dungan, rf
Buck Ewing, rf	"Uncle" Adrian Anson, 1b
Jake Virtue, 1b	Bill ("Little Eva") Lange, lf
Jimmy McAleer, cf	George Decker, 2b
Patsy Tebeau, 3b	Tom ("Tacky Tom") Parrott, 3b
"Chief" Zimmer, c	Willie ("Kid") McGill, p
Cy Young, p	Malachi Kittredge, c

Cleveland batted first, but failed to score when McKean was robbed of a terrific long hit to right when Sam Dungan made a circus catch.

Chicago drew first blood in the second inning. Left fielder Lange put a ball into right that went to the fence, and he went to third. Decker came up and hit a ball right at the mid-section of Young, who just got out of the way, and Lange scored. One run.

Cleveland's first runs showed up in the third. The famous heavy-hitting Buck Ewing scared McGill into walking him. Virtue sacrificed him over to second, and McAleer beat out a grounder to first. Catcher Kittredge, leery of a possible double steal, hesitated as McAleer made a move to snatch second. His throw down there was a weak one that gave McAleer an easy base and allowed Ewing to run in from third. Tebeau went out on a ball he lifted to center. Zimmer hit a grounder to "Jiggs" Parrott at third and was safe on another bad throw by a Colt. Young hit a ball straight up in the air, and while Kittredge and McGill stared at it, it fell at their feet, and McAleer ran home. Two runs.

The second run of the game for Chicago was earned in the third. With a man down, Dahlen beat out a bunt to first. Manager Anson smashed the ball against the left field fence, a drive that Burkett did manage to get a tiny piece of glove on, but the double sent Dahlen home. One run.

Chicago broke the tie in the fourth. Decker got a free pass to first, Parrott hit a hard single to center, and Decker scored when the light-hitting Kittredge drove him in with a hit. One run.

Cleveland came up and retied the game in the fifth: McAleer got his third hit of the game, promptly stole second, and came in when Young helped his own cause with a run-scoring base hit. One run.

The next runs came with Chicago at the bat in the seventh. Kittredge singled and was bunted over by Dahlen, who was safe at first when Virtue dropped the ball. Dungan hit a smoker past the shortstop position into left, and Kittredge scored. Anson hit his second double to the outfield fence, and Dahlen danced his way to the plate. Two runs.

Down by two runs, Cleveland mounted a rally in the eighth, but with the bases loaded and but one out they couldn't muster a single run. And that turned out to be the story of the game — Chicago taking the opener with a 5–3 victory.

Inning	1	2	3	4	5	6	7	8	9	Final
Cleveland	0	0	2	0	1	0	0	0	0	3
Chicago	0	1	1	1	0	0	2	0	*	5

Young allowed 10 base hits as well as did McGill. Umpire: Mr. Lynch. Time of game: 1:50.

Baseball Notes of a Local Nature

• A frequent user of the old Brotherhood grounds this year was the amateur Outwaites; they had games against the Mayflowers and Gordons.

• The Old Leaguers were still the featured team at Forest City Park.

• Former sandlotters Ed Delahanty, "Princeton Charlie" Reilly and Lave Cross all hit home runs in a May game for their Philadelphia N.L. team.

• The Erie, PA, team, managed by Ohio native Charley Morton, won the Eastern League championship. The superb pitching of left-handed Cleveland native Charlie Dewald was the reason why.

• Akron's catcher Ed McFarland (the former C.A.C. catcher) signed a contract as a back-up catcher for Cleveland. He would appear in eight games in 1893.

The Longview horse racetrack on the west side was to be converted to other uses. Upon hearing this news, the east-side Newberg Athletic Company that featured many sports, including horse racing, baseball games and now bicycle racing, decided to remodel. Details of the improvements came from the offices of President W. F. Thompson, Secretary F. M. Brady, and Treasurer Charles Norris.

A new half-mile, egg-shaped horse track, fifty feet wide, was planned, and inside this a quarter-mile bicycle track was to be laid out. A new grandstand to hold 1,200 would be built, and the horses were to have 300 feet of new and roomy stalls.

At the Albion ball club grounds on the west side, a new informal Sunday sport was introduced by the fans: it was called "throw the cop in the creek."

A series of Sunday games, that had been played at the Albions' grounds earlier this year, had been stopped by the police and some arrests of players had been made. However, no conclusive court ruling had come out of this, so attempts to stage the well-attended games continued.

The Albion grounds, located in the Brookside valley, were on land the team owned, and were between Brooklyn Village and South Brooklyn, two towns whose legal status over the property was not clear.

On Sunday, June 18, a game between the new Yucatan team and the Albions was about to begin. The law-and-order folks of the area—opposed to the games—showed up with Justice Maxfield of Lindale, and swore out a warrant in front of him for the arrest of the players, and presented it to Constable J. B. Williams to serve.

Williams had arrested players and closed down some of these games in the past without resistance. Today the large crowd wanted their game. When he walked onto the diamond, shouts of:

> 'Duck him in the creek,' 'Drive him back up the hill,' 'Slug him with a bat,' were heard. There was a wild scramble for sticks and stones. The lone officer of the law was rolled in the dust, his coat was nearly torn off, a big piece of slag struck him in the head and he was clubbed about the leg:
> Then he was forced to retreat with his revolver drawn to protect himself but the game stopped, as it was announced that the city police force had been called upon. It was a very mad crowd that dispersed for the high grounds.[4]

In early May, Jake Virtue was given a good-luck ring for his little finger by a local waitress named Bridget. He claimed it was the reason why the team pulled two wins out of the fire against Chicago. Jake was still wearing the ring on May 22 when the team record of 9 and 3 had them in first place.

June Fun

The Spiders had some unforgettable games in June. In Boston on June 6, Cy Young and Jack Stivetts were pitching, and after eight innings Boston had a cushy 11–5 lead. Stivetts' arm came undone in the ninth, giving up seven hits, including two home runs. McKean hit the first round-tripper. Then the "Chief" hit one: "Zimmer's home run, which brought in the last three runs, went over the left field fence to foul ground but struck the telegraph wires and disappeared out of sight in fair ground."[5]

Zimmer's homer concluded an eight-run uprising that put Cleveland ahead 13–11. Boston went down quietly in their turn, and a most incredible win went into the record books for Cleveland.

Cy Young was the June 26 hero in a home game against Washington. In the sixth inning Young came to the bat against Duke Esper. Two accounts of what happened — the first from the *Cleveland Leader* and the second from the *Cleveland Press*— show a marked difference in writing styles:

> "Cy" came rushing on the scene with a big bludgeon of oak. He rapped the heavy villain amidships and the sound of the blow crashed out on the limpid air like the explosion of a cannon cracker under the chair of a sleeping man. The h. v. departed from the scene with the rapidity of a meteor through space, and the last seen of the objective point of "Cy's" blow it was speeding beyond the fence with two citizen's of Washington gazing wistfully at its sight ... the good-natured and manly pitcher jogged home with a grin on his face and delight in his eyes.[6]
>
> Cy landed on the ball and it sailed over the left field fence scoring three runs and setting the crowd wild. The Cleveland players, including Cy himself were nearly tickled to death because of the hit.[7]

Young was also the winning pitcher. Score: Cleveland 8, Washington 4.

A fire in Pittsburgh, across the river from Exposition Park, was said to have grown threatening towards the ball grounds in the seventh inning of a Cleveland — Pittsburgh game June 18. This, it was said, explained the large exit of the patronage at that time. The fact that Cleveland had just racked up its seventeenth run against Pittsburgh's four probably had nothing to do with it. George Cuppy won the 17–4 game over Adonis Terry and Hank Gastright.

Fourth Coming

In the week before Independence Day, the *Cleveland Plain Dealer* and the *Cleveland Press* were busy trying to cash in on the baseball excitement engendered by the upcoming Fourth of July doubleheader. The *Plain Dealer*, however, earned the enmity of "Scorecard Harry" Stevens when they printed a free scorecard in their paper. The flap ended with the *Plain Dealer*'s pulling its ad in Stevens' scorecard.

The *Press* came up with an idea that was popular with both fans and players. An ad painted on the left field fence was in the form of a circle; any player on either team hitting the Cleveland Press Circle on a fly would win a $25 cash prize.

Brooklyn at Cleveland—Game One

Pitchers: Ed Stein for Brooklyn and John Clarkson for Cleveland. The *Press* counted a crowd of 5,000 but the *Leader* felt it was closer to 7,000. Cleveland sent "Kid" Childs to the plate to start the game. After four pitches he was walking down to first. During the time Burkett was going out on strikes Childs got to second, because Richardson dropped the throw to catch him stealing; he then came home on Ewing's single. One run.

The next runs came in the Cleveland second, when with two out Ed Stein was seized with a spasm of wildness that ended after five straight walks and 2 Cleveland tallies. Two runs.

In the third Tebeau singled, stole second, was sacrificed to third and plated by a long fly ball. One run. Brooklyn's Richardson doubled and was singled home by pitcher Stein in inning three.

Cleveland scored 4 in the fourth. A Clarkson hit, a Childs walk, and a safe bunt by Burkett loaded the sacks. The runners held their place on a McKean fly out to Shoch in right, then a double by Ewing brought in 2, and a single by Tebeau sent 2 more in. Four runs.

In inning five, the action for the visitors began with a Richardson single and a run–producing double by Stovey. Next, a bad throw by McKean gave Foutz his base, and the second double of the frame, this one by Brouthers, gave Brooklyn 2 more. Three runs.

The score after five was Cleveland 8, Brooklyn 4.

One run was scored in the top of the sixth inning when Cleveland earned it with back-to-back doubles off the bat of Ewing and Tebeau. On the second double Tebeau re-injured his bad knee: "In sliding back to second base his knee was caught in such a way that it was badly twisted and it will be some time before it mends so that he can use it again. He pluckily tried to walk off the field with the assistance of the players but it was not to be. The pain was such that he could not bear his weight upon his leg and he was carried slowly away while the crowd sat in silent sympathy."[8]

It was thought that Patsy might be lost to the team for the year. Zimmer moved to third, O'Connor came in to catch, and the bench man, Williams, went into center.

More runs went up on the scoreboard in the bottom of the sixth when Richardson doubled, Stovey walked, and Foutz brought them in with a triple. Two runs.

"Déjà vu all over again": there were back-to-back doubles in the seventh, these by Burkett and McKean. One run.

The holiday fun was spoiled when Brooklyn tied the game up in the seventh. Daly walked, Corcoran hit for a base, Richardson walked, and the pitcher Stein, with a single to right, added 2 runs to his cause. Stovey then knotted the game at 10 apiece with a double. Four runs.

Cleveland got a run in the eighth on a Williams walk, an O'Connor hit, and a Virtue double. One run. Brooklyn also scored once in the eighth, they did it with singles in sequence by Con Daily, Tom "Tido" Dale, and George Shoch. One run.

Childs got things going in the ninth for Cleveland by a base on balls, Burkett bunted safe, and McKean sacrificed the runners into scoring position. Ewing came up with the intention of giving his side the lead, but Stein wisely decided to take his chances with the substitute Williams and walked Ewing. Williams fouled out, but on the play the crafty Childs caught Brooklyn napping, and he hot-footed it home for a run to give Cleveland the lead and hopefully the win. One run.

Bottom of the ninth: "In Brooklyn's half another base on balls to Stovey did the business and he again tied the score when hits came. At the end of the ninth the umpire called the game as it was too near time for the afternoon game and the players needed a little rest."[9] One run. The tie was to be played off at a later date.

Inning	1	2	3	4	5	6	7	8	9	Final
Cleveland	1	2	1	4	0	1	1	1	1	12
Brooklyn	0	0	1	0	3	2	4	1	1	12

Umpire: Mr. Seward. Time: 2:40.

Cleveland	Hits	Runs	Brooklyn	Hits	Runs
Childs, 2b	1	3	Stovey, cf	3	3
Burkett, lf	3	2	Foutz, lf	2	1
McKean, ss	1	0	Brouthers, 1b	3	0
Ewing, rf	3	2	Daily, c	2	1
Tebeau, 3b	3	1	Daly, 2b	1	1
Williams, cf	0	1	Shoch, rf	1	0
O'Connor, of-c	1	0	Corcoran, ss	1	1
Zimmer, c-3b	0	0	Richardson, 2b	3	4
Virtue, 1b	2	1	Stein, p	2	1
Clarkson, p	1	2			
Totals	15	12	Totals	18	12

BROOKLYN AT CLEVELAND—GAME 2

Pitchers: George "Gentleman George" Haddock, rhp for Brooklyn, and George Cuppy, rhp for Cleveland. The *Plain Dealer* counted about 9,000 for the afternoon game; the *Leader's* math said 10,000. The noise level in game two was definitely in keeping with the spirit of the Fourth of

July: "About every other man on the bleachers and on the field had a revolver loaded with blank cartridges and every time a cripple made a hit there was a flashing of pistols and sharp firing. The thwack, thwack of base hits and the cracking of the pistol shots harmonized famously."[10]

Brooklyn, batting second, got the first run in the first, as Stovey singled and a couple of hits drove him in. One run. Cleveland earned their first run in the second on an O'Connor double followed by a Zimmer single. One run.

Cleveland put up 3 in the third. Burkett walked and Ed McKean walloped one over the right field fence for a homer. Ewing singled, Alvord singled, and when Ewing tried to score on O'Connor's single he was out at the plate. Zimmer's hit knocked in Alvord with the last run. Three runs.

In the fourth Cleveland scored for the third inning in a row. Burkett walked, McKean plated him with a double, McKean took third on a long Ewing fly out to center, and on a high throw to first, McKean scampered home. Two runs.

Brooklyn, after putting up three consecutive round numbers on the scoreboard, had a little run rally in the fifth. Stovey coaxed a one-out walk, he took second on a passed ball, moved to third on a sacrifice, and came on home when Brouthers doubled. Kinslow got a base, Daly doubled, and Brouthers and Kinslow ran in with 2 more Brooklyn runs. Daly touched the home base when Shoch hit safely. Four runs.

The *Cleveland Leader*:

Cleveland got seven runs in the sixth inning. With one man out Burkett hit for two bases to right field, McKean followed with a single, Ewing with another, and Alvord and O'Connor with one each. Zimmer varied the monotony by hitting for two bases. Virtue got a base on balls and Cuppy hit safely. Childs ought to have had a hit but put the ball right in Stovey's hands. Burkett made his second hit of the inning, a bunt this time, and McKean flied to short.

The remainder of the Cleveland and Brooklyn runs during the game came in about the same way. It would be tedious to try to tell about it.[11]

Inning	1 2 3	4 5 6	7 8 9	Final
Cleveland	0 1 3	2 0 7	1 1 1	16
Brooklyn	1 0 0	0 4 0	2 0 1	8

Home run: McKean. Umpire: Mr. Seward. Time: 2:20.

"Chief" Zimmer was the first to win $25 by hitting the Cleveland Press Circle on the Fourth of July.

Cleveland	Hits	Runs	Brooklyn	Hits	Runs
Childs, 2b	1	1	Stovey, cf	0	2
Burkett, lf	3	3	Foutz, lf	1	0
McKean, ss	4	3	Brouthers, 1b	2	2
Ewing, rf	2	1	Kinslow, c	3	1
Alvord, 3b	2	2	Daly, 3b	3	2
O'Connor, cf	4	4	Shoch, rf	2	1
Zimmer, c	5	1	Corcoran, ss	3	0
Virtue, 1b	0	1	Richardson, 2b	0	0
Cuppy, p	1	0	Haddock, p	3	0
Totals	22	16	Totals	17	8

Sizing Up the Season

Due to injuries, and in order to protect the pitching staff from overuse, Cleveland made a number of transactions during the season.

John Stafford was added in early June. However, in his only major league year he would go 0 and 1 in two games. George Washington Davies, who showed promise for Cleveland in '92, was released in late June after going 0 and 2 in three tries.

John Scheible of Youngstown was signed in early September. It was a pleasant surprise when he shut out Washington 7–0 shortly after joining the team. His career, however, lasted but two more games and then he was heard of no more. Charlie Hastings, in his only year with Cleveland, ate up some innings. In 15 appearances he went 4 and 5 in 92 innings of work.

With third baseman Tebeau disabled, Cleveland got lucky when it found Chippy McGarr playing in the Southern League, and was able to sign the thirty-year-old former veteran of six major league seasons to a contract. In 63 games he put up a .309 batting average. Chippy would become the regular Cleveland third baseman for several years into the future.

After eleven seasons of pitching John Clarkson's arm was starting to show some wear. After a number of ineffective appearances in June and July the papers began calling for his dismissal. Clarkson, however, still had a few surprises left in him. At the end of August, when the Spiders had really gone into the tank with nine straight losses, it was Clarkson who stopped the slide. In a 7–2 win at Boston he defeated his old club and former teammate Harry Staley. On September 18 he came to his own rescue when he again defeated Boston by hitting a solo home run in the tenth to win the game 7–6. A few days later it was announced that Clarkson was scheduled to coach at Yale next year. Clarkson in spite of his critics managed a record of 16 and 17 in 36 games.

Cleveland was criticized for not playing very hard in the last game of the regular season down in Cincinnati, losing by a score of 11–5.

Despite their injuries the Spiders still earned respectability in the standings by finishing in third place, twelve and a half games behind the pennant winner Boston. There was no League post–season series this year.

Add-ons

An Ohio post–season series between Cleveland and Cincinnati, billed as the state championship, took place in October. A few games were played in Cincinnati and then the show was taken on the road.

On October 11, the players were reported nixing President Robison's plan for the Spiders to play his favored amateurs, the Cleveland Athletic Club. The men bluntly stated that they were going home because their contracts had expired and so had their desire to play any more games for Mr. Robison.

However, some players wintering in Cleveland, in order to stay in shape, did join the Pythians' indoor baseball league that had games at the Red Cross and Cadillac rinks.

1894

Hot-Stove League

As winter drew to an end, and talk of the upcoming season began, the baseball public learned some interesting facts about the private lives and personalities of their Cleveland Spiders.

Readers discovered:
- Ed McKean, now that his winter work as a wrestler was over, planned to continue as a part-time ghostwriter of sports columns, and that he has once considered full time work in the ministry.
- "Peach Pie" O'Connor had spent the cold weather in Cleveland playing football.
- Chief Zimmer, despite the recession, had done well in the off-season selling indoor-base

ball devices, and that his patented catcher's glove — without a thumb — was selling well nationally and in Cleveland was available at Larwood & Day.

• John Clarkson had left coaching at Yale when President Robison offered him a chance to pitch one more season for the Spiders.

• George Cuppy sent a large consignment of chickens to the hotel he was building in Logansport, Indiana.

• Clarence "Kid" Childs, later known as "Cupid," went "Hollywood" long before that term existed: "'Kid' Childs sported, but did not 'wet,' a knobby new street suit, Sunday. He looked a real swell as he galumped down the avenue in a handsome barouche, his yellow shoes high up on the seat and his necktie of a color to match floating in the breeze. Clarence sauntered about the Hawley house like an alderman, scarcely deigning to speak to the other boys. He also ate yellow custard pie. Kid is a crank on colors."[1]

The *Cleveland Press* this year paid more attention to the amateur game around town than did the other dailies. We learned that the one-time Forest Citys' ambidextrous pitcher, Harry Campbell, had just given up, after three years, a second career as a Cleveland stage manager. Harry was now devoted full time to religious work at the Disciple church on Canal St. and had retired from all sport.

The *Press* also notified its public that "Billy" Zimmer, a regular on amateur rosters around Cleveland, had left town:

> We are fortunate in having with us Mr. Will Zimmer of Cleveland, brother of the now famous catcher for the Cleveland League club, a gentleman of pleasant address, a thorough base ballist, and who has already made many friends here.[2]
>
> —*Marietta Register.*

"Billy" was now the new player/manager of the Marietta team that would play at the newly enclosed College Athletic grounds. Marietta, starting in June, planned to play games against the leading clubs of Ohio and West Virginia.

In the spring, the *Cleveland Press* printed scorecards in the paper for the use and convenience of amateur teams. They also paid tribute to the sandlotters in town with short biographies of the best players.

The players profiled were Andrus; Baehr; Black; Charley; Boyle, ss; Briggs, "Buttons," p (future major leaguer); Brower, Elgie, 1b; Carrol, Jack, p; Cavell, Charley, p; Cleve, George; Delahanty, Tom, 2b (future major leaguer); Doolan, Jim, p; Flood, Will; Fry; Gatch; Ganns, Billy; Gibbons, c; Hartwick, "Bottle"; Kaufman; Kelly, Tom, p; Kendall, Nate, p; Koehl, p; Male, Jimmy, 3b; Mapes; McFarland, Ed, c (major leaguer in 1893); McGinty, Tom; Miller, "Billy," lf; Miller, "Bud"; O'Donnell, Tom, 1b; Rettger, George, p (major leaguer in 1891–1892); Roach, Bob, p; Russell, 1b; Schwab, Eddie, c; Scott, 2b; Siegrist; Snyder, "Ollie,"1b; Spurney, Ed, c (a Cleveland lawyer); Strief, George (a former major leaguer and current Cleveland policeman); Weber, Jack, lf; Wilson, Jack.

These men played for the best teams in town. The local competition to get any one of these superior players to change teams from year to year was keen — that is, unless one of the professional clubs across the country got hold of a favored player first.

The best amateur teams were Albions, C.A.C., Forest City, Iron Wards, Kinsmans, Main Stars, Malleables, Nancy Hanks, Nationals, Old Leaguers, Quinns, Shamrocks, Unions, Woodlands, Young Woodlands, and Yucatans.

Exercise Club

It was hoped that some of these amateur teams might play practice games against the Spiders, because their training trip to the South had been nixed due to a still-sluggish economy. The Cleveland Athletic Club's new gymnasium became the Cleveland team's primary training site, where the main exercise engaged in by the players was handball.

An extra workout for some of the men took place in early April on a downtown stage. The

C.A.C. club presented four shows of an entertainment at the Euclid Opera House, called "Moses Cleaveland up to Date."[3]

About a dozen of the Spiders performed in a five-minute skit written for them: In a reproduction of a game Burkett hits a home-run ball but is called out at the plate, a decision which is followed by verbal and physical fireworks involving the umpire and all the players.

The terrible cold and stormy weather in Cleveland in March and early April kept the team in the gym and away from games with the local amateurs. Complaints from the players that the team should have gone south led to a short trip in the second week of April to Grand Rapids, Michigan. The nice weather there allowed for a few extra games, as well as a few more at Toledo on the way home.

The official League schedule of 1894 started in mid–April. Cleveland started its season on the road. Two weeks later, when they boarded the St. Louis train bound for Cleveland, they were sporting a 7 and 2 record.

The Opener

"The game was preceded by a cable car street parade, brass band and usual adjuncts to such an occasion, but it needed no such demonstration to inform the public that there was to be a base ball game in town. The subject was the general topic of conversation, and just about 3 o'clock many a desk was quietly locked and many an owner thereof boarded a car that displayed a blue lettered placard inscribed: 'This Car to the Baseball Grounds.'"[4]

The huge blue flag flying over the Cuyahoga Building was also a reminder that a game was scheduled for the day.

THE LOUISVILLE COLONELS VERSUS THE CLEVELAND SPIDERS

Pitchers: Jocko Menefee for the Louisvilles and Cy Young for the Clevelands.

Inning one: The crowd of 5,400 applauded as "Kid" Childs walked up to the plate and started the season off with a line-drive single. Burkett then hit a dribbler in front of the plate and was safe when a hurried Menefee hit Burkett in the face with the ball. Both runners advanced into scoring position on the miscue and scored on a hit by McKean. Two runs.

Tim O'Rourke sent a ball at Virtue in center who misjudged it, giving O'Rourke a triple. Tom Brown's sacrifice grounder to Tebeau at first sent in O'Rourke. One run.

Innings two and three: No scoring. Inning four: McKean's ground out went Brown in center to Menefee at first. Buck Ewing smoked a drive off the outfield fence for a double, and moved over to third on a Tebeau single. Tebeau stole second, and on the throw down to second an alert Ewing dashed home. Virtue was a fly ball out. McGarr reached on a Richardson miscue that allowed Tebeau to grab third. McGarr swiped second, and O'Connor lifted a high fly that landed against the left field fence, sending in both runners. Three runs.

The only action for Louisville was a walk to Twitchell who was picked off first with a great throw from the catcher Ewing.

Innings five and six: no runs. Inning seven: Childs got on with a single after Young had fouled out to the catcher. Burkett's out at first moved Childs to second. A hard smash single by McKean sent Childs to third, and once again catcher Grim's throw to second to catch a would-be base thief, in this case McKean, allowed the man on third to run home. One run.

Burkett ran down a Tom Brown hit to the left field fence, and promptly dropped it, giving Brown second. Twitchell wasted no time in bringing Brown around to score with a single. One run.

Inning eight: Blanks for both sides. Inning nine: One more run for Cleveland, on a triple by Childs and a single by McKean. One run. Young retired Louisville without a run in the ninth to win a brilliant three-hitter. Score: Cleveland 7, Louisville 2.

Cleveland	Runs	Hits	Louisville	Runs	Hits
Childs, 2b	3	3	O'Rourke, rf	1	1
Burkett, lf	1	1	T. Brown, cf	1	0
McKean, ss	0	3	Twitchell, lf	0	2
Ewing, rf	1	1	W. Brown, 1b	0	0
Tebeau, 1b	1	2	Pfeffer, 2b	0	0
Virtue, cf	0	1	Richardson, ss	0	0
McGarr, 3b	1	1	Denny, 3b	0	0
O'Connor, c	0	1	Grim, c	0	0
Young, p	0	0	Menefee, p	0	0
Totals	7	13	Totals	2	3

Inning	1	2	3	4	5	6	7	8	9	Final
Cleveland	2	0	0	3	0	0	1	0	1	7
Louisville	1	0	0	0	0	0	1	0	0	2

Young struck out six and walked one. Menefee struck out two. Cleveland stole four bases. Umpire: Swartwood.

Amateur Adventures

Black teams of record this year included the Kennard House team under the management of Amos Taylor.

The McKinleys were the best black team this year. The roster on May 4 was Bigben, 1b; Griffin, 2b; Pettie, 3b; Sommers, p; Craig, ss; Lindsey, lf; Mitchell, c, cf; Brooks, rf; Cole or Hall, c.

Some McKinley games: They won a game over the Handy Athletic team 17–7 and lost the follow-up game, the second in as many days, 23–11.

The McKinleys also played a game with the crack colored club the Hustlers; darkness ended the contest in a tie. The McKinleys' battery was W. H. Cole and A. Try while the Hustlers' combination was Scott and Nickens.

Ball Players Not White or Black

"The base ball club of Indians that has been playing throughout the Pennsylvania coal regions got stranded at Ashland [PA] last Monday, because their manager had skipped with $220, the receipts for the week. A collection was taken by Ashland people, and enough raised to send the unfortunates back to their homes in Akron."[5]

This *Boston Herald* story appeared in the *Cleveland Press* July 31 and may well have been referring to a baseball team called the "Chippewa Indian Club." On August 21, they were beaten by the "Butlers" of Carrollton, OH. A few days later they sent a dispatch from New Lisbon, OH, that challenged the "Main Stars" of Cleveland.

The battery for the Indians in the game with the Butlers was listed as Shelafo, p; Wautigo, p; and Pecoe, c.

May Play

Cleveland was in first place and had been since the first day of May. On Saturday, May 26, a "monster" crowd of 9,000 passed through the turnstiles hoping to watch the Spiders whip the Smoky City boys, come over from Pittsburgh.[6] Things went well for Cleveland's pitcher George Cuppy into the fifth inning, at which time his arm gave out. His replacement, Chauncey "Whoa Bill" Fisher, continued to give up more runs and soon Pittsburgh had a commanding lead.

The attendance, of which a sizable number were required to stand on the field, was made up of a number of irregulars: "There was also a mob of hilarious urchins there, imbued, evidently, with the idea that they were on the river bed grounds. They began the cushion throwing act and soon had plenty of company."[7]

With the game as good as lost, the disruptive elements in the crowd encroached upon the playing field. The umpire ordered the crowd to move back, but they weren't in a moving-back mood, so Umpire Emslie gave the game to Pittsburgh by the forfeit score of 9–0.

The wild forfeit loss notwithstanding, Cleveland remained in first place as it headed out on the road to play a twin bill in New York City for Decoration Day on May 31.

In the middle of May, Cleveland played an exhibition game in Oil City, PA. They then continued sneaking in extra games between regular ones, with a Sunday stop at the Ontario Beach of Rochester, New York, where their opponent was Troy, NY, of the Eastern League. Troy used the old Cleveland pitcher "Hen" Gruber, but he wasn't good enough and Cleveland took the showcase game 6–2.

At home, Case and Adelbert colleges booked League Park for their Decoration Day game. The big local crowd for the holiday, however, was at Willoughby, where the inaugural game for the Willoughby club on their home grounds drew a crowd of 2,000. The batteries were Sheppard and Sorter for the home team and Stakes and Porter for the visiting team from Nottingham. Nottingham knocked off Willoughby 11–5.

The Decoration Day games with the Giants in New York City set attendance records. A count of 8,000 was made for the morning game and an unbelievable turnout of 24,000 showed up for the afternoon affair.

George Cuppy and Amos Rusie were the moundsmen in the first game, and pitched scoreless ball until the fifth. With one out Childs walked, Burkett and McKean hit back-to-back singles into left, and on the latter hit Eddie Burke booted the ball allowing Childs to score.

New York tied the score in the lower half of the fifth. Rusie had a lead-off hit but was forced by Murphy, former Cleveland player George Davis whacked a double over the head of Tebeau at first and Murphy sprinted home.

No more scoring took place until New York's turn in the bottom of the eighth. Doyle popped out to Childs, and Ewing made a sensational catch in right that probably robbed Van Haltren of a home run. Ward was walked and Mike Tiernan picked this moment to hit one of his signature triples. This triple, to left center, plated Ward to give New York a one-run lead. And when Cleveland went up and down in order in the ninth, New York was the 2–1 winner.

Inning	1	2	3	4	5	6	7	8	9	Final
Cleveland	0	0	0	0	1	0	0	0	0	1
New York	0	0	0	0	1	0	0	1	*	2

Winner: Rusie. Loser: Cuppy. Time: 2:15. Umpire: Lynch.

* * *

John Clarkson pitched for the Spiders and Les German for the Giants in the second game.

Childs led off with a single into left, Burkett then got his base with a hit to center. An infield error by Murphy on a McKean grounder sent Childs home. Ewing doubled in Burkett with a drive into center for the second run. Cleveland then loaded the bases but made three outs in a row without getting a run.

No more runs went up on the board till the New York seventh. Ewing misjudged a Davis fly and when he caught up with it, near the outfield crowd-retaining rope, he muffed it. By the time he got the ball away from the crowd, Davis was standing on third. Doyle got first on a grounder to third when McGarr tried to catch Davis off the bag at third and missed him. Van Haltren bunted out to Tebeau but on the play Davis scored and Doyle took second. Doyle on a close play stole third. The Cleveland manager thought he was out: "Tebeau came rushing in his face as red as a boiled lobster. He argued with Umpire Lynch for several minutes."[8] Ward bounced a high one over the pitcher's head and the game was tied.

Chippy McGarr's superb fielding at several critical junctures kept New York off the board. Les German, however, also kept Cleveland from the scoring ledger and the game went into extra innings. The first run came in the eleventh for Cleveland. O'Connor beat out a slow roller to third to lead off. Zimmer hit to Ward at second, but in his hurry to get the lead runner Ward's bad throw allowed all hands to be safe. The runners moved up on a wild pitch and O'Connor scored the go-ahead run on a McGarr single.

Davis weakly went out to Tebeau at first. McGarr continued his day of fielding gems with a sensational running catch of a Doyle foul ball for out number two. Van Haltren's high infield fly came down and landed in the hands of Childs to give Cleveland a hard-fought victory. Final: Cleveland 3, New York 2.

Inning	1	2	3	4	5	6	7	8	9	10	11	Final
Cleveland	2	0	0	0	0	0	0	0	0	0	1	3
New York	0	0	0	0	0	0	2	0	0	0	0	2

Winner: Clarkson. Loser: German. Umpire: Lynch.

Different Greens

On Sunday, June 3, Cleveland was at Newark, NJ, to play an exhibition game with the semi-pro "Ironclads." They won 6–0. The stop-over drew a 4,000-plus crowd—not bad for a little Sunday scratch.

A few weeks earlier, on May 15, boys set fire to a pile of rubbish under one of the stands at the South End Grounds ballpark, home of the Boston League team. In a few hours the blaze destroyed the grandstand, the bleachers, and a good piece of the surrounding neighborhood—over 150 buildings were lost.

With what was often called the most beautiful ballpark in the country now gone, Boston transferred its games to the Congress Street Grounds, the former home of the Boston Players League team of 1890.

Cleveland came to town on June 2 and its batsmen found the change of venue and the pitching of Kid Nichols to their liking. They rang up 10 runs with the help of four home runs—two by Burkett and one each by McGarr and Zimmer. Unfortunately Boston found John Clarkson's pitching to be rather tasty too. Duffy hit the only home run for the Bean Town boys, but it was the difference in an eleven to ten victory for Boston.

Anemic pitching was a complaint heard throughout the League this year. Hoping to find some pitching help where no one else was already looking, Cleveland in the middle of June signed Frank Knauss, currently of the Old Leaguers. In two appearances he was ineffective. Cleveland continued to slide in the standings through June and early July.

The Fourth of July Doubleheader

NEW YORK AT CLEVELAND

The closing of the streets around Public Square, and the free hoopla for the grand opening of the Soldiers and Sailors Monument, was blamed for a relatively small holiday crowd at the Spiders' doubleheader at League Park.

George Cuppy and Jouett Meekin pitched the morning game in front of a patriotic gathering of 5,500. The crowd was heavily armed with revolvers and blank cartridges and used them freely whenever something went well for Cleveland.

A ground rule that allowed hits into the crowd behind the ropes on the field to be counted as triples was believed to have given the visitors at least four triples that were, at best, maybe good for doubles.

Since the streetcars couldn't pass through Public Square during the war monument dedication festivities, a very small crowd of 2,000 saw John Clarkson pitch for Cleveland and Huyler Westerveldt for the Giants in the second game. Cleveland lost both games.

Early game:

Inning	1	2	3	4	5	6	7	8	9	Final
Cleveland	1	0	0	1	0	1	0	0	0	3
New York	0	0	1	1	1	1	0	0	*	4

Time: 2:05. Umpire: Stage.

Late game:

Inning	1 2 3	4 5 6	7 8 9	Final
Cleveland	2 3 0	0 4 1	0 1 0	11
New York	0 3 0	2 0 2	3 1 1	12

Ed McKean and Mike Tiernan hit home runs in the second game. Time: 2:00. Umpire: Stage.

The sports columnist at the *Press* brought out his poison pen following the loss of the Independence Day games: "It's about time that Prest. Frank DeHaas Robison, of the Cleveland club had taken 'a tumble' to the fact that his team is playing a decidedly yellow game of ball.... If he finds any disgruntled players who are purposely playing rank ball, or who wish to get away from here Robison should see to it that they are disposed of at once. If the fault is in the management, Tebeau's official head should be allowed to drop into the basket forthwith."[9]

Tebeau in Action

On July 5 the Spiders were in seventh place with a record of 29 and 26. Pat Tebeau tried to bolster his team's sagging position in the pennant race with the addition of some new blood. He gave local pitcher "Buttons" Briggs a try-out but found the youngster was not yet ready for fast company.

Patsy also got his brother George "White Wings" Tebeau to leave the Washingtons after their series in Cleveland. Washington as usual was competing for the cellar in the standings and readily agreed to cash. The deal was announced July 10. George, the elder of the two Tebeaus, filled in for forty games in the outfield, hitting .313.

Also on July 10 it was announced that twenty-year-old outfielder Harry Blake had been signed off an Atlanta roster where he had played well. Blake turned out to be a solid addition in his role as a platoon outfielder for 73 games.

July 10 was a "newsy day"—Patsy Tebeau had hit a double off the Press Circle in a 16–15 win the day before over the Washington club: "Pat was an early caller at this office Tuesday. He entered timidly, but left carrying a broad smile and his $25. He sent a box of fine cigars to the office later."[10]

Cleveland's fortunes made a turn for the better at this point. The next day Cleveland set a team record with 29 hits off of Washington pitcher Duke Esper (12–28). Cy Young held the visitors to but a handful of tallies. Score: Spiders 23, Senators 4. It was too bad that only a tiny crowd of 300 saw the historic game.

The leadership of manager Tebeau kept the Spiders playing sharp and smart ball most

Over the eight-plus seasons that Patsy Tebeau was player-manager, the Cleveland Spiders compiled a .570 winning percentage and never finished below .500 (Library of Congress)

of the time, and they were winning games. One of the times that less-than-smart play occurred however was when "Jess Burkett called down the wrath of the crowd by a silly play. Because two strikes were called on him, Jess dropped his bat and began to argue. Another nice one came over the plate and Hurst very properly called Burkett out."[11]

Cleveland made another pitching move in the last week of July. They replaced an erratic John Clarkson. Clarkson announced he had quit the game and was going into the tobacco business in Michigan. His replacement was another old veteran, Tony Mullane. Mullane proved to also be at the end of the line. His 1 win and 2 losses in 4 games for Cleveland were his last appearances in a major league career that had lasted thirteen seasons.

At the end of July Cleveland had crawled back into fourth place with a 45 and 33 record.

Moon of Blood

A wild fracas of a ball game went down in Pittsburgh on August 9. Troublemakers waited for the Spiders on the streets, "Cleveland players being pelted with ancient fruit, sticks and stones on their way to the grounds."[12]

The toughs made their way into the stands and kept up a vicious harangue against Cleveland throughout the affair. Pittsburgh took advantage of new pitcher Charlie Petty, scoring 3 runs in the bottom of the first, and a total of 10 by the end of the eighth. In the meantime, Cleveland had made but 3 runs, as the curtain lifted for the drama that was to be the Spider ninth.

Cleveland felt that all through the game umpire Hoagland had been partial to Pittsburgh. In a last hurrah, with two out and Zimmer on third, O'Connor slammed the ball into left field only to have Hoagland declare it foul. Tebeau at this point had had enough and confronted the umpire. He went so far as to remove the umpire's mask and to Hoagland's credit he ignored this.

Tebeau went back to his coaching position. However, the Cleveland players were still milling around the edge of the field and refused to disperse, so Hoagland walked out to the pitcher's box to call the last out from there.

Tebeau then said to his men, "Come boys, let's go home."[13] With the game as good as lost already, Zimmer decided to break up the impasse and save his manager a fine for pulling the players from the field. He started a dogtrot in from third, hoping to make the last out of the game. The pitcher Ehret threw the ball to Hartman at third, who then threw it to the plate:

> O'Connor, however, didn't let the ball pass. He reached up, caught the ball with one hand, and then heaved the ball with all his might over the stands and out of sight.
>
> "That'll cost you $25," shouted Hoagland, "and I'll give the game to Pittsburg."
>
> Then pandemonium did reign surely. The crowd surged on the field and Tebeau and Hoagland were brushing clothes. Patsy was so mad he could not talk. His face looked like a moon of blood. He wanted to fight. It looked as if he had the umpire in as clever a toll as ever spider wove around the body of a struggling fly.
>
> "I'll take you in the dressing room and whip you till you can't stand," said Hoagland, and suiting the action to the word, he immediately made for that place through the exit in the grand stand.
>
> But Cleveland only had a few minutes to catch the train, and of course there was no fight. The Clevelands took their 'bus, with the assistance of the entire park police, and made their departure amidst showers of dust, catcalls and hisses.[14]

Official score:

Inning	1	2	3	4	5	6	7	8	9	Final
Pittsburgh	1	1	1	1	1	1	1	1	1	9
Cleveland	0	0	0	0	0	0	0	0	0	0

Unofficial score:

Inning	1	2	3	4	5	6	7	8	9	Final
Pittsburgh	3	0	1	0	2	2	0	2	*	10
Cleveland	1	0	0	1	1	0	0	0	0	3

Exhibition Players

The day after the crazy Pittsburgh game the Norwalk-based team, the Peters Clothing Company, went up to Sandusky for an exhibition game with the Spiders. Petty and Cuppy pitched and O'Connor caught for Cleveland against the Norwalk battery of Gallup and M. Flanagan.

Score: Cleveland 15, Norwalk 7.
Audience: 1,000.

Findlay's Great Team.

Findlay. O., Aug. 11 — Spl. — The Findlay ball team has played 59 games and has won 52. There is no other team in the country with such a record. The team is made up as follows: Fowler 2b, Brandenburg rf, Johnson ss, Woods c., Cooke 3b, Ogden lf, Swartz cf, Derby 1b, Reidy and Pastorius pitchers. Reidy is a Cleveland boy and formerly played with the Albions.[15]

The Brooklyn League club, after its series against Cleveland in September, stopped in Findlay for an exhibition game and found out just how good Findlay was. They barely pulled out a 7–6 win. Findlay's J. W. "Bud" Fowler and Findlay native Grant "Home Run" Johnson, were a novel sight to the Brooklyn players; they were black ball players, and perhaps the two best ball players on an otherwise all-white team.

At League Park at the end of August a game reminiscent of the old-style "muffin" games of the late 1860's took place. Players from the Murray-Lane Opera Company challenged the members of the Young Men's Hebrew Association.

The actors, wearing stage costumes in lieu of regular uniforms, surprised their opponent when some of the troupe proved to have a modicum of hitting and fielding ability.

Both teams showed they were skilled in another less strenuous sport: "It was noticed during the progress of the game that players on both sides showed a tendency to linger about third base on reaching that point, and upon investigation it was discovered that the dark colored object which rested close to the bag was a keg. And it did not contain nails, either. Each runner who succeeded in making third was rewarded by being permitted to interview the barrel. The spectators enjoyed the game immensely."[16]

Final: Murray-Lane 18, Hebrew Association 17.

End Games

The last home game was on September 29 against Philadelphia. A spring-like day brought out a very large crowd for the finale. Mike ("Big Mike") Sullivan won the game for Cleveland and Jack ("Brewery Jack") Taylor took the loss for the visitors.

Inning	1	2	3	4	5	6	7	8	9	Final
Cleveland	0	2	0	0	0	6	0	3	0	11
Philadelphia	0	0	0	0	0	0	1	2	0	3

The last game was at Cincinnati on September 30, Cincinnati had a 16–3 lead after six innings. In the seventh they let Cleveland get back into it by giving up 11 runs. A run for Cleveland in the bottom of the eighth and one in the ninth tied the game. O'Connor, with two out, knocked the ball out of Merritt's hands at third and ran home with what many fans thought was the winning run. Umpire McQuaid, however, called O'Connor out for interference and called the game over due to darkness. The tie game made the last game in Cleveland the last official one that counted.

Inning	1	2	3	4	5	6	7	8	9	Final
Cincinnati	4	0	8	0	0	4	0	0	0	16
Cleveland	1	0	0	0	0	2	11	1	1	16

George Cuppy and Wittrock pitched the tie.

The Spiders throughout this month of September stumbled and sank in the standings, ending up 21 and a half games behind the winner Baltimore, in sixth place, with 68 wins and 61 losses.

Cleveland then had to play some post-season exhibition games in October before they could go home. They drew a large crowd at Massillon, beating one of the best amateur clubs in the state, the Massillon Russells, 11–3.

The high point of the extra-season games was the game between the Pittsburgh League team and the Spiders held at Canton, Ohio, on Sunday, October 7. Two thousand people watched Pittsburgh prevail by a score of 5–3. Chief Zimmer, who had been put in charge of the exhibition series, brought his brother Billy along to play for Cleveland.

Patsy Tebeau was fortunate to avoid the second season in more than one way. He was given permission to leave the team to take care of personal business. He had been left $2000 by the estate of Billy Robinson.

1895

Workout

In February basketball was being played at the YMCA gym, and at the Cadillac and Red Cross rinks — the indoor baseball season was nearing an end. Cleveland in March went to Hot Springs, Arkansas, for a real spring training. They ventured over to Little Rock for a game before wrapping up the spring training pennant against Pittsburgh at Hot Springs. The road home included games in Tennessee, and then on into the North for a number of exhibitions in Indiana — at Evansville, Terre Haute, Ft. Wayne, and Logansport (George Cuppy's home town).

George Cuppy had rebuilt his new hotel after a damaging fire the previous autumn. When he arranged an exhibition game with the Spiders, at Logansport, his popularity reached new heights. Cuppy pitched seven innings against the hometown team, giving up only four hits. In the third, as he headed to the plate for his first at-bat, he was stopped by Mayor McKee, and presented with a nice gold-headed walking stick, a gift from his Logansport friends. The Spiders, however, showed no such sentimentality, as they went about their business of whipping Logansport 18–0.

Cleveland opened its National League championship schedule for 1895 at Cincinnati on the eighteenth of April. A parade was held to advertise the Queen City opener. An electric train pulling three cars was decorated with flags, flowers, and bunting. The first car carried Weber's Band, the second the Red Stockings, and the third the Spiders.

It was called the largest Opening Day crowd in Cincinnati history. Fifteen thousand were there to watch pitchers Thomas "Tacky Tom" Parrott of the home team and Michael "Big Mike" Sullivan of the visitors battle it out for the day's honors. Cincinnati won the close game 10–8. They then spoiled the start of the Spiders' season by also winning the next two games of the series.

Cleveland had an exciting game at St. Louis on the twenty-fifth of April. Burkett hit a homer early in the contest, but Cleveland was still trailing 2–1 when McKean came to bat in the eighth with a man on. McKean was ordered to move his man into scoring position, but he missed the bunt sign. Instead, he put Cleveland ahead — with a home run over the fence. Cleveland added a fourth run and won 4–2. The victory went to George Cuppy and the loss to hard-luck Red Ehret (W.6 — L.19).

Cy and Red Start Things Off

May 2 brought the St. Louis Browns to town for the Cleveland home opener. St. Louis was late in getting into town, so the traditional parade of decorated streetcars and a band made its morning rounds without the players. The two teams, however, did an abbreviated tour before game time and were cheered along the way.

The sun kept skipping in and out of some dark clouds as the crowd filed in, but, by the start of game at 3:30 the sun looked like it was out to stay.

Red Ehret and Cy Young were the choice of pitchers for the day. Young went to the mound, and Miller stepped up to the plate for the Browns to start the fun.

Miller scorched one at third base; McGarr handled it and threw him out. Cooley also grounded out to third. Now the trouble started — Connor and Lyons coaxed Young into giving up a couple of free passes, and Quinn hit one so far to center that he was able to turn it into a 3-run inside-the-park home run. Three runs. Cleveland fought back in their turn. Burkett, on via a lead-off single, scored on a McKean double that reached the left field fence. McKean was out at third on a fielder's choice that put Childs at first. Patsy Tebeau hit a fly out, but his brother George tied the score when he tripled to plate Childs, and came home himself on the play when the pitcher Miller threw the relay over the third baseman's head. Three runs.

Nothing happened in the second inning except Chief Zimmer's getting a gift of flowers, followed by his striking out.

Cooley dropped the ball about a foot in front of the plate, and beat it out for a hit to start the third. Connor doubled, and a red-hot smash off the bat of Lyons, into and out of the hands of McKean, brought in 2 runs. Quinn singled, but on Dowd's hard hit to third, McGarr tagged Lyons at third and threw out Dowd at first. Quinn came around on an Ely single, and when Peitz also singled, Tebeau went to the mound for a conference. In an unusual move, Tebeau pulled his pitcher in an early inning, and summoned Cuppy to take Young's place. Cuppy struck out Ehret to close the inning. Three runs.

Cleveland got on the board again in the fourth. Zimmer had a one-out single and McGarr hit a double to the fence in left. Zimmer, with a good slide into the home plate, was called safe, and on the close play McGarr advanced to third.

Cuppy doubled in McGarr, and when Quinn at second missed the relay, Cuppy went to third. A single from Burkett and Cuppy came in. Three runs.

Zeroes went up in the next four innings with both teams avoiding some dicey situations along the way.

The St. Louis ninth began with the first two men going out. Cuppy then earned an error on Ehret's foul pop up that he dropped. The St. Louis pitcher then hit a single. Miller negated Ehret's hit and closed the St. Louis ninth by flying out to Burkett in left. Burkett took first on balls to open the Cleveland ninth. Catcher Peitz's bad throw to catch Burkett stealing second ended up putting Jesse on third. McKean fouled out to Peitz. Childs showed patience at the plate, and he was rewarded with a single — sending Burkett home with the game winner. One run.

Score: Cleveland 7, St. Louis 6. Attendance: 5,000.

CLEVELAND	AB	H	R	E	ST. LOUIS	AB	H	R	E
Burkett, lf	3	2	3	0	Miller, rf	6	0	1	1
McKean, ss	5	0	2	0	Cooley, cf	5	1	2	0
Childs, 2b	4	1	1	0	Connor, 1b	4	2	3	0
O. Tebeau, 1b	4	0	0	0	Lyons, 3b	3	1	2	0
G. Tebeau, rf	4	1	1	0	Quinn, 2b	5	2	3	1
McAleer, cf	4	0	1	0	Dowd, lf	5	0	1	0
Zimmer, c	4	1	1	0	Ely, ss	5	0	2	1
McGarr, 3b	4	1	1	1	Peitz, c	5	0	1	1
Young, p	1	0	0	0	Ehret, p	5	0	1	0
Cuppy, p	3	1	2	1					
Totals	36	7	12	2	Totals	43	6	16	4

Inning	1	2	3	4	5	6	7	8	9	Final
St. Louis	3	0	3	0	0	0	0	0	0	6
Cleveland	3	0	0	3	0	0	0	0	1	7

Doubles: Cuppy (2), McKean, McGarr, Connor (2). Triple: G. Tebeau. Home run: Quinn. Time: 2:15. Umpires: Betts and Stage.

Groundskeeper Tom Lawrence claimed the victory was due to the new mascot he was in charge of: a young black street-waif named "Rastus" who had hooked up with the team at Louisville.[1] Rastus was done up in a new set of "dude" clothes and did his thing to entertain the Opening Day crowd for his benefactors. The Cleveland players were shortly thereafter threatened with arrest for abduction if they showed up in Louisville with Rastus, because he was wanted there as a vagrant. However, if Rastus was sent back to his original home in Little Rock, Arkansas, the whole matter could be dropped.

Rastus got word and bolted town with his new sponsor, pugilist Charley Slusher, who coincidentally was also from Louisville. The kid got a second set of dude clothes, courtesy of Slusher, only this time he also got a nice pair of lucky yellow shoes. Rastus was gone, but Ed McKean found someone he could play mentor to; Ed was teaching a young newsboy how to box. The boy was undefeated in a number of fights—even beating the king of the fighting newsboys, the redoubtable "Piggy."[2]

School Ball, Black Ball, and Show Ball

At Oberlin College, George Cowan got knocked to the ground when a group of "scrubs" played the varsity. Cowan, one of the scrubs and a senior at the school, went to the plate against Vorhees, the regular varsity pitcher. Mr. Cowan was playing ball in spite of warnings by doctors that his poor eyesight could impair his judgment on tricky pitches. Cowan turned his back on a fastball—inside and a little wild.

"It struck him back of the left ear and felled him to the ground. Soon afterward he recovered enough to walk, but when about halfway to the city he was seized with convulsions and was taken to the nearest house. He soon became unconscious and remained so until death."[3]

George was the son of W. L. Cowan, a farmer living near Oberlin. He was 21 years young: "His death has cast a gloom on the college. No blame is attached to Vorhees."[4]

ADELBERT COLLEGE '98 VERSUS UNIVERSITY SCHOOL

The Cleveland School Association game for the championship trophy: "After the fracas, 26 Colts had crossed the rubber, while only six 'Adelbertians' had managed to lumber around the circuit. There was joy in the 'Varsity' camp, Saturday evening, and the event was celebrated in true schoolboy fashion. Frankfurters and ginger ale were freely dispensed, and a new epoch started in the school's history."[5]

The history of black baseball in Cleveland included two outstanding teams in 1895 that received substantial coverage for an unprecedented number of games against white teams. They were named the Hollendens and the H.A.C.s.

Hollenden roster: Poindexter, 2b; Denny (Dennie), lf; Turner, 3b, p; Storie, cf; Fry (Frye), c; Griffin, 1b; Williams, p, 3b; Taylor, ss; Jackson, p; Jackson, c; Yates, ss; Stone, lf; Lurkins, cf.

H.A.C. roster: Dean (Deans), 2b, rf; Brooks (Brook), 1b, 3b; Adams, 1b, 3b; William Cole, capt., c, lf; Kelley (Kelly), ss, c, rf; Craig, cf, rf, lf; McPherson (McPhearson), lf; Jack, p; Miller, cf; Goodman, 3b, p, rf; Zimmer (Zimmerman), ss; Stump, p; Lions (Lines, Line, Lime), 2b, cf; Thomas, sub.; Hellez, c; Ed Williams, p; Paul, p. (Names in parentheses are least-likely spelling of surnames appearing in box scores.)

The Murray-Lane theatrical group had a game against the newspaper boys at League Park on July 31. Because Cleveland was on the road, Manager Tebeau extended the courtesy of allowing the newsboys to wear the Spiders' white home uniforms for the game. To increase interest, the actors' troupe played and dressed as characters from the play *Trilby*, which they were currently performing. They also brought many props from the play, including guns and knives.

The batting order of the Trilby characters: "The Laird cf, Taffy lf, Little Billy 1b, Gecko 2b, Zow Zow rf, Svengali ss, Trilby 3b The Altogether p., Dodor c. Rev. Mr. Baggott, dispenser of spiritual comfort; Trilby De Lune, dispenser of physical comfort. Subs. A. Du Maurier, Harper Bros., a.m. Palmer, Paul Potter."[6]

Six hundred lovers of baseball-as-theater watched the actors beat the paper carriers 22–18. Comedians David and Felix Rosenberg played the role of umpire.

Pen and Bat

A letter from Manager Pat Tebeau:

What Patsy Says.
  The following special was received at the "Press" office from Patsy Tebeau, Monday morning:
  "If 'Press' reports give Sunday's game to St. Louis by score 5 to 4 they are wrong, as they give them credit for one run which does not count, according to section 12, rule 60. I claim the game 4 to 4 and nine innings. Entered protest and placed our men in their position to finish the game, but St. Louis left the field. I claimed the game 9 to 0, and Umpire Wallace, after five minutes, decided it such. It is our game if the rules count for anything."
  "O. TEBEAU."[7]

Cleveland put on an impressive display of power hitting in a doubleheader in Boston on June 18. In the first game Cleveland trailed 8–5 when Chief Zimmer capped off a 5-run eighth with a grand slam to put Cleveland ahead to stay. He also had a solo homer in the fourth. Score: Cleveland 10, Boston 9.

In the second game Cleveland was trailing 9–1. The 1 run for Cleveland had come on a McGarr home run in the seventh. It was the ninth and Cleveland got 2 runs on five singles by McGarr, O'Connor, McAleer, Young, and Burkett. McKean stepped in, and soon the Spiders' fourth home run, and second grand slam on the day, went flying out of the Congress Street grounds. Unfortunately, 6 runs in the ninth were not enough to catch Boston. Score: Boston 9, Cleveland 7. All four home runs of the doubleheader went over the left field fence.

Freedom's Day

The League schedule sent Cleveland to Pittsburgh this year for a Fourth of July twin bill. It was a lucrative day for the Pittsburgh owners. A crowd of 14,000 came out for the early game, and another crowd of 16,000 showed up for the later contest. Cleveland played well, but it was all Pittsburgh's day in the run column. Young and Wallace took the losses for Cleveland, and Hart and Hawley were the Pittsburgh winners.

Inning	1	2	3	4	5	6	7	8	9	Final
#1 Pittsburgh	2	0	0	0	1	0	0	3	*	6
Cleveland	1	0	0	0	0	0	0	0	1	2
Inning	1	2	3	4	5	6	7	8	9	Final
#2 Pittsburgh	0	2	1	0	2	1	1	3	*	10
Cleveland	0	0	0	0	2	0	0	0	3	5

Winning Streak

A few weeks after the double dip on the Fourth at Pittsburgh, the Baltimore Orioles were in town. Baltimore was the reigning pennant champion of 1894, and they were slated to play back-to-back doubleheaders with the Spiders on the sixteenth and seventeenth.

Game one: Phil Knell kept Baltimore scoreless for the first eight innings. George Hemming was down by six runs when Baltimore brought in rookie pitcher Arlie Pond, recently off the campus of the University of Vermont, to make his first League appearance in the seventh. He worked two scoreless innings.

Knell missed his chance for a shutout when he weakened in the ninth and gave up three runs before Brodie popped out to the catcher to end it.

Inning	1	2	3	4	5	6	7	8	9	Final
Baltimore	0	0	0	0	0	0	0	0	3	3
Cleveland	0	1	0	1	0	4	0	0	0	6

Winner: Phil Knell. Loser: George Hemming.

Game two: Cleveland scored a run in the bottom of the fifth. Cy Young singled, advanced on an out by Burkett, and on McKean's hit into left field he scored. It was all Young would need, as he crafted a four-hit masterpiece over the champions, shutting them out for the first time this year.

Inning	1	2	3	4	5	6	7	8	9	Final
Baltimore	0	0	0	0	0	0	0	0	0	0
Cleveland	0	0	0	0	1	0	0	0	0	1

Winner: Cy Young. Loser: Duke Esper. Attendance: 4,000.

Game three: Cleveland was trailing eight to six in the eighth inning with two outs. McKean got on by a throwing error, and O'Connor and Childs singled to load 'em up for Chief Zimmer. Esper put one over the plate hip-high: "It cleared the high fence in left field by twenty feet, struck the roof of a house and bounded back into the grounds. The ball was fielded in, but it was a home run just the same and the bases were cleared."[8] Two singles followed by two doubles gave Cleveland three more, to complete a two-out, seven-run rally. And that was enough.

Inning	1	2	3	4	5	6	7	8	9	Final
Baltimore	0	0	0	4	3	0	1	0	1	9
Cleveland	0	0	2	0	1	0	3	7	*	13

Winner: Phill Knell. Loser: Duke Esper. Home run: Zimmer.

Game four: "Pitcher Cuppy has a wearisome way of pitching. He should pay less attention to his cap and belt, and pitch ball. Through his senseless pulling and tugging at his belt, arranging his cap, and posing for the grandstand...."[9]

All of Cuppy's posing won him the fourth game in a row over the formerly-in-first-place Orioles, who now trailed Pittsburgh by a percentage point, with third-place Cleveland only seven percentage points back.

Inning	1	2	3	4	5	6	7	Final
Baltimore	0	0	2	0	0	1	1	3
Cleveland	2	1	1	0	0	2	*	6

Winner: George Cuppy (in seven — due to darkness). Loser: Arlie Pond.

NOTE ON THE DARKNESS

According to the July 18 *Baltimore Sun*, the game was "called back to the sixth inning on account of darkness when Baltimore had played her half of the seventh inning and secured one run." "Everybody but the Baltimores wanted the game called at this stage," wrote the *Cleveland Press*. "When McKean began Cleveland's half with a slashing single that could not be seen until it struck ground McDonald called the game and McKean's hit was wasted."[10]

When Cleveland made it seven wins in a row at home by taking the three-game series against Brooklyn, they moved into first place, six percentage points ahead of Baltimore.

A Rough Time

Cleveland won a game August 20 at Washington, with a little help from the umpire. The game started late at 4:35, and by the seventh inning darkness was rapidly descending on the grounds. The Senators, in order to preserve their 7–4 lead, started stalling tactics in the top of the seventh, hoping to get the game called due to darkness. Umpire O'Day didn't care for the trick and allowed Cleveland to bat in a pretty dark eighth inning. McKean's three-run homer, in the night, put Cleveland ahead by one and O'Day called the game over. The ruffians in the crowd, encouraged by the Washington players, decided to take their anger at the results out on the umpire:

The mob in the stands and scores of boys made a grand rush for the unfortunate umpire. They were in dead earnest, and but for the timely arrival of a detail of police, they might have killed him. As it was, one of the rocks hurled at O'Day struck pitcher Maul, giving him a nasty scratch.

Even women tried to strike the umpire, and one portly lady did manage to break a handsome parasol in striking at Hank. Cries of 'Robber!' 'Thief!' and the like, filled the air, with an occasional chunk of coal or rock interspersed.

The Cleveland players had a rough time of it trying to leave the ball grounds. Their 'bus was surrounded by the angry multitude, and the most disgusting epithets were hurled at Tebeau's men.[11]

Post-Season Play

Cleveland stayed near the top of the standings throughout August and September. Baltimore also played excellent ball, and Cleveland ended up having to settle for second place, three games behind the pennant-wining Orioles, but that earned them an appearance against Baltimore in the post-season Temple Cup series.

Cleveland clobbered Pittsburgh in front of a huge partisan crowd, 17–3, to close out the season on September 12. During the game, Jesse Burkett was presented with a gold medal with a diamond setting in the center for having won the League's batting title with a .423 average.

There would be a delay of two weeks before the start of the Temple Cup series, scheduled to start in Cleveland on October second. To stay in fighting form Cleveland went up to Detroit for some exhibition games.

The Temple Cup Series

GAME ONE

"The gates at League Park registered 7,000 people for game one of the Temple Cup championship series. The enthusiasm vent in noises of all conceivable varieties, fish horns, whistles, rattles, and plain but strenuous voices being in the ascendancy."[12]

Batting orders:
Baltimore: McGraw, 3b; Keeler, rf; Jennings, ss; Kelley, lf; Brodie, cf; Gleason, 2b; Carey, 1b; Robinson, c; McMahon, p.
Cleveland: Burkett, lf; McKean, ss; Childs, 2b; McAleer, cf; O. Tebeau, 1b; Zimmer, c; Blake, rf; McGarr, 3b; Young, p.

With the exception of the pitchers and Clarke (who filled in at catcher for Robinson in two games), the batting orders stayed the same throughout the entire series.

Pitchers Cy Young and Sadie McMahon had it their way through the first four innings, neither team being able to put up a run. The icebreaker came in the bottom of the fifth for Cleveland. McGarr singled to left, Young beat out his bunt for a hit, and Burkett sacrificed both runners to the next base. McKean popped out to second baseman Gleason in short right, and McGarr tagged up and ran in from third ahead of the throw. One run.

Baltimore got the run back in their next turn at the bat. McGraw, on via a single, was moved to second and then to third by a Keeler ground-out and a Jennings fly-out to center. Kelley got an infield scratch hit, and McGraw scored. One run. Cleveland answered back in the bottom of the inning. Tebeau singled, Zimmer beat out a grounder he hit at second, and Patsy crossed the plate when Blake knocked a double off the fence boards in left. One run.

The seventh was a blank. In the Oriole eighth, McGraw singled, moved to second on Keeler's infield out, and came in on Jennings' single. Kelley dropped one into center, good for a base, and Jennings advanced to third. When Brodie forced Kelley out at second, Jennings was able to score when the relay to double up Brodie at first was late. Two runs. Tebeau was not given a base when McMahon hit him with a pitch, because the umpire felt he made no effort to get out of the way.

Tebeau's answer to that decision was to hit a double, and come home to tie the score when Blake rapped out a single. One run.

Robinson hit a double in the ninth, and McGraw delivered a two-out single to send him home with the go-ahead run. One run.

Burkett led the charge for the Spiders to get back into the game with a lead-off double. The loud crowd got louder when McKean's hit fell safe in right to send Burkett home with the tying run. Childs worked the count carefully and got a pitch he turned into a single. McAleer's job of moving the runners over with a bunt turned into a hit that loaded the bases. The infield moved in for a possible play at the plate. Tebeau's grounder was quickly sent to the plate for the first out. The crowd froze when Zimmer hit what looked like an inning-ending double-play ball right at second baseman Gleason. Gleason got his first man sure enough, and his throw to first was a straight one, but the umpire signaled the runner safe — just as Childs scampered across the plate to give the Spiders game one. Two runs.

Final: Cleveland 5, Baltimore 4.

Game #1

BALTIMORE	AB	R	H	E	CLEVELAND	AB	R	H	E
McGraw, 3b	4	2	3	0	Burkett, lf	4	1	1	0
Keeler, rf	5	0	1	0	McKean, ss	4	0	3	1
Jennings, ss	4	1	1	0	Childs, 2b	5	1	1	1
Kelley, lf	4	0	3	0	McAleer, cf	5	0	1	0
Brodie, cf	4	0	0	0	Tebeau, 1b	5	2	2	1
Gleason, 2b	4	0	2	0	Zimmer, c	4	0	2	0
Carey, 1b	4	0	0	0	Blake, rf	4	0	2	0
Robinson, c	4	1	2	0	McGarr, 3b	4	1	1	0
McMahon, p	4	0	0	0	Young, p	4	0	1	0
Totals	37	4	12	0	Totals	39	5	14	3

Inning	1	2	3	4	5	6	7	8	9	Final
Baltimore	0	0	0	0	0	1	0	2	1	4
Cleveland	0	0	0	0	1	1	0	1	2	5

Triple: McKean. Doubles: Burkett, McKean, O. Tebeau, Blake, McGraw. Stolen bases: McGarr 2, McGraw. Time: 2:15. Umpires: McDonald and Keefe.

GAME TWO

An audience of 10,000 came to League Park on Thursday, October 3. They filled the stands and a good part of the field: "The first row next the ropes was composed of sitting spectators while those next behind were kneeling. Then came a row stooping and behind these the mass stood peering over shoulders, elbowing, jostling, crowding for a glimpse on the field."[13]

The battle of Jericho may have had fewer noisemakers brought to the scene than the fans of Cleveland brought to game two of the fight for the Temple Cup. In addition to all the fish horns, tin horns, rattles, etc., of yesterday: "There were bells large enough for a fire engine house, but the greatest musical instrument was an invention of the tin horn species that was fully eight feet long and had a dozen tubes attached through which as many fans blew at once."[14]

To keep order tighter than the day before, President Robison offered $25 to the police for arresting those throwing things onto the field. One thrown pop bottle, and one rowdy with firecrackers, were the only incidents reported.

Bill Hoffer pitched for the visitors and Cy Young for the home team. Baltimore went to the bat first. McGraw hit a slow grounder, Keeler hit a regular grounder, Jennings hit a fast grounder, and in order Childs, Cuppy and McKean threw them out.

Burkett's liner into center was good for a base, a wild pitch gave him second, and McKean's liner over Gleason at second sent Burkett in. McKean took second on the throw home, and moved to third on a sacrifice by Childs. The pitcher hit McAleer, and Tebeau's fly-out to Keeler drove in McKean. On the play, McAleer ran all the way to third, and walked home on a double off the bat of Zimmer into left field. Three runs.

Baltimore in the second had a hit past McKean off the bat of Kelley, Brodie fouled out to Zimmer, Scoops Carey hit a hard one at Cuppy, that he missed, and the ball went into center, where McAleer misplayed it, allowing Kelley to score from first. One run.

No more scoring occurred until the Cleveland fifth. Burkett slow-rolled a hit in front of McGraw, McKean put one in the air that the catcher grabbed, and Childs put Burkett out on a force. The pitcher Hoffer tried to catch Childs napping at first, but his throw was so errant Childs chugged into third. McAleer's hard bounder to short handcuffed Jennings and Childs ran home. One run.

Keeler hit an ankle-high ball that McKean dove and caught for the first out in the Oriole sixth. Jennings sliced a single into left. Kelley went down on strikes. Brodie moved Jennings to third with a hit. Brodie broke for second, stopped, and was caught in a run down. The strategy enabled Jennings to sneak home. One run.

Cleveland started their end of the sixth when Zimmer got a free pass to first. Blake couldn't get a bunt down to move the runner and was called out on strikes. Carey made a fielding gem on McGarr's smash to first and retired him unassisted, Zimmer taking second. Cuppy helped his cause with a run-producing double to center. Burkett blasted a follow-up double into left field, sending Cuppy to the dish. With men on second and third, Childs fouled to Hoffer to end the inning. Two runs.

Cleveland got its seventh run in the seventh. Tebeau singled with one out. Zimmer singled to center, but the throw in caught him off first, and he was caught in a run down. Tebeau adroitly made it to the home base during the run down. One run.

McKean made quick work of Baltimore in the ninth. He threw out Kelley and Brodie, and caught Gleason's fly to retire the Orioles in order — and the game ended.

Final: Cleveland 7, Baltimore 2. Winner: Cy Young. Loser: Bill Hoffer.

Game #2

BALTIMORE	AB	R	H	E	CLEVELAND	AB	R	H	E
McGraw, 3b	4	0	0	0	Burkett, lf	5	1	4	0
Keeler, rf	3	0	1	0	McKean, ss	4	1	1	1
Jennings, ss	4	1	1	1	Childs, 2b	3	1	0	0
Kelley, lf	3	1	0	0	McAleer, cf	3	1	0	1
Brodie, cf	4	0	1	0	Tebeau, 1b	4	1	1	0
Gleason, 2b	4	0	0	0	Zimmer, c	3	1	2	0
Carey, 1b	3	0	2	1	Blake, rf	4	0	0	0
Clarke, c	3	0	0	0	McGarr, 3b	4	0	2	0
Hoffer, p	3	0	0	1	Cuppy, p	3	1	1	0
Totals	31	2	5	3	Totals	33	7	11	2

Inning	1	2	3	4	5	6	7	8	9	Final
Baltimore	0	1	0	0	0	1	0	0	0	2
Cleveland	3	0	0	0	1	2	1	0	*	7

Doubles: Zimmer, McGarr, Cuppy, Burkett. Stolen Bases: Burkett, McKean, Jennings. Time: 2:15. Umpires: McDonald and Keefe.

GAME THREE

Wild estimates of crowd size ran from fifteen to twenty-five thousand for game three. Though it was the largest and loudest crowd of the three games played in Cleveland, the number on hand was more likely closer to the fifteen thousand estimate: "When all the choice positions on the ground had been filled the crowd began to rise. The fences were topped off with a fringe of fans. Every ledge that gave a foothold had a rooter's foot upon it. The scoreboard gave space for a score of spectators who sat on it, hung over and to it. Then there was the crowd outside. Every window, every roof, every tree was full. The cross-trees on the telegraph poles held all that could perch upon them, while the climbing braces were occupied wherever they were high enough to admit of a glance into the grounds."[15]

Also, after about five dozen people had climbed on top of the grandstand and sat dangling their legs over the edge, an order came to allow no more for fear of a roof collapse.

This crowd was perhaps the best-armed of the Cleveland crowds in terms of cheering devices: "There were gongs large enough and loud enough to equip an electric railroad; monster rattles made after the pattern used in the nursery and filled with rocks; there were the remnants of a dozen defunct brass bands, and, in fact, everything that could make noise without exploding."[16]

As part of the entertainment, George Cuppy was summoned to the grandstand where he was presented with a new shotgun. He raised the gun to his shoulder and each barrel discharged a blast. A young boy immediately ran out of the crowd from the direction Cuppy had fired, and handed the pitcher a recently deceased pigeon. The crowd was delighted.

Sadie McMahon took the mound for Baltimore and Cy Young for Cleveland. John McGraw started the game off with a bunt single, but was out stealing second. Keeler grounded out. Jennings hit one into the crowd on the field and was awarded a ground-rule double. Kelley ended the threat with a roller to McGarr at third.

Cleveland put up some runs in their first try. Burkett hit a solid single but was forced out by McKean. Hits by Childs and McAleer sent McKean home. Tebeau smacked the ball between short and third and Childs came in with the second run. McAleer was dancing around second, and when catcher Robinson threw to catch him, he took off for third and made it. Zimmer put the ball in play to the shortstop, and on the out McAleer scored. Three runs.

The pitchers held both teams scoreless through the sixth inning. Cleveland broke though the scoring impasse in the bottom of the seventh. Blake got a ground-rule double to center on a drive that, on an ordinary day, might have been a home run. Consecutive singles by McGarr and Young sent Blake in. Burkett nicely sacrificed the runners into scoring position. The game was momentarily halted to pass out some more stuff from admiring fans. McKean collected a diamond stud. A grateful McKean then lifted a sacrifice fly to Kelley in left to plate McGarr. Kelley's throw in on the play eluded the catcher and Young scored. Three runs.

Baltimore scored for the first time in the eighth. McMahon went out on a nice assist by McKean. McGraw, on via a single, was forced out by Keeler. Jennings got a single past Tebeau at first, and Kelley dropped one into right that brought Keeler around. One run.

Cleveland got the Baltimore run back in the bottom of the inning. With one out Zimmer doubled, with two men down McGarr came through with a two-bagger into left, and Zimmer scored. One run.

The Baltimore ninth was short-lived—a fly to McAleer in center from Gleason, a ground-out by Carey went Childs to Tebeau, and the game-ender by Robinson was a fly ball out with Tebeau again doing the glove work.

Final: Cleveland 7, Baltimore 1.

The *Cleveland Plain Dealer*:

> When the victory was finally won several hundred wild spectators wild with enthusiasm marched around the diamond and tooted and sang and rattled their loudest....
>
> With all the crowd and all the noise nothing occurred that need be regretted by the audience or the management.[17]

Many Baltimore fans, however, believed the stories of outrage against their players, penned by some of their town's more sensationalist writers. Trouble awaited the Spiders in "Oysterville."

Game #3

BALTIMORE	AB	R	H	E	CLEVELAND	AB	R	H	E
McGraw, 3b	4	0	2	0	Burkett, lf	3	0	2	0
Keeler, rf	4	1	0	0	McKean, ss	4	1	0	1
Jennings, ss	3	0	2	0	Childs, 2b	4	1	2	0
Kelley, lf	4	0	1	1	McAleer, cf	4	1	3	0
Brodie, cf	4	0	0	0	Tebeau, 1b	4	0	1	0
Gleason, 2b	4	0	0	0	Zimmer, c	3	1	1	0
Carey, 1b	4	0	1	0	Blake, rf	3	1	1	0
Robinson, c	4	0	1	0	McGarr, 3b	4	1	2	0
McMahon, p	3	0	0	0	Young, p	4	1	0	0
Totals	34	1	7	1	Totals	33	7	12	1

Inning	1	2	3	4	5	6	7	8	9	Final
Baltimore	0	0	0	0	0	0	0	1	0	1
Cleveland	3	0	0	0	0	0	3	1	*	7

Doubles: Blake, Childs, McGarr, and Zimmer. Umpires: Hurst and McQuaid. Time: 1:45.

GAME FOUR

"Mr. Van der Horst of the Baltimore team was led to apologize to President Robison for the conduct of one of the writers, and assured him that nothing would prevent Cleveland from having a fair show in the games in Baltimore."[18]

In this promise the owner of the Baltimore club was wrong.

The *Cleveland Plain Dealer* gave some examples of the alleged fabrications penned by some Baltimore scribes, and gave its opinion of the level of sportswriting talent at Baltimore in general: "One of the papers asserts that the audience was composed of nothing but thugs and rowdies and that the Baltimore players did not dare win the game for fear of their lives."[19]

One Baltimore writer was quoted as saying that the noisemaking was in bounds as far as that went, but concerning the Baltimore players: "It was the pelting they received with missiles, the bold interference of the crowd and the vile imprecations heaped upon them that the Orioles objected to. Robinson, McGraw and Kelley were the worst sufferers, perhaps, as the crowd was chiefly on the left hand side of the field. Pecks of potatoes seemed to have been distributed along the line, and every time Robinson went after a foul fly a shower of them were hurled at him. McGraw and Kelley were hit in the head with potatoes."[20]

A *Cleveland Plain Dealer* man wrote: "The literary style of visiting Baltimore ball writers reminds one of the way the editor of the Bagtown Clarion would wade into the editor of the Puckerbrush Astonisher. For billingsgate they cannot be beaten.... The vituperative tongues of fish women are proverbial. The Baltimore ball writers easily outclass fish wives and descend to the level of Oyster pirates so far as veracity and vocabulary are concerned."[21]

Cleveland Plain Dealer: "Baltimore. Oct. 8 — The crowd at Monday's game was large, and there was an exhibition of rowdyism of the sort that the Baltimore writers said they saw, but did not see, at Cleveland last week. When the players started from the hotel for the grounds their 'bus was pelted with rotten apples, eggs and potatoes."[22]

Union Park was the site of the first game in Baltimore on Monday, October 8. George Cuppy pitched for Cleveland and Duke Esper for Baltimore. The crowd numbered about 9,000.

The first run of the game came for Baltimore in the bottom of the second. Brodie singled and Carey doubled him home. Baltimore scored again in the third on singles by McGraw, Keeler and Jennings with McGraw coming home. Kelley got a walk to load the bases and Keeler scored on a sacrifice fly by Brodie. Esper kept Cleveland off the plate through seven. Baltimore's 2 insurance runs, by Keeler and Jennings in the seventh, proved unnecessary with Cleveland being shut out in the eighth and ninth.

Final: Baltimore 5, Cleveland 0.

Outside the park was a group not satisfied with a mere shutout of the Spiders; they wanted a more physical payback:

> It was on the return home that the worst rowdyism of the day occurred. After the game a mob of about 1,500 rowdies started at the Cleveland players, but the police beat them back. As soon as the players reached their wagon they were greeted with a shower of missiles. It was a crazy mob that the players had to fight their way through, and it took five minutes to cross the sidewalk and get to the wagon. Rocks, slag brickbats and chunks of dirt were thrown at the players in a perfect bombardment, and the boys had to lay down flat in their wagon. This lasted for ten minutes, and the mob tried to cut the harness and unhitch the horses, but did not succeed.
>
> Police were on the top, sides and steps of the vehicle but they were practically powerless against the attack. When the team finally got a start through the mob, the crowd followed and continued the fusillade till the wagon was out of reach. Three arrests were made by the police for the riotous proceedings.
>
> Kid Childs had a bad lump on his head, caused by a stone, and nearly all the players are more or less bruised.[23]

Game: #4

CLEVELAND	AB	R	H	E	BALTIMORE	AB	R	H	E
Burkett, lf	4	0	0	0	McGraw, 3b	4	1	1	0
McKean, ss	4	0	1	0	Keeler, rf	3	2	1	0
Childs, 2b	4	0	0	0	Jennings, ss	4	1	3	0
McAleer, cf	4	0	1	0	Kelley, lf	3	0	2	0
O. Tebeau, 1b	3	0	1	0	Brodie, cf	4	1	1	0
Zimmer, c	3	0	0	1	Gleason, 2b	4	0	0	1
Blake, rf	3	0	1	0	Carey, 1b	4	0	1	0
McGarr, 3b	3	0	1	0	Robinson, c	4	0	0	0
Cuppy, p	3	0	0	0	Esper, p	3	0	0	0
Totals	31	0	5	1	Totals	33	5	9	1

Inning	1	2	3	4	5	6	7	8	9	Final
Cleveland	0	0	0	0	0	0	0	0	0	0
Baltimore	0	1	2	0	0	0	2	0	*	5

Doubles: Carey, Jennings. Stolen bases: Jennings, Kelley. Time: 1:55. Attendance: 9,000. Umpires: Hurst and Keefe.

Game Five

Cy Young and Bill Hoffer faced each other as moundsmen in front of the series' smallest crowd so far. Only 4,100 fans came to the game.

It was all pitching for six scoreless innings. Cleveland broke through in the top of the seventh. Young doubled to the fence in left center, but Keeler's strong throw kept him at third after Burkett had slapped a single into right. Kelley in left was given an easy chance on Childs' fly ball, but in his hurry to throw home, he failed to catch it, and Young scored easily. Singles by McAleer and Tebeau sent Burkett and Childs in with the second and third run of the inning. Baltimore got a run back in the bottom of the inning. Clarke singled, stole second, went to third on Hoffer's ground-out, and scored on McGraw's out at first.

Cleveland cushioned its lead in the eighth with a run by McGarr and another by Young to go up 5–1. Cleveland drew a blank in the top of the ninth, but during the inning the bad blood that was brewing between John McGraw and Patsy Tebeau surfaced. A sliding Tebeau was out at third when McGraw tagged him out by shoving the ball into his face and giving him a bloody lip that drew cheers from the bleacher crowd. Baltimore came up for their last chance. Clarke was an easy grounder to short for the first out. Hoffer fouled out to Zimmer, and the Spiders could taste the Temple Cup — now but an out away. Then things got sticky. Young suddenly couldn't find the plate, and he walked McGraw and Keeler. Cy didn't walk Jennings — he hit him instead to load the bases. The possible winning run now came to the plate in the person of Joe Kelley, the team leader in home runs. Kelley hit an easy grounder to McKean at short. McKean, however, booted it and McGraw ran home. Brodie now took his turn at the bat with the bases loaded. Brodie's swing topped the ball and it one-hopped right in front of the pitcher. Young snared it and threw successfully to Tebeau at first — and the Temple Cup was Cleveland's.

Score: Cleveland 5, Baltimore 2.

Cleveland now had the job of getting out of town with their bodies intact: "The players 'bus was surrounded by police when the game was over and as soon as the boys had entered the vehicle a platoon of mounted police barged back through the crowd and made way for the 'bus. A few stones were thrown, but nobody was hurt."[24]

Game: #5

CLEVELAND	AB	R	H	E	BALTIMORE	AB	R	H	E
Burkett, lf	5	1	3	0	McGraw, 3b	4	1	2	1
McKean, ss	4	0	1	0	Keeler, rf	4	0	1	1
Childs, 2b	4	1	1	1	Jennings, ss	4	0	0	0
McAleer, cf	5	0	1	0	Kelley, lf	5	0	1	1
O. Tebeau, 1b	4	0	1	1	Brodie, cf	4	0	2	0
Zimmer, c	5	0	1	0	Gleason, 2b	4	0	0	1
Blake, rf	5	0	1	0	Carey, 1b	4	0	1	0
McGarr, 3b	4	1	1	1	Clarke, c	4	1	2	0
Young, p	4	2	1	0	Hoffer, p	4	0	0	1
Totals	40	5	11	3	Totals	37	2	9	5

The 1895 Cleveland Spiders, winners of the Temple Cup.

Inning	1	2	3	4	5	6	7	8	9	Final
Cleveland	0	0	0	0	0	0	3	2	0	5
Baltimore	0	0	0	0	0	0	1	0	1	2

Doubles: Blake, McGraw, and Young. Attendance: 4,100. Time: 2:30. Umpires: Hurst and Keefe.

At the Cleveland Elks club on Friday, October 11, 1895, a crowd of over two hundred attended the ceremonies honoring the Temple Cup winners. Toastmaster Harley, after some introductory business, called the manager of the Spiders to the stage: "Capt. Tebeau exhibited the famous Temple cup, and in his own style told how it all happened.... The little captain was several times interrupted by applause."[15]

1896

Hot Springs: Spring Training

The Spiders arrived in Arkansas by train on March 8, 1896, for spring training. They stayed at the Avenue Hotel in Hot Springs.

The next day at 10 A.M. the players gathered in the courtyard of the hotel and as a unit began the mile run to Whittington Park. Arriving at the field, they sprinted around the bicycle track a few times. They then settled into practicing their batting, fielding, and pitching until 11:30 A.M., at which time they walked back to the hotel for dinner. After filling their bellies at the hotel restaurant, they walked back to the ballpark for the afternoon session. The veterans ("Vets") and the rookies ("Colts") played a practice game.

The youngsters were helped when Cuppy, Wallace, and Zimmer were assigned as their pitchers. They managed to win 12–8. One of the new players was second baseman Tom Delahanty, brother of Ed Delahanty. The day's work finished up with another run, this time back to the hotel.

Once again Pittsburgh was the co-training partner of Cleveland. On Saturday, March 23—a particularly entertaining game for the local fans—Cleveland came from behind with 2 runs in the eighth and 1 in the ninth to pull out a 9–8 win. Monday was payback day—Pittsburgh came back with a 12–5 victory. Cleveland, however, once more won the majority of games and carted away the spring pennant flag. Colonel Harridge of Kalamazoo, Michigan, presented the Spiders' banner—provided by the ladies of Hot Springs—to Jesse Burkett. Jesse then handed the prize over to Manager Tebeau.

In April Cleveland undertook a series of exhibition games in the Middle South and Midwest prior to its first season game on April 17 in St. Louis. In Missouri, Cleveland showed up Jefferson 16–0, Kansas City 7–3, and the St. Joe "Saints" 5–2. In Iowa, the Cleveland club beat Burlington 16–7, but at Des Moines the battery of Figgemer and Burell led the local team to a surprise upset of the Spiders 11–6. In the Prairie State, at Peoria, Illinois, a crowd of 2,200 saw their heroes lose 6–2. Also in the land of Lincoln, in its last exhibition game of the spring, Cleveland bested Quincy 7–1.

Cleveland opened the championship season on the road: "St. Louis, April 16.—(Special)—Fast and faultless fielding, brilliant stick work, and, in fact, a general exposition of how to play baseball were the chief factors that enabled the St. Louis Browns to utterly rout the blue hosed young men from the Forest City today in the inaugural game of the championship season of 1896. Nearly 13,000 persons witnessed the contest, many more than the number who patronized the opening game a year ago."[1]

Score: St. Louis 5, Cleveland 2.

Opening at Home

"Lawn boxes" were an addition in front of the grandstand this year.[2] Among the opening day notables entertaining parties in the new elite seats were Myron T. Herrick, Marcus A. Hanna,

William Whitehead, Ralph Worthington, William Rhodes, Addison Hough, Charles Otis, Harvey H. Brown, Howard White, J. H. Wade, William Chisholm, W. H. Crawford and George W. Howe.

The home season was scheduled to start on Tuesday, April 30, with Cy Young trying to even the Spiders' record at 5 and 5. Due to inclement weather it took three tries to get the first game in. Though rain clouds hung around Thursday morn and throughout the game they kept their moisture to themselves.

University School was represented by 200 of its more vocal students. Of the 4,100 people at the game they were the ones yelling and shouting the loudest.

Tom Delahanty, one of the younger brothers of Cleveland baseball great Ed Delahanty, was the new second baseman for the Spiders and a natural favorite of the home crowd.

Twice, to the beat of clapping hands and loud cheering, he was presented with floral gifts. First, a giant horseshoe made of flowers made its appearance, to be followed, a short time later, by a basket of roses mixed in with various other flowers. The final red flush on the face of the young Delahanty came with the presentation of a diamond stickpin, from yet another group of admiring friends.

Despite all the attention, Delahanty played a solid game in the field with the exception of one somewhat wild throw to first. He made no hits, but hit the ball solid three times, though three times he also went after the first pitch.

Inning	1 2 3	4 5 6	7 8 9	Final
Cleveland	1 0 0	1 0 0	0 0 *	2
Cincinnati	1 0 0	0 0 0	0 0 0	1

After winning the opener Cleveland's .500 record of 5 and 5 put them in seventh place behind a proud Pittsburgh, the leader with a 9 and 2 mark. Pittsburgh was a pretender, but a serious contender was two places behind the Spiders in ninth place with a record of 5 and 7, and their name was Baltimore. By the beginning of June the cream-teams of the league would be fighting it out at the top of the standings.

Cleveland played well enough in the first half of May to move into a tie with Pittsburgh on Friday, May 15. They were in first alone the next day when they defeated New York at League Park 8–3. They followed up that win with two more at home against the bad boys from Baltimore 4–3 and 12–7.

Cleveland went 7 and 1 on its home stand. They won 6 straight before losing 1 to Boston, but came back in the final game as Cy Young, in front of a farewell crowd of 6,000, led the Spiders to a 13–5 victory over Jack Stivetts and Boston.

Cleveland now took its 18 and 9 record on the road.

On the Road Chasing Baltimore

Cleveland was in first place over Baltimore by percentage points on the first of June. On the second of June they were in second behind Baltimore by 5 percentage points.

Cleveland was in Washington on the third. Cleveland managed a run in the first off of George "Win" Mercer, but both teams were unable to score in the next six innings. Cleveland went up by 2 in the eighth when Burkett walked and McKean knocked him in with a scorching triple. It looked like that would be enough for Young to secure a win, but in the ninth he weakened and gave up two singles and a double and the score was tied. In the tenth a triple by Bobby Wallace and a put-out gave Washington the lead. In the bottom of the inning Burkett saved Wallace's bacon with a tying home run to the center field fence. Umpire Emslie's play calling was questioned all day long by Captain Joyce of the Senators and by Manager Tebeau. In the tenth, Emslie had had enough of Tebeau and sent him to the bench; O'Connor took over his coaching spot at first. After a scoreless eleventh, Emslie declared the affair a 3–3 tie due to darkness.

Unable to gain ground on Baltimore in Washington, the Spiders headed up the road about thirty miles to take on Baltimore at Baltimore. In Cleveland, for a quarter, the three-game series would be reenacted—as it happened—via telegraph at the Euclid Avenue Opera House. George Cuppy put Cleveland back in first place with a 7–6 victory over Sadie McMahon.

Cy Young made up for the game in Washington with a win over his Baltimore rival Joe Corbett (brother of the famous prizefighter Gentleman Jim Corbett) 10–4.

Cleveland used three pitchers, Wilson, Wallace, and Cuppy, in game three but still lost 11–6. Tebeau had a home run for Cleveland and Kelley had one for Baltimore.

Cleveland then headed up the East Coast again—destination Philadelphia. The Athletics scored the first run in the bottom of the first. Cleveland put their first run on the board in the third. In the fifth and sixth they came up with 3 and 2 runs respectively to go up by a safe margin of 6–1.

Young had a very bad seventh as Philadelphia helped themselves to a tying share of runs, getting 5. Nothing happened in the eighth but in the ninth "Brewery Jack" Taylor allowed Cleveland a run to retake the lead. Cy Young returned the favor in the bottom of the ninth and sent the game into overtime. "Peach Pie" O'Connor, pinch-hitting for pitcher Young in the top of the tenth, drove in the go-ahead run. With George Cuppy's solid relief in the tenth, that run, proved to be the winner.

Score: Cleveland 8, Philadelphia 7.

Umpire: Tim Hurst.

The exciting game featured four home runs. Jesse Burkett and Ed McKean of Cleveland, and Joe Sullivan and Mike Grady of Philadelphia each got to make a circuit of the bases. Live reenactments via telegraph of the games in Philadelphia also drew large crowds to the Cleveland Opera House.

Ballparks

The Euclid Avenue Opera House received a little competition for the entertainment quarter this year from an amusement park out by the Rocky River off of Detroit Avenue. Scenic Park was promoting quite a number of attractions for the season of 1896: a dance pavilion, Ferris wheel, boats, picnic grounds, two house bands, and a miniature railroad—the largest "scenic" railroad in existence. They had also booked Kedah, the sacred elephant, for an appearance, and put up a new grandstand for watching horse racing, bicycling, and amateur baseball games.

Some amateur teams around Cleveland were getting the royal treatment, facility-wise, this year. The recently built sports complex of the City League at Woodland Hills was first rate. There was, however, some talk of a boycott when the City League raised its admission price by a dime.

Baseball was still being played over on the southeast side of town at the well-tended Forest City Park facilities, where the city's two best black teams, the Hollendens and the H.A.C.s (renamed the Keystones), occasionally put in an appearance.

Summer Spiders

Action on the major league diamond had a competitive Spiders club trading places with Baltimore for the top spot in the standings during June. As a result Manager Tebeau's popularity around Cleveland continued to grow and, some said, may have even surpassed that of a very popular governor from Canton. The governor did something about Patsy Tebeau's fame when he went down to St. Louis—Tebeau's hometown.

In the eighth inning on June 17 the ball game in Cleveland was stopped by Umpire Lynch to make a public announcement. The National convention of the Republican Party, meeting in St. Louis, had just nominated Governor William McKinley of Ohio as their candidate for president of the United States. The crowd cheered for five minutes. Pat Tebeau, a staunch Republican, was among those cheering the loudest. Cy Young celebrated the happy occasion with a 5–3 victory over Adonis Terry of Chicago.

Cleveland split two games at home against Pittsburgh. W. C. Temple, the donor of the Temple Cup, and a loud crowd of Pittsburgh people were at the game.

Outlaws in Louisville

A quite memorable series of games at Louisville and Chicago followed the games with Pittsburgh. In the first game against the Louisville Colonels the umpiring of Umpire Weideman was severely questioned. At one point "Burkett took Weideman by the shoulders and gave him a good shaking for one raw decision."[3] (He did not hit him — a fine distinction — or he'd have been thrown out of the game.

Cy Young gave up 2 runs in the bottom of the first. He was hit hard throughout the game, but by yielding no walks and with fine fielding behind him, he allowed but one more run in the eighth. He gave up ten hits.

A McGarr triple and an error gave Cleveland a run in the third. In the fifth McGarr singled, and Cy Young made up for the 2 runs he allowed in the first by belting the ball over the left field fence for a two-run homer. In the sixth, with the help of walks and illegal deliveries (balks), and but a solitary hit, Cleveland scored 3 off Louisville rookie Chick Fraser. Young led off the seventh with a triple, and Burkett convinced the umpire that a pitch had hit him on the foot, and he was sent to first. Both men came around to score. In the bottom of the inning Louisville got the last run of the game, on a hit, two sacrifices, and another hit.

Score: Spiders 8, Colonels 3.

Inning	1	2	3	4	5	6	7	8	9	Final
Cleveland	0	0	1	0	2	3	2	0	0	8
Louisville	2	0	0	0	0	0	1	0	0	3

Attendance: 1,000. Time: 2:20.

Cleveland had its problems in the "City of the Falls" with a particular umpire named Weideman and a certain Doctor Stucky of the Colonels: "Louisville. June 26.—(Special)—In the history of baseball probably no more disgraceful scene has been enacted on the diamond than at League park today. Weideman was the cause of it all, and the sooner he is relegated to some minor and unheard of league the better it will be for baseball."[4]

George Cuppy was in the pitcher's box for Cleveland and "Still Bill" Hill for Louisville. Despite the questionable calls by Weideman throughout the contest, the game was an exciting seesaw battle. Cleveland got 2 in the second. Louisville went up by a run with 3 in the bottom of the third, only to watch Cleveland tie the game with a run in the fourth. The Colonels went up by a run once again in the fifth. The sixth, seventh, and eighth saw much arguing with the umpire but no scoring. In the ninth Burkett saved Cleveland's day with a home run to knot the game at 4 each. Cuppy earned Cleveland a tenth inning at bat by stranding two Louisville runners in the ninth.

With all the arguing, the protracted game was encroaching upon nightfall by the tenth. Tebeau led off and gained first via an error. McGarr then brought in 2 runs with a home run over the left field fence. Blake singled but was forced out on a Cuppy grounder. One out. Burkett flied out to Clarke in left. Two outs. McAleer hit a fly ball to left that Clarke had difficulty seeing, or chose not to see, and McAleer had himself a 2-run homer. McKean decided that Louisville was playing for darkness in order to have the game called, in order to revert to the score of the last full inning, and get off with at least a tie. He hit an easy grounder to O'Brien at second who let the easy chance elude him.

McKean, seeing this, refused to run to first base and eventually Louisville fielded the ball in and threw it to first to end the inning, with Cleveland up by four. Cuppy, in too much of a hurry to retire the Colonels, loaded the bases on a single and two walks. At this point, Weideman — to the disgust of both teams — declared the game a tie due to darkness:

> The entire Cleveland team surrounded Weideman. The Louisville team also got in the "push." The crowd surged on the diamond and it was with difficulty that the police kept them from attacking some of the players. Weideman was not the object of physical attack, but he was intimidated to such an extent that his usefulness as an umpire is forever ended.[5]

After the game a crowd of boys stoned the Cleveland players but no damage was done. Attendance 1,000.[6]

In the box score of the tie game Burkett's home run in the ninth was listed but those of McGarr and McAleer in the tenth were not.

Inning	1	2	3	4	5	6	7	8	9	Final
Cleveland	0	2	0	1	0	0	0	0	1	4
Louisville	0	0	3	0	1	0	0	0	0	4

Manager Tebeau protested the game, claiming there was light enough in the tenth for the game to continue. The *Cleveland Press* backed his claim by saying that it had asked the telegraph operator at the ball park, just before the game was called, if it was getting 'to dark to go on. The *Press* wrote: "He answered that there wasn't the slightest danger, as there was still plenty of light."[7]

The next day a crowd of 2,000 was disappointed when the rainy weather forced the game to be called off. The owner of the Louisville franchise, Doctor Stucky, had a little surprise for the Spiders before they left town to play an exhibition game at George Cuppy's home town of Logansport, IN.

Stucky, who did not care for the Spiders' style of play, secured a warrant for their arrest for breach of the peace:

At 3:20 o'clock the warrants were served on the Cleveland team and all the newspaper men and many others were subpoenaed. Policeman rode in the front and rear of the Clevelands' bus, which was taken direct to police headquarters.[8]

—*Plain Dealer.*

After the Cleveland players had been arrested in Louisville, Saturday afternoon, they were dragged off before a magistrate and given in Kentucky what is called a hearing.

All but Tebeau, McKean, Burkett and McAleer were discharged. Tebeau was fined $100, McKean and McAleer $75 each, and Burkett $50, for what in hospitable Kentucky is called disorderly conduct. The men did not pay their fines, but gave bond and will contest the case. It will be up for hearing again in August, when Cleveland plays in Louisville again.[9]

—*Cleveland Press.*

If ever a foolish break was made by a league manager [owner], it was this move on the part of the fellow Stucky. On its face, it was simply a spiteful trick made because of ill report about the Spiders. By making it he not only hurt the Cleveland club, but Stucky gave baseball the severest kind of a body blow. And now comes Jim Hart, the Chicago catspaw of Al Spalding, with a little 'me too' story, in which he says that he will do just what Stucky did if the Spiders do not behave themselves in the games at Chicago this week. This man Hart is the same man who some years ago, when Chicago finished second to Boston in the League race, charged other teams in the league with throwing games to Boston for the sake of keeping Chicago out of the pennant. He is a tall fellow with a head about the size of a peanut.[10]

—*Cleveland Press.*

Jim Hart put a large contingent of police in place, intended to intimidate the Spiders, for the games at Chicago. Cleveland didn't seem to notice as Young took the first game 9–6.

Cuppy cruised to a 19–7 win in game two. The Chicago lefty, Danny Friend, was so disgusted with himself that, late in the game, he simply stormed out of the pitching box, without permission, and abandoned the game. The regular catcher Malachi Kittredge had to come off the bench to finish the game. In a career covering 1,215 games over a span of 16 years, it was the only game Kittredge ever played a position other than catcher.

In game three, Zeke Wilson was the winner 10–7. Following game three —*The Cleveland Press*: "Did Jim Hart have Anson arrested when he purposely spiked Tebeau, Wednesday? Or will he swear out a warrant for Tebeau on the charge of destroying property in willfully dulling one of Anson's spikes?... Jim Hart must feel proud of himself about these times. The Weddell house collection of rooters, Wednesday evening joined in a telegram of about 50 words in which they thanked Hart for ordering the police to the Chicago grounds and asking him to detail 50 extra coppers for Thursday's game. 'We want to make it four straight,' said the telegram."[11]

Chicago managed to salvage the finale in a close battle, 8–7. It took a Cleveland boy, rookie Buttons Briggs, to do it. Young took the loss for Cleveland.

Meanwhile plans were afoot in Cleveland to give the Spiders a glorious welcome home. A huge throng estimated at over two thousand assembled on the Public Square at 7:30 in the morning. Led by a brass band, they marched to the Union Depot on the lakefront to meet the Spiders' train. "Banners inscribed 'Hurrah for the heroes. The people are with you,' 'Welcome home; we are proud of your victories,' etc., were conspicuous in the parade."[12]

The ball players were placed in a coach drawn by six white horses, followed by more carriages carrying the town elite. The tally-ho parade, led by the same band, marched back to the square where the heroes were breakfasted at the Forest City House by Mayor McKisson, President Robison, and guests.

Badges worn by supporters, and a poem:

OUR CHAMPIONS,
Cleveland
B.B.C.
Against the World
1896

The Return of the Victors.

Ring out the horns, bring out the drums,
   Let all the cymbals sound -
The Cleveland men are home again,
   So dauntless, so renowned!

They come with laurel on their bats,
   They come with courage high -
They know no fear, oh, give them cheer,
   And sing their praises high.

The mighty Tebeau leads the way,
   So stalwart on the field -
Oh, lift the bat to fearless Pat,
   Who knows not how to yield.

Then hail McKean, the agile short,
   And cheer the gentle Zim,

And gladly shake with Harry Blake,
   And Cuppy, here's to him.

Then greet the aldermanic youth,
   And shout for honest Chip,
And Burkett's bat, hooray for that -
   It hasn't lost its grip.

Then give a whoop for anxious Jack,
   And one for Wilson too,
And lift a cheer for McAleer,
   So fleet of foot and true.

Oh, sound the horns and beat the drums,
   And make a joyful noise -
Let every cheer show far and near
   We're with the Cleveland boys![13]

All this hoopla and hyperbole was just in time for the weekend Fourth of July series with St. Louis, scheduled to start later that same afternoon, Friday, July 3. Cleveland went on to win the Friday game on what turned out to be a very rain-drenched field, 8–3.

Independence Day, 1896

THE MORNING GAME

As in recent years, the Fourth of July twin bill was nerve-rackingly noisy, as fans armed with blanks-firing revolvers and firecrackers were plentiful.

Red Donahue did the pitching for the visitors and Zeke Wilson for the Clevelands.

Cleveland	St. Louis
("The Crab") Burkett, lf	("Buttermilk Tommy") Dowd, 2b
Jimmy McAleer, cf	("Shang") Kissinger, lf
Ed McKean, ss	("Tacky Tom") Parrott, cf
("Kid") Childs, 2b	Roger Connor, 1b
("Peach Pie") O'Connor, c	Bert Meyers, 3b
"Patsy" Tebeau, 1b	"Klondike" Douglas, rf
"Chippy" McGarr, 3b	Monte Cross, ss
"Bobby" Wallace, rf	Ed McFarland, c
"Zeke" Wilson, p	"Red" Donahue, p

The Brown Stockings led off, and after three ground balls Cleveland headed for the bench. Burkett, up first, went out first, but the Irish trio of McAleer, McKean, and O'Connor walked, singled, and singled again, to score the game's first run.

St. Louis in the second went three up and three down. Cleveland, after McGarr was out, got five straight singles and 2 runs. The run damage was limited as Wilson was thrown out at the plate as well as McAleer, when he was caught on the relay after breaking for home on the McKean steal.

In the third, the former Cleveland amateur star catcher, Ed McFarland, got the first run for St. Louis when he singled, and came home on a walk and a single. His good slide beat a fine throw in from right field by Bobby Wallace. Cleveland failed to score in the third.

In the fourth, Wilson got out of a one-out bases-loaded jam, with the help of a home to first double play. Wallace struck out, Wilson did the same, and Burkett put Cleveland out in order with a ground-out to Meyers at third.

The pitcher Donahue doubled in the fifth, and when Tebeau put Kissinger out at first on a grounder, his throw around the horn went errant to McGarr at third, so Donahue seized the opportunity and ran home. Cleveland did not score in their turn.

St. Louis started the sixth by going out in order. Cleveland's half of the frame started with a McGarr single, Wallace sacrificed him to second, McGarr helped himself to third, and sprinted home when Wilson put the ball in play to his counterpart Donahue.

Three men to the plate and three back to the bench for the Browns in the seventh. Childs, the Spiders' "aldermanic"-looking second baseman, walked to begin the seventh for the home team. He was pushed along the bases by singles from O'Connor and Tebeau. The sacks were left full when McGarr popped out to the pitcher. Wallace was able to solve Donahue's delivery and knocked in two men with a double. Tebeau also came in on an error by Cross who threw wild to the plate. Wallace alertly grabbed third on the throw and Burkett drove him in with a single.

Both clubs went out without a run in the eighth. One solitary run crossed the plate in the St. Louis ninth, on successive singles by Meyers, Douglas, and Cross, after which Wilson finished the Browns off to secure his victory.

Inning	1 2 3	4 5 6	7 8 9	Final
Cleveland	1 2 0	0 0 1	4 0 *	8
St. Louis	0 0 1	0 1 0	0 0 1	3

Score: Cleveland 8, St. Louis 3. Strikeouts: by Wilson 3, by Donahue 5. Time: 1:45. Umpire: Sheridan.

THE AFTERNOON GAME

Cleveland	St. Louis
("The Crab") Burkett, lf	("Buttermilk Tommy") Dowd, 2b
Jimmy McAleer, cf	Ted Breitenstein, lf
Ed McKean, ss	("Tacky Tom") Parrott, cf
("Kid") Childs, 2b	Roger Connor, 1b
("Peach Pie") O'Connor, c	Bert Meyers, 3b
"Patsy" Tebeau, 1b	"Klondike" Douglas, rf
"Chippy" McGarr, 3b	Monte Cross, ss
"Bobby" Wallace, rf	Ed McFarland, c
"Cy" Young, p	Bill Hart, p

Pitchers: for Cleveland — Cy Young, for St. Louis — Bill Hart.

Dowd, the first man up in the game, singled off Young and then got himself thrown out stealing by a very wide margin at second. Breitenstein next went on strikes, Childs let Parrott's grounder elude his grasp, Connor hit safely, but the damage was undone when Meyers smacked one back to the box, and Tebeau was able to hold on to a bad throw to first from his pitcher. A triple off the bat of Burkett opened the Cleveland first. McAleer grounded out to short, McKean got a hit and Jesse jogged in from third. Childs got a free pass only to be forced by O'Connor. Tebeau then sent McKean across the plate with a single, and when Tebeau's theft of second drew a throw, O'Connor quickly headed home and on a wild relay in from second he made it.

No trouble from St. Louis in the second. Burkett led off for the second inning in a row and knocked a double, but his over-anxious teammates went out on three fly balls.

A Dowd single, that had a wild pitch and a bad throw from McKean tacked on to it, gave the Browns a run in the third. For Cleveland, McKean singled and moved over when Childs almost beat out a bunt; he advanced to third on a wild pitch, but got nailed at home on an O'Connor grounder. O'Connor stole second and on a bad throw from catcher McFarland advanced to third. Tebeau doubled in O'Connor, and McGarr singled in Tebeau.

In the fourth all that St. Louis got was a man on, when Burkett lost one in the sun. All that Cleveland got in their turn was a walk to Burkett.

In the top of the fifth Dowd hit safely, Breitenstein walked and Parrott was safe when Young had a miscue on a grounder. With the bases loaded Connor fouled to O'Connor for out number two. Young, however, ran out of luck when Meyers failed to cooperate and let him off the hook. Meyers' triple cleared the bases and the Browns added 3 runs. Cleveland in their turn failed to score.

Cleveland went out in the sixth. With two on and one out in the sixth the Browns' man, Dowd, smoked a hopper to Childs, who tagged the runner Hart off of second and returned the ball to first to get Dowd and end the threat. With Cleveland still up by a run after the sixth, each club continued to put up zeroes in the final frames until it was over — allowing Cleveland to claim its second victory on the day.

Inning	1	2	3	4	5	6	7	8	9	Final
Cleveland	3	0	2	0	0	0	0	0	*	5
St. Louis	0	0	1	0	3	0	0	0	0	4

Score: Cleveland 5, St. Louis 4. Time: 1:45. Umpire: Sheridan. (No official attendance was given — crowd for the day only referred to as large.)

There were two memorable games played at the end of July. The first one had Philadelphia in town on July 23: "The poetry of motion was blank verse compared to the motion of Cy Young's arm Thursday. There was the swing to it that foretold trouble for the other fellows. The motion was easy and unhesitating, and when the hand at the end of that mighty arm let loose the ball, there could be heard that whistling noise that accompanies a cannon ball in flight through the air."[14] Cy Young pitched a brilliant two-hit shutout; his opponent Harry ("Beans") Keener yielded two runs on seven hits to take the loss.

Inning	1	2	3	4	5	6	7	8	9	Final
Cleveland	1	0	1	0	0	0	0	0	*	2
Philadelphia	0	0	0	0	0	0	0	0	0	0

The second exciting game was at St. Louis, July 31. Cleveland made all of its four runs in the seventh on a couple of fluke plays including the two from the episode below:

> One tally was in and Chief Zimmer was on first base when Cuppy came to the bat. He hit a long fly to left. Sullivan after a mighty run got under the ball near the rail of the race track. He had his hands up ready to clasp the sphere when his foot struck a long rail, such as is used by traction companies.
>
> Sullivan fell and the ball rolled under the fence and was counted a home run.... Sullivan's head barely missed coming in contact with an electric light pole. He injured his knee and was obliged to retire from the game.[15]

Inning	1	2	3	4	5	6	7	8	9	Final
St. Louis	0	0	0	0	0	0	1	2	0	3
Cleveland	0	0	0	0	0	0	4	0	0	4

Winner: Young. Loser: Kissinger.

Cleveland ended July in third place behind the leader Baltimore and second place Cincinnati. August was a so-so month for Cleveland until the end, when they started to get hot.

Warming Up

On August 21 they had taken three in a row on the road from Washington and headed up the coast a short distance to challenge the leader Baltimore. Cuppy beat Esper and Flemming in the first game 10–3. The next day was rained out and a doubleheader was scheduled for the twenty-fifth. Young beat Corbett 12–2 in game one, and Cuppy and Pond fought to a 4–4 tie in game two that was called after nine innings due to darkness. Cleveland lost three straight in Philadelphia, but Cincinnati, in second place, helped keep Cleveland close behind them by also losing three in a row. The Spiders finished August in third place.

Cleveland played well in September. Starting on September 9 they took three games from St. Louis in Cleveland. Ed McFarland, a product of the Cleveland sandlots, played catcher for St. Louis in the first game; he received a nice round of applause from the audience. Ed hit a double, scored a run, and in the seventh drove in Meyers. Ed McKean of Cleveland hit a round-tripper in the Spiders' 8–3 win. McKean's homer was the first of the year to go over the right field fence at League Park.

With Bobby Wallace pitching in game two, Cleveland moved into second place ahead of Cincinnati with a 5–2 victory over Ted Breitenstein and the Browns. Cleveland percentage: .619; Cincinnati percentage: .611.

It was a very exciting game three. The decisive moment came after Zimmer had tripled and Wallace had gone in to run for him. Tebeau hit a short pop-out; Wallace tagged up and ran home and somehow slid under the tag of McFarland at the plate—to win the game 3–2 in ten innings.

Cleveland next went to Chicago. They won 2–0 in the first game. In the second game they came from behind to tie it with 3 runs in the ninth, but had to settle for a tie due to that spoiler called darkness. They took the third game 4–1, loaded up their bags, and headed home for a four-game showdown with Cincinnati.

A doubleheader was scheduled on Saturday against Cincinnati. Cleveland scored 21 runs and Cincinnati 2 in the early contest. Cy Young contributed to the run outburst with a home run of his own. Umpire Sheridan, however, decided at the close of the seventh that the first game was over and that a second would not be played. The double header was rescheduled for Tuesday. Cincinnati ran down to Louisville for a single Sunday game and back to Cleveland to finish the series. Cleveland won the Monday game 4–1. Cleveland now needed one more win to clinch a berth in the Temple Cup series. The Red Stockings prevented that by winning 7–2. The second game was called off, once again, due to darkness. Cleveland and its fans would now have to wait to celebrate another day. Louisville, the franchise responsible for the Cleveland players' arrested down there, was due up here for 4 games.

Bobby Wallace pitched for Cleveland and "Chick" Fraser for Louisville in the first game. Cleveland won 2–0 and "cinched" second place and an appearance in the Temple Cup series with Baltimore.[16] Louisville won the next two games but Cleveland bounced back in the season finale with a win for good luck 3–2.

The local amateur teams in the City League also closed out their season in September, but unlike the Spiders they were not scheduled for post-season play in October:

CITY LEAGUE ENDED.

The City Base Ball League closed the season with last Sunday's games, the Quinns winning the championship of the city and the Collister [*sic*] & Sayle cup, which will be on exhibition in their store in a day or two. The following is the standings of the clubs:

	W	L	Pc
Quinns	8	0	1.000
Baehrs	5	2	.714
West Ends	5	3	.625
Standards No.2	4	3	.571
Standards No.1	5	4	.555
Pabst	4	4	.500
Diamond Rocks	2	4	.333
Athletics	3	6	.333
Resolutes	1	6	.143
Centrals	0	5	.000[17]

"THE TEMPLE CUP"

"For the benefit of those who may not know the conditions of the Temple cup, they are given below: The cup was presented to the League by Mr. W. C. Temple, of Pittsburg, to be played for by the clubs finishing first and second at the end of the year, the grounds to be furnished free by the management of the clubs contesting. The receipts all go to the players. The team that wins a majority of seven games will receive 60 per cent of the net receipts, and the losing team will receive 40 per cent. All the money taken in at these games is for the benefit of the players. Any club which wins the cup three years in succession is entitled to retain the trophy as its property, and the Clevelands, if they can win it again this year, will have the 'call' on the chance of ultimately possessing it."[18]

Several heated letters were exchanged between managers Tebeau and Hanlon over how to set up the seven-game series for 1896. Because in 1895 the first three games were played in Cleveland, it was finally agreed to play the first three games, this year, in Baltimore on October 1, 2, and 3. The fourth, and fifth and sixth games if needed, would be in Cleveland on October 7, 8, and 9. Should a seventh game be required, it would be played at a neutral site in Pittsburgh in honor of Mr. Temple, the date to be determined later.

The train trip to Baltimore almost ended the Temple Cup series before it began:

BELATED PILGRIMS.

Special Dispatch to the Leader.

Baltimore, Md., October 1.—Yesterday afternoon at 2:50 o'clock a happy little band of nineteen pilgrims, whose numbers increased to twenty at Youngstown, left on a trip to witness or take part in the Temple cup games. To-night at 5:50 o'clock, just twenty-seven hours later, twenty weary muddy, grimy people drew a long breath of relief as their train drew into the city of oysters, Orioles and Hanlon. They had been on the road long enough to have gone to Omaha or Newfoundland, or some other remote part of the earth; had walked part of the way, changed cars three times, and gone through several other harrowing experiences, which the players vow it was never their lot to encounter before, and hope it never will be again. They had crept over a piece of track in the night, where there had been a washout, and they had followed close behind a freight train, which was utterly wrecked in a fearful head-end collision just ahead of them. If the time table had been so arranged that the passenger had run ahead of the freight, there would have been no Temple cup games this year, unless Baltimore played them alone. The Cleveland pilgrims had footed it over a muddy, rocky country road for half a mile or so around the wreck, and exchanged their special car for a day coach the rest of the way. They had ridden over numberless washouts; through towns where the water was at the windows, and the only people going about the streets were in row boats. They had crept across

TWO HIGH TRESTLE BRIDGES

Both of which were badly damaged, and undergoing repairs, and which the trainmen themselves admitted were likely to drop train and passengers a hundred feet into a raging torrent in the one case or a rocky gulch in the other. It was enough to turn their hair gray.

All the old Temple cup team were in the train when it left Cleveland except McAleer, and he, after bidding adieu at the Youngstown depot to 237 bosom friends, joined the party. The ride to Pittsburg was uneventful enough, and that city was left at 9 o'clock. A dangerous washout was crossed in safety, but at 2 A.M. the train came to a stop and moved no more. At 3:30 the conductor reported a freight wreck on the track ahead, and said the passengers would have to walk around it in the morning. The players got a fair night's rest in the motionless train, and at 6 o'clock were routed for breakfast. It was fully two hours later before the train pulled them up as close to the wreck as possible.

It was a frightful wreck, two engines and a dozen cars being absolutely broken to bits and piled in a heap as big as a two-story house. Engines and cars were ground to fragments the former being scattered about in the debris like bits of scrap iron. Two mangled corpses, both of tramps, had been taken out when the Cleveland party passed the wreck, and four or five more were reported to be in the debris, as half a dozen tramps were known to be in one of the foremost cars. The trainmen saved their lives by jumping. The players footed it around the mass of debris

THROUGH ANKLE DEEP MUD,

and across little rivulets, but thanking their lucky stars they were still able to walk. Jack O'Connor trudged through the drizzling rain with a nice new mackintosh tucked under his arm to keep it out of the wet.

It was just noon when Cumberland was reached and dinner eaten. Then came the two trestles. The first of them was jacked up on temporary supports and tied together with ropes and cables, and creaked and groaned under the weight of the train. The second was enough worse than the first to scare anyone, and as Oliver Tebeau gazed into the depths below while the train crept cautiously inch by inch over it, he remarked: "If we ever go through here we'll be below Louisville before we stop." At Cumberland the players saw their first glimpse of sunshine for a week and the skies grew clearer as Baltimore was approached. The team had borne up well under their misfortunes, but as they realized they had missed a beautiful day and a big crowd in Baltimore their spirits fell. As a matter of fact 3,000 people went out to the grounds here this afternoon and were disappointed. A bus with four white horses was at the depot to receive the players in the morning, but not when they finally came.

Manager Tebeau is a trifle depressed over the fact that the club has not played for five days. "Of course it's a rest," he says, "but their eye is apt to get just a little rusty. Young is all right, though. The longer the rest, the better he is, and, rusty or not, the Baltimore's will do well to get one game from us. Young will pitch on Friday and Cuppy or Wallace Saturday, depending on the state of Cuppy's finger, which has not been healing quite as well as had been expected. Wilson has been under the weather for a day or two and is not likely to take part in any of the games here. The third game will be on Monday."

The Orioles are chock full of confidence and Hanlon is wearing a broad smile which he says means something. Hoffer is slated to pitch Friday with Pond on Saturday.[19]

The Temple Cup Series of 1896

The Cleveland Spiders began the series against the Baltimore Orioles on Tuesday, October 2, 1896, at Union Park in Baltimore.

GAME ONE

Denton True ("Cy") Young of Cleveland: age 29, throws right, height 6'2" and weight 210 lbs., versus Bill ("Wizard") Hoffer of Baltimore: age 25, throws right, height 5'9", and weight 155 lbs.

The players

Baltimore	*Cleveland*
John "Mugsy" McGraw, 3b*	Jesse ("The Crab") Burkett, lf
Joe Quinn, 2b	Ed McKean, ss
Willie ("Wee Willie") Keeler*, rf	Clarence ("Kid") Childs, 2b
Hughie ("Ee-Yah") Jennings*, ss	Jimmy McAleer, cf
Joe Kelley, lf*	"Chief" Charles Zimmer, c
Jack ("Dirty Jack") Doyle, 1b	"Chippy" James McGarr, 3b
Heinie Reitz, 2b	"Patsy" Oliver Tebeau, 1b
Steve Brodie, cf	Jack ("Peach Pie") O'Connor, 1b
Wilbert ("Uncle Robbie") Robinson, c*	Harry ("Dude") Blake, rf
Bill ("Wizard") Hoffer, p	"Cy" Denton Young, p
	Bobby Wallace, ph

* Baltimore players in the Hall of Fame.

The Orioles batted first and in front of their 3,995 fans, and did not score. Cleveland in their first try started the game off with a single off the bat of Burkett, McKean showed patience and earned a walk, "Kid" Childs laid down a fine sacrifice bunt to move the runners into scoring position, McAleer smacked a smoker on the ground to McGraw at third, and Burkett got caught off the base at third for the second out. Zimmer was outwitted by "Wizard" Hoffer and struck out to end the threat.

Baltimore went out in the second. The Cleveland second: three up and three out on flies.

The hometown boys' first runs came in the third. McGraw singled to center, Keeler went out on a high one to Blake in left, Jennings singled into right and McGraw decided to try for third on the play. Young got the relay from Blake and had a sure out on Jennings, who was trying for second. However, Young's poor throw caromed off the ground and past McKean; McGraw alertly tried for the plate. Childs tracked down the loose ball, and in his hurry, fired it home and over Zimmer's head and McGraw scored with Jennings taking third. A wicked line smash back to the pitcher's box off the bat of Kelley hit and stunned Young, who could not find the ball hiding a foot away, and by the time he did, Jennings had scored the second run. Cleveland threatened in the third, when with two out, McKean put a triple against the fence in center. Childs hit a hot hummer to Doyle at the first base position, and in a foot race to the bag Childs lost — end of inning.

Young kept Baltimore off the board in the fourth and fifth innings, and Hoffer made easy work of Cleveland in their fourth and fifth turn at the bat.

The Orioles put up a tally in the sixth when Brodie, on via a force-out of Reitz, stole second and came in on a Robinson hit to left that Burkett took his time fielding in. Cleveland had two outs in the sixth when Childs dropped a lazy fly into short left. McAleer moved the "Kid" over with a walk, and Zimmer put the ball in play for the first time on the day, with a hit down the third base line to bring in Childs.

The Baltimore seventh put a serious crimp into the Cleveland chances for victory. It started out well enough with a ground-out by Quinn. "Wee Willie" Keeler followed with another grounder, but Keeler, who had 67 stolen bases on the year, was fast and he beat it out. Jennings doubled, but Cleveland held Keeler at third. Keeler, however, scored easily when he ran on contact as Kelley grounded out to Childs. A double by Doyle and a single by Reitz earned 2 more. The home team went up 6–1 and "after that Cleveland was easy fruit until the ninth inning."[20]

Baltimore added a run in the eighth with triples by Hoffer and Keeler, then went out without a run in the top of the ninth, and Cleveland came up for their last try. Zimmer kept the faith by starting things out with a walk; McGarr broke faith with a dinky fly to second. O'Connor stepped up and rapped out a single but Blake forced him at second. Young was due to bat, but Bobby Wallace came out to pinch hit for him. Hoffer, as he had done at a number of critical junctures in the game, once again set the last man down on strikes.

Score: Baltimore 7, Cleveland 1.

Inning	1	2	3	4	5	6	7	8	9	Final
Baltimore	0	0	2	0	0	1	3	1	0	7
Cleveland	0	0	0	0	0	1	0	0	0	1

First base on balls: Hoffer 4, Young 1. Strikeouts: Hoffer 5. Stolen bases: Kelley (2), Brodie, and McAleer. Hits: Baltimore 13, Cleveland 5. Time: 1:45. Umpires: Emslie and Sheridan. Attendance: 3,995.

Notes: • Quinn replaced McGraw when he became ill and O'Connor replaced Tebeau when he hurt his back while at bat in the second. Wallace pinch-hit for Young.

GAME TWO

Bobby ("Rhody") Wallace of Cleveland: age 22, throws right, height 5'8" and weight 170 lbs., versus Joe Corbett of Baltimore: age 20, throws right.

Batting orders

Baltimore	Cleveland
McGraw, 3b	Burkett, lf
Keeler, rf	McKean, ss
Jennings, ss	Childs, 2b
Kelley, lf	McAleer, cf
Doyle, 1b	O'Connor, 1b
Reitz, 2b	Zimmer, c
Brodie, cf	McGarr, 3b
Robinson, c	Blake, rf
Corbett, p	Wallace, p

John McGraw led off the game for Baltimore and hit a hard one at McKean, but a bad throw from McKean let him get to second. Keeler hit a solid drive into center and McGraw walked home. A pitch hit Jennings. A single into center by Kelley plated Keeler and on the play McAleer mishandled the ball and Kelley took second. Jennings scored when Doyle was safe on a high chopper to short, and a bounce-out by Brodie to O'Connor at first allowed Kelley to score. Four runs.

Burkett tried to get Cleveland out of its 4-run hole in their first turn at the bat with a hit down the first base line. His teammates yelled and hollered when the umpire called it foul. Burkett hung in and got to first on an ugly hop hit over second baseman Reitz's head. McKean forced out Burkett, Childs walked and McAleer grounded out second to first. With two out and two on, O'Connor came up and went down on a slow roller to short to cancel any threat. The second frame was uneventful.

Jennings led off the third with a liner into left, and Kelley's hit into right put him on third. Doyle put another single into right to drive in Jennings. Reitz bunted the runners over. Brodie flied out to O'Connor at first and Kelley smartly tagged up and scored, but Doyle on the same play got caught between third and home to end the inning. Two runs. In the bottom of the inning the running speed of pitcher Bobby Wallace got him to first ahead of the throw from Jennings to Doyle; a wild pitch gave him second. Burkett was set down on strikes. McKean placed one down the left foul line for a double that brought in Wallace. Reitz retired the next two Spiders on consecutive plays with some great glove work from second to first. One run.

Neither team scored in the fourth. Wallace, however, got out of a jam in the top of the inning. He had hit Jennings in the ribs to load up the sacks, but then Kelley kindly ended the trouble by flying out to McAleer in center.

Baltimore rang up run number 7 in the fifth inning of play. Burkett was able to hold on to Doyle's low liner for the first out. The pitcher hit Reitz and then Brodie batted the ball on the ground to third and was thrown out, as Reitz took second on the play. He scored on Robinson's single over second. One run. For Cleveland in the fifth, Wallace knocked one way over into the right field corner, but Keeler made a circus catch of it. Burkett got an infield scratch hit and moved up on a wild pitch. McKean struck out and Childs grounded out.

Baltimore did no damage in the sixth. Cleveland led off with McAleer hitting a long fly to left field, but Kelley made a fine running catch of it. O'Connor hit a ball to third but Jennings once again had throwing problems, and O'Connor made it to second. Zimmer bounced out to Corbett but O'Connor advanced. Jennings, who was having a day full of problems in the field, booted an easy chance off the bat of McGarr, and O'Connor scored. One run.

Baltimore did not score in the seventh. Cleveland in their half was the victim of two sensational plays. Another great outfield play by Kelley retired Blake, then Wallace grounded out. The Spiders, however, threatened when Burkett walked and McKean singled. Unfortunately, Jennings at this point got a grip on his defense, and made a "beautiful backward run" and catch on a fly from Childs to close the inning.[21]

Wallace made quick work of Baltimore in the eighth, no scoring. With one out in the eighth Cleveland got a single to center from O'Connor, and another one, this time into left, from Zimmer. But as bad luck would have it Chippy McGarr hit into a double play.

In the ninth Jennings got on via a bad throw from McGarr, and Kelley beat out an infield nubber. The runners moved over on a wild pitch and came home on Doyle's single into right. Two runs.

The umpire decided that with darkness looming there was no way Cleveland could plate 7 runs in the ninth while there was still any light left—so he called the game over.

Because the ninth was not completed the score officially reverted to the last full inning of play, making the Orioles 7–2 winners.

Inning	1	2	3	4	5	6	7	8	Final
Baltimore	4	0	2	0	1	0	0	0	7
Cleveland	0	0	1	0	0	1	0	0	2

Strikeouts: Corbett 4, Wallace 4. Walks: Corbett 2, Wallace 2. Wild pitches: Corbett 2, Wallace 1. Attendance: 3,100. Time: 2:00. Umpires: Emslie and Sheridan.

GAME THREE

Bill ("Wizard") Hoffer of Baltimore: age 25, throws right, height 5'9" and weight 155 lbs., versus George Cuppy of Cleveland: age 27, throws right, height 5'7" and weight 160 lbs.

Batting orders

Baltimore	Cleveland
McGraw, 3b	Burkett, lf
Keeler, rf	McKean, ss
Jennings, ss	Childs, 2b
Kelley, lf	McAleer, cf
Doyle, 1b	O'Connor, 1b
Reitz, 2b	Zimmer, c
Brodie, cf	McGarr, 3b
Robinson, c	Blake, rf
Hoffer, p	Cuppy, p

Patsy Tebeau was still unable to play because of his bad back, and it looked like he would sit out game four also. Tebeau had the company of the famous actor De Wolf Hopper, who sat behind him the entire game and cheered loudly for the Spiders; in an off-field incident, Hopper had become disenchanted with the Orioles.

The weather was perfect and the ticket price for the game was cut in half: "The attendance at twenty five cents was 4,250, a very sorry showing, indeed. If all the games were played in Baltimore, the players could about come out even in their hotel bills and expenses."[22]

George Cuppy, somewhat recovered from a split hand, waited in the pitcher's box for John McGraw to arrive at the plate to begin the game. McGraw grounded out to McGarr at third, Keeler flied out to Burkett in left, and McGarr caught a fly at third off the bat of Jennings. Burkett led off for Cleveland by lining a Hoffer pitch over the head of McGraw, but he was caught trying to pilfer second. McKean hit an out to Doyle at first. Childs smacked the ball off of the shin of McGraw and was safe, but McAleer forced him with a grounder to Jennings at short.

Kelley got a base on an infield hit to McKean at short to start the second. A hit-and-run was attempted and Childs fielded the ball and forced out Kelley, but was unable to turn two when Kelley came in high and disrupted his throw to first. Doyle then stole second. Reitz hit the ball to Burkett for out number two. Brodie popped a single into right and Doyle scored. McKean made a brilliant stab and return throw on a high bounder over Cuppy's head for the last out. One run. Cleveland didn't score in the second, but during the inning Zimmer, on via a single, enlivened the crowd when trying to avoid being forced out at second: "'Big Chief' played Doyle's trick of a few minutes before nearly knocking Reitz over. The crowd hissed like all the geese and snakes in Christendom though the other time they had nearly died of joy."[23]

In the third a triple to the center field fence, by the pitcher Hoffer, turned more than a few heads in the crowd. Keeler hit a short fly to left, Hoffer tagged up and broke for the plate—he was safe when Burkett's rushed throw was off the mark. One run. Burkett got a one-out single, and McKean's hit put him at third, from where he scored when Childs forced out McKean at second. One run.

The fourth saw Baltimore down on three consecutive flies, but one of the catches made by Burkett actually drew applause from the partisan crowd. Kelley, however, upstaged Burkett with two sensational catches of his own on hits by Zimmer and McGarr. Cuppy ended the fourth by fouling out.

In the Baltimore fifth Cuppy retired the last two men on strikeouts—using only seven pitches. Cleveland scored a run in the fifth on a two-out walk to Childs, followed by singles from McAleer and O'Connor. One run.

In the sixth Baltimore got a run when McGraw hit for a base, stole second, and took third on the wild throw from Zimmer. Keeler sent McGraw home with a fly to McAleer in center. One run.

Both teams went out in order in the seventh. Robinson started the eighth with a double, was moved over by the pitcher, and came home on a McGraw single. Keeler on a hit-and-run managed a scratch hit that sent McGraw to third. When Jennings lifted a fly to Blake in left McGraw tagged and scored. Keeler stole second, and when Kelley's grounder was thrown wild to first, Keeler crossed the plate. Three runs. Cleveland put O'Connor on base with a single and he was forced. They put McGarr on via an error and he was forced. And Cuppy fouled out.

The ninth started with Baltimore up and down in order. Burkett led off for Cleveland with a sizzling liner at left field, but right into the hands of a waiting Kelley. McKean whiffed and Childs grounded out to Jennings at third. And Cleveland lost.

Score: Baltimore 6, Cleveland 2.

Inning	1	2	3	4	5	6	7	8	9	Final
Baltimore	0	1	1	0	0	1	0	3	0	6
Cleveland	0	0	1	0	1	0	0	0	0	2

Stolen bases: Doyle, Hoffer, McGraw (3) and Keeler. Strikeouts: Hoffer 5, Cuppy 2. Attendance: 4,250. Time: 2:00. Umpires: Emslie and Sheridan.

> Three games they lost for the Temple cup;
> Three games right at the start;
> So Tebeau leaves with a pain in his back
> And another in his heart.
> Oh, where is Cleveland's pennant pole?
> In the town of the oyster stew.
> And where is the blooming Temple cup?
> I'm afraid they'll get that, too.[24]

Game Four

Joe Corbett of Baltimore versus George Cuppy of Cleveland.

Batting orders

Cleveland	Baltimore
Burkett, lf	McGraw, 3b
McKean, ss	Keeler, rf
Childs, 2b	Jennings, ss
McAleer, cf	Kelley, lf
O'Connor, 1b	Doyle, 1b
Zimmer, c	Reitz, 2b
McGarr, 3b	Brodie, cf
Blake, rf	Robinson, c
Cuppy, p	Corbett, p
Wallace, ph	

The cold weather kept the Cleveland crowd down to two thousand. It also tightened Tebeau's muscles in his injured back, so much so that he had to substitute O'Connor at first once again. "Cy" Young was also not available; after having been hit hard by a batted ball early in game one, he had finished the contest with a very swollen pitching hand, and he was still not ready for game four.

The game through six innings was a great pitcher's duel between Cuppy and Corbett, with neither team able to get a run up on the board. Cleveland had a chance in the fifth: "McGarr hit a liner to center for a base in the fifth, and Jennings error gave Blake a chance, putting two men on the base for the first time in the game. A double steal took place just as Cuppy struck out. Burkett's grounder resulted in McGarr being thrown out at the plate by Jennings, but Burkett got to second. McKean was thrown out at first by Reitz and Baltimore was out of a bad hole. No runs."[25]

Cuppy came undone in the Baltimore seventh:

Kelley [sic] started out with a clean two-bagger between left and center and scored the first run of the game on Doyle's single over McKean's head. Reitz was out on a fly to McAleer. Doyle stole second and went to third on Zimmer's wild throw. Brodie was out from Childs to O'Connor, but Doyle scored on the play. Cuppy threw Robinson out. Two runs.

The eighth started well. Cuppy hit safe over Jennings head. Burkett forced Cuppy, Jennings to Doyle. Childs hit safe two feet from the plate and Burkett went to third. Childs stole second. McAleer struck out. No runs.

The Spiders' last chance was soon over. O'Connor hit a sharp one to Doyle, but Corbett covered the bag and he was out. Zimmer got a base on balls, but McGarr struck out, and after Blake had walked Wallace, who had batted for Cuppy, was thrown out by Corbett.[26]

Score:

Inning	1	2	3	4	5	6	7	8	9	Final
Cleveland	0	0	0	0	0	0	0	0	0	0
Baltimore	0	0	0	0	0	0	2	3	*	5

Strikeouts: Corbett 7, Cuppy 2. Walks: Corbett 5. Stolen bases: McKean, McGarr, Blake, Childs, Doyle. Time: 2 hours. Umpires: Sheridan and Emslie. Attendance: 2,000.

The *Cleveland Leader:*

FAREWELL TO THE CUP

The Cleveland players said farewell to the Temple cup at the Hollenden Hotel last evening. At 7 o'clock the players of both clubs, together with Messrs. Frank DeHaas Robison and Harry Von der Horst, gathered about the bar, upon which Mr. Temple's trophy was placed and filled with champagne by the Cleveland club, in honor of the team which had three times won the pennant, and finally the cup. The champagne was soon disposed of, and the Orioles took possession of their trophy.[27]

BLAMING BALTIMORE

A Case of Swelled Head

There is a reason for the poor attendance at the Temple cup games at Baltimore. A Baltimore writer in a out-of-town special gives some of the inside points about the Baltimore public as follows: "In speaking of the poor attendance at the Temple cup games, a well known local newspaper man, who, for obvious reasons, does not want his name mentioned, said: 'Don't blame the Baltimore public. The players have a great deal to do with the latent interest in baseball. They were treated too well for the first year, and now they expect too much. You know there is such a thing as looking a gift horse in the mouth, and that is what the Baltimore players have been doing. They have disgusted a great many of their friends by their actions.' Some funny stories are told about the Baltimore players in this respect, and De Wolf Hopper tells about as an amusing story as could be imagined. As everyone knows, De Wolf Hopper is a ball crank. He is always at the games, and almost every ball player of note in the country knows the comic opera star. He was playing at the Academy of Music last week, and he thought: it would be a clever thing to invite the champions to occupy a couple of boxes for one of the performances. He also extended an invitation to the Cleveland players. Thursday night was the night the Orioles were invited, and Mr. Hopper wrote a personal letter inviting the boys to be present. Imagine his surprise the next day when he received a letter from the three times champions, saying that if he would give the champions a percentage of the receipts, they would accept the invitation; otherwise they would have to decline it.

Hopper answered that he was not running a dime museum, and had not invited them as freaks, but that he might make arrangements for them to appear as curios in some of the museums in other cities that he visited.

It is said that the business of getting a rake-off became so strong that when McGraw took a fainting spell in the first Temple cup game, and a doctor was called to prescribe for him, that Mugs said before the doctor touched him: "Remember we get 10 percent of the gross for letting you attend me."

Another story is to the effect that the European players of the team went to one of the newspaper offices and demanded $50 to help pay their expenses in Europe. It is said that all the newspapers were "touched" and for that reason the newspapers did not go wild advertising the Temple cup games.

It is said that some of the players objected to the begging business, and it is known that Manager Ned Hanlon and Treasurer Vonderhorst were much opposed to it, but some players did it on their own hook. Vonderhorst gave the players the ballpark for the first three days of last week and gave them all the receipts, amounting to $1,200, although the men were under contract until Oct. 1.

The Orioles have not yet completed all their arrangements for their trip abroad, but they expect to make a little money in dear old "Hingland." Joe Campbell of Washington met Joe Kelley here Saturday, and said: "You had better look out if you go to England, as it is a cinch that McGraw, Jennings and yourself will be picked out as dynamiters and members of the Tynan gang. Why, all they need to do is to hear your names over there in England, and nobody will go to the games. You ought to make a tour of Limerick, but it is a great mistake to go to England." Kelley said he would think it over, and is sort of concerned that an Irish team of ball players will not be a great attraction in England at the present time.[28]

The finish of some unfinished business

STUCKY HAS REPENTED

Louisville Ky., October 14.— The case of the Cleveland base ball players who were fined in the police court last summer ... Dr. Stucky the president of the Louisville base ball club, and chief prosecuting witness, wrote Judge Noble that the trouble arose in the heat of excitement, and that, as the men were non-residents, the matter had best be settled. Kinney, Gregory & Kinney, their attorneys, confessed fines of $11 each for breach of the peace, and the cases were disposed of.[29]

The legal business in Kentucky was the last business of the Cleveland Spiders for the season of 1896.

Some baseball pundits felt that Cleveland needed to add some hitting power in the off-season if it was to compete for the pennant and the Temple Cup. Mr. Temple, however, withdrew the Temple Cup from competition due to the poor attendance at the post-season matches. There would be no form of "world series" until 1903, by which time the American League had established itself as the second major league. The next time a Cleveland team won a pennant and played in any post-season series, they would be in the American League, and the year would be 1920. In a touch of irony, they would win the World Series that year by defeating the Brooklyn National League team managed by the 1896 Baltimore Orioles catcher, Wilbert Robinson. This Brooklyn team would become best known by the nickname of "Dodgers"; however, in 1920 they were called "Robins" in honor of their beloved manager, Wilbert "Uncle Robbie" Robinson.

1897

The Cleveland "Indians"

The American Indian in the 1890's began to be viewed in popular culture more sympathetically, as the noble red man rather than the uncivilized savage of the past. The mass urbanization brought on by the Industrial Revolution contributed to this longing for lost scenes of a more pastoral and colorful past.

Publishing tapped into this desire with its stories and drawings of the Western frontier and things Indian. Individuals like Buffalo Bill Cody, Pawnee Bill, and others also exploited this interest in the ways of the West, by bringing their Wild West shows—featuring real live Indians—to eager eastern audiences.

Even some baseball club executives were not without their touch of Indian fever: "This year, President Hart of the Chicago base ball club planned to dress his ball players in colorful robes to emulate the look of a tribe of Indians—ready for fearsome combat on the field of play: It is thought that it will be a picturesque scene when eighteen animated "rainbows" strut solemnly across the field from the dressing rooms to the benches. After a little procession up and down in front of the grand stand, the team will emerge from the depths, cast off the bath robes in one glowing, blazing heap, and prepare to win the championship. The idea is borrowed from the football teams."[1]

Cleveland capitalized on this sentiment for things Indian, by signing major league baseball's first full-blooded Native American to play right field. He was born in Old Town, Maine, and was a descendant of the Penobscot tribe. His name was Louis Sockalexis, recently of Holy Cross and Notre Dame colleges:

Tebeau's New Indian
Tebeau, the Cleveland manager, has secured the services of the much sought Sockalexis, a full blooded Indian.
— Baseball Note.

Sock-alexis, Sock-alexis
  Sock-alexis tall,
Down to wild and wooly Texas
  Soon will knock the ball:
And the crank, whate'er the sex is,
  Soon will raise the stock,
Just to prove spry Sock-alexis
  Worthy of his sock.

Soon will he, until he's sore, whoop
  On the coaching line,
And the music of his war whoop
  Will be very fine.
Yea, the glamour of his war paint
  Will delight the crowd,
Though it be but common store paint

Laid on thick and loud.
When he grabs the flying leather
  By the batter sped,
It will add another feather
  To his feathered head:
And a sense of the romancing
  Methods of his race
Will be felt when he is dancing
  On the umpire's face.

Oh, it's gayly
  That we'll daily
All amid the hullabaloo
  Hear the sock-a-doodle-doodle
  Of his sock-a-doodle-doo.[2]

Cleveland manager Patsy Tebeau got word in early March that his little boy was dangerously ill with pneumonia. He took the boy and his other child to Denver where it was believed the western climate had health benefits, as opposed to Cleveland. His brother George, who had lost a child of his own suddenly a year or so previously, was in Denver to meet them. Patsy's boy survived his bout with pneumonia, and his uncle landed a job as manager of the ball club in Columbus, Ohio.

In the off-season, two Cleveland players had jobs as part-time instructional coaches of college teams. Zeke Wilson coached at Auburn in Alabama and Jesse Burkett at Holy Cross, in his wife's home town of Worcester, MA. Jesse also made some money over the winter in his native city of Wheeling, WV — playing ice polo, for $20 a week.

The Indians' New Mascots

Following the tradition of the 1890's the team again went to Arkansas for spring training:

Hot Springs, Ark., March 18.—
An effort to secure a new variety of mascots caused quite a joke on some of the players. The chameleon is said to possess more good luck giving qualities than the left hind feet of all the graveyard rabbits that the moon ever shone on, and a day or so ago Jess Burkett, Bobby Wallace and Harry Blake made a ten strike. In going through the woods they ran onto a whole settlement of queer little reptiles, and Burkett and Blake started for the high ground. Wallace recognized the bonanza, and told the others what they had found.

"We'll get some for every member of the team," he said, and the capture began. Burkett got his handkerchief full, Blake filled a tobacco bag and Wallace tied half a dozen on a string.

Filled with pride they returned to the hotel. "They'll change to the color of anything you put them on," said Wallace. "The colts can have little ones, and they'll turn green."

To the office of the Avenue hotel the remaining players were called to receive their mascots, and Burkett's handkerchief was spread before their astonished eyes.

"What t'hell!" was the unusual exclamation.
"Chameleons," said Wallace.
"Mascots," said Blake.
"Beat rabbits' feet," said Burkett.

Now Zeke Wilson is a native of this southern clime, and the way he went at those mascots was something fierce. He seized a railroad guide and cut loose at them to demolish the lot, that began scurrying in all directions.

"Don't!" roared the trio; "they're good luck. They are chameleons. They'll change any color you—"

"Chameleons, thunder!" roared Wilson; "they're lizards. They'll bite the life out of you. Kill the little devils."

It is a belief that the species of lizard that the three gathered is venomous, but, if so, the three players must have charmed lives for not a scratch did they get. Poisonous or not, it was a bad day for the lizards, and the team is still without mascots.

WALTER M. ROBISON.[3]

Shown here at age 41, as manager of the 1909 Worcester Busters (New England League), Jesse Burkett was in the 1890s a hard-hitting member of the Cleveland Spiders (Library of Congress).

Cleveland left Hot Springs in late March and spent the next few weeks touring cities in the old Northwest Territory. Sockalexis joined the team at this time following a brief stay in Cleveland working out at the C.A.C. gym and doing photo-shot publicity. Sockalexis was quite the novel draw in the training games, which took place in Columbus, Dayton, Indianapolis, Ft. Wayne, Grand Rapids, and Toledo.

Cleveland opened in Louisville on April 22. There was a parade from the Louisville hotel out to the ballpark. The First Regiment Band led the way, and six trumpeters of the First Regiment State Guard pulled up the rear.

The overflow crowd of 10,010 watched as their man Chick Fraser out-dueled Cy Young to win a 3–1 victory for the home folks.

Time: 1:45.

Umpire: McDermont.

Cleveland lost 5 in a row to start the season. In game 6 at St. Louis a crowd of about a thousand came out in the threatening weather, which caused a rain delay in the fourth inning.

Cleveland was up by 2 in the ninth inning when St. Louis tied the game at 6. A spectacular catch by Sockalexis kept the score tied, and because it was near seven o'clock, and dark, the umpire declared the game a tie.

The Indians then won 3 in a row before heading home for the Cleveland opener.

Cy Young Opens

It was cold and chilly for the 4,500 Cleveland fans out at League Park. Cy Young was the pitcher for the opener and he faced off against Ted Breitenstein of Cincinnati.

Cleveland got on the board in the bottom of the first. McKean singled, and O'Connor walked. With the help of a couple of stolen bases, a bad throw, and a single by Blake, Cleveland had 2 tallies.

In the second Tebeau singled, Wallace bunted him over, and Cy Young drove his manager in with a double.

THE CLEVELAND BASEBALL TEAM. 1897

A pen and ink depiction of the 1897 Cleveland team, newly nicknamed Indians. Louis Sockalexis, the game's first full-blooded Indian, is shown center top row (George Mears Scrapbook, Cleveland Public Library).

The next runs came in the Cleveland sixth. Zimmer singled, Wallace walked, and a single by Burkett sent Zimmer on home. Young got on when he forced out Wallace, and came on to score when McKean rapped a single.

Cincinnati's first runs came in the seventh. A walk to Irwin, a Peitz single, a sacrifice by Breitenstein, and a hit by Burke into left gave the Red Stockings their first 2 runs.

In the eighth, Wallace doubled, Young sacrificed him to third, and on Burkett's fly-out he scored. In the cold and twilight of the ninth, Cincinnati went easy — in one, two, three fashion.

Score: Cleveland 6, Cincinnati 2.
Time of game: 1:45.
Umpires: McDonald and McDermont.

Sox and Sundays

"Peach Pie" O'Connor and "Chief" Louis Sockalexis had become fast friends. In the gym they had proven themselves to be the best duo of handball players on the entire roster. A few days after a May win over Chicago Sockalexis and O'Connor mysteriously both developed bad charley horses in their legs that prevented them from playing.

The episode was a clue concerning some serious problems that were to develop for Mr. Louis Sockalexis as the season unfolded and his fame skyrocketed.

Amateur teams were catching Indian fever. It was reported that a team in Galion, Ohio, was named the "Sockalexis," and that "Sockalexis" and "Indians" were the names of two Cleveland teams made up of boys below thirteen years in age.

Cleveland owner Frank Robison was not satisfied with the attendance in 1896. Robison, perhaps a bit jealous of the large crowds in cities that were allowed to have Sunday baseball (the crowds on Sunday often doubled those of the rest of the week combined), pushed for Sunday ball in Cleveland. Robison threatened to move the franchise, or at least play many home games at more lucrative neutral sites, if he did not get his way. With the help of the *Plain Dealer*, he also renamed the Spiders the Indians, hoping the name change and the addition of Sockalexis would increase attendance.

In the matter of Sunday ball he received bitter opposition from the ministers' association. One fan gave his response to the anti — Sunday ball clergy with a poem:

Cleveland is nearly done for,
It's on the toboggan slide,
And when Patsy's aggregation,
Sanctimoniously denied,
Leaves the town of non-supporters
It will more than once be said
That the preachers' little racket
Left it practically dead.

We will never part with Patsy,
That's as sure as we're alive,
For Patsy holds the ribbons
And he knows just how to drive.
De Haas refused a million,
And we're not surprised at that,
For the famous tricky thinker
Under Patsy Tebeau's hat.

If the team must go up to Detroit
Or somewhere else to play.
They'll be still known as the Cleveland's,
Even though they're far away.
But I rather think that Robison

Won't take that pulpit bluff.
For Sunday is the day that dough
Is recognized as stuff.

We've got a team of hustlers,
That are always in the game,
And if deer speed Sockalexis
Proves a credit to his name,
For that little piece of bunting
We will make a gallant fight.
With the only scalper in the biz
A-running around in right.

The preachers claim that cycling
Is a very rank disgrace,
And that boxing don't become
The enlightened Caucasian race;
Nor is football in the Bible.
You'll not find it if you search,
But if Sunday games are not allowed
We'll stop our going to church.[4]

While Sockalexis was a good draw on the road and at home, the real chunk of change that was to be had for President Robison was with Sunday home games—if he could find a way to get away with them.

Thinking that he had a deal with Mayor McKisson to do just that, while at the same time creating a test case in the courts, he went ahead with plans for a Sunday game against the Washington Senators on May 16. When the Ministers' Association, and an unlikely ally in the liquor league, came out against the game, the mayor suddenly had second thoughts about allowing a professional ball game on a Sunday.

The saloons around town were open on Sunday in spite of the law against it (most suspected graft). However, the thought of losing ten to twenty thousand mostly male blue-collar drinkers to a ball game for a few hours on Sunday motivated many bar owners to action. Concerning the issue the *Plain Dealer* said: "It is certainly a delicate satire on the city authorities to prevent one alleged evil for the benefit of a greater one...."[5]

Mayor McKisson, Law Director Abbott, and Prosecutor T. M. Kennedy huddled on Saturday in order to decide which statute would permit arrest without the need of a citizen's complaint first.

Robison advertised that a full refund would be given if the game were not played at least the official five innings.

To expedite a possible refund, $4000 in silver halves and quarters was made available for the cashiers. Judge George B. Solders, acting as Mr. Robison's attorney, was confident that any arrest of players would not take place until after the fifth inning. Acting on this belief, President Robison wired the Washington management to bring the club over early after the final game in Pittsburgh. That way they could get a good night's sleep, because the Sunday game was as good as a done deal.

The gates for the three o'clock game opened at 12:30, but it was not until 2:30 that a policeman brought the mayor's message that the men would be arrested after one inning of play: "'What

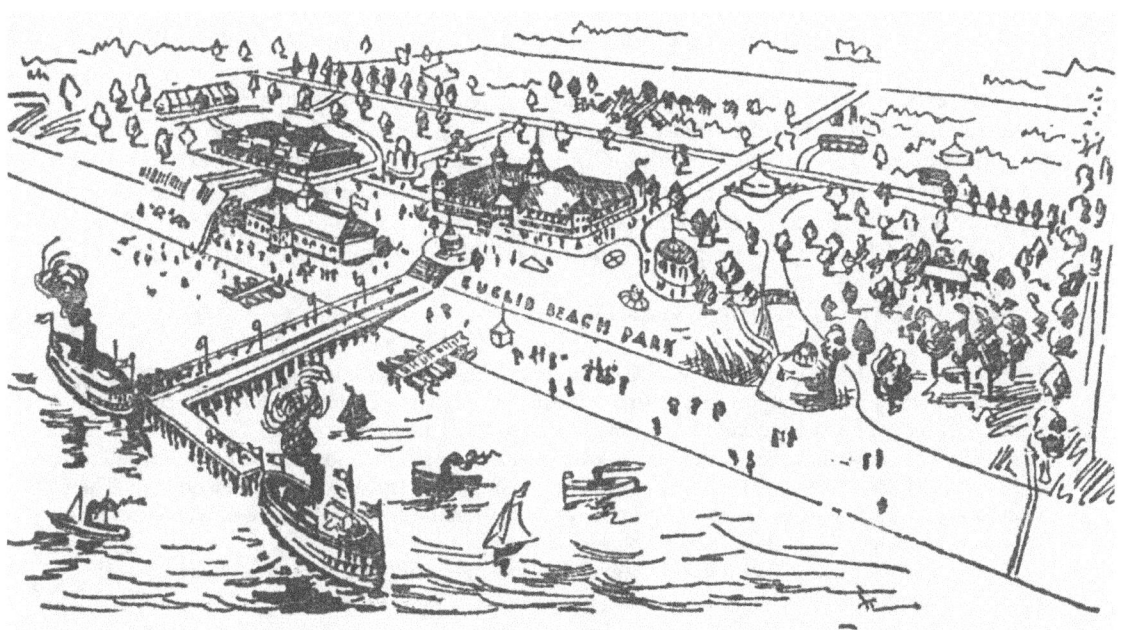

An 1897 drawing of Euclid Beach Park in the City of Collinwood. Euclid Park, an amusement park built in 1895, was the site of 1897 Indians' home games on Sunday. The illustration is from the August 10, 1897, edition of the *Cleveland Press*.

if they return and attempt to finish the game?' asked President Robison. 'They will be arrested again,' replied the officer who did the warning. 'That is not according to the law,' said President Robison. 'It is according to orders,' replied the officer."[6]

There were nine thousand people on the grounds at this time and an equal number on the outside anxious to get in.

At this point, in order to save his personnel additional refund work and further inconvenience to the public not already inside, Robison ordered the ticket windows and gates closed.

Lester German for Washington and Zeke Wilson for Cleveland pitched the first inning without allowing a run. When Farrell lined out to Tebeau to end the first inning the proceedings were called to a halt.

Captain English of the Cleveland police, with President Robison and a reporter from the *Leader* newspaper at his side, approached the home plate area. Robison gestured to the hissing crowd to be heard. "Ladies and gentlemen: We are ordered by the police to refrain from fracturing a State law. The law must be respected. I will take this case into the State courts, and I believe yet that we will be victorious."[7]

The two managers were given a choice of going to jail in a "hoodlum wagon" or a 'bus.[8] They chose the latter. Cleveland was allowed to change into civilian clothes in the clubhouse, but Washington had to go in uniform because their street clothes were back at the Hollenden Hotel. The crowd dispersed without incident.

President Robison posted $100 bonds each for Umpire Hurst, the Senators, and the Indians, all of whom were expected in police court the next day.

A jury trial in police court was asked for, and by arrangement John Powell was put on trial. The jury in Judge Fiedler's courtroom found him guilty, and the conviction was appealed to the common pleas court. The decision of that court would be handed down in July.

Sockalexis' Skyrocketing Fame

On May 17 the Cleveland record stood at 9 and 10, good for seventh place. Baltimore at 16 and 3 was in first.

Sockalexis by the end of May had hit enough triples to be thought of as a serious challenger for the all-time season record in that department. In early June the *New York World* featured an action illustration of Sockalexis—in full uniform shading his eyes with his glove as he prepares to snag a fly ball in right. A few days later a large crowd of New Yorkers went out to see the Indian novelty. Sockalexis right away gave them something to look at, as he blasted a line drive over the ropes in right field in the first inning for a homer, and the first run of the game—a game Cleveland went on to win 7–2.

By mid–June it was written of Sockalexis:

No player in the National league is attracting as much attention these days as Louis Sockalexis, the Indian, who covers right green for Patsy Tebeau. In the east he is the center of attraction and columns after columns are devoted to telling of his wonderful playing.

A New York writer has also made this discovery, and he says: 'The most talked of baseball player in the country is Sockalexis, the full blooded Indian playing the outfield for the Cleveland club. The red man has scored a sensational success in the very fast National league company, and with experience promises to be one of the most valuable players in the land.'[9]

In the east the fact that Sockalexis is highly educated and an interesting and intelligent talker seems to be overlooked....[10]

A *New York Sun* man was hence somewhat surprised to get the following interview:

"If the small and big boys of Brooklyn and other cities find it a pleasure to shout at me, I have no objections," said Sockalexis. "No matter where we play, I go through the same ordeal, and at the present time I am so used to it that at times I forget to smile at my tormentors, believing it to be part of the game. But I do love to play ball. Ever since I was so high" (lowering his hand to within three feet of the ground) "I have played the game. Out at Old Town, Me., where I was born, I used to join other Indians and some white boys, and it has been my ambition to become a great player.

"Will I succeed? Why of course, I will. You have no idea how anxious I am to learn every point and trick of the game. There are many little things that come up in nearly every game which are new to me, but the white players are good to me and are always ready to advise me.

"I have seen printed in several papers that the Cleveland players are likely to freeze me out of the club because I am an Indian. That is all bosh, for the white players can't do enough for me, especially Burkett, who is said to be jealous because I lead him in batting. Jesse is proud of me because I made such a good showing, he having recommended me to Manager Tebeau. It was while I was playing with the Holy Cross college team at Williamstown, two years ago, that John M. Ward told a league manager to sign me. Burkett who coached the Holy Cross team, finally got Tebeau to let me have a trial."[11]

The standings on June 17 showed Cleveland in fifth place with a win-loss record of 22 and 20. Baltimore still held the top spot with a 32 and 9 record.

Sockalexis in Chicago on June 24 was a big hit. The bleacher bums kept up a chorus of war-whoops throughout the game but Sockalexis' demeanor throughout was all business.

At Chicago Manager Tebeau offered his candid analysis of his new right fielder's abilities: "He's a bit weak on judging those shooting flies and not perfect on the bounders, but he'll learn all that. He's a great sticker and far above the average of intelligence for ball players. As a matter of fact, the Indian is valuable to Cleveland outside of his advertising purposes. He hits the ball harder than most left-handers and seems to lose

SOCKALEXIS BREAKING FOR THIRD

The May 4, 1897, issue of the *Cleveland Plain Dealer* included this cartoon of rookie Louis Sockalexis in action on the base paths.

no time in getting started because of his vicious swing. He is not a good fielder but up to the average."[12]

Sockalexis was also described in one quarter as a batter who goes at the ball from a rather unorthodox stance, and as an impatient batter, who in spite of that is a very good bad-ball hitter.

Sockalexis in the June 26 game at Chicago, while attempting to chase down the home run drive off the bat of Bill "Little Eva" Lange, ran into the fence so hard that he injured his arm to the point that when he retrieved the ball he had to lob it back in.

Fortunately for him he was back in the lineup in short order, because there was soon to be no chance of McAleer returning to the outfield. McAleer, who was on the hospital list, quit the team, packed his bags, and headed home to Youngstown. He was upset with newspaper stories about "his time honored charley horse"[13] and Tebeau's refusal to grant his request for a contract release. McAleer, the occasional politician and real estate dealer, had recently purchased an interest in a clothing store at Youngstown. Presumably, he would now pursue a more active role in those off-field activities.

Scenic Park

The management of the Indians was hoping a decision on the constitutional legality of the statute used by Cleveland authorities to stop their Sunday ball game in May would be forthcoming before the Fourth of July, which this year happened to fall on a Sunday, and was but a few days away. It was not.

However, if one wished to take in a ball game that holiday Sunday, the newly renovated amusement park along the eastern shore of the Rocky River by Detroit Street had one on tap — along with many other interesting diversions for your "day of rest."

Scenic Park could be accessed direct from Public Square via the Cleveland City Railway Company. The seven-mile ride along beautiful Detroit Street — with its handsome homes, green lawns, towering trees and gardens beautiful — would take no time at all. And in but a few more days, four miles of Detroit Street were to be illuminated by electric arc light, adding further to the charm of an evening ride out to the park. The grounds themselves were lit by thousands of electric lights "which give a fairyland appearance to the whole."[14]

On the Fourth of July a military band was scheduled to perform an afternoon and an evening concert. And the public, if it chose, could take a ride on the popular "Scenic Railway," as well as enjoy "Merry-go-rounds, the Ferris wheel, old Aunt Sally, swings, shooting the chute and other innumerable harmless sports" including baseball.[15] The park also hosted a first-class restaurant.

And in the evening, to top off your holiday adventure, "there will be a grand pyrotechnical display, including Niagara Falls in fire."[16]

A Win in Court

Judge Walter C. Ong, of the common pleas court, made his ruling on July 9 concerning the constitutionality of statute 7032a, under which the arrest and prosecution was made of the players for playing Sunday ball on May 16. He found the statute unconstitutional because it prohibits the playing of ball on Sunday, and the law can not protect a religious day, but can only set aside a day of rest. As an example he said the state can allow Saturday to be the Jewish day of rest, in which case they can play baseball or conduct business on a Sunday. The state can allow Sunday to be the day of rest in general, and that would include most Christians, but the state cannot compel any particular day for all people, because that would be a violation of religious freedom.

Judge Ong stated: "I hold that the legislature under the constitution has no right to compel the citizens of the state to refrain from playing ball on Sunday simply because it is Sunday, and since there was no other ground that could be claimed under the statute I held the law invalid."[17]

The judge was asked to comment further on a different statute — the common labor law — as it applied to Sunday: "'I have not thought of the matter before,' he said, 'and would not like to express the opinion, but I would not say that the act of playing ball for hire on Sunday would not be a violation of the law.'"[18]

President Robison immediately scheduled a game for the upcoming Sunday, the eleventh. As luck would have it the weather was terrible: "The game was played in mud, slush and drizzle."[19] The small crowd of 1,500 that showed up to watch Cleveland whip Washington 15–4 enjoyed the game, and was reasonably quiet and well behaved.

The following Sunday a crowd of 8,241 watched Cleveland beat Brooklyn 8–1. An exciting ten-inning game on Sunday, July 25, ended up in the Baltimore win column 6–5. In addition to the 15,000 inside there were many neighbors outside — watching from the rooftops and the windows.

Paint the Town Red

In the second week of July, Sockalexis was benched. He had hurt his toe and had difficulty running out his hits, and his fielding was described as that of a wooden Indian.

It was said that the faculty of Notre Dame warned Sockalexis that if he left before his term was up to join the Indians he would not be taken back. That was the story out of Cleveland. In John Phillips' book about the Cleveland Indians of 1897 a different account of events is revealed.

According to the story, Louis Sockalexis and another student decided to paint the town red one night. After trashing the establishment of "Popcorn Jenny," the hostess of a local bordello, they ended up in the calaboose — where they had a chance to sleep off the effects of a bottle of "Old Oscar McGroggins" whiskey.

Father Andrew Morrissey, the president of the college, expelled Sockalexis and the other student. Patsy Tebeau hurriedly went to South Bend after an informant gave him the news, and brought the troubled Indian to Cleveland, amidst much fanfare and glowing praise in the Cleveland papers.

Sockalexis' problems with alcohol continued to plague him behind the scenes in Cleveland. His hurt toe was legitimate enough, but his method of treating it with a good drunk on the town was questionable. Sockalexis would make a comeback at the end of July, after being benched supposedly for the bad toe but in reality more so for his drinking.

Stories about the popularity of Sockalexis on as well as off the field continued to appear. The *Cleveland Plain Dealer*: "They tell me that Sockalexis has more mash notes from the ladies than any matinee favorite the diamond has ever seen, not even barring Len Viau."[20]

Sox returned to the lineup on July 24 against the visiting Philadelphia Phillies for what would turn out to be one crazy game. Sitting in the stands were a number of Indians, who claimed to be relatives of Sockalexis—come down from Maine to see their now-famous kinsman.

The umpire for the game was a no-show but league president Nick Young said, when wired by Manager Tebeau, that it would suffice if a man from each team took turns as umpire. Tebeau claimed the substitution rule said a man from the home club, only, should umpire. Philadelphia, however, refused to play unless one of their men also umpired. Tebeau conceded for the sake of the crowd, and McGinty of Cleveland and Boyle of Philadelphia assumed the umpiring chores.

During the game Sockalexis showed off his skills with two solid hits in three official turns at the bat. In the ninth inning Cleveland came to bat trailing by a run. McGinty sent the first two batters to their base with a walk. Sockalexis was due next: "When the Phillies thought that they had been robbed to the extent of two bases on balls in the ninth they set up a howl that would have done credit to a pack of prairie wolves and finally refused to go on with the game."[21]

McGinty, who had been harassed for his decisions throughout the game by Philadelphia, waited five minutes for the Phillies to resume play. He then pulled out his pocket watch and counted the ticks for sixty seconds, at which point he declared a 9–0 forfeit in favor of Cleveland.

Two days later a game was stopped in the third inning so that admirers of Sockalexis could present him with a gift. Sockalexis expressed his thanks for the present — a three-foot-tall wooden Indian carved in his likeness.

Shortly after this Sockalexis, again, found himself on the bench (until August 16) when he was hospitalized and details of his drinking escapades became public knowledge. He was described as a fallen idol, who had to be taken to the Huron Street hospital with a very bad case of blood poisoning due to neglect of his injured toe. His doctor blamed his drinking for the serious condition of his foot, but believed any amputation should not be necessary.

It was reported that: "President Robison had a long talk with the Indian yesterday and again showed his generosity to his men. Sox has been under suspension for some time but that was due to his too frequent indulgence in the flowing bowl. He was warned that one more outbreak would give him a steady job on the bench without pay for the rest of the season."[22]

The foot problems of Sockalexis persisted and on September 4 he was sent back to the doctor: "Yesterday afternoon the X-rays were applied to Sockalexis' lame foot. The trouble was in the toe next to the great one on his right foot, and it was thought the bone had been broken and not properly knit together. The experiment was made by Dr. George S. Giddings, No. 168 Huron street. It was found that there were no broken bones in the foot, but the raw condition prevailed, as in Criger's [sic] hand, that a swelling of the muscles caused the pain."[23]

Sockalexis made but a handful of appearances in the lineup the rest of the season. In 1898 and 1899 he made short-lived attempts at a comeback. In but four short months the 25-year-old American Indian who had walked onto the national baseball stage had gone from star to star dust, never to be a star again. When the spirit of the genie got out of the bottle, it put Louis Sockalexis into the bottle, a place from which escape would take its time and its toll. Louis Sockalexis died on December 14, 1913, in Burlington, Maine. He was 42.

The record of Sox in 1897: Games 66; at bat 278; hits 94; doubles 9; triples 8; home runs 3 (at St. Louis, at Cleveland versus Cincinnati, and at New York); runs 43; runs batted in 42; walks 18; stolen bases 16; batting average .338; slugging average .460, and played right field 66 games.

Cleveland managed to keep a strangle hold on fifth place most of the year. On July 24 they were at 41 and 32, by August 10 their record dipped to 45 and 43, due to a dismal road trip that saw them go 2 and 8.

Another Sunday game at home came off on August 15. Cleveland beat last-place St. Louis 13–2. It was reported that the rain kept the crowd at Saturday's size.

Cleveland took the Buffalo boat east, for exhibition games in Toronto on Monday, and in Buffalo on Wednesday. At Toronto they drew 4,000 but the crowd was disappointed that Sockalexis didn't play. Buffalo beat the Indians 5–1.

Cy Young shocked Buffalo on Thursday, August 18, by shutting them out in front of their fans 3–0. It was the first shutout of the year for Buffalo. John Powell, Cleveland's rookie pitching sensation (15–10), was so inspired by Young that he went out and blanked Buffalo the next day 5–0 for their second shutout of the year. Cleveland started September in their favorite place, fifth, the record was 54 and 50.

Corbett and Cy

In the first week of September, the famous boxer and ex-heavyweight champion of the world, Jim Corbett, was in the northeast Ohio area. He appeared as a guest player for a number of teams. The amateur Cleveland Marquettes featured him in a game at Forest City Park against the team from Wheeling, West Virginia. Two thousand were on hand to see Corbett play first base and get two doubles in the Marquettes' 3–2 victory.

W. J. Connor, representing W. A. Brady, Corbett's manager, was in town the week prior to Corbett's appearance and got the boxer some free publicity. He said he was authorized to buy the Indians for Mr. Corbett, who would spare no amount of money in bringing a championship to Cleveland. President Robison, however, said of the $50,000 offer, thanks but no thanks.

The highpoint of 1887 — Saturday, September 18 at League Park:

A fair-sized crowd came out for a scheduled double header against Cincinnati. Cy Young faced Billy Rhines in the opening game at 1 o'clock.

Cleveland quickly got 2 runs in the first. Childs doubled and O'Connor singled him in. With two out, O'Connor, running on the fly off McKean's bat, scored when Burke dropped the ball in left. In the fourth, Belden singled, was moved over on a sacrifice by Zimmer, and was plated by a single off the bat of Burkett. In the seventh, Childs walked, O'Connor and Pickering got hits, and all three figured in the scoring.

Cincinnati for the day had put a man on via a walk, and three more reached on errors—two off of Wallace and one more charged to McKean. This was the extent of the visitors' offense up until the ninth inning. Pitcher Rhines was asked to take a seat, and Claude ("Little All Right") Ritchey came up as a pinch hitter. He hit it hard, right back to the mound, but Cy was calm, and he snagged it nicely and threw him out. "Bug" Holliday grounded one over to Wallace at third, and he was out number two. "Dummy" Hoy was next, and in his anxiety to get his team a hit, he struck out, and Cy Young went into the record books with Cleveland's second no-hitter.

The last no-hitter by a hometown pitcher was fourteen years earlier when "One Arm" Daily put the magic feat over on Philadelphia in 1883. Cy's, however, was sweeter, being done in front of the hometown crowd.

Young's no-hitter was the National League's nineteenth since its founding in 1876: "A record which has stood since Hawke [sic] was in his prime as a star pitcher for Baltimore was made by Cy Young in the first game yesterday afternoon — a record of shutting out a team without a base hit. [Bill Hawke had pitched the previous no-hitter in August of 1893.] That Cy's arm was in old form this result shows and nobody ever saw better ball pitched since ball pitching began. The nearest thing to a base hit was a sort of a scratch that Wallace would have taken had he not considered it too easy; as it was it got through him. Again Holiday hit a hard one at Wallace but he knocked it down. It fell at his feet and he had plenty of time to throw the runner out but his throw took O'Connor off the bag. Besides these cases there was not even a suspicion of a hit and besides this pitching record the game was featureless, at least all other features faded into insignificance. Rhines pitched a pretty fair sort of a game himself but it was not a day when pretty fair pitching cut any figure."[24]

Cleveland	Cincinnati
Burkett, lf	Holiday, rf
Childs, 2b	Hoy, cf
Wallace, 3b	McPhee, 2b
O'Connor, 1b	Beckley, 1b
McKean, ss	Corcoran, ss
Pickering, cf	Irwin, 3b
Belden, rf	Burke, lf
Zimmer, c	Schriver, c
Young, p	Rhines, p
	Ritchey, ph

Inning	1	2	3	4	5	6	7	8	9	Final
Cinicinnati	0	0	0	0	0	0	0	0	0	0
Cleveland	2	0	0	1	0	0	0	3	*	6

Final: Cleveland 6, Cincinnati 0. Time: One hour and thirty-five minutes (the fastest game at home on the year). Pitching: Young walked one and struck out three. Umpire: Kelley.

John Powell won the second game over Ted Breitenstein by a score of 4–3. He allowed six hits.

Umpire Kelley received notice from League headquarters following the double-header that he was fired. He was an apparent victim of the politicking of a number of East Coast magnates who did not care for his game-calling.

Amateurs and Exhibitions

Among the amateur teams of 1897, the Pragues, Bohemians, Grotzingers, Brachwitz, and others testified as to the ethnic nature of Cleveland's people in 1897. Also, the Keystones, Cleveland's best team of black ball players, won so many games this year against good white amateur teams across the Western Reserve that at the end of the season they crowned themselves colored champions of Ohio.

Ira Belden, a local ballplayer playing for the house team at the Euclid Beach Amusement Park, was doing so well that he was called — "The Peach of Euclid Beach." In September Pat Tebeau gave him a tryout with the Indians and he played eight games in the outfield that fall, including Cy Young's no-hitter. Ira was well liked by the players; when his father died at the end of September the club postponed an intra-squad game to attend the funeral as a group.

In addition to the regular games, Cleveland played exhibition games at home and on the road during the last weeks of the season and on into October. At League Park the games were split-squad affairs. In one game on the nineteenth of September the Indians, with Cy Young pitching, beat the Red Men, who pitched John Powell (10–5). A crowd of 1,500 came out in the cold to watch it.

On the twenty-fourth of September the Indians went to Mansfield and won a close one 7–6. The Cleveland home schedule was closed out on September 26, a Sunday — a nice day brought out a crowd of 3,000. Cleveland had its hitting shoes on that day as they defeated Louisville 8–4. McKean had two triples; Blake, Wallace, and Zimmer each had a double.

Cleveland pitched Powell and used its first string in a 10–4 exhibition win at Geneva on September 28. Irwin took the loss for the Genevas. It was a nice day and two thousand people went to the game. The official League season for Cleveland ended in a 7–4 loss in front of 2,000 of the Pittsburgh faithful.

The Cleveland record for the year was 69 wins and 62 losses, good for fifth place. One consolation on the season was that Boston edged out Baltimore for the pennant by 2 games. No postseason championship series was played this year.

Cleveland closed out its exhibition season with a game at Canton and two at Toledo. Cy Young pitched on Sunday, October 3, and defeated Reisling of Canton 9–4 in front of 3,000. On the fifth and sixth Cleveland was at Toledo. They lost game one 6–3, but Cy Young struck out eight to win the second contest 8–2. Pat Tebeau left the team on October 9 to go on tour with Al Spalding's All Americans and the season for the Indians' players was finally over.

1898

"Remember the Maine"

On February 15, the recently commissioned battleship *Maine*, the pride and joy of the U.S. Navy, was blown up in the harbor at Havana, Cuba. Two hundred fifty-six American sailors died. Though the cause was never proven, it served as a rallying call for intervention on the side of the Cuban patriots, now fighting in their fourth year for independence from Spain.

When the Cleveland Indians' train left for Hot Springs on March 6 the looming specter of war was on all the players' minds. George Cuppy may have been the most anxious of all. Previously he had fought with a volunteer unit for Cuban independence in the off-season of '96 and had gotten a bullet in his foot for the effort. Cuppy, though born in Indiana, was of Latin ancestry, his name at the time of birth being George Maceo Koppe.

Hot Water

Missing in action of another sort was Louis Sockalexis. He disappeared after dinner on Friday at the Hawley House. He was found at a "downtown resort" the next day, after having missed the team train.[1] He had to appeal to Secretary Muir for train fare, because all of his own money was gone. After a consultation by telegraph with President Robison, who had gone with the team, Sockalexis was given a ticket to Hot Springs and taken to the depot.

Hot Springs, because it is nestled in a valley below a mountain and surrounded by heavy forest and lakes, has a unique geography that gives it a year-round mild climate. In addition it has dozens of hot springs, making the place a popular resort destination for over a century.

H. O. Price, a native Clevelander, operated Whittington Park where the players trained. Mr. Price had staged a prizefight there, which was technically illegal. The sheriff came looking for him after the bout, but George Cuppy helped him escape by pulling him in the back window of his room. After a few days the sheriff lost interest in pursuing the matter.

The ball club was booked at the Avenue Hotel. A typical day had the men up by 7:30 for a half-hour breakfast — each player ordering what he wanted. Following breakfast, a fifteen-minute stroll was taken along the hotel's many wide verandas. Next, the players would quickly get into uniform and start a brisk two-mile walk up a gradual incline to the ballpark.

The ball field was on a plateau surrounded on one side by a mountain, on another side by an artificial lake (made by damming the flow of a number of springs); a third side was where the U. S. government was putting up a new park, and on the last side were a large number of vacation cottages.

A non-stop practice of batting and fielding would go on for two straight hours; the players would then put their jackets on and run back to the hotel for lunch. Some of the players would take a quick sponge bath, rub down, and short rest during the break. They then headed back to the park for the afternoon exhibition game, after which: "The game once out and the players walk to the hotel for there is now no need to run to 'keep up a sweat.' In a few moments the baths are full of ball players. They take a nine-minute dip in the pure hot spring water, a three-minute rub from an attendant, few breaths in the vapor cells and then lounge in the hot rooms until they have had enough."[2]

The evening hours belonged to the players. Many engaged in some form of physical activity or another. Cy Young and Jimmy McAleer usually headed into the mountains to hunt — Young had even brought his favorite hunting dog down to camp with him. One writer commented that even though the two men used up a lot of powder only one turkey ever made it to the ball club's dinner table.

Chief Zimmer brought a bicycle with him and went mountain biking, an activity, he thought more beneficial than running on the hard roads. Some rode horses and yet others would take but a simple stroll: "Some take a bottle of ale before retiring, and some drink it before meals, but that is all the drinking that is being done except a most liberal indulgence in the hot spring water and that the men regard as wonderful stuff. Nearly every player has his little folding pocket cup and as they walk along the streets they lineup and drink their fill ... for of course the water is as free as that of Lake Erie as far as cost is concerned, and a heap freer when it comes to a few things that trouble the health department."[3]

At the hotel card-playing, reading the paper, billiards, and bed by 10:30 closed out the typical day.

Some odds and ends concerning the players: Jimmy McAleer came out of his self-imposed retirement. Chief Sockalexis claimed his communing with nature in Maine during the off-season had cured his drinking problem. Chief Zimmer's cigar emporium at Euclid and Erie St. (E. 9th) was broken into while he was in camp. George Cuppy got word that a city surveyor had found the front of his hotel in Logansport, Indiana, to be two feet over the property line: "'A pretty hotel I would have with the front out of it' says Cuppy."[4]

The best game of the training schedule was the one at Hot Springs on March 25 against Pittsburgh. The game was tied in the ninth at 6 apiece. In the bottom of the tenth, Burkett hit a drive so far that it would have been an inside-the-park homer if George Kelb hadn't crossed the plate first with the wining run.

Score: Cleveland 7, Pittsburgh 6.

Cleveland broke camp in early April and headed north with some games in Indiana prior to opening on the road. Cleveland had a memorable road game at St. Louis on the twentieth of April, winning 10–5 and knocking out 4 home runs. Tebeau and O'Connor had a home run each, and the winning pitcher, Cy Young—he hit two home runs!

Leaving on Opening Day

The home opener against St. Louis on Friday the twenty-ninth just happened to coincide with the departure of Cleveland's Fifth Regiment—on their way to the Cuban front in the Spanish-American War.

The families of the soldiers were allowed to visit them at the Central and Grays armories in the early morning. The troops were then assembled, and with an escort of bands playing patriotic songs they headed down the flag-lined streets with people clapping and cheering from every window. At Erie and Superior the columns of four across swung onto Superior for the final march to Public Square for the official speeches and farewell. The soldiers then marched down to the waiting cars, in the Erie railway yards, across the river south of Superior.

At 10:45 A.M. the train, carrying Cleveland's finest, released a cloud of steam and started to move. Thousands watched as it slowly pulled away—headed toward war. It was not surprising therefore, considering the events of the morning, that the crowd at the afternoon opener was smaller and more somber than might have been the case in any other year.

The League put a policy of not kicking (arguing with the umpire) in place for 1898. Walter M. Robison, the sports editor at the *Cleveland Plain Dealer*, related some of the players' sillier thoughts on the subject:

Jack O'Connor has a little speech that he says will fix the umpires. 'Pardon the intrusion, my dear Mr. Umpire, but do you not agree with me that your decision is a slight injustice? I have no desire to question your ability or fairness, but merely suggest that under some misapprehension you have inadvertently wronged us in a slight degree.'

Sockalexis says he has the list of all other players under the new rule. 'I'll cuss the umpire in Penobscot,' says the Indian, 'and if they call me, I'll say I was telling them they are just right and that you fellows are dead wrong in kicking.'

Jesse Burkett is taking lessons from Socks in the latter's native tongue and can already say 'hickehowgo' (robber), 'kanylanyee' (green lobster) and several adjectives that fit in quite nicely.[5]

Cy Young took the mound for Cleveland and Kid Carsey for St. Louis. The day was very cold and the sky held dark clouds. Two thousand people came to the opening game. At 3:15 Umpire McDonald, with the help of assistant Umpire O'Day, called for the start of play.

St. Louis hit three ground-ball outs and the Indians came to bat. Burkett walked, moved up on a McKean out, went to third on a passed ball, and was plated by a Childs single over second.

St. Louis got a single from Sugden; and that was it in their second inning. Cleveland added a run in their turn, with a Tebeau hit, an O'Connor sacrifice, and a hit off the bat of pitcher Young.

St. Louis went out one, two, three, in the top of the third. Then Cleveland put on a hitting show in the lower third. A single and a walk, sandwiched between doubles by Wallace and O'Connor, netted 3 runs.

A single, errors by McKean and Childs, and a sacrifice fly gave St. Louis its first 2 runs in the fourth. Cleveland got one of those runs back in the bottom of the inning. McKean stroked a nice double into the heart of the open area in left center and singles by Childs and Wallace brought him around.

St. Louis failed to score in the fifth, and decided to bring in a change pitcher. They sent southpaw Pete Daniels to the mound. The lefty kept Cleveland off the board for three innings. Young, however, continued to pitch a masterpiece, giving up but one more hit in a scoreless last five innings, to notch the win by a 6–2 score. With a little more support in the field his three-hitter would have been a shutout.

Inning	1 2 3	4 5 6	7 8 9	Final
Cleveland	1 1 3	1 0 0	0 0 *	6
St. Louis	0 0 0	2 0 0	0 0 0	2

Hits: St. Louis 3, Cleveland 13. Time: 1:55. Umpire: McDonald.

Notes: • President Robison was peeved at the powers that be in the Little Consolidated — the new company containing his old cable car line. In revenge he closed the ballpark's access door to that route; thus many of the fans rode the rival Wade Park line home instead. • The *Cleveland Press* distributed free baseball schedules to all the ticket holders on the way into the game. They also had their paperboys out in force after the game to catch the downtown streetcar riders at the corner of Dodge St. (E. 12th) — where the boys were actively peddling the sports extra. • When President Robison was asked about the possibility of a game for the upcoming Sunday he said: "Sunday? What day is Sunday?"[6] • Cleveland had added some new seating to League Park in the off-season. The contractor had used non-union labor, a fact that President Robison claimed he had no control over. The Central Unions disagreed and threatened a boycott of games.

May Days

Cleveland played well in May and by the middle of the month their 16 and 6 record had them in second place. Attendance throughout the League was down this year. This was blamed on the war and on the magnates' greed and attitude of arrogance in general. Despite Clevelands ending the month in second place at 24 and 12, attendance figures were disappointing in management's view. Robison was confident that if he could stage Sunday games without problems from the law, he could turn the minimal profit he needed to go on.

At the beginning of his major league career, Bobby Wallace spent parts of five seasons with the Spiders, the first three primarily as a pitcher (Library of Congress).

He said that stories (which he claimed he was not connected to) about a possible franchise shift to another town would go away with the advent of Sunday ball in the Cleveland baseball market.

Robison was thus positioning himself to shift blame onto the politicians, other opposing forces, and the fans if his political leverage did not lead to his getting the money he wanted out of his baseball investment. Don't hold it against him, it was implied, if the unenlightened of Cleveland forced him to move the team, in search of greener pastures where an honest businessman could make an honest buck.

The idea of playing Sunday games at Euclid Beach Park in the village of Collinwood — starting in June — now took on the air of an item that could very well make or break National League baseball in Cleveland.

Beach Party

SUNDAY: THE PITTSBURGH AND CLEVELAND GAME

Collinwood, June 12, 1898:

To-day the Cleveland club will quietly put out its paw and feel of the Sunday base ball law. The law will be touched in a new place this time and it is expected by the club owners the result will not be disastrous, that the team will be permitted to play with it, and leave unharmed.[7]

Judge Dissette allowed a temporary lifting of his injunction against the Big Consolidated Streetcar Co. Streetcars would be allowed to run along Euclid Avenue and out to Euclid Beach Park for the Sunday game. The steamboat line out of Cleveland that ran boats to the park added a boat for Sunday. The Painesville electric streetcar company would run Sunday cars to the park along its lakefront route. Fans from Pittsburgh were also expected to come up by train.

Operatives of the Indians' management put up a ballpark in one week. It went up in the southwest corner of the park in a mud-hole recently occupied by the German Village attraction.

The park stands were still without roofs the day of the first Sunday game, but a clubhouse for the players had something resembling the early stages of a roof on it.

John Powell of Cleveland and Jim Gardner of Pittsburgh warmed up under a heavy rain-cloud sky. In the audience were Mr. Clarke of the YMCA and the Reverend Barry of the Congregational Church. They were the Collinwood village leaders of the anti–Sunday ball movement.

Clarke was alleged to have said that he did not intend to see "the discarded filth of Cleveland dumped upon the village," a quote he denied.[8] One of the "discarded" Clevelanders was said to have expressed a desire, upon seeing Mr. Clarke, for a strong club and a dark alley—this in spite of his being in the company of his wife and son.

It would remain to be seen if the opposition group could meet a new state law that required a two thousand dollar bond to be posted before any arrest for Sunday ball playing could be made.

Cleveland batted first and went down without a run. Pittsburgh followed their example. The rain came down in the second and never stopped after that. Tebeau and Robison wanted a five-inning official game no matter how much rain fell. At the start of the fourth a massive downpour sent everyone scuttling for any form of shelter.

Most of the crowd took advantage of their ticket, that gave admission to the entire park, and found the rest of their Sunday entertainment under some roofed activity or another.

When the teams returned, the wet ball slipped from the pitchers' hands, the wet bats slipped out of the batters' grip, and the fielders fell down if they moved with the least bit of urgency through the ankle-deep mud. The conditions gave Cleveland a run, but in the bottom of the inning Pittsburgh took advantage of the same elements and scored three. Both teams played out the fifth without a run; Umpire Snyder at once called the game official and over. He was last seen running away at full-slog looking for dry land.

Game end: Pittsburgh 3, Cleveland 1.

With short notice of added transportation, as well as looming bad weather conditions, the crowd of 6,000 that showed up was seen as a major victory for the proponents of Sunday baseball. The opponents' failure to make good on their threats to stop the game encouraged President Robison. That week he ran the first ads for Sunday ball.

On Thursday, June 16, Cleveland played exhibition ball at Ashtabula against the highly regarded local team —1,500 came out to watch.

Cleveland: Cowboy Jones and Chief Zimmer
Ashtabula: Wilhelm and Murphy

Inning	1	2	3	4	5	6	7	8	9	Final
Cleveland	0	3	2	0	0	0	1	0	*	6
Ashtabula	0	3	1	0	0	0	0	0	0	4

Hits: Cleveland 10, Ashtabula 9. Errors: Cleveland 1, Ashtabula 2.

Second Sunday

Cleveland vs. Pittsburg
At Beach Park,
JUNE 19th
Game called at 3:15 standard time.[9]

More than 3,000 were at Euclid Beach Park to watch Cleveland overcome a three to nothing deficit to win. Jim Gardner walked the bases full of Indians in the top of the eighth, and

Cleveland got the go-ahead run when a pitch hit Criger. In their turn Pittsburgh failed to score — and by "mutual agreement" the game was ended after eight innings ("mutual agreement" meant the police had moved in and arrested the players).[10]

Cleveland	AB	R	H	E	Pittsburgh	AB	R	H	E
Burkett, lf	4	0	1	0	Donovan, rf	4	0	3	0
O'Connor, 1b	3	0	1	0	O'Brien, cf	1	1	0	0
Wallace, 3b	3	0	0	0	Gray, 3b	3	1	0	1
McKean, ss	2	0	0	0	McCarthy, lf	4	1	2	0
Tebeau, 2b	1	1	0	0	Davis, 1b	4	0	1	1
Blake, rf	4	0	0	0	Padden, 2b	4	0	1	0
McAleer, cf	3	0	0	0	Bowerman, c	4	0	3	0
Criger, c	2	2	1	0	Ely, ss	4	0	1	0
Wilson, p	1	1	1	1	Gardner, p	3	0	0	0
Totals	23	4	4	1	Totals	31	3	11	2

Inning	1	2	3	4	5	6	7	8	Final
Cleveland	0	0	0	0	2	0	1	1	4
Pittsburgh	2	0	1	0	0	0	0	0	3

Collinwood, June 26, 1898:
The boats and cars took about 7,500 people out to Euclid Beach park, Sunday afternoon, to see the championship game scheduled to be played between the Cleveland and New York league clubs. No game was played, however, nor were the gates to the park thrown open.

Mayor Hall, of Collinwood, notified Vice President M. S. Robison as early as 2:15 p. m. that if a game was started all the players would be arrested immediately. As he spoke he pointed to 25 special officers who were on hand to enforce his orders. The game was at once called off, and the players did not don their uniforms.

The action of Justice of the Peace Elton, of Collinwood, Saturday, in fining the players taking part in the game Sunday before but $1 and costs each, was taken to mean that the authorities of the village were disposed to be lenient towards the ball club.

Mayor Hall's action was evidently a complete surprise to the Cleveland club officials, who had, at considerable expense, made complete arrangements for the game.[11]
—*Cleveland Press.*

Cleveland, June 27 — Editor "Sporting Life" — The old cry about the transfer of the Indians to some other city will no doubt be revived with great vigor now that the second attempt to bring off Sunday games in or near Cleveland has ended in failure. The action of the Collinwood authorities in threatening the Cleveland and New York players with arrest immediately if a game was begun was

A COMPLETE SURPRISE

to President Robison. He had been led to understand, so I am told to-day, that the officials of the township in which Euclid Beach Park is located were inclined to be lenient if not entirely friendly. They had been abused like so many pickpockets for their failure to ride rough-shod over the players two weeks ago, and were naturally indignant. When the case against the players was called at Collinwood Saturday the venerable Justice of the Peace had smilingly imposed

AN INSIGNIFICANT FINE

of $1 and cost in each case. This was taken to mean that the authorities did not believe that any fearful crime had been committed in playing an orderly game of base ball in a park remote from the thickly inhabited part of the township. In fact President Robison had the absolute assurance of those in a position to give it that the game yesterday could be played. During Saturday night and Sunday morning, however

AN ENORMOUS PRESSURE

was brought to bear upon the Mayor of the village. An indication of the "influence" is afforded to-day by the statement of a preacher named Berry, who saw in the playing of a League game in Collinwood the whole kingdom of Heaven tottering, although the amateur games, played on that day with barrels of beer as prizes, did not ruffle his feelings. Berry declares that had Mayor Hall refused to act he would probably have been

TARRED AND FEATHERED.

As between being treated to this Puritanical method of enforcing a foul law and stopping the game the Mayor decided on the latter. It was a bitter disappointment to a big crowd. There were 17 car loads of enthusiast here from towns in Indiana, and plans had been made to care for 10,000 people. What will be done next is an open question. It is safe to say, however, that Sunday games between League clubs cannot be played

IN OR NEAR CLEVELAND.

To even mention them is to drive the sensational preachers to the verge of distraction. Strange to say, however, these same ministers can see no harm to the cause they claim to espouse in the howling, hooting mobs that congregate on the back lots and vacant places about the city, often within a few yards of their churches, and

MAKE A MOCKERY

of the national game by putting up nine drunken men against nine other drunken men, and promising the victors more liquor. In opposing a League game, attended by orderly people and played by orderly players, however, in an enclosure where no liquor of any kind can be had for love or money there is a glorious opportunity for

ADVERTISING THEIR WARES

that must not be ruthlessly thrown away. It is the same old crowd of fanatics and nobodies that have been so successful in keeping Cleveland in the background for years. The highlight of their lives is to parade up and down the highways and byways after such a victory (?) as that of yesterday, as if to say: "See, how much better am I than thou."[12]

* * *

The latter part of the nineteenth century was called by some the age of the monopoly trust. The National League had once been humorously referred to collectively as the diamond trust. By 1898 there was nothing funny about the monopolistic practices of League ownership.

The magnates' arrogance was such that the teams might as well have been named after them rather than the cities they were supposed to represent. Transfers of home games to the visitors' city or a neutral site occurred whenever a change of venue promised more revenue. In addition to this, there were now interlocking directorates of ownership, to such an extent that players were moved from team to team on a whim, because the same owner or owners had large amounts of stock in a number of other franchises.

President Robison blamed the shut-down of Sunday ball and the boycott by the trade unions (for using non-union contractors at the ball park) for low attendance; he forgot to mention that there was also a war going on.

"The Transferring Business"

Robison, in July, started transferring Cleveland home games out of town. Cleveland played so many games in Philadelphia at one point the press called them the "New Phillies" versus the "Old Phillies."[13]

His friends down at the fire station on St. Clair and Phelps Street in Cleveland did not forget Ed Delahanty, one of the Old Phillies. Ed played sandlot ball as a little kid on the lot by the station and the firemen were proud of his success. Every time "Big" Ed got an extra-base hit during a Phillies game the news would be telegraphed to the station and the men would set off fireworks from the roof. In 1898 the neighborhood sky was lit up forty-nine times.

With almost all the Indians' games now being played on the road the team earned a number of new nicknames in the papers. In order of first appearance, they were variously called "vagrants,"[14] "outcast,"[15] "tramps,"[16] "wanderers,"[17] "pothunters,"[18] and "nomads."[19] With the addition of a number of rookies in the lineup, by October they became "Tebeau's wandering yanigans."[20]

On July 21, Pat Tebeau reverted to his character of years past when he threw a bat — that just missed — at a fan who was unmercifully hurling epithets in his direction from the stands at Baltimore. Tebeau had to go to the police station and put up collateral to guarantee a court appearance the next morning. But the aggrieved fan was too scared to show up and so charges were dropped.

Despite living on the road, Cleveland on August eighth was in second place with a record of 58 and 35. But this was going to be a very long year. In addition to several exhibition games around the country including Atlantic City, NJ, and Richmond, IN, this season would be the longest on record—a total of 154 games. This number would become the norm for the next sixty years.

To make matters more difficult for the players, additional travel was incurred when a number of regular season games were played at neutral sites. These included Cleveland and the Brooklyn Trolley Dodgers—at Rochester, NY, for three; a Cleveland and Washington game—at Philadelphia; as well as Cleveland playing Cincinnati—at St. Louis.

This last-named game, played in St. Louis at the close of September, drew a large crowd because it was rumored that Frank Robison had closed a deal to buy the St. Louis franchise. The local fans, therefore, wanted a look at the good players of Cleveland who might very well be transferred to their city to replace the aggregation of stiffs currently wearing St. Louis uniforms.

In October, at Chicago, a three-team doubleheader saw Cleveland lose the first game to St. Louis 4–3. That game was cut short after the seventh so Cleveland could catch its train for Cincinnati.

St. Louis stuck around for nine innings in the second contest only to lose to Chicago 4–3:

St. Louis, Oct. 2 — The National League has discussed and decided to apply a method to improve the baseball situation in St. Louis. This determination, it is stated, will result in the elimination of Chris Von der Ahe and all the interest allied with him in the present organization and will give the St. Louis franchise to Frank DeHaas Robison of Cleveland, who will transfer the Cleveland club to this city bodily next year.

The league holds that a franchise consist merely of the consent of the different clubs to play with one another, and if eleven of the clubs agree to withdraw this consent to play with one another, the twelfth club has no redress. Under this ruling a franchise is considered to be a thing of no tangible value, and each so-called franchise, or agreement to play games is the property of the whole league and not of any individual baseball club.

This description of a value of a franchise was advanced by John T. Brush during his visit to this city last week, during a discussion as to the fate of St. Louis. Mr. Brush said that the interest in the league demands a championship club and to bring this about they have determined to withdraw their consent to play with the present St. Louis club, and transfer it to Mr. Robison and his Cleveland team, when they are located in St. Louis.[21]

—*Cleveland Plain Dealer*

The reckless practices of baseball's magnates earned some pithy, tongue-in-cheek comments from one sports columnist writing in the pages of the *Plain Dealer*:

The transferring business if not prohibited, will cause the public to lose all faith in the purity of baseball. If schedules can be rearranged so as to give a certain club the best chance of winning simply because the most money can be made in that way, why not decide upon the club that should win the pennant and pass a rule providing that the games that club loses don't count? Then let the other clubs be picked for certain places and arrange games so as to let them finish there.

Then too, magnates might award the pennant and arrange the standing at the finish according to the financial showing of the clubs, and remove the element of sport altogether.[22]

Cleveland ended the year in Louisville with a doubleheader on the fourteenth and a solo game the fifteenth. They split the doubleheader, losing the early match 14–2 and bouncing back in the afternoon game to win 6–4.

In the last game Cleveland was down 5–0 when they mounted a come-back in the sixth and seventh with 2 runs in each inning. But that was the end of the run-making and shortly the end of the season.

Notes: • Final: Louisville 5, Cleveland 4. • Attendance: 900. • Umpires: Emslie and Warner.

The 1898 Cleveland Spiders included the likes of Cy Young, Bobby Wallace, Jesse Burkett and Patsy Tebeau, but the club could do no better than a fifth-place finish, ending the season 21 games behind the pennant-winning Boston Beaneaters.

Cleveland had five unknown players in the lineup for the last game of the year: Frank Bates pitched, Fred Frank played center, Jimmy Burke was at third, John Heidrick was in right and Ossee Schreckengost was the catcher. The only four familiar faces were Bobby Wallace, Jesse Burkett, Ed McKean and Jack O'Connor. Only Frank Bates and Ossee Schreckengost would ever wear a Cleveland uniform again.

On October 16 a benefit game for the Cleveland and Chicago players was held at Chicago. In a fast game of an hour and twelve minutes Chicago defeated Cleveland 4–0. Cleveland received one third of the $4,500 contributed by the six thousand Chicago fans.

With the exceptions of McKean, Zimmer and McAleer, all of the Cleveland regulars allowed themselves to be transferred to the hoped-for greener pastures of St. Louis in 1899. The team with Cleveland's name on it in 1899 would experience the biggest disaster of a season that any major league baseball team had ever had — or would ever have.

1899

Misfits

Cleveland's team in 1899 was a complete joke, even before the season started, and everyone who knew anything about the game of baseball knew it.

The National League's contracted agreement that bought out four and merged four American Association teams into the League in 1892 was up in 1901. Reduction of the unwieldy twelve-team National League to an eight-team outfit was just a matter of time. Louisville and Washington of the old Association were perennial tail-enders, and Baltimore, with its transfer of half its players to the Brooklyn team, was another original Association team now fallen from grace. These teams looked to be likely candidates for a not-too-distant chopping block. St. Louis, however, was the Association market the National League had always wanted. With the ouster of the eccentric Chris Von der Ahe from the team's ownership, and the installation of Frank De Haas Robison as the new owner, the League was confident of turning a healthy profit there.

Robison couldn't get rid of his Cleveland holdings on the terms he wanted, so, in a sense he beat the other owners to a reduction of the League circuit by turning his League team at Cleveland into a St. Louis farm team. St. Louis now had most of the Cleveland Indians of 1898. Cleveland's new roster was seven regular position players and a pitcher from last year's last-place (W.39—L.111) St. Louis team, as well as four marginal minor-league pitchers.

The *Cleveland Press* renamed the Indians the "Misfits"—an accurate, if not flattering, choice of nickname. The Cleveland Misfits, without the benefit of spring training, opened on the road at St. Louis and lost 10–1.

A week later they won their first game. In a doubleheader they squeaked out a 6–5 victory in game one against a poor Louisville team. Louisville, however, looked a lot better than the Misfits in the second game, winning 15–2.

While Cleveland was on the road, Harry Hamilton, the man who had replaced the veteran Tom Lawrence as groundskeeper, had the outfield fence at League Park painted a dark green. This was supposed to help the batters see the ball better. In the case of the Misfits, one might have wondered if that didn't mean help the visiting batters *see better.*

Bad weather on the first of May turned the Cleveland opener into a doubleheader on the second. When the game started there were a hundred people watching. As the day progressed and the weather warmed the number neared five hundred. Cleveland beat Louisville 5–4 and lost the second game 2–1.

As small as the opening day attendance was a few days later it was worse: "It was a very poor imitation of the national game that the 150 spectators—score-card, lemonade, and peanut boys counted—saw at League park, Friday. It was too cold for errorless playing, and when the people in the stands did any rooting they did it to keep warm. Carsey essayed to pitch for Cross's Raw Recruits, but had nothing up his sleeve wherewith to deceive Tom Burns' boisterous Orphans. Callahan on the contrary, after starting off poorly, steadied down and pitched a pretty fair game. The contest was featureless. The visitors from Chicago got 11 runs all told: the visitors from St. Louis [a disparaging reference to the Misfits] only, two."[1]

Cleveland continued to draw crowds counted in the hundreds.

Sad "Sox"

If Cleveland hadn't been so bad Louis Sockalexis would never have played this year; as it was, he appeared in only seven games. His work in the field left little doubt as to his right to be called a Misfit too: "Sox gave the scorers a little trouble several times as to whether his performance in the outfield should be scored as errors or the batters given hits. On two occasions Sox fell down when he had the ball in his hands. He made the plays look very hard, and there is no doubt but when he got to the ball each time it was a hit, but he was very slow. Once after he turned a complete somersault, going after a ball, which went for three bases, he was cheered by the grandstand when he came in. The Indian did not wait to ask whether it was sarcasm or not, but lifted his cap just the same."[2]

It was no real surprise then that, a few days after this performance on May 13, Sox was once again bailed out of jail at the Central Police station for drunkenness. This time the chore of springing him fell to player-manager Lave Cross.

The cops of Cleveland had now seen the last of Louis Sockalexis. After the middle of May the Misfits' games for the remainder of the 154-game schedule were all transferred out of town.

The National League franchise that came to Cleveland in 1889 had now played its last home game in Cleveland—forever.

Town Ball

With the Misfits being a Cleveland team in name only, local fan attention now turned more to the amateur game. In Cleveland the best two clubs may well have been the Cleveland Athletic Club (C.A.C.) and the team from the bicycle club, the Cleveland Wheel Club (C.W.C.). The Standards and the Baehrs were also popular with the fans. One amateur game of interest was the city championship between University and Central high schools, held at League Park at the end of May. Central won the game 8–5. And two additional Cleveland teams of note had there own special followings: the black team the Keystones and the Y.M.J.A. (the Young Men's Jewish Association).

One particular barnstorming ball club, known throughout the Midwest, played a good portion of its schedule for 1899 in Ohio. They were the Nebraska Indians (a team of Native Americans from the state of Nebraska). They won 26 games in Ohio this year while losing only 6. Appearances included games at Akron, Ashtabula, Canton, Elyria, Findlay, Lisbon, Medina, Painesville, Salem, Urbana, Wadsworth, and Warren.

On the Western Reserve the Oberlin and Painesville clubs received a lot of coverage. However, the premier club, the one everyone who had any sense picked as best in Ohio this year, was the incredibly talented club of Ashtabula.

Three good barnstorming base ball clubs—the national colored champion Cuban Giants; the American Indian team from Cattaraugus, NY; and the previously mentioned Nebraska Indians—played and lost games to the Ashtabulas in 1899.

At the end of the year the record of Ashtabula was 44 and 6—a winning percentage of .880—and this after playing the best teams of northeast Ohio, western Pennsylvania and western New York, while refusing none.

Home on the Road

The Misfits continued to lose throughout the summer. They lost games in which they had big leads and little leads, and games they had come back from behind in—only to lose in late innings.

The players at one point in September hadn't been paid in two weeks and they threatened to strike. When President Robison promised to schedule a Sunday game in the upcoming series with St. Louis—and give them the receipts—the strike talk ended.

Most of the characters making up the Misfits were on the St. Louis team that in 1898 won only 39 games. This team would not even come close to that winning number. To their credit the Misfits played all of the 154-game schedule. Their record of 20 wins and 134 losses still stands as the worst record in major league baseball history. They were 84 games behind pennant-winning Brooklyn.

The Western League had roots going back to the minor league circuit that had a franchise in Cleveland in 1885. A former Cincinnati sportswriter, Ban Johnson, was its president; under his leadership it had become the strongest minor league in the country. In 1900 Johnson planned to transfer many of his franchises into the large city markets that the League was not in. With the four-team reduction the National League would orchestrate over the winter of 1899, one of those cities would be Cleveland.

1900

The Western Goes American

His Honor Mayor John H. Farley walked down the grandstand steps carrying a brand new baseball in his hands. He then entered one of the private boxes near the field. Without fanfare, or even a speech, he simply hesitated a moment, "Then he pressed the ball to his lips, said 'Good luck.' And threw it to the umpire."[1]

Umpire Cantillion then handed it to the Cleveland catcher Harry Spies, who fired it to pitcher Zeke Wilson, and a cheer went up. George Hogriever then stepped into the batter's box for Indianapolis, and Zeke went into his windup and let loose. "'One strike' called the umpire, another cheer went up and the season of nineteen hundred was opened."[2]

One hundred and some years ago, in 1900, Cleveland joined baseball's American League. The American League was the renamed Western League, the latter name having been dropped the previous November, and the less regional sounding American League adopted in its place.

Cincinnati sportswriter Byron "Ban" Johnson had become the league's president in 1892. Eight years of moving franchises, under the direction of "Ban," from small cities to ever-larger market cities accomplished two important things for the Western League. First, the strongest minor league of the nineteenth century was established, and second, the league's management gained a great deal of baseball business expertise.

Experience would be indispensable to the league's officials, as Ban and the boys prepared to make a serious run in 1900 at the National League's monopoly on major league baseball. American League cities franchised for the year 1900 were Buffalo, Chicago, Cleveland, Detroit, Indianapolis, Milwaukee, and Minneapolis. At the beginning of the twenty-first century only Chicago, Cleveland and Detroit remained as continuous members of the original 1900 circuit.

In 1900 the American League called itself a major league. Most baseball historians, as well as Major League Baseball itself, for at least the last fifty years have both claimed that that status occurred in 1901—the first year of the twentieth century. A review of the caliber of players on the rosters of the 1900 versus the 1901 American League teams gives the latter date more credibility.

The Cleveland Americans

Grand Rapids, Michigan, was a team in the Western League of 1899. Tom Loftus owned it and George "White Wings" Tebeau managed it. Tom, a former major league manager, including Cleveland (1888 A.A. and 1889 N.L.), and George, a one-time player with the old Cleveland Spiders, were given an assignment by Mr. Johnson. They were to take the Michigan franchise a step higher by moving it into Cleveland for 1900.

At the last minute control of the ball club was turned over to Clevelanders with far greater resources. Charlie Sommers and John Kilfoyl—both well-heeled and well connected to Cleveland's upper class—became the owners of the American League franchise in Cleveland. Mr. Kilfoyl owned a clothing store downtown near Cleveland's Public Square. He had also been the business agent and manager for the Cleveland Athletic Club's great baseball teams of the 1890's. Mr. Sommers was the heir to a coal fortune. His millions bankrolled baseball in Cleveland, and his money eventually kept the entire American League solvent in its early years.

Ban Johnson was acutely aware of Mr. Sommers' financial resources and his fanatical passion for the game of baseball. In March he came to Cleveland. His mission was to woo Charlie for his wealth and personally negotiate with Frank Robison for the use of the old Cleveland Spiders' National League field—League Park. He succeeded.

The owners of the Cleveland baseball company now had a field. Next on their agenda was finding a manager and some players to put on that field, as well as develop an overall operating policy. Jimmy McAleer was for many years a fan favorite with the old Spiders' team. Signing the Youngstown native to the job of player/manager was a good public relations move.

Jimmy's fame came not from a bat — he was an average hitter — but from his glove. In center field he had no peer. Jim's sure route to a ball, as he ran after it, caught it, and in the same fluid motion delivered the ball quickly and accurately to the right place, was legendary. Manager McAleer set up shop in Room 535 of the Cuyahoga Building on Public Square (imploded for the B. P. Tower site in 1981).

Fourteen players made the original squad — most were over thirty. Some had once been stars but most were veteran journeyman of the major league or minor leagues. The roster would add and subtract about a dozen players over the course of the season. That elusive "diamond in the rough," around which a franchise could be built, was not to be found in season 1900.

Two veterans of the National League, Ollie Pickering and Candy LaChance, would contribute most to Cleveland's new team. They as well as a few of the roll players would see action in 1901. The rest would be gone and forgotten.

Eventually the starting field positions solidified around the usual batting order of center fielder Ollie Pickering; right fielder Charlie Frisbee; left fielder Frank Genins; shortstop Charley Buelow; first baseman Candy LaChance; second baseman Tim Flood; third baseman Suter Sullivan (a Cleveland player in 1899); and catcher Harry Spies. Players named "Buck" Weaver and Lou Bierbauer, and others surnamed Chrisham, Cross, Diggins, Shay, Tansett, and White, made appearances in the box scores fairly often at different points in the year.

The most notable of the pitching staff were big league veterans Bill "Wizard" Hoffer and the Alabama native and former Cleveland Spider, Zeke Wilson. They were assisted by the very-forgettable Baker, Braggin, Chech, "Rip" Egan, Fauver, Bumpus Jones, McKenna, and Reust.

The "Lakeshores" Open

Nicknames for baseball teams in this era, as was mentioned earlier in this book, were, with or without the encouragement of management, most often the creation of sportswriters. When a particular name caught the public's fancy it stayed; if not, it went. The nickname most heavily promoted for the team was the "Lakeshores." It was created by the *Cleveland Press*, which used it frequently in illustrations and in bold-face headlines throughout the year.

Another popular pet name used this year was "babes"— usually in small letters. Once again as stated earlier, this nickname was an often-used generic term to denote that the team in question was either new to the league or had a roster full of rookies.

Fans came out in the cold weather to watch the Lakeshores warm up at League Park before the start of the season. New American League management — in a departure from the old National League Spiders' owner — treated its patronage well.

During workouts and for practice games there was no admission charge, and during these sessions the fans were allowed to sit in the good seats— the ones in the grandstand.

Some National League owners, commenting to the national press, called Cleveland a dead town for baseball. In answer to this charge —following a huge turnout at a pre-season game — a *Plain Dealer* writer wrote: "Cleveland showed yesterday that it is about the liveliest corpse that has ever been found in history."[3]

ROAD OPENER

Cleveland's first American League game was played on the road against Indianapolis, Indiana. This Indianapolis team had won the Western League championship in 1899.

It had rained for quite awhile before the game, and the field was quite soggy. By start of game, the rain had stopped, but for the entire nine innings the sky stayed a dark gray. Win Kellum was the Indy pitcher and Bumpus Jones the Cleveland ball-tosser.

Cleveland took to the bat first. Ollie Pickering, the center fielder, stepped into the batter's box, but he soon bounced a weak one — out, pitcher to first. The next man up, right fielder White,

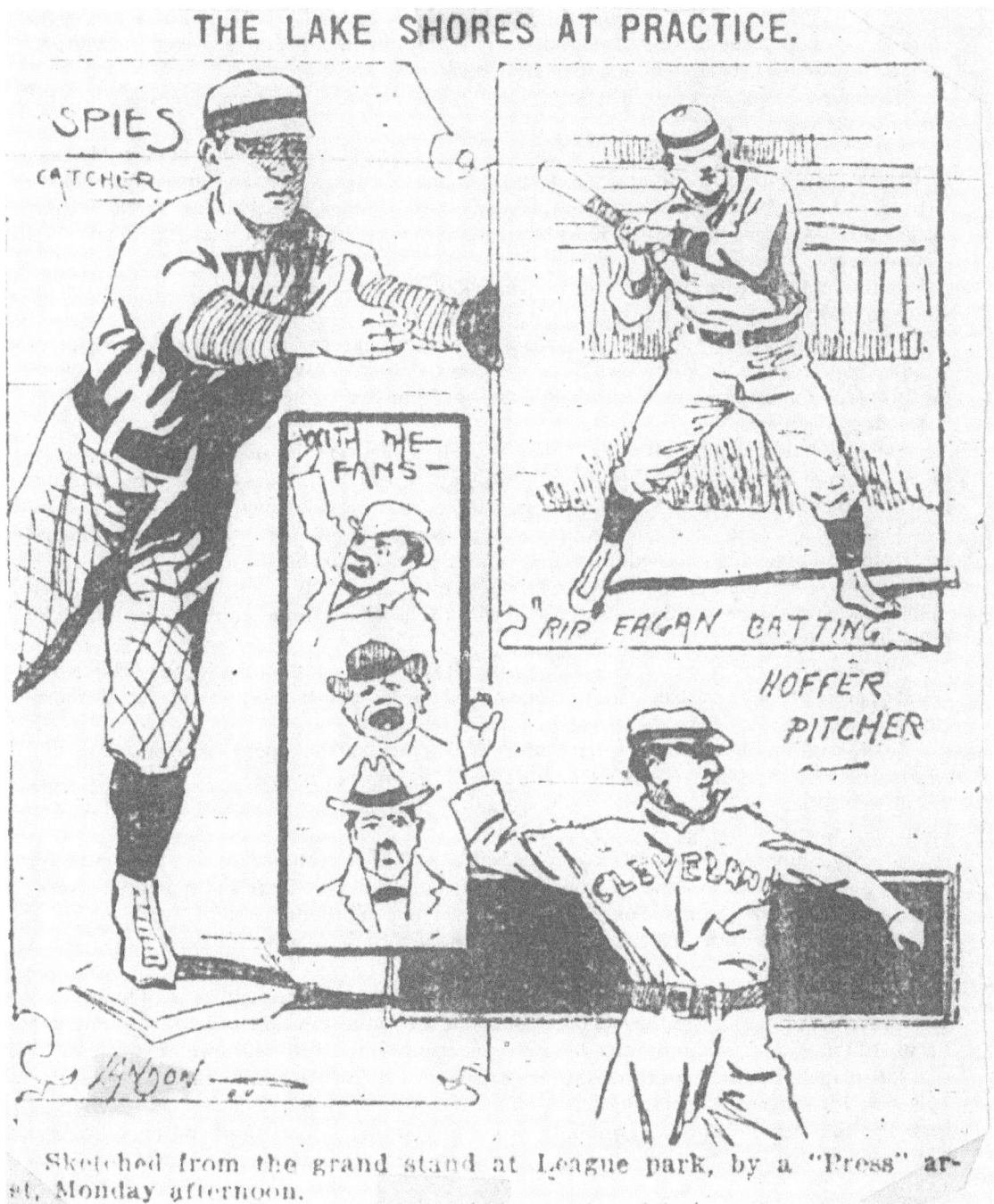

A *Cleveland Press* action drawing of the 1900 Cleveland Lakeshores practicing at League Park.

did exactly the same thing — out, pitcher to first. Now Charley Buelow, the third baseman, got his chance.

He let a few of Win's offerings go by before he found one to his liking. He lined it to left past Hartzell in the outfield. The ball bounded to the fence, where it stuck itself in the mud. Hartzell ran after it, dug it out of the wet ground, and fired it to shortstop Madison for the relay home.

Buelow was puffing hard as he rounded third. Just as he sighted his goal — an inside-the-park home run — he hit a slick spot and went down in a heap. By the time he recovered his wits and his feet, he was one very muddy, and very dead, duck — out at the plate!

Therefore, Cleveland's first hit as American Leaguers, instead of a home run, went into the record books as a triple.

For Indianapolis, Hogriever led off and went out; Hartzell, up next, hit a double; Madison then made the second out, and now the clean-up batter was due. Up to the plate stepped heavy-hitting "Socks" Seybold, the darling of the partisan crowd. Unlike Charley Buelow, he didn't come up short. It didn't take long before Socks blasted a Bumpus pitch far over the left field fence — a 2-run homer.

Indianapolis added a third run, then pitchers Kellum and Jones earned their pay, both teams failing to tally in the second, third, and fourth innings.

Cleveland's first big inning would be the fifth inning. Lou Bierbauer led off with a single and Diggins followed with one of his own. Viox made an out and the number nine batter was scheduled. It was Bumpus Jones, the Cleveland pitcher — and he had a determined look on his face as he strode to the plate.

Stepping into the batter's box, he waited for Kellum's delivery; he didn't offer at the first few pitches. Kellum again went into his windup, and Jones just knew this was the one — he banged it hard and straight into left center. It was a two-bagger — scoring Bierbauer.

This was Cleveland's first run as American Leaguers. It also gave Mr. Bumpus Jones, a pitcher, the distinction of having knocked in the first run for the new franchise.

Diggins scored the second run, when Pickering hit a sacrifice fly to left. White then doubled in Jones, tying the score at 3. White was plated with the go-ahead run when Hartzell muffed a fly off the bat of Buelow.

In the bottom of the frame, Pickering proved it was not a good inning for left fielders. His counterpart Hartzell hit the ball at him, and he played it into a two-base error. Indianapolis shortstop Madison then singled in the tying run.

In the seventh, Cleveland was given 3 gift runs. They were at the expense of pitcher Damman, who had come in to relieve Kellum in the sixth. A walk, a couple of booted bunts, and Viox scored. A walk to Pickering was followed by two outs. Frank Genins then drove a vicious liner past third — scoring Jones and Pickering. Cleveland now led 7–4.

Charley Sommers and John Kilfoyl could not be with their team for the first game. Charley was out of town on business and John had stayed in Cleveland. One Cleveland sportswriter speculated on boss Kilfoyl's thoughts on game day: "He sat long in his office yesterday and wondered. 'I don't dare go look at the scoreboard,' he said, 'I hope they don't make monkeys of us right at the jump.'"[4]

It was said that eventually he could contain his curiosity no longer, and he went to a nearby scoreboard/ticker to discover the fate of his boys. He arrived just in time to get the results from the top of the seventh, and was quite pleased to see that his team had rallied to take the lead.

Indianapolis bounced back with 2 runs in their turn at bat. Pitcher Damman led off with a strikeout. The proverbial wheels then came off the cart. Hartzell was walked, Madison then lifted a lazy fly ball to center that Genins promptly dropped — putting runners on second and third. Seybold then put a ball right into the hands of Pickering. It was too easy, so he dropped it — 2 runs scoring.

The Hoosier State boys had now pulled within a run of the Buckeye State boys.

Mr. Jones buckled down to the task ahead of him, and in the eighth and then in the ninth he kept the champions off the plate. The Cleveland players were absolutely jubilant as they celebrated their unexpected 7–6 victory.

Game: One hour and fifty minutes.

Umpire: Cantillion.

Sports note: • Following the opener Cleveland penned "Buck" Weaver and "Candy" LaChance to contracts. LaChance would become one of the team's best.

Home Opener

The *Plain Dealer* reminded its readers that for the home opener, as well as during the regular season, tickets for "Private boxes and reserved seats are on sale at the American House; Collister & Sayles and P. J. Pushaws. They can also be secured by telephoning Main 149."[5]

Crowds descended upon League Park early April 26, a Thursday, for the afternoon season opener. Some came on foot while others rode their bicycles — checking them at the park for a nickel. The majority, however, arrived by electric streetcar — that was something new.

In the past, most patrons rode the San Francisco–style cable cars; Frank DeHaas Robison, whose Spiders were the previous occupant of League Park, had owned the cable line. In January of 1900, after a run of but ten years, the very-expensive-to-build cable car system had its final run — a victim of the much more efficient electrical lines.

The fans filed into the park through the gates behind the grandstand, near the northeast corner of the lot. They then entered one of the three attached wooden stands.

Shortly before three o'clock, the attention of the crowd was drawn toward the southern fence where the gate had just opened.

It hit the ears and then the eyes: It was the Great Western Band, leading the march of freshly uniformed and waving ball players from both teams. The aggregation crossed the field and took up positions in front of the grandstand. The crowd continued to cheer as the band played on.

Prior to their grand entry at the ballpark, the band and the players had ridden through the principal streets in a parade to promote the opening game. They had started out at the Stillman House.

No sooner had the Great Western Band stopped playing, than the sounds of a second band could be heard in the not-too-far distance. Suddenly, in through the outfield fence marched the Cleveland Outing Club — with Mayor Farley and the group's leader President J. J. Buckley in the lead of the sixty-strong membership and band. They had marched all the way from downtown. Amidst a continuous cacophony of cheers, they continued across the field, stopping in front of the grandstand. The Cleveland Outing Club would serve as the Lakeshores' unofficial booster club in 1900.

Following a short musical interlude by the club band, attention was directed to a familiar figure in the grandstand. It was George Howe — a beloved fixture in Cleveland baseball management and ownership for decades. George had been given the honor of sounding the bell. This bell signaled the start of warm-up practice.

The visitors took the field first. Cleveland followed, and for fifteen minutes there was continuous applause and shouts of encouragement for the new players. The Lakeshores then sprinted off the field to await the official ceremony.

A caricature of fans at the 1900 Cleveland Lakeshores (A.L.) home opener at League Park.

Zeke Wilson was the Cleveland pitcher and Harry Spies his catcher. Indianapolis countered with pitcher Dale Gear assisted by catcher Hayden.

The Cleveland Lakeshores was about to host a team that — in what would become a twist of irony — was called the "Indians." From 1915 on, the Cleveland American League franchise would itself be nicknamed "Indians."

The Indians of Indianapolis went down quickly in the first inning. Cleveland now came to bat. Ollie Pickering stepped to the plate. He found a pitch that met his need and bunted it down the third base line. Hickey, at third, charged it, grabbed it, and fired to Kelly at first. Not in time! Ollie now laid claim to the Lakeshores' first hit at League Park.

Next man up, Buck Weaver, made a nice bunt of his own — sacrificing Pickering over to second. Now it was Charlie Buelow at the bat. He smoked one past the shortstop, driving in a run and earning the first run batted in for Cleveland, and giving Ollie Pickering the honor of scoring the first run at the home park.

Indianapolis was blanked in the second but Cleveland was not. Bierbauer led off with an easy fly-out. Then a bit of luck — Spies should have fouled out to the catcher, but when the backstop backed up, he tripped over the home plate broom. With a second life, Spies lined a single to right. Viox was out number two on a fly to center. Wilson came up, and the pitcher took matters into his own hands; he smacked a double into right field, scoring Spies. Pickering earned first on a Madison error, Wilson going to third. Gear then balked Zeke home. Score after two: Home 3, visitors 0.

The visitors tallied a run in the third. A walk to Magoon followed by a Hogriever triple did the damage. This ended the scoring until the Cleveland fifth.

Buck Weaver, with two outs, hit a double. Buelow then hit an anemic infield fly that looked like an inning-ender. Hayden the catcher, and Kelly the first baseman, both drew a bead on it, but they never got their signals straight — they collided and the ball fell safe. Weaver in the confusion scored all the way from second. Score after five: Cleveland 4, Indianapolis 1.

In the sixth inning, Indianapolis earned a run: Socks Seybold doubled and Magoon singled him in. Cleveland responded in their half of the sixth with a run. A "sun hit" single by LaChance started the inning.[6] Bierbauer's bunt was overrun by third baseman Hickey, allowing him to gain first and LaChance to advance to third, and Spies' sacrifice scored LaChance with the fifth run.

In the seventh, the visitors had a double off the bat of Hogriever, followed by a Hartzell single. Madison's fly ball plated Hogriever. The score at the close of the inning stood 5–3 in favor of the home team.

Cleveland came up empty in the run department in the seventh and the eighth. Indianapolis failed to score in the eighth, but they would not go quietly in the ninth.

The inning started out well enough for Cleveland. Gear, the number nine man, went out, and lead-off man Hogriever was also soon retired. Next it looked like a simple single to center by Hartzell, but it quickly escalated into something more.

In the words of a writer on the scene: "Genins ran in on it, the ball struck something, probably the remains of a hole dug in some fierce football scrimmage last fall, and bounded merrily away. By the time it had been recovered and fielded in Hartzell had made the circuit of the bases."[7] The potential tying run, in the person of Madison, now came to bat.

Zeke Wilson decided there would be no more merrily bounding balls in this game. He quickly fired three strikes. Game over!

The crowd cheered! And cheered some more! The upstart Cleveland Lakeshores had now beaten the champion Indianapolis Indians in two openers.

* * *

On May 1, Cleveland was in first place with a 6 and 3 record. In mid–May some cuts to shave payroll were made. Infielder Buck Weaver went to Syracuse and pitcher Rip Egan went without a job.

The American League standings on June 1 showed Cleveland to be in third place, trailing Indianapolis and Milwaukee. The Lakeshores were two games over the .500 mark at 17 and 15.

The prognosticators of baseball events, in 1900, had early declared that the cream of the crop in the American League resided in Chicago. By July 1, the cream had finally risen to the top. Charley Comiskey's White Stockings, with a record of 37 and 24, now held the top spot. Cleveland, with a record of 30 and 29, was in fourth place — seven back. However, they were only five behind in the all-important loss column.

Indians and Independence

The series of games wrapped around the Fourth of July were, as was generally true, the most important of the year in terms of box office potential.

It was hoped a good showing in this series would fill the team's coffers and turn some of the holiday visitors into regular customers. All that was needed was for the weather to cooperate and the fans to show up.

The opponent for the holiday series was the Indianapolis Indians. On July 3, Cleveland pitcher Bill Hart put the team in a holiday mood. He beat the Hoosier team 5–2. Mr. Bares was the losing pitcher for the visiting Indians.

The Fourth of July, a Wednesday, was scheduled as a doubleheader. The games, however, would be separate-entry affairs. In its lead-in, recapping the day's games, the *Plain Dealer* said: "The morning game was the better base ball but the afternoon game was a whole lot more fun."[8]

Morning game

Six thousand two hundred and ninety-one people rotated the numbers in the turnstiles for the early game. One of them had left Chicago early. It was still dark when Ban Johnson, the American League president, caught the train for Cleveland. He took in both games. His very presence, on this Independence Day, illustrated just how important Cleveland was in the league's plans.

It was written that at least two thousand, or one-third of the crowd, came with noisemakers. As in previous years, that meant revolvers and pockets full of supposedly blank ammo. The rest of the crowd each brought a pair of strong lungs.

Win Kellum was the pitcher for Indianapolis and Bill "Wizard" Hoffer for Cleveland. The visitors led off but did not score. Ollie Pickering led off for Cleveland and singled to left, Frisbee sacrificed him over to second, and then Genins drove him home with a hit to left. A deafening volley of shots and loud shouts greeted Ollie as he crossed the plate.

Buelow made a hard-hit out to Flynn in right. Candy LaChance followed with a feeble bouncer back to the pitcher. In his attempt to run it out, LaChance tripped and fell down hard on his shoulder. He was so hurt that he remained on the ground, grimacing in pain, for ten minutes, while a doctor and the players ministered to him. He was removed to the dressing room and Crisham took his place in the field. Miraculously, he was back in the lineup about a week later.

Both teams scored a run in the second. Cleveland made 2 runs in the fourth and eighth frames, and took what looked like a safe 5–1 lead into the ninth.

Hoffer had pitched a masterful game for Cleveland through eight. In the ninth, "poor or rather dumb playing allowed the visitors to fill the bases without a man out. An infield error, a walk and a double play attempt that caught no one, accounting for the dumb playing."[9]

The pitcher Kellum was due up, representing the tying run. Socks Seybold, the Indians' heavy hitter, had been sitting out the morning game, but now he came off the bench to pinch hit — but soon the mighty Socks had struck out! George Hogriever then hit a powerful drive to left that Genins made a terrific play on, but it went as a sacrifice, plating Gray. With two on and two out it was Hartzell's turn. The "Wizard" got him to hit it on the ground toward third; Suter Sullivan scooped it up, stepped on third for the force on Flynn — and the Lakeshores had a 5–2 victory.

Then things got very noisy!

Afternoon game

Seven thousand fans bought tickets for the second game. With McKenna pitching for Cleveland and Damman for Indianapolis, a high-scoring game was not unexpected. At 3:15 P.M.,

Indianapolis went to bat but did not score. Cleveland wasted no time; in their first try, they exploded for 7 runs.

Pickering led off with a single, Frisbee followed with one of his own, and Genins reached on an error to load the bases. A missed force-out on a Buelow grounder scored Pickering, and kept the bases filled. Shortstop Madison, arguing the call concerning his botched force-out, got himself thrown out of the game. Flynn came in from right to play shortstop and Seybold went into the game in right.

The *Cleveland Leader*: "With the bases full Crisham sent one to deep center for the first home run made by a Cleveland player at League Park this season."[10] The grand slam earned Crisham a box of fifty cigars. They had been offered by a local merchant as a prize for the Lakeshores' first round-tripper at home.

No scoring occurred in the second, third, or top of the fourth, but in the bottom of the fourth Cleveland had another offensive outburst. Pickering singled, and Frisbee promptly hit the second homer of the day, to deep center. Genins singled to left, and Buelow doubled him home. Crisham took first on an error, but was forced out by Flood, Buelow scoring in the process. Flood stole second, but the throw to get him was so wild, he came all the way around to score the fifth and final run of the fourth.

In the fifth, Buelow hit a double and was driven in by a Crisham single — his fifth run batted in on the day, and Cleveland's thirteenth unanswered run.

In the sixth, McKenna decided to take it a wee bit easy on his pitching arm. Two singles, a double, and a triple later his shutout was gone, Gray, Hickey, Seybold, and Flynn, in order, doing the damage. The Indians now had 3 runs. Cleveland did not score in the bottom of the inning.

In the seventh, McKenna relaxed so much he allowed Indianapolis to get back in the game. Hartzell walked, Geier singled and Power was hit by a pitch to load the sacks. Seybold, Gray, and Flynn hit singles, and 3 runs were in, and the bags were still juiced. McKenna then hit Hickey to force in a run. The pitcher Dammann helped his desperate cause with a single, good for a run. Buelow booted a Hartzell grounder and Flynn scored. Exit McKenna and enter Chech in relief. A Geier single and a messed-up double play allowed Dammann and Geier to score runs 7 and 8 of the inning. The laugher was no longer a laugher. The Lakeshores, to their credit, buckled down to work in the bottom of the frame. Genins led off with a single, Crisham, Flood, and Sullivan followed with singles of their own, and Cleveland had 2 more runs.

Neither team managed a run in the eighth. Indianapolis came to bat in the ninth with the score standing at 15–11 for the good guys. The bad guys refused to go easily.

Hartzell earned a walk to start the Indians' half of the ninth. Geier then forced him at second for the first out. Powers was not as cooperative in his turn at bat; he doubled in Geir for the visitors' twelfth run. Seybold was patient and earned a walk. Gray, the sixth batter of the inning, grounded out easily, pitcher to first, for the second out. Shortstop Flynn refused to end it, as he singled in Powers with run 13, bringing Hickey to the plate with the potential go-ahead run. Hickey put the ball in play and Flynn headed for second at full speed, but he wasn't quite quick enough. He was forced out and the game was over.

Score: Cleveland 15, Indianapolis 13. Flynn now held the dubious distinction of having been forced out to end both games of the doubleheader.

The fans fired their noisemakers and shouted themselves hoarse as they joyfully filed out of the ballpark. In two openers, and for the biggest crowd of the year on the Fourth of July, they had beaten the champions of Indianapolis every time.

July and August

Following the holiday series of ballgames, Cleveland was within 3 games of first place. Unfortunately for the Lakeshores, from this high point in the season, they now headed in a decidedly southern direction as far as the standings were concerned. On August 1, they had slipped a notch into fifth place, with a record of 2 games under .500 at 41 and 43. Chicago was flying high in first with a 51 and 33 record.

In the first week of August, Cleveland lost its manager. He was also flying high, in Chicago, if his comments on his return were meant to be anything but humorous. He had gone to Chicago for a medical operation: "'The operation did not amount to much,' said McAleer. 'I have known for some time that the doctors would have a slash at me but it was nothing serious. I only wanted to get to the town in which I have a friend who handles the knife pretty well, then I told them to cut me open and carve out as much as I do not need. They did it quite well and I am all right again.... I am in good shape now and will join the team at once.'"[11]

In mid-August, Cleveland lost the services of Sutter Sullivan when they released him to Buffalo. What they had also lost by September 1 was another notch in the standings. With a 56 and 61 record they had moved into sixth, the place they would close out their year in.

Closing Contest

The *Cleveland Plain Dealer*: "The final curtain was rung down on the first act of the American League play in Cleveland yesterday...."[12]

Cleveland, due to the American League schedule, closed its home season early on Thursday, September 6, versus the "Millers" of Minneapolis.

Minneapolis decided — as was their right — to play a single game rather than make up an earlier postponed game as part of a doubleheader.

The cold weather and prospects of a small share of the gate receipts may have had more to do with that decision than did their claim to be shorthanded in the pitching department.

The old veteran Red Ehret pitched for the Millers, and someone named Baker for Cleveland.

Minneapolis broke the ice in the home finale with a run in the third. Mr. Lally, on board via a force-out, scored with the help of a single, an error, and a sacrifice fly.

Cleveland was held at bay until the fifth. Second baseman Tim Flood earned a walk, advanced on a passed ball, and scored on a single by Baker to knot the score at a run each.

Cleveland forged ahead in the sixth. LaChance bunted for a hit, and a wild throw by Ehret, after Cleveland's third baseman Tansett had placed a sacrifice bunt, put Candy at third and Tansett at first. Tim Flood then delivered a double, scoring both runners. The Lakeshores now had a 3–1 lead.

The Millers closed the run gap in the seventh. Singles by Fisher, Bandelin, and Lally netted the visitors a run.

In the eighth, Cleveland earned a solo run, when Shay, with two men down, doubled home Tansett. This gave Baker a 2-run cushion going into the ninth.

Minneapolis gave up the ghost in the ninth. Cleveland's frozen fans had a warm feeling this final day, as they bid a fine farewell to season one of the American League in Cleveland.

Notes: • Score: Cleveland 4, Minneapolis 2. • Ehret, the loser, allowed 10 hits, walked 4, and struck out 2. • Baker, the winner, allowed 7 hits, walked 0, and struck out 0. • Attendance: 1,200. • Time: 1 hour and 30 minutes. • Umpire: Cantillion.

A review of the team's finances, on this the final home date, was not a rosy one. Cleveland, however, did prove one thing — it was not as dead a ball town as some had claimed. The owners believed a longer home schedule in September, and a strengthening of the product on the field, would help the bottom line in 1901. They had deep pockets that they were willing to reach into — and the patience to wait for success.

The final series of ball games for Cleveland in 1900 was in Milwaukee. The series started on Sunday, September 16 — a doubleheader was on tap against the "Brewers."

The weather that day was bitterly cold: "Every fan had an overcoat and the players were obliged to wear sweaters."[13] The cold led Manager McAleer and his counterpart, Connie Mack, to predict a crowd of less than 500.

Perhaps because it was the final Sunday game of the year, and a doubleheader, a surprise flash crowd of 3,000 showed up.

Native Clevelander Bill Reidy was the man in the pitcher's box for the Brewers in game one.

Cleveland used Baker to oppose him. It took thirteen cold innings but Cleveland prevailed in game one, 3–2.

In the second game, Pete Dowling faced the Lakeshores' man Billy Hart. Cleveland was leading 8–1 in the seventh, when both managers agreed to call it a game — approaching twilight and a long day in the cold made it an easy decision.

The weather was not much better on Tuesday, September 18, than it had been on Sunday, as the Brewers and Lakeshores each prepared to play their last game of the year. Only 355 dedicated fans bought tickets. They were rewarded with a well-played game.

Milwaukee had another Cleveland sandlotter on their roster. His name was George Rettger; he pitched for the home team. Curve-ball specialist Reust pitched for the Cleveland visitors.

The Lakeshores' man Pickering was the game's first batter. Ollie, on the game's first pitch, rapped it to third and beat it out for an infield scratch. Genins singled him over to third, and a smoker off the bat of Jones handcuffed shortstop Conroy — plating Pickering with the last game's first run.

In inning two, Tim Flood hit an easy bounder to Conroy, and what should have been an easy out turned into a three-base error, when the shortstop inexplicably launched a throw way past first baseman Abbey. Another easy chance was hit by Cross to Conroy; Flood broke for the plate, beating Conroy's throw, "although it was by a hair breadth escape."[14]

The Lakeshores went up 3–0 in the fifth, when a free pass to Shay was followed by a hit to the center field fence by Flood. It was good for a triple and a run batted in.

Milwaukee got back into the game in the seventh. An Abbey single, a Fultz triple, and a Burke single netted the Brewers 2.

Milwaukee came to bat in the bottom of the ninth trailing 3–2. Fultz was first and he took a walk. Conroy and Burke then bowed out. The potential go-ahead and wining run came to the plate. It was Harry Spies, the former Cleveland catcher from earlier in the season.

Would Harry be friend or foe? The question was rendered moot. Fultz, trying to get into scoring position, headed for a swipe of second. He didn't make it. Game over! Year over!

Score: Cleveland Lakeshores 3, Milwaukee Brewers 2.

Notes: • Losing pitcher: Rettger — he walked two, struck out none. • Winning pitcher: Reust — he walked one, hit a batter, and struck out two. • Time: One hour and fifteen minutes. • Umpire: Sheridan.

Afterword

An organization of experienced baseball men, headed by H. D. Quinn, had been called the American Association. In 1900 it changed its name to the National Association. What they intended was to form a new major league to compete with the National League's so-called "diamond monopoly." The Association had contacted Ban Johnson about combining forces in an attack on the National League's markets and upon its status as the only major league. Conflicts of interest between the two groups' principals in Milwaukee and Chicago kept Ban from considering the proposal.

The National League forces, fearing an invasion from two rival leagues—especially in its lucrative East Coast cities—reached a gentlemen's agreement with the Americans to share the seaboard markets. This effectively muscled the National Association out of the major league baseball business before they were even in it.

Indianapolis, Kansas City, Minneapolis, and Buffalo were dropped from the American League lineup, and the cities of Boston, Philadelphia, Baltimore, and Washington became the new members of the 1901 circuit.

A temporary peace concerning markets having been achieved, the two leagues now chose to go to war on other fronts. Over the next few years they raided each other's franchises for star players. Sportswriters were only too happy to keep the public informed of all the sensational details.

Cleveland would be right in the thick of this combat. When Cleveland obtained future Hall of Fame players Napoleon Lajoie and Elmer Flick in 1902, the success of their franchise would be secured for the next decade.

Peace and unity would eventually come to the two leagues, but even the passage of one hundred-plus years has not erased all the differences between Major League Baseball's Americans and Nationals.

Chapter Notes

Introduction

1. *Cleveland Herald*, April 15, 1841. Water St. (W. 9th) is in the Warehouse District in downtown Cleveland. North of St. Clair between Water Street and Bank Street (W. 6th), and now intersected by Johnson Court, was land used in 1841 as a park — it was the only place on Water Street large enough for a ball game.
2. A "poole" is a form of betting.

1865

1. *Lorain County News*, April 5, 1865.
2. *Lorain County News*, April 12, 1865.
3. *Lorain County News*, April 19, 1865.
4. *Lorain County News*, October 11, 1865.
5. *Cleveland Leader*, October 2, 1865.

1866

1. *Cleveland Leader*, July 5, 1866.
2. *Cleveland Leader*, August 27, 1866.

1867

1. *Portage County Democrat*, June 26, 1867.
2. *Ibid.*
3. *Ibid.*
4. *Geauga Democrat*, August 7, 1867.
5. *Mansfield Herald*, July 31, 1867.
6. *Cleveland Leader*, August 16, 1867.
7. *Cleveland Herald*, August 16, 1867.
8. *Canton Repository*, May 15, 1867.
9. *Ibid.*
10. *Ibid.*
11. *Canton Repository*, July 10, 1867.
12. *Medina Gazette*, October 4, 1867.
13. *Medina Gazette*, September 3, 1867.
14. *Ibid.*
15. *Mansfield Herald*, May 29, 1867.
16. *Mansfield Herald*, June 12, 1867.
17. *Norwalk Reflector*, August 13, 1867.
18. *Ibid.*
19. *Norwalk Reflector*, August 27, 1867.
20. *Ibid.*
21. *Cleveland Herald*, May 31, 1867.
22. *Ibid.*
23. *Ibid.*
24. *Cleveland Plain Dealer*, September 30, 1867.
25 *Cleveland Plain Dealer*, August 21, 1867; *Cleveland Herald*, August 22, 1867.
26. *Cleveland Herald*, August 31, 1867.
27. *Cleveland Herald*, August 23, 1867.
28. *Ibid.*
29. *Ibid.*
30. *Cleveland Herald*, September 5, 1867.
31. *Cleveland Herald*, September 13, 1867.
32. *Cleveland Herald*, September 5, 1867.
33. *Cleveland Leader*, September 27, 1867.
34. *Cleveland Herald*, September 27, 1867.
35. *Cleveland Leader*, October 21, 1867.
36. *Mansfield Herald*, October 30, 1867.
37. *Norwalk Reflector*, October 15, 1867.
38. *Mansfield Herald*, October 30, 1867.
39. *Cleveland Leader*, October 26, 1867.
40. *Norwalk Reflector*, October 29, 1867.

1868

1. *Cleveland Herald*, June 18, 1868.
2. *Cleveland Leader*, May 29, 1868.
3. *Cleveland Leader*, June 18, 1868.
4. *Cleveland Herald*, June 16, 1868.
5. *Cleveland Leader*, June 18, 1868.
6. *Ibid.*
7. *Cleveland Plain Dealer*, June 18, 1868.
8. *Cleveland Herald*, June 18, 1868.
9. *Cleveland Herald*, June 25, 1868.
10. *Ibid.*
11. *Ibid.*
12. *Ibid.*
13. *Lorain County News*, July 22, 1868.
14. Oberlin College Archives.
15. *Cleveland Herald*, August 1, 1868.
16. *Cleveland Herald*, August 3, 1868.
17. *Sandusky Register*, August 15, 1868.
18. *Cleveland Herald*, October 13, 1868.
19. *Ibid.*
20. *Cleveland Leader*, March 23, 1881 [reprint from files of late July 1868].
21. *Ibid.*

1869

1. *Cleveland Herald*, May 19, 1869.
2. *Cleveland Herald*, April 8, 1869.
3. *Cleveland Herald*, June 1, 1869.
4. *Cleveland Herald*, May 27, 1869.
5. *Cleveland Herald*, June 1, 1869.
6. *Cleveland Leader*, June 2, 1869.
7. *Ibid.*
8. *Ibid.*
9. *Ibid.*
10. *Cleveland Plain Dealer*, June 3, 1869.
11. *Cleveland Leader*, June 3, 1869.
12. *Ibid.*

13. *Ibid*
14. *Cleveland Herald*, June 30, 1869.
15. *Ibid*.
16. *Ibid*.
17. *Ibid*.
18. *Cleveland Herald*, July 6, 1869.
19. *Ibid*.
20. *Ibid*.
21. *Ibid*.
22. *Ibid*.
23. *Cleveland Herald*, July 9, 1869.
24. *Cleveland Plain Dealer*, July 9, 1869.
25. *Cleveland Herald*, July 9, 1869.
26. *Cleveland Plain Dealer*, July 10, 1869.
27. *Cleveland Herald*, August 2, 1869.
28. *Ibid*.
29. *Ibid*.
30. *Cleveland Herald*, August 3, 1869.
31. *Cleveland Herald*, August 26, 1869.
32 *Cleveland Herald*, August 9, 1869.
33. *Cleveland Herald*, August 6, 1869.
34. *Cleveland Herald*, August 7, 1869.
35. *Ibid*.
36. *Ibid*.
37. *Cleveland Herald*, August 9, 1869.
38. *Cleveland Herald*, August 13, 1889.
49. *Ibid*.
40. *Ibid*.
41. *Cleveland Leader*, August 24, 1869.
42. *Cleveland Leader*, October 11, 1869.
43. *Ibid*.
44. *Cleveland Herald*, October 11, 1869.
45. *Cleveland Herald*, October 7, 1869.

1870

1. *Cleveland Leader*, February 11, 1870.
2. *Cleveland Herald*, April 25, 1870.
3. John Erardi and Greg Rhodes. *The First Boys of Summer*. Cincinnati: Road West Pub. Co., 1994.
4. *Cleveland Herald*, May 13, 1870.
5. *Cleveland Herald*, May 16, 1870.
6. Erardi and Rhodes, p.87.
7. *Cleveland Herald*, May 16, 1870 [reprint from the *Buffalo Express*].
8. *Cleveland Herald*, August 2, 1870.
9. *Cleveland Herald*, June 3, 1870.
10. *Ibid*.
11. *Cleveland Herald*, June 1, 1870.
12. *Ibid*.
13. *Ibid*.
14. *Ibid*.
15. *Ibid*.
16. *Cleveland Plain Dealer*, June 4, 1870.
17. *Cleveland Plain Dealer*, June 7, 1870 [reprint from the *Chicago Journal*].
18. *Cleveland Plain Dealer*, June 1870.
19. *Cleveland Plain Dealer*, June 7, 1870 [reprint from the *Chicago Journal*].
20. *Cleveland Plain Dealer*, June 4, 1870.
21. *Cleveland Herald* June 21, 1870.
22. *Cleveland Herald*, July 30, 1870.
23. *Ibid*.
24. *Ibid*.
25. *Cleveland Plain Dealer*, July 30, 1870.
26. Erardi and Rhodes, p.125.
27. *Cleveland Plain Dealer*, October 8, 1870 [reprint from the *Cincinnati Commercial*].

28. *Cleveland Plain Dealer*, November 7, 1870.
29. There is a direct line from the original Cincinnati Red Stockings to the Atlanta Braves of the National League today. According to author Michael Gershman, the original Cincinnati Red Stockings (Ind.) have been called the Boston Red Stockings (N.A.); Boston Red Caps, Beaneaters, Doves, Rustlers, Braves, Bees, and Braves (N.L.); Milwaukee Braves (N.L.); and Atlanta Braves.

1871

1. *Fort Wayne Daily Democrat*, June 2, 1870.
2. *Fort Wayne Daily Gazette*, May 4, 1871.
3. *Ibid*.
4. *Fort Wayne Gazette*, May 5, 1871.
5. *Ibid*.
6. *Cleveland Leader*, May 5, 1871.
7. *Cleveland Leader*, May 8, 1871.
8. *Cleveland Herald*, May 6, 1871.
9. *Fort Wayne Gazette*, May 5, 1871.
10. *Cleveland Leader*, May 8, 1871.
11. *Cleveland Leader*, May 12, 1871.
12. *Ibid*.
13. *Ibid*.
14. *Cleveland Plain Dealer*, May 12, 1871.
15. *Cleveland Leader*, May 12, 1871.
16. *Ibid*.
17. *Cleveland Herald*, May 25, 1871.
18. *Cleveland Herald*, July 7, 1871.
19. *Ibid*.
20. *Ibid*.
21. *Cleveland Herald*. August 11, 1871.
22. *Cleveland Herald*, August 14, 1871.
23. *Ibid*.
24. *Cleveland Herald*, August 11, 1871.
25. *Cleveland Herald*, August 14, 1871.
26. *Cleveland Herald*, August 11, 1871.
27. *Cleveland Herald* , October 11, 1871.
28. *Ibid*.
29. *Ibid*.
30. *Ibid*.
31. *Ibid*.

1872

1. *Cleveland Herald*, April 30, 1872.
2. *Cleveland Herald*, May 14, 1872.
3. *Cleveland Leader*, May 23, 1872.
4. *Cleveland Leader*, May 25, 1872.
5. *Cleveland Leader*, June 1, 1872.
6. *Cleveland Plain Dealer*, June 3, 1872.
7. *Ibid*.
8. *Cleveland Leader*, June 3, 1872.
9. *Ibid*.
10. *Ibid*.
11. *Cleveland Herald*, June 24, 1872.
12. *Ibid*.
13. *Ibid*.
14. *Cleveland Leader*, August 20, 1872.
15. *Ibid*.
16. *Ibid*.

1873–1877

1. *Cleveland Herald*, June 9, 1873.
2. *Cleveland Leader*, August 24, 1874.

3. *Cleveland Leader*, August 25, 1874.
4. *Cleveland Herald*, August 25, 1874.
5. *Cleveland Plain Dealer*, September 10, 1874.
6. *Cleveland Leader*, May 30, 1877.
7. *Cleveland Herald* June 1, 1877.

1878

1. *Cleveland Leader*, May 7, 1878.
2. *Ibid.*
3. *Cleveland Leader*, May 10, 1878.
4. *Cleveland Leader*, May 8, 1878.
5. *Cleveland Leader*, May 11, 1878.
6. *Ibid.*
7. *Cleveland Herald*, May 6, 1878.
8. *Cleveland Plain Dealer*, June 12, 1878.
9. Ibid.
10. *Ibid.*
11. *Ibid.*
12. *Ibid.*
13. *Cleveland Leader*, May 13, 1878.
14. *Cleveland Leader*, August 7, 1878.
15. *Cleveland Leader*, September 4, 1878.
16. *Ibid.*
17. *Ibid.*

1879

1. *Cleveland Leader*, April 23, 1879.
2. *Cleveland Leader*, May 19, 1879.
3. *Cleveland Leader*, May 1, 1879.
4. *Cleveland Leader*, May 3, 1879.
5. *Cleveland Leader*, May 5, 1879.
6. *Ibid.*
7. *Ibid.*
8. *Cleveland Plain Dealer*, May 22, 1879.
9. *Cleveland Leader*, June 13, 1879.
10. *Cleveland Leader*, June 11, 1879.
11. *Ibid.*
12. *Cleveland Leader*, July 18, 1879.
13. *Cleveland Leader*, June 18, 1879.
14. *Cleveland Leader*, July 27, 1879.
15. *Ibid.*
16. *Cleveland Herald*, August 13, 1879.
17. *Cleveland Herald*, August 16, 1879.
18. *Ibid.*
19. *Cleveland Leader*, August 16, 1879.
20. *Cleveland Leader*, August 28, 1879.
21. *Cleveland Herald*, August 16, 1879.
22. *Cleveland Leader*, August 29, 1879.
23. *Ibid.*
24. *Ibid.*
25. *Ibid.*
26. *Ibid.*

1880

1. *Cleveland Leader*, March 3, 1880.
2. *Cleveland Plain Dealer*, April 16, 1880.
3. *Ibid.*
4. *Cleveland Plain Dealer*, May 3, 1880.
5. *Cleveland Leader*, June 14, 1880.
6. *Cleveland Leader*, June 14, 1880.
7. *Cleveland Plain Dealer*, July 19, 1880.
8. *Cleveland Plain Dealer*, July 6, 1880.
9. *Cleveland Plain Dealer*, August 12, 1880.

1881

1. Umpire Doesher's name also appears as "Doscher" in various box scores. The Cleveland player of 1881 named Herm Doscher (5 games) may well be the same person.
2. *Cleveland Leader*, May 6, 1880.
3. *Ibid.*
4. *Cleveland Herald*, May 6, 1881.
5. *Cleveland Leader*, May 6, 1881.
6. *Akron Daily Beacon*, Sept. 4, 1881 [reprint from the *Cincinnati Enquirer*].
7. *Akron Beacon Journal*, September 7, 1881 [reprint from a St. Louis paper].
8. *Cleveland Leader*, July, 5, 1881.
9. *Cleveland Herald*, July 5, 1881.
10. *Cleveland Plain Dealer*, July 20, 1881.
11. *Ibid.*
12. *Cleveland Plain Dealer*, August 2, 1881. Mother Shipton was supposedly an English prophetess born in 1488; stories about her predictions have surfaced over the centuries. In 1861, a document attributed to her was circulated — it said that the world would end in 1881!
13. *Cleveland Plain Dealer*, August 4, 1881.
14. *Cleveland Plain Dealer*, August 8, 1881.
15. *Cleveland Leader*, August 26, 1881 [reprint from the Louisville Commercial].
16. *Ibid.*
17. *Cleveland Plain Dealer*, September 1, 1881.
18. *Cleveland Plain Dealer*, September 28, 1881.
19. *Encyclopedia Americana* (New York, 1951), vol. XII, p.290.

1882

1. Michael Gershman, *Diamonds* (Boston, Houghton Mifflin, 1993), p. 32.
2. *Cleveland Plain Dealer*, April 10, 1882.
3. *Cleveland Herald*, May 2, 1882.
4. *Cleveland Plain Dealer*, May 2, 1882.
5. *Cleveland Herald*, September 12, 1882.
6. *Cleveland Herald*, July 5, 1882.
7. *Ibid.*
8. *Cleveland Leader*, July 5, 1882.
9. *Ibid.*
10. *Cleveland Herald*, July 5, 1882.
11. *Cleveland Plain Dealer*, March 18, 1889 [reprint from the *Leader* files].
12. *Cleveland Plain Dealer*, July 14, 1882.
13. *Cleveland Plain Dealer*, July 12, 1882.
14. *Cleveland Plain Dealer*, July 27, 1882.
15. *Cleveland Plain Dealer*, July 25, 1882.
16. *Cleveland Leader*, July 25, 1882.
17. *Cleveland Herald*, July 25, 1882.
18. *Cleveland Plain Dealer*, July 25, 1882. Lord Dundreary, a character in the play *Our American Cousin*, was a nobleman whose head was full of "trivialities" and "whimsicalities." Written by English playwright Tom Taylor (1817–1880), the play made its American debut in New York City in 1858. Abraham Lincoln was watching a performance of it at Ford's Theater the night he was assassinated.
19. *Cleveland Herald*, July 25, 1882.
20. *Cleveland Plain Dealer*, July 28, 1882.

1883

1. *Cleveland Leader*, April 14, 1883.
2. *Cleveland Leader* , May 2, 1883.

3. *Ibid.*
4. *Cleveland Leader*, July 23, 1883.
5. *Ibid.*
6. *Ibid.*
7. *Cleveland Leader*, April 27, 1883.
8. *Cleveland Leader*, July 25, 1883.
9. *Cleveland Leader*, May 4, 1883.
10. *Cleveland Leader*, May 5, 1883.
11. *Cleveland Leader*, July 11, 1883.
12. *Cleveland Leader*, May 10, 1883.
13. *Ibid.*
14. *Ibid.*
15. *Ibid.*
16. *Ibid.*
17. *Ibid.*
18. *Cleveland Leader*, July 3, 1883.
19. *Cleveland Leader*, April 19, 1883.
20. *Cleveland Leader*, August 5, 1883.
21. *Cleveland Leader*, July 18, 1883.
22. *Cleveland Leader*, May 5, 1883.
23. *Cleveland Leader*, May 23, 1883.
24. *Cleveland Leader*, August 10, 1883.
25. *Cleveland Leader*, August 14, 1883.
26. *Ibid.*
27. *Cleveland Leader*, August 23, 1883.
28. *Cleveland Leader*, September 14, 1883.
29. *Cleveland Herald*, September 14, 1883.

1884

1. *Cleveland Herald*, June 13, 1884.
2. *Cleveland Herald*, July 4, 1884.
3. *Cleveland Herald*, July 5, 1884.
4. *Ibid..*
5. *Ibid.*
6. *Cleveland Herald*, July 18, 1884.
7. *Cleveland Herald*, July 28, 1884.
8. *Cleveland Herald*, August 9, 1884.
9. *Ibid.*
10. *Cleveland Herald*, August 10, 1884.
11. *Cleveland Herald*, August 9, 1884.
12. *Ibid.*
13. *Cleveland Herald*, August 10, 1884.
14. *Cleveland Herald*, August 9, 1884.
15. *Cleveland Herald*, September 14, 1884.
16. *Cleveland Herald*, August 23, 1884.

1885–1886

1. *Cleveland Plain Dealer*, April 20, 1885.
2. *Ibid.*
3. *Cleveland Leader*, May 17, 1885.
4. *Ibid.*
5. *Cleveland Plain Dealer*, May 28, 1885.
6. *Cleveland Plain Dealer*, June 5, 1885.
7. *Cleveland Herald*, April 11, 1886.

1887

1. *Sporting Life*, March 2, 1887.
2. *Ibid.*
3. *Cleveland Plain Dealer*, April 26, 1887.
4. *Cleveland Herald*, February 27, 1887.
5. *Cleveland Plain Dealer*, April 4, 1887.
6. *Cleveland Plain Dealer*, April 8, 1887.
7. *Cleveland Plain Dealer*, April 12, 1887.
8. *Cleveland Plain Dealer*, April 19, 1887.
9. *Cleveland Plain Dealer*, April 20, 1887.
10. *Cleveland Plain Dealer*, May 5, 1887.
11. *Ibid.*
12. *Ibid.*
13. *Ibid.*
14. *Ibid.*
15. *Ibid.*
16. *Ibid.*
17. *Cleveland Plain Dealer*, May 3, 1887.
18. *Cleveland Plain Dealer*, July 5, 1887.
19. *Cleveland Plain Dealer*, May 2, 1887.
20. *Cleveland Plain Dealer*, April 30, 1887.
21. *Cleveland Plain Dealer*, July 16, 1887.
22. *Cleveland Plain Dealer*, September 14, 1887.
23. *Cleveland Plain Dealer*, April 21, 1887.
24. *Cleveland Plain Dealer*, August 26, 1887.
25. *Cleveland Plain Dealer*, August 22, 1887.
26. *Ibid.*
27. *Cleveland Plain Dealer*, May 8, 1887.

1888

1. *Cleveland Plain Dealer*, March 21, 1888.
2. *Cleveland Plain Dealer*, April 15, 1888.
3. *Ibid.*
4. *Cleveland Plain Dealer*, April 11, 1888.
5. *Cleveland Plain Dealer*, April 17, 1888.
6. *Cleveland Plain Dealer*, May 3, 1888.
7. *Cleveland Plain Dealer*, June 9, 1889.
8. *Ibid.*
9. *Cleveland Plain Dealer*, May 30, 1888.
10. *Cleveland Plain Dealer*, July 13, 1888.
11. *Cleveland Plain Dealer*, April 24, 1888.
12. *Cleveland Plain Dealer*, June 9, 1888.
13. *Cleveland Plain Dealer*, June 16, 1888.
14. *Ibid.*
15. *Cleveland Plain Dealer*, June 19, 1888.
16. *Sporting Life*, July 1888.
17. *Cleveland Plain Dealer*, June 17, 1888.
18. *Ibid.*
19. *Cleveland City Record*, September 17, 1888, p. 145.
20. *Cleveland Plain Dealer*, September 26, 1888.
21. *Ibid.*
22. *Cleveland Leader*, July 23, 1888.
23. *Chagrin Falls Exponent*, July 26, 1888.
24. *Cleveland Leader*, July 30, 1888.
25. *Ibid.*
26. *Cleveland City Directory*, 1885 & 1886 editions.
27. *Cleveland Press*, September 10, 1888.
28. *Cleveland Plain Dealer*, September 10, 1888.
29. *Cleveland Plain Dealer*, October 26, 1888.

1889

1. *Cleveland Plain Dealer*, March 18, 1889.
2. *Ibid.*
3. *Cleveland Plain Dealer*, April 6, 1889 [reprint from the *St. Louis Star Sayings*].
4. *Cleveland Plain Dealer*, April 18, 1889.
5. *Cleveland Plain Dealer*, March 20, 1889.
6. *Cleveland Leader*, May 27, 1889.
7. *Cleveland Leader*, September 13, 1889.
8. *Cleveland Plain Dealer*, April 25, 1889.
9. *Cleveland Plain Dealer*, May 4, 1889.
10. *Sporting Life*, May 22, 1889.
11. *Cleveland Plain Dealer*, June 23, 1889.

12. *Cleveland Plain Dealer*, June 28, 1889.
13. *Cleveland Plain Dealer*, June 28, 1889.
14. *Ibid.*
15. *Ibid.*
16. *Ibid.*
17. *Cleveland Plain Dealer*, October 16, 1889.
18. *Cleveland Plain Dealer*, October 17, 1889.

1890

1. *Cleveland Press*, March 5, 1890.
2. *Cleveland Plain Dealer*, January 27, 1890.
3. *Cleveland Plain Dealer*, January 6, 1890.
4. *Cleveland Plain Dealer*, February 7, 1890.
5. *Akron Daily Beacon*, March 25, 1890.
6. *Cleveland Plain Dealer*, May 6, 1890.
7. *Cleveland Plain Dealer*, April 28, 1890.
8. *Cleveland Leader*, April 13, 1890.
9. *Cleveland Press*, April 26, 1890.
10. *Cleveland Plain Dealer*, April 26, 1890.
11. *Ibid.*
12. *Sporting Life*, May 3, 1890.
13. *Sporting News*, April 12, 1890.
14. *Cleveland Plain Dealer*, April 12, 1890.
15. *Cleveland Leader*, May 1, 1890.
16. *Cleveland Plain Dealer*, May 1, 1890.
17. *Cleveland Leader*, May 1, 1890.
18. *Cleveland Plain Dealer*, May 18, 1890.
19. *Cleveland Plain Dealer*, May 1, 1890.
20. *Cleveland Leader*, May 1, 1890.
21. *Ibid.*
22. *Ibid.*
23. *Cleveland Plain Dealer*, June 6, 1890.
24. *Cleveland Press*, June 6, 1890.
25. *Cleveland Leader*, June 6, 1890.
26. *Cleveland Leader*, June 20, 1890.
27. *Cleveland Plain Dealer*, July 5, 1890.
28. *Ibid.*
29. *Cleveland Plain Dealer*, August 7, 1890.
30. *Cleveland Plain Dealer*, October 5, 1890.

1891

1. *Cleveland Press*, April 22, 1891.
2. *Cleveland Leader*, May 2, 1891.
3. *Cleveland Plain Dealer*, May 2, 1891.
4. *Ibid.*
5. *Cleveland Leader*, May 2, 1891.
6. *Ibid.*
7. *Cleveland Plain Dealer*, May 2, 1891.
8. *Cleveland Leader*, May 2, 1891.
9. *Cleveland Plain Dealer*, May 9, 1891.
10. *Cleveland Plain Dealer*, June 22, 1891.
11. *Cleveland Plain Dealer*, June 7, 1891.
12. *Cleveland Plain Dealer*, July 5, 1891.
13. *Ibid.*
14. *Ibid.*
15. *Cleveland Plain Dealer*, June 8, 1891 [reprint from the *New York World*].
16. *Cleveland Plain Dealer*, August 22, 1891.
17. *Sporting Life*, July 18, 1891.
18. *Sporting Life*, September 26, 1891.
19. *Cleveland Plain Dealer*, September 18, 1891.
20. *Cleveland Plain Dealer*, September 30, 1891.
21. *Cleveland Leader*, October 15, 1891.
22. *Cleveland Plain Dealer*, October 15, 1891.

1892

1. *Cleveland Press*, March 25, 1892 [Reprint from the *Tuscarawas Chronicle*].
2. *Ibid.*
3. *Ibid.*
4. *Cleveland Press*, June 11, 1892.
5. *Cleveland Press*, June 7, 1892.
6. *Cleveland Press*, July 5, 1892.
7. *Ibid.*
8. *Cleveland Press*, July 6, 1892.
9. *Cleveland Gazette* August 3, 1892.
10. *Cleveland Press*, July 16, 1892.
11. *Cleveland Press*, July 24, 1892.
12. *Cleveland Press*, July 16, 1892.
13. *Cleveland Press*, August 26, 1892.
14. *Cleveland Press*, July 7, 1892.
15. *Ibid.*
16. *Cleveland Press*, August 2, 1892.
17. *Cleveland Press*, September 6, 1892.
18. *Cleveland Leader*, October 12, 1892.
19. *Cleveland Leader*, October 17, 1892.
20. *Cleveland Leader*, October 18, 1892.
21. *Ibid.*
22. *Cleveland Plain Dealer*, October 19, 1892.
23. *Cleveland Plain Dealer*, October 20, 1892.
24. *Cleveland Plain Dealer*, October 22, 1892.
25. *Cleveland Plain Dealer*, October 23, 1892.
26. *Cleveland Plain Dealer*, October 25, 1892.
27. *Ibid.*

1893

1. *Cleveland Leader*, April 28, 1893.
2. *Cleveland Leader*, May 6, 1893.
3. *Cleveland Press*, May 5, 1893.
4. *Cleveland Press*, June 19, 1893.
5. *Cleveland Leader*, June 7, 1893.
6. *Cleveland Leader*, June 27, 1893.
7. *Cleveland Press*, June 27, 1893.
8. *Cleveland Leader*, July 5, 1893.
9. *Ibid.*
10. *Cleveland Plain Dealer*, July 5, 1893.
11. *Cleveland Leader*, July 5, 1893.

1894

1. *Cleveland Press*, May 7, 1894.
2. *Cleveland Press*, May 21, 1894.
3. *Cleveland Press*, April 2, 1894.
4. *Cleveland Plain Dealer*, May 4, 1894.
5. *Cleveland Press*, July 31, 1894.
6. *Cleveland Press*, May 28, 1894.
7. *Ibid.*
8. *Cleveland Press*, July 5, 1894.
9. *Cleveland Press*, July 5, 1894.
10. *Cleveland Press*, July 10, 1894.
11. *Cleveland Press*, July 25, 1894.
12. *Cleveland Press*, August 9, 1894.
13. *Cleveland Press*, August 10, 1894.
14. *Ibid.*
15. *Cleveland Press*, August 12, 1894.
16. *Cleveland Press*, August 24, 1894.

1895

1. *Cleveland Press*, May 6, 1895.
2. *Cleveland Press*, May 15, 1895.

3. *Cleveland Press*, April 17, 1895.
4. *Ibid.*
5. *Cleveland Press*, June 10, 1895.
6. *Cleveland Press*, July 31, 1895.
7. *Cleveland Press*, July 15, 1895.
8. *Cleveland Plain Dealer*, July 18, 1895.
9. *Cleveland Press*, June 26, 1895.
10. *Cleveland Press*, July 18, 1895.
11. *Cleveland Press*, August 21, 1895.
12. *Cleveland Press*, October 3, 1895.
13. *Cleveland Plain Dealer*, October 4, 1895.
14. *Ibid.*
15. *Cleveland Plain Dealer*, October 6, 1895.
16. *Ibid.*
17. *Ibid.*
18. *Cleveland Plain Dealer*, October 5, 1895.
19. *Ibid.*
20. *Ibid.*
21. *Ibid.*
22. *Cleveland Press*, October 8, 1895.
23. *Ibid.*
24. *Cleveland Plain Dealer*, October 9, 1895.
25. *Cleveland Press*, October 13, 1895.

1896

1. *Cleveland Plain Dealer*, April 17, 1896.
2. *Cleveland Plain Dealer*, May 3, 1896.
3. *Cleveland Plain Dealer*, June 26, 1896.
4. *Cleveland Plain Dealer*, June 27. 1896.
5. *Cleveland Plain Dealer*, June 27, 1896.
6. *Ibid.*
7. *Cleveland Press*, June 28, 1896.
8. *Cleveland Plain Dealer*, June 28, 1896.
9. *Cleveland Press*, June 29, 1896.
10. *Cleveland Press*, June 29, 1896.
11. *Cleveland Press*, July 3,1896.
12. *Cleveland Plain Dealer*, July 4, 1896.
13. *Ibid.*
14. *Cleveland Press*, July 24, 1896.
15. *Cleveland Press*, July 31, 1896.
16. *Cleveland Leader*, September 24, 1896.
17. *Cleveland Leader*, September 10, 1896.
18. *Cleveland Leader*, September 28, 1896.
19. *Cleveland Leader*, October 2, 1896.
20. *Cleveland Plain Dealer*, October 3, 1896.
21. *Cleveland Plain Dealer*, October 4, 1896.
22. *Cleveland Leader*, October 6, 1896.
23. *Ibid.*
24. *Cleveland Plain Dealer*, October 8, 1896.
25. *Cleveland Plain Dealer*, October 9, 1896.
26. *Ibid.*
27. *Cleveland Leader*, October 9, 1896.
28. *Cleveland Plain Dealer*, October 9, 1896.
29. *Cleveland Leader*, October 15, 1896.

1897

1. *Cleveland Leader*, March 2, 1897.
2. *Cleveland Plain Dealer*, March 15, 1897 [poem by R. K. Munkittrick reprinted from the *New York Journal*].
3. *Cleveland Plain Dealer*, March 19, 1897.
4. *Cleveland Plain Dealer*, April 9, 1897.
5. *Cleveland Plain Dealer*, May 17, 1897.
6. *Ibid.*
7. *Washington Post*, May 17, 1897.
8. *Ibid.*
9. *Cleveland Plain Dealer*, June 14, 1897.
10. *Ibid.*
11. *Ibid.*
12. *Chicago Tribune*, June 25, 1897.
13. *Cleveland Plain Dealer*, July 1, 1897.
14. *Cleveland Plain Dealer*, July 4, 1897.
15. *Ibid.*
16. *Ibid.*
17. *Cleveland Plain Dealer*, July 12, 1897.
18. *Ibid.*
19. *Cleveland Press*, July 13, 1897.
20. *Cleveland Plain Dealer*, August 6, 1897.
21. *Cleveland Plain Dealer*, July 25, 1897.
22. *Cleveland Plain Dealer*, August 17, 1897.
23. *Cleveland Plain Dealer*, September 5, 1897.
24. *Cleveland Plain Dealer*, September 19, 1897.

1898

1. *Cleveland Plain Dealer*, March 2, 1898.
2. *Cleveland Plain Dealer*, March 11, 1898.
3. *Ibid.*
4. *Cleveland Plain Dealer*, March 26, 1898.
5. *Cleveland Plain Dealer*, March 25, 1898.
6. *Cleveland Plain Dealer*, April 30, 1898.
7. *Cleveland Leader*, June 12, 1898.
8. *Cleveland Leader*, June 13, 1898.
9. *Cleveland Plain Dealer*, June 17, 1898.
10. *Cleveland Press*, June 20, 1898.
11. *Cleveland Press*, June 27, 1898.
12. *Sporting Life*, July 2, 1898.
13. *Cleveland Plain Dealer*, August 5, 1898.
14. *Cleveland Plain Dealer*, July 12, 1898.
15. *Cleveland Plain Dealer*, July 15, 1898.
16. *Cleveland Plain Dealer*, July 18, 1898.
17. *Cleveland Plain Dealer*, July 21, 1898.
18. *Cleveland Plain Dealer*, July, 24, 1898.
19. *Cleveland Plain Dealer*, August 16, 1898.
20. *Cleveland Plain Dealer*, October 10, 1898.
21. *Cleveland Plain Dealer*, October 3, 1898.
22. *Ibid.*

1899

1. *Cleveland Press*, May 6, 1899.
2. *Cleveland Plain Dealer*, May 14, 1899.

1900

1. *Cleveland Leader*, April 27, 1900.
2. *Cleveland Plain Dealer*, April 27, 1900.
3. *Ibid.*
4. *Cleveland Plain Dealer*, April 21, 1900.
5. *Cleveland Plain Dealer*, April 25, 1900.
6. *Cleveland Plain Dealer*, April 27, 1900.
7. *Ibid.*
8. *Cleveland Plain Dealer*, July 5, 1900.
9. *Cleveland Leader*, July 5, 1900.
10. *Ibid.*
11. *Cleveland Plain Dealer*, August 7, 1900.
12. *Cleveland Plain Dealer*, September 7, 1900.
13. *Cleveland Plain Dealer*, September 17, 1900.
14. *Cleveland Plain Dealer*, September 19, 1900.

Bibliography

Books

Baseball Encyclopedia. New York: Macmillan, 1974.

Baseball's First Stars. Cleveland: Society for American Baseball Research, 1996.

Cramer, C. H. *Case Western Reserve: A History of the University, 1926–1976.* Boston: Little, Brown and Co., 1976.

Encyclopedia Americana. New York: Americana Corporation, 1955.

Erardi, John, and Greg Rhodes. *The First Boys of Summer.* Cincinnati: Road West Pub. Co., 1994.

Gershman, Michael. *Diamonds.* Boston: Houghton Mifflin, 1993.

Guide to Cleveland Architecture. Cleveland: Cleveland Chapter of the American Institute of Architects, 1997.

Hetrick, J. Thomas. *Misfits! The Cleveland Spiders in 1899: A Day by Day Narrative of Baseball Futility.* Jefferson, NC: McFarland, 1991.

Kelly, Thomas. *The Cleveland 200.* Cleveland: Archives Press, 1996.

Lansche, Jerry. *Glory Fades Away.* Dallas: Taylor Publishing, 1991.

Lewis, Franklin. *The Cleveland Indians.* New York: G. P. Putnam's Sons, 1949.

Lowry, Philip. *Green Cathedrals.* Cooperstown, NY: Society for American Baseball Research, 1998.

Miller, Carol Poh, and Robert Wheeler. *Cleveland: A Concise History, 1796–1990.* Bloomington: Indiana University Press, 1990.

The Negro Leagues Book. Ed. Dick Clark and Larry Lester. Cleveland: Society for American Baseball Research, 1994.

Nemec, David. *The Beer and Whiskey League.* Guilford, CT: Lyons Press, 2004.

Phillips, John. *The Astonishing Cleveland Babes of 1889.* Cabin John, MD: Capital Pub. Co., 1994.

Pietrusza, David. *Major Leagues: The Formation, Sometimes Absorption, and Mostly Inevitable Demise of 18 Professional Baseball Organizations, 1871 to Present.* Jefferson, NC: McFarland, 2006.

Rosenberg, John M. *The Story of Baseball.* New York: Random House, 1962.

Rucker, Mark. *Base Ball Cartes: The First Baseball Cards.* Sarasota Springs, NY: Self-published, 1988.

Ryczek, William J. *Blackguards and Red Stockings: A History of Baseball's National Association, 1871–1875.* Jefferson, NC: McFarland, 1992.

_____. *When Johnny Came Sliding Home: The Post–Civil War Baseball Boom, 1865–1870.* Jefferson, NC: McFarland, 1998.

Seymour, Harold. *Baseball: The Early Years.* New York: Oxford University Press, 1989.

Sowell, Mike. *July 2, 1903: The Mysterious Death of Hall-of-Famer Big Ed Delahanty.* New York: Macmillan, 1992.

Sullivan, Dean A. *Early Innings: A Documentary History of Baseball, 1825–1908.* Lincoln: University of Nebraska Press, 1995.

Total Baseball. Ed. John Thorn and Pete Palmer with David Reuther. 2d ed. Warner Books, 1991.

Newspapers (local circulation)

City	Newspaper	Source
Akron	*Summit County News*	University of Akron
Berea	*Grindstone*	Baldwin Wallace College
Canton	*Repository*	Canton Public Library
Chagrin Falls	*Exponent*	Chagrin Falls Public Library
Chardon	*Geauga Democrat*	Chardon Public Library
Cleveland	*Gazette*	Cleveland Public Library
Cleveland	*Herald*	Cleveland Public Library
Cleveland	*Leader*	Cleveland Public Library
Cleveland	*Plain Dealer*	Cleveland Public Library
Cleveland	*Town Topics*	Cleveland Public Library
Cleveland	*World*	Cleveland Public Library
Erie, PA	*Daily Dispatch*	Erie Public Library

City	Newspaper	Source
Erie, PA	*Weekly Observer*	Erie Public Library
Ft. Wayne, IN	*Democrat*	Ft. Wayne Public Library
Ft. Wayne, IN	*Gazette*	Ft. Wayne Public Library
Ft. Wayne, IN	*Sentinel*	Ft. Wayne Public Library
Geneva	*Times*	Geneva Public Library
Mansfield	*Reflector*	Mansfield Public Library
Medina	*Gazette*	Medina Public Library
Norwalk	*Reflector*	Norwalk Public Library
Oberlin	*Lorain County News*	Oberlin College
Painesville	*Telegraph*	Painesville Public Library
Ravenna	*Portage County Democrat*	Kent State University
Sandusky	*Register*	Sandusky Public Library
Youngstown	*Mahoning Courier*	Youngstown State University
Youngstown	*Mahoning Register*	Youngstown State University

Newspapers and Magazines (national circulation)

American Street Railroad Association (ASRA)
Brooklyn Eagle
Chicago Tribune
Harper's Weekly
Leslie's Illustrated
New York Clipper
New York World
Spirit of the Times
Sporting News
Sporting Life
Vintage & Classic Baseball Collector (December 1995)
Washington Post

Archives

Cleveland	Case Western Reserve University
Cleveland	Cleveland City Hall
Cleveland	Western Reserve Historical Society
Hudson	Hudson Historical Society
Oberlin	Oberlin College

Baseball Collections

Charles W. Mears Baseball Collection, Cleveland Public Library.
Eugene C. Murdock Collection, Cleveland Public Library.

Nineteenth Century Baseball Guides

Brotherhood: 1890
Reach: all
Spalding: all

Maps

Cleveland Public Library (main branch)
Birds Eye View
City Atlas
City Directory
Sanborn

Pamphlets

Cuyahoga County Soldiers' and Sailors' Monument: Centennial Issue, 1894–1994. Cleveland: Published by the Monument Trustees, 1994 [Reprint of 1896-edition].

(Sources for the above: Cleveland Public Library, main branch)

Sources by Chapter

1865

Cleveland Herald, 1865–October 10
Cleveland Leader, 1865–September 18; October 16, 21
Cleveland Plain Dealer, 1865–October 21
Lorain County News (Oberlin), 1865–April 5, 19; October 11, 18, 25

1866

Cleveland Herald, 1866–April 20, 28; May 15, 18; June 11, 18, 25, 27, 28; July 5, 13; August 27; September 5
Cleveland Leader, 1866–July 5; August 27
Cleveland Plain Dealer, 1866–July 3, 5; August 27
Erie Daily Dispatch, 1866–May 3, 8, 21; June 18, 22, 26
Erie Weekly Observer, 1866–July 5; August 3, 23
Lorain County News (Oberlin), 1866–June 27; July 11, 18; August 1
Mansfield Herald, 1866–August 8; September 5, 12
[Oberlin — see *Lorain County News*]
Painesville Telegraph, 1866–June 21, 28; September 6; October 18, 25

1867

Akron Beacon Record [Most of this file is lost. Akron information comes mostly from Cleveland papers.]
Canton Repository, 1867–May 15; June 10
Chardon — see *Geauga County Democrat*
Cleveland Herald (Akron), 1867–August 16
Cleveland Herald, 1867–April 30; May 22, 24, 31; June 29; July 1, 2, 27; August 22, 23, 30, 31; September 2, 5, 13, 21, 27, 28; October 21
Cleveland Leader (Akron), 1867–August 16
Cleveland Leader, 1867–September 19, 27; October 4, 21, 25, 26
Cleveland Plain Dealer (Akron), 1867–August 16
Cleveland Plain Dealer, 1867–May 31; August 12; September 30; October 26
Geauga County Democrat (Chardon), 1867–June 5; July 24; August 7, 14, 28; September 11, 18; October 9
[Kent — see *Portage County Democrat*]
Mansfield Herald, 1867–May 1, 29; June 12; July 3, 31; August 21; October 23, 30

Medina Gazette, 1867–July 26; August 30; September 3, 20; October 4
Norwalk Reflector, 1867–August 6, 13, 20, 29; September 3, 17, 24; October 1, 15, 20, 22; November 5
Painesville Telegraph, 1867–May 23
Portage County Democrat (Kent and Ravenna), 1867–June 19, 26; July 31; August 14; September 11, 25; October 16, 30
[Ravenna — see *Portage County Democrat*]
Youngstown Courier, 1867–May 15, 29; June 26; July 3, 24; August 7, 21; September 25
Youngstown Register, 1867–May 16, 30; August 13

1868

Cleveland Herald, 1868–May 3, 8, 25; June 4, 5, 16, 17, 18, 19, 25; July 14, 21, 22, 24, 27; August 1, 2, 3, 5, 7, 10, 13, 14, 26, 27; September 6, 15; October 7, 12
Cleveland Leader, 1868–May 29
Lorain County News (Oberlin), 1868–April 22; June 24; July 15, 22, 26, 29; August 6, 12; September 16, 30; October 7.
Mansfield Herald, 1868–April 22; June 24; July 15, 22, 26, 29; August 6, 12; September 16, 30; October 7
[Oberlin — see *Lorain County News*]
Painesville Telegraph, 1868–August 20
Sandusky Register, 1868–August 5, 15
Youngstown Register, 1868–July 9, 15; August 17, 27; September 2

1869

[Chardon — see *Geauga County Democrat*]
Cleveland Herald, 1869–May 8, 19, 22, 27; June 1, 2, 3, 30; July 1, 6, 9; August 2, 3, 6, 7, 9, 10, 13, 23, 24, 26; September 4, 28, 30; October 7, 11
Cleveland Leader, 1869–June 2, 3; October 11
Cleveland Plain Dealer, 1869–June 3; July 2, 7, 9, 10; August 2, 27
Geauga County Democrat, 1869–August 18.
Painesville Telegraph, 1869–September 9, 16, 30; October 4, 14, 21

301

1870

Cleveland Herald, 1870–April 25; May 2, 11, 13, 16, 18, 21, 24, 27, 30, 31; June 1, 3, 4, 17, 21, 28; July 5, 6, 8, 12, 14, 15, 28; August 2, 5, 7, 19, 26; September 1, 5, 7, 19, 24; October 17

Cleveland Plain Dealer, 1870–June 2, 4, 7; July 30; October 8; November 5, 7

Fort Wayne Daily Democrat, 1870–June 2, 16, 29

Fort Wayne Gazette, 1870–June 16, 20; July 4

1871

[Akron — see *Summit County Beacon*]

Cleveland Herald, 1871–April 24; May 3, 4, 6, 10, 11, 12, 22, 25, 27, 30; June 13; July 6, 7, 10, 21, 22 23, 25, 28; August 11, 14; September 4, 5, 23, 28; October 2, 10, 11

Cleveland Leader, 1871–April 5; May 4, 5, 8, 9, 12, 19

Cleveland Plain Dealer, 1871–May 5, 12

Fort Wayne Gazette, 1871–May 4, 5, 9

Fort Wayne Sentinel, 1871–April 10, 19; May 4, 10

Spirit of the Times, 1871–April 8; May 13

Summit County Beacon (Akron), 1871–August 2

1872

Cleveland Herald, 1872–January 3; February 2; March 19, 21; April 20, 30; May 14, 16, 17; June 3, 6, 17, 24; August 3, 5, 10, 19, 20

Cleveland Leader, 1872–May 23, 25; June 1, 3; August 19, 20

Cleveland Plain Dealer, 1872–June 3; July 8, 12, 26; August 2, 20; September 2

Spirit of the Times, 1872–March 9

1873–1877

Cleveland Herald, 1873–June 7, 9; August 9

Cleveland Plain Dealer, 1873–July 10

Cleveland Herald, 1874–June 2; August 24, 25

Cleveland Leader, 1874–August 24, 25

Cleveland Plain Dealer, 1874–August 25; September 10

Cleveland Herald, 1875–June 10, 26

Cleveland Herald, 1876–May 19, 23, 24, 30

Cleveland Plain Dealer, 1876–August 23, 25

Cleveland Herald, 1877–May 17, 28, 29; June 1

Cleveland Leader, 1877–May 29, 30, 31

1878

Cleveland Herald, 1878–May 3

Cleveland Leader, 1878–May 7, 8, 9, 10, 11, 16, 18, 25, 30, 31; June 1, 4, 5, 11, 12, 13, 15, 19, 20, 25, 26; July 2, 5, 15, 19, 24, 25, 27, 31; August 1, 2, 7, 15, 21, 22, 24, 26, 27, 28, 29; September 4, 16, 17, 18, 19, 20; October 4

Cleveland Plain Dealer, 1878–May 2, 6

1879

Cleveland Herald, 1879–August 13, 16

Cleveland Leader, 1879–March 11, 12, 13, 18; April 3, 23, 24, 25, 26, 28, 29, 30; May 1, 2, 3, 5, 19, 26, 28; June 7, 11, 13, 16, 18, 23; July 18, 22, 25, 27; August 26, 28, 29; September 11, 25, 26

Cleveland Plain Dealer, 1879–March 31; May 3, 22

1880

Cleveland Leader, 1880–March 3, 31; April 2, 8, 14, 27; May 1

Cleveland Plain Dealer, 1880–March 16, 30; April 5, 6, 9, 12, 16, 19, 22; May 3, 14, 18, 28; June 3, 11, 12, 14, 15, 17, 23; July 1, 15, 19; August 12, 31; September 4, 9, 11, 23, 25; October 21

1881

Cleveland Herald, 1881–May 6; July 5

Cleveland Leader, 1881–March 11, 16; May 6; June 27; July 5; August 3, 4, 8, 13, 16, 17, 30; September 1, 2, 19, 20, 29

Cleveland Plain Dealer, 1881–March 23, 25; April 11, 15, 16, 23, 27; May 7, 9 30; June 24, 25; July 5, 6, 18, 20; August 3, 4, 8, 13, 16, 17, 30; September 1 2, 19, 20, 29

1882

Cleveland Herald, 1882–May 2; July 25; August 30; September 12, 14, 19, 23; October 2, 3, 4, 5, 7, 20, 24

Cleveland Leader, 1882–March 29; April 10, 19; July 5, 25; August 31; September 1, 2, 4, 6; October 10

Cleveland Plain Dealer, 1882–April 7, 10, 21, 22, 25; May 6, 24; June 8, 15; July 14, 17, 19, 25, 28

1883

Cleveland Gazette, 1883–September 8, 29; October 13, 27

Cleveland Herald, 1883–September 14

Cleveland Leader, 1883–March 13, 15, 28, 30; April 12, 19, 23, 26, 28, 30; May 2, 4, 5, 7, 9, 10, 11, 16, 18, 23, 29, 30; June 4, 28; July 3, 10, 18, 20, 25; August 5, 8, 9, 10, 12, 14, 16, 18, 20, 23; September 11, 14, 23, 24, 28; October 28

New York Clipper, 1883–October 13

1884

Cleveland Gazette, 1884–April 12

Cleveland Herald, 1884–March 28; April 3, 5, 6, 9, 10, 11, 21, 23, 24, 25, 27, 29; May 3, 4, 9, 18, 22, 28, 29; June 4, 10, 13, 14, 18, 19, 22, 27; July 3, 4, 17, 18, 28, 30; August 9, 10, 23; September 7, 14; October 1, 9, 13

Cleveland Plain Dealer, 1884–March 3, 18, 21; May 22

1885–1886

Cleveland Leader, 1885–March 2, 27; April 12, 21, 23; May 1, 2, 17, 18, 24; June 5, 7, 27; September 11, 19
Cleveland Plain Dealer, 1885–April 12, 20, 21; May 18, 20, 21, 25, 29; June 17
Cleveland Press, 1885–September 4, 8, 17
Sporting Life, 1885–April 8
Cleveland Herald, 1886–April 11
Cleveland Leader, 1886–August 18

1887

Cleveland Leader, 1887–January 30; February 22, 27; April 4; July 3; August 21
Cleveland Plain Dealer, 1887–April 2, 4, 5, 8, 10, 11, 12, 13, 14, 16, 17, 19, 20, 21, 25, 26, 28, 30; May 1, 4, 5, 6, 7, 9, 22; June 15, 18, 21, 22, 27, 28, 29; July 1, 3, 5, 15, 16, 23, 25; August 19, 22, 23, 24, 26; September 2, 14; October 4, 10, 15, 17, 25, 27, 28
Cleveland Press, 1887–January 4, 21
Cleveland Town Topics, 1887–December 17
Sporting Life, 1887–January 5, 12; February 9; March 2, 16, 30; April 6, 7, 20; May 4; August 24

1888

Cleveland Leader, 1888–July 19, 22
Cleveland Plain Dealer, 1888–March 1, 12, 19, 20; April 7, 8, 10, 11, 12, 14, 15 21, 23, 24, 28; May 1, 2, 3, 6, 8, 9, 11, 19, 20, 21, 23, 25, 26, 27, 29, 30, 31; June 1, 7, 8, 9, 10, 13, 16, 17, 18, 19, 21, 22, 23, 27, 30; July 1, 2, 4, 7, 9, 10, 11, 13, 14, 15, 16, 17, 21, 23, 24, 25, 27, 28; August 1, 3, 5, 6, 10, 11, 15, 16, 19; September 1, 2, 3, 6, 17, 21, 22, 24, 25, 26, 29; October 2, 8, 10, 12, 15, 22, 23, 28
Sporting Life, 1888–July 18

1889

Cleveland Gazette, 1889–June 1
Cleveland Leader, 1889–April 3, 6, 8, 9; May 9, 27; August 4, 10, 22; September 13, 21; November 11, 20, 22
Cleveland Plain Dealer, 1889–January 20; March 3, 9, 11, 12, 13, 14, 16, 17, 18, 19, 20, 21, 22, 25, 26; April 1, 3, 6, 11, 13, 18, 23, 25, 27, 28; May 2, 4, 5, 6, 8, 12, 13, 15, 27; June 10, 23, 28, 29; July 4, 5, 7, 16, 23; August 11, 12, 23; September 8, 9, 10, 12, 14, 16, 17, 26, 29; October 5, 15, 17, 18, 19, 20, 22, 25, 27
Cleveland Press, 1889–May 9; September 24, 27, 30
Sporting Life, 1889–May 1, 22

1890

Akron Daily Beacon, 1890–March 25
Cleveland Leader, 1890–March 1, 9, 13, 15; April 9, 12, 13, 18; May 1; June 6, 20, 26; August 16; October 11, 12, 17
Cleveland Plain Dealer, 1890–January 5, 6, 8, 9, 14, 22, 26, 27; February 7, 8, 9, 17, 28; March 6, 11, 15, 16, 17, 18, 19, 22, 24, 25, 26; April 1, 5, 6, 7, 9, 10, 11, 12, 14, 17, 18, 19, 24, 26, 28, 30; May 1, 6, 8, 13, 18, 20, 22, 23, 24, 25, 29; June 1, 2, 3, 5, 6, 14, 16, 23, 26; July 2, 3, 4, 5, 7, 14, 18, 25, 27, 29; August 2, 7, 14, 18, 29; September 2, 16; October 5, 7, 8, 9, 24; November 1, 22; December 17
Cleveland Press, 1890–January 10, 11; February 17; April 11, 12, 18, 19, 25; August 7
Cleveland World, 1890–May 1, 2
Sporting Life, 1890–May 3
Sporting News, 1890–January 11; March 1, 22; April 5, 12; May 3; September 6; August 2, 9, 23

1891

Cleveland Leader, 1891–April 12, 15, 27; May 2; August 3; October 15
Cleveland Plain Dealer, 1890–November 25; December 3
Cleveland Plain Dealer, 1891–February 12; March 25, 26; April 14, 28; May 1, 2, 9, 16, 21, 22, 23; June 4, 7, 8, 13, 20, 22, 23; July 12, 28; August 19, 22; September 18, 26, 29, 30; October 11, 14, 15
Cleveland Press, 1891–April 16, 20, 28; May 1
Sporting Life, 1891–April 18; May 2, 23; June 13; July 18; August 8, 15, 27; September 19, 27; October 31

1892

Cleveland Gazette, 1892–August 6
Cleveland Leader, 1892–October 12, 16, 17, 18
Cleveland Plain Dealer, 1892–February 24; March 8, 11, 13, 15, 19, 22, 27; April 21; July 5; August 1, 2, 30; October 12, 16, 18, 19, 20, 21, 22, 23, 25
Cleveland Press, 1892–February 24; March 13, 17, 25, 28, 29; April 21; May 10, 11, 23, 24; June 7, 11, 16, 17, 18, 20; July 5, 6, 7, 24; August 2, 15, 16, 17, 18, 26; September 1, 6; October 1, 12, 16, 18

1893

Cleveland Leader, 1893–April 28; May 5, 6; June 7, 27; July 5
Cleveland Plain Dealer, 1893–July 4
Cleveland Press, 1893–March 14, 16, 22, 28, 29; April 7, 8, 14, 28; May 4, 5, 8, 10, 11, 13; June 1, 9, 19, 25, 26, 27, 29; July 4, 6, 7, 11, 19, 25; August 14, 28; September 2, 19, 20, 22, 24, 26; October 3, 5, 7, 9, 11, 15

1894

Cleveland Leader, 1894–May 3
Cleveland Plain Dealer, 1894–May 4, 31; July 5; September 30; October 1

Cleveland Press, 1894–March 12, 13, 15, 18, 20, 22, 23, 27; April 2, 3, 11, 15, 16; May 3, 5, 6, 7, 17, 21, 26, 28, 31; June 1, 2, 4, 11, 17; July 5, 25, 31; August 6, 9, 10, 12, 24; September 14, 19, 24; October 4, 11
Cleveland World, 1894–May 4

1895

Cleveland Plain Dealer, 1895–May 2; June 25; July 5, 17, 18, 21; August 22, 26, 31; October 4, 5, 6
Cleveland Press, 1895–February 9; March 15, 29; April 8, 11, 14, 17, 19, 25; May 1, 6, 15, 23; June 6, 10, 12, 14, 17, 18, 20, 24, 26; July 5, 15, 17, 22, 31; August 21, 31; September 9, 13, 15; October 8, 9, 13, 15

1896

Cleveland Leader, 1896 -September 18, 26, 27, 28; October 2, 6, 9, 15
Cleveland Plain Dealer, 1896–April 17, 30; May 3; June 26, 27, 28; July 1, 3, 4, 5; October 3, 4, 6, 8, 9
Cleveland Press, 1896–March 10, 16, 24, 27, 30; April 6, 8, 10, 11, 13, 14, 17; May 2, 16, 30; June 4, 5, 9, 16, 18, 22, 24, 25, 26, 29, 30; July 1, 2, 3, 4, 18, 22, 24, 31; August 21, 26, 29; September 1, 3, 10, 13, 15, 16, 17, 20, 22, 24, 27

1897

Chicago Tribune, 1897–June 25, 27; July 4
Cleveland Leader, 1897–March 2; April 30
Cleveland Plain Dealer, 1897–March 4, 5, 6, 10, 14, 15, 16, 17, 19, 20, 24, 28, 31; April 5, 6, 11, 13, 15, 16, 18, 19, 21, 22, 23, 24, 30; May 6, 10, 11, 13, 15, 16, 17, 22, 29; June 2, 5, 7, 10, 11, 14, 18; July 1, 4, 10, 12, 13, 18, 19, 24, 25, 27, 31; August 2, 6, 17, 19, 24, 27, 31; September 5, 6, 14, 19, 30; October 2, 6, 7, 9
Cleveland Press, 1897–July 12
New York Times, 1897–June 17
Washington Post, 1897–May 17

1898

Cleveland Leader, 1898–June 13, 19, 25, 26
Cleveland Plain Dealer, 1898–March 2, 6, 7, 11, 20, 21, 22, 25, 26, 28, 30; April 30; June 12, 13, 17, 27; July 1, 12, 15, 18, 21, 24, 25, 31; August 5, 12, 14; September 8, 14, 30; October 2, 3, 9, 10, 12, 13, 15, 16, 17
Cleveland Press, 1898–April 11, 18, 19, 21, 30; May 28, 31; June 15, 20, 27
Sporting Life, 1898–June 18; July 2

1899

Cleveland Leader, 1899–May 6, 16
Cleveland Plain Dealer, 1899–April 16; May 2, 6, 8, 10, 14, 16, 18, 31; June 8, 10, 17, 19, 20; July 12; August 27, 28, 30, 31; September 9; October 11, 14
Cleveland Press, 1899–April 1; May 16

1900

Cleveland Leader, 1900–April 27; July 5
Cleveland Plain Dealer, 1900–April 21, 25, 27; May 10; July 3, 5, 23; August 3, 7; September 3, 7, 17, 19, 23
Cleveland Press, 1900–July 5

Index

For Cleveland baseball teams see listing: Cleveland baseball clubs.
For any other baseball team see specific city BBC (Base Ball Club).

A. Du Maurier (actor/role) 232
"A la militaire" 12
A.A.U. *see* American Amateur Union
Abbey, ____ 290
Abbott, ____ (Cleveland law director) 263
Abecco, Sig 83
"Academy" BBC *see* Collamer "Academy" BBC
Academy of Music (Baltimore) 257
Accommodation Line Co. (paddle wheeler) 39
"Active" BBC *see* Kent "Active" BBC; Lowellville "Active" BBC
Ad: baseball 186
Ada College BBC 122
Adams, ____ 11
Adams, ____ (black) 232
Adams, C. (black) 173
Adams & Ford 74
Addison, May 93
Adelbert College 225
"Adelbert College" BBC *see* Cleveland baseball clubs
"Adelbertians" 232
"Adventures in Baxter Street" 151
"Aetnas" BBC *see* Chicago "Aetnas" BBC
A. F. Drake Co. 146, 155, 157, 158, 173, 185
Agricultural Society (Ashtabula County) 29
A. I. Root Co. 14
Ainsworth, ____ 14
Akron "Akrons" BBC 12, 13, 15, 19, 26, 132
Akron BBC 76, 96, 102, 109, 113, 133, 134, 184, 217
Akron "Chipewa Indian Club" BBC 224
Akron depot 135
Akron "Excelsiors" BBC 12
Akron—new grandstand (1890) *see* Baseball grounds: Akron Grounds—new grandstand (1890)
Akron, OH 12, 15, 101, 132, 135, 147, 179, 183, 224, 280
Akron "Orientals" BBC (black) 39

Akron-Cleveland "Colts" Reserve BBC 132, 135
Akronites 12
Al Spalding's "All Americans" 270
Alabama Street (E. 28th) 203
Alaska 17
Alaska (steamship) 83
Albany BBC (NY) 96
Albany, NY 160
Albert Spalding Co. 78, 98, 18, 184
Albert Spalding tours 169–171, 270
Alberts, Gus 156, 158, 165
"Albions" BBC *see* Cleveland baseball clubs
Alcorn, ____ 9, 10
Alden, ____ 14
"Alerts" BBC *see* Bellevue "Alerts" BBC; Cleveland baseball clubs; Detroit "Alerts" BBC; Rochester, NY "Alerts" BBC
Alexander, ____ 12, 93
"All America" *see* Albert Spalding tours
"All American" BBC *see* Cleveland baseball clubs
All girls' team 173
"All Irish" BBC *see* Cleveland baseball clubs: "All Irish" BBC
"All on Account of Eliza" (song) 107
Alle, ____ 11
"Alleged Clevelands" BBC *see* Cleveland baseball clubs
"Allegheny" BBC *see* Pittsburgh "Allegheny" BBC
Allegheny Mountains 33
Allen, Clarence (doctor) 75
Allen, Florence 75
Allen, Myron 148–151, 153
Allentown, PA 159
"Alliance" *see* National "League Alliance"
Alliance, OH 13
Alliance, OH BBC 209
Alligator tooth *see* Mascottes
Allison, ____ 42
Allison, Arthur 33, 34, 36–38, 42, 48–52, 56–59, 61, 69, 70, 77, 78
Allison, Douglas 34, 48
The Altogether (actor/role) 232
Altoona, PA 135

Altoona, PA BBC (UA) 130, 135
Alvord, Billy 197, 198, 220
A.m. Palmer (actor/role) 232
Amateur Ball 199
Amateur Champions 172
"Amazonian affliction" 92
America (U.S.) 23, 27, 54, 75, 93, 94, 135, 183
"America" BBC *see* Cleveland baseball clubs
"American" 33
American (Seville restaurant) 14
American Amateur Union 203, 206, 207
American Association 113, 122, 130–132, 134, 138, 139, 144, 146, 147, 153, 155, 159–162, 166–169, 179–181, 193, 204, 278, 279, 291
American culture 152
American flag(s) 169, 196, 203
American House (hotel) 285
American House (Norwalk restaurant) 17
American Indian 259, 268, 280
American League 140, 207, 258, 281, 282, 287, 289
American League cities 281
American League president 287
American Leaguers 284
American public 62
American Revolution 15
American Sportsman 190
American Wire Works Co. 200
Americans in Europe 169, 170
"Anchors" BBC *see* Berea "Anchors" BBC
"Anchors" BBC *see* Seville "Anchors" BBC
Andrews, Jim 186
Andrus, ____ 222
Angel, ____ 12
Ann Arbor College BBC (MI) 109
Anson, Adrian ("Cap;" "Pop") 59, 62, 80, 81, 107, 108, 121, 133, 134, 170, 174, 185, 186, 215, 216, 245
Antietam, GA 66
Anti–Sunday ball movement 274
Anti–Sunday games 262, 263
Appomattox, VA 5
"Arcade" BBC *see* Cleveland baseball clubs

305

Index   306

The Arch (tavern) 105
"Arctics" BBC *see* Norwalk "Arctics" BBC
Ardner, Joseph 114, 132–135, 186
Arkansas 242, 260
"Article 47" (play) 158
Arundel, ____ 114, 132
Ashland, OH 15
Ashland, PA 224
Ashland "Washingtons" BBC 15
Ashtabula "Ashtabulas" BBC 274, 280
Ashtabula County 11, 29, 100
Ashtabula, OH 7, 15, 274, 280
Ashtabula "Union(s)" BBC 29
Association *see* National Association of Base Ball Players; Western Reserve Base Ball Association
Association Grounds *see* Baseball grounds: Case Commons (1868–1870); Baseball grounds: Forest City Grounds (1871, 1872, NA)
Association headquarters 67; *see also* National Association
Association Park *see* Baseball grounds: Cleveland Base Ball Park (1887, 1888 AA; 1889, 1890 NL)
"Asylum" BBC *see* Newberg "Asylum" BBC
Athey, Jay L. (attorney/councilman/umpire) 142, 164
Athletic Park *see* Baseball grounds: East Madison (E. 79th) and Cedar Grounds
Athletic Park (Indianapolis IN) *see* Baseball grounds
"Athletics" BBC *see* Cleveland baseball clubs; Hartsville "Athletics" BBC; Indianapolis "Athletics" BBC; Painesville "Athletics" BBC; Philadelphia "Athletics" BBC
"Athletics-second" BBC *see* Painesville "Athletics-second" BBC
Atlanta, GA 140, 196, 215, 227
Atlantic City, NJ 277
"Atlantics" BBC *see* Brooklyn, NY "Atlantics" BBC; Cleveland baseball clubs; London, Can. "Atlantics" BBC
Auburn College (AL) 260
Austin, ____ 28
Austin, TX 183
Austinburg, OH 29
Aveline House (hotel) 55
Avenue Hotel (Hot Springs, AR) 242, 260, 271

Babcock, ____ 12
Babcock & Wilcox Co. 195
"Babes" *see* Cleveland baseball clubs: "Blues" (AA-1887), "Lakeshores" (AL-1900), "Spiders" (NL-1889)
"Babies" *see* Cleveland baseball clubs: "Blues" (AA-1887), "Lakeshores" (AL-1900), "Spiders" (NL-1889)
Bachelor, J.E. 154
Baehr, ____ 222
"Baehrs" BBC *see* Cleveland baseball clubs
Baggott, Mr. *see* Mr. Baggott (actor/role)
Bagtown Clarion 239
Bakely, Edward "Jersey" 156, 157, 159, 160, 165–167, 173–175, 182, 190
Baker, ____ 18, 282, 289, 290
"Balance of Power" BBC *see* Cleveland baseball clubs
Baldwin, Charles "Lady" 170, 171
Baldwin, Clarence "Kid" 148, 149
Balks 244
"Ball Game Today" (banner) 148
Balloon ascension (manned) 8, 189
Baltimore and Potomac train station 113
Baltimore BBC (AA) 113, 131, 164, 165, 168, 204
Baltimore BBC (AL) 291
Baltimore BBC (NL) 209, 211, 229, 233, 234–236–244, 250–258, 264, 265, 267, 269, 270, 276, 279
Baltimore BBC (UA) 130, 139
Baltimore, Lords BBC 66–71
Baltimore, MD 56, 139, 251, 252, 276, 291
Baltimore "Pastimes" BBC 53, 62
Baltimore players (1896 NL team) 257
Baltimore public 257
Bancroft, Frank 12, 124
Bandelin, ____ 289
Bands 230, 271; brass 187, 205, 206, 223, 247; military band 266; sixteen-piece brass band 196, 197; *see also* Brainard's Band; Great Western Band; Messer's Band; Papworth's Band; "Southern colored boys;" Weber's Band (Cincinnati); White Sewing Machine Band
Bank Street (W. 6th) 67, 74, 129
"Bannakers" BBC *see* Cleveland baseball clubs (black)
Bares, ____ 287
Barn ball 3
Barnum, G. W. (umpire) 173, 175
Barnum, Phineas T. 152
Barnum's elephants 147
Barr, ____ 55
Barr, ____ (doctor) 180
Barron, O. G. 183
Barrows, ____ (professor/umpire) 10
Barry, ____ (reverend) *see* Berry, ____ (reverend)
Bascom, ____ (scorer) 31
"Base Ball" (poem) 29
"Base Ball Grand Championship Game!" 69
Base Ball in a Farm Town 14

Baseball clubs (BBC) *see* individual city
Baseball Encyclopedia 103
Baseball grounds: Akron Grounds–new grandstand (1890) 184; Albions Grounds 217; Association Grounds *see below* Case Commons (1868–1870 IND) *and* Forest City Base Ball Grounds (1871, 1872 NA); Association Park *see below* Cleveland Base Ball Park; Athletic Park *see below* East Madison (E. 79th) and Cedar Grounds; Athletic Park (Indianapolis) *see below* Indianapolis Athletic Park; Baltimore Union Park 239, 252; Berea Fair Grounds 99; Beyerle Amusement Park 151, 163, 167, 168, 171–173, 184, 191; Bicycle Park *see below* East Madison (E. 79th) and Cedar Grounds; Boston Congress Street Grounds 226; Boston South End Grounds 213, 226, 233; Brighton Grounds 172; Brooklyn, NY Eastern Park 203; Brooklyn Park (Cleveland) 140–144; Brotherhood Park 185–187, 189, 190, 193, 194, 200, 217; Buffalo Brotherhood Park 193; C.A.C. Grounds *see below* Cleveland Athletic Club Grounds; Canton Pastime Park Grounds 170; Capitoline Grounds (Brooklyn, NYC) 48; Case Commons (1868–1870 IND; Association Grounds #1) 23, 32, 33, 36, 39, 41, 50, 52, 54, 74–76, 84, 88, 93, 116; Chagrin Falls Washington Park 166; Chicago Grounds 247; Cincinnati Union Grounds 40, 55; Cleveland Athletic Club Grounds 203, 206; Cleveland Base Ball Grounds (League Park #3, 1891–1899, NL, 1900, AL) 194, 195, 197, 202, 205, 207, 209–211, 216, 225, 226, 232, 235, 236, 238, 243, 250, 261, 268, 270, 273, 276, 279–283, 286, 288; Cleveland Base Ball Park (Association Park 1887, 1888 AA; League Park #2 1889, 1890 NL) 144–147, 155, 160, 163, 186, 189, 190, 192, 193; Cleveland Driving Park *see below* East Madison (E. 79th) and Cedar Grounds; Detroit Recreation Park 111; East Madison (E. 79th) and Cedar Grounds (a.k.a. Athletic Park, Bicycle Park, Cleveland Driving Park and YMCA Park) 75, 140, 146, 153, 203; Eastern Park (Brooklyn, NY) *see above* Brooklyn, NY Eastern Park; Euclid Beach Amusement Park 263, 270, 273–275; Exposition Park (Pittsburgh) *see below* Pittsburgh Exposition Park; Forest

Index

City Base Ball Grounds (1871, 1872, NA; Association Grounds #2) 59, 60, 63, 71 74, 84; Forest City Park (formerly Beyerle Park) 209, 217, 268; Foster's Grounds 162, 171; Geauga Lake Grounds 164–166; Grand River Grounds (Lake County) 7; Hedges Grove-East Market Street Grounds (Mansfield) 14, 15; Hot Springs, AK Whittington Park 242, 271; Indianapolis Athletic Park 173; Jefferson Fair Grounds (Ashtabula County) 29; Kansas City "Cowboys" Grounds (1888 AA) 161; Kennard Street Base Ball Park (1878 IND, 1879–1884 NL; League Park #1 1879–1884) 86, 87, 88, 91, 92, 96, 102, 105, 116, 123, 126–128, 132, 139, 140, 142, 143; Kinsman Grounds (1865–1867) 5, 7, 8, 12, 19–21, 33; League Park #1 (1879–1884) *see above* Kennard Street Ball Park (1878 IND 1879–1884 NL); League Park #2 (1889, 1890) *see above* Cleveland Base Ball Park (1889, 1890 NL); League Park #3 (1891–1900) *see above* Cleveland Base Ball Grounds (1891–1899 NL, 1900 AL); Louisville, KY League Park 245; Madison and Cedar Grounds *see above* East Madison (E.79th) *and* Cedar Grounds; Marietta College Athletic Grounds 222; National Association Grounds *see above* Forest City Base Ball Grounds (1871, 1872, NA); Newberg Athletic Grounds 162, 217; Norwalk Fair Grounds 16, 22; Old-River Bed Grounds 146, 171, 224; Pittsburgh Exposition Park 215, 218; Presque Island Grounds 157; Ravenna Driving Park Grounds (racetrack) 9, 10; Ravenna Fair Grounds 10; Ridgewood Park NJ 168; Rubber Works Grounds 172; Scenic Amusement Park 244, 266; Seville Grounds 14; Shamrocks Grounds 171; South End Grounds (Boston) *see above* Boston South End Grounds; Stones Flats Grounds 84; Union Park (Baltimore) *see above* Baltimore Union Park; Washington Park (Chagrin Falls, OH) *see above* Chagrin Falls Washington Park; West Federal Street *see below* Youngstown Baseball Grounds; West Side Park *see below* Youngstown West Side Park; Willoughby Grounds 225; Woodland Hills Park 84, 244; YMCA Park *see above* East Madison (E. 79th) and Cedar Grounds; Youngstown Baseball Grounds (West Federal Street) 136; Youngstown West Side Park 179

Baseball tournaments: Bucyrus 121, 122; Cincinnati 23; Fremont 52; Jefferson 29; Medina 23; Norwalk 21; Ravenna 10; Seville 14
Basketball 230
Bass, John E. 56, 58, 61
Bastian, Charley 188, 189
Bates, Elmer E. 164
Bates, Frank 278
Battering ram Bob 112
Battin, Joe 140–143
Bauer, Al (umpire) 154
"Bay City" BBC *see* Sandusky "Bay City" BBC
Bay Citys (soccer) 193
B.B.A. *see* Boston Athletic Association
Bean Town boys (Boston) 226
"Beaneaters" BBC *see* Boston "Beaneaters" BBC (NL)
Beatin, Ed 159, 174, 176, 185, 186
Beckley, Jake 269
Beckman, Henry 142
"Bed Ticks" BBC *see* Painesville "Bed Ticks" BBC
Bedford "Ivanhoes" BBC 20
Bedford "Mayflowers" BBC 20
Beecher Street 197, 205
Beefsteak Club 186
Beeman, Doc 181
Beeman Chewing Gum Co. 181
Beer and Whiskey League 113
Belated Pilgrims 251
Belden, Ira 269, 270
"Belfast Spider" *see* Weir, Ike "Belfast Spider" (pugilist)
Bell, _____ 164, 172
Bell, _____ (senator) 216
Bell, George (umpire) 157
Bell, Georgia 93
Bell, J. 15
Bell, Robert 160
Bell, William 161
Bellevue "Alerts" BBC 21
Bellevue, OH 213
Benett & Fish Co. 185
"Benicia" BBC *see* Cleveland baseball clubs
Bennedict, Platt 15
Bennett, _____ 17
Bennett, Charlie 100, 111, 115, 120, 176, 214, 215
"Benton, Myers and Canfield" BBC ("Pills") *see* Cleveland baseball clubs
Berchtold, _____ 172
Berea "Anchors" BBC 99
Berea "Stars" BBC 93
Berea "Zephyr" BBC 84
Berry, _____ (reverend) 274–276
Berry, Tom 27
Bestor, G. 11
Bestor, H. 11
Betts, (umpire) _____ 231
Beyerle, George William 167, 172
Beyerle Amusement Park *see* Baseball grounds

Bible 262
Bickle, _____ 11
Bicycle Park *see* Baseball grounds: East Madison (E. 79th) and Cedar Grounds
Bierbauer, Lou 157, 158, 282, 284, 286
Big Bonanza Beerguzzling Association 102
Big Consolidated Streetcar Company 274
"Big four" (ball players) 169
Bigben, _____ (black) 224
A Big-Time Social Game 13
Bill, Pawnee 259
Billings, _____ 38
Billingsgate 239
"Billy Voltz's Luck" 134
"Birds" BBC (Lord Baltimores) 68
Birdsall, Dave 28
Birmingham, AL 140
Birthplace of the Players League 181
"Bisons" BBC *see* Buffalo "Bisons" BBC (NL)
Black, Charles (black) 163, 172
Black, Charley 222
Black crepe 157
"Black list" 136
"Black Maria" (hearse) 68
Black River (Elyria, OH) 83
"Black Stockings" BBC *see* St. Louis "Black Stockings" BBC (black)
"Blackberriwyne row" (booster club) 125, 129
Blackstone Building 191
Blake, Harry 227, 235–241, 244, 247, 252–256, 260, 261, 270, 275
Blake, S. L. (reverend) 92
Blanchard, _____ 17
"Bloody Lions" BBC *see* Wapokeneta "Bloody Lions" BBC
"Blue Stockings" BBC *see* Cleveland baseball clubs (black); Philadelphia "Blue Stockings" BBC (female); Toledo "Blue Stockings" BBC
"Blue Stockings" Forest City BBC *see* Cleveland baseball clubs
"Blues" BBC (1901 AL) *see* Cleveland baseball clubs
"Blues" BBC (AA) *see* Cleveland baseball clubs
Blymer, G.W. 15
Boake, John L. (umpire) 56, 57
Boats 210
"Bohemians" BBC *see* Cleveland baseball clubs
Bohen, _____ 74
Bohn, _____ 78, 79
Bohn, Billy 84, 93, 98, 132, 133, 159
Bohn, Charley 98, 152, 162
Bohn, Johnny 44
Bolton Avenue 154
Bond, _____ 91
Bond Street (E. 6th) 181
Bordeaux, France 135

Index

Boston Athletic Association 210
Boston BBC (AA) 204
Boston BBC (AL) 291
Boston BBC (UA) 131, 136, 139
Boston "Beaneaters" BBC (NL) 81, 84, 91, 96, 100, 113, 130, 131, 139, 151, 159, 176–178, 201–204, 211–215, 217, 218, 221, 226, 233, 243, 246, 250, 270, 278
Boston Congress Street Grounds *see* Baseball grounds
Boston franchise 215
Boston Herald 224
Boston "Lowells" BBC 63
Boston, MA 65, 68, 86, 91, 160, 177, 196, 211, 217, 221, 233, 291
Boston "Red Stockings" BBC (NA) 55, 62, 63, 65, 71, 72
Boston "Reds" BBC (PL) 226
Bouse, _____ 25
Bowerman, Frank 275
Bowler, _____ 37
Bowman, George H. 15
Boyle, _____ 222
Boyle, Jack "Honest Jack" 166, 188, 189, 267
B P Tower site 282
"Brachwitz" BBC *see* Cleveland baseball clubs
Bracy, _____ (black) 127
Bradbier, _____ 25
Bradley, G. H. (umpire) 101, 102, 110
Bradley, George "Grin" 106, 110, 111, 117, 122, 124
Brady, F.M. (secretary) 217
Brady, W. A. 268
Braggin, _____ 282
Brainard, Asa 34, 35, 44, 46, 48, 54
Brainard's Band 160
Branch, _____ 28, 31, 33
Brandenberg, _____ 229
Brass bands *see* Bands
Brassel, _____ 93
Bratt, _____ 40
Brayton, Charles A. 85, 113, 204
Breitenstein, Ted 248–250, 261, 262, 269
Breks, _____ 12
Brennan, Jack 182
Brennan, Jim 189
Brennan, John (umpire) 141, 142
Briar-Hill block coal 9
Bridgeport, CT 147
Bridgeport, CT BBC 147
Bridget, _____ (waitress) 217
Bridgewater, _____ (black) 125
Briggs, Herbert "Buttons" 222, 227, 247
Brighton "Brighton" BBC 17, 27
Brighton Grounds *see* Baseball grounds
Briody, Charles "Fatty" 113, 116–118, 121, 122, 125, 126, 133, 135, 136, 138, 139
British 15
British thread 60
Broadway Avenue (Cleveland) 84, 162

Broadway, New York 83
Broadway Street *see* Broadway Avenue (Cleveland)
Brodie, Steve (ballplayer) 233, 234, 236, 237, 239–241, 252–257
Brodie, Steve (swimmer) 172
Brooklyn (Cleveland area) 140
Brooklyn, NY 56, 258, 264
Brooklyn, NY "Atlantics" BBC 24, 45, 48, 53, 66, 68, 71; flag 24
Brooklyn, NY BBC (AA) 131, 140, 142, 150, 151, 160, 168
Brooklyn, NY "Eckfords" BBC 52, 53, 61, 66, 68, 71
Brooklyn, NY "Stars" BBC 53
Brooklyn, NY "Trolley Dodgers" BBC (NL) 203, 210, 218–220, 229, 234, 258, 267, 279, 280
Brooklyn Park (Cleveland) *see* Baseball grounds
Brooklyn Street Railway (streetcar line) 125, 171, 186
Brooklyn Township 140
Brooklyn Village 140, 217
Brooks, (Brook) _____ (black) 224, 232
Brooks, Lizzie 93
"Brooks Academy" BBC 99
Brooks School 75
Brookside Park 162
Brookside valley 171, 172, 217
Brooksmith, _____ 172
Brotherhood *see* Brotherhood of Professional Base Ball Players
Brotherhood Amateur League 184
Brotherhood Guide *see* Players' League Guide
"Brotherhood Headquarters" 187
Brotherhood magnates 192
Brotherhood of Professional Base Ball Players (Players League) 180–184, 190, 192, 193, 200
Brotherhood Park *see* Baseball grounds
Brotherhood parks 193
Brotherhood players 192
Brotherhood "Quakers" BBC *see* Philadelphia "Quakers" (PL)
Brotherhood War 181
Broughton, Cecil 122
Brouthers, Dan "Big Dan" 123, 169, 176, 178, 218–220
Brower, _____ 172
Brower, Elgie 222
Brown, _____ 12, 16, 93
Brown, _____ (Detroit) 37
Brown, Charles 27
Brown, Harvey 25, 28, 30, 43, 50
Brown, Harvey H. 243
Brown, Lew "Blower" 89, 91
Brown, Tom 170, 171, 176–178, 222, 224
Brown, W. 224
"Brown Stockings" BBC *see* Cleveland baseball clubs; St. Louis "Brown Stockings" BBC (AA)
Brown University 93, 100, 101
Browning, Pete "Gladiator" 147, 181, 182, 188, 189

Brownlee, _____ (manager) 135
Bruce, _____ 11
Bruce's (drug store) 97
Brunell, Frank E. 144, 146, 175, 187, 190, 191
Brunner Bros. of Cleveland 127
Brush, John T. 277
Brush Company (electric) 200
Brussels carpet 185
"Bryan's Bill Posters" BBC *see* Cleveland baseball clubs
Buchtel, _____ 12
Buchtel College 75
Buchtel Hotel 184
Buckenberger, _____ 141, 142
Buckeye State boys 284
"Buckeyes" BBC *see* Cincinnati "Buckeyes" BBC; Streetsboro "Buckeyes" BBC
Buckley, J. J. (president) 285
Buckley, Jim 169
Bucyrus, OH 121, 122; *see also* Baseball tournaments
Buelow, Charley 282–284, 286, 287, 288
Buffalo BBC (AL) 281, 289, 291
Buffalo BBC (IL; 1878) 82
Buffalo Bill *see* Cody, Buffalo Bill
Buffalo Bill Cody *see* Cody, Buffalo Bill
Buffalo "Bisons" BBC (NL) 96, 98, 99, 104, 105, 109, 113, 120, 123, 124, 130, 131, 268
Buffalo "Bisons" BBC (PL) 181, 183, 189, 192
Buffalo boat 268
Buffalo Express 44, 138
Buffalo "Firemen" BBC 84
Buffalo, NY 52, 86, 138, 268
Buffalo "Niagaras" BBC 18, 19, 23, 53
Buffett, _____ 164
Buffington, Charles 190
Bulkely, Charles H. 66, 84, 113, 116
Bulkely, Morgan 86
Bulkely family 113
Bullas, _____ 172
Bullas, Sim "Derby" 162
"Bulletinized" 91
Bumboat women 177
Burch, Ernie 139, 150
Burdock, Jack 91
Burell, _____ 241
Burke, _____ 171, 290
Burke, Eddie 225, 262, 269
Burke, Jimmy 278
Burke, Mike 77
Burkett, Jesse "The Crab" 201, 202, 203, 206–208, 212–214, 216, 218–220, 223–226, 231, 233–241, 242–249, 252, 253, 256, 257, 260, 262, 265, 269–272, 275, 278
Burlington, IA BBC 242
Burlington, ME 268
Burns, _____ 25, 36
Burns, J. H. 184
Burns, Thomas "Oyster" 165, 170
Burns, Tom 108, 121, 174, 186

Burt, _____ 30, 34, 36–38, 40, 42, 43
Burwell, Anson 27
Burwell, Austin 27
Bus 264
Bushong, Albert "Doc" 122–124, 130, 135, 152
"Business" BBC see Oberlin "Business" BBC
"Busters" BBC see Worcester, MA "Busters" BBC
Butcher, J.J. 172
Butler, _____ 9
Butler, PA 163
"Butlers" BBC see Carrollton, OH "Butlers" BBC
Byrne, _____ 164

C & P Railroad see Cleveland & Pittsburg Railroad
Cable car line 185, 273
Cable car parade 215
Cable car powerhouse 206
Cable car train 209
Cable cars 192–194, 195, 196, 205, 223, 285; last run 285
Cable Park 194
"C.A.C." BBC see Cleveland baseball clubs
C.A.C. gymnasium see Cleveland Athletic Club gymnasium
Cadillac Rink 221, 230
Cady, Charles 122
Cairo short line (railroad) 183
"Cal" the scorer 21
"Calamity water" (alcohol) 94
California 96
Callahan, James "Nixey" 279
Cameron, C. (black) 173
Cameron, O.C. 172
Camp, _____ 78
Campbell, _____ 9
Campbell, Harry 222
Campbell, Joe 258
Canada 77
Canal Street 222
"Canaries" (Lord Baltimore BBC) 68
Canfield, (#1)_____ 11
Canfield, (#2)_____ 11
Canter, _____ (black) 127
Cantillion, _____ (umpire) 281, 284, 289
Canton BBC 152, 170, 184, 191, 270
Canton — Champion of 1889 184
Canton "Duebers" BBC 209
Canton, NY 39, 43, 56
Canton, OH 13, 191, 230, 244, 270, 280
Canton Pastime Park see Baseball grounds
Canton Repository 12, 13
Canton "Stark" BBC 12, 13
"Capital" BBC see Indianapolis "Capital" BBC
Capitoline Grounds (Brooklyn, NY) 48
Carabin, _____ 16
"Cardinals" BBC (Western League,

1885) see Cleveland baseball clubs
Carey, George "Scoops" 235–241
Carey, Thomas John 56, 57, 58, 68, 69, 87, 91, 93
Caricature of fans 285
Carleton, James 43, 48, 49, 50, 56, 58, 59
Carpenter, Warren "Hick" 148, 149
"Carpet Baggers" BBC see Cleveland baseball clubs
Carr, _____ 171
Carr, E. A. (general) 143
Carr, Joe (umpire) 160, 161
Carran, T. J. (city attorney) 33
Carrol, Jack 222
Carrol, Mike 86
Carroll, Cliff 136, 186
Carroll, Fred 170, 171
Carroll, John E. 141, 142
Carroll, John "Scrappy" 153, 154
Carroll, Samuel "Cliff" 186
Carrolton, OH "Butlers" BBC 224
Carsey, Wilfred "Kid" 272, 279
Carter, Art "Ike" (black) 127
Cartwright, Alexander 3
Case, _____ 17
Case, Leonard, Jr. 23
Case, Leonard, Sr. 23
Case College 225
"Case College" BBC see Cleveland baseball clubs
Case Commons (1868–1870; Association Grounds #1) see Baseball grounds
"A Case of Swelled Head" (article) 257
Case Street (E. 40th St.) 5, 23, 186
Caskin, John 103
Cassidy, John 80, 103
Castor, _____ 74
Castor's stable 83
Cattaraugus, NY 280
Cattaraugus, NY BBC (Native American) 280
Catoir, Danny 105
Caucasion race 262
Cavell, Charley 222
"C.C.C." BBC see Cleveland baseball clubs
Cedar Avenue 77, 146
Center Street (Ft. Wayne) 55
Central Armory 272
"Central High School" BBC see Cleveland baseball clubs
Central Police Station 83, 142, 279
Central police station (Wheeling, WV) 156
Central Unions 273
"Centrals" BBC see Cleveland baseball clubs
Chadwick, Henry 55
Chagrin Falls Exponent 165, 166
Chagrin Falls "Invincibles" BBC 166
Chagrin Falls, OH 166
Chagrin Falls "Quicksteps" BBC 44
Chamberlain, Elton "Icebox" 205, 206

Chameleons see Mascottes
Champion (dog) 124
"Champion Club of the United States" 41
Champion Jumper and Swimmer of the United States see Brodie, Steve
Champion of 1889 (Canton) see Canton — Champion of 1889
"Champion Young Ladies' base ball club No. 1" 191
Champions of America 25
Champions of Indianapolis (Western League 1899) 288
Champions of the United States 112
Championship banner (newspaper men) 164
Championship baseball game (Press newsboys) 209
Championship of Ohio 215
Championship of the City 250
"Change pitcher" 88
Charleston, SC 159, 183, 215
Charlie 80
Charley Notry's barber shop 125
Chattanooga, TN 215
Chech, _____ 282, 288
"Chester" BBC (Geauga County) 12
Chewing gum sign 175
Chicago BBC "Aetnas" 63, 64
Chicago "Excelsiors" BBC 30
Chicago fans 278
Chicago fire see "Great Chicago Fire"
Chicago Grounds see Baseball grounds
Chicago, IL 43, 48–50, 53, 59, 63, 65, 66, 69, 86, 96, 98, 120, 134, 138, 139, 159, 170, 173, 185, 215, 245, 246, 265, 266, 277, 287, 289
Chicago Journal 49
Chicago (my kind of town...the town that Billy Sunday couldn't shut down) 134
Chicago "Pirates" BBC (PL) 183, 184, 186–189
Chicago players benefit 278
Chicago Tribune 201, 203
Chicago "White Stockings" BBC (AL) 281, 287, 288
Chicago "White Stockings," "Colts," "Orphans" BBC (IND, NA, NL) 48, 49, 50, 53, 55, 59–61, 63, 64, 65, 67, 81, 86, 93, 94, 96, 100, 102, 107–109, 112, 113, 121, 122, 129–131, 133, 134, 155, 170, 171, 174, 179, 185, 186, 191, 201–203, 205, 211, 215–217, 244, 246, 247, 265, 266, 279
Chicagoan 60
Chicagoens 66
"Chicagoed" 52, 94
Chicago-Milwaukee BBC (AA) 204
Chicago-Pittsburg BBC (UA) 131
Chicago's flag (Brotherhood PL) 187

Index

Children's Aid Society 91
Childs, Clarence "Kid" 197–199, 202, 205–208, 211, 213–216, 218–220, 222–226, 231, 235–241, 248, 249, 252–257, 269, 272
"Chin music" 70
"Chipewa Indian Club" BBC 224
Chisolm, William 243
Christendom 255
Churchill, _____ 21
Cigar emporium 200
"Cinched" 250
Cincinnati BBC (AA) 113, 122, 131, 148–150, 155, 168, 179, 180
Cincinnati BBC "Red Stockings" (NL) 81, 84, 85, 86, 95, 99, 104, 105, 192, 193, 196–199, 205, 206, 211, 215, 221, 229, 230, 243, 250, 261, 262, 268, 269, 277
Cincinnati BBC (UA) 131, 132, 138, 139
Cincinnati "Buckeyes" BBC 31, 40, 41
Cincinnati Commercial 58
Cincinnati Enquirer 138, 147, 182
Cincinnati "Live Oaks" BBC 57
Cincinnati native 182
Cincinnati, OH 31, 33, 39, 44, 48, 53, 56, 64, 135, 138, 145, 180–182, 191, 193, 198, 201, 221, 229, 230
Cincinnati "Red Stockings" BBC (IND) 31, 33–35, 39, 40, 44, 45, 48, 53, 54, 67, 90
Cincinnati sportswriter 280
Cincinnati tournament 23
Cincinnati way (railroad) 46
Citizens Purse ($200 22-city atlas) 87
City Base Ball League *see* City League
City championship 200
City Hall (Cleveland) *see* Cleveland City Hall
City League (baseball) 163, 167, 171, 172, 184, 244, 250
City of Brotherly Love 193
City of Collinwood 263
City of Detroit (steamship) 110
City of oysters (Baltimore) 251
"City of the Falls" (Louisville) 245
"City of the Straits" (Detroit) 110
Civil War 3, 5, 9, 27, 55, 66
Civil War camp 6
Clapp, _____ 11
Clapp, John 6, 26, 36, 105, 106, 108–110, 123
Clark, _____ 11, 18, 27, 43
Clark Avenue 162, 168
Clarke, _____ 274
Clarke, Fred 245
Clarke, James 18
Clarke, William "Boileryard" 235, 237, 240, 241
Clarkson, John 176, 177, 204, 210, 212–214, 218, 219, 221, 222, 225, 226, 228
Cleve, George 222
Cleveland, Grover (president) 147
Cleveland American League club 215
Cleveland & Pittsburg Railroad 18
Cleveland Association Grounds (1868–1870 IND) *see* Baseball Grounds
Cleveland Association Park (1871–1872 NA) *see* Baseball grounds
Cleveland Athletic Club (C.A.C.) 193, 203, 205, 210, 223
Cleveland Athletic Club (manager/business agent) 281; *see also* Kilfoyl, John
Cleveland Athletic Club gymnasium (C.A.C.) 222, 260
Cleveland BBC (1901 AL) *see* Cleveland baseball clubs: "Blues" (AL-1901)
Cleveland Base Ball Amateur Association 90
Cleveland Base Ball Association 23, 24, 32, 33, 86, 113
Cleveland Base Ball Grounds (1891–1899 NL, 1900 AL, League Park #3) *see* Baseball grounds
Cleveland Base Ball Park: clubhouse 192; description of 145
Cleveland Base Ball Park (1887, 1888 AA; Association Park; 1889, 1890 NL; League Park #2) *see* Baseball grounds
Cleveland baseball clubs: "Adebert College" 144, 184, 189; "Albions" 162, 171, 193, 200, 222, 229; "Alerts" BBC 6, 90; "All American" (Cleveland; spring training) BBC 183; "All Irish" (spring training) 183; "Alleged Clevelands" (Spiders derisive) 207; "Amateur(s)" 19, 44; "Athletics" 19, 44, 159, 184, 251; "Atlantics" 45, 84; "Baehrs" 251, 280; "Balance of Power" 199; "Benicia" 19; "Benton, Myers and Canfield" ("Pills") 76; "Blue Stockings" Forest City *see all below* Forest City Blue Stockings; "Blues" (AA; 1887, 1888) also called "babes," "babies" and "infants" 146–148, 205, 281; "Blues" (1901 AL) 162; "Bohemians" 269; "Brachwitz" 269; "Brooks School" 144; "Brotherhood" ("Electrics;" PL)—(a.k.a. "Infants") 180, 183, 184, 186–189, 191, 192, 193, 201, 216; "Brown Stockings" 75, 84; "Browns" 166; "Bryan's Bill Posters Co." 199; "C.A.C." 203, 217, 221, 222, 280, 281; "Cardinals" (Western League, 1885) 140–143, 155; "Carpet Baggers" 44; "Case College" 189; "C.C.C." 74; "Central High School" 280; "Centrals" 251; "Charter Oaks" 27; "Cleveland Athletic Club" *see above* "C.A.C."; "Cleveland Burial Case Co." 184, 200; "Cleveland, Columbus and Cincinnati" (railroad) *see above* "C.C.C."; "Cleveland Court House Base Ball Club" 39; "Cleveland Twist Drill" 184; "Cleveland Wheel Club" *see below* "C.W.C."; "Colts" (spring training) 242; "Colts" Reserve (Akron-Cleveland) *see* Akron-Cleveland "Colts" Reserve BBC; "Comet"19; "Contest" 19; "Crescents" 144; "Crickets" 90; "Cuyahogas" 19; "C.W.C." 280; "Dailies" (newsmen) 164; "Dashes" 72; "Defiance" 6; "Diamond Rocks" 251; "Dramatics" 19; "Eagle" 6; "East Cleveland" 75; "East High" 75; "Eastern Rocks" 44, 63, 74, 84; "Electrics" 190; "Electrics" Brotherhood (PL) *see above* Brotherhood ("Electrics;" PL); "Eries" 44; "Eurekas" 6; "Excelsiors" 44; "Fakirs" 199; "Fats" 32; "Favorites" 84, 199; "Fifth Ward Snakes" 90; "Fighters" (Spiders' NL nickname) 201; "Fire Department" 99; "Firemen" 84; "Forest City" (amateur) 90, 91, 96, 142, 143, 171–173, 184, 189, 191, 222; "Forest City" (1865–1867 amateur) 5–8, 12, 18–23; Forest City "Blue Stockings" (1868–1870 IND) 23, 25, 26, 28, 30, 31, 33, 34, 36–46, 49–54, 88; Forest City "Blue Stockings" (1871,1872 NA) 55–61, 66–72, 74; Forest City "Blue Stockings" (1878 IND) 77–85; Forest City "Blue Stockings" (1879–1884 NL) 88–92, 94–107, 113, 114, 102, 103, 109, 110, 116–125, 128–140, 142; "Forest City Juniors" *see above* "Eastern Rocks"; "Forest City Troop" 91; "Gattling Gun Nine" (military reserve) 91; "George Worthington Co" 84; "Germania" 152; "Goldsmith, Joseph, Feiss & Co." 184; "Gordons" 217; "Graphics" 144, 151; "Grays" 116; "Grotzingers" 269; "Grove Boys" 90; "Grove Citys" 44, 52; "Growlers" 199; "Gymnasium" (picked nine) 157; "H. R. Jacobs" theatre 171; "Hand-Me Downs" BBC (NL Spiders) 170; "Heavy Bobs" 32; "High School" 75, 99; "High School "Occidentals" *see below* "Occidentals" High School; "Hower and Higbee Co." 84; "Hudsons" 163; "Idlers" 99; "Indians" (AL) 285; "Indians" (amateur) 262; "Indians" (NL 1897, 1898) 259–277, 278, 279, *see also below* "Spiders" (1889–1896 NL) *and* "Misfits" (1899 NL); "Infernals" (Internal Revenue) 18; "Iron Wards" 26, 222; "Ironclads" (Plain Dealer) 26; "Jewelers" 116; "Kennard &

McKinney" 74; "Kennard House" 184; "Kinsman Street" 166; "Kinsmans" 184, 222; "Lakeshore Railroad" 18; "Lakeshores" (AL-1900) 281–290; "Lakesides" 144; "Leans" 32; "Light Bobs" 32; "Little Tycoons" 152; "Main Stars" 222, 224; "Malleable Iron Works" (Malleables) 74, 90, 99, 144, 148, 151, 222; "Marquettes" 268; "Mayflowers" 217; "Mechanics" 19; "Mets" 184; "Misfits" (1899 NL) 278, 279, 280, *see also below* "Spiders" (1889–1896 NL) *and* "Indians" (1897, 1898 NL); "Mohawks" 6; "Murray-Lane Opera Company" (theatre) 229; "Mystics" 19; "Nancy Hanks" 222; "National City Bank Co." 184; "Nationals" 222; "New" 42, 43; "New Phillies" (Cleveland "Indians" NL nickname) 276; "Newsboys" (Plain Dealer) 160, 161; "Niagaras" 44, 84; "Nine Snides" 91; "Nomads" (Cleveland "Indians" NL nickname) 276; "Occidentals" High School 6, 17, 19, 21, 24, 27, 33; "O'Hare, Petty & Bruce" 18; "Old" 42, 43; "Old Leaguers" 209, 217, 222, 226; "Orientals" 39; "Outcast" (Cleveland "Indians" NL nickname) 276; "Outwaites" 217; "Pabst" 251; "Park Theatre troop" 152; "Peconic" 6, 24; "Picked nine" 74, 75, 88, 92, 98; "Picked nine" (spring training) 170; "Pills" (Benton, Myers and Canfield) Co. *see above* "Benton, Myers and Canfield" ("Pills"); "Pinafores" 93; "Pothunters" (Cleveland "Indians" NL nickname) 276; "Pragues" 269; "Press Nine" 90; "Printers" (Cleveland Herald) 26; "Prospects" 184; "Puzzlers" 199; "Quinns" 222, 250, 251; "Railway" *see below* "Union Railway"; "Rattlers" 99; "Red Hots" 25; "Red Jackets" 39; "Red Men" (Indians NL split-squad game) 270; "Red Stockings" 84, 93, 116; Reserve "colts" (Cleveland-Akron) *see* Akron-Cleveland "Colts" Reserve BBC; "Resolutes" 251; "Rhodes Co." BBC 84; "Robison & Sanford Co." 74; "Rocks" 184; "Rockwells" 99; "Rolling Mills" (steel company) 84; "St. Clair machine shop" 74; "St. Edward's" 172; "St. Ignatius" 184; "St. Patrick's" 184; "Sanfords" 144; "Shakespeare" 19; "Shamrocks" 144, 146, 148, 159, 161, 163, 171, 200, 222; "Slow & Easy" 75, 84; "Snide Nine" 91; "Society for Savings Co." 184; "Sockalexis" 262; "Southern Rocks" 90; "Spiders" (1889–1896 NL) 36, 169, 170, 173–181, 183, 185, 186, 189–193, 196–199, 201, 203, 205–215, 217–223, 225–240, 241, 242–251, 253–258, 260, 262, 281, other nicknames: "Clevelands," "babies" and "infants" 175, *see also above* "Indians" (1897, 1898 NL) *and* "Misfits" (1899 NL); "Standard Oil Co." 84, 184; "Standards" 189, 193, 203, 280; "Standards No. 1" 251; "Standards No. 2" 251; "Stars" 6, 90, 202; "Strong Cobb & Co" ("Bad Medicine") 76; "Sunsets" 184; "Tebeau's wandering yannigans" (Cleveland "Indians" NL nickname) 276; "Tramps" (Cleveland "Indians" NL nickname) 276; "Troys" 184; "Union Railway" 6, 18–23, 25, 26, 28, 29, 42; "Unions" 184, 222; "University" 6; "University School" 232, 280; "Vagrants" (Cleveland "Indians" NL nickname) 276; "Vets" (spring training) 242; "Wanderers" (Cleveland "Indians" NL nickname) 276; "Warner & Swasey Co." 184; "Weddell House" 184; "Weeklies" (newsmen) 164; "West End Grays" 143; "West Side Reds" 90; "Western Union Telegraph" 72; "White Caps" 84, 90, 93; White Sewing Machine Co. "Whites" *see below*; "Whites" (White Sewing Machine Co.) 99, 102, 106, 111, 114, 116, 127; "Wideawakes" 199; "Woodlands" 171, 172, 184, 222; "Work House Nine" 90; "X Y Z's" 90; "YMJA" 280; "Young America" 6, 184; "Young Men's Hebrew Association" 229; "Young Clevelands" 184; "Young Green Flags" 199; "Young Idlers" 99; "Young Mens Jewish Association" *see above* "YMJA"; "Young Rattlers" 99; "Young Woodlands" 222; "Yucatans" 217, 222; "Zouves" 19; *see also* Cleveland baseball clubs (black)

Cleveland baseball clubs (black): "Bannakers" 39; "Blue Stockings" 127; "Blue Stockings" (Geneva) *see* Geneva "Blue Stockings" (black) BBC; "Excelsiors" 39; "HAC's" 232, 244; "Handy" 224; "Hollendens" 232, 244; "Hustlers" 224; "Kennard House" 224; "Keystones" 244, 269, 280; "Manhood" 19; "McKinleys" 224; "New colored nine" 93; "Olympics" 74, 76; "Orientals" (Akron) *see* Akron "Orientals" (black) BBC; "Southern Stars" 116; "Twilight" 19; "Unions" 144; "Z's" (Zulus) 163, 171–173, 184, 200

Cleveland baseball company 281
Cleveland baseball team — pen and ink 261
Cleveland Board of City Improvement 32
Cleveland Brotherhood (Players League) 216
Cleveland Burial Case Co. 184
Cleveland Burial Case Co. BBC *see* Cleveland baseball clubs
Cleveland City Council 3, 31, 91, 116, 153, 164
Cleveland City Hall 39, 97, 187
Cleveland City Railway Company 266
"Cleveland Comet" 46
Cleveland Cuyahogan 164
Cleveland Driving Park *see* Baseball grounds: East Madison (E. 79th) and Cedar Grounds
Cleveland Elks club 242
Cleveland Euclid Avenue Opera House 83, 115, 123, 223, 244
Cleveland football team 193
Cleveland Forest City Cricket Club 116
Cleveland franchise slot 140
Cleveland Gazette 209
Cleveland Grand Arcade 128
Cleveland Graphic 164
Cleveland Grays (reserve military) 116
Cleveland Grip 164
Cleveland Herald 3, 12, 18, 20, 21, 29, 33, 36–38 41, 42, 46, 48, 59, 63, 64, 66, 67, 74, 92, 94, 107, 110, 116, 120, 121, 129, 133, 134, 136, 138, 164
Cleveland Indian 73
Cleveland Indians of 1897 267
"Cleveland is nearly done for" (poem) 262
Cleveland jayhawkers (derisive) 170
Cleveland Lacrosse club 200
Cleveland lady cyclist 203
Cleveland lakefront station *see* Cleveland Union Terminal (train depot)
Cleveland "Lakeshores" BBC (AL) 281
Cleveland Leader 8, 18, 22, 33, 42, 58, 72, 74, 76, 81, 89, 90–94, 107, 108, 110, 115, 116, 120, 125, 127–129, 164, 166, 187, 189, 190, 218, 219, 251, 257, 264, 288
Cleveland National Bank 128
Cleveland native 271
Cleveland, OH 3, 5–8, 12, 18–23, 28, 33, 37–39, 42, 44, 46, 54, 59–61, 65, 66, 68, 69, 70, 72–75, 77, 84–86, 93, 95–97, 99, 100, 107, 110, 112, 113, 116, 122, 123, 127, 128, 132, 135–137, 140, 143, 146, 152, 159, 162, 163, 165, 167, 169, 170, 173, 175, 184, 191–193, 201, 202, 211, 215, 221, 223, 227, 232, 235, 237, 239, 243, 244, 247, 251, 260, 262, 267, 268, 273,

274, 279, 280, 282, 284, 287, 289
Cleveland Opening Day (home) 60, 69, 70, 78, 88, 89, 90, 98, 107, 108, 114, 123, 133, 134, 148–150, 157, 158, 174, 185–189, 196–199, 205, 206, 215–217, 223, 224, 230-232, 242, 243, 261, 262, 272, 279, 281, 285, 286
Cleveland Opening Day (road) 67, 78, 107, 132, 173, 196, 205, 215, 223, 230, 242, 261, 272, 279, 282–284
Cleveland Opera House *see* Cleveland Euclid Avenue Opera House
Cleveland Outing Club 285
Cleveland Plain Dealer 19, 25, 33, 38, 49, 54, 81, 90, 97, 98, 110–112, 114–116, 120, 121, 127, 141, 144, 145, 148, 154, 158–161, 163,169, 172, 173, 175, 177, 178, 181, 183, 186, 187, 190, 191, 193, 195, 218, 219, 238, 239, 262, 263, 265, 267, 272, 277, 282, 285, 287, 289
Cleveland players' benefit 278
Cleveland Police 127, 264
Cleveland Police Department 152
Cleveland policemen 102
Cleveland Press 164, 189, 196, 198, 206, 207, 209, 218, 222, 224, 227, 233, 246, 263, 273, 275, 279, 282, 283
Cleveland Press Circle 218, 220, 227
Cleveland Public Library 261
Cleveland School Association 232
Cleveland "Spiders" name (origin of) 175
Cleveland "Spiders" pen and ink illustration (1890) 182
Cleveland stage manager 222
Cleveland style 64
Cleveland Sun & Voice 164
Cleveland Sunday News Leader (illus.) 73
Cleveland Town Topics 164
"Cleveland Twist Drill" BBC *see* Cleveland baseball clubs
Cleveland Twist Drill Co. 200
Cleveland Union Station *see* Cleveland Union Terminal
Cleveland Union Terminal (train depot) 46
Cleveland Universe 164
Cleveland Wanderers (soccer) 193
Cleveland Wheel club 280
"Cleveland Wheel Club" BBC *see* Cleveland baseball clubs: "C.W.C."
Cleveland White Sewing Machine Band 148
Cleveland World 164
Clevelander(s) 37, 46, 48, 49, 66, 71, 88, 111, 119, 148, 168, 281
"Clevelands" *see* Cleveland baseball clubs: "Spiders" (NL)
Cleveland's Fifth Regiment 272
Cleveland's flag (Brotherhood PL) 187

Cleveland's people 269
Cleveland's upper class 281
Clever Inventions 138
Cley, _____ 30
Clifford, _____ 93
Clinton, Massachusetts BBC 92
Clough, _____ (secretary AA) 168
The Club (sports bar) 123
Clubhouse 196
Clugston, _____ 26, 38
"Clumsy" BBC *see* East Cleveland "Clumsy" BBC
Clyde "McPherson" BBC 17
Clyde, OH 17
Coal fortune 281
Cobean, J. 15
Cobean, Jimmy 26
Cobleigh, N. S. 90
Codding, C. G. 14
Cody, Buffalo Bill 143, 144, 259
Cogswell, Ed 102
Cohen, B. 161
Cohen, J. 161
Cole, _____ (black) 224
Cole, W. H. (black) 224
Cole, William (captain; black) 232
Coleman, J. J. 181, 200
Coleman, John 130
"Collamer" (now in Cleveland) 20
Collamer "Academy" BBC 128
Collamer, OH 128
"Collamer Reds" BBC 99
College Athletic Grounds (Marietta, OH) *see* Baseball grounds
Collier's pub 55
Collins, _____ 9, 37
Collins "Hub" 167
Collinwood neighborhood 128
Collinwood Village 274, 275
Collister & Sayle Co. 250, 285
Collister & Sayle cup 250
"Colonels" BBC (NL) *see* Louisville "Colonels" BBC (NL)
Colorado 68
Colored champions of Ohio 270
"Colored spectacles" 153, 199
"Colts" 260.
Columbia "Dexters" BBC 38
Columbiana County 96
Columbus BBC 122
Columbus BBC (AA) 131, 132, 139, 169, 179
Columbus Day parade 213
Columbus "Independents" BBC 79, 91
Columbus, OH 79, 93, 147, 155, 184, 215, 261
Columbus OH BBC 260
"Comets" BBC *see* Cleveland baseball clubs
"Comets" second-nine BBC *see* Cleveland baseball clubs
Comic opera star 257
Comiskey, Charles "The Old Roman" 166, 188, 189, 205, 206, 287
Common labor law 266
Commons (Canton) 13
Company A (military) 200

Company B (military) 200
Confederacy 5
Confederate forces 5
Congregational Church 274
Congress Street Grounds (Boston) *see* Baseball grounds: Boston Congress Street Grounds
Connecticut 15
Connor, Roger 103, 231, 248, 249
Connor, W. J. 268
Connotton Valley Depot 167
Conroy, _____ 290
Consens, _____ (black) 200
Constantinople 127
"Contest" BBC *see* Cleveland baseball clubs; Painesville "Contest" BBC
Cook, _____ 141, 142
Cooke, _____ 229
Cooley, Duff 231
Coolman, _____ 9
Cooner, _____ 16
Cooney, Jim 186
Co-op plan 210
Cooperstown (Hall of Fame) 104
Cora (character) 158
Corbett, James "Gentleman Jim" (pugilist) 244, 268
Corbett, Joe 244, 250, 253–257
Corcoran, Larry 121, 133, 134
Corcoran, Tommy 219, 220, 269
Corkhill, John "Pop" 148, 149
Cotter, _____ 9
County Prize ($50) 22
Courier (Youngstown) *see* *Youngstown Courier*
Covered wagon specials 186
Cowan, George 232
Cowan, W. L. 232
"Cowboys" BBC (AA) *see* Kansas City "Cowboys" BBC
Cowles, Converse (umpire) 11
County Democrat (Portage County) *see* *Portage County Democrat*
"Crack" (ball club) 9, 20, 25, 45, 93, 109
"Crack open" 107
Craig, _____ (black) 224, 232
Crane, _____ 25
Crane, Edward "Cannonball" 170, 171
Crane, Sam 98
"Cranks" *see* "Kranks"
Craver, _____ 49, 50
Craver, William 67, 69, 70
Crawford, W. H. 243
Crescent football team 193
"Crescents" BBC *see* Cleveland baseball clubs
Cricket *see* Toledo "Maumees" (cricket)
"Crickets" BBC *see* Cleveland baseball clubs; Newberg "Crickets" BBC
Criger, Lou 268, 275
Crisham, _____ 282, 287, 288
Crittenden Jewelry 148
"Croakers" (fans) 125

Index

"Croghans" BBC *see* Fremont "Croghans" BBC
Cross, ____ 282, 290
Cross, Amos 137, 162, 168
Cross, Frank 162
Cross, Joe 162
Cross, Lave 162, 167, 168, 217, 279
Cross, Monte 248
"Cross's Raw Recruits" 279
Crowell, Bill 98, 159, 160, 167
Crowley, Bill 122, 129, 130
Crumbie, ____ 25
Cuba 146
Cuban front 272
Cuddy, Ed 161
Cudell & Richardson Co. (architects) 194
Culp, ____ 16, 17
Cumberland, MD 252
Cummings, Andy 77, 80, 81, 83
"Cupid" *see* Childs, Clarence "Kid"
Cuppy, George 207, 208, 211, 213, 218–220, 222, 224–226, 229–231, 233, 237–240, 241, 242, 244, 246, 249, 250, 252, 255, 256, 257, 270, 271
Curry, ____ 132
Curry, Wesley (umpire) 177, 178
Cushman, Ed 153
Cuthbert, E. E. (umpire) 148
Cuthbert, Edgar (Ned) 26, 27, 49, 50, 70
Cutter, W. H. (umpire) 17
Cuyahoga Building 223, 282
Cuyahoga River 68, 146
Cuyahogan (weekly newspaper) 164
"Cuyahogas" BBC *see* Cleveland baseball clubs
"C.W.C." BBC *see* Cleveland baseball clubs
Czechoslovakia 162

D.A.C. *see* Detroit Athletic Club
Dahlen, Bill 216
"Dailies" BBC (newsmen) *see* Cleveland baseball clubs
Daily, Cornelius "Con" 219
Daily, Hugh "One Arm" 122, 127, 129, 130, 151–153, 269
Daily, Vince 186
Dallas, TX 183
Dalrymple, Abner 107, 108, 121, 133, 134
Daly, ____ (councilman) 146
Daly, Tom 17, 203, 219, 220
Damman, ____ 284, 287, 288
Daniels, Pete 272
Dark glasses *see* Colored spectacles
Darragh, ____ 132
Darsey, ____ 161
Darwin's theory 64
Dave Price's 32
Davenport, IA 93
Davidson, ____ (manager) 162
Davies, George 204, 220, 225
Davis, ____ 18, 40, 172
Davis, ____ (black) 127
Davis, George 186, 197, 198, 199, 201, 207, 208, 211–213, 215, 226
Davis, Harry 275
Davy Jones ("Davy Jone's locker") 196
Dayton, BBC 184
Dayton, BBC (Ohio League) 132
Dayton, OH 261
Deagle, Ren 140, 142
Dean, ____ 54
Dean, (Deans) ____ (black) 200, 232
Decker, George 216
Declaration of Independence 86
Decoration Day 116, 135, 143, 175, 225
"Defiance" BBC *see* Cleveland baseball clubs
Deitz, "Japanese Tommy" 26, 36
DeKoven Street (Chicago) 65
Delahanty, Edward "Big Ed" 147, 156, 159, 182, 183, 188–190, 192, 217, 242, 243, 276
Delahanty, Tom 160, 161, 222, 242, 243
Delaware College, OH BBC 109
Delaware "Lenape" BBC 15
Delhman, H. J. (umpire) 81
De Lune, Trilby *see* Trilby De Lune (actress/role)
Democrat(s) 91, 116
Democratic Councilman 158
Dempsey, ____ 184
Dennis, ____ (black) 200
Denny, (Dennie) ____ (black) 232
Denny, Jerry 110, 117, 118, 136, 224
Denver BBC 183
Denver, CO 259, 260
Derby, ____ 229
Derby, George H. 111, 115, 123
Des Moines BBC 242
Despard, Lena 158
Detroit "Alerts" BBC 37
Detroit Athletic Club 210
Detroit Avenue 92, 244, 266
Detroit Base Ball Club 85
Detroit BBC (AL) 281
Detroit City Council 91
Detroit "Detroits" BBC 21, 31
Detroit Evening Journal 161
"Detroit Fire Department" BBC (Detroit) 99
Detroit franchise 174, 191
Detroit Free Press 111
Detroit "Jewelers" BBC (Detroit) 116
"Detroit Light Guard" BBC (Detroit; reserve military) 116
Detroit, MI 18, 20, 31, 36, 37, 85, 144, 235, 262
Detroit "Newsboys" BBC (*Evening Journal*) 160, 161
Detroit Opera House 37
Detroit police 152
Detroit Post & Tribune 110 152
Detroit "Printers" BBC (Detroit) 26
Detroit Recreation Park *see* Baseball grounds
Detroit Street *see* Detroit Avenue
Detroit "Wolverines" BBC 47
Detroit "Wolverines" BBC (NL) 109–111, 113–115, 122, 130, 131, 154, 159, 169
Detroiters 110, 116
Dewald, ____ 164
Dewald, Charlie 217
Dewey, ____ 93
Dexter Park (Chicago) 69
Dexter Trotting Park (Chicago) 48
"Dexters" BBC *see* North Madison "Dexters" BBC
"Dhundeen" 125
Diamond Court 185
"Diamond in the rough" 282
"Diamond monopoly" 291
Diamond Park Street 180, 187
"Diamond Rocks" BBC *see* Cleveland baseball clubs
Diamond stud 238
Diamond trust 276
Dickerson, Louis "Buttercup" 103
Dietz, "Japanese Tommy" 26
Diggins, ____ 282, 284
Dime museum 258
Dinsmore, ____ 161
Disciple church 222
Dissette, (judge) 274
District Prize ($75) 23
Dixie 215
Dixwell, General 177
Dobson, ____ 12
Doctor, ____ 93, 116
Doctor, Edward W. (black) 126, 127
Doctor, Frank (black) 172
Dodge (E. 12th) 273
"Dodgers" (Brooklyn) 258
Dodor (actor/role) 232
Donahue, Francis "Red" 247, 248
Donahue, Jim 153
Donelly, T. J. 56
Donovan, Patsy 275
Donovan, T.D. 184
Doolan, Jim 222
Dooley, Ed 125
Doolittle, Clay H. 66
Dorman, ____ 78
Doscher, Herm 106, 107, 114
Doubleday, ____ 18, 25
Double-pump handcar 169
Dougherty, W. 15
Douglas, William "Klondike" 248
Douglas Street (E. 36th) 144
Dover Station 200
Dowd, Tommy 207, 208, 231, 248, 249
Dowling, Pete 290
Downer, ____ 161
Downs, Mr. ____ 16
Downtown resort (bar) 270
Downtown stage 222
Doyle, Harry 145, 152, 155
Doyle, Jack ("Dirty Jack") 225, 226, 252–257

Index

Drake's 186 Superior Street *see* A. F. Drake Co.
Drake, A.F. Co *see* A. F. Drake Co.
Drake, Lyman D. 132
"Dramatics" BBC *see* Cleveland baseball clubs
Draper, John (Doctor) 48, 54
Driving Park (Cleveland) *see* Baseball grounds: East Madison (E. 79th) and Cedar Grounds
Driving Park *see* Baseball grounds: Ravenna Driving Park Grounds
"Drop curve" 100
Dubuque, IA 160, 162
"Duebers" BBC *see* Canton "Duebers" BBC
Dufee, Charlie 207, 208
Duffy, Ed 61
Duffy, Hugh 170, 174, 188, 189, 214, 226
Duhamel, George 158
Du Maurier, A. *see* A. Du Maurier (actor/role)
"Dundreary" 120
Duncan C. Ross' saloon 137
Dungan, Sam 216
Dunham (E. 66th) 192, 195, 197
Dunlap, Fred ("Sure Shot") 96–98, 100, 102–104, 106, 108, 110 114, 115, 117, 118, 121–124, 129, 131
"Duplex" BBC *see* Toledo "Duplex" BBC
Duryea, James "Jesse" ("Cyclone Jim") 197, 199
Dutch birth 67
Dwyer, Frank 188, 189
Dwyer, John 114, 116
Dynamiters 258

Eagan, "Rip" *see* Egan, "Rip"
"Eagles" BBC *see* Cleveland baseball clubs
Earle, Billy ("The Little Globetrotter") 170
East 129, 175, 185
East Cleveland (original) 59, 60
East Cleveland BBC *see* Cleveland baseball clubs
East Cleveland "Clumsy" BBC 20
East Cleveland line (streetcar) 24, 59, 88
East Cleveland Street Railway Company 106, 116
East Coast 67, 178, 207, 244
East Coast cities 291
East Coast games 168
East Coast magnates 269
East Coast trip 71
East End League (baseball) 184
East Madison (E. 79th) 146, 194
East Market Street ball field *see* Baseball grounds: Hedges-East Market Street Grounds
E. 36th *see* Douglas Street
E. 38th *see* Putnam Street
E. 39th *see* Osborne Street
E. 40th *see* Case Avenue

E. 55th *see* Wilson Street
Easter bonnets 187
"Eastern" (circuit) 86
Eastern League 225
Eastern League championship 217
Eastern Park (Brooklyn, NY) *see* Baseball grounds
"Eastern Rocks" BBC *see* Cleveland baseball clubs
Eastern seaboard 3
Eastern Tour of 1872 (first) 67
Eastman Hotel 183
Eaton, ____ 17
Eb 14
"Eckfords" Brooklyn, NY BBC 53
Eclipse (of the sun) 41
"Eclipse" BBC (AA) *see* Louisville "Eclipse" BBC (AA)
Eden, Charley 77–80, 83, 88–90, 92
Edinborough, PA BBC 9
Edith (prose) 3
Egan, "Rip" 282, 283, 286
Eggler, Dave 51
Eggleston, ____ 11
Ehret, Philip "Red" 228, 230, 231, 289
Eighteenth ward 91
El Paso, TX 169
Electric arc light 266
Electric cars (streetcars) 186
Electric light pole 249
Electric lights 183, 266
Electric streetcar 285
Electric train 230
"Electrics" BBC (amateur) *see* Cleveland baseball clubs
"Electrics" Brotherhood BBC (PL) *see* Cleveland baseball clubs
Elizabeth, NJ "Resolutes" BBC (NA) 62
Ellicke, ____ 11
Ellis, ____ 54, 71
Ellis, W. R. (umpire) 46, 48
Ellser, John 37, 158
Elton,____ (justice of the peace) 275
Ely, Frederick "Bones" 77, 78, 231, 275
Elyria, OH 280
Elyria "Western Rocks BBC 74
Emerald cadet drum and fife corps 183
Emerson, Billy 82, 83
Emerson's Minstrels 82
Emmett, ____ 38
Empire City (NYC) 52
Empire Hotel (Akron) 102
Emslie, ____(umpire) 211–214, 225, 243, 253, 255–257, 277
England 258
England, ____ 152
England on Euclid (store) 185
English, ____ (police captain) 264
English F over C 60
English lord 53
English-style F C 24
English-type F C 33

"Enterprise" BBC *see* Hudson "Enterprise" BBC
Erie (great lake) 52
Erie (E. 9th) and Superior 272
Erie County 15
Erie, PA 78, 148
Erie, PA BBC 217
Erie, PA "Eries" BBC 77, 79–81
Erie railway yards 272
Erie Street (E. 9th) 271, 272
"Eries" BBC *see* Cleveland baseball clubs; Erie, PA "Eries" BBC
"Erratic curve" 149
Esper, Charles "Duke" 201, 218, 227, 234, 239, 240, 250
Essig, ____ 12
Esterbrook, Thomas Jefferson "Dude" 98, 113, 117–119, 121
Etlein, A. J. 76
"Etlein" BBC *see* Warren "Etlein" BBC
"Etnas" BBC *see* Warren "Etnas" BBC
Euclid and Erie Street (E. 9th) 271
Euclid Avenue 87, 146, 160, 206, 271, 274
Euclid Avenue and Wilson Street (E. 55th) train station 49, 88
Euclid Avenue Opera House *see* Cleveland Euclid Avenue Opera House
Euclid Beach Amusement Park *see* Baseball grounds
Euclid Beach Park *see* Baseball grounds: Euclid Beach Amusement Park
Euclid Block 144
Euclid Opera House *see* Cleveland Euclid Avenue Opera House
"Eureka" BBC *see* Cleveland baseball clubs; Fremont "Eureka" BBC; Hamden "Eureka" BBC
Europe 258
Europe *see* Americans in Europe
Evans, Jake "Bloody Jake" 122, 123, 125, 133–138
Evans, James Ford 53, 66, 67, 85, 88, 96, 97, 99, 107
Evans, Van Epps & Co. 85, 86, 88, 97
Evansville, IN 135, 230
Evening Journal see *Detroit Evening Journal*
Ewell, ____ 164
Ewing, William "Buck" 175, 215, 216, 218–220, 223–225
Excelsior Clothing 127, 150
"Excelsiors" BBC *see* Akron "Excelsiors" BBC; Chicago "Excelsiors" BBC; Cleveland baseball clubs: "Excelsiors" BBC; Cleveland baseball clubs: "Excelsiors" BBC (black); Rochester "Excelsiors"
"Exercise Club" BBC *see* Mansfield "Exercise Club" BBC
"Experts" BBC *see* Philadelphia "Experts" BBC

Exposition Park (Pittsburgh) *see* Baseball grounds

Faatz, ____ 142
Faatz, Jay 141, 156, 158, 160, 165, 173–178, 192
Faatz, Mrs. 156
Fair Grounds (Norwalk) *see* Baseball grounds: Norwalk Fair Grounds
Fair Grounds (Ravenna, Portage County) *see* Baseball grounds: Ravenna Fair Grounds
Fair Street (Ft. Wayne, IN) 55
"Fairchilds" BBC *see* Oberlin "Fairchilds" BBC
"Fakirs" BBC *see* Cleveland baseball clubs
"Fan" 150
"Fanning" 149
Farley, John H. (mayor) 281, 285
Farmers Exchange 22
Farrar, Sid 130
Farrell, Charles "Duke" 174, 175, 188, 189, 264
Farrell, Jack "Moose" 91, 110, 117, 118, 136, 137, 165
Farrell, Joe 115
Father Time 73
Fauver, ____ 282
"Favorites" BBC *see* Cleveland baseball clubs
Fawcett, J. A. 181
Fay, C. V. 16
"Female base ballist" 92
Female baseball clubs 92, 93, 173, 191
Female Seminary (well-to-do girls boarding school) 5
Fenian Cadets 8
Fenn, ____ 14
Fennelly, Frank 148, 149
Fenney, ____ (fireman) 83
Ferguson, Bob ("Death to Flying Things") 25, 80, 102, 130, 157
Ferguson, Bob (umpire) 166, 167, 189
Ferris wheel 244, 266
Ferry, D. M. (umpire) 21
Ferson, Alex (colonel) 189
Fiedler, ____ (judge) 264
Fiel, Nate 184
Fifth Infantry 200
"Fifth Ward Snakes" BBC *see* Cleveland baseball clubs
Figgemer, ____ 242
"Fighters" BBC (Spiders' NL nickname) *see* Cleveland baseball clubs
Findlay, OH 215, 280
Findlay, OH BBC 229
"Fire Department" BBC *see* Cleveland baseball clubs
Firecrackers 236
Firelands (Western Reserve area) 15
"Firelands" BBC *see* Norwalk "Firelands" BBC
Firemen 276

"Firemen" BBC *see* Cleveland baseball clubs
"Firemen" Buffalo BBC *see* NY "Firemen" Buffalo BBC
First American League road game (Cleveland) 282
First American League home game (Cleveland) 281, 285, 286
The First Grand Game of the Season (Cincinnati 1870) 44
First major league game 55
First major league home game (Cleveland) 60, 65
First major league home run 59, 65
First major league player from Cleveland 162
First major league Sunday game (Cleveland) 153
"First nine" 5
"First no-hitter" (Cleveland) 130
First perfect game 100, 101
First Prize ($300) 23
First Regiment Band (Louisville) 261
First Regiment State Guard (Louisville) 261
First soccer game 193
First "world series game" (Cleveland) 211
Fish horns 235, 236
Fish women 239
Fisher, ____ 8, 289
Fisher, Chauncey ("Whoa Bill") 224
Fisher, Harry C. 184
Fisher, William "Cherokee" 26, 59, 62, 68, 69–70
Fisk House 7
Fitch & Fairchild 27
Flanagan, M. 229
Flats 74, 84
"Fleetwood" (paddle wheeler) 39, 40
Flemming, ____ 250
Flick, Elmer 291
Flint, Silver 108, 121
Flood, Tim 282, 288–290
Flood, Will 222
Florida 163
"Flower" BBC *see* Rochester, NY "Flower" BBC
Floyd, ____ 14
Flynn, ____ 49, 50, 287, 288
Fogerty, Jim 170
Folder, ____ 11
"Folding opera chairs" 185, 193, 200
Foley, Tom 61
Football 221
Foote & Company 144
Foran, James H. 56, 57, 58
Force, ____ 38
Force, Davy 98, 120, 123
Ford, A. F. 15
Forepaugh (circus owner) 125
Forest City (Cleveland nickname) 23, 242
"Forest City" BBC *see* Cleveland baseball clubs

"Forest City" BBC (amateurs) *see* Cleveland baseball clubs
"Forest City" BBC (1865–1867) *see* Cleveland baseball clubs
"Forest City" BBC flag (Cleveland) 24
Forest City ballplayers (illus.) 73
Forest City Base Ball Association 84
Forest City Base Ball Club *see* Cleveland baseball clubs
Forest City Base Ball Grounds (1871, 1872 NA) *see* Baseball grounds
Forest City "Blue Stockings" BBC (1868–1870 IND) *see* Cleveland baseball clubs
Forest City "Blue Stockings" BBC (1871, 1872 NA) *see* Cleveland baseball clubs
Forest City "Blue Stockings" BBC (1878 IND) *see* Cleveland baseball clubs
Forest City "Blue Stockings" BBC (1879–1884 NL) *see* Cleveland baseball clubs
Forest City Cricket Club 5, 6, 84
Forest City "Green Stockings" BBC (Rockford, ILL) 45
Forest City House 88, 244, 247
"Forest City Juniors" BBC *see* Cleveland baseball clubs
Forest City Park 39
Forest City Park (formerly Beyerle Park) *see* Baseball grounds
Forest City Picked Nine 69
"Forest City Troop" BBC *see* Cleveland baseball clubs
Fort Wayne City Council 55
Fort Wayne Gazette 57–59
Fort Wayne, IN 55, 58, 63, 65, 206, 230, 261
Fort Wayne, IN BBC 210
Fort Wayne, IN "Kekiongas" BBC (NA) 55, 56, 57, 58, 63, 65, 66; flag 55
Fort Wayne Journal 216
Fort Worth, TX 183
Foster, ____ 164
Foster's Grounds *see* Baseball grounds
Fountain, E. G. (umpire) 89
Fourth of July 7, 8, 13, 20, 36, 52, 102, 103, 109, 116–118, 120, 135, 136, 150, 151, 162, 176, 190, 191, 200, 201, 207, 218, 220, 226, 227, 233, 247, 266, 287, 288
Foutz, Dave 203, 218–220
Fowler, J. W. "Bud" (black) 229
Frame, ____ 25
"Framed hangers" (billboards) 123
Franchise: defined 277
Frank, Fred 278
Frankfurt Street 105, 125
Frankfurthers 232
Franklin, ____ (manager) 191
Fraser, Charles "Chick" 245, 250, 261

Frazee, J. N. 66
Frazier, ____ 14
Freaks 258
"Free list" 116
Fremont "Croghans" BBC 16, 17
Fremont "Eureka" BBC 17
Fremont, OH 16
French dancing master 188
Frey, ____ 172
Friend, Danny 246
Fringer, ____ 172
Frisbee, Charlie 282, 287, 288
Fry, ____ 222
Fry, (Frye) ____ (black) 232
Fuller, Charles 111
Fulmer, Chick 43, 51, 52
Fulmer, Chris 165
Fulton Avenue see Rhodes Avenue
Fulton, IL 56
Fultz, ____ 290
Furlong, W. E. (umpire) 124

Gabriel (angel) 110
Gaffney, ____ 160, 161
Gaffney, ____ (umpire) 157, 211–213, 215
Galion, OH 15, 262
Galion, OH BBC 122
Galion "Resolutes" BBC 15, 22
Galion "Sockalexis" BBC 262
Gallagher, J. 161
Gallagher, M. 161
Gallup, ____ 229
Galvin, James "Pud" 179
Gambier "Gambier" BBC 76
Gamble, Bob 157
Game bell 148
"The Game versified" (poem) 52
Gann, ____ 16
Ganns, Billy 222
Ganz, ____ 164
Ganzel, ____ 177, 178
Ganzel, Charlie 214
G.A.R. see Grand Army of the Republic
Garden line (streetcar) 33
Garden Street (Central Avenue) 23, 59, 74
Garden Way (streetcar) 78
Gardiner, ____ 9
Gardner, Gid 101, 102
Gardner, Jim 274, 275
Gardner, "Pony" 37
Garfield, James Abram (president) 113
Garfield, Will 181
Garland, Joseph 83
Garretts Hall (restaurant) 6
Garrettsville, OH 91
Garrettsville "White Stockings" BBC 84
Gastright, Hank 218
Gatch, ____ 222
"Gattling" BBC see Cleveland baseball clubs
Gear, Dale 286
Geauga County 11
Geauga County "Chester" BBC 12
Geauga Democrat 11

Geauga Lake see Baseball grounds: Geauga Lake Grounds
Gecko (actor/role) 232
Geier, ____ 288
Geneva BBC 270
Geneva "Blue Stockings" BBC 78
Geneva "Grays" BBC (black) 172, 173
Geneva, OH 78, 93, 100, 101, 172, 270
Geneva "Spencer" BBC 29
Geneva "Times" BBC 29
Genins, Frank 282, 284, 287, 288, 290
"Gentleman player" 42
George Mears Scrapbook 261
George Worthington Co. BBC see Cleveland baseball clubs
Gerhardt, Joe "Move Up Joe" 111, 153
German 154; celebration 37; communities 36; immigrant 134; surnames 171
German, Les 225, 226, 264
German Village 274
"Germania" BBC see Cleveland baseball clubs; Sandusky "Germania" BBC
Getzein, Charles "Pretzels" 173
Giants (Cincinnati IND) 40
Giants (Providence NL) 90
"Giants" BBC (NL) see New York "Giants" BBC (NL)
The Giants Felled 90
Gibbons, ____ 222
Gibson House 40
Giddings, George (doctor) 268
Gifts: alcohol 139; boat ride 46, 83; cheese bread and lemonade 46; diamond stick pin 243; diamond studded watch charm 205; fruit 83; gold headed walking stick 230; flowers 48, 123,178, 188, 197, 198, 231, 243; pie 159; shotgun 238; shows 37, 82, 83, 115, 158; silver trophy 178; watch in gold case 188; wooden Indian 268; see also prizes
Gilbert, ____ 93
Gilbo M. J. 184
"Gilded Age" 122
Gilks, Bobby 156, 157, 165, 166, 174, 182
Gillespie, Pete 102
Gillette House (restaurant) 10
Gilligan, Barney 92, 94, 96, 103, 118, 136, 137
Gilman, J. 171
"Gilt-edged" 122, 128, 129, 130
Ginger ale 232
Girard "Social" BBC 9
Girl baseball clubs see Female baseball clubs
Glasgow, Scotland 133
Glasscock, John "Pebbly Jack" 77, 80, 81, 88–91, 94, 99, 103, 106–108, 110, 114, 115, 117, 118, 121–124, 126, 129, 133, 134, 136, 138, 139

Gleason, William "Kid" 158, 201, 235–241
Glenville "Hungry Men" BBC 90
Glenville "Independents" BBC 44
Glenville, OH (now in Cleveland) 112
"Globetrotters" BBC (Spalding tour of Europe) 170
Glouchester, NJ 168
Goat and terrier see Mascottes
Goff & Kirby Co. 185
Goggin, ____ 164
Goldie, ____ 28, 29
Goldsmith, Fred 108, 112
Goldsmith, Wallace 56–58
"Goldsmith, Joseph, Feiss & Co." BBC see Cleveland baseball clubs
Gong 238
Good, ____ 27
Goodfellow, Mike 156, 165
Good-luck ring see Mascottes
Goodman, ____ (black) 232
Goodrich, ____ 30
Goodrich Co. 27
"Goose eggs" 30
Gordon, ____ (black) 127
Gordon, J. (black) 173
Gordon, William (black) 172
"Gordons" BBC see Cleveland baseball clubs
Gore, George 108, 121, 133, 134
Gorham, ____ 18, 43
Gould, ____ 34, 35, 48, 54
Gould plant 146
Governor (Ohio) 244
Grady, Mike 244
Grafton, OH 148, 192, 199
Graham, Billy 134
Graham, D. M. (scorer) 37
Grand Arcade see Cleveland Grand Arcade
Grand Army of the Republic (G.A.R.) 13
"Grand Duchess" (Ft. Wayne, IN) 55
"Grand Duchess" (Cincinnati) 44, 53
Grand Hotel (Cincinnati) 163
Grand Rapids, MI 137, 223, 261, 281
Grand Rapids, MI BBC (Northwest League) 132
Grand River BBC 29
Grand River Grounds (Lake County) see Baseball grounds
Grand slam home run 175
Grannis, ____ 27
Grant, Annie 191
Grant, Lulu 191
"Graphic" (hot air balloon) 151
Graphic (weekly newspaper) 164
Gray, ____ 287, 288
Gray, Bill see Grey, Bill
Gray, Laura 93
Grays (reserve military) see Cleveland Grays (reserve military)
Grays Armory 272

Grays Band 68, 143
"Grays" BBC *see* Cleveland baseball clubs: "Grays" BBC (reserve military); Geneva "Grays" BBC (black); Providence, RI "Grays" BBC (NL)
"Great Chicago Fire" 66, 69
Great Depression 101
The Great Eastern Tour (1870) 52
Great Fire 66, 69
Great Western Band 285
Greater Cleveland 3, 92
Greatest musical instrument (giant tin horn) 236
Green, ____ 78
"Green Stockings" Forest City BBC *see* Rockford, ILL "Green Stockings" Forest City BBC (NA)
Greenwood, Bill 165
Greer, Ed 150, 151
Gremminger, Ed 241
Grey, Bill 275
Griffin, ____ (black) 200, 224, 232
Griffin, C. (black) 172
Griffin, Mike 165
Griffith, Frank 241
Griffith Bros. & Kennard Co. 18
Grim, John 223, 224
"Grip" 194; *see also* Cable cars
Gross, Emil M. 77–81, 83, 109, 110, 129
Gross, R. (black) 173
"Grotzingers" BBC *see* Cleveland baseball clubs
"Grove Boys" BBC *see* Cleveland baseball clubs
"Grove Citys" BBC *see* Cleveland baseball clubs
"Growlers" BBC *see* Cleveland baseball clubs
Gruber, Henry "Hen" 174, 175, 182, 188, 189, 193, 225
Guiteau, Charles 113
"Gymnasium" BBC *see* Cleveland baseball clubs
Gymnastic appliances 185

"HAC" BBC (black) *see* Cleveland baseball clubs (black)
Hackett, Charley (manager) 132, 137, 139
Hade, "Farmer" 26, 36
Hade, J. 15
Haddock, George "Gentleman George" 219, 220
Hague, Bill 88, 89
Halford, ____ 169
Hall, ____ 37, 164
Hall, ____ (black) 224
Hall, ____ (mayor) 275, 276
Hall, Al 99
Hall, George 69, 70
Hall, O. (black) 173
Hall, Webb C. *see* Webb C. Hall's store
Hall of Fame *see* National Baseball Hall of Fame
Halligan, William "Jocko" 205, 206

Ham, ____ 62
Hamden Center 11
Hamden "Eureka" BBC 11, 29
Hamilton, Harry (groundskeeper) 279
Hamilton, John (black) 172
Hamilton Field (Ft. Wayne, IN) 55
Hamilton, OH 134, 135
Hamms, ____ 18
"Hand Me Downs" BBC *see* Cleveland baseball clubs
Handy, T. P. 91
Hanford, F. 12
Hanford, Fred 12
Hankinson, Frank 80, 99, 103, 153
Hanlon, Ned 96–98, 103, 104, 111, 114, 115, 170, 171, 251, 252, 258
Hanna, L. C. 6, 28, 30, 36–38, 43, 97
Hanna, Marcus 6, 66, 242
Hannis, ____ (black) 127
Hanssom, ____ 12
Harbidge, William 80, 129
Hard, ____ 14
Hardenberg, ____ 18, 25
Harding, Nellie 93
Hardwick, ____ 172
Harkins, John "Pa" 139, 140, 151
Harkness, ____ 17
Harley, ____ (toastmaster) 242
Harper Bros. (actor/role) 232
Harridge, ____ (colonel) 242
Harris, ____ 9
Harrison, Benjamin (U. S. president) 169
Hart, Bill 233, 287, 290
Hart, Jim (president) 246–249, 259
Harter, ____ 12
Hartford, CT 86
Hartford, CT BBC (NL) 86, 106
Hartman, ____ 93
Hartman, Fred 228
Hartsgrove "Athletics" (Ashtabula County) BBC 29
Hartsgrove BBC (Ashtabula County) 12
Hartwick, "Bottle" 222
Hartzell, ____ 283, 284, 286, 288
Harvard University 101
Harvey, Frank (recording secretary) 31
Hastings, Charlie 221
Hastings, Scott 67, 69, 70
Hatfield, ____ 17, 51
Hattersly, ____ 18
Havana, Cuba 270
Haverly, J. H. *see* J. H. Haverly booking agency
Haverly's Consolidated Mastodon Minstrels *see* J. H. Haverly's Consolidated Mastodon Minstrels
Hawke, Bill 269
Hawley, Davis 144, 147, 152, 155, 162, 203, 204
Hawley, Davis, Jr. 152
Hawley, Emerson "Pink" 233

Hawley House 148, 150, 155, 222, 270
Hawthorne, Grace 158
Hayden, ____ 286
Hayden, ____ (professor) 151
"Haymakers" Union BBC *see* Troy, NY "Haymakers" Union BBC (NA, NL)
Haynie, James (secretary, umpire) 60–62
"Heart" BBC *see* Painesville "Heart" BBC
Heat stroke 163
Heckman, ____ 12
Hedges Grove-East Market Street Grounds (Mansfield) *see* Baseball grounds
Heidrick, John 278
Hellers League (baseball) 184
Hemming, George 182, 233, 234
Henderson, ____ 93
Henderson, ____ (manager) 139
Henrietta, Lorain County (OH) 5
Herald see *Cleveland Herald*
Herr, Ed 148, 149
Herrick, Myron (mayor, governor, ambassador) 91, 242
Herse, ____ 30
Heuble, George 43, 46, 49–51
Heyman, ____ (captain) 183
Heywood, Charles 83
Hexter's (news depot) 155, 185
Hi! Hi! Hi! Hi! 177
"Hickehowgo" (robber) 272
Hickey, ____ 286, 288
"High School" BBC *see* Cleveland baseball clubs; Painesville "High School" BBC
High School "Occidentals" BBC *see* Cleveland baseball clubs
Higham, ____ (umpire) 114
Higham, Dick 69, 70
Hill, Bill ("Still Bill") 245
Hillsdale College BBC (MI) 109
"Hingland" (England) 258
Hines, Paul A. 88, 110, 117, 118, 136, 137
Hiram College 75
Hiram College BBC 184
"H.M.S. Pinafore" (play) 93
Hoagland, ____ (umpire) 227
Hobart, ____ 14
Hodes, ____ 42, 49, 50, 60, 61
Hofer, ____ 172
Hoffer, Bill ("Wizard") 236, 237, 240, 241, 252, 253, 255, 256, 282, 283, 287
Hogan, Ed 140–142, 153, 155–158
Hogan & Harris ambulance 129
Hogriever, George 281, 284, 286, 287
Holbert, Bill 103
Holden, L. E. (*Plain Dealer* president) 160
Holden pennant 160
Holdsworth, James "Long Jim" 67, 69, 70
Holiday, James "Bug" 197–199, 205, 269

Holland, R. (black) 172
Hollenden Hotel 179, 196, 205, 257, 264
"Hollendens" BBC (black) *see* Cleveland baseball clubs (black)
Hollinger, William 22, 77, 81, 83, 85
Holloway, Charles M. (captain) 39
"Hollywood" 222
Holy Cross College 259, 260, 265
"Home and home match" 16
Home Opener *see* Cleveland Opening Day (home)
"Hoodlum wagon" 264
Hoodoo rabbit ears 214
Hoosier State boys 284
Hoosier team 287
Hoosiers 173
"Hope" BBC *see* Wooster "Hope" BBC
Hopper, De Wolf 255, 257, 258
Horan, E. 161
"Hornells" BBC (IL) *see* Hornellsville, NY "Hornells" BBC
Hornellsville, NY "Hornells" BBC (IL) 81, 82
Hornung, Joe "Ubo Ubo" 98
"Horribles" BBC *see* Norwalk "Horribles" BBC
Horse-drawn rollers 146
Horse-drawn streetcars 193
Horse-hitching post 187
Horses 210
Horseshoes *see* Mascottes
"Hospital list" 120, 266
Hot Springs, AR 155, 169, 182, 183, 204, 205, 230, 242, 260, 270, 271
Hotaling, Pete "Monkey" 98–100, 102, 103, 122, 123, 124, 128, 129, 133, 134, 136, 140, 148–151, 153, 154, 156, 158, 165, 166
Hot-Stove League Stories 147
Hough, A. B. 85, 113
Hough, Addison 243
Hough Avenue 194
Houk, "Sadie" 91, 111
Houston, ____ 16
Houston, TX 183
How Shall We Receive Them? 68
How the Resolutes Won the Junior Championship 27
Howard, Earl 186
Howard, Hattie 93
Howard, Josie 93
Howard, May 191
Howard, Retta 93
Howard Street 162
Howe, George W. 113, 123, 135, 138, 144, 153, 155, 169, 196, 203, 204, 243, 285
Hower and Higbee Co. BBC *see* Cleveland baseball clubs
Hoy, William "Dummy" 208, 269
Hoyle, ____ 132
Hoyt, ____ 16, 17
H. R. Jacobs theatre 171
"H. R. Jacobs" theatre BBC *see* Cleveland baseball clubs
Hudson, ____ 12, 24

Hudson, G. B. (umpire) 11
Hudson, William 18
Hudson "Enterprise" BBC 9, 10
Hudson, OH 6, 10
Hudson "Reserve" BBC *see* Hudson "Western Reserve College" BBC
Hudson "Reserve-second-nine" BBC 19
Hudson "Western Reserve College" BBC 6, 9, 10, 19, 20 24, 36, 75, 76, 96, 109
"Hudsons" BBC *see* Cleveland baseball clubs
Hughes, ____ 172
Hughes, Sam T. 164
Hulbert, William A. 86, 113
Humberger, ____ 12
Hummel, O. 172
Hundley, C. M. 184
"Hungry Men" BBC *see* Glenville "Hungry Men" BBC
Hunt, ____ 26
Hunter, Lem 122
Huntington, ____ 172
Hurlbut, ____ 8, 18, 21, 43
Huron County 15, 21
Huron Street hospital 268
"Hurrah for the heroes" (banners) 247
"Hurrah for the pennant winners! ..." (cheer) 211
Hurst, Tim (umpire) 207, 208, 228, 239, 240, 242, 244, 264
Husten, ____ 116
"Hustlers" BBC (black) *see* Cleveland baseball clubs (black)
Hutchins, John E. (judge) 142, 154
Hutchinson, William "Wild Bill" 174, 175, 185, 186, 191, 205
Hutchison *see* Hutchinson, William "Wild Bill"
Hyberger, Emma 168

Ice polo 260
Ice skating 43
Ice-skating rink 96
"Idlers" BBC *see* Cleveland baseball clubs
"Ile and turpentine" 94
Ilg, August S. 148
Illinois 45, 55, 59, 94
"In Memoriam" 68
Incorporation (Brotherhood team) 180
Independence Day *see* Fourth of July
Independence Street 167
"Independents" BBC *see* Chardon "Independents" BBC; Cleveland baseball clubs; Columbus "Independents" BBC; Mansfield "Independents" BBC
Indian (Native American) 259, 265, 268, 272, 279
Indian ancestry 154
Indian BBC (Native American) 224
Indian clubs 97

Indian corn dance 123
Indian fever 259, 262
Indiana 102, 182, 230, 270, 271, 276
Indiana Legislature 216
Indianapolis BBC (AA) 131
Indianapolis BBC (AL) 281, 282, 284, 286–288, 291
Indianapolis BBC (NL) 84, 86, 173, 174, 179
Indianapolis BBC (Western League) 140
Indianapolis "Capital Citys" BBC 79
Indianapolis, IN 155, 173, 261, 282
Indians (Native Americans) 224, 259
"Indians" BBC (AL) *see* Cleveland baseball clubs; Indianapolis "Indians" BBC (AL)
"Indians" BBC (amateur) *see* Cleveland baseball clubs
Indoor-baseball devices 221
Indoor baseball season 230
"Infants" *see* Cleveland baseball clubs: "Blues" (AA; 1887–1888), "Brotherhood" (electrics; PL) *and* "Spiders" (NL)
"Infernals" Internal Revenue BBC *see* Cleveland baseball clubs
Inks, Bert ____ 203
International League 80, 81, 84, 147
International Order of Odd Fellows 63
"Invincibles" BBC *see* Chagrin "Invincibles" BBC
Irish 92; brogue 116; team 258; uprising 213
"Iron" BBC *see* Newberg "Iron" BBC
Iron City House (restaurant) 9
Iron Mountain & Southern Railroad 183
"Iron Wards" BBC *see* Cleveland baseball clubs
"Ironclads" BBC *see* Newark, NJ "Ironclads" BBC
"Ironclads" *Cleveland Plain Dealer* BBC *see* Cleveland baseball clubs
"Ironsides" BBC *see* Newberg "Ironsides" BBC; Youngstown "Ironsides" BBC
Irwin, ____ 270
Irwin, Arthur 100, 136
Irwin, Charlie 262, 269
"Island" BBC *see* Kent "Island" BBC
"Ivanhoes" BBC *see* Bedford "Ivanhoes" BBC

Jack, ____ (black) 232
Jackson, ____ (black) 200
Jackson, #1 ____ (black) 232
Jackson, #2 ____ (black) 232
Jackson, James (black) 172
Jackson, John (black) 173
Jacksonville, FL 163, 196

Index

Jacobs, H. R. theatre *see* H. R. Jacobs theatre
Jacobs, S. B. 15
Japanese acrobats 210
Jayhawkers *see* Cleveland jayhawkers
"Jed Prouty" (character) 191
Jefferson BBC (Ashtabula County) 11
Jefferson Fair Grounds (Ashtabula County) *see* Baseball grounds
Jefferson, MO 242
Jefferson, MO BBC 242
Jennings, Hughie 235–241, 252–258
Jericho (battle of) 236
"Jerk" 41
"Jewelers" BBC *see* Cleveland baseball clubs; Detroit "Jewelers" BBC
Jewett, _____ 42
Jewish: ancestry 63; day of rest 266
Jewish Orphan Asylum 5
J. H. Haverly Co. (booking agency) 115
J. H. Haverly's Consolidated Mastodon Minstrels 115
J. H. Murch & Co. 67
Joe Haverly booking agency 96
"John Brown's Body" 68
John McCullough acting company 123
Johnson, _____ 30, 33, 78
Johnson, _____ (black) 200
Johnson, _____ (sergeant) 142
Johnson, Al 125, 140, 141, 152, 180, 181, 183, 185–189, 192, 193, 200, 202
Johnson, B. (scorer) 57
Johnson, Byron "Ban" 280, 281, 287, 291
Johnson, Caleb Clark 56
Johnson, F. (black) 172
Johnson, Grant "Home Run" (black) 229
Johnson, J. (black) 173
Johnson, R. (black) 200
Johnson, Ralph 197–199, 201
Johnson, Richard 147
Johnson, Tom 83, 125, 140, 152, 186
Johnson, Will 183, 184
Johnson House (hotel) 97, 99
Johnson's bride (Al Johnson) 202
Johnston, Dick 176–178
"Jonah" 125
Jones, _____ 109, 116, 147
Jones, _____ (umpire) 188, 190
Jones, Albert "Cowboy" 274
Jones, "Bumpus" 282, 284
Jones, Charley 148, 149, 153
"Josh Whitcomb" (character) 191
Joyce, J. P. (secretary of Cincinnati BBC) 45
Joyce, William (captain) 243
J. P. Martins (restaurant) 9
"Jump," "jumped," or "jumping" 131, 138, 183

"Junior championship" 24
"Junior" organization 26
Junior trophy 21

Kalamazoo, MI 53, 147, 242
Kalamazoo, MI BBC 53, 147
Kansas City BBC 170
Kansas City BBC (AL) 291
Kansas City BBC (UA) 131
Kansas City BBC (Western League) 140, 143
Kansas City "Cowboys" BBC (AA) 161, 168
Kansas City "Cowboys" Grounds (AA-1888) *see* Baseball grounds
Kansas City, MO 144, 242 161
Kanylanyee (green lobster) 272
Kaufman, _____ 222
Kaufman, H. 171
Keas, Ed 156
Kedah (sacred elephant) 244
Keefe, _____ (umpire) 237, 240, 242
Keefe, Timothy 1 79
Keeler, Willie ("Wee Willie") 235–241, 252–256
Keenan, Jim 197, 199
Keener, Harry ("Beans") 249
Kehres, Wilamina 187
"Kekionga" 56
"Kekiongas" BBC (NA) *see* Ft. Wayne, IN "Kekiongas" BBC (NA)
Kelb, George 271
Kelley, _____ (umpire) 269
Kelley, (Kelly) _____ (black) 232
Kelley, Joe 235–241, 244, 252–258
Kelley, William 56–58
Kellogg, _____ 161
Kellogg, _____ (umpire) 11
Kellogg, T. H. 15
Kellum, "Win" 282–284, 287
Kelly, _____ 286
Kelly, C. A. (umpire) 13
Kelly, Michael "King" 120, 121, 133, 134, 176–178, 212
Kelly, Tom 222
Kelly, William ("Father") 114–117
Kemmler, Rudy 106
Kendall, Nate 222
Kennan, _____ (captain) 16, 17
"Kennard & McKinney" BBC *see* Cleveland baseball clubs
"Kennard" BBC *see* Cleveland baseball clubs
Kennard Grounds *see* Baseball grounds: Kennard Street Base Ball Park (1878 IND, 1879–1884 NL)
Kennard House 8, 12, 19, 21, 66, 201
"Kennard House" BBC *see* Cleveland baseball clubs
Kennard Street (E. 46th) 77, 78, 80, 87, 86
Kennard Street (E. 46th) and Cedar 80, 87
Kennard Street Base Ball Park

(1878 IND, 1879–1884 NL) *see* Baseball grounds
Kennedy, Michael "Doc" 88, 89, 91, 92, 98, 100, 109, 114–116, 123, 124, 140–142
Kennedy, T. M. (prosecutor) 263
Kent, _____ 164
Kent "Active" BBC 11
Kent House 166
Kent "Island" BBC 10, 11
Kent, OH 116
Kentucky 39, 40, 182, 246, 258
Kenyon College 75
Kenyon College BBC 109
Kenzie, Walt 133, 134
Keokuk, IA BBC (Western League) 140
Kerns, James N. 66
Keystone Kops 207
"Keystones" BBC (black) *see* Cleveland baseball clubs (black); Pittsburgh "Keystones" BBC (black)
"Kicker" *see* "Kicking pen"
"Kicking pen" 145
Kiernan, J. 161
Kilfoyl, John 206, 281, 284
Killen, Frank 208, 215
Kimball, Eugene 43, 46, 48–51, 56–64
King, Charles "Silver" 166
King, Mart 9, 49, 50, 60
"King of exercise" 96
Kingdom of Heaven 275
Kingston, NY 148
Kinney, Gregory & Kinney (law firm) 258
Kinslow, Tom 220
"Kinsman" BBC *see* Cleveland baseball clubs
Kinsman Grounds (1865–1867) *see* Baseball grounds
Kinsman line (omnibus) 18, 19
Kinsman line (streetcar) 24, 33
Kinsman Street (current) 187
Kinsman Street (Woodland Ave.) 5
"Kinsman Street" BBC *see* Cleveland baseball clubs
Kirkwood, _____ 28
Kirtland (at Waite Hill) "Pioneers" (Lake County) BBC 12
Kirtland Street (E. 49th) 194
Kissinger, Bill ("Shang") 248, 250
Kittredge, Malachi 186, 216, 246
Kline, _____ (attorney) 142
Knapp, _____ (umpire) 18
Knauff, Ed 160
Knauss, Frank 159, 197, 226
Knell, Phil 207, 208, 233, 234
Knickerbockers *see* New York City "Knickerbockers" BBC
Knight, Lon (umpire) 111, 114, 115, 188, 190
Knights of Labor 166
Knights of Pythias Band 150
"Knights of the Crimson Hose" 45
Knocktown 112
Knouff, Ed 156

Index

Koehl, ____ 222
Koll, ____ 171
Koppe, George Maceo *see* Cuppy, George
Koppler, Oliver 80
"Kranks" (fans) 145, 147, 150, 152, 153, 177, 191, 196, 199, 222, 257, 259
Kuhn, ____ 12
Kurtz, ____ 93

"Labor Day" 184, 211
Labor movement 97, 180
Labor union 130, 131, 180
LaChance, George "Candy" 282, 284, 286, 287, 289
Lacrosse 74, 75; *see also* Cleveland Lacrosse club
Lacrosse "Victoria" (London, Canada) *see* London, Canada "Victoria" Lacrosse
The Laird (actor/role) 232
Lajoie, Napoleon 291
Lake County 11, 29, 72
Lake Erie 83, 186, 271
Lake Michigan 94
Lakeshore line *see* Lakeshore Railroad
Lakeshore Railroad 46
"Lakeshore Railroad" BBC *see* Cleveland baseball clubs
"Lakeshores" BBC (AL) *see* Cleveland baseball clubs
Lakeshores' unofficial booster club 285
Lakeside Hospital 193
"Lakesides" BBC *see* Cleveland baseball clubs
L'Allemand, Pauline 158
Lally, ____ 289
Lamprecht, ____ (councilman) 91
Land of Lincoln (Illinois) 242
Landis, John 15
Landy, ____ 171
Lane, Frank (umpire) 123
Laney, ____ (manager) 133
Laney, Ben 133
Lange, Bill 216, 266
"Lantern parade" 210
Larkin, Henry 182, 188, 189, 208
Larkin, Terry 80, 81
Larson, ____ 14
Larwood & Day Co. 185, 222
Latham, Arlie ("The Freshest Man on Earth") 166, 188, 189, 197–199, 205, 206, 215
Latin ancestry 270
Lauer, "Chuck" 140–142
Lavelle, ____ 184
"Lawn boxes" 242
Lawrence, Thomas (groundskeeper, manager) 123, 140, 141, 143, 155, 190, 195, 232, 279
Leach, Tommy 209
Leadley, Bob (manager) 191, 197, 201, 210
League *see* National League

League clubs (National League) 276
League game (National League) 276
League headquarters (National League) 91
League Park *see* Cleveland Base Ball Grounds; Cleveland Base Ball Park; Kennard Street Base Ball Park
League Park (Louisville) *see* Baseball grounds: Louisville, KY League Park
League race (National League) 246
League's "Alliance" *see* National League's "Alliance"
League's batting champion *see* National League's batting champion
"Ledge" BBC *see* Nelson "Ledge" BBC
Lee, Robert E. (general) 5
Leech, ____ 38
Leffingwell, ____ 9
Le Marche, Charles 125
Lemonade boys 279
Lenahan, ____ (patrolman) 142
"Lenape" BBC *see* Delaware "Lenape" BBC
Lennon, ____ 30
Lennon, William F. 56–58
Leonard, ____ (councilman) 91
Leonard, Andrew 34, 35, 48, 54
Lester, G. S. (umpire) 13
"Let me hit him for his mother" 69
Lewis, ____ 16, 40
Lewis, Lillian 158
Lex, ____ 30
Lexington and Dunham (E. 66th) 192
Lexington Avenue 192, 194–197
Liberty Bell 63, 215
Library of Congress 106, 119, 227, 260, 273
License 97, 146
"Light Guard" BBC *see* Detroit "Light Guard" BBC (reserve military)
Lightening 189
Lightening rods 190
"Lightfoot" BBC *see* Chardon "Lightfoot" BBC
Lima, OH 159, 215
"Limberger" BBC (humorous nickname) 171
Limerick, Ireland 258
Lincoln, Ezra 181
Lindale, Oh 217
Lindell House (hotel; St. Louis) 169, 183
Lindsay, ____ (black) 200
Lindsay, J. (black) 172
Lindsey, ____ 224
Lindsey, Jim (black) 209
Lions (Lines, Line, or Lime), ____ (black) 232
Liquor league 263
Lisbon, OH 280

"Little Big Horn" 144
Little Billy (actor/role) 232
"Little Consolidated" (transit company) 273
Little Rock, AR 183, 230, 232
"Little Tycoons" BBC *see* Cleveland baseball clubs
Littler, ____ 36
"Liver pad" 138
Lizards (unlucky) 260
Loftus, Tom (manager) 162, 163, 168, 169, 196, 197, 281
Logansport, IN 222, 230, 246, 271
London "Atlantics" BBC (Canada) 79
London, Canada 79, 121
London, Canada "Victoria" Lacrosse 74, 75
London, England 63
London "Tecumsehs" BBC (Canada amateur) 121
London "Tecumsehs" BBC (Canada IL) 81, 82
Long, Herman 212, 214
Long Island, NY 43
Longview horse racetrack 217
Lorain County News 5, 27
Lord 68
Lord's Day 154
Lostabum, Georgia 93
Louisville "Colonels" BBC (NL) 86, 211, 223, 245, 250, 261, 270, 277, 279
Louisville Commercial 112
Louisville "Eclipse," "Colonels" BBC (AA) 109, 111, 113, 131, 147, 162, 167, 168, 181, 204
Louisville franchise 246
Louisville hotel 261
Louisville, KY 109, 112, 135, 140, 152, 181, 232, 245, 246, 250, 252, 258, 261, 277
Louisville, KY League Park *see* Baseball grounds
Lowe, Bobby 212
Lowell, MA 62
Lowellville "Active" BBC 9
Lucas, Henry 130, 131, 139
Lucky-jack-rabbit ears *see* Mascottes
Luff, Henry 77, 80
Lurkins, ____ (black) 232
Lyman Building 33
Lyn, ____ (umpire) 215
Lynch, ____ (umpire) 205, 206, 217, 225, 226, 244
Lyons, Denny 231
Lyons, Harry 166

M.A.A. *see* Michigan Athletic Association
Macbeth quote 41
Mack, ____ 93
Mack, A. J. (umpire) 9
Mack, Connie (manager) 289
Mack, Joe H. (manager) 86, 91, 96, 115
Mack, Reddy 147
Macon, GA 140, 215

Madison, ____ 283, 284, 286, 288
Madison (E. 79th) and Cedar Grounds (a.k.a. Athletic Park, Bicycle Park, and YMCA Park) *see* Baseball grounds: East Madison (E. 79th) and Cedar Grounds
Magoon, ____ 286
Mahon, ____ 37, 172
Mahoning & Pittsburg Railroad 46
"Mahoning" BBC *see* Warren "Mahoning" BBC
"Mahoning second-nine" BBC *see* Warren "Mahoning second-nine" BBC
Mahoning valley 9
"Mahonings" BBC *see* Youngstown "Mahonings" BBC
Main 149 (phone number for tickets) 285
"Main Stars" BBC *see* Cleveland baseball clubs
Main Street 76
Main Street (Norwalk) 16
Main Street station 142
Maine 267, 271
Maine (battleship) 270
Major League Baseball 281
Major League Baseball's Americans and Nationals 291
Male, ____ 172
Male, Jimmy 222
"Maleables" *see* "Maleables Iron Works" BBC
"Maleables Iron Works" BBC *see* Cleveland baseball clubs
Malone, ____ 38
Malvern Junction, AK 169
Manchester, ____ 36
Manger, ____ 17
"Manhood" BBC (black) *see* Cleveland baseball clubs (black)
Mann, Fred 148, 149
Manning, Jack 129
Manning, Jimmy 170
Mansell, Mike R. 140–142
Mansfield, Joseph (general) 66
Mansfield BBC 6, 12, 14, 15, 147, 152, 170, 184, 270
Mansfield "Exercise" BBC 6, 14
Mansfield "Independents" BBC 6, 15, 22, 23, 26, 31, 34, 36, 38
Mansfield, OH 6, 12, 14, 22, 77, 147, 270
"Mansfields" BBC (Middleton, CT; NA) 66, 68
Mansion House (restaurant) 10
Mapes, ____ 222
"Maple City" BBC *see* Norwalk "Maple City" BBC
Marble Block 8
Marble plunge bath 185
Marietta College 222
Marietta College BBC 109
Marietta, OH 222
Marietta Register 222
Marlboro, MA 174
"Maroons" BBC *see* St. Louis "Maroons" BBC (UA)

"Marquettes" BBC *see* Cleveland baseball clubs
Marr, Charles "Lefty" 197–199
Marshall, Maggie 191
Marshalltown, IA 59
Martin, ____ 28, 41, 42, 172
Martin Luther King Blvd. 112, 194
Martin, Mast 82
Marvin, Walter 184
Mascot *see* Mascottes
Mascottes: alligator tooth 124; black youth 152; chameleons 260; dogs 124; goat and terrier 192; good-luck ring 217; horseshoes 124,192; lucky charms 124; lucky-jack-rabbit ears 213; mules 192; old broom 93; young boy 199
Maskrey, ____ 109
Mason, ____ 9
Mason, GA 196
Massachusetts 113, 123
Massillon, OH 12, 230
Massilon "Russells" BBC 209, 230
Massilon "Sippo" BBC 12, 13
Mat Wolford's tavern 105
Match game 5, 6, 8, 9, 14, 26
"Match play" 5
Mather, Margaret 158
Mathews, Robert T. 56–58, 68–70
Maul, Al 235
"Maumees" (Toledo; cricket) *see* Toledo "Maumees" (cricket)
Maxfield, ____ (justice) 217
"Mayflowers" BBC *see* Bedford "Mayflowers" BBC
"Mayflowers" BBC (Cleveland) 217
Mayres, Edith 191
Mays, Al 153
McAleer, Jimmy 136, 173–179, 181, 182, 188, 189, 197–199, 205–208, 213, 216, 231, 235–241, 245–249, 251–257, 266, 271, 275, 282, 289
McArthur, ____ 142
McAtee, ____ 49, 50, 60, 61
McBride, Dick 26, 27, 63, 70
McCarthy, Jack 275
McCarthy, Tommy 166, 213, 214
McClellan, Bill 80, 110, 129, 150, 151, 156
McCluskey, C. E. 15
McCluskey, J. 15
McClusky, ____ 15
McClymonds, ____ 12
McCormick, Jim 88, 89, 92, 94, 98–100, 103, 105–110, 111, 114, 115, 118, 120, 122–124, 127, 130, 133, 134, 136–139
McCoy, ____ 164
McCreary L. A. 37
McCrosky F. B. 128
McCullough, John *see* John McCullough acting company
McDermith, W. H. 184
McDermont, Joseph 56–58
McDermott, ____ (umpire) 191, 261, 262
McDonald, ____ 25, 141, 142, 161

McDonald, ____ (umpire) 234, 237, 273 262, 272
McEwen, ____ 8, 18, 21, 43
McFarland, Ed 217, 222, 248–250
McGarr, James "Chippy" 221, 223–226, 231, 233, 235–241, 245–249, 252–257
McGeary, Mike 88, 106–108
McGill, William "Kid" 189, 216, 217
McGinley, Tom 77, 78
McGinty, ____ 267
McGinty, Tom 222
McGlone, John 156, 158, 165
McGraw, John "Mugsy" 235–242, 252–256, 258
McGuire, James "Deacon" 156, 208
McGunnigle, William "Gunner" 98, 99, 114
McKay ____ (captain) 37
McKean, Ed 148–151, 153, 154, 156–158, 65, 167, 173–179, 181, 186, 192, 197–199, 201, 202, 204–208, 212–214, 216, 218–221, 223–225, 227, 230–241, 243, 245–250, 252–257, 261, 262, 269, 270, 272, 275, 278
McKee, ____ (mayor) 230
McKeesport, PA 184
McKenna, ____ 282, 287, 288
McKinley, William (governor, president) 6, 244
"McKinleys" BBC (black) *see* Cleveland baseball clubs (black)
"McKinney" BBC *see* Cleveland baseball clubs
McKisson, ____ (mayor) 247, 263
McMahon, ____ 51, 52
McMahon, John 161
McMahon, John "Sadie" 235, 236, 238, 239
McNerney, ____ 184
McPhee, John "Bid" 148, 149, 197, 199, 205, 206, 269
McPherson (McPhearson), ____ (black) 232
"McPherson" BBC *see* Clyde "McPherson" BBC
McQuaid, Jack (umpire) 151, 186, 212, 213, 215, 229, 239
McTammany, ____ 150, 151
McVey, Cal 34, 48, 54
McVicker's Theatre (Chicago) 48
Meadville, Cricket, (PA) 5
Meadville, Pennsylvania 5
Mears, George 187; *see also* George Mears Scrapbook
Mears, Thomas (major domo) 187
"Mechanics" BBC *see* Cleveland baseball clubs
Mechanicsville, OH 162
Mechanicsville "Tuscan" BBC 29
Medina County 14
Medina Gazette 14
Medina "Medina" BBC 14
Medina, OH 280
Medina tournament 23

Medina Village 14
Meekin, Jouett 226
Melain, ____ 12
Melton, ____ 18, 25, 43
Memphis, TN 140
Menefee, John "Jocko" 223, 224
Mercer, George "Win" 243
Merrick, Mercy 158
Merrimac (iron-side ship) 143
Merritt, Bill 229
Merry-go-rounds 266
Mesner's Band 136
Metcalfe, ____ 11
"Mets" BBC *see* Cleveland baseball clubs
Meyer & Glein Co. 185
Meyerle, ____ 49, 50
Meyerle, Levi 63, 70, 71
Meyers, Bert 248–250
Meyers, George (black) 126
Michigan 132, 228
Michigan Athletic Association 210
Michigan franchise 281
Middle South 242
Middleberg BBC 12
Middletown, CT 66
Midwest 242, 280
Miles, L. C. 184
Military band *see* Bands
Miller, ____ 12, 25
Miller, ____ (black) 232
Miller, A. 172
Miller, A. E. 184
Miller, "Billy" 222
Miller, "Bud" 222
Miller, G. 172
Miller, George "Doggie" 231
Miller, R. (black) 172
Milligan, John "Jocko" 208
Milligan, W. (black) 93, 116, 126
Mills, Charley (captain) 51
Milwaukee BBC (AA) 204
Milwaukee BBC (AL) 281, 286, 289, 290
Milwaukee BBC (NL) 81, 82, 86
Milwaukee BBC (UA) 131
Milwaukee BBC (Western Association) 170
Milwaukee BBC (Western League) 140
Milwaukee, WI 289
Mincher, Edward John 56–58
Mini-baseball tournament (Ravenna) 10
Minister's Association 263
Minkitttrick R. K. 298
Minneapolis BBC (AL) 281
Minneapolis "Millers" BBC (AL) 289, 291
Minneapolis, MN hospital 137
Minor, ____ (doctor) 163
Miracle mineral water 192
Missouri 27, 170
Mrs. O'Leary's cow 65
Mr. Baggott (actor/role) 232
Mr. J. P. Martins *see* J. P. Martins (restaurant)
Mitchell, ____ (black) 200, 224
Mitchell, Bobby 88

Mitchell, Rose 191
Mitchell, S. (black) 173
M.L.K. Boulevard (formerly Liberty Blvd.) *see* Martin Luther King Blvd.
Mobile, AL 183
Moderwell & Fowler's shop 55
Moffett, Sam 139
"Mohangahela river water" 209
Mohawk, NY 148
"Mohawks" BBC *see* Cleveland baseball clubs
Monahan, ____ (*Fort Wayne Journal*) 216
"Monarch of Minstrelry" 83
Monitor (iron-side ship) 143
Monroeville "No Names" BBC 16, 17
Monroeville, OH 22
"Monster" crowd 224
Monster rattles 238
"Moonlighting" 97
Moore, Charles 83
Moore, Kate 93
Moran, ____ 171
Morgan, Charles (umpire) 79
Morris, J. 93
Morris, James (black) 126
Morris, W. 93
Morrisania "Unions" BBC *see* NYC Morrisania "Unions" BBC
Morrisey, Andrew (father) 267
Morrison, ____ 132, 142
Morrison, Dave 91
Morrison, Mike 148–151, 156, 157
Morrow, Alice 191
Morton, Charles 77, 78, 80, 81, 217
Morton, Johnny 82
"Moses Cleaveland up to Date" (play) 223
Mother Shipton (prophetess) 110
Mouks, Geiger (manager) 172
Mouks, Tom E. 172
"Mound City" (St. Louis) 154
Mount Pleasant, OH 112
Mount Union College 75, 184
Mountain, Frank 121
Mowry, J. N. (doctor) 15
Moynahan, Mike 106, 108, 110, 135
Muffdom 112
"Muffin game" 26, 32, 164, 229
"Muffin nines" 16, 102
Muir, ____ (secretary) 270
Muldoon, Mike 114, 115, 117, 118, 121–123, 128, 130, 133, 136
Mules *see* Mascottes
Mulholland, ____ 132
Mullane, ____ 78
Mullane, Tony "Count" 148–150, 228
Mul'y, ____ 164
Munsell, ____ 11
Murch, J. H. 67
Murphy, ____ 171, 274
Murphy, E. C. 160
Murphy, Morgan 205
Murphy, William ("Gentle Willie") 133, 136, 137
Murphy, William "Yale" 225

"Murray-Lane Opera Company" BBC *see* Cleveland baseball clubs
"Muscle" BBC *see* New Lyme "Muscle" BBC
Muskegan, MI BBC (Northwest League) 132
Musson, ____ 9
"Mustard legs" BBC (Lord Baltimore) 68
"Mutes" *see* New York "Mutuals" BBC
"Mutual agreement" (police arrest) 275
"Mutuals" BBC *see* Pittsburgh "Mutuals" BBC; New York "Mutuals" BBC
"Mystics" BBC *see* Cleveland baseball clubs

N.A.B.B.P. *see* National Association of Base Ball Players
"Nail City" (Wheeling, WV) 159
"Nameless" BBC *see* Plymouth "Nameless" BBC
"Nancy Hanks" BBC *see* Cleveland baseball clubs
Nash, Billy 176–178
Nashville, TN 140
"National" BBC *see* Cleveland baseball clubs
National Association 55, 57, 60, 62, 66, 67, 72, 75, 85, 86, 291
National Association of Base Ball Players 3, 5, 15, 18, 28, 30, 31, 55
National Association Grounds *see* Baseball grounds: Forest City Base Ball Grounds (1871–1872 NA)
National Baseball Hall of Fame 28, 59, 88, 89, 96, 97, 103, 104, 108, 117, 136, 154, 169, 170, 175, 176, 179, 252, 291
National City Bank Building 59
"National City Bank Co" BBC *see* Cleveland baseball clubs
National Convention of the Republican Party 244
National League 47, 75, 84–86, 87, 94, 95, 98, 99, 101, 103, 105, 106, 109, 113, 114, 120, 121, 123, 127, 130–132, 138–140, 146, 154, 158, 169, 170, 180, 181, 183, 184, 190, 192, 193, 200, 204, 205, 215, 230, 233, 235, 264, 269, 272, 273, 275–282, 291
National League pennant 179
National League owners 282
National Leaguer(s) 90, 209
National League's "Alliance" 106
National League's batting champion 134
National Pastime 123
National streetcar magnate 181
"Nationals" BBC *see* Cleveland baseball clubs; Washington "Nationals" BBC
Native American 259, 280
Nava, "Sandy" 117

Nebraska 280
"Nebraska Indians" BBC (NE) 280
Negro Leagues Book 140
Negroe(s) 40, 111, 124
Neil, J.P. 184
Nelson, _____ 42, 51
"Nelson Ledge" BBC *see* Nelson "Nelson Ledge" BBC
Nelson "Nelson Ledge" BBC 10
Nevil, _____ 172
Nevins, S. P. 123
"New" BBC *see* Cleveland baseball clubs
New Castle, PA BBC 9
"New colored nine" BBC (black) *see* Cleveland baseball clubs (black)
New England League 92, 260
New Haven, CT 132
"New Jerusalem" 112
New Lisbon, OH 224
New London, "Stars" 23 BBC 17, 22
New Lyme "Muscle" BBC 29
New Orleans, LA 183
"New Phillies" BBC (Cleveland "Indians" NL nickname) *see* Cleveland baseball clubs
New York BBC 105
New York chewing gum firm 182
New York, Chicago & St. Louis Railroad (Nickel Plate) 187, 200
New York City 14, 21, 33, 53, 55, 56, 65, 67, 68, 105, 148, 170, 201, 206, 211, 225
New York City "Knickerbockers" BBC 3
New York City "Unions of Morrisania" 28, 29
New York City "Unions" of Tremont 53
New York "Giants" BBC (NL) 86, 130, 175, 178, 179, 181, 190, 203, 211, 225–227, 243, 268, 275
New York "Hornells" (IL) BBC *see* Hornellsville, NY "Hornells" BBC
New York Journal 298
New York "Metropolitans" BBC (AA) 131, 132, 153, 154
New York "Mutuals" BBC 30, 50–53, 55, 62, 63, 65, 68, 70, 71
New York, Pennsylvania & Ohio Railroad 165
New York "Red Stockings" (female) BBC 92
New York Sun 264
New York World 264
New Yorkers 264
Newark, NJ 226
Newark, NJ "Ironclads" BBC 226
Newberg "Asylum" 18 BBC
Newberg Athletic Company 162, 217
Newberg Athletic Grounds *see* Baseball grounds
Newberg BBC 76
Newberg "Iron" BBC 19
Newberg "Ironsides" 19 BBC

Newberg "Crickets" BBC 84
Newberg, OH 18, 19, 162
Newfoundland, Canada 251
"Newsboys" BBC (*Evening Journal*) *see* Detroit "Newsboys" BBC
"Newsboys" BBC (*Plain Dealer*) *see* Cleveland baseball clubs
Newsboys Championship 160
Newton, _____ 150
Ney, _____ 9
"Niagara" BBC *see* Buffalo "Niagara" BBC; Cleveland baseball clubs; Monroeville "Niagara" BBC
Niagara Falls 52, 53, 172
Niagara Falls in fire (pyrotechnics) 266
Nichols, Charles "Kid" 213–215, 226
Nickel Plate (railroad) *see* New York, Chicago & St. Louis Railroad
Nickel Plate depot 187
Nickens, _____ (black) 224
Nicol, Hugh 121, 148, 149
"Nine Snides" BBC *see* Cleveland baseball clubs
"No game" 104
"No Names" BBC *see* Monroeville "No Names" BBC
Noble, _____ (judge) 258
No-hitter *see* First no-hitter (Cleveland)
No-hitter (Cy Young's first) 269
Nolan, Sylvester "The Only" 105
"Nomads" BBC (Cleveland "Indians" NL nickname) *see* Cleveland baseball clubs
Non-union contractors 276
Non-union labor 273
Norris, Charles (treasurer) 217
North 230
North Kingsville, OH (Ashtabula County) 77
North Madison "Dexters" BBC 29
Northeast, Ohio 268
Northern Ohio Athletic Association 184
Northern Ohio Fair Association 112
Northern Ohio Fair Grounds 74
Northerners 147
Northwest (steamship) 110
Northwestern Association 93
Norwalk "Arctics" BBC 17
Norwalk Base ball tournament *see* Baseball tournaments
Norwalk, CT 15
Norwalk Fair Grounds *see* Baseball grounds
Norwalk "Firelands" BBC 17, 18
Norwalk "Horribles" BBC 16
Norwalk "Maple City" BBC 17, 22, 27
Norwalk, OH 15–18, 22, 23, 229
Norwalk, OH "Peters Clothing" BBC 229
Norwalk Reflector 15, 16
Norwalk "Terribles" BBC 16

Norwalk tournament *see* Baseball tournaments
Notre Dame College 259, 267
Notry, Charley *see* Charley Notry's barber shop
Nottingham, OH 225
Nottingham, OH BBC 225
N. S. Wood cup 160
Number 9's house (fire station) 83
No. 68 Croton Street 129
No. 168 Huron street (doctor's office) 268
N.Y.C. *see* New York City
Nypano *see* New York, Pennsylvania & Ohio Railroad

Oakley, _____ 9
Oberlin BBC 280
Oberlin "Business" BBC 27
Oberlin College 28, 75, 100, 109, 111, 127, 232
Oberlin College Archives 28
Oberlin College BBC 232
Oberlin College BBC (1890) 184
Oberlin depot 8
Oberlin "Fairchilds" BBC 27
Oberlin, OH 5, 44, 49, 109
Oberlin "Penfields" BBC 5, 6, 8, 21
Oberlin "Penfields-second" BBC 8
Oberlin "Resolutes" BBC 27, 42, 44, 49, 63
Oberlin, "Scrubs" BBC 232
Oberlander, _____ 30
Oberlander, Hart 156
Obouvan, _____ (black) 127
O'Brien, _____ 160
O'Brien, John ("Chewing Gum") 245
O'Brien, John F. "Darby" 155, 156, 159, 160, 163, 166, 169, 174–176–178, 182, 190, 205
O'Brien, Tom 275
O'Brien, William D. "Darby" 160
"Occidentals" High School BBC *see* Cleveland baseball clubs
O'Connor, John "Peach Pie" 204–206, 208, 212, 215, 219–221, 223–226, 228, 229, 233, 234, 241, 243, 244, 248, 249, 252–257, 261, 262, 269, 272, 275, 278
O'Day, _____ (umpire) 234, 235, 272
Odell, _____ 17
O'Donnel, _____ 172
O'Donnell, Tom 222
Oergel, _____ 172
Ogden, _____ 229
"O'Hare, Petty & Bruce Co." BBC *see* Cleveland baseball clubs
Ohio 3, 6, 9, 15, 30, 31, 109, 113, 132, 139, 170, 182, 215, 222, 280
Ohio & Erie Canal 3
Ohio Association of Base Ball Players 31
Ohio Centennial Commission 162
Ohio League 147, 179
Ohio natives 217
Ohio post-season series 221
Ohio River 39

Ohio series 179, 180
Ohio Supreme Court 75
Oil City, PA 45, 71, 99, 225
"Oil City" PA BBC 45
Oil City, PA "Senecas" BBC 71
Old Aunt Sally (amusement ride) 266
Old English letter C 157, 158
"Old Glory" 187, 197
"Old Leaguers" BBC see Cleveland baseball clubs
Old Northwest Territory 260
"Old Oscar McGroggins" (whiskey) 267
"Old Phillies" BBC (NL nickname) see Philadelphia "Old Phillies" BBC
Old-river bed grounds see Baseball grounds
"Old Sol" 199
Old Town, ME 259, 265
Olmsted "Rough and Ready" BBC 38
"Olympics" BBC see Washington "Olympics" BBC
"Olympics" BBC (black) see Cleveland baseball clubs (black)
Omaha, NE 142, 251
Omaha (Western League) 140, 142
"One dark and stormy night..." (short story) 124
One-eyed-cat 3
O'Neil, ____ 164
O'Neil, James "Tip" 166, 188, 189, 205, 206
One-price doubleheader 191
Ong, Walter (judge) 266
Ontario Beach, Rochester, NY 225
Ontario Street 125, 137
Opening Day (home) see Cleveland Opening Day (home)
"The opening day..." (poem) 196
Opening Day (road) see Cleveland Opening Day (road)
Ordinance No. 269 146
"Organized club" 5
"Orientals" BBC 39
"Orientals" BBC see Cleveland baseball clubs
"Orientals" BBC (black) see Akron "Orientals" BBC (black)
"Orioles" see Baltimore BBC (NL)
"Ornate" alligator tooth 124; see also Mascottes
O'Rourke, James 88, 89, 123, 124, 132, 138
O'Rourke, Tim 223, 224
"Orphans" BBC (NL) see Chicago "Orphans" BBC (NL)
Osborne Street (E. 39th) 32
Oswalt, ____ 93, 116
Oswego, NY 62
Otis, Charles 243
Ottawa County 15
Our Champions (badge) 247
"Ours" BBC see Philadelphia "Ours" BBC
"Outcast" BBC (Cleveland "Indians" NL nickname) see Cleveland baseball clubs
"Outwaites" BBC see Cleveland baseball clubs
Owl Club (black) 125
Oyster pirates 239
Oyster stew 256
"Oysterville" (Baltimore) 238

Pabor, Charles ("The Old Women in the Red Cap") 28, 56–58, 60–62, 69–71
"Pabst" BBC see Cleveland baseball clubs
Padden, Dick 275
Paddy Rooney (character) 197
Paige, R. K. (umpire) 8
Painesville "Athletics" BBC 7, 8, 11
Painesville "Athletics-second" BBC 7
Painesville BBC 74, 280
Painesville "Bed Ticks" BBC 44, 52
Painesville "Contest" BBC 7
Painesville electric streetcar company 274
Painesville "High School" BBC 7
Painesville, OH 7, 44, 280
Painesville "Red Hearts" BBC 99
Painesville "Remnant" BBC 7
Painesville "Rough and Ready" BBC 29
Painesville Telegraph 7
Pain's Wondrous Fireworks 143
Palmer, a.m. see A.m. Palmer (actor/role)
Pancoast, ____ 15
Panhandle train 182
Panic of 1893 (economic recession) 215
Papworth's Band 32, 68
Parades 8, 160, 170, 173, 174, 180, 183, 185, 186, 196, 205, 209, 215, 223, 230, 247, 261, 272, 285
Park Theatre 150, 158
"Park Theatre troop" BBC see Cleveland baseball clubs
Parker, ____ 17, 43, 50, 54, 132
Parma "Reds" BBC 93
Parrott, Tom "Tacky Tom" 216, 230, 248, 249
Parsons, Charlie 181
"Parti-colored" hats 133
"Pass to de bleacher" 187
Pasteboard tickets 196
"Pastime" BBC see Baltimore "Pastime" BBC; Canton "Pastime" BBC
Pastime Grounds (Canton) see Baseball grounds: Canton Pastime Grounds
Pastorius, ____ 229
Patchin, E. (umpire) 11
"Patented air punching bag" 96, 97
Patented catcher's glove 222
Patterson, ____ 42, 51
Patterson & Brunell 97
Paul, ____ (black) 232

Paul Potter (actor/role) 232
Pawnee Bill see Bill, Pawnee
Payne Avenue 76, 185, 194, 203, 207
Payne Avenue and Alabama Street (E. 28th) 203
Payne Avenue grounds see Baseball grounds: Cleveland Athletic Club Grounds
Payne cable car 192, 194; see also Cable cars
"The Peach of Euclid Beach" see Belden, Ira
Peacocks 210
Peake, Frank 64
Peanut boys 279
Pearce, Dickey 63, 117, 121
Pearl (steamboat) 83
Pecoe (Indian) 224
"Peconic" BBC see Cleveland baseball clubs
"Peerless" BBC (Sharon, PA) 9
Peitz, "Heinie" 231, 262
Penfield, ____ 16, 17
Penfield, ____ (professor) 5
"Penfields" BBC see Oberlin "Penfields" BBC
"Penfields-second" BBC see Oberlin "Penfields-second" BBC
Pennant pole 256
Pennant-winning Orioles 235
Pennington, ____ 43
Pennsylvania line 9
Penobscot language 272
Penobscot Tribe 259
Peoria, IL BBC 139, 242
Perfect game 152
Perkins, ____ 12, 16, 17
Perkins, Grant (black) 172
Perkins Avenue 144, 145
Perfect game 100, 101
Perfect pitcher 101
Perry Street (Cleveland) 83
Peru, BBC 17
"Petee" 80
"Peters Clothing Co." BBC see Findlay, OH "Peters Clothing Co." BBC
Petrie Street 167
Pettie, ____ (black) 224
Petty, Charlie 229
Pfeffer, Fred ("Dandelion") 133, 170, 171, 174, 188, 189, 224
"Phantom" (yacht) 46
Phelan, ____ 29
Phelps, F. J. (umpire) 31, 49
Philadelphia "Athletics" BBC 26, 27, 43, 48, 53–55, 62–64, 68, 70, 71
Philadelphia BBC (AA) 113, 131, 148, 157, 158, 168, 204
Philadelphia BBC (AL) 291
Philadelphia BBC (UA) 131
Philadelphia "Blue Stockings" BBC (female) 92
Philadelphia "Experts" BBC 62
Philadelphia "Old Phillies" BBC (nickname) 276
Philadelphia "Ours" BBC 36

Philadelphia, PA 33, 56, 63, 66, 71, 131, 148, 159, 168, 211, 215, 244, 250, 276, 277, 291
Philadelphia "Phillies" BBC (NL) 86, 124, 129, 130, 157, 159, 178, 183, 193, 201, 203, 211, 217, 229, 244, 249, 267, 269
Philadelphia "Quakers" BBC (PL) 190, 193
Phillips, Bill 77, 80, 81, 88–90, 92, 94, 98, 103, 106–108, 110, 114–118, 121–124, 129, 133, 136, 137, 140, 150
Phillips, G. 9
Phillips, John (author) 267
Phillips, M. 9
Phoenix club 126
Photographs 25, 46, 53, 95, 155, 197, 260
"Picked nine" BBC *see* Cleveland baseball clubs
Pickering, Ollie 269, 282, 284, 286–288, 290
Pierce, Maud 93
Piercy, ____ 109
Piero, ____ 12
Pierong, ____ 12, 13
"Pietro Gladiatorio" 188
"Piggy" (newsboy) 232
Pike, Lip 68, 69, 70
"Pikey" Captain *see* Smith, Austin R. "Pikey" (captain)
"Pills" Benton & Canfield BBC *see* Cleveland baseball clubs
"Pinafores" BBC *see* Cleveland baseball clubs
Pinckney, George 139, 140, 150
Pine Bluff, NE 183
Pinkham, ____ 41, 42, 49, 50, 61
"The pins" 97
"Pioneer" BBC *see* Kirtland "Pioneer" BBC
"Pirates" BBC (PL) *see* Chicago "Pirates" BBC (PL)
Pitching rubber 215
Pittsburgh "Alleghenies" BBC (AA) 113, 131, 155 132
Pittsburgh "Alleghenies" BBC (IND, IL) 13, 53, 80, 81, 82
Pittsburgh BBC (NL) 174, 178, 179, 196, 203, 211, 215, 218, 224, 225, 228, 229, 230, 233–235, 242–245, 270, 271, 273–275
Pittsburgh-Chicago BBC (UA) *see* Chicago-Pittsburgh BBC (UA)
Pittsburgh "Keystones" BBC (black) 163, 209
Pittsburgh Leader 13
Pittsburgh "Mutuals" BBC 31
Pittsburgh, PA 13, 55, 64, 99, 137, 170, 196, 209, 215, 218, 224, 228, 233, 251, 263
P.J. Pushaws Co. 285
Plate glass mirrors 185
Plateau Hotel 169
Platt, L. B. 27
Platt map 87
Players League *see* Brotherhood of Professional Ball Players

Players' League Guide 187
Players' League's publicist 190
Players National League *see* Brotherhood of Professional Ball Players
Plymouth "Nameless" BBC 17, 22
Pneumonia 205
Poems 27–30, 52, 111, 128, 196, 201, 202, 206, 211, 247, 256, 259, 262; *see also* Prose
Poindexter, ____ (black) 232
Poland "Resolutes" BBC 9
Poland "Stars" BBC 9
Police 199, 217, 235, 236, 240, 241, 245, 247, 264, 275, 279; headquarters 246; station 276
Policemen 197, 246, 263, 264
Pond, Erasmus "Arlie" 234, 250, 252
"Poole(s)" 92, 105, 125
"Poole halls" 3, 68
Pooler, O. E. (wrestler) 137
Poorman, Tom 158
Pop bottle 236
"Popcorn Jenny" (bordello operator) 267
"Porkopolitans" (Cincinnati) 40
Portage County 9
Portage County Democrat 9, 10
Porter, ____ 225
Portland, ME 147
Portland, ME BBC 147
Portsmouth, OH 40
Portsmouth "Riversides" BBC 40
Post-season 235; championship 192, 204; exhibition games 230; matches 258; play 250; series 258
"Pothunters" BBC (Cleveland "Indians" NL nickname) *see* Cleveland baseball clubs
Potter, Paul *see* Paul Potter (actor/role)
Powell, John 264, 268–270, 274
Powell, Martin J. 111, 114, 115
Powers, ____ 288
Powers, Phil 106
Powers, Phil (umpire) 198
"Pragues" BBC *see* Cleveland baseball clubs
Prairie State (Illinois) 242
Pratt, Albert "Uncle Al" 25, 33, 34, 36–38, 40–45, 48–54, 56–62, 64, 69–71, 92, 98, 99
Prentice, N. B. "Doc" 66, 77, 80
Prentiss, ____ 17
Presbyterian Church 16
Presque Island Grounds *see* Baseball grounds: Presque Island, OH
Press Circle *see* Cleveland Press Circle
"Press Nine" BBC *see* Cleveland baseball clubs
Price, H. O. 271
Price's, Dave *see* Dave Price's
"Printers" BBC *see* Cleveland baseball clubs; Detroit "Printers" BBC

"Printers" BBC (*Cleveland Herald*) *see* Cleveland baseball clubs
Private boxes 281, 285
Prize medals *see* Prizes
Prizes: cigars 199, 288; diamond on a gold-and-platinum scarf pin 148; diamond stud 148; pair of solid-gold sleeve buttons 148; "pass to de bleacher" 187; Press Circle $25 218, 227; prize medals 127, 235; spiked brogans 48; *see also* Gifts; Baseball tournaments
Proceedings of the Board of Councilmen 164; *see also* Cleveland City Council
Proeser, George 156
"Professional" player 42
Prose 41, 59, 68, 69; *see also* Poems
Prospect Street 105
Prospect Way (streetcar) 78
"Prospects" BBC *see* Cleveland baseball clubs
Prouty, Jed *see* "Jed Prouty" (character)
Providence "Grays" BBC (NL) 84, 88–90, 95, 96, 104, 109, 110, 113, 117, 118, 122, 130–132, 136, 137, 139
Providence, RI 88, 93, 100, 101, 135
P.S. Ryder studio (photographer) 95
Public Square 3, 8, 88, 116, 125, 160, 163, 186, 194, 226, 247, 266, 272, 281, 282
Puckerbrush Astonisher 239
Purcell "Blondie" 95, 106, 108, 129, 165
Puritanical method 276
Pushaws, P. J. Co. *see* P. J. Pushaws Co.
Putnam Street (E. 38th) 23
"Puzzlers" BBC *see* Cleveland baseball clubs
Pythians' indoor baseball league 221

Quail (birds) 168; hunting 182
Quaker City (Philadelphia) 26
"Quakers" BBC (PL) *see* Philadelphia "Quakers" BBC (PL)
Queen City (Cincinnati) 39, 155, 230
Quest, Joe 102, 108
"Quicksteps" BBC *see* Chagrin "Quicksteps" BBC; Toledo "Quicksteps" BBC
Quincy, IL 185
Quincy, IL BBC 185, 242
Quinn, H. D. 291
Quinn, Joe 176, 212, 214, 230, 252, 253
"Quinns" BBC *see* Cleveland baseball clubs

Radbourn, Charles "Old Hoss" 109, 110, 117, 118, 136, 137, 176–178
Radcliff, John 26, 69, 70
Radcliffe, J. (umpire) 11

Index

Radford, Paul 136, 174–178, 207, 208
Railroad guide 260
Rain Forest building *see* Zoo
A Rainbow for all the Baseball Tomorrows 59
Rainey, _____ 17, 141, 142
Raleigh, NC 15
Ramsey, Thomas "Toad" 167
Randall, H. 11
Randall, W. 11
Randolph, _____ 16
Ranney, _____ 9
"Rastus" (black mascotte) 232
"Rattlers" BBC *see* Cleveland baseball clubs
Rattles 235, 236
Ravenna Driving Park Grounds (racetrack) *see* Baseball grounds
Ravenna Fair Grounds *see* Baseball grounds
Ravenna, OH 9
Ravenna "Star Club Juniors" BBC (second nine) 11
Ravenna "Star second-nine" BBC *see* Ravenna "Star Club Juniors" BBC (second nine)
Ravenna "Stars" BBC 9, 10
Rawson, _____ 12, 31
Rawson, E. B. (umpire) 14
Rawson's book store 33
Reach, Al 26, 38, 63, 159
Reach & Co *see* Reach sporting goods
Reach sporting goods 63, 173, 184
Read, _____ 16
Reccius, Phil 150
Recreation Park (Detroit) *see* Baseball grounds: Detroit Recreation Park
Red Cross Rink 221, 230
"Red Hearts" BBC *see* Painesville "Red Hearts" BBC
"Red Hots" BBC (*Cleveland Herald*) *see* Cleveland baseball clubs
"Red Jackets" BBC (Cleveland) 39
"Red Men" BBC (Cleveland; Indians NL split-squad game) 270
"Red Stockings" BBC *see* Cincinnati "Red Stockings" BBC; Cleveland baseball clubs; New York "Red Stockings" BBC (female)
"Reds" BBC *see* Collamer "Reds" BBC; Parma "Reds" BBC
Reed, _____ 17, 27
Reese, _____ 14
Refrigerating car 170
Reid, Will A. 140–142
Reidy, Bill 229, 289
Reilly, Charles "Princeton Charlie" 217
Reilly, John "Long John" 149, 197, 199
Reipschlager, Charlie 149, 153
Reisling, _____ 270
Reitz, Heinie 252–257

"Remnant" BBC *see* Painesville "Remnant" BBC
Remsen, Jack 80, 81, 107, 110
Renaissance Hotel 88
Renegade seating 145
Republican 91, 244
Republican Party 244
Republicans 116
"Reserve" BBC (Hudson) *see* Hudson "Western Reserve College" BBC
"Reserve clause" (form of) 105
Reserve "colts" BBC (Akron-Cleveland) *see* Akron-Cleveland "colts" Reserve BBC
"Reserve" teams 131, 132
"Resolutes" BBC *see* Cleveland baseball clubs; Elizabeth, NJ "Resolutes" BBC (NA); Galion "Resolutes" BBC; Oberlin "Resolutes" BBC; Poland "Resolutes" BBC
"Resorts" (bars) 211
Rettger, George 208, 209, 222, 290
"The Return of the Victors" (poem) 247
Reust, _____ 282, 290
Rhines, Billy 199, 269
Rhode Island 88
Rhodes, William 243
Rhodes Avenue (Fulton Avenue) 140
"Rhodes Co." BBC *see* Cleveland baseball clubs
Rice, Walter (architect) 195
Richardson, Danny 218–220, 223, 224
Richardson, Hardy 98, 99, 120, 123, 176–178, 208
Richardson, John (architect) 206
Richmond, IN 277
Richmond, John H. 114, 117, 118, 120
Richmond, John Lee 93, 100, 101
Richmond Twp. Settlement BBC 99
Richmond, VA BBC (AA) 131, 132
Rider, _____ 12
Ridgewood Park NJ *see* Baseball grounds
Riley, _____ 172
Riley, _____ (umpire) 21
Riley, John 25, 31, 34, 36–38, 40, 42, 43
Riley, William ("Pigtail Billy") 77, 78, 80, 81, 88, 89
"Ringer(s)" 30
Ritchey, Claude ("Little All Right") 269
River-bed grounds *see* Baseball grounds: Old River-bed Grounds
"Riversides" BBC *see* Portsmouth "Riversides" BBC
R.N. Rice (steamer) 37
Roach, _____ 172
Roach, Bob 222
Road opener *see* Cleveland Opening Day (road)

"Robins" BBC (Brooklyn NL 1920) 258
Robinson, _____ 38
Robinson, Billy 230
Robinson, Wilbert "Uncle Robbie" 235, 236, 238–240, 252, 254–258
Robinson, William "Yank" 166, 207, 208
Robison, Frank De Hass 144, 145, 155, 163, 169, 181, 182, 185, 191–195, 202–204, 206, 207, 210, 215, 216, 221, 222, 227, 236, 239, 247, 257, 262–264, 267, 268, 271, 273–277, 279–281, 285
Robison, M. Stanley (vice president) 204, 275
Robison, Marie (Frank's daughter) 216
Robison, Mrs. (Frank's wife) 216
Robison, W. S. Co. City Directory *see* W. S. Robison Co. City Directory
Robison, Walter M. 260, 272
"Robison & Sanford" BBC *see* Cleveland baseball clubs
Rob'n, _____ 164
Rochester "Alert" BBC 18, 43
Rochester BBC 154
Rochester BBC (IL) 81, 82
Rochester "Excelsiors" BBC 23
Rochester "Flower City" BBC 52, 53
Rochester, NY 48, 56, 160, 225, 277
Rochester, NY (Ontario Beach) *see* Ontario Beach, Rochester, NY
Rochester "Newsboys" BBC 160
Rock Creek 11
Rock Creek BBC 11
Rock Island, IL 135
Rockefeller, John D. 87
Rockefeller Park lagoon 194
Rockford, IL 65
Rockford, IL "Forest City Green Stockings" BBC (IND, NA) 49, 55, 59, 62, 63, 65, 66, 67
Rockhill, Wright (scorer) 57
Rockhill Addition (Ft. Wayne) 55
Rockland, IL 181
Rockport, OH (Lakewood and Rocky River area) 128
"Rocks" BBC *see* Cleveland baseball clubs
"Rockwells" BBC *see* Cleveland baseball clubs
Rocky River 92, 128, 244, 266
Rodgers, _____ (black) 127
Rogers, _____ 172
Rogers, Zachariah 200
"Rogues March" 68, 178
Roller rink 132
Rolling mills (steel co.) 66
Room 535 of the Cuyahoga Building 282
Room No. 15 (Rumsey's Gym) 96
Rooney, Paddy *see* Paddy Rooney (character)
Rose, _____ 164
Rose, Peter 63, 64, 66, 67

Roseman, James "Chief" 153
Rosenberg, David (actor-umpire) 233
Rosenberg, Felix (actor-umpire) 233
Rosewood bat and silver ball: "junior" 21; "senior" 7
Ross, Duncan C. *see* Duncan C. Ross' saloon
"Rough and Ready" BBC *see* Painesville "Rough and Ready" BBC; Youngstown "Rough and Ready" BBC
Rouse, ____ 18
Rowe, Dave E. 114, 120, 121
Rowe, Jack 98, 99, 123, 169
Rowland, ____ 22
Rowland, "Banker" 26
Rowland, R. H. (umpire) 15
Royalton Twp. 38
"Royaltons" BBC 38
R.T.A. rapid tracks 180
Rubber Works Grounds *see* Baseball grounds
Ruffen, ____ 93
Rumsey, ____ (professor) 96
Rumsey's Gym 96
Ruprecht, Edward 144
Rusie, Amos 225
Russell, ____ 222
Russell, Daniel 5
Russell hotel 37
"Russells" BBC *see* Massillon "Russells" BBC
Russian leather 127
Ryan, ____ 172
Ryan, Jimmy 170, 174, 216
Ryder, Mr. 6
Ryder, P.S. *see* P.S. Ryder studio (photographer)
Ryn, ____ 152

Sabb, William (black) 126, 127
SABR *see* Society for American Baseball Research
St. Clair and Phelps Street 276
St. Clair Avenue *see* St. Clair Street
"St. Clair machine shop" BBC *see* Cleveland baseball clubs
St. Clair neighborhood 159
St. Clair Street 112
St. Cloud Hotel 13
"St. Edward's" BBC *see* Cleveland baseball clubs
"St. Ignatius College" BBC *see* Cleveland baseball clubs
St. Joe, MO BBC (1889) 170
St. Joe, MO "Saints" BBC 242
St. John, New Brunswick, Canada 106
St. John, Roll (umpire) 11
St. John's Day 109
St. Louis BBC 109, 135, 125, 126, 127
St. Louis BBC (IND) 86
St. Louis "Black Stockings" BBC (IND; black) 125, 126, 127
St. Louis "Brown Stockings" BBC (AA) 113, 126, 130, 131, 134, 154, 159, 160, 168, 170, 184, 204
St. Louis farm team 279
St. Louis franchise 277
St. Louis "Maroons" BBC (UA) 97, 131, 135
St. Louis "Maroons," "Brown Stockings" BBC (NL) 140, 205, 211, 230, 231, 233, 242, 247–250, 261, 268, 272, 273, 279, 280
St. Louis, MO 109, 126, 131, 135, 169, 182, 183, 242, 244, 261, 268, 272, 277, 278
St. Louis "Olympics" BBC 183
St. Louis Sayings 170
St. Louis streetcar company 183
St. Louis train 223
St. Malachi's Hall 105
St. Mary's River 55
"St. Patrick's" BBC *see* Cleveland baseball clubs
St. Patrick's Day 55, 183
"Saints" BBC *see* St. Joe, MO "Saints" BBC
Salem, OH 280
Salen, Charles P. 164
Salisbury, Harry 77, 78, 80, 81, 84
San Francisco style cable cars 285
Sanders, Ben 190
Sandusky "Bay City" BBC 17, 29
Sandusky "Germania" BBC 29
Sandusky, OH 27, 193, 229
Sandusky, OH BBC (1887–1888) 152, 159
Sandusky Register 29
Saner, H. A. 15
Saner, L. S. 15
"Sanfords" BBC *see* Cleveland baseball clubs
Sanskrit 64
Sargent, John 7
Sargent's store 8; *see also* John Sargent
Savannah, GA 215
Sawyer, Will 122, 127, 130, 137
Say, Jimmy 142, 153
Scates, ____ 18, 21
Scenic Amusement Park *see* Baseball grounds
"Scenic" railroad (Scenic Amusement Park) 266
Scheible, John 221
Schlee, H. 171
Schreckengost, Ossee 278
Schriver, William "Pop" 269
Schwab, Eddie 222
Scoreboard/ticker 284
Scorecard(s) 199, 216, 218
Score-card boys 279
Scott, ____ 222
Scott, ____ (black) 224
Scotten, ____ (umpire) 18, 52
Scottish Games 36, 116
Scoville electric (streetcar) 186
Scoville Street (Community College Avenue) 19, 23, 74
"Scrubs" BBC *see* Oberlin "Scrubs" BBC

"The Seasons Over" or "The Short Stops Reverie" (poem) 202
Second-half championship 211
Secretary of State's Office 53
Seipel, ____ 172
Selden Farm 140, 144
"Senators" BBC (NL) *see* Washington "Senators" BBC (NL)
Seneca Falls, NY 56
"Senecas" BBC *see* Oil City, PA "Senecas" BBC
"Senior" BBC 26
Sensendorfer, "Count" 26
Seville "Anchors" BBC 99
Seville Grounds *see* Baseball grounds
Seville, OH 91
Seville "Stars" BBC 14
Seward, ____ (umpire) 219, 220
Seward, Ed 137, 168
Seward, William (secretary of state) 17
"Seward's Folly" 17
Sexton, ____ 14
Seybold, "Socks" 284, 286–288
Seymour, S. E. (president) 184
Shaffer, George "Orator" 98, 102, 103, 107, 108, 110, 114, 117, 118, 120, 121, 123, 124
"Shakespeare" BBC *see* Cleveland baseball clubs
"A Sham Sham Battle" 200
"Shamrocks" BBC *see* Cleveland baseball clubs
Shamrocks Grounds *see* Baseball grounds
"Shams" *see* "Shamrocks" BBC (Cleveland)
Sharon, PA "Peerless" BBC 9
Sharpnack, ____ 12
Shay, ____ 282, 289, 290
Shea, ____ 184
Shearon, ____ 37
Sheehan, ____ 161
Sheffield, ____ 28, 30, 36–38, 40, 42, 43
Sheffield, Charles J. 97, 204
Sheffield Twp., OH 99
Shelafo (Indian) 224
Shelby "Union(s)" BBC 17
Sheldon, Tillie 93
Shelly, ____ 28
Sheppard, ____ 225
Sheppard, ____ (umpire) 156
Sheridan, ____ (umpire) 248–250, 253, 255–257, 290
Sheriff Street (downtown) 203
Sherwin, N. B. 66
Shindle, Bill 165
Shippy, ____ 132
Shipton, Mother *see* Mother Shipton (prophetess)
Shoch, George 218–220
"Shoo Fly" BBC (Geauga County) 52
Shoot the chutes 266
Shop baseball league 200
Short & Foreman (ticket agents) 97

Index

Shotgun 238; see also Gifts
Sibley Street (Carnegie Avenue) 77, 86
Siegerist, C. 171
Siegrist, ____ 222
Silver ball and rosewood bat (junior trophy) see Rosewood bat and silver ball: junior
Silver ball and rosewood bat (senior trophy) see Rosewood bat and silver ball: senior
Silver ball and silver bat (Ravenna) 10
Simmons, ____ 30
Simmons, Joe 61, 67, 69, 72
Sinatra, Frank 134
Sioux Indian chief 144
"Sippo" BBC see Massillon "Sippo" BBC
Sitting Bull 144
Sixth Avenue ears 178
Skating rink 107
Skeets, E. 15
"Skin" diamond (all dirt) 145, 157, 164
"Sky raker" 70
Skylight 102
Slager, John 129
Slattery, Mike 197
Slattmeyer, ____ (contractor) 185
Sliney, George 200
"Slow & Easy" BBC see Cleveland baseball clubs
Slusher, Charley (pugilist) 232
Smalley, Will 186
Smeltz, Gus 181, 191
Smith, ____ 12, 18, 25, 28, 30, 30, 36, 93, 116
Smith, Austin R. "Pikey" (captain) 6, 8, 19–21, 34, 36–38, 42, 43
Smith, Bill 144
Smith, Billy 82
Smith, C. B. (mayor) 163
Smith, Charles "Pop" 106
Smith, Eb 36–38, 42, 43, 45, 46, 48–50, 64, 75
Smith, George "Germany" 135, 137, 140, 150, 197, 205
Smith, H. 132, 136
Smith, Harold (black) 127
Smith, John "Phenomenal" 165
Smith, Sam (black) 127
Smith, W. 171
Smith, Walter (news dealer) 199
"Smokey City" (Pittsburgh) 155
Smokey City boys (Pittsburgh NL) 224
"Snide Nine" BBC see Cleveland baseball clubs
Snider, ____ 172
"Snides" BBC see Cleveland baseball clubs
Snyder, ____ (umpire) 212–214, 274
Snyder, Charles "Pop" 91, 150, 153–156, 165, 174, 175
Snyder, Charley 189
Snyder, George 15
Snyder, "Ollie" 222

Soccer game see First soccer game
"Social game" 14
Society for American Baseball Research (SABR) 140
"Society for Savings" BBC see Cleveland baseball clubs
Sockalexis, Louis 259–261–264, 265–268, 270–272, 279
"Sockalexis" BBC see Cleveland baseball clubs; Galion "Sockalexis" BBC
"Sock-Alexis, Sock-Alexis" (poem) 259
Soft-cushion concession 216
Solders, George (judge) 263
Soldiers and Sailors Monument 226
Sommer, ____ 132
Sommers, ____ 142
Sommers, ____ (black) 224
Sommers, Charlie 281, 284
Sommers, J. A. 140
Sommers, Joe 143, 186
"Song of the Haymaker" 42
Sorter, ____ 225
"Sorters" BBC see Willoughby "Sorters" BBC
South 124, 140, 183, 215
South Bend, IN 267
South Brooklyn (Cleveland area) 140, 217
South End grounds see Baseball grounds: Boston South End Grounds
"South Side" (Cleveland neighborhood) 38, 39
"Southern" BBC (black) see Cleveland baseball clubs (black)
Southern cities 183
Southern city 112
"Southern colored boys" (band) 209
Southern League 221
Southern League of Baseballist (black) 144
"Southern Rocks" BBC see Cleveland baseball clubs
"Southern Stars" BBC (black) see Cleveland baseball clubs (black)
"Sox" (nickname for Sockalexis) see Sockalexis, Louis
Spade, ____ 18
Spain 270
Spalding, Al 85, 170, 181, 192, 246
Spalding base ball 198
Spalding Sporting Goods Co. see Albert Spalding Co.
Spalding sporting-goods empire see Albert Spalding Co.
Spalding tours see Albert Spalding tours
Spalding uniforms 85
Spanish 146
Spanish-American War 272
Sparrow House (restaurant) 9
"Special police" 141
"Specials" (omnibuses) 24
"Specials" (security guards) 18
"Spencer" BBC see Geneva "Spencer" BBC

"The Spider came smiling..." (poem) 201
"Spiders" BBC (NL) see Cleveland baseball clubs
Spies, Harry 281, 282, 283, 286, 290
Split-season 21
Split-season format 204
Sporting Life 175, 182, 202, 275
Sporting News 187
Sprague, ____ (Detroit) 37
Sprague, Charlie 174
Spring pennant flag 242
Spring training 88, 96, 97, 105, 114, 132, 146, 147, 155, 156, 169, 170, 182, 183, 184, 196, 204, 205, 215, 222, 223, 230, 242, 260, 261, 270, 271, 279, 282, 283; pennant 205
Springfield, OH 133, 184
Springfield, OH BBC 133
Springfield, MA "Springfields" BBC (IL) 82
Spurney, ____ 172
Spurney, Ed 222
Square see Public Square
"Square" 49
Squire, ____ 11
Stacy, Mirnie 93
Stafford, John 220
Stage, ____ (umpire) 226, 227, 231
Stakes, ____ 225
Staley, Harry 212, 221
Stanard, W. (black) 173
"Standard Oil Co" BBC see Cleveland baseball clubs
"Standards" BBC see Cleveland baseball clubs
"Standards No.1" BBC see Cleveland baseball clubs
"Standards No.2" BBC see Cleveland baseball clubs
Standish, F. D. (umpire) 37
Stanford, ____ 160, 161
Stanley, ____ 116
Stanley, Charles (black) 126, 127
"Star Club Juniors" BBC (Ravenna second-nine) 11
Stark, ____ 17
"Stark" BBC see Canton "Stark" BBC
"Stars" (nickname for Boston NL-1889) 176, 177
"Stars" BBC see Berea "Stars" BBC; Brooklyn, NYC "Stars" BBC; Cleveland baseball clubs; New London "Stars" BBC; Poland "Stars" BBC; Ravenna "Stars" BBC; Seville "Stars" BBC; Syracuse, NY "Stars" BBC (1888); Youngstown "Stars" BBC
"Stars-second nine" BBC see Ravenna "Stars-second nine" BBC
Start, Joe "Old Reliable" 25, 80, 88, 89, 110, 117, 118, 136, 137
"Startling English" 187
State championship 221

State courts 264
State Fair 5
State law 264
State Prize ($100) 23
Statute 7032a (Sunday ball law) 266
Steam fire department 8
Steamboat line 274
Stearns, G. 30
Stearns, W. 30
Stein, Ed 218, 219
Stemmyer, Bill 141–143, 151, 152, 156, 157, 159, 160
Stentz, _____ 16
Stephens, George 92
Sterling Avenue (E. 30th) 200
Sterling estate *see* Sterling and Williamson (estates)
Sterling and Williamson (estates) 146
Steubenenville, OH 147, 163
Stevens, _____ 27
Stevens, Harry "Scorecard Harry" 216, 218
Stewart, _____ 78
Stillman House 285
Stivetts, Jack 212–214, 217, 243
"Stocking fever" 45
Stockley, _____ 8, 18, 43
Stone, _____ (black) 232
Stones Flats *see* Baseball grounds
Storie, _____ (black) 232
Stovey, Harry 218–220
Streetsboro "Buckeyes" BBC 10
Strick, _____ 78, 79
Stricker, George "Cub" 146, 149–151, 153, 154, 156, 158, 165, 166, 174–176–178, 182, 188, 189
Strief, George 77, 80, 81, 83, 88, 126, 127, 222
Strong, L. A. 15
Strong, "The Man From Morgan County" 26
"Strong Cobb & Co." BBC ("Bad Medicine") *see* Cleveland baseball clubs
Stubbs, J. C. 15
Stucky, _____ (doctor) 245, 246, 258
"Stucky Has Repented" (article) 258
Stump, _____ (black) 232
"Subscription plan" 105
Suburbia 153
Suburbs 84, 144
Sugden, Joe 272
Sullivan, _____ 158
Sullivan, Joe 244, 249
Sullivan, John L. (pugilist) 144
Sullivan, Marty 170
Sullivan, Michael "Big Mike" 229, 230, 241
Sullivan, Suter 282, 287–289
Sullivan, W. H. 38
Summit County 9
Sun & Voice (weekly newspaper) 164
"Sun baths" 157
"Sun hit" 286

Sunday, Billy 133, 134,
Sunday baseball 109, 153, 154, 163–168, 172, 173, 184, 230, 250, 262, 266, 273–276, 280
Sunday games *see* Sunday baseball
"Sunflowers" BBC (nickname Lord Baltimore BBC) 68
"Sunsets" BBC *see* Cleveland baseball clubs
Superior & Bond Street 181
Superior and Payne cable car employees 207
Superior cable line *see* Superior Street cable
Superior Court of Warren, County IN 102
Superior Street 8, 33, 76, 150, 160, 181, 185, 194, 199, 200, 205, 272
Superior Street and Payne Avenue 76, 185
Superior Street cable 194, 202; *see also* Cable cars
Sutcliffe, Edward "Sy" 174, 176, 182, 192
Sutton, _____ (black) 127
Sutton, Ezra Ballou 43, 48–51, 54, 56, 58, 59, 61, 62, 65, 69, 70
Swain, _____ 9
Swandell, _____ 51
Swartwood, _____ (umpire) 223, 224
Swartwood, Ed 109, 150
Swartz, _____ 229
Swartzenberg, _____ 88
Swartzenberg Cigar Emporium (cigar store) 88, 97
Sweasy, Charles 34, 35, 48, 54, 67, 69
Sweeney, _____ 140, 141
Sweeney, Charlie 150, 151
Syracuse, NY 91, 100, 286
Syracuse, NY BBC (1885) 152
Syracuse, NY BBC (NL-1879) 86, 91, 92, 95, 96
Syracuse, NY "Central Cities" BBC 39
Syracuse, NY "Stars" BBC (1888) 163
Syracuse, NY "Stars" BBC (IL) 82

Taffy (actor/role) 232
Tansett, _____ 282, 289
Tappan Hall 28
Tappan Square 5, 27
"Ta-ra-ra Boom-de-ay" (song) 206
Taylor, _____ 30
Taylor, _____ (black) 232
Taylor, Amos (black) 224
Taylor, Bill 106
Taylor House 40
Taylor, Jennie 93
Taylor, John "Brewery Jack" 229, 244
Tebeau, George "White Wings" 227, 231, 241, 260, 281
Tebeau, Oliver Wendell "Patsy" (player and manager) 174–178, 182, 188, 189, 201, 205, 206, 208,
211–214, 216, 218, 219, 221, 223–226, 227, 228, 230–233, 235–241, 242–252, 253, 255–257, 259–262, 264, 265, 267, 270, 272, 274–276, 278
"Tebeau's Wandering Yannigans" BBC (Cleveland "Indians" NL nickname) *see* Cleveland baseball clubs
"Tecumsehs" BBC *see* London, Canada "Tecumsehs" BBC
Tello, _____ 164
Temple, W. C. 244, 251, 258
Temple Cup 236, 240–242, 244, 250, 251, 256–258; series 235
Tener, John 174
Tennessee 230
Tenney, Fred 170
Tent (structure) 8
Terre Haute, IN 230
"Terribles" BBC (Norwalk) 16
Terry, William "Adonis" 150, 151, 211, 218, 244
Texarkana, AR 183
Texas 259
"That's the way the money goes..." 69
"This Car to the Baseball Grounds" (streetcar placard) 223
Thomas, _____ (black) 232
Thomas, G. 15
Thompson, _____ (police lieutenant) 154
Thompson, Mervin (pugilist) 137
Thompson, Samuel "Big Sam" 169
Thompson, W. F. (president) 217
Thorn, John 73, 188
Thorner, President 138
"Three games they lost..." (poem) 256
Ticket windows 197
Tiernan, Mike 225, 227
Tiffany(s) of New York 7
"Tight board" fence 162
Tilley, John C. 114
"Times" BBC *see* Geneva "Times" BBC
Tin horns 236
Toledo BBC 134, 157, 223, 270
Toledo BBC (Western League) 140–143
Toledo "Blue Stockings" BBC (Northwest League AA) 127, 131, 132, 139, 162, 163
Toledo "Duplex" BBC 72
Toledo "Maumees" (cricket) 116
Toledo, OH 22, 72, 101, 123, 133, 157, 159, 223, 261, 270
Toledo "Quicksteps" BBC 18, 20, 22
Toledo "Unions" BBC 22, 23
Toledo University 101
"Tonsorial department" (barber shop) 125
Toronto BBC (1886) 152
Toronto, Canada 144, 163, 268
Toronto, Canada BBC (IL) 147
Torreyson, Frank W. 184
Total Baseball 103

Index

"Touched" 258
"Tourist" BBC (Al Spalding tour) 170
Tournament *see* Baseball tournaments
Town Topics (weekly newspaper) 164
Toy, James 150, 151, 154
Tracey, _____ 30, 42
Trade unions 276
Train wreck 252
"Tramps" BBC (Cleveland "Indians" NL nickname) *see* Cleveland baseball clubs
Trappist Monks 201
Travelers Protective Association 150
Treacy, _____ 49
Treat, _____ 172
Trembly, _____ 22
Tremont 38
Tremont "Unions" (NYC) BBC 53
Trenton, NJ 132
Trilby (actor/role) 232
"Trilby" (play) 232
Trilby De Lune (actress/role) 232
Trip, _____ (black) 126, 127
Tri-State League 159, 184
Troy, NY 65
Troy, NY BBC 225
Troy, NY "Haymakers" BBC *see* Troy, NY "Union Haymakers" BBC
Troy, NY "Union Haymakers" BBC (NA, NL) 42, 53, 55, 62, 65, 68, 86, 90, 96, 99, 102, 103, 113, 116, 120
"Troys" BBC *see* Cleveland baseball clubs
Truesdale, _____ 43
Try, A. (black) 224
Tucker, Tommy 165, 212–214
Turkish bath massages 204
Turkish carpet 127
Turner, _____ (black) 232
Turnstile(s) 87, 176, 184, 187, 196, 205, 224, 287
"Tuscan" BBC *see* Mechanicsville "Tuscan" BBC
"Tuscarora Indians" Lacrosse (Canada) 74
T.W.&W. (railroad) 55
Twain, Mark 122
Twelve-team league 204
Twenty-fifth Ward 185
Twitchell, Larry 174–177, 178, 182, 188, 189, 223, 224
"A $2-a-week brain" 112
Tyler, W. S. Co. *see* W. S. Tyler Co.
Tynan gang (Ireland) 258
Typhoid fever 137

Underhill, _____ 12
Uniforms 8, 12, 24, 26, 34, 42, 50, 53, 56, 60, 78, 89, 90, 98, 107, 113, 114, 120, 133, 141, 146, 147, 148, 157, 158, 160, 171, 173–175, 184, 186–188, 191, 196, 202, 205, 209

Union *see* Labor union
Union Association 94, 97, 131, 138
Union Depot (Cleveland) *see* Union Terminal (train depot)
Union Depot (St. Louis) 183
Union Grounds (Cincinnati) *see* Baseball grounds: Cincinnati Union Grounds
Union "Haymakers" BBC (NA, NL) *see* Troy, NY Union "Haymakers" BBC (NA, NL)
Union Park (Baltimore) *see* Baseball grounds: Baltimore Union Park
Union Railroad Terminal *see* Union Terminal (train depot)
"Union Railways" BBC *see* Cleveland baseball clubs
"Union Railways" BBC flag (Cleveland) 24
Union Terminal (train depot) 6, 194, 196, 247
"Unions" BBC *see* Ashtabula "Unions" BBC; Cleveland baseball clubs; Cleveland baseball clubs (black); Shelby "Unions" BBC; Toledo "Unions" BBC
"Unions" of Morrisania BBC *see* NYC "Unions" of Morrisania BBC
"Unions" of Tremont BBC *see* NYC "Unions" of Tremont BBC
United States 28, 113, 121, 244
United States Circuit Court of Appeals 75
United States Colored Troops 27
United States Congress 75
U. S. government 271
U. S. Navy 270
Universe (weekly newspaper) 164
"University" BBC *see* Cleveland baseball clubs
University Circle 192, 194
University Heights (original city of) 38
University Heights "Red Jackets" *see* Cleveland baseball clubs
University of Vermont 233
University School 243
University School BBC *see* Cleveland baseball clubs
"Unripe bug juice" 209
Urbana, OH 280
U.S.C.T. *see* United States Colored Troops
Utah 75
Utah legislature 75
Utica, NY 92
Utica, NY "Uticas" BBC 84

"Vagrants" BBC (Cleveland "Indians" NL nickname) *see* Cleveland baseball clubs
Van Wert, OH 45
Vance, _____ 9
Vanduzer, A. M. 37
Van Epps & Company 136, 170
Van Haltren, George 174, 225, 226
Van Valsor, John (umpire) 18

Van Zunt, Dick 156
Veach, William ("Peek-A-Boo") 186
Vernon, James (scorer) 37
"Vets" BBC (spring training) *see* Cleveland baseball clubs
Viau, Leon "Len" 201, 267
"Victoria" Lacrosse (London, Canada) 74, 75
Vilas, _____ 18
Vincennes, IN 135
Virtue, Jake 197–199, 205, 206, 208, 213, 214, 216, 217, 219, 220, 223, 224
Viox, _____ 284
Voeike, L. 172
Vogele, C. H. 184
Voltz, Billy 132, 133, 134
Voltz, Edward C. (umpire) 36, 38
Voltz, W. H. (umpire) 91, 123
Von der Ahe, Chris 134, 135, 277, 279
Von der Horst, Harry 239, 257, 258
Vonderhorst *see* Von der Horst, Harry
"Voodoo" 124
Vorhees, _____ 232

Wabash Avenue (Chicago) 48
Waco, TX 183
Wade, B. F. 113
Wade, J. H. 243
Wade Park line (electric trolley) 196, 273
Wadsworth, _____ 9
Wadsworth, John 181
Wadsworth, OH 280
Wagner, _____ 78
Wagner, Chris 139
Waiz, Fred 83
Wakefield, _____ (manager) 160
Wakeman, OH 121
Wakeman, OH BBC 121
Wald'ke, _____ 164
Waldron, Dan 82
Walker, Moses Fleetwood 109, 111, 112, 127, 140–142, 163
Walker, Oscar 98, 99
Walker, Walter 140
Walker, Weldy Wilberforce 109, 140, 163
Wallace, _____ (umpire) 233
Wallace, Bobby 233, 241, 242–244, 248, 250, 252–257, 260–262, 269, 270, 272, 273, 275, 278
Walnut Street (Ft. Wayne) 55
Walsh Zouves 183
"Wanderers" (soccer) 193
"Wanderers" BBC (Cleveland "Indians" NL nickname) *see* Cleveland baseball clubs
Wapokeneta "Bloody Lions" BBC 52
Ward, C. 37
Ward, John Montgomery 33, 34, 36, 37, 42, 43, 46, 48–52, 54, 88, 89, 110, 117, 118, 170, 171, 225, 265

Ward, M. 37
Warden, ___ 93
Ware, Arthur (doctor) 164
Warehouse District 74
Waring Block Building 96
Warner, ___ (umpire) 277
Warner, Fred 88, 89, 91, 130
Warner & Swasey Co. 184
Warner & Swasey Co. BBC *see* Cleveland baseball clubs
Warren "Etnas" BBC 84
Warren "Mahoning" BBC 9, 10
Warren "Mahoning second-nine" BBC 10
Warren, PA 100
Warren, OH 9, 280
Washington BBC (AA) 131, 137, 204
Washington BBC (AL) 291
Washington BBC (UA) 31
Washington, D.C. 65, 67, 113, 169, 175, 244, 258, 291
Washington "Nationals" BBC 53, 62, 67, 98, 106
Washington "Olympics" BBC 38, 53, 55, 62, 65, 67
Washington Park (Chagrin Falls, OH) *see* Baseball grounds
Washington "Senators" BBC (NL) 175, 207–209, 211, 218, 221, 227, 234, 243, 250, 263, 264, 267, 277, 279
"Washingtons" BBC *see* Ashland "Washingtons" BBC
Water Cure (health retreat) 5
Water Street (W. 9th) 74, 125, 160, 165, 194, 205, 209
Waterman, Fred 35, 48, 54
Watson, Bobby 93
Wautigo (Indian) 224
Wayne BBC 14
"We are a merry little crew…" (poem) 206
Weaver, "Buck" 282, 284, 286
Webb C. Hall's store 155
Webber, ___ 9, 26
Webber, Jack 222
Weber, ___ 172
Weber's Band (Cincinnati) 230
Weddell estate 144
Weddell House (hotel) 24, 33, 42, 46, 53, 90, 94, 102, 105, 123, 125, 143, 144, 170, 246
"Weddell House" BBC *see* Cleveland baseball clubs
"Weeklies" BBC (newsmen) *see* Cleveland baseball clubs
Weideman, ___ (umpire) 245
Weidman, George "Stump" 122, 153
Weir, Ike "Belfast Spider" (pugilist) 175
Welch, ___ 169
Welch, Curt 158
Welker, ___ 17
Welkers 169
Welsh, Michael "Smiling Mickey" 103, 175
"Went back" 38

Wesley, ___ 86
Wesley, C. 85
Wesley, Charles F. 113
West 129, 135, 201, 259
West Dover, OH 200
"West End Grays" BBC *see* Cleveland baseball clubs
West Federal Street–Youngstown ball grounds *see* Baseball grounds: Youngstown Ball Grounds (West Federal Street)
West Indies Emancipation 39
West Side Park (Youngstown) *see* Baseball grounds: Youngstown West Side Park
"West Side Reds" BBC *see* Cleveland baseball clubs
West Troy, NY 205
West Virginia 222
"Western" (circuit) 86
"Western" BBC *see* Elyria "Western" BBC
Western Association 170
Western frontier 259
Western League 140, 141, 280, 281
Western League championship (1899) 282
Western New York 280
Western Pennsylvania 100, 280
Western Reserve 3, 7, 9, 27, 29, 91, 121, 270, 280
Western Reserve Base Ball Association 21, 22
"Western Reserve" BBC (Hudson) *see* Hudson "Western Reserve College" BBC
Western Reserve College *see* Hudson Western Reserve College
Western Reserve Junior Clubs 21
"Western Rocks" BBC *see* Elyria "Western Rocks" BBC
"Western Unions" BBC *see* Cleveland baseball clubs
Westerveldt, Huyler 226
Wheal, F. C. (supt.) 207
Wheeler, Harry W. 140–142
Wheeling, WV 147, 156, 260, 268
Wheeling, WV BBC (1888, 1890) 159, 184
Whiskey Island 146, 171
Whistles 235
Whitcomb, Josh *see* "Josh Whitcomb" (character)
White, ___ 282
White, Bertha 191
White, Elmer 43, 52, 56–58, 59, 61
White, Howard 155, 199, 204, 243
White, James "Deacon" 28, 30, 31, 33, 39, 40, 42–47, 48–52, 54, 56–58, 60, 61, 63–65, 67, 69–71, 85, 123, 138, 169
White, John M. 138
White, Will 85
"White Caps" BBC *see* Cleveland baseball clubs
White House 6, 169
White Motors Company 106
White Mountain hotels 183
White Sewing Machine Company

"Whites" BBC *see* Cleveland baseball clubs
"White Stockings" BBC (NA, NL) *see* Cleveland baseball clubs
"White Stockings" BBC *see* Garrettsville "White Stockings" BBC
Whitehead, William 243
"Whites" White Sewing Machine Co. BBC *see* Cleveland baseball clubs
"Whitewashed" 40
Whitman, Walt (poet) 205
Whitney, ___ 100, 172
Whitney, ___ (captain) 200
Whitney, Art 111
Whittington Park *see* Baseball grounds: Hot Springs, AR Whittington Park
Whittlesey, Elisha 15
Wickham, ___ 16, 17
Wickoff, ___ (president AA) 168
"Wideawakes" BBC *see* Cleveland baseball clubs
Wild West Show(s) 143, 259
Wilhelm, ___ 274
Willard, ___ 60
William Wright (steam boilers) 195
Williams, ___ 12, 116, 164
Williams, ___ (black) 232
Williams, ___ (Spiders 1893) 219
Williams, Ed (black) 232
Williams, Frank 56–58
Williams, J. B. (constable) 217
Williams, James (doctor) 162
Williams, Jimmy 145, 155, 159, 162
Williams, Nellie 191
Williams College 113
Williamsberg "Eckfords" BBC (Brooklyn) *see* Brooklyn, "Eckfords" BBC
Williamson, Ned 21, 108, 133, 134
Williamson estate *see* Sterling and Williamson estates
Williamstown, MA 265
Willigrod, Julius 114, 121
Willoughby BBC (1872) 74
Willoughby BBC (1894) 225
Willoughby Grounds *see* Baseball grounds
Willoughby, OH 225
Willoughby "Sorters" BBC 11, 24, 33
Willoughby "Yankee" BBC 12
Wilmington, DE BBC (UA) 131
Wilmot, Walt 186
Wilson, ___ 93, 116
Wilson, ___ (black) 200
Wilson, Edward 126, 127
Wilson, George 125
Wilson, Jack 222
Wilson, W. (black) 173
Wilson, William (black) 200
Wilson, William W. (black) 126, 127, 144
Wilson, Zeke 244, 246–248, 252, 260, 264, 275, 281, 282, 286
Wilson Avenue *see* Wilson Street (E. 55th)

Wilson Street (E. 55th) 69, 77, 139, 180, 185–187, 194
Wilson Street (E. 55th) and Diamond Court 185
Windmills 210
"Windsor" Cricket Club (Canada) 6
"Winning post" 61
Wire screen 87, 202
Witter, _____ 9
Wittrock, _____ 229
Wolford, Mat 105, 125
Wolters, Rynie 50, 51, 67, 71, 72
"Wolverines" BBC (NL) see Detroit "Wolverines" BBC (NL)
Women baseball clubs see Female baseball clubs
Wood, George "Dandy" 111, 114, 115, 170
Wood, Jimmy (captain) 62, 64
Wood, N. S. see N. S. Wood cup
Wooden Indian 267, 268
Woodland Avenue Presbyterian Church 96
Woodland Hills Park see Baseball grounds
"Woodlands" BBC see Cleveland baseball clubs
Woods, _____ 38, 42, 50, 229
Woods Gym 203
Woodward, S. B. 14
Woolrich, Michael 180
Wooster, OH 14
Wooster College, OH BBC 75, 109
Wooster "Hope" BBC 14
Worcester, MA 100, 260
Worcester, MA BBC (NL) 100, 101, 104, 113, 121
Worcester, MA "Busters" BBC (New England League 1909) 260
"Work House Nine" BBC see Cleveland baseball clubs
World (weekly newspaper) 164
"World Series" 96, 154, 258
World's Championship 213, 214
"World's Championship Games" 211
World's Fair (Chicago) 215
Worthington, George Co. see George Worthington Co.
Worthington, Ralph 243
Wright, _____ 141, 164
Wright, Frank 90
Wright, Frank B. 38
Wright, George 28, 34, 35, 48, 54, 88, 117, 118
Wright, Harry 34, 35, 46, 48, 54, 63, 90
Wright, William see William Wright (steam boilers)

W. S. Robison Co. City Directory 60
W. S. Tyler Co. 200

"Xenia" BBC (Xenia, OH) 31
Xenia, OH 31
X-rays 268
"XYZ's" BBC see Cleveland baseball clubs

Yale College 221, 222
Yale College BBC (New Haven CT) 79, 93, 109, 132,
Yale University BBC see Yale College BBC
"Yankee" BBC see Willoughby "Yankee" BBC
Yates, _____ (black) 232
Yellow fever 163
YMCA see Young Mens Christian Association
YMCA gymnasium 230
YMCA Park see Baseball grounds: East Madison (E. 79th) and Cedar Grounds
"YMJA" (Young Mens Jewish Association) BBC see Cleveland baseball clubs
York, _____ 191
York, Tom 70, 88, 110, 117, 118, 122–124, 129
York BBC 14
Young, _____ 38
Young, Denton True "Cy" 154, 191–193, 197–199, 204–206, 211–218, 223, 224, 227, 231, 233–236, 238–241, 242–250, 252, 253, 257, 261, 262, 268–272, 278
Young, Nick (president) 267
"Young America" BBC see Cleveland baseball clubs
"Young Cleveland" BBC see Cleveland baseball clubs
"Young Green Flags" BBC see Cleveland baseball clubs
"Young Idlers" BBC see Cleveland baseball clubs
Young Mens Christian Association 92, 274
"Young Mens Hebrew Association" BBC see Cleveland baseball clubs
"Young Mens Jewish Association" BBC see Cleveland baseball clubs: "YMJA"
"Young Rattlers" BBC see Cleveland baseball clubs
"Young Woodlands" BBC see Cleveland baseball clubs
Younger, Charles H. L. 27
Younger, Elizabeth 27
Younger, Katherine 27
Younger, Simpson Charles 21, 27, 42
Youngstown (new park of 1889) see Baseball grounds
Youngstown BBC 142, 185
Youngstown baseball association 179
Youngstown baseball grounds see Baseball grounds: Youngstown Baseball Grounds (West Federal Street)
Youngstown Courier 9
Youngstown depot 251
Youngstown "Ironsides" BBC 9
Youngstown "Mahonings" BBC (1872) 75
Youngstown minor league franchise 136
Youngstown native 179, 282
Youngstown, OH 9, 75, 135, 221, 251, 266
Youngstown Register 9
Youngstown "Rough and Ready" BBC 9
Youngstown "Stars" BBC 9
Youngstown streetcar company 136
Youngstown West Side Park see Baseball grounds
"Yucatans" BBC see Cleveland baseball clubs

"Z" BBC (Zulus; black) see Cleveland baseball clubs (black)
Zanesville, OH 147
Zanesville, OH BBC 147
Zeke 14
"Zephyrs" BBC see Berea "Zephyrs" BBC
Zettlein, George "Charmer" 24, 25, 60, 61
Zimmer (Zimmerman), _____ (black) 232
Zimmer, Billy 222, 230
Zimmer, Charles "Chief" 154, 156, 158, 163, 166, 174, 175, 177, 178, 181, 186, 196, 197, 199, 205–208, 212, 214, 216, 218–221, 225–227, 230, 231, 233–241, 242, 247, 249, 250, 252–257, 262, 269–271, 274, 278
Zimmerman, _____ (captain) 200
Zoo 171
"Zouaves" BBC see Cleveland baseball clubs
Zow Zow (actor/role) 232